LABOR ECONOMICS: A Comparative Text

LABOR ECONOMICS: A Comparative Text

Robert F. Elliott
University of Aberdeen

The McGraw-Hill Companies

London · New York · St Louis · San Francisco · Auckland · Bogotá · Caracas
Lisbon · Madrid · Mexico · Milan · Montreal · New Delhi · Panama · Paris
San Juan · São Paulo · Singapore · Sydney · Tokyo · Toronto

Published by
McGRAW-HILL Book Company Europe
Shoppenhangers Road, Maidenhead, Berkshire SL6 2QL, England
Telephone : 01628 23432
Fax: 01628 770224

British Library Cataloguing in Publication Data

Elliott, Robert F.
    Labor economics: a comparative text.
    1. Labour market
    I. Title
    331.12
    ISBN 0-07-707234-0

Library of Congress Cataloging-in-Publication Data

Elliott, R.F.
    Labor economics: a comparative text / Robert F. Elliott.
       p.   cm.
    ISBN 0-07-707234-0
    1. Labor economics.   I. Title.
HD4901.E45   1990
331—dc20   90-32458

Reprinted 1997

Typeset by Times Graphics, Singapore
and printed and bound in Great Britain
at the University Press, Cambridge
Printed on permanent paper in compliance with ISO Standard 9706

For
Sue and Andrew

CONTENTS

PREFACE

Labor economics is now firmly established as an area of theoretical and empirical inquiry in the mainstream of economics. The issues addressed by the subject have always been among the most important confronting economists but the manner in which they have been addressed has changed substantially over the last quarter of a century. The tools that labor economists use to explain and investigate economic phenomena display the same theoretical rigor and require application of the same degree of econometric expertise as other major areas of the subject. Twenty-five years ago, particularly in the United Kingdom, labor economics was a much more descriptive area of economics. Relatively little use was made of econometric techniques in empirical work and the formal analytical content of the subject was sparse.

The change in the approach of labor economists reflects in part changes that have occurred in labor markets themselves. In his pioneering analytical treatment of wages and employment, Allan Cartter reminds us that the depression of the 1930s saw an outburst of work on wage and employment problems[1] in which the treatment of these issues was in a formal manner 'reasonably abreast of modern economic knowledge'.[2]

The subsequent post-war period saw the growth of collective bargaining in both Europe and North America and the focus of attention changed to reflect this. The

---

1. The principal examples are Hicks, John R. (1932) *The Theory of Wages*, Macmillan, London; Douglas, Paul H. (1932) *The Theory of Wages*, Macmillan, New York; and Pigou, A.C. (1933) *The Theory of Unemployment*, Macmillan, London.
2. Cartter, Allan M. (1959) *Theory of Wages and Employment*, Richard D. Irwin Inc., Homewood, Illinois, p. 1 quoting Hicks, John R. (1932), *op. cit.* p. v.

descriptive nature of much of the work of this period reflected what was then perceived to be the relative intractability of institutions to formal economic analysis. The formal model building and application of advanced econometric techniques by the modern labor economist perhaps reflects the fact that in the 1980s, as in the 1930s, collective bargaining was no longer seen as a principal concern. Such a view may have some validity in the United States but it is certainly a mistaken one to hold in Europe. Although collective bargaining was in retreat during the 1980s we ignore the institutions of the labor market at our peril. The institutions of the labor market are more extensive and their influence extends beyond that of collective bargaining. They encompass the belief systems, the social customs and practices and the rules that influence and constrain individual behavior in labor markets. One of the purposes of this book is to emphasize the important role of these institutions in labor market analysis in order illustrate how these constrain and sometimes determine choice.

In some respects North America and Europe lie at opposite ends of the spectrum with regard to the institutions of collective bargaining. Other countries chosen for analysis—Australia, Japan and Germany—lie at points in between. Each country is chosen to illuminate important features of the modern labor market and to illustrate the different ways in which labor markets adjust. A further objective of this book is to reveal, often to advocate, the insights that comparative analysis offers. Comparative analysis offers the prospect of discerning how differences in the tastes and attitudes of the population and differences in labor market institutions affect market outcomes.

The book pays particular attention to explaining why wages and employment often do not adjust rapidly to changes in market conditions. One reason for this is the prominence of life cycle dimensions in labor supply. These have an important impact on the participation, mobility and human capital investment decisions of individuals. A second and associated reason is that substantial transaction costs now confront economic agents wishing to make quantity adjustments in labor markets. Many of the decisions taken in modern labor markets amount to investment decisions and it is therefore no longer appropriate to regard labor as a flexible factor of production in many contexts.

Labor economics illustrates perfectly that amalgam of logic and intuition, together with a wide knowledge of facts, which was emphasized by Keynes as 'required for economic interpretation in its highest form'.[3] In economics that logic finds expression in the models that economists construct to explain the world. Again to quote Keynes 'economics is a science of thinking in terms of models joined to the art of choosing

---

3. Keynes was reporting a conversation with Max Planck, the physicist–mathematician responsible for the quantum theory. Keynes reported that Planck 'once remarked to me that in early life he had thought of studying economics but had found it too difficult! Professor Planck could easily master the whole corpus of mathematical economics in a few days. He did not mean that! But the amalgam of logic and intuition and the wide knowledge of facts, most of which are not precise, which is required for economic interpretation in its highest form is quite truly overwhelmingly difficult for those whose gift mainly consists in the power to imagine and pursue to their furthest points the implications and prior conditions of comparatively simple facts which are known with a high degree of precision' Keynes, J.M. (1972) *Essays in Biography* Macmillan, p. 186.

models which are relevant to the contemporary world'.[4]

In modern economics these models are frequently specified in a mathematical and highly abstract form surrounded by a large number of simplifying assumptions that are required to make the models tractable. This textbook is set at an intermediate level, it is aimed predominantly, but not exclusively, at those with some knowledge of introductory economic concepts. Mathematical models will occupy only a small part of this text and in general are confined to appendices and footnotes, for it remains true that at this level many economics students in Europe and the United States are uncomfortable with the extensive use of mathematics. In almost all cases the ideas developed in these formal models can be conveyed by use of diagrams, and this practice is adopted here. Yet mathematics, even at its most simple, casts new and revealing light on familiar problems. Where they afford such insights, mathematical techniques should not be eschewed and they are not avoided here. The technical skills required to master this text are therefore those possessed by a student who has completed an introductory economics course. Many other individuals of equivalent ability but without exposure to an introductory economics course will also find the text accessible.

In common with other areas of economics the techniques used to investigate empirical phenomena arising in labor markets have advanced substantially in recent years. An understanding of the appropriateness of the different techniques—on the one hand of the robustness of simple ordinary least squares estimation and on the other of its unsuitability for another class of problems that frequently confront the researcher—is an essential precondition for appraising the results of the voluminous empirical literature that has emerged in this field in recent years. The intention of this text is to acquaint the student with the results of this research; to provide a theoretical context for their interpretation; and to facilitate some understanding and an appreciation of the appropriateness of the different techniques now available.

Throughout this text, and despite the urgings of some of those who read the text, the neoclassical paradigm represents the maintained hypothesis. This hypothesis, grounded in a view of rational maximizing behavior on the part of the individual, a group of individuals or a firm, provides a logical framework with which to interpret and to predict behavior in labor markets. It focuses our attention on the constraints and opportunities that confront individuals, building on a clearly defined set of individual tastes and objectives. Until an alternative and superior analytical framework is proposed, I am reluctant to abandon the one we have. Yet this analytical perspective will not receive unqualified or unquestioning support. There will be points in the text at which my doubts about the appropriateness of this paradigm will be all too evident.

Finally, a request to the readers of this text, be they students, faculty members or informed laypersons. I should appreciate your comments on this book as they will help me to produce an even better product next time round to the benefit of future students. To you all, good reading.

---

4. *The Collected Writings of John Maynard Keynes*, Vol 14. Moggridge, D. (ed.), Macmillan, 1973, pp. 296–7.

ACKNOWLEDGMENTS

I have accumulated many intellectual debts during my study of labor economics over these past 15 or so years. In my formative years Rodney Crossley, as a stimulating teacher, and Donald Mackay, within the Scottish tradition of applied labor economics, had an important influence on my thinking about the subject. Earlier still my interest in the application of quantitative methods in economics was awakened by Roy Moore and in economics more generally by Peter Donaldson, Andrew Graham, John Hughes and Avinash Dixit. Some of the limitations of the subject were brought home to me during my studies in quite different areas and for this I have to thank Bill Weinstein and Steven Lukes. More recently, in his capacity as friend and colleague, the work of John Pencavel has served as a model for that blend of theoretical rigor and empirical inquiry that is the hallmark of all that is best in modern labor market analysis. To all the above I owe a considerable debt.

The idea for this text germinated in discussions with Bob Smith and Ron Ehrenberg while I was a visitor to Cornell University. I have long regarded their text *Modern Labor Economics* as a model of clarity and as an excellent survey of the theoretical foundations and empirical literature in this field. However, their book focuses on the United States and, understandably perhaps, makes little reference to the substantial body of empirical and some theoretical work that has accumulated over the years outside the United States. Initially I proposed to 'anglicize' their text, but the more I began to define the form that such anglicization would take, the more I realized that I proposed quite a different product. Cornell, and the School of Industrial and Labor Relations in general, provided an excellent environment in which my ideas could take shape. I am grateful to Ron and Bob and to all my other friends at Cornell for playing their part in making the School one of the most friendly yet stimulating academic environments North America has to offer the labor economist.

A large number of my friends and colleagues have read parts of the text. Richard Disney, Derek Leslie, Gavin Mooney, Ali MacGuire, John Pencavel and Bob Hart, all read large sections of the manuscript and provided extensive comments, while Rod Cross, Mark Killingsworth, Ed Lazear, Jacob Mincer, Kevin Murphy, Phil Murphy, Kathryn Nantz, Andrew Oswald, Sherwin Rosen, Paul Ryan, Ioannis Theodossiou, Kip Viscusi and Glen Withers read and provided comments on particular chapters. To all the above my profound thanks. Though you may not all approve of the product that has emerged, your critical comments and encouragement have proved invaluable.

It is customary to acknowledge the assistance of those who helped in the production of this text. I do so here with more than the usual degree of enthusiasm. As the resources at the disposal of academics in UK universities are reduced still further, I have had to trade more than usual on the goodwill of the secretaries who typed drafts of this text. To all who played a part in the typing of this manuscript my sincere thanks. However, I reserve my warmest thanks for Trish Pope, for the uncomplaining and cheerful way she prepared the final manuscript, and Winnie Sinclair without whose energy and commitment this project would have been much delayed. Finally, without the wholehearted support of the two most important people in my life this project would not have been possible. To them I dedicate this book.

PART 1

AN OVERVIEW OF THE LABOR MARKET

Modern labor economics employs the basic concepts of neoclassical price theory to analyze behavior in labor markets. The strength of this approach is that it provides an integrated explanation of behavior and gives rise to testable propositions. However, before it can account for much of what we observe in labor markets the basic theory requires substantial modification. The factor of production labor has many distinctive characteristics that set it apart from other factors of production. One purpose of the first chapter is to identify some of these distinguishing characteristics. This first chapter provides an overview of the labor market and introduces some of the principal concepts that will be encountered later in the book.

All markets comprise buyers and sellers and the market for labor is no exception. A simple model of the labor market is therefore constructed in which the behavior of buyers is summarized in the form of a labor demand curve and that of sellers in a labor supply curve. This analytical framework, which most readers will have encountered in an introductory economics course, is then used to offer an insight into the movement of wages and employment in the labor markets of a number of major industrial nations in recent years. This chapter will reveal the quite different paths that these key variables have taken in these countries over the last quarter of a century. It is not intended as an empirical chapter, the experience of these countries is examined to illustrate the insights that simple market models can provide, and to remind the reader of the methodology of economics. The reader who has completed an introductory economics course will find this easy reading. For such readers it is designed to introduce key concepts and to inform them of some of the key outcomes in labor markets in recent years.

THE NATURE OF LABOR MARKET ANALYSIS

Man's character has been moulded by his every-day work and the material resources which he thereby procures. . . . The business by which a person earns his livelihood generally fills his thoughts during by far the greater part of those hours in which his mind is at its best; during them his character is being formed by the way in which he uses his faculties in his work, . . . and his relations to his associates in work, his employers or his employees.[1]

Of the many markets that exist in a modern economy the market for labor is the most important. It is from selling their services in this market that most families derive their income, it is also in this market that they spend the single largest part of their waking hours. When not working many individuals devote a large part of the remaining time to acquiring the skills necessary for effective performance in this market. The education and training individuals undertake during their lives is chiefly designed to equip them with skills which enhance their performance in the labor market. It is moreover from their activities in the labor market that individuals derive a large part of their self-esteem and form friendships and ties that determine many of the parameters of their social life.

For most people work is undertaken primarily for pecuniary gain. For the vast majority work is essential to secure the income necessary to buy the goods and services that support their standard of living. Work is undertaken because it is a means to this end and, although many individuals find aspects of their work and the social environment in which they work enjoyable, few find it so enjoyable that they would be prepared to pay for the privilege. For most people work is, in the main, a source of

1. Marshall, A. (1890) *Principles of Economics*, Macmillan, London, pp. 1–2.

disutility and they therefore require payment to compensate them for the time they devote to it. In the market for labor the essential transaction is therefore the exchange of work for pay. The conditions governing this exchange, determining the quantity of labor which is bought and sold and the price at which these transactions take place, is the subject matter of labor economics.

The efficiency with which exchange in labor markets is accomplished is a principal determinant of the efficiency of the economy as a whole. Delays in exchange result in costs which take the form of output that is forgone, output that could have been produced had labor been available. Mistakes in and impediments to exchange can similarly result in forgone output. These occurrences diminish the volume of goods and services available to support the standard of living of the citizens of a country and therefore the efficiency of labor market exchange is of vital concern to us all.

In this chapter we outline the simple analytical framework that will be used to analyze the labor market and we illustrate some of the outcomes of labor market exchange in a sample of industrial nations. We also provide an overview of the concepts and issues that will be encountered in the rest of the book.

THE LABOR MARKET

The market for labor is an abstraction; it is an analytical construction used to describe the context within which the buyers and sellers of labor come together to determine the pricing and allocation of labor services. Before exchange can take place in any market there have to be both buyers and sellers of the required service. Much of our subsequent analysis will therefore be concerned to detail the tastes, motivation, characteristics and constraints on the two parties to the transaction. In free markets parties come together as willing buyers and sellers, in a less free environment one or both of the parties may be forced or compelled to conduct the exchange. In the markets we analyze such compulsion is absent. In civilized countries the state has prohibited slavery, the right of one individual to acquire the rights to another's labor, and has ensured that employees have freedom of mobility and choice of job.

The market for labor usually has a distinct geographical dimension—a single town, a region or a country. Typically we are concerned with the labor market for a particular skill or occupation, region or industry, but we shall also consider *the* market for labor. Such an abstraction ignores the complexity and heterogeneity of labor supply but is necessary for some purposes. Furthermore, it emphasizes that through the process of mobility each of the separate submarkets is linked.

For analytical purposes it is helpful to think of the terms of any labor market exchange being specified in a labor contract. These contracts can take the form of either an explicit written agreement or an implicit verbal 'understanding', about the price that is to be paid and the quantity of labor that is to be bought. The terms of the contract may have been drawn up as the result of bargaining between a trade union and employer or between an employer and single employee. In the former case we view the trade union officials who negotiate the terms as the agent acting on behalf of the principal, the union member. One problem that emerges in such a relationship is to write the rules so as to ensure that the principal acts in a way that maximizes the utility of the members. Bargaining only occurs where both parties possess some degree of market power and the relative magnitudes of this influence the eventual outcome. In contrast competitive labor markets are distinguished by the absence of such power.

In both competitive and monopolized labor markets exchange will often be governed by rules, by informal understandings or practices, often of a customary nature, which influence the behavior of both parties. These rules often emphasize considerations of fairness but the meaning of such a concept is likely to differ substantially between countries. Few of the terms and conditions under which labor is exchanged can be stated explicitly in written labor contracts. A price for labor services may be agreed, but the quality and often the quantity of these is left unspecified.[2]

What is so special about labor services?

Workers may exercise considerable discretion over the quantity and quality of the services they offer and thus often over the quality of the final product. Sustained delivery of the right quality of labor services depends on the continued co-operation of labor. Machines may be temperamental and at times appear to be uncooperative, but this results from mechanical failure. It is not a result of the exercise of 'free will' as is the case with labor. Because labor often has considerable discretion over the extent to which it cooperates to provide the services required, profit maximizing firms establish mechanisms to induce cooperation. Either payment systems can be structured to induce appropriate performance or firms can monitor employee performance, penalizing slacking and rewarding appropriate behavior. Piecework systems, group bonus system and profit-related payment systems are all examples of payment systems structured to induce the desired performance by workers. More recently it has been recognized that some firms pay above the market clearing wage to induce appropriate performance; this is known as efficiency wage theory. This same theory proposes that the need to motivate workers is one explanation for involuntary unemployment.

The quality of labor services that employees deliver depends on their attitudes and dispositions: in a word, it depends on their morale. In this respect labor services are quite unique for the quantity and quality of the services offered by other factors of production, capital and land, do not depend on their morale. Again, while the services of capital frequently require a particular working environment, for example, a dust-free 'clean' environment for mainframe computers and for microchip manufacture, these conditions can be determined objectively. The machine itself forms no subjective

2. For the contents of collective agreements in Britain see Oswald, A.J. and Turnbull, P. (1985) 'Pay and employment determination in Britain: what are labor contracts really like?', *Oxford Review of Economic Policy*, **1**, Summer, 80–97. Hanami, T. (1981) *Labor Relations in Japan Today*, Tokyo, Kodansha International, notes that Japanese collective agreements are short and abstract, indeed that 'the detailed enumeration of specific contract provisions would be fatal to this flexibility'. In Japan management and labor depend on consultations conducted in good faith should disagreements arise or circumstances change.

judgment as to whether the appropriate standards have been met. In contrast, the worker delivers the labor services in person and it is therefore the subjective judgment of the supplier of labor services that determines whether the appropriate working environment has been created. Reciprocally it is the subjective judgment of the demander of labor services which determines whether the appropriate quantity and quality have been delivered.

The labor services offered for sale in most labor markets exhibit a considerable degree of heterogeneity. Individuals differ in drive and motivation, in their aptitude for certain tasks, in their willingness to take risks and in their ability. Yet, perhaps the single most important way in which the services offered by different individuals are distinguished is by the qualifications and training they possess. Individuals choose whether or not to enhance their qualifications through education and training and both firms and individuals have an incentive to incur the initial costs associated with this. Education and training raise individuals' productivity and therefore can offer substantial financial rewards. Accordingly we talk of investment in human capital in a manner analogous to investment in physical capital. This investment takes one of two forms. It either raises a worker's productivity in a range of different firms or the skills acquired are demanded by one firm only. The skills acquired are described, respectively, as general skills and specific skills—a distinction that has profound implications for the subsequent pricing and allocation decisions. The more specific are the skills the more heterogeneous is the workforce but the more heterogeneous the workforce the less mobile it becomes and it is mobility that provides the link between different labor markets.

The price of labor services

The returns workers receive from selling their labor can take a number of forms. The real wage is calculated by deflating the money wage, W, by an appropriate price index for final goods and services, P. In this manner the money wage is expressed in terms of the goods and services it will buy. Workers also receive fringe benefits, goods and services provided directly by the employer, such as medical insurance, use of a car, meals and sports facilities. Together with pay these comprise the total compensation package and constitute the pecuniary rewards from work. In addition to these there are non-pecuniary rewards from work, some of which are commodities produced as a by-product of the firm's production. An example of such a commodity is a pleasant and safe working environment. No explicit prices are charged for such commodities but they are in effect purchased by workers who receive lower wages than they would otherwise. Together these pecuniary and non-pecuniary aspects of different jobs constitute the net advantages of different jobs. The theory of equalizing differences suggests that when we standardize for all of the differences in the types of reward offered by different jobs, the net advantages tend to equality.

The price the firm pays to obtain labor services often differs according to whether the firm satisfies its labor demand by hiring more people or by buying extra hours from existing employees. The cost to a firm of an additional hour will be the hourly wage and any addition to fringe benefits that occurs but it will encounter further costs if it attempts to acquire the same number of hours by employing more people. Every time a firm takes on additional employees it incurs a set of once-and-for-all hiring and training costs. These constitute fixed labor costs which do not vary with the number of hours the employee subsequently works. Such costs represent an investment by the firm in its workers and in these circumstances it is no longer appropriate to regard labor as a variable factor of production. Labor now incorporates both a fixed and a variable element. It is for this reason that labor has been called a quasi-fixed factor of production.

The fixed element in total labor costs has grown significantly in most advanced industrial nations in recent years.[3] In many circumstances it is cheaper for a firm to expand output by inducing its existing employees to work longer or harder than it is to hire additional employees. Firms are no longer indifferent to whether they use their existing employees or employ people outside the firm. They have invested in their own employees and therefore offer inducements to them to stay. Certain types of fringe benefits and payments for long service, known as seniority payments, constitute such inducements. The quasi-fixity of labor leads to a distinction between workers with appropriate skills and in possession of jobs, that is insiders, and those who are no longer considered by firms to be part of the effective labor supply, that is outsiders.

AN ANALYTICAL FRAMEWORK FOR INTERPRETING LABOR MARKET DEVELOPMENTS

An analytical framework for interpreting labor market behavior is provided by the microeconomic concepts of supply and demand. Consider how these can be employed to describe the simultaneous determination of price (the wage) and quantity (employment) in labor markets. A supply function representing the behavior of the sellers of labor (individual workers or their representatives) and a demand function representing the behavior of the demanders of labor (individual firms or their representatives) are developed for each labor market. The price and quantity of labor exchanged are determined by the point of intersection of the two functions.

Labor supply

A supply curve is drawn to indicate the amount of labor that individuals or groups of individuals are willing to supply at each wage rate. A seller is one who is in a position to determine the amount of labor that is to be offered for sale. There can be many sellers, and therefore competition in supply, or just one seller, a monopolist. A monopoly may arise because a single individual possesses a unique talent or because

3. In a most detailed study of fixed and variable labor costs Hart, R.A., Bell, D.N.F., Frees, R., Kawasaki, S. and Woodbury, S.A. (*Trends in Non-Wage Labour Costs and their Effects on Employment*, Commission of the European Communities, Brussels, 1988) conclude that fixed costs 'account for up to 20 per cent of total labour costs in most countries and a considerably higher percentage in Japan', p. 203.

a number of individuals combine to act as one, for example when they form a trade union or professional association. There will be some wage below which individuals will not wish to work. The highest wage at which individuals will not work is termed the reservation wage; at wages above this they offer some labor supply. One determinant of the reservation wage will be the system of welfare support and the resulting level of income individuals would enjoy if they were not working.

A supply function may be drawn for each labor market as illustrated in Fig. 1.1(a). The price of labor is represented by the real wage rate W/P (we ignore other pecuniary and non-pecuniary rewards), drawn on the vertical axis, and the quantity by the number of individuals who are willing to work, shown on the horizontal axis. Quantity supplied is shown to be a positive function of the wage rate.

The determinants of the supply of labor can also be specified in a more general functional form as in Eq. (1.1):

$$L^s = L^s(W/P, Y, \tau) \tag{1.1}$$

where labor supply, L^s, is shown to be a function of the real wage rate, W/P, as in Fig. 1.1 but also of non-labor income, Y, and tastes, τ. Changes in non-labor income and in individuals' tastes for leisure will shift the position of the supply curve in Fig. 1.1, while changes in the wage rate result in movements up and down the curve.

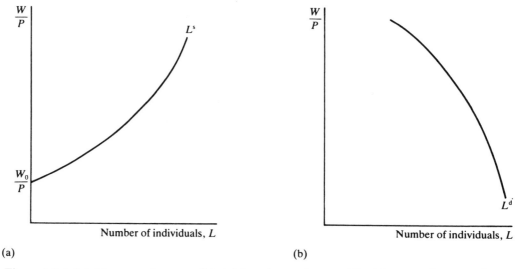

(a)   (b)

Figure 1.1 (a) A labor supply curve; (b) A labor demand curve. The labor supply curve drawn above informs us that the number of individuals willing to work increases as the real wage rises although no individuals are willing to work if the real wage falls below W_0/P. The labor demand curve indicates that as the real wage falls employers are willing to take on more workers. The reasons for this behavior on the part of buyers and sellers in the labor market will be explained more fully in later chapters

Labor demand

A labor demand curve representing the demand for labor by a single firm or number of firms can also be drawn. Buyers of labor require the services of labor not as an end in itself, but in order to produce commodities, that is, goods or services that are for sale or delivery in some product market. The demand for labor is therefore a derived demand, derived from the demand for the final commodity that labor produces and the price that the buyer of labor is willing to pay is related to the market value of an employee's output (the revenue that the firm obtains from selling the output of labor). Often a commodity can be produced by using a machine—capital—as an alternative to hiring the services of labor and thus the price that the buyer of labor is willing to pay is also affected by the price of substitute factors of production such as capital. A single firm may on occasion be the sole buyer of one type of labor service, it is then a monopsonist; on other occasions there may be numerous buyers and the demand for labor will be competitive.

Figure 1.1(b) illustrates the proposition that the demand for labor is inversely related to the price of labor and this can again be represented in a more general functional form as in Eq. (1.2):

$$L^d = L^d(W/P, K/P) \tag{1.2}$$

Where K/P is the real price of capital.

The downward slope of the labor demand curve reflects the arguments of marginal productivity theory. This theory, formalized by J.B. Clark,[4] proposed that as more of a variable factor is used in conjunction with a fixed factor of production—capital—the output of each successive unit of the variable factor will eventually diminish. Originally marginal productivity theory was offered as the theory of wages but Marshall emphasized that 'there is no valid ground for any such pretension. ... demand and supply exert coordinate influences on wages; neither has a claim to predominance; any more than has either blade of the scissors. ... Wages are governed by the whole set of causes which govern demand and supply.'[5]

Labor market equilibrium

The two blades of the scissors taken together illustrate the determination of equilibrium price and quantity. Such a point is given by the point of intersection of the labor supply and labor demand schedules as in Fig. 1.2. This results in an equilibrium real wage, W^*/P and level of employment L^* at which the amount of labor that sellers wish to supply is exactly equal to the amount of labor that is demanded. Unimpeded competitive forces will establish such an equilibrium. Thus if the real wage were initially set too low at W_0/P only L_0 workers would be willing to work although employers would demand L_1. Competition among employers for the available labor would lead them to bid up money wages and at an unchanged general level of prices,

---

4. Clark, J.B. (1900) *The Distribution of Wealth*, Macmillan, New York.
5. Marshall, A. (1890), *op. cit.*, pp. 42.

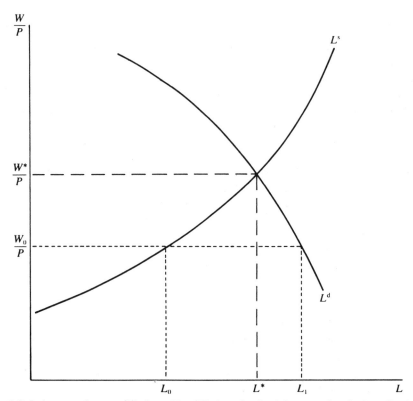

Figure 1.2 Labor market equilibrium. Equilibrium in the labor market is described by the point at which the labor supply and the labor demand curves intersect. $W*/P$ and $L*$ represent the equilibrium real wage and level of employment respectively. If the wage were initially established below this, at a level W_0/P, there would be an excess demand for labor, equal to $L_1 - L_0$. Competition among buyers of labor would then bid up the wage until it reached $W*/P$. Only at $W*/P$ and $L*$ is there no tendency for the wage and employment to change

P, this would result in a rise in real wages. The effect of the rising real wage rate would be both to reduce the excess demand for labor and to induce additional labor supply. Labor demand would fall back below L_1 and labor supply would rise above L_0. Equilibrium would thus be established as a result of employers cutting back their labor requirements in the face of rising wages and more individuals being attracted to work by the higher wages on offer. Only at $L*$, $W*/P$ is there no tendency for wages or employment to change: there is a position of equilibrium.

LABOR MARKET FLOWS

The equilibrium depicted above comprised a stock of individuals with jobs and when out of equilibrium a further stock of individuals who were involuntarily unemployed.

Lying behind these two was a further stock, the population of working age, and the positive slope to the labor supply function suggested that as the real wage rose an increasing proportion of this stock sought work. The size of each of these stocks differs substantially from country to country and they are in a constant state of flux. There are continuous flows of individuals between employment and unemployment and into and out of the labor force. In any one year in both the United Kingdom and the United States approximately one-quarter of all jobs change hands. Most individuals who leave one job take another immediately but some people have no job waiting, and either retire from the labor force or enter unemployment. Still other individuals join the labor force for the first time or re-enter after a period of absence.

For the most part analysts of the labor market rely on information that offers only a one-off snapshot or at best a series of snapshots of the state of the labor market at different points in time. The analysis therefore tends to focus on stocks rather than flows although a series of such snapshots helps us to build up a picture of such flows. Figures 1.3(a) and (b) present snapshots of the magnitude of the major labor market stocks (the employed, the unemployed, and the labor force) for the United States and the United Kingdom respectively in 1986, but also detail the major flows between each of these stocks in this year. Consider these figures in more detail.

In the United Kingdom and the United States all individuals aged 16 and over constitute the *population of working age*, although it is not uncommon to find this term used to describe only that part of the 16 and over population which has not reached retirement age. The size of the 16 and over population is increased by flows of immigrants and is diminished by deaths and migration from among its ranks. There is a considerable difference between the size of these populations in the two countries and the differences have grown more pronounced over the past 25 years. In 1960 the working age population numbered around 125 million in the United States, just over three times the size of that in the United Kingdom which stood at 40 million. By 1986 the population of working age had increased to almost 190 million in the United States but stood at 46 million in the United Kingdom. As a result the population of working age in the United States was by 1986 over four times as large as that in the United Kingdom.

The working age population of each country splits into those in the *labor force*, the *economically active*, and those not in the labor force. The three largest groups among the economically inactive comprise those retired from the labor force (predominantly the elderly), a significant proportion of married women whose work in the home goes unrecorded and those people, predominantly the young who are in full-time education. The labor force comprises all those with a job for which they receive some recorded payment (the employed), together with those looking for a job (the unemployed).

In any one year there will be a change in labor market status of a substantial proportion of the population of working age. Those leaving full-time education for the first time constitute the majority of *new entrants* to the labor force. Alongside these new entrants there will be many *re-entrants* among whom married women, returning to the labor market after a temporary absence, perhaps due to childbearing, are most

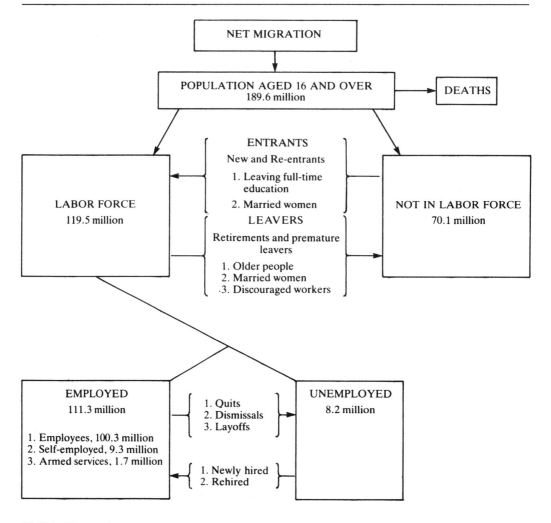

(a) United States of America

Figure 1.3 Labor market flows in (a) the United States of America and (b) the United Kingdom in 1986

prominent. Again there will be some returning after a temporary absence due to further education or retraining. There are also large flows in the other direction reflecting similar arguments to those above. Retirement figures prominently among those leaving the labor force but there will also be premature leavers, predominantly married women who leave to have children or perform other forms of non-market work and

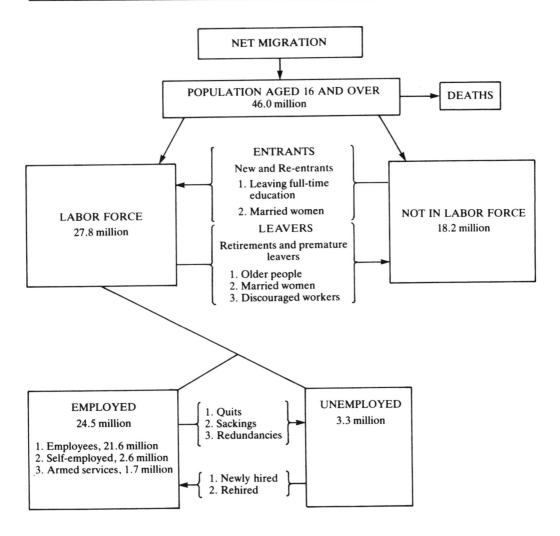

(b) United Kingdom

individuals of both sexes who either re-enter full-time education or drop out of the labor force because they cannot find work. These latter are referred to as *discouraged workers*.

Within the labor force there is constant turnover as workers voluntarily leave one job—before entering another: these are called *quits*. Some of these quits will experience an intervening period of unemployment. Quits are one of the routes by which people enter unemployment. However, a much more significant route in the United Kingdom during the 1980s was involuntary job loss due to redundancy (permanent layoff). In the United States workers are frequently laid off for temporary periods, *laid off awaiting recall*,[6] and hence recalls account for a large part of the flow out of unemployment into employment. In the United States it is accordingly necessary to distinguish between temporary and permanent layoffs; for the latter there is no job to return to, employment has been terminated. In the United Kingdom there is no system of temporary layoffs, and therefore the distinction between temporary and permanent layoffs or redundancies is seldom made.

LABOR MARKET DEVELOPMENTS IN SELECTED INDUSTRIALIZED NATIONS

Equilibrium wages and employment are constantly changing. Take the quarter of a century after 1960. Over the period from 1960 to 1985 there was a rise in real wages and employment in almost all countries. What is most striking about the experience of these 25 years is the differences between the new and the old 'equilibrium' prices and quantities in different countries. We can use the simple analytical framework we detailed above to cast light on differences in the rates of growth of pay and employment in a sample of major industrialized countries, over this period.

Real and money wages

First consider the changes in real wage rates that have occurred over the period 1960–85. These are detailed in Table 1.1. The most striking thing about the general advance in wages over the 25 years shown is the difference between the experience of the countries. In the United States money wages in 1985 were three times higher than they were in 1960; in Germany they were five times higher; in Australia seven times higher; while in Japan and the United Kingdom they were respectively ten and eleven times higher than in 1960. The rate of change of wages was highest during the 1970s and early 1980s but since 1982 the rate has dropped substantially below that of the 1970s.

In all countries the change in money wages, W, has evidently been accompanied by a change in prices, P, in the same direction, for the change in real wages, W/P, over the same period is dramatically less. Nevertheless real wages have more than doubled in Germany and Japan, and increased by in excess of 66 percent in Australia and the United Kingdom. In stark contrast they increased by a mere 13 percent in the United States over this 25-year period!

Why have real wages advanced so little in the United States and so rapidly in Germany and Japan? The analytical framework we developed above suggests

6. Topel, R.H. (1982) 'Inventories, layoffs and the short-run demand for labor', *American Economic Review*, **72**, 769–87, suggests that temporary layoffs account for almost one-half of all employer initiated layoffs in the United States. Feldstein, M.S. (1975) 'The importance of temporary layoffs: an empirical analysis', *Brookings Papers on Economic Activity*, **13**, 725–45 and Lilien, D. (1980) 'The cyclical importance of temporary layoffs, *Review of Economics and Statistics*, **62**, 24–31, suggest about two-thirds of all layoffs in US manufacturing were temporary in that workers subsequently returned to their original employers.

Table 1.1 The growth of pay: 1960–85 (% per annum)

	United States		Australia		Germany		United Kingdom		Japan	
	Money	Real	Money	Real	Money	Real	Money	Real	Money	Real
1960–67[†]	3.3	1.6	3.2	1.0	8.4	5.5	5.2	1.7	9.3	3.5
1968–73	6.6	1.7	9.7	4.7	9.9	5.3	10.9	3.8	15.0	8.5
1974–78	7.0	– 1.0	13.7	0.5	7.6	2.9	16.9	0.7	14.1	2.3
1979–82	8.2	– 1.9	13.0	3.0	5.3	0.0	14.8	2.0	5.5	0.7
1983–85	4.8	1.3	7.7	1.1	3.0	0.4	7.6	2.4	3.9	1.8
Total percentage increase 1960–85	307.5	13.2	740.9	68.4	500.5	131.5	1153.1	69.4	1058.3	152.3

Sources: OECD *Economic Surveys* for each country, various issues and OECD *Main Economic Indicators*, 1960–75, OECD, Paris.

Earnings series:
United States   Wages and salaries per person.
United Kingdom   Average earnings all employees monthly series.
Australia   Average weekly earnings. From 1983 onwards, average weekly earnings all employees.
Germany   Gross wages and salaries per employee.
Japan   Total cash earnings.

[†] Prior to 1968 these are earnings in manufacturing industries only.

that changes in the relative magnitudes of labor supply and demand provide the explanation. Thus a rise in wages will result from any increase in labor demand that outstrips the growth of labor supply, for such a development will have the effect of tightening the market. Under these circumstances *both* wages and employment will increase. The market will also tighten, and wages rise, where there is a reduction in labor demand which is exceeded by a reduction in labor supply, but note under these circumstances the rise in wages will be accompanied by a fall in employment. The changes in employment that have occurred in each of the above countries are reported in Table 1.2.

Changes in employment

Over the quarter of a century from 1960 employment has increased by over 60 percent in the United States and Australia and by 30 percent in Japan. Among the European nations represented here, employment growth has been negligible, less than 2 percent in the United Kingdom while employment actually fell in Germany. In the United States alone more jobs were created over this period (over 40 million) than were created in the whole of Western Europe!

Table 1.2 Employment growth: 1960–85

	Total (millions)			Percentage change		
	1960	1974	1985	1960–74	1974–85	1960–85
United States	67.64	88.52	108.90	30.9	23.0	61.0
Australia	4.16	5.96	6.75	43.3	13.3	62.3
Germany	26.25	26.57	25.54	1.2	– 3.9	– 2.7
United Kingdom	24.18	25.13	24.62	3.9	– 2.0	1.8
Japan	44.36	52.37	58.07	18.1	10.7	30.9

Sources: OECD, *Labour Force Statistics*, Table 4, OECD, Paris.

The magnitude of the rise in employment and the accompanying much more modest rise in real wages suggests that both labor supply and labor demand have risen substantially in the United States but that the increase in labor demand barely exceeded the increase in labor supply. Again, in both Australia and Japan there must also have been a sharp rise in labor supply for employment increased sharply but in both these countries this must have been accompanied by a relatively greater rise in labor demand than occurred in the United States, for both real wages and employment rose sharply in these countries. There was in contrast little employment growth in the United Kingdom although a not inconsiderable rise in real wages. While there appears to have been a modest rise in labor supply therefore this would seem to have been accompanied by a more substantial rise in labor demand. Finally, employment in Germany fell while real wages rose sharply. Labor demand therefore appears to have risen substantially but here it appears that labor supply might actually have declined.

These outcomes can be depicted in a series of supply and demand diagrams. In order to do this it is generally necessary to know whether we are to depict any increase in labor supply as a movement along a curve or a shift in a curve, for an increase in labor supply can be depicted in both these ways. Take the case of the United Kingdom. Does the increase in employment from approximately 24 million in 1960 to 24.5 million in 1985 reflect a rise in the number of people who would have been willing to work even if there had been no rise in real wages; or does it reflect the fact that only the rise in real wages induced more people to work? The former would be depicted as an outward shift in the labor supply curve while the latter constitutes a movement up a single supply curve. For the moment we shall suppress this distinction and depict these changes in terms of a single long-run labor supply curve for each country.

Depicting the changed equilibrium

Developments in each of these countries can be summarized in a series of supply and demand diagrams. Changes on the supply side can be depicted in terms of the long-run labor supply curves and developments on the demand side by shifts in the labor demand curve against this. Thus we have seen that while Australia and the United

States enjoyed similarly sized increases in employment, the rise in real wages was much more substantial in Australia than in the United States. In Australia the rise in labor demand must therefore have exceeded the rise in labor supply by a much more substantial margin than in the United States. The magnitude of the rise in wages that accompanied the rise in employment in Australia suggests that the long-run labor supply curve is substantially shallower (more elastic) in the United States than in Australia. Figures 1.4(a) and (b) depict the position in the United States and Australia. The labor supply curve in Japan would in turn appear to be more steeply sloped than that of Australia for Japan enjoyed the largest rise in real wages of any country and, although not insubstantial, a more modest rise in employment than Australia. The long-run supply curve suggested by these developments is depicted in Fig. 1.4(c). There was little employment growth in the United Kingdom over this period although real wages rose by a comparable magnitude to those in Australia. The absence of employment growth in the United Kingdom suggests that over this period the long-run labor supply curve was almost vertical as Fig. 1.4(d) illustrates. Finally, Germany enjoyed the second largest rise in real wages but this was accompanied by a reduction in employment. In Germany the long-run labor supply curve is therefore depicted as backward sloping in Fig. 1.4(e).

The above analysis is of course premised on the assumption that the labor market in each of these countries was in equilibrium at the start and at the end of the period shown and that the long-run labor supply curves and labor demand curves intersect. As we shall see in later chapters there are reasons to doubt the appropriateness of this assumption to some of these countries, for some were experiencing large-scale and involuntary unemployment by the mid-1980s. In Germany in particular the conclusion that the long-run labor supply was backward sloping should be treated with caution. More probably it was similar to that of the United Kingdom, very steeply sloped if not vertical. Yet having cautioned interpretation, striking differences are still apparent. The long-run labor supply curve appears most elastic in the United States and least elastic in the Western European countries shown while Japan and Australia fall in between these two extremes, with the supply curve in Australia relatively more elastic than in Japan.

Changes in labor supply

The long-run changes in labor supply depicted above can result from either a change in the number of people of working age or a change in the proportion of individuals of working age wishing to work or both these reasons. So consider each of these dimensions in more detail. Table 1.3 details the number of individuals of working age in each of the five countries since 1960. Evidently the United States has by far and away the largest population of working age. It is almost twice as large as that of Japan, the next largest, and over three times as large as that in Germany and the United Kingdom. Moreover, the population of working age in the United States has expanded by over 50 percent since 1960, although in this respect it is not alone for in Australia

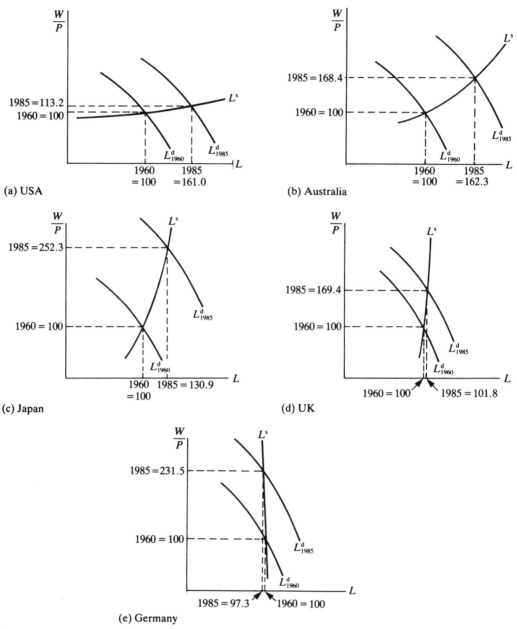

Figure 1.4 A graphical illustration of labor market developments in selected OECD countries over the period 1960 to 1985. (a) USA: The growth in real labor demand in the USA in the 25 years to 1985 was almost wholly channeled into the creation of more jobs; (b) Australia: In Australia the growth in real labor demand led to a substantial rise in both employment and real wages; (c) Japan: The relatively inelastic nature of labor supply in Japan meant that while employment grew by 30 percent, the majority of the growth in real labor demand in this country went into higher real wages; (d) UK: The modest growth in real labor demand was channeled almost wholly into a growth in real wages. Labor supply appears to be highly inelastic; (e) Germany: The whole of the substantial growth in real labor demand has been channeled into higher real wages. Unlike the other four countries employment actually fell over the quarter century to 1985

18

Table 1.3 Size of the population of working age[†]: 1960–85

	Total (millions)			(Percentage change)		
	1960	1974	1985	1960–74	1974–85	1960–85
United States	124.6	158.7	187.4	27.4	18.1	50.4
Australia	7.8[‡]	9.8	12.1	25.6	23.5	55.1
Germany	43.6	48.4	51.8	11.0	7.0	18.8
United Kingdom	40.3	42.9	45.7	6.5	6.5	13.4
Japan	65.2	83.4	94.6	27.9	13.4	45.1

Source: OECD, *Labor Force Statistics*, Country Tables, OECD, Paris.
[†] Population aged 15 and over.
[‡] 1964.

the population of working age has grown by 55 percent and in Japan by 45 percent. In this respect there emerges a clear distinction between the experience of the two European countries and that of the United States, Australia and Japan. In the latter countries the population of working age has expanded by around 50 percent in each case while in the two European nations it has grown by less than 20 percent.

There are two principal reasons for this rapid expansion in the United States, Australia and Japan. In the United States and Australia there has been substantial in-migration and, as we shall see later, this in-migration has been concentrated among individuals of working age. In the case of Japan and again the United States there was a higher birth rate than in other countries in the immediate post-war years and this was reflected in an expansion of the population of working age in the early 1960s.

These increases in the numbers of people of working age represent only an increase in *potential labor supply*, for some from among these may not wish to work. The size of the labor supply depends on both the size of the population of working age and the proportion of that population who choose to join the labor force. The *participation rate*, *PR*, expresses the number of individuals who choose to join the labor force, *LF*, as a proportion of the total population of working age, *PW*, in any particular period. At time t the participation rate, $PR_t = (LF_t/PW_t) \times 100$.[7] The participation rates for each country are detailed in Table 1.4 and relate to the entire population beyond secondary school leaving age. They reveal that at the outset of the period the rates were lowest in the United States and Australia but that over the period to 1985 they have grown in both these countries while they have fallen in Germany, Japan and for a period in the United Kingdom. The reduction in participation rates has been most

7. A rise in the participation rate can be depicted as either a shift in the labor supply curve or a movement up the curve. Thus a positive change in tastes for work shifts the labor supply curve to the right, while if more people want to work due to higher wage rates this is represented by a movement up the labor supply curve. Note that an increase in the population of working age at unchanged participation rates results in a shift in the labor supply curve.

Table 1.4 Participation rates[†]

	Percentage rate			Change over period		
	1960	1974	1985	1960–74	1974–85	1960–85
United States	57.9	59.3	62.8	1.4	4.0	5.4
Australia	59.0[‡]	61.8	60.5	2.8	– 1.3	1.5
Germany	60.8	56.1	53.8	– 4.7	– 2.3	– 7.0
United Kingdom	62.2	59.9	60.4	– 2.3	0.5	– 1.8
Japan	69.2	63.7	63.0	– 5.5	– 0.7	– 6.2

Source: OECD, *Labor Force Statistics*, Country Tables, OECD, Paris.
[†] Labor force as a proportion of the population aged 15 and over.
[‡] 1964.

marked among those aged over 65; indeed this has been a feature common to all countries shown. In the United States and Australia the rise in participation among those aged between 16 and 65 has more than offset the fall among the older age group, this has not happened in Germany and Japan. Indeed in both these countries participation rates are also falling among those aged between 16 and 65. In Germany little over half the population aged 16 and over are now in the labor force, a figure some six percentage points below the next lowest—the United Kingdom.

The rise in the size of the population of working age accounts for the major part of the substantial growth in labor supply in the United States, Australia and Japan. In the case of the United States and Australia, the contribution to the growth in labor supply of the rise in the working age population exceeded the contribution resulting from the rise in participation rates. In the case of Japan the rise in the working age population offset the consequences of the fall in the participation rate for this would otherwise have resulted in a substantial reduction in the labor supply. Again, in the United Kingdom labor supply grew only because the modest increase in the size of the working population offset the effects of the fall in participation rates. In Germany, however, the

Table 1.5 Labor productivity growth (Real GDP per person employed in % per annum)

	United States	Australia	Germany	United Kingdom	Japan
1960–68	2.6	2.7	4.2	2.7	8.8
1968–73	1.0	2.3	4.1	3.0	7.3
1973–79	0.0	1.7	2.9	1.3	2.9
1979–85	1.1	1.4	1.6	1.8	3.0
1960–85	1.3	2.1	3.2	2.2	5.6
Total increase	38.1	68.1	119.8	72.3	290.5

Sources: OECD, *Historical Statistics*, Table 3.7.

Table 1.6 Real growth in labor demand 1960–85 (Index values, 1960 = 100)

	Real wage growth (1)	Employment growth (2)	Real growth in labor demand $(1) \times (2) \div 100$
United States	113.2	161.0	182.3
Australia	168.4	162.3	273.3
Germany	231.5	97.3	225.2
United Kingdom	169.4	101.8	172.4
Japan	252.3	130.9	330.3

Source: Tables 1.1 and 1.2.

fall in participation rates may have been of a sufficient order of magnitude to offset the rise in the population of working age.

Changes in labor demand

Substantial increases in labor demand were required to accommodate the increases in labor supply we have seen above. What was the magnitude of the outward shifts in the labor demand schedule in each of the countries shown? One element of the growth in labor demand is labor productivity, output per unit of labor employed. An increase in the amount of output each person produces will result in an outward shift in the labor demand schedule and, at unchanged wage rates, will result in more people being employed.

It is evident from Table 1.5 that the rate of productivity growth has varied substantially across the five nations. It has grown most in Japan and least in the United States. Indeed the total increase in productivity in Japan is over seven times as large as in the United States. The United Kingdom and Australia, after the United States, are the next poorest performers. The rate of productivity growth in Germany is approaching double that of Australia and the United Kingdom, but is still less than half that of Japan.

However, as we have seen from Tables 1.1 and 1.2, in the majority of the five countries both real wages and employment rose. The growth in productivity has therefore facilitated an increase in both real wages and employment. Indeed in two of the countries, Australia and the United States, the growth in both wages and employment when taken together has substantially exceeded the growth in labor productivity. A measure of the growth in real labor demand can be obtained by taking the product of an index of the values for real wage growth, reported in the final row of Table 1.1, and an index of the values for employment growth derived from the figures in the final column of Table 1.2. Thus in the United States the growth in real labor demand was sufficient to support a rise in real wages of 13.2 percent over the period 1960 to 1985 (to a new index value of 113.2 in 1985) and a rise in employment of 61.0 percent (to a new index value of 161). The product of these two indexes [(113.2 × 161.0)/100 = 182.3] results in a third index measuring the change in real labor demand over the period. This indicates that the real growth in labor demand over these 25 years was 82.3 percent. Similar calculations for the remaining countries result in the values reported in Table 1.6.

The results emphasize the striking differences in the experience of the five countries. Thus the real growth in labor demand in the United Kingdom was only slightly less than in the United States. But while in the latter this growth largely went into creating extra jobs, in the United Kingdom it was almost wholly channeled into extra pay. We have seen that in part this was because the extra workers were more readily available to the United States: (a) as a result of the growth in US population; and (b) as a consequence of US willingness to admit more immigrants—factors we shall study in greater detail in Chapter 5. In the United Kingdom large wage rises captured almost completely the gains from the real growth in labor demand. Similarly Germany seems to have chosen real wage growth as opposed to employment growth and even in Japan the major part of the growth in labor demand has been translated into real wage rises.

Only in Australia and the United States was a large part of the real growth in labor demand translated into creating extra jobs. But it was only in the United States that a majority of the growth in labor demand was channeled into new jobs. What are the factors that account for this split between pay and employment growth? What is so different about the labor markets in each of these countries that has led to these strikingly different outcomes? These are issues which the techniques of labor market analysis to be developed in the following chapters will enable us to explain.

SUMMARY

It is evident from the above that labor supply and demand curves provide useful summary statements of the many factors determining employment and wage outcomes. Depicting these many and complicated factors in a concise graphical form affords us illuminating insights into the processes at work. Yet it is equally evident that our simple propositions about the shape of these curves and our unstated assumptions about the existence of labor market equilibria are unlikely always to hold. Certainly during the 1980s substantial departures from equilibrium seemed to occur for in many countries there appeared to be a large rise in involuntary unemployment. The more exact specification of the nature of the labor supply and demand curves in many contexts in which they are employed is one of the two major tasks of the rest of this book. Evaluating the explanations of developments in the labor markets of a number of the major Western industrialized nations, which are offered by this analytical framework, is the other task.

PRINCIPAL CONCEPTS

In this chapter we have introduced the following terms and concepts, students should make sure that they understand each of them before proceeding:

1. The population of working age.
2. The labor force.
3. The economically active population.
4. New entrants and re-entrants to the labor market.
5. Discouraged workers.
6. Quits and layoffs.
7. A labor supply function.
8. A labor demand function.
9. Labor market equilibrium.
10. The participation rate.

QUESTIONS FOR DISCUSSION

1. Distinguish those changes in labor market conditions that lead to shifts in, as distinct from movements along, the labor supply curve.
2. Distinguish changes that result in shifts in, rather than movements along, the labor demand curve.
3. Starting from an initial position of equilibrium show diagrammatically the various combinations of shifts in labor supply and demand curves that produce increases in both employment and real wages.
4. In what manner do changes in labor force participation rates affect the labor supply curve?
5. Discuss the possible reasons why the increases in real labor demand have been split between employment and real wage growth in the manner shown in the five countries covered in this chapter.

FURTHER READING

The most useful and concise source of statistics on labor market developments in the countries discussed here is produced by the OECD in its annual publication *Employment Outlook*. This presents standardized statistical series for each OECD country. In addition, the OECD produces an *Economic Survey* for each member country which often contains a useful commentary on labor market developments in that country. The principal source of information on the labor market in the United Kingdom is contained in the monthly *Employment Gazette* produced by the Department of Employment and available from HMSO, London. The comparable publication in the United States is the *Monthly Labor Review*, produced by the US Department of Labor, Bureau of Labor Statistics, Washington. Both these publications report all the main statistical series available for the labor market and contain articles that comment on recent labor market developments.

LABOR SUPPLY

What is labor supply, how do we measure it and what determines the manner in which it changes through time? These are the questions we set out to answer in Part 2 of this book.

Labor supply is the term used to describe the human input into the production process; it is the term used to describe the supply of that factor of production which results from the activity of individuals. Labor supply can be measured in a number of ways, but is most commonly measured either at the individual level in terms of the number of hours an individual is willing to work, or in terms of the number of individuals willing to work. It can also be measured in terms of efficiency units, for none of the first two measures takes account of the quality of the supply, that is how intensively or effectively individuals are willing to work. This last measure is rather more abstract and requires us to develop a uniform measure of the efficiency of each hour of work supplied by each individual. Evidently it is difficult to operationalize and in our discussion of labor supply we tend to focus on the first two.

What determines the magnitude of each dimension of labor supply? The number of individuals willing to work is a function of both the size of the population of working age and the proportion of this population that is willing to work. The size of the population of working age is, in turn, determined by demographic factors and migration—both long-run considerations. The number of hours each individual is willing to work is determined by a complex set of social and economic factors. The quality of the labor supply is a function of the skills and abilities and the attitudes and motivation of individual members of the working population. We shall distinguish and focus on the most important of each of these.

For analytical purposes economists distinguish between the long and the short run. In the context of labor supply the short run is the period in which the size of the population of working age and the skills they possess are held constant and the long run is the period over which these are allowed to vary. In the first chapter in Part 2 of the book, we shall look at the labor market opportunities that confront the individual in the short run and at how an individual's labor supply changes as these opportunities change. In Chapter 3 we shall analyze the way in which tax and welfare benefit policies restrict or expand the opportunities available to individuals and at the probable labor supply responses that changes in these will induce. Chapter 4 considers the empirical evidence on labor supply revealing how labor supply has changed in recent years and how well the simple theory developed in the previous two chapters explains these changes. In Chapters 5 and 6 we move on to the long run. In Chapter 5, we look at the population of working age and at the role of economic analysis in understanding the determinants of changes in this. In Chapter 6 we consider the quality of the labor force. We analyze the process of investment in education and training and the incentives for individuals and firms to undertake such investment.

In the last decade economists have increasingly focused on the supply side of the economy. In trying to explain why the generation of wealth and the growth in income have been more rapid in some countries than in others, they have focused on the constraints that exist to productive and enterprising activity on the part of economic agents. They have sought to explain the differential economic performance of nations by the different restrictions that societies have placed on the productive performance of their populations. Labor input represents the most important part of the supply side of the modern economy. In the following chapters we therefore develop an understanding of the single most important market in the modern economy. In so doing, we enhace our understanding of the wider question of the determinants of the relative growth and prosperity of nations.

THE SHORT-RUN THEORY OF LABOR SUPPLY

In this chapter we are concerned with the basic theory of labor supply in the short run. A simple model will be developed to illustrate the determinants of an individual's decision to work and of the total number of hours supplied. Subsequently we shall aggregate across all individuals in order to distinguish the total supply of labor in the short run.

The theory builds on the everyday maxim that individuals do the best they can under the circumstances! Stated more formally this amounts to the proposition that individuals maximize their utility subject to the constraints that confront them in the labor market. We therefore need to know something about an individual's preferences (what it is that gives him or her satisfaction or utility) and to distinguish the opportunities for realizing them that exist in the labor market. We shall argue that individuals derive utility from the consumption of commodities and that in order to buy these commodities they have to obtain an income. Undertaking paid work is one of the ways of obtaining an income but the size of this income is limited by the opportunities that confront the individual in the labor market. In the following pages we build from the position of a single individual to that of all the individuals who populate a particular labor market. The simple model of individual behavior we construct assumes that individuals work in order to be able to buy commodities. It also assumes that as a result of their work individuals obtain the commodities they want to buy; it is as if they were operating in a barter economy swapping their labor directly for commodities. The act of offering to supply labor therefore constitutes a simultaneous demand for commodities and, accordingly, there ought to be no deficiency of aggregate demand in such a world. In practice, however, in a monetary economy individuals work for money and only later do they translate this money into a demand for commodities. In some of the last chapters of this book we shall encounter models that explore some of the macroeconomic consequences of these features of a monetary economy and in the next chapter we shall discuss the consequences for labor supply when individuals are unable to translate their income into commodities. First we provide a more formal statement of and derive a way of illustrating, the individual's decision of hours of work.

THE DECISION TO WORK

The decision to work and consequent upon working how many hours to work are inseparably linked and in the following analysis we shall therefore consider these issues together. Whether or not individuals work and for how long they work depend on their preferences and the opportunities that confront them in the labor market. Consider each of these in turn.

An individual's preferences

An individual's preferences can be summarized in terms of:

1. The *objects of choice*, the commodities from which they derive satisfaction.
2. The *marginal rate of substitution*, which indicates the relative intensity of the satisfactions.

Commodities, understood in the widest possible sense, are the objects of individuals' choices. Commodities may take the generally recognized form of goods—tangible commodities such as compact disc players or a bottle of 1979 Chambertin—or they may be intangible commodities—such as courteous service on the airline or attendance at a performance of a Schubert string quartet. They may be commodities that are traded in formal markets and therefore have an explicit price or they may have only implicit prices. An example of this latter would be the price we pay for certain forms of leisure such as relaxing in the hot tub, sunbathing or sleeping late. Commodities are those things that ultimately enhance, or detract from, an individual's satisfaction.

Some commodities will be more desired than others. One way of stating the intensity of our preferences for particular commodities is to state the rate at which we are willing to swap, to trade off or substitute, one commodity for another. The more of one commodity we are willing to give up in order to secure an extra unit of another commodity the more highly we prefer the latter commodity. Identifying both the objects of choice and the rate at which an individual is willing to trade off one against another, enables us to represent an individual's preferences, diagrammatically. Consider both of these aspects further.

The objects of choice What are the objects of choice? In the simple theory we develop here they are assumed to be goods and services, G, and leisure, L. Formally we can construct a utility function:

$$U = U(G,L) \tag{2.1}$$

G, is used to describe all the tangible and intangible commodities available to the individual, with the single exception of time. The amount of goods and services we consume also constitutes a measure of our real income, and hence the term real income, I, is often used interchangeably with that of the volume of goods and services, $G = I$. We adopt the approach of aggregating all commodities into a single *composite commodity*. It is of course an extreme simplification, for a complex array of goods and services confronts most individuals. However, it has been shown by Hicks (1946) that it makes no difference to our subsequent analysis, how many different commodities there are within the composite provided their relative prices do not change.[1]

L, is used to describe all hours not spent working. At this stage in our analysis it is the generic title for hours spent relaxing as well as hours spent either doing unpaid work (termed *non-market work*) or studying or training which we shall later describe as hours devoted to human capital investment. Again, and for purposes of analytical convenience, it is a considerable simplification of a complex reality.

The objects of choice (G and L) are mapped along the vertical and horizontal axes respectively in each of Figs. 2.1(a), (b) and (c) and we represent the individual's preferences for G and L in a family of indifference curves in this G,L space. Each indifference curve details all those combinations of G and L which produce the same level of utility and between which an individual is therefore indifferent. Higher indifference curves, curves lying to the north-east, represent higher levels of utility, that is $U_3 > U_2 > U_1$. They are assumed to display the usual properties of smoothness, convexity with respect to the origin and transitivity—this latter property means that they cannot cross. In Fig. 2.1 we represent the preferences of three different individuals. Evidently the indifference curves have quite different slopes in each case, so what sort of statement are we making about each individual's preferences?

The marginal rate of substitution Consider the slope of an indifference curve. First note that the marginal utility of leisure, MU_L, is the rate of change of utility with respect to a unit change in L, when all other independent influences on utility are held constant. It is therefore the partial derivative of U with respect to L, $MU_L = \partial U/\partial L$. Similarly, the marginal utility associated with the consumption of goods and services, MU_G, is the rate of change of utility with respect to a unit change in the consumption of goods and services when all other independent influences on utility are held constant, $MU_G = \partial U/\partial G$. What then does the slope of the indifference curve represent? Suppose that at point Y in Fig. 2.1 there is a small change in G, the magnitude of the change is measured by dG and the magnitude of the associated change in L is given

1. Hicks, J.R. (1946) *Value and Capital*, 2nd edn, Oxford University Press, Oxford, pp. 312–13.

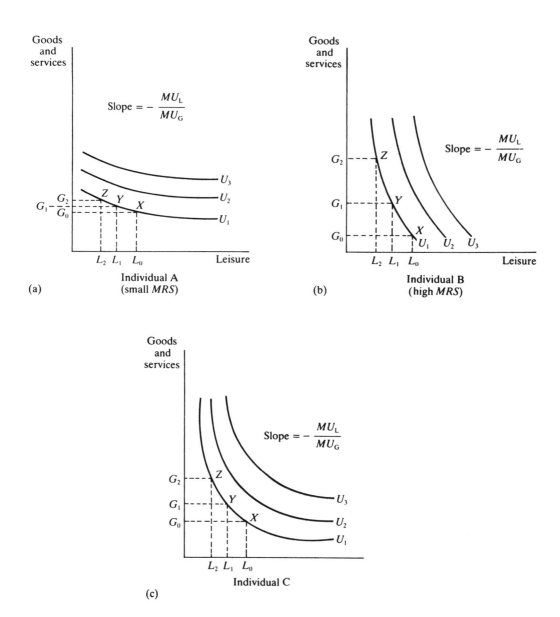

Figure 2.1 Individual preferences for goods and services and leisure. (a), (b) The indifference maps indicate that individual A has a marked preference for goods and services, while at the other extreme individual B has a strong preference for leisure. Individual A has a low *MRS*, a low rate at which he or she is willing to substitute goods and services, *G*, for leisure, *L*, while individual B has a high *MRS* and is willing to forgo a lot of *G* in order to obtain a little more *L*; (c) Individual C falls in between these two extremes

by dL. Then the total change in utility, dU resulting from these changes in G and L is represented by:

$$dU = dG \left(\frac{\partial U}{\partial G} \right) + dL \left(\frac{\partial U}{\partial L} \right) \tag{2.2}$$

The total change in utility is found by taking the total derivative of Eq. (2.1). Now of course a single indifference curve represents a constant level of U so that dU = 0, that is:

$$dU = dG \left(\frac{\partial U}{\partial G} \right) + dL \left(\frac{\partial U}{\partial L} \right) = 0 \tag{2.3}$$

by rearranging (2.3) above we find that:

$$\frac{dG}{dL} = - \left(\frac{\partial U/\partial L}{\partial U/\partial G} \right) = - \frac{MU_L}{MU_G} \tag{2.4}$$

Now the slope of the indifference curve is given by the ratio of the change in the consumption of goods and services to the change in leisure, that is dG/dL, so that it follows from the above that the slope of the indifference curve is equal to the negative of the ratio of the marginal utility of leisure to the marginal utility of consumption of goods and services. The negative, in turn, of this ratio (we add a negative to make MU_L/MU_G positive) is called the *marginal rate of substitution, MRS.*[2] The marginal rate of substitution reflects the rate at which the individual is willing to trade off goods and services for leisure in order to sustain a particular level of utility. The higher the *MRS* the more goods and services are required to substitute for a unit change in leisure.

It is evident that the assumption of convexity implies that the *MRS* changes as we move along an indifference curve. As we reduce L by equal amounts, moving from L_0 to L_1 to L_2 in each of the three parts of Fig. 2.1 we move from point X to point Y and from Y to Z. In all three cases the increase in G as we move from Y to Z is larger than that associated with the move from X to Y. The less we have of L the more we value it, that is the larger the increment to G we require to compensate for any reduction in L and still leave the individual no worse off than before. Reciprocally the more we have of L the less we value an additional increment. The assumption of convexity implies that both L and G display *diminishing marginal utility.*

Evidently the marginal rate of substitution of leisure for goods differs considerably between the three individuals shown in Fig. 2.1. Individual A exhibits the smallest *MRS*, demands a smaller increase in G, to compensate for any reduction in L than

---

2. This is sometimes qualified by the addition of the phrase 'in consumption' to distinguish it unambiguously from the marginal rate of substitution in production, otherwise known as the marginal rate of technical substitution. However, conventional usage employs the marginal rate of substitution to describe its use here while the marginal rate of technical substitution is used to distinguish the marginal rate of substitution in production. We shall stick with this convention.

does either individual B or C. Looked at another way, individual A is willing to give up a much smaller amount of goods and services to obtain an additional unit of leisure than is either individual B or C. Individual A has a strong preference for goods and services. On the other hand, individual B has a very high *MRS* and demands a very large increment to goods before he or she will sacrifice any leisure. Conversely, individual B is willing to give up a large amount of goods and services to obtain an additional unit of leisure. Individual B can be said to display a strong preference for leisure. Individual C falls midway between these two extremes.

An indifference map represents a statement about an individual's preferences but what of the constraints that confront the individual in the market place?

Constraints

The real income that individuals have at their disposal imposes a constraint on their choice. In the simple model considered here an individual's expenditure on goods and services cannot exceed his or her real income, I, that is $G \leq I$. How many of the objects of choice a given real income can purchase is determined by the price of these objects, which in our simple model means the price of goods and services, *and* the price of leisure.

What determines the size of an individual's real income? The total real income the individual has at his or her disposal comprises first unearned income, Y_u/P, perhaps resulting from the yield on wealth or from transfer payments made by government, and second income from work. This latter is the product of the real hourly wage rate, W/P, and the number of hours devoted to work, H. Thus total real income, I, is given by total nominal income $(Y_u + WH)$ deflated by the price of goods and services, P:

$$I = (Y_u + WH)/P \tag{2.5}$$

The constraints on individuals' choices are therefore their real unearned income, the real hourly wage rate they can earn when working and any constraint on the number of hours they are able to work. Consider this last aspect further. The amount of time individuals have at their disposal in a particular period is limited—limited to the number of hours in the day, days in the week, weeks in the year, etc. If we call this total, T, then H cannot exceed T, that is, $H \leq T$. It also follows that:

$$H = T - L \tag{2.6}$$

Thus T in conjunction with P, Y_u and W determine the size of the real income, I, an individual can attain. They determine the budget constraints confronting the individual which can now be found by substituting Eq. (2.6) into Eq. (2.5) which if $G = I$ gives:

$$G = [Y_u + W(T - L)]/P \tag{2.7}$$

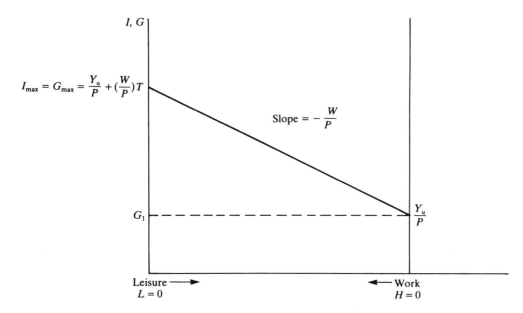

Figure 2.2 Constraints influencing an individual's labor supply. The constraints on an individual's choice are real unearned income, Y_u/P, the real hourly wage rate, W/P, and the number of hours available to work H. These give rise to the budget constraint of slope $-W/P$. Full income, I_{max}, is where all hours available are worked

The equality reflects the assumption that individuals purchase the maximum amount of goods and services permitted by their income.[3]

It follows from Eq. (2.6) that an hour more devoted to leisure is an hour less worked, and accordingly an hour's less pay. The opportunity cost, the price, of an hour of leisure is the hourly wage rate that is forgone by taking an extra hour's leisure. Therefore W represents the price of a unit of leisure while P represents the price of goods and services.

Now consider a diagrammatic representation of the budget constraint confronting the individual as in Fig. 2.2. The horizontal axis is the same as in Fig. 2.1, as we move from left to right we enjoy increasing amounts of leisure. However, the amount

3. Under the assumption that the individual consumes the maximum amount attainable, Eq. (2.7) can be manipulated to show the composition of the individual expenditures. An individual's full income [the income attained if all hours available were worked, and shown by $(Y_u + WT)/P$] is spent on either goods and services, or leisure. That is

$$G + \frac{W}{P}L = \frac{Y_u}{P} + \frac{W}{P}T \tag{2.7a}$$

In Eq. (2.7a) the right-hand side indicates the sources of real income while the left-hand side represents the pattern of expenditures. In this example the individual purchases, L, amount of leisure, at price, W/P, and G, amount of goods and services. Expressing this relation as an equality can be interpreted as making the simplifying assumption that the individual does not save.

of leisure time available is now bounded by T, the time constraint. If all the time at our disposal is taken as leisure, then $T = L$, and $H = 0$, and the only source of income is unearned income Y_u/P. Y_u/P therefore represents the intercept on the vertical axis above point $H = 0$ and with Y_u/P the individual can only purchase goods and services equal to G_1. At the other extreme if all the time is devoted to work, then $T = H$; and $L = 0$ and maximum income $[Y_u/P + H(W/P) = Y_u/P + T(W/P)]$ is obtained. This gives the intercept above point $L = 0$. This level of real income has been termed *full income*[4] for it is the maximum attainable if individuals, rather unrealistically, worked every hour at their disposal. In turn this would enable them to buy goods and services, equal to G_{max}.

The line joining G_{max} and Y_u/P represents the boundary of the feasible set of opportunities confronting the individual; it represents the budget constraint confronting the individual.[5] This budget constraint is frequently known as the *wage ray* and it is shallower the lower is the wage on offer to the individual. Evidently those individuals who receive only low wage offers have a more restricted set of opportunities.

To what extent does the individual represented in Fig. 2.2 exercise any control over these constraints? In the short period represented here the individual has none, all three factors are taken as exogenous. The number of hours at his or her disposal is, indisputably, fixed. Unearned income reflects past endeavors (industry and thrift, or lack of it) or good fortune (inheritance or a win in a lottery) and is given in the short run. Again, the wage rate, which reflects the best offer for labor services that the individual can obtain from an employer, is also assumed outside his or her control.

The wage rate that the individual is offered in the short run reflects the employer's evaluation of the individual's productivity but over the longer term the individual is able to influence this. This can be achieved either by investing in schooling and training or by providing evidence of an appropriate attitude and motivation. The short period model developed here assumes that the slope and position of the budget constraint are exogenously determined but in later chapters we shall have something to say about how the employee can influence each of these.

Having identified the preferences of individuals and the constraints that confront them in the labor market the next step is to consider the optimization process.

---

4. See Becker, G.S. (1965) 'A theory of the allocation of time', *Economic Journal*, **75**, 493–517.
5. Note that the slope of this line is negative for it is given by the ratio of the change in goods and services, dG, to change in hours of leisure, dL. Equation (2.7) shows that

$$G = \frac{Y_u}{P} + (T - L)\left(\frac{W}{P}\right)$$

from which

$$\frac{dG}{dL} = -\frac{W}{P}$$

the slope of the budget constraint is negative and is given by the real wage rate.

Optimization

The optimum for individuals is realized by doing the best they can under the circumstances, that is by maximizing their utility subject to the budget constraint. Formally this amounts to reaching the highest indifference curve they can subject to the budget constraint. This is illustrated in Fig. 2.3 as the point of tangency between the indifference U_1 and the budget constraint, with slope $-W_1/P$. It is shown as point A. Confronted by a budget constraint of slope $-W_1/P$ the individual chooses to work H_1 hours, and consume $T - H_1 = L_1$ hours of leisure. This produces income

$$I_1 = \frac{Y_u}{P} + \left(\frac{W_1}{P}\right)H_1$$

Formally this problem amounts to maximizing Eq. (2.1), the utility function, subject to Eq. (2.7), the budget constraint. That is maximize

$$U = U(G,L) \tag{2.1}$$

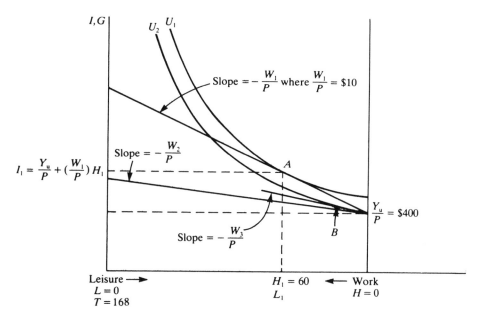

Figure 2.3 The determination of an individual's hours of work. Of the $T = 168$ hours that are available in the week the individual chooses to work $H_1 = 60$ hours at $W_1/P = \$10$, resulting in $T - H_1 = 108$ hours of leisure, and real income, I_1 of $\$1000$. I_1 comprises $Y_u/P = \$400$ and $H_1 \times W/P = \$600$. Note that at this wage full income is $\$400 + \$10 \times 168 = \$2080$. This income is used to purchase 108 hours of leisure at $\$10$ per hour, total cost $\$1080$, and to buy goods and services equal to $\$1000$

subject to

$$G = \frac{Y_u}{P} + \frac{W_1}{P}(T - L) \qquad (2.7)$$

Equation (2.7) can be rearranged as follows

$$PG = Y_u + W_1(T - L) \qquad (2.8)$$

which indicates that utility is to be maximized subject to total expenditure PG equalling total money income $Y_u + W_1(T - L)$. The above is an exercise in constrained optimization.[6] The optimum is at the point of tangency, A, at which the slope of the budget constraint, W_1/P, is equal to the slope of the indifference curve MU_L/MU_G. At this point the slope of the wage ray equals the marginal rate of substitution.

What then are the determinants of this optimal solution and of the number of hours the individual will wish to work? They are of course those arguments which affect the slope and position of the budget constraint and the nature of the indifference map. At their most fundamental they are the real wage, real non-labor income and tastes, τ. Thus an individual's hours of work, H, are given by:

$$H = H\left(\frac{W}{P}, \frac{Y}{P}, \tau\right) \qquad (2.9)$$

6. The above is a constrained extremum problem with utility maximization as the objective. Mathematically this is most simply solved by the Lagrangian multiplier method, in which the first step is to write out the Lagrangian function Z thus:

$$Z = Z(\lambda, G, L) = U(G, L) - \lambda[PG - Y_u - W_1(T - L)] \qquad (2.8a)$$

where λ is the Lagrangian multiplier. This enables us to obtain the first-order conditions for a constrained maximum which is that $Z_\lambda = Z_G = Z_L = 0$. Therefore:

$$\frac{\partial Z}{\partial \lambda} = Z_\lambda = PG - Y - W_1(T - L) = 0 \qquad (2.8b)$$

$$\frac{\partial Z}{\partial G} = Z_G = \frac{\partial U}{\partial G} - \lambda P = 0 \qquad (2.8c)$$

$$\frac{\partial Z}{\partial L} = Z_L = \frac{\partial U}{\partial L} - \lambda W_1 = 0 \qquad (2.8d)$$

The solution to which gives

$$\frac{\partial U/\partial L}{\partial U/\partial G} = \frac{\lambda W_1}{\lambda P} \text{ or, by substituting in Eq. (2.4) above, } \frac{MU_L}{MU_G} = \frac{W_1}{P} \qquad (2.8e)$$

Upon rearranging this gives

$$\frac{MU_L}{W_1} = \frac{MU_G}{P} \qquad (2.8f)$$

From Eq. (2.8f) it is clear that the ratio of the marginal utility of goods to the price of goods is equal to the ratio of the marginal utility of leisure to the price of leisure, under the assumption that expenditure equals money income.

Given tastes, hours worked are a function of the real wage rate and real non-labor income.

Equation (2.9) is subject to the restriction that $H > 0$. Consider this point further. Note that the decision to supply H_1 hours is taken simultaneously with the decision to work. In this model no distinction is made between what might initially be thought of as two quite distinct dimensions of labor supply; the decision whether or not to work, the participation decision, and conditional on a decision to work the decision how many hours to supply. In this analysis if individuals decide to work they simultaneously decide to supply hours. Suppose however that the wage rate fell to (W_2/P), in Fig. 2.3 now U_2, would represent the highest indifference curve that the individual could reach but this involves a corner solution whereas the above assumed an interior solution. The budget constraint reflecting W_2/P is just tangent to U_2 at Y_u/P where $H = 0$ and $L = T$. In this case the implicit value of the individual's time, as given by the slope of the indifference curve, *exceeds* the value placed on his or her time by the labor market, W_2/P, at all points to the left of $H = 0$. That is

$$\frac{\partial U/\partial L}{\partial U/\partial G} > \frac{W_2}{P}$$

so the individual decides not to participate in the labor market. If W_2/P were the wage rate on offer the individual would not work.

Figure 2.3 reveals that it requires only a very small increase in the real wage rate from W_2/P to, say, W_3/P to induce the individual to work once again and move to tangency point B. In Fig. 2.3, W_2/P can therefore be said to represent the highest wage at which the individual will not work and W_3/P the lowest wage at which he or she is prepared to work. The slope of the wage ray to W_2/P shows the individual's *reservation wage*, W^*/P, for it distinguishes the highest wage at which $\frac{\partial U/\partial L}{\partial U/\partial G} > \frac{W}{P}$. W_3/P is therefore the lowest wage—the wage that just exceeds the individual's reservation wage—which is necessary to induce this individual to work. Thus if $W/P > W^*/P$ then $H > 0$. If $W/P \le W^*/P$ then $H = 0$. The reservation wage represents the highest wage rate at which the individual will not work.

THE INDIVIDUAL'S LABOR SUPPLY CURVE

Point A in Fig. 2.3 represents one point on the labor supply curve, for it represents the amount of labor H_1, the individual is willing to supply at real wage rate W_1/P. Point B represents another unique combination of hours of work and real wage rate.

Consider the individual's reaction to a rise in the real wage from W_1/P to W_2/P as illustrated in Fig. 2.4.[7] As the wage rate rises the ray from Y_u/P pivots upwards

---

7. Throughout the following analysis we shall focus on changes in nominal, that is money, wages the price level remaining unchanged. But note that a rise in real wages will also result from a fall in prices if nominal wages remain unchanged. However, because such a fall in prices will also affect real non-labor income, Y_u/P, we shall for reasons of simplicity focus on changes in nominal wages.

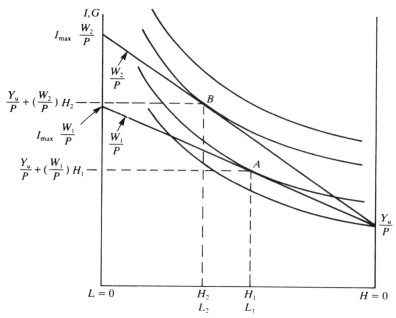

Figure 2.4 The effect of a change in the wage rate on an individual's labor supply. An increase in the wage from W_1/P to W_2/P pivots the wage ray, the budget constraint, at point Y_u/P. The higher real wage produces a more steeply sloped wage ray. The optimum for the individual has now changed from point A to point B. At point B they are on a higher indifference curve, and this new optimum is associated with working extra hours $H_2 - H_1$, taking less leisure, $L_1 - L_2$ and produces a higher income $(Y/P_u + (W_2/P)H_2)$ instead of $(Y/P_u + (W_1/P)H_1)$

reflecting the greater W at a given P. The line becomes steeper reflecting the fact that a rise in the real wage produces a higher full income $[I_{max} (W_2/P)]$ as indicated by the point at which the wage rays intercept the I axis. In the example shown the individual reaches a new optimum at point B on a higher indifference curve. At this point hours of work have been increased from H_1 to H_2 and hours of leisure have been decreased from $L_1 = T - H_1$ to $L_2 = T - H_2$. The individual's real income has also increased from $Y_u/P + (W_1/P)H_1$ to $Y_u/P + (W_2/P)H_2$.

The relationship between the change in the real wage rate and the hours of work can be mapped explicitly as in Fig. 2.5. Here the horizontal axis is drawn to the same scale as the horizontal axis in Fig. 2.4, but now the vertical, I, G, axis has been removed and we measure the changes in the wage rate on the vertical axis. We have also turned the horizontal axis through 180° and map only hours of work on the horizontal axis. Now the origin represents zero hours of work and hours of work become positive and increase as we move to the right along the axis. If we now map the new and the old wage rates on the vertical axis of Fig. 2.5 and draw a line joining the coordinates of the points W_1/P and H_1 and W_2/P and H_2, the line representing the locus of these points is the labor supply curve, L^s. It tells us how much labor is supplied at each real wage rate. Note that the proportional distance $(W_2/P - W_1/P)/W_1P$ on the vertical axis

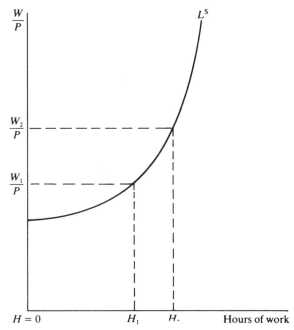

Figure 2.5 The labor supply curve. The move from H_1 to H_2 in Fig. 2.4 is mapped against the wage rate. The rise in the wage rate from W_1 to W_2, a proportional increase of $(W_2/P) - (W_1/P)/(W_1/P)$, resulted in a rise in hours worked from H_1 to H_2. The locus of these points results in a positively sloping labor supply curve, L^s. Initially, small rises in the wage rate produce large increases in hours worked, but eventually the curve steepens considerably, reflecting the fact that further rises in the wage rate are likely to produce only small increases in hours worked

of Fig. 2.5 measures the proportional change in the real wage which was represented in Fig. 2.4 by the distance $[I_{max}(W_2/P) - I_{max}(W_1/P)]/I_{max}(W_1/P)$.

Will a rise in the wage rate always lead to a rise in the number of hours of work supplied as shown above? This aspect is considered further in Figs. 2.6(a) and (b).

INCOME AND SUBSTITUTION EFFECTS

In Figs. 2.6(a) and (b) there has been an increase in the real wage of the same magnitude, from W_1/P to W_2/P. However, while in Fig. 2.6(a) more hours of work are offered (hours supplied rise from H_1 to H_2), in Fig. 2.6(b) fewer hours of work are supplied, they fall from H_1 to H_2. The shape of the labor supply curve that is associated with each of these developments is detailed in the lower half of each figure. In the first case the rise in wages gives rise to a positively sloping labor supply curve, but in the latter the supply curve is backward sloping. Both of these developments are theoretically possible but how can they be explained?

Two forces are at work as a result of the rise in the real wage. The first of these, termed the *income effect*, results from the fact that the rise in the wage rate increased the individual's real income. The magnitude of the potential increase in the

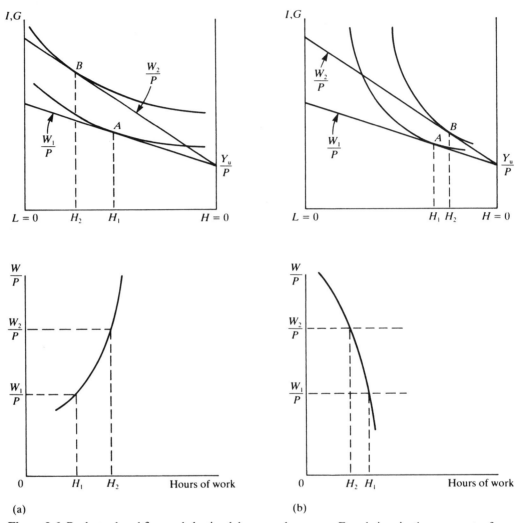

Figure 2.6 Backward and forward sloping labor supply curves. Equal rises in the wage rate, from W_1/P to W_2/P, produce (a) an increase in hours of work and (b) a decrease in hours of work. The result is a positively sloping supply curve in the first case and a backward sloping curve in the latter.

individual's income, consequent upon the rise in the wage rate, is given by the increase in the individual's full income. This increase in income enables the individual to purchase more of all commodities and if leisure is a normal good more will be purchased. If more leisure is purchased, fewer hours are worked. Therefore, contingent on leisure being a normal good, the income effect of a wage rise results in fewer hours of work.

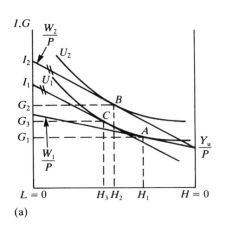
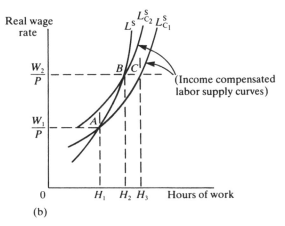

(a)   (b)

Figure 2.7 The positively sloping labor supply curve. (a) The pure change in relative prices, the increase in the price of leisure the price of goods and services remaining unchanged, results in the move from A to C with the individual offering more hours of work, an increase from H_1 to H_3. This produces the shallow income compensated labor supply curve, $L^s_{c_1}$ shown in (b). In addition, the rise in the real wage, produces a rise in real income, and this results in the purchase of more leisure (leisure being a normal good) and the move from C to B. As a result the compensated labor supply curve shifts inwards to $L^s_{c_2}$ for at W_2/P fewer hours of work are offered, they fall from H_3 to H_2. The net effect of these two moves produces a labor supply curve L^s which represents the locus of the points on the two compensated labor supply curves. In this example it is positively sloping

Working in the opposite direction is the *substitution effect*. Recall that the price of leisure is the wage rate. Hence a rise in the wage rate increases the opportunity cost, or price, of leisure. We buy fewer of those goods whose prices have risen and so when wages rise we buy less leisure, that is we work more. Obviously we have two opposing tendencies at work. A substitution effect reflecting the argument. 'It's worth my while to work more hours now' and an income effect reflecting the argument 'but I don't need to work as many hours now'.[8]

To discover more precisely the relative magnitude of these income and substitution effects, consider Fig. 2.7, in which there has been a rise in the wage rate from W_1/P

8. The opposing tendencies of what we now term the income and substitution effects were recognized many years ago as the following quotation illustrates: 'If a workman can earn ninepence an hour instead of sixpence may he not be induced to extend his hours of labour by this increased result? This would doubtless be the case were it not that the very fact of getting half as much more than he did before lowers the utility to him of any further addition. By the produce of the same number of hours he can satisfy his desires more completely: and if the irksomeness of labour has reached at all a high point, he may gain more pleasure by relaxing that labour than by consuming more products. The question thus depends upon the direction in which the balance between the utility of further commodity and the painfulness of prolonged labour turns. In our ignorance of the exact form of the functions either of utility or of labour it will be impossible to decide this question in an *a priori* manner.' Jevons, W.S. (1888) *The Theory of Political Economy*, Macmillan, London, quoted in Pencavel, J. (1986) 'The labor supply of men: a survey', in Ashenfelter, O. and Layard, P.R.G. (eds.), *Handbook of Labor Economics*. North-Holland, New York and Oxford.

to W_2/P and a move from an initial equilibrium position A to a new equilibrium position B.[9] First we focus on the substitution effect.

Substitution effect

The substitution effect captures the individual's reaction to the change in the relative price of leisure holding constant the individual's real income. To measure the substitution effect we abstract from the change in real income that resulted from the price rise. Recall that around an indifference curve the individual's real income, the satisfactions produced by differing combinations of goods and services and leisure, is unchanged. In order to hold constant the individal's level of real income we therefore focus on points around a single indifference curve and we choose to focus on the original indifference curve U_1. Now the change in the relative price of leisure and goods that resulted from the wage rise is depicted by any line drawn parallel to the new wage ray W_2/P. Thus we draw such a line just tangent to original indifference curve U_1 and this gives us point C. The individual shown has reacted to the change in relative prices, represented by the steepening of the wage ray by moving from original point A, supplying H_1 hours of work, to new position C, supplying H_3 hours of work. A rise in the wage rate means a rise in the opportunity cost or price of leisure, and as a result, at unchanged real income, the individual now buys less of the good whose price has risen, and supplies more hours of work. Provided indifference curves are convex this will always be the case and thus there is a positive association between the rise in the wage rate and in hours of work; the substitution effect of a wage rise is therefore positive.

The pure substitution effect can also be illustrated as a movement up a labor supply curve which holds the level of real income constant. Such a labor supply curve is known as an *income compensated labor supply curve* and is shown in Fig. 2.7(b) as $L^s_{c_1}$. This curve abstracts from the rise in real income consequent upon the wage rise and is accordingly more shallowly sloped than the uncompensated labor supply curve L^s. When we focus only on the substitution effect the rise in the wage produces a larger increase in hours of work from H_1 to H_3, than will occur when we allow real income to vary. The income compensated labor supply curve is a useful analytical device, for it reveals what happens to labor supply when wages change but real income does not.

---

9. In the figures we shall employ Hick's compensating variation, as distinct from the Slutsky approximation we employ in Appendix 2B to distinguish the income and substitution effects. [See Hicks (1932) *The Theory of Wages*, Macmillan, London.] In conventional consumer demand theory, the income or substitution effects work in the same direction, here they work in opposite directions. In conventional consumer demand theory we are only concerned with the individual as a consumer of the good whose price has risen. Here we are concerned with the individual both as a consumer and a seller of the good. The good in question is leisure. This fact introduces a new dimension into the theory of labor supply for the rise in the price of leisure makes individuals still better off should they choose to sell more leisure, that is to work more. For this reason the income effect of a rise in the wage rate can work in the opposite direction to that in conventional consumer demand theory.

Income effect

The income effect captures the individual's reaction to the change in real income occasioned by the change in the wage rate, and holds constant the change in the relative price of leisure. To measure this we now focus on the movement between the two indifference curves in Fig. 2.7. The rise in the real wage evidently increased the individual's utility as the move from indifference curve U_1 to indifference curve U_2 in Fig. 2.7(a) clearly indicates. The magnitude of the change in real income is represented by the vertical distance between the indifference curves. Confronted by an increase in real money income of $I_2 - I_1$, the individual chose to 'spend' this on $H_2 - H_3$ additional hours of leisure and $G_2 - G_3$ additional goods and services as indicated by the move from C to B. Provided leisure is a normal good more leisure will always be purchased out of rising income, but we cannot say, *a priori*, how large these additional purchases of leisure will be. The income effect is described as negative, for the rise in the wage rate results in fewer hours of work. The income effect in turn can be illustrated in Fig. 2.7(b), where it can be seen that the income effect results in an inward shift in the income compensated labor supply curve. For now we have abstracted from the change in relative prices and are focusing exclusively on the effects of the change in income. Less labor is supplied at any wage rate and at the new higher real wage W_2/P fewer hours, $H_3 - H_2$, are worked and so $L^s_{c_1}$ shifts back to $L^s_{c_2}$. The total change, incorporating both the income and the substitution effects, is of course illustrated by the move from point A to B in both parts of the diagram.

Evidently the income effect works in the opposite direction to the substitution effect but in this example, on balance, the hours worked increased. This was due to the relative magnitudes of the two effects. The move from H_1 to H_3, the increase in hours worked due to the substitution effect, was greater than the reduction in hours worked due to the income effect, the move from H_3 to H_2. In this example therefore the net effect was to increase the supply of hours and produce a positively sloping labor supply curve. Evidently the labor supply curve, L^s, is the locus of the points on the underlying income compensated labor supply curves, as shown in Fig. 2.7(b).

Contrast the relative magnitude of the income and substitution effects in Fig. 2.7 with those shown in Fig. 2.8. Again in Fig. 2.8 the positive substitution effect of the rise in the real wage rate leads to a move around the initial indifference curve, U_1 from A to C in Fig. 2.8(a) and to hours of work rising from H_1 to H_3. Again this pure substitution effect is captured by the movement up the income compensated supply curve, $L^s_{c_1}$, detailed in Fig. 2.8(b). However, in this case the rise in real income, reflected in the vertical distance between U_1 and U_2, now gives rise to substantial purchases of leisure, as evidenced by the size of the reduction in hours of work as we move to point B. The move from C to B now results in a substantial reduction in hours from H_3 to H_2 and is equivalent to a substantial backward shift in the income compensated supply curve, from $L^s_{c_1}$ to $L^s_{c_2}$ as illustrated in Fig. 2.8(b). Indeed the move is so substantial that it overwhelms the substitution effect. The increase in hours worked as a result of the positive substitution effect is overwhelmed by the decrease in hours worked as a result of the negative income effect, so that the move from H_1

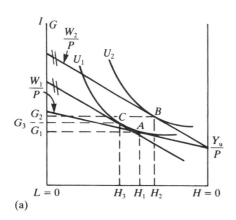
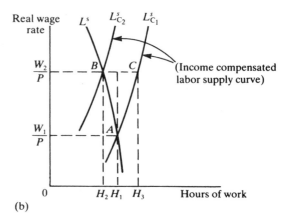

(a)   (b)

Figure 2.8 The backward sloping labor curve. The rise in the price of leisure relative to the price of goods and services at the initial level of utility, U_1, results in an increase in hours of work from H_1 to H_3, and produces the positively sloped income compensated labor supply curve, $L^s_{C_1}$. The income effect produces a backward shift in this income compensated labor supply curve and results in a reduction in hours of work from H_3 to H_2. In this example the income effect overwhelms the substitution effect with the net result that hours of work fall from H_1 to H_2 and the labor supply curve slopes backwards

to H_3 is more than offset by the reduction in hours from H_3 to H_2. The net result is that the labor supply curve, L^s, reflecting the total move from A to B, is backward sloping.

In Fig. 2.7 the labor supply curve, L^s, is positively sloping; in Fig. 2.8 it is backward sloping. In both cases the substitution effect works in the same direction—it results in more hours of work and fewer hours of leisure. In both cases the income effect works in the same direction—it results in fewer hours worked and more hours of leisure. The difference between the two is in the magnitude of the income effect, more precisely, in the relative magnitude of the income and substitution effects. In Fig. 2.7 the substitution effect is greater than the income effect, which results in a positively sloping labor supply curve. In Fig. 2.8 the substitution effect is less than the income effect, which results in a backward sloping labor supply curve. These results are derived more formally in Appendix 2B.

At an intuitive level the reason for the results we have derived in our discussion of income and substitution effects is evident from a comparison of Figs. 2.7 and 2.8. The individual represented in Fig. 2.7 exhibited a strong preference for goods and services as reflected in the slope of the indifference curves. That individual's indifference curves were relatively shallowly sloped revealing a low *MRS* and reflecting the fact that the employee was willing to give up a considerable amount of leisure to achieve a small increase in goods and services. As a result the individual availed himself or herself of the opportunities to increase his or her purchases of goods and services, afforded by the increase in the wage, and G rose from G_1 at A to G_2 at B. In contrast the individual whose preferences were represented by the indifference map in Fig. 2.8 displayed a marked preference for leisure. That individual displayed a high *MRS*, reflecting the fact that a large increment to G was demanded if he or she were to forgo an increment to leisure. This was represented by steeply sloped indifference curves. Faced with the rise in the real wage and the increased opportunities this afforded, the individual represented in Fig. 2.8 opted to consume considerably more leisure and for the most part to forgo the opportunity to increase G. Accordingly in this case, while leisure increases by the difference between H_1 and H_2, purchases of goods and services increase by the amount G_1 to G_2. Differences in individual tastes determine the relative strength of the income and substitution effects and determine whether the individual's labor supply curve will be positively or backward sloping.

THE BACKWARD BENDING LABOR SUPPLY CURVE

An individual's tastes for leisure and goods may change over time as income grows. It is also possible that these tastes differ between different segments of the population distinguished according to their income level. If individuals with low levels of income have a low *MRS*, then a rise in the wage rate at low income levels might lead to an offer of increased hours of work. However, as we move up the income distribution the *MRS* increases, and beyond some level a rise in the wage rate may result in a reduction in hours of work. At low incomes the substitution effect might dominate while at high incomes the income effect might dominate. This possibility is illustrated for a single individual in Fig. 2.9. Up to W_5/P, the substitution effect dominates and the rise in the wage rate from W_1/P to W_5/P results in an increased supply of hours of work from H_1 to H_5. Over this region the labor supply curve is positively sloped as illustrated in Fig. 2.9(b). However, beyond W_5/P further rises in the wage rate result in a decrease in hours worked as the individual purchases more leisure. This is the result of a relative steepening of the indifference curves, evidence of an increasing *MRS*, and this produces the backward sloping segment of the labor supply curve shown in Fig. 2.9(b). Taken together this change in tastes as the individual's income increases, or the change in tastes as we move up the income distribution, produces the backward bending labor supply curve shown in Fig. 2.9(b). Individual tastes are evidently of crucial importance in determining labor supply.

Now we move on to consider the way in which we measure the changes in hours worked that result from changes in the wage.

ELASTICITY OF INDIVIDUAL LABOR SUPPLY

To date the discussion has been in terms of the absolute magnitude of the changes in hours worked as a result of changes in the real wage rate, but are we to consider a reduction in hours worked of one hour consequent upon a rise in the wage of £1 per week the same when the rise in the wage is from £100 to £101 as when it is from £1000 to £1001? Surely not. We therefore need to standardize our measures of the changes in the variables in some way. Converting the changes into proportional terms is the

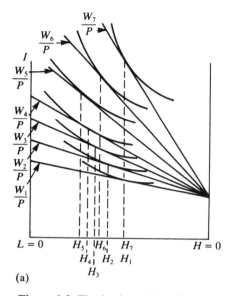
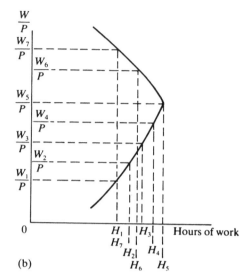

Figure 2.9 The backward bending labor supply curve. The tastes of the individual represented above change as income increases. At wage rates below W_5/P this individual displays a marked preference for goods and services and the labor supply curve is positively sloping. Beyond W_5/P, however, the individual displays an increasing preference for leisure. Accordingly, any further rise in the wage rate results in a reduction in hours worked, and the labor supply curve is backward sloping.

general method of accomplishing this. By so doing we construct a measure of the elasticity of labor supply which, as we shall see in the next chapter is a concept which is of principal concern to policy-makers.

The elasticity of labor supply, ε^s, is defined as the proportional change in the quantity of labor supplied divided by the proportional change in the wage rate. Expressed in terms of hours of work for individual i this is:

$$\varepsilon_i^s = \frac{\partial H_i / H_i}{\partial w_i / w_i}$$

or, on rearranging

$$\frac{\partial H_i}{\partial w_i} \cdot \frac{w_i}{H_i} \tag{2.10}$$

where $w = W/P$. This informs us that we are concerned with the slope of the labor supply curve $\partial H_i / \partial w_i$ measured at a particular point on the supply curve, that point give by w_i/H_i, the ratio of the means of the two variables which is the reciprocal of the slope of a line from the origin to that point on the supply curve. Elasticity can assume the following numerical values with the following consequences for hours worked.

Value of elasticity	Description	Consequences for hours of work
$\varepsilon^s = \infty$	Infinitely elastic	A rise in the wage rate results in an infinitely large rise in hours worked.
$\infty > \varepsilon^s > 1$	Elastic	A rise in the wage rate results in a larger proportional rise in hours of work.
$\varepsilon^s = 1$	Unit elastic	A rise in the wage rate results in an equal proportional rise in hours worked.
$0 < \varepsilon^s < 1$	Inelastic	A rise in the wage rate results in a less than proportional rise in hours worked.
$\varepsilon^s = 0$	Completely inelastic	No change in hours worked

It should be evident from our earlier discussion of the determinants of the slope of the labor supply curve that the elasticity of labor supply depends on the relative magnitude of the income and substitution effects. In Appendix 2B this is shown more formally.

The magnitude of the elasticity of labor supply has important implications for policy, for it determines how labour supply reacts to changes in nominal wages, prices and taxes—all of which determine the real wage rate the individual receives from work.

CHANGES IN UNEARNED INCOME

So far we have looked at changes in the wage rate, which manifested themselves in changes in the slope of the budget constraint and changes in tastes, which were reflected in changes in the slope of the indifference curves, but we have yet to look at changes in unearned income. This we do now. Recall that in Figs. 2.7 and 2.8 the income effect of a rise in the wage rate displaced the individual's compensated supply curve. In the same way a change in unearned income at a given wage rate displaces the labor supply curve. A rise displaces it to the left and a fall displaces it to the right provided that leisure is a normal good. The causes of changes in unearned income are many and varied. One source of unearned income may be the return on an individual's wealth. Alternatively, unearned income may take the form of transfer payments or supplements to income paid by the government to those in work. For example, many countries pay some grant toward the maintenance of children. Again, where the individual is a member of a household, it is often appropriate for analytical purposes to count the earned income of other members of the household as constituting in part

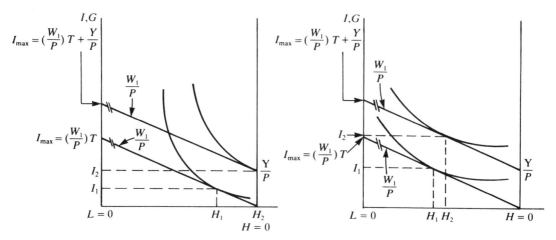

Figure 2.10 Changes in unearned income. Individual A exhibits a high *MRS*, while individual B exhibits a small *MRS*. In both cases the effect of introducing unearned income Y/P is to cause a reduction in hours of work supplied from H_1 to H_2. In the case of individual A, this leads to quitting work altogether. Both individuals consume more leisure and have a higher income, I_2, as a result of the introduction of Y/P

or in whole the unearned income of remaining family members. The term Y/P therefore covers a wide range of different contingencies, but common to all the above cases is the fact that Y/P is independent of hours worked, for that is how it has been defined in our theory.

What happens to hours worked if there is an increase in any one of these elements or the introduction of a new source of unearned income? Two possibilities are illustrated in Fig. 2.10, in which individuals A and B display, respectively, a marked preference for leisure and a marked preference for goods and services. Suppose in the first instance that they are each confronted by the same wage rate W_1/P and neither has any unearned income, then full income is identical at $I_{max} = (W_1/P)T$. Now suppose that some form of unearned income, Y/P, is introduced, and their income from this source remains independent of the number of hours worked.[10]

The effect of the introduction of unearned income is to displace vertically the wage ray. Now at $H = 0$, $I = Y/P$ and at full income when $H = T$, $I_{max} = Y/P + (W_1/P)T$. As a result of the rise in income both individuals A and B reduce their hours of work and the points of tangency between the new budget constraint and the higher indifference curves lie to the north-east of the original point. This reduction in hours at an unchanged wage rate has the effect of shifting the labor supply curve to the left. Indeed in the extreme case of individual A, this person quits work altogether. The difference

10. In practice this is unlikely to be strictly accurate for under most progressive tax schemes (a scheme with either a non-zero threshold at which the individual starts paying tax, or progressively steeper marginal tax rates), earned and unearned income are cumulated. The effect of the unearned income may then be to raise the individual's tax liability in work and hence to lower the effective post-tax wage rate.

between the behavior of individuals A and B is a consequence of the shape of their indifference maps and the differences in tastes that these reflect.[11] In general therefore a rise in unearned income leads unambiguously to a reduction in hours worked, provided leisure is a normal good.

AGGREGATE LABOR SUPPLY CURVE

Our theory so far has focused on the behavior of a rational individual but for most empirical purposes analysis focuses on the behavior of groups of individuals: all those individuals who taken together comprise the labour supply to a particular market. It is therefore necessary to aggregate across all those individuals who constitute the effective labor supply to a particular market to describe labor supply in the short run.

At this level it is important to distinguish between *notional* and *effective* labor supply. The former includes all those who are willing to supply labor to a particular market; the latter includes only those who have the characteristics, qualifications and aptitudes, essential to gain employment should it be offered. The former measure of labor supply may be larger than the latter, and the effective labor supply curve may therefore lie inside the notional labor supply curve. In later chapters it emerges that this distinction plays an important part in some explanations of unemployment.

Skill is one characteristic that determines an individual's suitability for a job. But more subjective characteristics such as attitude and motivation are also likely to be important. However, these are rather imprecise notions, involving as they do subjective judgments on the part of labor market participants. For the moment we assume that we can distinguish applicants of appropriate quality, in which case the supply of hours in labor market, 0, comprises the sum of the labor supply of all the $1, \ldots, n$ individuals of the appropriate quality who offer to work at different wage rates. Thus, summing across $1, \ldots, n$ individuals, Eq. (2.9), revealing the determinants of the number of hours supplied, becomes:

$$H^0 = \sum_{i=1}^{n} H_i \left(\frac{W^0}{P}, \frac{Y_i}{P}, \tau_i \right) \tag{2.11}$$

Diagrammatically this involves the horizontal summation of each of the individual labor supply curves. For some individuals a change in the wage rate will confront them with a discrete choice, to work or not to work; for others it will be a question of whether to supply more or fewer hours. Even though both effects may be present together it will still be possible to describe a smooth and continuous supply curve if there are a sufficiently large number of individuals. However, if there are few individuals the labor supply will be stepped as depicted in Fig. 2.11.

---

11. When indifference curves are convex, where the $MRS > 0$, a rise in unearned income will *always* lead to a fall in hours of work. The new equilibrium will always be to the right of the old equilibrium. This is a function of the negative slope and convexity of the indifference curves, which results from the positive MRS.

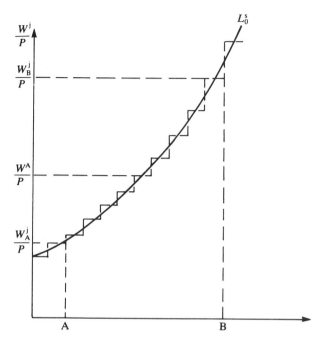

Figure 2.11 The supply of individuals to a firm. Individual A is willing to work in firm j at wage W_A^j/P which is below the wage W^A/P which could be earned in an alternative firm. Individual A has a taste for this type of work. Individual B, however, dislikes this type of work. It takes a wage rate W_B^j/P, considerably higher than could be earned elsewhere, to induce this person to work in this firm. Individuals A and B are merely two from a continuum of individuals who together comprise the labor supply to firm j and produce a smooth and continuous labor supply curve.

The shape of the aggregate labor supply curve is determined by the shape of the underlying individual labor supply curves. At the one extreme they may be identical miniature versions of the aggregate curve where τ is identical for all individuals. If there are a sufficiently large number of such individuals this will result in a perfectly elastic aggregate labor supply curve. For although each individual's labor supply curve may be positively sloped, a trivial rise in the wage rate from its existing level will attract into the market so many additional individuals that the wage returns to its former level: the labor supply curve is horizontal. If, on the other hand, the pool of labor on which we draw is fixed, the schedule will be positively sloping—again a mirror image, although much larger, of the shape of each underlying curve. Again, the aggregate supply curve will be positively sloping where there are differences in tastes between individuals, if for no other reason than that such differences in tastes are likely to be reflected in differences in reservation wages and hence in the point at which each underlying curve intersects the vertical axis.

Opportunity wages

The labor supply curve in Fig. 2.11 represents the supply to a particular firm, call this j, and is drawn under the assumption that the wage rates in all the other firms for which the individuals described here are qualified are fixed. These alternative wage rates represent the opportunity costs of supplying labor to firm j, and for a given level of tastes determine the minimum wage rate necessary to induce individuals to supply labor to firm j. The highest wage rate an individual can command in the best alternative employment is known as the individual's *opportunity wage*.

Individuals may differ substantially in their tastes for the work in firm j and therefore be willing to work at different wage rates. If W^A/P in Fig. 2.11 represents the opportunity wage for both individuals A and B, individual A may be said to exhibit a taste for firm j since A is willing to work in firm j at a wage rate below that which could be obtained elsewhere; B may be said to display an aversion to such work for he or she demands a considerably higher wage than could be earned elsewhere. A rise in the alternative wage, W^A/P, would increase the costs to individual A of exercising a taste for firm j and accordingly would reduce the labor supply to this firm. Equally such a rise would now mean that wage rate W_B^j/P offered individual B insufficient compensation for working in this firm and this employee too would cut back labor supply.[12] A rise in the wage rate in an alternative job therefore results in a backward shift in the labor supply curve: a reduction in labor supply at all wage rates.

It is evident from the above that when describing the aggregate labor supply curve for a particular firm we must enter the wages in alternative occupations as an explicit argument. Thus we now write:

$$H_j = \sum_{i=1}^{n} H_i\left(\frac{W_j}{P}, \frac{W^A}{P}, \frac{Y_i}{P}, \tau_i\right) \tag{2.12}$$

Changes in wages in alternative jobs are one cause of shifts in the aggregate labor supply curve while changes in unearned income and tastes are others.

Finally, note that although this discussion of aggregate labor supply curves has been in terms of the supply to a particular labor market the discussion has general application. The labor supply to a regional, urban or industrial labor market will be the aggregate of the supply to each of the underlying submarkets.

SOME LIMITATIONS OF THE STATIC THEORY

The static theory of labor supply we have developed above represents a simplified and abstract view of the world and accordingly it has not been without criticism. A number of the principal criticisms are reviewed below. First it has been objected that the simple dichotomy between work and leisure is too crude for all practical purposes. Most individuals have to perform some non-market work, such as digging the garden,

---

12. We explore the implications of differences in individuals' tastes more fully in Chapter 11.

looking after the children, washing the car, cleaning the house, which it would be inappropriate to classify simply as leisure.

Table 2.1 indeed suggests that individuals devote a considerable part of their 'leisure' time to non-market work. Indeed, women working full time appear to devote more hours to non-market than to market work. In the United Kingdom in 1985 women working full time spent some 45.1 hours on essential non-market work while they devoted 40.8 hours to market work. If we similarly included personal care in the figures for non-market work by women in the United States, it is likely that they too would exceed the figures for market work. For men working full time in the United Kingdom, non-market work accounted for three-quarters as many hours as market work, which appears to be a larger proportion than for men in the United States. (US males are evidently less keen on DIY.) Of course, the categories used in the two studies

Table 2.1 (a) Allocation of time in a typical week in the United Kingdom in 1985

	Full-time employees		Housewives
	Men	Women	
Weekly hours spent on:			
Employment (including travel to and from work)	45.0	40.8	—
Essential non-market work (cooking, washing, childcare, etc., including personal care)	33.1	45.1	76.6
Total work time	78.1	85.9	
Sleep (excluding personal care)	56.4	57.5	59.2
Leisure time	33.5	24.6	32.2

(b) Allocation of time in a typical week in the United States in mid-1970s

Weekly hours spent on:			
Employment (including travel to and from work and education)	48.6	39.1	
Essential non-market work (cooking, washing clothes, childcare, etc., excluding personal care)	12.7	24.6	44.0
Sleep (including personal care)	75.1	74.0	81.7
Leisure time	31.7	30.4	37.8

Source: UK, CSO *Social Trends*, 1987.
USA, Hill, M.S. (1983), 'Pattern of time use', in Juster, F.T. and Stafford, F.P. (eds.), *Time, Goods and Well-being*, University of Michigan, Survey Research Centre.

are different and there is a difference of 10 years between the two surveys. US males are recorded as working longer hours than their UK counterparts, although as we shall see in Chapter 4, the opposite now appears to be the case. The different categories employed and different dates of the surveys make cross-country comparisons difficult but two points emerge which are worth commenting on. First, in the mid-1970s women in the United States enjoyed considerably more 'true' leisure than did women in the United Kingdom a decade later. Second, US women enjoy only marginally less leisure than men, while in the United Kingdom there is a considerable disparity between the sexes. The greater leisure of US females does not appear to be achieved at the expense of sleep, rather it appears to be at the expense of non-market work. This result is intuitively plausible and probably reflects the greater technology at the disposal of women in the United States.

Once we begin to distinguish between the different constituents of leisure time it is clear that all hours of 'leisure' do not add equally to an individual's satisfaction. However, the simple model we have developed above recognizes this for it proposes a diminishing marginal utility of leisure. Each hour of leisure time is not assigned equal value, and we might interpret this to mean that we are looking at a spectrum of different activities which make claims on our time and are ordered in terms of the satisfaction they produce with work at one end of the spectrum and pure leisure at the other.

Second, the theory makes no distinction between permanent and transitory changes in labor market opportunities. Part of most individuals' leisure time is set aside to enable them to increase their income and hence the flow of goods and services they enjoy in the future. Part of their non-market working time is devoted to investing in themselves. This investment in human capital can take the form of going to college or studying at home, but individuals have to choose at which point during their lives they are going to undertake such investment. Similarly women, or men, may at some time during their lives choose to leave the labor market to raise a family. In order to decide which is the best time to undertake such activities individuals may take a view about the labor market opportunities that confront them now and in the future. In so doing they will need to distinguish between permanent and transitory changes in opportunities. These are aspects of the life cycle dimensions of labor supply which we shall develop more fully in Chapter 4. The model we have developed above works well if we recognize that it is essentially describing changes that are believed to be permanent.

Third, the theory appears to rest on the proposition that work is a source of disutility and that only the offer of a wage to compensate for this disutility will induce individuals to work. However, at the start of the first chapter it was acknowledged that work is often valued in itself, as a vehicle around which we structure our time and organize our lives. It provides a social environment in which we associate with other people and strike up friendships. It may be an activity which we value because we believe that it determines our self-worth. We may see our job as the main determinant of our status among our peers and believe that it is through our jobs that we convey the most important image of ourselves to others. All of these views have been well documented by psychologists and explain why long-term unemployment can be such a damaging phenomenon. In the next chapter we shall suggest that such arguments can be incorporated into the theory by drawing indifference curves which are positively sloped over some range. Over this range individuals are willing to forgo income in order to work. However, the fact remains that, on balance, it is employers who pay individuals to work, not the other way round. The institution of a wage in return for work did not arise from the benevolence of employers, but from recognition on their part that only by doing so could they attract the labor they required. While aspects of work are undoubtedly valued in themselves, on balance work is a source of disutility which must be compensated by a wage.

Finally, it is objected that there are institutional limits on workers' choices. Individuals, it is argued, do not have the degree of choice over their hours of work that our theory implies. They cannot opt to work 30 hours or 60 hours a week, nor can they find themselves a job which enables them to take every first Monday in the month off to recover from the 'night out with the lads'. In fact, the theory makes none of these claims. Certainly some firms have technologies which require their employees to work a fixed number of hours per day and per week. For these firms the budget constraint facing the individual reduces to two points. The 'take it' point of, say, 45 hours per week and the 'leave it' point of no work, but firms are rarely this inflexible. Indeed, if individuals were faced with the requirement in their principal occupation that they work X and only X hours per week, and this did not coincide with their preferences, they would find ways of circumventing these restrictions. They would 'moonlight', that is take a further job, if they wanted to work longer hours or they would go sick or appear among the absentees if they wished to work less.[13] We might also expect to see them taking action to change the situation. The length of the working week and the number of weeks worked per year have indeed changed dramatically over the years as we shall see in Chapter 4. Firms have a strong incentive to respond to workers' preferences. If they fail to do so, they will be faced with higher turnover or may only be able to attract lower quality workers.

SUMMARY

In this chapter we have analyzed the determinants of the individual's supply of labor in the short run. It was shown that a rise in the wage rate could produce either an increase or decrease in the supply of labor but that this could not be determined, *a priori*, it was an empirical question. We also developed the concept of the elasticity of labor supply which provided a measure of the strength and direction of the income and substitution effects.

13. Moonlighting is most prevalent in Japan. The number of workers holding two or more jobs at the same time—multiple job holders—expressed as a proportion of total employment, has been estimated at 2.6 percent in Australia, 1.7 percent in Germany, 3.3 percent in the United Kingdom, 4.9 percent in the United States and 6.3 percent in Japan in the early 1980s. See 'Self-employment in OECD countries', *OECD Employment Outlook*, September 1986.

The analysis in this chapter was based on the maxim 'that individuals do the best they can under the circumstances'. For some the opportunities that the market presents may be limited. Some individuals are offered only very low wage rates while others will be able to command extremely high wages. Just why this disparity should arise is a matter of substantial social and economic concern. In subsequent chapters, Chapter 6 in particular, we shall be looking in more detail at some of the determinants of the labor market opportunities that confront individuals in the short run and the manner in which they can relax these. In the next chapter we use the concepts we have developed here to provide further insights into labor market behavior in the short run.

PRINCIPAL CONCEPTS

In this chapter we have developed the following concepts. The student should ensure that they have a clear grasp of these before they proceed to the next chapter.

1. The indifference map as a diagrammatic representation of the individual's preferences.
2. The marginal rate of substitution.
3. Full income.
4. The diagrammatic and/or mathematical analysis of the optimum for the individual supplier of labor.
5. The reservation wage.
6. Income and substitution effects.
7. The explanation of a backward bending supply curve.
8. The elasticity of individual labor supply.
9. The causes of shifts in an individual's labor supply curve.
10. The construction of the aggregate labor supply curve.

QUESTIONS FOR DISCUSSION

1. What do we mean when we talk of some individuals having a strong preference for goods and services while others have a strong preference for leisure? Explain how such preferences are reflected in the marginal rate of substitution and the individual's indifference map.
2. Illustrate the effects of each of the following on the daily budget contrast facing an individual:
   (a) an increase in unearned income;
   (b) a reduction in the wage rate;
   (c) the offer of employment for eight hours a day, nothing more nothing less;
   (d) the introduction of 'double time', twice the hourly rate, for all hours worked in excess of eight per day.

3. Detail the construction of a labor supply curve for an individual. What shape will it take if the size of the substitution effect always exceeds the size of the income effect?
4. Illustrate the possible effects of a rise in the price level on the labor supply of an individual.
5. Describe the shape of an indifference map that might give rise to a negative substitution and positive income effect. Are such preferences plausible?
6. What are the relative magnitudes of the income and substitution elasticities that are associated with the different segments of a backward bending labor supply curve?
7. How appropriate is the simple distinction between work and leisure which lies at the heart of the static theory of labor supply?

FURTHER READING

For a comprehensive treatment of this area the modern student need do no more than read the excellent survey produced by Mark Killingsworth. The above treatment draws on this in places. Titled *Labor Supply,* Killingsworth's book is a volume in the Cambridge Surveys of Economic Literature, published by Cambridge University Press, London and New York, in 1983. This takes the student well beyond the treatment in this chapter but is essential reading for those looking for a concise (493 pages) treatment of the modern theory of labor supply.

APPENDIX 2A   DIRECT AND INDIRECT UTILITY FUNCTIONS

The object of the optimization process detailed above was to maximize the individual's utility. At the start of this chapter we identified the arguments in the individual's utility function. Utility we stated was a function of goods and services and leisure. Thus we wrote the individual's direct utility function as

$$U = U(G,L) \tag{2.1}$$

and because by rearranging Eq. (2.6) above:

$$L = T - H$$

Eq. (2.1) above can be redefined by substituting the rearranged Eq. (2.6) into Eq. (2.1) to give:

$$U = U(G, T - H) \tag{2A.1}$$

Above we have seen, Eq. (2.9), that hours of work are a function of W/P and Y/P and the individual's tastes for goods and services or leisure, τ. Similarly, we have seen that the amount of goods and services, G, available to the individual is a function of these same arguments, namely W/P, Y/P and τ, and so we may write

$$G = G(W/P, Y/P, \tau) \tag{2A.2}$$

Now on substituting (2.9) and (2A.2) into (2A.1) we obtain the expression for maximized utility U^*. Thus:

$$U^* = U[G(W/P, Y/P, \tau), T - H(W/P, Y/P, \tau)] \tag{2A.3}$$

This equation identifies the variables that determine the individual's maximum utility. The *direct* determinants of the individual's utility were identified in Eq. (2.1), while here the determinants of the variables appearing in Eq. (2.1) have been detailed. This equation is therefore known as the *indirect utility function*. It is utility functions of this type that generally form the basis of empirical estimates of labor supply as we shall see later.

APPENDIX 2B   THE SLUTSKY DECOMPOSITION AND THE ELASTICITY OF LABOR SUPPLY

The income and substitution effects can be derived more formally by differentiating the first-order conditions with respect to the real wage rate. This produces the Slutsky equation

$$\frac{\partial H}{\partial w} = \left.\frac{\partial H}{\partial w}\right|_{U\,=\,\text{const}} - H\left(\frac{\partial H}{\partial y}\right) \tag{2B.1}$$

$$\quad ? \qquad\quad + \qquad\qquad\quad -$$

where $w = W/P$ and $y = Y/P$. The first term on the right-hand side is the equation measuring the substitution effect and the direction of this effect is shown by the sign below. That is

$$\left.\frac{\partial H}{\partial w}\right|_{U\,=\,\text{const}} = \text{substitution effect}$$

This measures the change in hours worked as a result of the change in the real wage rate, real income remaining constant, and it captures the income compensated effect of a wage increase. The second term on the right-hand side is the equation measuring the income effect that is induced by the wage change, again the sign below shows the direction of the effect.

Thus

$$- H\left(\frac{\partial H}{\partial y}\right) = \text{income effect}$$

In turn this effect is composed of two parts, $-H$ which measures the magnitude of the reduction in hours of work and the pure income effect:

$$\frac{\partial H}{\partial y} = \text{pure income effect}$$

Given that leisure is a normal good this results in a fall in hours worked. The signs on these partial derivatives shown below Eq. (2B.1) emphasize that the total change in hours worked cannot be signed, *a priori*.

The Slutsky decomposition can also be used to reveal the determinants of the magnitude of the elasticity of labor supply. A measure of the elasticity of the income and substitution effects can be calculated by multiplying Eq. (2B.1) by the ratio of the means of the variables thus

$$\frac{\overline{w}}{\overline{H}} \times \frac{\partial H}{\partial w} = \left(\frac{\overline{w}}{\overline{H}}\right)\left(\frac{\partial H}{\partial w}\right)_{U=\text{const}} - \left(\frac{\overline{w}}{\overline{y}}\right)H\left(\frac{\overline{y}}{\overline{H}}\right)\left(\frac{\partial H}{\partial y}\right) \tag{2B.2}$$

So that $\varepsilon^s = \varepsilon_1 + \varepsilon_2$ where

$$\varepsilon_1 = \left(\frac{\overline{w}}{\overline{H}}\right)\left(\frac{\partial H}{\partial w}\right)_{U=\text{const}} \quad \text{and} \quad \varepsilon_2 = -\left(\frac{\overline{w}}{\overline{y}}\right)H\left(\frac{\overline{y}}{\overline{H}}\right)\left(\frac{\partial H}{\partial y}\right)$$

Elasticity therefore depends on the relative size of the substitution elasticity, or income compensated elasticity, ε_1, and the income elasticity, ε_2 which is sometimes called the 'marginal propensity to earn out of non-labor income'.

3

APPLICATIONS OF THE STATIC THEORY OF LABOR SUPPLY

In the previous chapter we developed the static theory of labor supply. In the present chapter we show how this elementary theory can be used to provide a number of useful insights into current policy issues in both the United States and the United Kingdom. We explore the consequences for individuals' labor supply of the several ways in which the modern state reduces or supplements the income that individuals earn in the market place. We explore the consequences of different tax and welfare systems. In recent years economic policy in both the United Kingdom and the United States has increasingly emphasized 'the supply side' of the economy. The relatively poor economic performance of the United Kingdom during the 1970s was attributed to rigidities on the supply side. Attention was focused on potential sources of rigidity in labor supply and on the tax/benefit systems which were suggested to have reduced the incentives to work and productivity. Here we explore the foundations of these beliefs which in large part arise from an application of the pedagogical devices we developed in the previous chapter. First however we recognize that individuals make their labor supply decisions in a household context and we therefore explore the implications of this for the model we shall employ in our subsequent analysis.

HOUSEHOLD LABOR SUPPLY

The theory developed in the previous chapter focused on individual labor supply. However, the vast majority of individuals in all societies are members of households and it has been objected that this fact alone will affect their labor supply. First, it is argued, it must be recognized that it is the household and not the market place which produces the commodities that most individuals consume. Second, the labor supply of each individual member of the household is likely to be contingent on the labor supply and non-market work of all other members of the household: labor supply decisions are interdependent. In this section we therefore consider how these two aspects—household production and household decision making—modify, if at all, the analysis developed to date.

Household production Many of the commodities that the household consumes require a substantial input of time by members of the household. Commodities such as reading a book, playing golf, sailing, cooking *cordon bleu* meals are all time intensive, indeed it seems that those commodities which have the greatest income elasticity of demand also require the greatest input of household time. If this proposition is correct it goes a long way toward explaining the strength of the income effect in empirical estimates of labor supply.

Recognition that all commodities require the input of time and goods and services leads naturally to the idea that in many respects the household is like a small firm: it combines various inputs to produce outputs. The household combines time and the goods and services purchased in the market to produce the commodities that the household consumes. We can think, in terms analogous to that of the firm, of a household production function, in which commodities, C, are produced by combining goods and services and leisure. So that

$$C = C(G, L) \tag{3.1}$$

We can also map a family of isoquants revealing the proportions in which G and L are combined to produce a particular level of commodities. Such an isoquant map is illustrated in Fig. 3.1(a) in which each isoquant represents a unique level of output. Imagine as a simplification that the household produces a single commodity to satisfy its needs—we shall call this food. At point A, level C_1 of food is produced by combining G_1 goods and services purchased in the market with leisure time L_1. At this point the production of C_1 may be described as relatively goods intensive. This could be food bought in a restaurant and the leisure time used is merely that necessary to consume the food. However, at point B it is evident that fewer goods and services are bought in the market and more leisure time is used. The household may be buying-in the produce and cooking and preparing it. Point C, in contrast, is relatively intensive in the use of time and requires relatively few goods and services to be purchased. The household might be cooking its own food, rearing its own chickens, growing its own vegetables, and merely purchasing the occasional fertilizer and feedstock to support these activities.

We cannot reduce the input of goods and services to zero, no matter how much of our time is substituted for bought-in items, nor can the time input be reduced to zero, no matter how much is spent on goods and services. Hence the isoquant displays the usual properties of a diminishing marginal rate of technical substitution. As usual those lying to the north-east represent higher levels of output. Of course households will differ in the degree of efficiency with which they combine G and L to produce C. If they

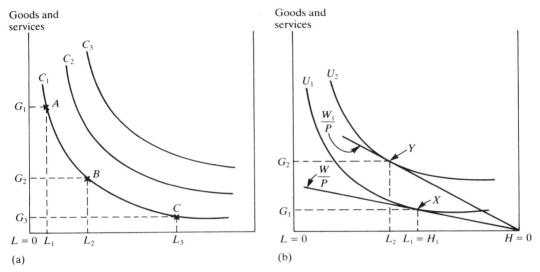

Figure 3.1 Household production. Households are like small firms combining goods and services and time to produce different commodities. Isoquants for a typical household, where each isoquant represents a unique level of output of a particular commodity, are detailed above. As an individual moves from point A to B, around isoquant C_1, they are substituting progressively more leisure time for market goods and services to produce C_1 of the commodity. If each level of output produces a unique level of satisfaction, the isoquants transform into the indifference curves of traditional theory as shown in (b). Now a rise in the wage rate from W/P to W_1/P leads to the offer of more market work and a reduction in the time spent producing commodities in the household. Commodities are now produced by more goods intensive methods

are poor cooks and burn the porridge it will take them longer and they will have to spend more on oats than the more efficient household. Households will presumably allocate tasks according to comparative advantage but even so households will still differ in efficiency.

The production of commodities is not of course an end in itself. It is the consumption of commodities from which consumers derive utility. Thus

$$U = U(C) \tag{3.2}$$

It will simplify matters if we assume that the processes of production and consumption take place simultaneously and that the satisfactions derived are strictly proportional to the 'expenditures' on time and goods and services required to produce the commodities (essentially we ignore the production by the household of assets which yield a flow of services through time, there are no deep freezers or home brewing in this world). We can then substitute Eq. (3.1) into Eq. (3.2) and a family of indifference curves of the same shape and bearing the same relationship to one another as the isoquants shown in Fig. 3.1(a) can be constructed. In this manner we arrive back at the family of indifference curves of conventional theory, that is

$$U = U[C(G,L)] \tag{3.3}$$

Such an indifference map is shown in Fig. 3.1(b) but now consider the interpretation of this. Take an individual facing a low wage rate W/P. The equilibrium of this individual is again given by the point of tangency, point X, but now this tells us not only that H_1 hours are being worked but also that L_1 hours are being devoted to the production of commodities. Evidently commodities are in this case produced by relatively time-intensive methods as we might anticipate, for the opportunity cost of the individual's time, the wage facing this individual, is low. If the wage rate rose to W_1/P this individual would devote less time to household production and more to market work.

The theory recognizes the role of the household as a producer as well as the ultimate consumer of commodities and in so doing facilitates a more realistic description of the allocation of time. However, has it provided any further insights into the determinants of labor supply in the market? In the conventional model the choice between goods and services and leisure is determined by their relative prices, P and W respectively, and although household production theory treats these as inputs, an individual's choice of inputs still depends on P and W. The opportunity cost of an individual's time remains W in all and any non-market activity, just as the price of goods and services remains P. Perhaps the most important implications of the model are for the consumer demand theory. The model reminds us that the purchase of goods and services in the market place is but a preliminary to combining these with the time necessary to produce commodities, and that therefore the demand for consumer goods and services depends both on the individual's wage rate, and the production time costs involved, as well as on the price of the goods and services themselves. Household production theory does not invalidate the conclusions that we shall draw from the model of individual labor supply developed in the previous chapter.

Household decision making The second aspect is potentially more important. Individuals' labor supply may be interdependent as a result of their membership of households. Even though a large and growing proportion of the households in both the United Kingdom and the United States comprise a single adult, it remains the case that the typical household from which we draw most of our labor supply comprises two adults: namely a married couple. In these circumstances the labor supply decisions of the partners are likely to be interdependent both because the partners' time may be regarded as substitutes in the production of certain commodities (although they will differ in the efficiency with which they can produce particular commodities) and because the earned income of one partner constitutes the unearned income of the other.

How then is this apparently more complex situation to be transformed into a form more tractable to analysis? One way is to treat the preferences of one partner as dominant and to describe the household's decisions purely in terms of the preferences embodied in the dominant partner's indifference map. Another way is to construct a household utility function, but in so doing we are then detailing the labor supplied by the household in total and are unable to distinguish the contributions of each of its members. Perhaps the simplest way is to consider the income earned and the goods and services produced in the household by the husband as constituting the unearned income of the wife, and vice versa. Then the point at which the wage ray facing either partner cuts the vertical axis in simple models of individual labor supply such as were depicted in Figs. 2.2 to 2.4 is determined by both the earnings and the scale of household production of the other partner. In this manner we can retain the simple diagrammatic apparatus we have employed to date. Throughout the subsequent analysis we shall employ this convention, recognizing that where the individual being analyzed is regarded as a member of a household containing at least two persons of working age, the labor supply decisions of the adult household members may be interdependent. This interdependence is captured in the magnitude of each partner's unearned income. Such interdependence can have important consequences for labor supply under certain types of welfare benefit systems which we now move on to discuss.

THE BENEFIT SYSTEM

Most industrial countries currently operate schemes that insure individuals against loss of income while out of work and schemes that provide income support for the least advantaged members of the community. They operate both *income replacement* programs, that is programs that replace or restore part of lost income and *income maintenance* or *income guarantee* programs, that is programs that exist to raise the incomes of the poor. Income replacement programs provide contingent benefits— benefits to which individuals become entitled if some particular event such as sickness, injury or unemployment occurs. Income maintenance programs exist to provide individuals with some socially acceptable minimum level of income. In the following pages we consider the consequences for work effort of the different forms that such schemes might take. First we consider income replacement programs.

Income replacement

Unemployment insurance Typically, individuals who are looking for work, having recently either lost or quit a job, are offered unemployment compensation from a public unemployment insurance scheme. Some schemes offer all eligible individuals the same fixed money sum while others tie the level of benefit to an individual's previous earnings and replace a fixed proportion of these.

The proportion of previous income that is replaced is known as the *replacement ratio*. Replacement ratios are calculated by taking previous earnings, net of income tax, and social security contributions and expressing the benefits received when unemployed (net of tax payments where appropriate) as a proportion of these. Figure 3.2 reports replacement ratios in four countries in the year 1981/82 for individuals unemployed for one year.

In Germany benefits were tied to previous earnings levels and were therefore constant at around 65 percent across different family sizes and previous earnings levels. In contrast, in Australia and the United Kingdom benefits are related primarily to family size and consequently for those on very low earnings, category A—less than

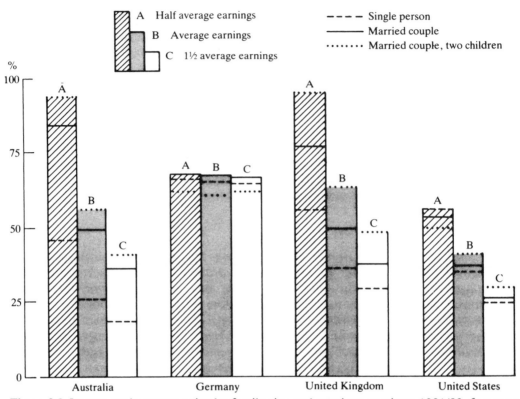

Figure 3.2 Income replacement ratios by family size and previous earnings: 1981/82, first year of unemployment (*Source*: OECD *Employment Outlook*, Sept. 1984). Reproduced with permission of the OECD.

half average earnings, the replacement ratio exceeded 90 per cent. However, few workers are on such low earnings, more representative is the situation of category B. In the early 1980s a married couple on average earnings but without any dependants enjoyed a replacement rate of approximately 65 per cent in Germany, 50 per cent in the United Kingdom and Australia and around 40 per cent in the United States. For single persons and those whose earnings were previously above the average, the replacement ratio is even lower, in all countries except Germany. On the face of it therefore most individuals who become unemployed are substantially worse off in money terms than when previously in work.[1]

1. The scale of the income loss consequent upon unemployment appears to be greater than that revealed here for Micklewright (1985) ('Fiction versus facts: unemployment benefits in Britain', *National Westminister Bank Review*) reports that in 1981 a quarter of those eligible for income replacement in the United Kingdom were not in receipt of it. However, he fails to distinguish whether they failed to claim because their entitlements would have been trivial or whether they were simply ignorant of their rights, and so the magnitude of the income and welfare loss is difficult to quantify.

One question commonly raised is why should individuals who become unemployed through no fault of their own be made so substantially worse off. Perhaps they became unemployed as a result of a necessary restructuring of industry, or as part of the ongoing process of reallocating factors of production in which intervening spells of unemployment are a feature. Why should the costs of adjustment bear so disproportionately on those who lose their jobs and might this not provide an incentive to resist job changes and restructuring? Should a much larger proportion of previous earnings be replaced? This is the issue we address in Fig. 3.3. Individual A, whose preferences are represented by indifference curves U_1, U_2 and U_3, is faced with wage rate W/P when in work. This is the wage the individual was earning before becoming unemployed and which he or she expects to earn when re-employed. Assume simply that this wage is subject to a proportional income tax, regardless of the level of the individual's income so that while pre-tax earnings are $(W/P)H_1$, post-tax earnings are

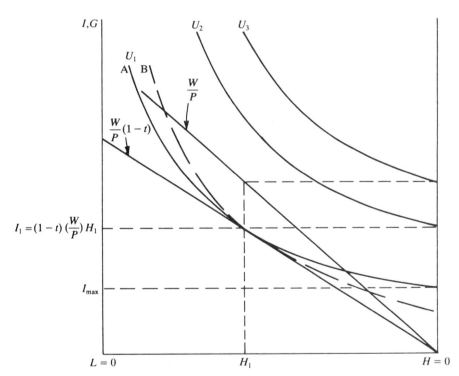

Figure 3.3 An income replacement program. Pre- and post-tax earnings while in work will differ by tax rate t. When in work individual A, whose preferences are represented by indifference curves U_1, U_2 and U_3 chooses to work H_1 hours and receives post-tax income $(1 - t)(W/P)H_1$. If this individual became unemployed, an income replacement program, which replaced either the whole of pre- or post-tax earnings, would place the individual on a higher indifference curve, U_3 or U_2 respectively. Only if income I_{max} is replaced is the individual no better off out of work than working. If a level just below I_{max} is established as the level of income replacement, then at present tax rates this results in the wage W/P becoming the reservation wage

$(1-t)(W/P)H_1$. (We shall discuss the effect of different income tax schedules and thus the likely shape of the post-tax wage ray later in this chapter.)

Now consider the position if this individual became unemployed. An unemployment compensation scheme which replaced the whole of gross income would enable the individual to reach indifference curve U_3 and would result in the individual being substantially better off out of work than in work. Replacing the whole of post-tax income would enable the individual to reach indifference curve U_2 and he or she would still be substantially better off out of work than before. Only if the proportion of earnings equal to I_{max} were replaced would the individual be no better off unemployed than when previously working. If the income replaced falls below I_{max} the individual is worse off out of work than in work and this provides an incentive to seek work. This would seem to be one of the reasons why unemployment compensation schemes typically replace only a relatively modest proportion of gross earnings.

Crucially the above conclusions depend on the nature of the individual's preferences. The individual in Fig. 3.3 was indifferent between working H_1 hours and receiving income $(1-t)(W/P)H_1$, and working zero hours and receiving the much lower income I_{max}. As a consequence of being unemployed the individual lost goods and services equal in value to $(1-t)(W/P)H_1 - I_{max}$, but this was adequately compensated by H_1 additional hours of leisure. The negative slope of the indifference curves reveals that individuals place a positive value on leisure and therefore even though their money income is lower when not working, they can still be better off out of work. From the above it seems clear that unemployment insurance schemes should replace only a fraction of lost earnings if they are to retain incentives to seek work.

Of course the rate at which individuals are willing to trade off goods and services for leisure, the *MRS*, will differ from one person to another. Older people may place a higher value on leisure, while workers of prime age may place a higher value on goods and services. This will be reflected in quite different indifference maps for the two groups. Suppose individual A in Fig. 3.3, whose preferences are represented by U_1, U_2 and U_3 is a prime age worker, while B is an older worker. The preferences of B might reasonably be illustrated as shown by the broken line. It is clear from this that we need only replace a smaller fraction of the earnings of B, than of A, if we wish to insure that they both enjoy the same level of utility in and out of work. If older workers place a higher value on leisure and the intention of the income replacement scheme is to compensate workers equally, then unemployment pay should be graduated inversely with age.

Tastes for leisure are unlikely to remain unchanged if an individual remains unemployed for a long period. Consider the effect that a long period of unemployment might have on an individual's tastes for leisure. It is probable that although the increased leisure associated with unemployment is initially valued, as the length of time spent unemployed increases, individuals come to place a negative value on some of this leisure time. They no longer require some increase in goods and services to induce them to work more, they are instead prepared to sacrifice goods and services, that is to pay for the opportunity to work. This is reflected in indifferences curves that are now positively sloping over some range as illustrated in Fig. 3.4.

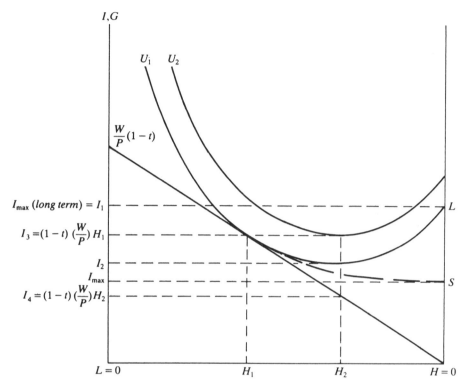

Figure 3.4 Income replacement for the long-term unemployed. When working and when initially unemployed the individual's preferences are represented by indifference curve U_1S. Continued experience of unemployment may result in a change in tastes which are now represented by indifference curve U_1L. Now the worker is willing to forgo income in order to secure up to H_2 hours of work. It is now possible to replace income to a level greater than previous earnings, up to I_1, without the worker being better off unemployed than working

As before we assume that the post-tax wage that faced the individual when in work is given by $(1 - t)W/P$. Previously the individual shown worked H_1 hours and received post-tax income $I_3 = (1 - t)(W/P)H_1$. Initially, upon becoming unemployed the individual's preferences for income and leisure are unchanged, and are represented by the indifference curve U_1S. However, as a result of a continuing inability to find a job individuals come to place a negative value on part of their leisure time, so that over the range from H_2 to $H = 0$, the indifference curve is positively sloping and preferences are now represented by the curve U_1L. The individual would now be prepared to forgo income $I_1 - I_2$ to obtain H_2 hours of work, that is he or she is willing to pay to obtain work.

What are the consequences of this change in tastes? First unemployment compensation can be increased above the level I_{max} without diminishing the incentives to seek work. The change in the worker's tastes means that there will no longer be the disincentive effects associated with the higher level of unemployment compensation which we noted before. Now only schemes which result in income greater than I_1 when without work will make the worker better off unemployed. If the purpose of the income replacement scheme is to compensate individuals equally, for the loss of a job, it is clear from this figure that the level of income provision for the long-term unemployed should be increased. Any level of income replacement below I_{max} (*long term*) makes the individual worse off unemployed than when previously employed. Moreover, it is also evident that it would be possible to make the worker better off, at a lower level of income replacement than I_1. This could be done, for example, by the state providing employment for H_2 hours each week together with a level of income support producing an income equal to I_3. Provided the individual regarded the work which the state provided as a perfect substitute for work in non-state employment he or she would now be better off. Note that I_3 comprises income from work, $I_4 = (1 - t)(W/P)H_2$ and an income supplement equal to $I_3 - I_4$. Such a combination of work and income replacement would place the worker on the higher indifference curve U_2 but could save the state income support costs equal to $I_1 - (I_3 - I_4)$. The total costs of such an exercise would of course depend on the costs of providing H_2 hours of work in addition to the income support, but as long as the cost of providing H_2 hours of work in addition to the income support, was less than $I_1 - (I_3 - I_4)$, it would be possible to increase the welfare of the long-term unemployed at a lower level of total outlay. If the net wage paid to the worker $((W/P)1 - t)$ equals their marginal product the state saves $I_1 - (I_3 - I_4)$.

The foregoing suggests that for the long-term unemployed all leisure can no longer be regarded as 'good', some at least assumes the characteristics of a 'bad'. Accordingly income replacement provision for the long-term unemployed can be more generous than for the recently unemployed, without diminishing incentives to seek work.

Up to now we have discussed the effects of income replacement schemes only on the person declared unemployed. However, income replacement schemes may affect the labor supply decisions of other family members in households where they are of working age. Thus, if the male in the household becomes unemployed, the reduction in male earnings will affect the unearned income of other family members. This can serve either to increase or reduce the labor supply of other family members. The alternative outcomes are illustrated in Fig. 3.5.

First consider the situation depicted in Fig. 3.5(a). Prior to the husband becoming unemployed the wife did not work, she located at point A, enjoying unearned income Y_0^A/P as a consequence of the husband's earnings. Once unemployed the husband's income consists only of unemployment compensation and the wife's unearned income therefore drops to Y_1^A/P. The wife therefore decides to work H_1 hours in order to increase family income which now comprises I_1 unemployment compensation and $I_2 - I_1$ wife's earned income. This outcome is known as the *added worker effect* for an additional person has been added to the labor force.

An alternative development is where the husband's entitlement to unemployment insurance payments is related to the level of family income. Prior to the husband becoming unemployed the wife worked H_1 and this is depicted in Fig. 3.5(b). Again, the unemployment of the husband results in a drop in the wife's unearned income

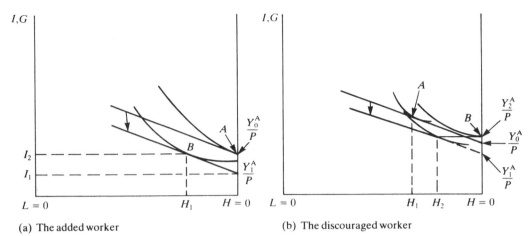

(a) The added worker   (b) The discouraged worker

Figure 3.5 Discouraged and added worker effects. The above diagrams show two alternative effects of unemployment insurance schemes on the labor supply of other family members. In both cases the wife's unearned income falls from Y_0^A/P to Y_1^A/P when the husband becomes unemployed. (a) This results in the wife taking a job and working H_1 to secure houshold income I_2, comprising $I_2 - I_1$, wife's earned income and Y_1^A/P unemployment insurance payments; (b) The situation illustrated here is different because the family's entitlement to supplementary unemployment insurance payments equal to $Y_2^A - Y_1^A/P$ is contingent on the level of family income. The supplement is withdrawn completely if family income equals or exceeds Y_2^A/P with the result that, given the limited earnings opportunities that confront the wife, the wife's utility is maximized if she ceases work altogether and moves to a point such as B

from Y_0^A/P to Y_1^A/P. But now if the wife is not earning the family also receives a further payment, $Y_2^A - Y_1^A$, provided the family has no other source of income. The wife who would otherwise have worked H_2 hours now stops work in order to insure eligibility for this additional source of income. This is one variant of the *discouraged worker effect*.[2]

Finally, a word of caution. In the foregoing analysis we reasoned that unemployed workers had an incentive to seek work if they expected to receive a higher post-tax income when in work than when unemployed. We assumed that the wage the unemployed workers expected to be offered if they obtained a job was equal to the wage rate received when last employed. This may be a reasonable assumption to make about workers who have recently become unemployed, but it may not accurately reflect the expected wages of the long-term unemployed. The continuing experience of unemployment will lead some workers to revise down their expectations of the wage rate they will be offered if they find a job. Accordingly the wage ray $(W/P)(1 - t)$ will

---

2. In the United Kingdom in 1987 unemployed workers were entitled to unemployment benefit for a maximum of a year. The full rate for the individual was £31.45 per week but this was increased by £19.40 for a dependant such as a husband or a wife. However, if the dependant earned more than £19.40 per week this addition to houshold income was withdrawn in full. Hence we might anticipate that dependants with relatively low earnings opportunities, those with earnings up to and only slightly in excess of £19.40 per week, would withdraw from the labor force. See Dilnot, A. and Kell, M. 'Male unemployment and women's work', *Fiscal Studies* **8**(3), 1–16.

pivot downwards leading to a new tangency position with a lower indifference curve. Such a development would warrant a lower level of income replacement than indicated above.[3] These downward revisions in the expected wage must be set against the reducing utility from leisure when determining the appropriate level of benefits for the long-term unemployed.

Lump sum severance payments One of the principal ways in which individuals become unemployed is through voluntary and involuntary severance, often termed voluntary and involuntary redundancy in the United Kingdom where statutory provisions require that many of those declared redundant receive a once-and-for-all lump sum payment. In addition, employers in both the United Kingdom and the United States often make additional provision both to compensate for the expected loss of income this entails and to induce voluntary severance.[4] Statutory and private provisions compensate individuals according to a formula which generally reflects previous earnings and length of service. Accordingly older workers tend to be among the principal beneficiaries of such schemes. The question arises as to the impact of such schemes on unemployment. Do such schemes diminish the incentive to find and accept work and do they therefore increase unemployment?

It might be thought that a once-and-for-all lump sum payment would have no effect on an individual's willingness to seek further work, for on the face of it, subsequently earned income is not adversely affected by the receipt of such a lump sum. However, such a view ignores the fact that an individual can convert the lump sum payment into either an annuity, by using it to purchase financial assets, or directly into a flow of consumption services, by using it to purchase consumer durables. Individuals can in this manner enhance their permanent income.

Consider Fig. 3.6 which reflects the situation confronting an unemployed worker in receipt of severance pay. It details the post-tax wage ray associated with the wage that the individual previously enjoyed and which he or she expects to be offered if a further job is secured. Assume for ease of exposition that a proportional tax rate, t, is applied at a uniform rate to all levels of earned income, while unearned income at the levels considered here is exempt from tax. Without the income stream provided by the severance pay the worker's full income is $(1 - t)(W/P)T$. With the permanent income stream, Y/P, it becomes $[(1 - t)(W/P)T] + Y/P$. Indifference curves U_1^A and U_2^A reflect the preferences of a prime age worker, while U_1^B and U_2^B reflect those of an older worker.

3. The student should pivot the wage ray $(W/P)(1 - t)$ in Fig. 3.4 to the left and consider the consequences of this for the level of utility of the long-term unemployed and the proportion of previous earnings that should now be replaced.
4. A 1981 survey revealed that around 70 percent of all workers declared redundant in the United Kingdom in that year were eligible for statutory redundancy payments; 40 percent of these also received an additional redundancy payment from their previous employers while employers made some payment to 30 percent of those who were ineligible under the state scheme. *Institute of Manpower Studies Manpower Commentary No. 13: Redundancy Provisions Surveys*, Institute of Manpower Studies, University of Sussex, Brighton, 1981.

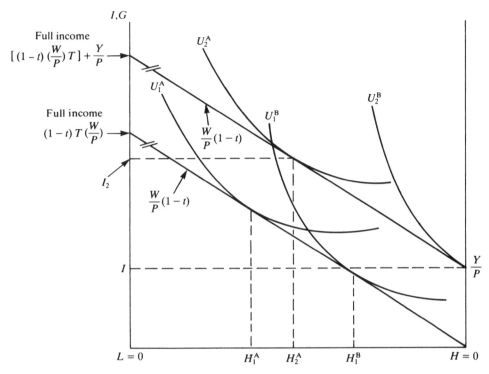

Figure 3.6 The effect of severance pay on hours subsequently worked. If a lump-sum severance payment is converted into à permanent income flow of magnitude Y/P, which we have assumed to be untaxed, this alters the constraints facing individuals. Above individual A reduces hours worked from H_1^A to H_2^A, while individual B, who has a marked preference for leisure, stops working altogether

Confronted with a wage offer of W/P in the absence of severance pay, individual A would work H_1^A hours and individual B, H_1^B hours. However, suppose that each had been awarded severance pay as a result of losing their previous jobs and had converted this lump sum into an income stream equal to Y/P. It is evident that this would affect the hours they are prepared to work in their new jobs. Individual A would wish to work only H_2^A hours producing total income I_2, while individual B would now stop working altogether and live off the unearned income.

Of course, the outcome will depend on the nature of each individual's preferences but provided individuals' preferences can be represented by indifference curves that are negatively sloped, provided leisure is a normal good, then hours worked will be reduced. It may be that as individuals approach retirement their preferences for leisure increase, as suggested by the more steeply sloped indifference map of individual B. Even younger individuals, those with a high personal discount rate, may 'blow the lot' on leisure and as a result stop work altogether.

Income maintenance

The poverty trap: the tax and benefit system Now we turn from income replacement to income maintenance schemes. In the United Kingdom there are now two main sources of income maintenance: Income Support which is available to those out of work and Family Credit which is available to those in work but with incomes below some socially agreed minimum. Income Support provides income maintenance for those who never worked, and is an additional source of income replacement for those who previously worked; Family Credit provides income maintenance for those in work. The size of these benefits is determined by comparing the 'need' of the family—taking into account family size, location and housing commitments—to its resources, that is income and wealth.

Prior to the introduction of these schemes in the United Kingdom benefits were available to individuals whose incomes fell below an agreed minimum; the state provided a *minimum income guarantee* to all its citizens. However, entitlement to benefits fell by £1 or more for every £1 extra earned. Thus, as individuals found work or increased their hours of work £1 or more was lost in tax payments and benefits for every £1 earned. This was because taxes became payable before the ceiling for benefits had been reached and thus taxes were being levied at the same time that benefits were being withdrawn. This system is very similar to the old system of welfare that existed in the United States prior to 1967. Here, again, a family's entitlement to welfare was assessed according to the size of the family, the area in which the family lived and, since welfare provision varies in the United States from state to state, according to the local welfare regulations. Consider the problems that are associated with this type of benefit system. An illustration of which is given in Fig. 3.7.

Suppose that the government establishes some minimum level of income, I_G, which it provides for all individuals whether they are working or not, call this the social minimum. Suppose further that this minimum is above the level of the tax threshold, that is the income level at which tax becomes payable, I_T. Up to this point the wage rate that an individual can earn from working is given by W/P but beyond the tax threshold, I_T, the individual starts to pay tax at rate t and the post-tax wage ray is therefore $W/P(1 - t)$. The government guarantees income level I_G but then effectively reduces income by withdrawing benefits and levying tax so that together they reduce income \$1 for every \$1 earned below the guaranteed minimum, I_G. This confronts the individual with the budget constraint represented by bold line *ABCD* in Fig. 3.7. Between income level 0 and I_G the individual is confronted with a horizontal tax schedule implying a marginal tax rate of 100 percent. Increasing hours of work by any amount from 0 up to H^P produces no increase in disposable income. Individuals are caught in something called '*the poverty trap*'. Even though they work additional hours they cannot increase their income. What effect does this have on individual work effort? As we might anticipate it substantially reduces it.

Individuals below the social minimum, such as individual B, who would have worked H^B hours for I^B income, in the absence of welfare entitlement, will now reach a much higher level of utility, U_2^B, if he or she ceases working altogether. There is no

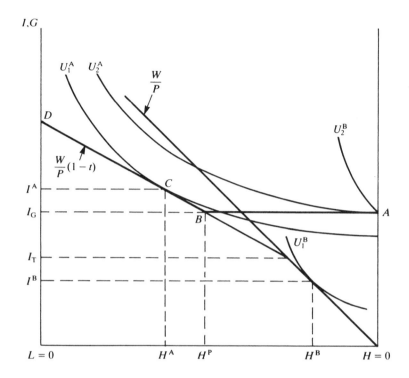

Figure 3.7 Guaranteed income levels. The government guarantees income level I_G to all individuals, but then withdraws welfare support on a $ for $ basis on all earnings up to this level. The effects of the tax system and the withdrawal of welfare support confront individuals with a marginal tax rate of 100 percent over the earnings range of 0 to I_G. The budget constraint is therefore represented by the solid line. Some individuals such as B whose earnings in the absence of the scheme (I^B) would have fallen below the guaranteed minimum, are now better off not working. Others with earnings which exceed the guaranteed minimum, such as individual A above, are also better off not working. Note that under such a scheme income remains at I_G regardless of how many hours in the range 0 to H^P individuals confronted by this wage rate work. These individuals are caught in the poverty trap

incentive to work for the minimum is received regardless, and if he or she works it means forgoing consumption of the 'good' leisure.

Such as system evidently provides no incentive to work to those individuals whose potential earnings fall below the I_G. But such schemes have other effects. They also induce some with earnings above the guaranteed minimum to stop working as well. Individual A, who in the absence of the scheme would have worked H^A hours for income I^A, is now able to reach a higher indifference curve U_2^A by stopping working altogether. In this case the extra income from work $I^A - I_G$ is insufficient to compensate for the forgone leisure of H^A hours.

It would appear that such schemes could offer substantial disincentives to a large number of people and it is therefore perhaps surprising that so many people continued to work when these schemes were in operation. One of the reasons that more people did not withdraw from work when confronted by such schemes was that the interaction of the several different types of benefits and the tax system made it extremely difficult for individuals to assess accurately the true marginal tax rates that confronted them. Another reason was that some individuals would have continued working for incomes below the minimum since they were investing in either human capital (which we shall discuss in Chapter 6), or work experience.

The above results again depend on both the tastes and preferences of individuals as well as on the opportunities that confronted them. If their tastes had been different, if they had displayed a stronger commitment to work, a more pronounced 'work ethic', the outcome might have been different. How would we represent the preferences or tastes of such an individual? A pronounced 'work ethic' need not represent a commitment to work as an end in itself by may instead reflect a strong preference for income and the goods and services this will buy. Clearly individuals with such preferences are less willing to trade off goods and services for leisure, they have a very low *MRS*, and their preferences are therefore represented by flatter indifference curves. The readers should be able to see for themselves that representing individual A's preferences by a series of flatter indifference curves in Fig. 3.7 could lead to this individual continuing to work H^A hours even after the introduction of the minimum income guarantee I_G.[5]

Yet such strong preferences for work might alone be insufficient to insure that the individual would be better off continuing to work, for the outcome depends on both tastes and opportunities. Suppose that the wage rate facing the individual in Fig. 3.7 were considerably lower than W/P, because the individual had no skills, or suppose that the imposition of a higher income tax rate flattened the post-tax wage ray. These developments would effectively extend the horizontal section of the budget constraint, increasing substantially the number of hours the individual would need to work before he or she could earn an income that exceeded I_G. Despite an individual's strong commitment to work it would now be far less likely that work would place him or her on a higher indifference curve than if he or she stopped working altogether.

The outcomes above were determined by the nature of the income maintenance scheme and its interaction with the tax system for together these determined the constraints confronting the individual. It was suggested that the combined effect of these was to offer only very small, if any, incentives to work, to certain individuals so that even in the face of a strong commitment to work on their part they were still better off not working. Are there tax systems which do not produce such marked disincentives to work?

---

5. Individuals who display an overwhelming commitment to work, who become restless and bored when not at work, have sometimes been described as workaholics. They regard no work as inferior to some work and are willing to trade off some of their income for hours of work. We have encountered such an individual before, in Fig. 3.4 when we discussed the enforced idleness of the unemployed. The same indifference map may be used to illustrate the preferences of the workaholic.

The negative income tax The disincentives to work inherent in the previous scheme could be reduced by lowering substantially the minimum income guarantee and reducing the rate at which benefits are withdrawn as income rises, that is by imposing a marginal tax rate which is substantially less than the 100 percent evident above. These are features of an alternative system of welfare support—the negative income tax system—but, in turn, this is not without its problems. Such a system is illustrated in Fig. 3.8.

In the absence of either taxes or transfers, the wage rate is shown as W/P in Fig. 3.8. There is a break-even level of income, B_1, beyond which individuals receive no benefits, but below which individuals receive a transfer payment, TR, determined as a fraction t_1, of the amount by which their earned income falls below this level. That is

$$TR = t_1[B_1 - (W/P)H] \tag{3.4}$$

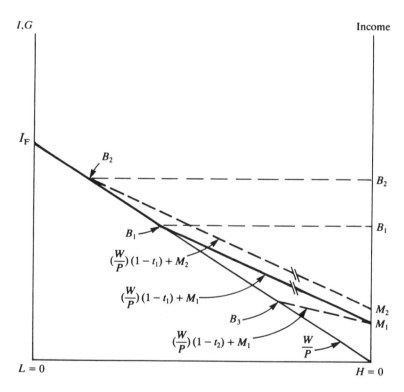

Figure 3.8 A negative income tax scheme. This provides a minimum income guarantee of M_1 then withdraws this income at a rate t_1 up to some break-even level of income B_1. The budget constraint confronting the individual is shown by the solid line, $M_1B_1I_F$. Raising the minimum income guarantee to M_2 keeping t_1 the same raises B_1 to B_2 and brings more people within the scope of the scheme. Raising t_1 to t_2, while holding M at M_1 reduces B_1 to B_3 and reduces the scope of the schemes

Effectively such schemes offer a lower guaranteed minimum income, M_1, which is then withdrawn at a rate t_1 for every $1 earned. If M_1 and t_1 are fixed, B_1 is then automatically determined thus

$$B_1 = \frac{M_1}{t_1} \tag{3.5}$$

Take the following example to illustrate the above points. Suppose that M = $20, per week and t has been fixed at 0.2, then the break-even point

$$B = \frac{M}{t} = \frac{\$20}{0.2} = \$100 \tag{3.6}$$

Now take individuals for whom W/P = $2.50 per hour. If they work 20 hours per week they earn $2.50 multiplied by 20 = $50 and from Eqs. (3.4) and (3.6) it can be found that they also received a transfer.

$$TR = 0.2[100 - (\$2.50)20] = \$10 \tag{3.7}$$

Their total income is $50 earned income plus the $10 transfer payment. Effectively the minimum income guarantee, M, of $20 has been withdrawn at a rate of 0.2 for every dollar earned. Income maintenance payments lost amount to

$$t[(W/P)H] = 0.2(\$50) = \$10 \tag{3.8}$$

Therefore $10 of the initial $20 per week guaranteed minimum income has been withdrawn when 20 hours have been worked. t is the tax rate confronting the individual and for every extra $1 earned, 0.2 or 20 cents is lost as the minimum income guarantee is reduced by 20 cents in each $1.

Again, an individual working 38 hours at the same wage receives a transfer payment

$$TR = 0.2[100 - (\$2.50)38] = \$1 \tag{3.9}$$

In this case the minimum guarantee, M, of $20 reduced at a rate of 0.2 for every $1 earned, results in a loss of income maintenance payments equal to

$$t[(W/P)H] = 0.2(\$95) = \$19 \tag{3.10}$$

and the individual is left with only a $1 transfer payment. This individual's income now comprises $95 earned income plus a $1 transfer payment.

Evidently the transfer payments made to each individual under such a scheme are in general lower than under alternative welfare schemes since the intention is to preserve the incentives to work. This intention is reflected in the low marginal tax rate, $t = 0.2$, in this example. A more generous scheme which raised M to M_2 as in Fig. 3.8 keeping t constant would raise the break-even level to B_2 and hence the number of people who became eligible for transfer payments. Suppose that in our example M were raised to $40, with t held at 0.2 then:

$$B = \frac{M}{t} = \frac{\$40}{0.2} = \$200 \tag{3.11}$$

B would double, and this would substantially broaden the scope of the scheme. On the other hand if t were raised, say to 0.4, while holding M constant at $M_1 = \$20$, then since

$$B = \frac{M}{t} = \frac{\$20}{0.4} = \$50 \qquad (3.12)$$

B would fall considerably and reduce the scope of the scheme, as indicated by the shallowest broken line in Fig. 3.8. In this latter case the higher rate, t_2, at which M is withdrawn, the higher marginal tax rate confronting those workers who remain within the scope of the scheme, would lower their incentives to work. In essence a negative income tax scheme insures incentives to work by lowering the minimum income guarantee and the rate at which this is withdrawn. It works by confronting those within the scope of the scheme by low marginal tax rates. But if the minimum income guarantee is not to be reduced to an absurdly inadequate level, lowering the marginal tax rate means increasing the scope of the scheme and this then affects the supply of hours of a far larger number of people than would a simple guaranteed income scheme.

Consider the supply of hours under a negative income tax (NIT) scheme as compared to both the 'no welfare' situation and a 'guaranteed income scheme', a scheme guaranteeing a higher minimum, but withdrawing this income support on a $1 for $1 basis as illustrated previously. Fig. 3.9 details these three situations. With no welfare support H_N^A hours of work are supplied and income level I_N^A is achieved by individual A. The introduction of a negative income tax scheme results in a higher income, I_{NT}^A, but some reduction in hours worked to H_{NT}^A for this individual. Under such a scheme, the level of utility, at U_2^A, is higher than in the absence of welfare support, but is still lower than under the guaranteed income scheme which enables the worker to reach indifference curve U_3^A. However, U_3^A was achieved by quitting work altogether, while at U_2^A the individual supplies H_{NT}^A hours of work. Under the negative income tax the individual reduced his or her dependency on the state compared to the guaranteed income scheme. The individual received a supplement equal to the vertical distance between W/P and U_2^A above H_{NT}^A, but also contributed to output by working. Thus the negative income tax has increased the supply of hours when compared to the guaranteed income system of welfare support.

Figure 3.9 also shows that the wider scope of the negative income tax scheme results in individual B, who was unaffected by the guaranteed income scheme reducing his hours of work from H_N^B to H_{NT}^B. Individual B is now in receipt of an income supplement equal to the vertical distance between W/P and U_2^B above H_{NT}^B whereas previously this individual received no welfare support. The wider scope of the NIT scheme results in a reduction in hours of work by individuals who were previously unaffected by the welfare system. The net effect of the negative tax scheme on hours of work therefore depends on the balance between two opposing tendencies. On the one hand it induces those previously affected by the old guaranteed minimum income level to increase their hours of work, but on the other it encourages some previously unaffected by welfare schemes to reduce their hours of work. It is an empirical question as to which effect dominates.

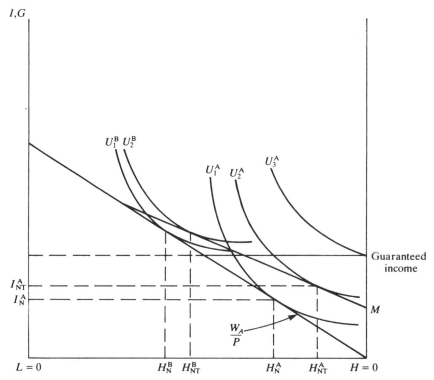

Figure 3.9 A negative income tax and guaranteed income scheme compared. The line W_A/P represents the 'no welfare' situation. In this situation individual A offers H_N^A hours of work. The introduction of a negative income tax scheme (NIT) results in some reduction of hours, from H_N^A to H_{NT}^A but results in a higher level of income I_{NT}^A and utility U_2^A. The introduction of a guaranteed minimum income scheme results in still higher income and utility U_3^A but complete withdrawal from the labor market. The negative income tax scheme therefore retains incentives to work while providing higher income than in the no welfare situation. However, the NIT also brings within its scope individuals, such as B, who were unaffected by the previous scheme. Under the NIT, individual B reduces hours of work from H_N^B to H_{NT}^B when there would have been no reduction in hours of work under the guaranteed income scheme. The NIT therefore only increases the supply of hours over those provided under a guaranteed income scheme if the reduction in hours by individuals such as B is less than the increase in hours of individuals such as A

It is clear from the above that when compared to a system of no welfare support a negative income tax scheme succeeds in raising the incomes of the low paid. The income of individual A rose from I_N^A to I_{NT}^A although this was still lower than the income level provided under the old guaranteed income scheme. The lower income provides the incentive for individuals to find work, but if this proves impossible the individual is worse off under the negative income tax scheme. Under the negative income tax scheme the individual can only achieve an adequate income by working.

The success of such a scheme is therefore dependent on the supply of jobs, that is on the demand for labor, an issue we shall consider in later chapters.

How large is the overall change in labor supply under a negative income tax scheme? This was a question a series of experiments, such as are seldom conducted, in the social sciences set out to answer in the United States over the period 1968–80. A series of experiments were mounted in New Jersey and Pennsylvania (1968–72), North Carolina and Iowa (1969–73), Gary, Indiana (1970–74) and Seattle and Denver (1970–80). In each of these a control group and an experimental group of households were selected. The budget constraint facing each of the experimental groups of households was then changed and their behavior contrasted with that of the control group and their own behavior before the experiment.[6]

Thus, for example, in the New Jersey and Pennsylvania experiment some 1400 families with incomes 150 percent or less than the social security defined poverty level were selected and these were split into a control and experimental group. Those in the experimental group were then further subdivided into four groups provided with different minimum income guarantees with M equal to 50,75,100 and 125 percent of the poverty line. In turn, each of these groups was subdivided into a further three groups, distinguished by the rate at which the minimim income guarantee was withdrawn. The minimum income guarantee was withdrawn at $t = 0.3$, 0.5 and 0.7 from each of the three groups. The control group received no welfare support.

So what happened? Invariably males in the experimental group were found to be working fewer hours than those in the control group, between 2 and 7 percent fewer hours per week. They were also found to be less likely to be employed midway through the experiment. These results reflect the effects of changes in both the slope and position of the budget constraint facing the experimental households, for both M and t were varied. The more important studies of the effects of these experiments on male labor supply are brought together and analyzed in Table 3.1, together with the results from a further three studies for females.

Table 3.1 details the overall wage elasticity of hours of work and the income and substitution elasticities from the various studies for men and women. The wage elasticity of hours of work (elasticity of labor supply) for men in these low income households ranges from -0.16 to $+0.21$. The income effect, the non-labor income elasticity of hours of work, ranges from a low of -0.29, suggesting more hours of leisure are purchased out of rising real income, to less plausibly $+0.02$, suggesting that for these households leisure is an inferior good. Estimates of the substitution effect are much narrower, ranging between 0.06 and 0.19, confirming the expected positive substitution effect in terms of hours of work, or negative substitution effect in terms of hours of leisure. On balance the studies suggest a positively sloping labor supply curve, because in general, the substitution effect exceeds the income effect but it is clear that this has not been measured with much precision. There is more agreement about

6. The negative income tax experiments are discussed in Pechman, J.A. and Tampane, P.M. (eds.) (1975) *Work Incentivies and Income Guarantees: The New Jersey Negative Income Tax Experiment*, Brookings, Washington.

Table 3.1 Estimated effects on labor supply of a negative income tax

	Elasticity of labor supply	Income elasticity	Substitution elasticity
Men			
Ashenfelter (1978)	0.21	0.02	0.19
	0.17	– 0.01	0.18
Burtless and Greenberg (1982)	0.08	– 0.04	0.12
	– 0.12	– 0.18	0.06
Hausman and Wise (1977)	0.10	– 0.01	0.11
Johnson and Pencavel (1982)	– 0.16	– 0.29	0.13
Johnson and Pencavel (1984)	0.02	– 0.17	0.19
Women			
Hausman (1980)	0.05	– 0.11	0.16
Burtless and Greenberg (1982)	0.19	– 0.18	0.37
Johnson and Pencavel (1982)	0.09	– 0.09	0.18

Sources: Pencavel, J.H. (1986), 'Labor supply of men: a survey' and Killingsworth, M.R. and Heckman, J.J. (1986), 'Female labor supply : a survey', both in Ashenfelter, O. and Layard, R. (eds.), *Handbook of Labor Economics*, vol. 1, North-Holland, London. Killingsworth, M.R. (1983) *Labour Supply*, Cambridge University Press, Cambridge, England.

the effects on women. Again, a positively sloping labor supply emerges, that is the substitution effect overwhelms the income effect. It is moreover noticeable that the magnitudes of the estimated income and substitution effects and hence of the overall elasticity differ little between men and women which is rather surprising given the generally larger claims on women's leisure time. These imprecise results for men and rather low estimates for women are due in no small part to the problems that plagued these experiments.

As we might expect, a controlled experiment involving human beings is difficult to conduct. Thus there were changes, outwith the control of the experiment, which affected the budget constraints of the selected households. For example, New Jersey reformed its welfare program midway through the experiment so that it now offered better opportunities than the experiment to a number of households with the result that they opted out of the scheme. Again the experiments were perceived to be of a temporary nature, for most households received the NIT payments for only three years. This would induce different behavioral responses from a permanent change in labor market opportunities. Some individuals perceiving a temporarily higher level of welfare support might withdraw from the labor market for the duration of the experiment, perhaps to invest in further schooling and return to the market on the cessation of the experiment.

Those individuals planning to be in and out of employment, for example married women contemplating childbearing, might concentrate their periods out of employment

during the experiment when benefits were highest. In contrast, workers with high paying steady jobs might be reluctant to quit these and move to other lighter jobs knowing
the income support to be of a temporary nature. For all these reasons it has been argued
that the results are best interpreted as those resulting from temporary changes in labor
market opportunities. In fact these ambiguous results tell us little about the effects of a
negative income tax scheme that we could not have deduced from other non-
experimental studies. A great deal of money was spent on these experiments from
which we have learnt little but, if nothing else, they testify to the almost insuperable
difficulties of conducting controlled experiments in the social sciences.

THE INCOME TAX SYSTEM

The effects of income tax on labor supply

We have already touched on the issues raised by the fact that an individual's earned
income is subject to income tax. The imposition of a tax affects the slope and possibly
the position of the budget constraint facing the individual and hence affects the
individual's labor supply. Tax is evidently necessary to finance government
expenditure—an important part of which will be chaneled into an income transfer
scheme such as we evaluated in the previous section. In that section we made no
mention of how such schemes are to be financed but at least part of the cost will be
borne by income tax and this will in turn have an effect on labor supply. In this section
we therefore look at the general form of the income tax regimes in the United Kingdom
and the United States and the implications of these for labor supply. Further, we
evaluate the consequences for labor supply of such changes in these schemes as have
recently been proposed and have in some cases taken effect.

First, consider the way that different income tax regimes affect the budget constraint:
consider the *post-tax wage ray*. If taxes have to be levied, one approach is to levy a
fixed proportional tax at all levels of income. This approach is illustrated by Schedule
(2) in Fig. 3.10, but in practice this never occurs. All the advanced industrial nations
levy taxes beyond a particular level. In all these countries there is a *tax threshold*, below
which income is exempt from tax and above which people start paying taxes—schedule
(3). In many countries the level of this threshold depends on individual circumstances.
Expenditures, such as those on housing and interest payments, can be offset against tax
in certain countries, thus effectively raising the tax threshold for individuals making
such payments. In the United Kingdom this threshold was until recently higher for a
married man than for either a single person or a married woman, but in both the
United Kingdom and the United States there is now no difference in the treatment of
married men and women.

Schedule (4) depicts a somewhat simplified version of the budget constraint facing
the typical worker in the United Kingdom and the United States today. At the end of
the 1980s the UK income tax structure comprised two marginal tax rates. The first of
25 percent was levied on all gross incomes up to a level approximately equal to twice

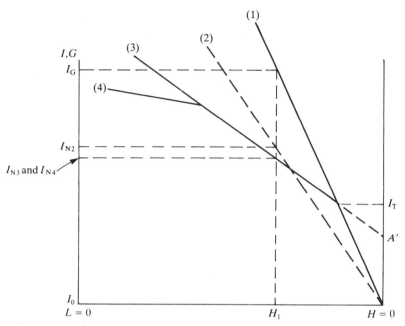

Figure 3.10 The slope of the budget constraint under different income tax regimes. The four schedules in the figure illustrate: (1) No income tax levied: slope = W/P; (2) Income tax at rate t, levied at all levels of income: slope = $(W/P)(1-t)$; (3) Income tax at rate t, on all incomes beyond the threshold I_T: slope = $((W/P)(1 - t_1) + A'$; (4) A tax schedule with successively higher marginal tax rates.

The amount of tax paid is given by the vertical distance between the ray reflecting the pre-tax wage and the appropriate post-tax ray. For an individual working H_1 hours this amounts to $I_G - I_{N2}$ if taxed according to schedule (2), or $I_G - I_{N3}$ or I_{N4} if taxed accordingly to schedules (3) and (4) respectively

average earnings and the second higher rate of 40 percent was levied on all incomes thereafter. In the United States there were three marginal rates of 15, 28 and 33 percent.[7]

A recent proposal to reform the tax system in the United States suggested a single marginal tax rate of 25 percent on all earned incomes after deduction of allowances. If this were to take effect the schedules in both the United States and the United Kingdom would have an initial slope of 0.75, but beyond some point the UK post-tax wage ray would have a further kink. (Fig. 3.11(a)).

7. The threshold beyond which individuals start paying tax does not differ dramatically between the two countries, but the allowances that can be set against tax (deductibles) do, so that the effective rate at which individuals start paying tax will differ according to family circumstances between the two countries. In addition, the effective budget constraint in the United Kingdom is affected by the structure of national insurance rate charges and in the United States by the structure of Old Age, Disability, Health and Social Insurance rates. (See Dilnot A, Kell, M. and Webb, S. 'The 1988 Budget and the structure of personal taxation', *Fiscal Studies*, **9**(2), 28–47 for the United Kingdom.)

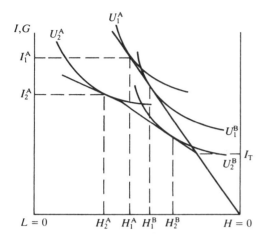
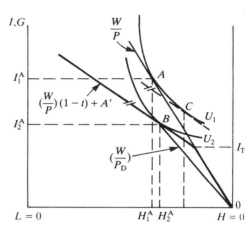

(a) Multiple marginal tax rates   (b) A single marginal tax rate

Figure 3.11 Budget constraints facing the typical worker in tax systems with single and multiple tax rates. In the United States a single marginal tax rate to apply to all earned income beyond permitted deductions, I_T, has frequently been advocated. This system is contrasted with one in which, there are multiple marginal rates. Which system reduces an individual's supply of hours most depends on the relative strength of the income and substitution effects and on the point on the tax schedule at which the individual is located

What might be the effects of a system with a single marginal tax rate on the typical individuals' labor supply? Levying tax rate, t, on all incomes beyond I_T might produce the bold kinked ray and lead to the new tangency position B, shown in Fig. 3.11(b), which would place the individual on a lower indifference curve, U_2. Prior to the levying of tax the individual was working H_1^A hours and receiving gross income I_1^A, he or she is now working fewer hours, H_2^A, and receiving lower income, I_2^A.

In this example the substitution effect (out of work and into leisure) as a result of the fall in the price of leisure overwhelmed the income effect. The move from A to C, the substitution effect, was greater than the move from C to B, the income effect, so that fewer hours were worked. Of course if individuals have different tastes from those suggested here, had they exhibited a high *MRS*, it is quite possible that rather different results might have emerged. The net effect might then have been to increase the supply of hours for the income effect might have overwhelmed the substitution effect. *A priori*, we cannot say which will dominate, it is again an empirical question.

Now what of the effects of a multiple marginal rate system? Again the consequence of a change in the slope of the budget constraint is to induce both an income and a substitution effect and as previously it depends on the nature of the individuals preferences as to which effect dominates. It is conceivable that individuals displaying a very high *MRS*, and confronted with the highest marginal tax rates are induced to work considerably longer hours. Thus individual A might increase hours of work from H_1^A to H_2^A, in order to 'protect his or her income' which, nonetheless, still falls from I_1^A to I_2^A (Fig. 3.11a). Here the income effect dominates the substitution effect.

Individuals with a very low *MRS* may reduce their hours of work as indicated by the move from H_1^B to H_2^B in which case the substitution effect dominates. Again, in the absence of knowledge about the precise nature of an individual's preference, we cannot say, *a priori*, which effect will dominate.

The effect of income tax reductions

In order to consider further the possible effects on labor supply of changes in income tax regimes consider those that were proposed and implemented in the United States and the United Kingdom in the early 1980s. In these countries the administrations of the 1980s advocated tax cuts as a method of increasing the incentive to work. The 1986 tax reform in the United States reduced marginal tax rates on all incomes above the threshold while in the United Kingdom the administration, which came to office in 1979, initially lowered the basic tax rate from 35 to 27 percent and the highest marginal tax rate from 83 to 60 percent, and subsequently simplified this further by lowering the top rate to 40 percent and introducing a single low rate of 25 percent. In addition, both administrations changed the income threshold at which tax became payable and the allowances (deductions) that could be set against tax. What are the probable effects of such reductions in marginal tax rates and changes in tax thresholds on labor supply? First consider a change in the tax threshold.

An increase in the tax threshold Suppose that the effective level of income at which individuals are required to start paying tax is increased, either by increasing the threshold itself or by increasing the allowances, the deductibles, that can be set against tax. Such a situation is illustrated in Fig. 3.12.

For the majority an increase in the threshold from T_1 to T_2 raises the level of income at which tax starts to be paid but does not change the slope of the post-tax wage ray. An increase in the threshold from T_1 to T_2 results in a parallel upward displacement of the post-tax wage ray $(W_1/P)(1 - t)$ indicated by the distance $A^2 - A^1$ at $H = 0$. For those paying tax before and after the change the slope of the post-tax wage ray is unchanged, reflecting no change in the relative price of income and leisure. For a minority who previously paid tax but now no longer do so there is a change in relative prices. This will induce some from among these to increase their labor supply, while a further group will now participate in the labor market when they did not do so before. This group comprises those individuals in two-person households who will no longer be taxed at the wages they can command if they work. However, for the majority the increase in the threshold produces a pure income effect and this leads to an increase in the amount of leisure purchased (under the assumption leisure is a normal good) and a reduction in hours of work from H_1 to H_2. In Fig. 3.12(b) this reduction in hours worked at the unchanged pre-tax wage W_1/P produces a backward shift in the labor supply curve from L_1^s to L_2^s. Whether, in aggregate, labor supply increases or decreases as a result of an increase in the tax threshold depends on whether the substitution effect, the additional workers and additional hours, is larger than the income effect illustrated here.

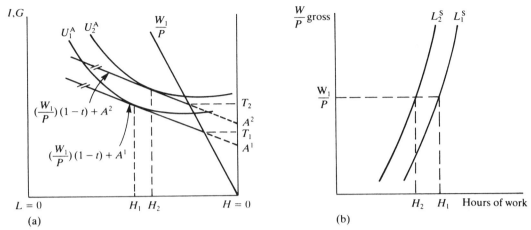

Figure 3.12 An increase in the income level at which individuals start paying income tax. An increase in the tax threshold from T_1 to T_2 leaves the relative price of goods and services and leisure unchanged for individual A. This produces a pure income effect, and if leisure is a normal good, a reduction in hours of work from H_1 to H_2 and a corresponding backward shift of the labor supply curve

A reduction in the tax rate Now consider the effects of a change in marginal tax rates, the income threshold at which tax becomes payable remaining unchanged. With a single marginal rate of tax as has been proposed for the United States, a reduction in the tax rate confronts the vast majority of wage earners with the same change in the relative price of goods and services and leisure. Where there is more than one marginal tax rate, it matters crucially which of those rates is reduced for these can produce quite different results. We focus on a reduction in the basic rate of tax, the tax rate in the lowest tax band, and assume that the size of this tax band and the marginal rate of tax in the next band remain unchanged. First consider this position where individuals are confronted by a single marginal tax rate as illustrated in Fig. 3.13(a).

The reduction in the tax rate results in a steepening of the wage ray $(W_1/P)(1 - t_1)$ to $(W_1/P)(1 - t_2)$ where t_2 is the new lower uniform tax rate. Recall that the post-tax wage ray illustrates the proportion of gross earnings that are retained after taxes have been levied, that is it illustrates disposable income. This change in the relative price of income and leisure produces both an income and a substitution effect. Individual A ends up working more hours, for him or her the substitution effect dominates the income effect. (The rise in the price of leisure leads to less leisure being purchased and this effect overwhelms the increased purchases of leisure as a result of the increase in income.) For individual A there is an increase in hours worked from H_1^A to H_2^A which results in an outward shift in the labor supply curve shown in the lower part of the figure, 3.13(a′). For individual B, however, there is a decrease in hours of work from H_1^B to H_2^B. In this case the income effect dominates the substitution effect and results in a backward shift in the individual's labor supply curve, which we do not show.

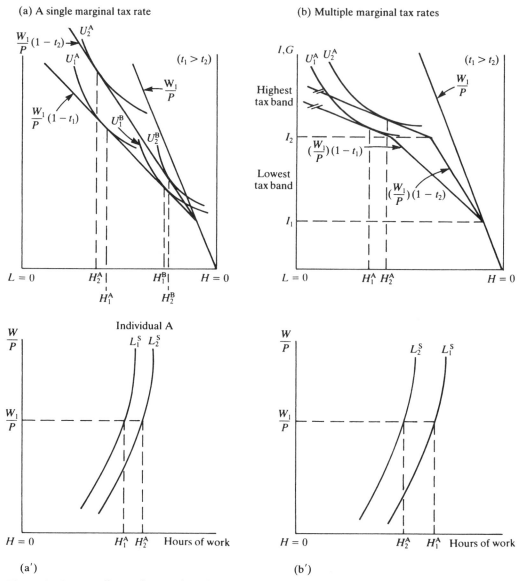

Figure 3.13 The effects of reductions in the lowest tax rates on high earners. (a) The effects of a reduction in the tax rate in a single rate system are ambiguous. A reduction in the single marginal tax rate from t_1 to t_2 results in an increase in the hours of work offered by individual A, shown as an outward shift in the labor supply curve in (a'), but a reduction in the hours of work of individual B. (This is not shown in (a').) (b) In contrast, a reduction in the tax rate in the lowest tax band in a multiple tax rate system, leaving the size of that band unchanged between I_1 and I_2, confronts higher earners with a pure income gain. There is no change in the relative price of goods and services and leisure that confronts them, and accordingly hours of work fall from H_1^A to H_2^A

Evidently either of these outcomes is possible, it depends again on individual preferences. The precise magnitude of the income and substitution effects and hence the net effect of a reduction in tax rates on labor supply cannot be determined, *a priori*.

Where there are multiple marginal rates the position is analogous to that just discussed for individuals in the lowest tax band. Whether individuals in this tax band reduce or increase their hours of work depends on their preferences. However, the position of the individuals in the higher tax bands is different. In this case with no change in the size of the lowest tax band the reduction in the lowest marginal tax rate from t_1 to t_2 pivots the wage ray from $(W_1/P)(1 - t_1)$ to $(W_1/P)(1 - t_2)$ as shown in Fig. 3.13(b). There is, however, no change in the relative price of goods and services and leisure for individuals in the higher tax band and consequently such a development confronts them with a pure income effect. The wage ray confronting such individuals is displaced in a vertical and parallel manner. As in the earlier case of the increase in the tax threshold, such a development results in a pure income effect and leads unambiguously to a reduction in hours worked. The individual decreases hours of work from H_1^A to H_2^A effectively displacing the labor supply curve from L_1^s to L_2^s as shown in Fig. 3.13(b'). Thus a reduction in the lowest rates of tax in a tax system with multiple marginal rates leads to a reduction in the labor supply of the more highly paid. While such a development may therefore increase the supply of hours of those in the lowest tax band it could be more than offset by a reduction in hours worked by the more highly paid. The overall effect of such tax reductions now depends on what proportion of the labor force falls into each tax band and on the tastes of individuals.

RATIONING IN THE GOODS MARKET: THE EASTERN EUROPEAN CASE

The objects of choice in our models of labor supply are goods and services and leisure. A constraint on the quantity of these that could be consumed is set by our full income. However, there are circumstances in which constraints are encountered at a level below full income, this is when there is rationing in commodity markets. Such a situation might arise due to the existence of state controlled prices at which prices there is an excess demand for commodities. This situation is depicted in Fig. 3.14.

Now we distinguish between a hypothetical full income—the amount of goods and services that individuals would command with their full income if they were available—and the *effective full income*—the amount of goods and services that are available for purchase. Suppose that the individual is confronted by wage ray W_1/P but there is a ceiling on the quantity of goods and services that the individual can purchase. This ceiling is given by I_E. The effective budget constraint facing this individual is therefore given by the wage ray up to the point at which it encounters the line I_E beyond which point the line I_E becomes the budget constraint. What are the effects of rising money wages under such a system?

Had there been no rationing in the goods market, then a rise in the money wage from W_1/P to W_2/P would enable the individual to reach indifference curve U_3 at tangency

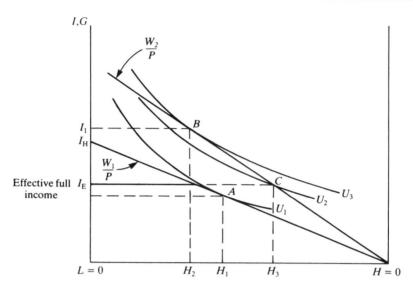

Figure 3.14 Rationing in the goods market. If goods and services are rationed this reduces the real income of workers. It places a ceiling on the goods and services individuals can purchase with their income from work as illustrated by 'effective full income'. Now a rise in the money wage rate from W_1 to W_2 results in a substantial reduction in labor supply from H_1 to H_3. Both labor supply and utility could be increased by improving the supply of goods and services, for at this wage rate, with no rationing, the worker would supply H_2 hours of work

point *B*. Such a point provides the individual with purchasing power I_1 but in the presence of rationing exceeds the supply of goods and services. Under rationing U_2 represents the highest indifference curve that can be reached. There is no longer a point of tangency between the effective budget constraint and the individual's indifference curves. The new location at point *C* represents a point of intersection of an indifference curve and the budget constraint.

In this example the rise in the money wage produced a very sharp cut-back in labor supply from H_1 to H_3. A corollary of this is that if firms wish to increase labor supply they cannot accomplish this by increasing wage rates; it is accomplished by removing the constraints on the supply of goods and services. At the new wage rate, individuals would be willing to supply more hours to increase supply from H_3 to H_2 if the constraint on goods and services were removed. Under these circumstances the price of leisure, the wage rate, no longer determines the supply of hours—it no longer determines the allocation of activity to market and non-market work. Rationing in the goods market now enters as a determinant of labor supply.

The above model provides a simplified but informative representation of the recent position in many Eastern European countries. Here price controls and consequent rationing in the goods market resulted in substantial disincentives to the supply of work. However, this often did not manifest itself in a reduction in hours of attendance at work as proposed above because individuals were, for the most part, formally constrained to attend for a standard workweek. However, under these circumstances individuals adjusted their effective hours through absenteeism and by taking leisure on the job. The response of managers to this was interesting. Some recognized that labor supply is contingent on both the wage they pay and the volume and nature of the goods and services that can be secured with these wages. Accordingly, they allowed their workforce to take time off during working hours to queue for desired commodities. In such a manner actual hours of work were reduced and the real incomes of their workforce raised. By raising the ceiling on the effective income of their workforce in this manner managers increased the incentives to effective labor supply, and allowed workers to move closer toward an equilibrium.

In the Western industrialized nations prices rather than queues are the mechanism by which commodities are distributed. Individuals increase their command over goods and services at a given price level, by increasing their money income. Offering individuals monetary incentives to greater productive performance is one of the ways that many firms in the industrialized world attempt to improve worker performance. In particular the payment system is designed to induce appropriate behavior.

PAYMENT SYSTEMS

Firms manipulate the level and structure of the wages they offer workers in order to induce them to supply the desired quantity and quality of labor. For example, firms frequently require employees to work longer than normal hours and induce them to do so by paying a higher hourly rate for all hours worked beyond normal hours.[8] Such a premium for overtime has the effect of introducing a kink into the budget constraint facing the employee. Again, firms need to ensure that hourly paid workers deliver work of the appropriate quality. One mechanism for achieving this is the offer of an hourly wage above the market clearing level (this is a version of efficiency wage theory which we shall explore in detail in Chapter 11). Another way is to monitor workers' performance and sack those who do not perform to the required standard. An alternative to all of these is to pay workers by results, that is to relate pay directly to output. What effects do such payment-by-results schemes have on labor supply and what are the associated effects on individual utility and worker productivity? These are the questions we address in this section.

The firm—the employer—requires the services of labor to enable it to produce the goods and services it wishes to sell; in turn the wage that it is prepared to pay its workers is related to the value of the output they produce. In the previous analysis in this chapter each hour of labor supplied was paid the same wage rate: to reflect this the wage rate was drawn as a straight line. This method of payment is known as *time rates*, for

---

8. Earlier it was found that as real incomes rose individuals bought more leisure. The corollary of this is that as real incomes have risen over the years it has been necessary to raise the premium for additional hours to induce individuals to work them. Evidence for the United Kingdom reveals that over the period from 1951–55 to 1981–82 the average overtime premium, measured as a ratio of the standard hourly rate of pay, has increased from 1.3 to nearly 1.5. (See Hart, R.A., Bell, D.N.F., Frees, R., Kawasaki, S. and Woodbury, S.A. (1987) *Trends in Non-Wage Labour Costs and their Effects on Employment*, p. 45, Commission of the European Communities, Brussels.)

payment is related directly to the workers' supply of time. Such a method of payment is appropriate where each hour of labor supplied is equally productive and the firm is confident that the number of hours contracted for will be delivered. However, in many jobs these conditions will not hold. The amount of output produced during the first hour of work each day, while employees are 'warming up' may be less than that produced during the middle hours of the day. Again, if workers work long hours output may increase at a slower rate towards the end of the day as workers suffer from fatigue and exhaustion.[9] Indeed, even within a much shorter working period output may increase more slowly towards the end of the day as workers 'get ready to go home' or 'slip off' early on a Friday afternoon. It seems probable therefore that output will initially rise at an increasing rate but that later the rate at which output increases will decline.

If firms pay workers according to the value, or the volume, of the output they produce they set a uniform price, W/P, for each piece of output produced and pay the worker according to the number of pieces produced. Under these circumstances the pre-tax wage schedule confronting a worker could take the form of the bold curved lines detailed in Fig. 3.15.

In Fig. 3.15 workers' output first increases at an increasing rate as each successive hour of work adds an increasing amount to total output—the marginal product of labor is increasing. However, beyond some point while total output continues to rise the contribution to output of each additional hour worked declines, the marginal product of labor declines. Thus while the marginal earnings per hour of work are always positive, the rate of change of those earnings becomes negative.

How will such a payment system affect the hours of work of the individual? It will depend on the preferences of the individual but it is instructive to compare this method of payment to that of a scheme in which pay is simply on the basis of hours worked. The hourly wage rate and price per unit of output is W/P in both cases as indicated in Fig. 3.15. In the case of payment for hours worked the hourly wage rate is set equal to the average hourly product of labor so that if maximum hours are worked or average hours worked = H^x the same level of total output is produced under either scheme. It is evident that the hourly wage scheme offers a higher income and hence higher utility to individuals such as A in Fig. 3.15(a) for, compared to payment by results, it affords them the opportunity to achieve a further reduction in hours of work, from H_1^A to H_2^A, without an accompanying reduction in income. Individual B, on the otherhand, the 'hard worker', would prefer to be paid by results for this would enable this individual to achieve a substantial increase in real income while working fewer hours: H_1^B to H_2^B.

Figure 3.15 also goes some way to explaining why employers may prefer to pay workers an hourly rate. If a firm is able to attract individuals such as B in Fig. 3.15(a), who produce output with a value equal to I_1 when they work H_1^B hours, payment of

9. In the United Kingdom in the nineteenth century many factory workers worked such long hours that their output would have increased had their hours of work been shortened. In terms of Fig. 3.15 their total product curves sloped downward over that part of the curve adjacent to its intersection with the vertical leisure axis. It is interesting to note that it was employers who at the end of the nineteenth century initiated the move to the eight-hour day. See Phelps-Brown, H. (1962) *The Economics of Labour*, Cambridge University Press, London.

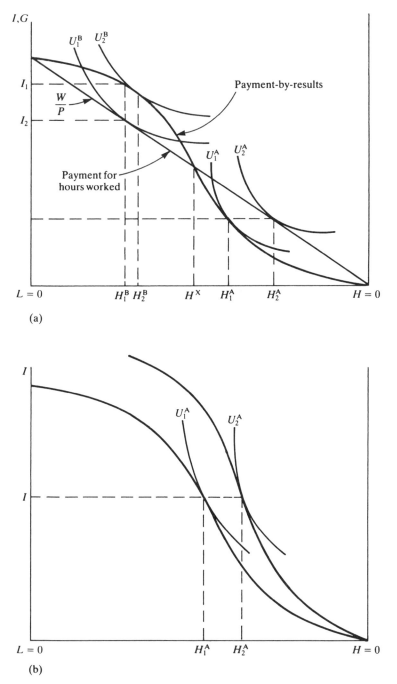

Figure 3.15 Piece rates compared to time rates. (a) Individuals' total product initially increases at an increasing rate, but eventually diminishing returns set in. Individuals such as A will be better off paid an hourly wage rate if this is set equal to the average product of all workers, while individuals such as B will be better off paid by results. If the firm pays individual B an hourly wage it obtains output worth I_1 when he works H_1^B hours in return for payment equal to I_2. The firm therefore secures a surplus equal to $I_1 - I_2$. On the other hand, the firm prefers to pay individual A by results, for to pay this individual an hourly wage would result in overpayment. (b) If workers' total productivity rises as depicted here, due to the introduction of payments-by-results, this need not result in additional output if workers use the increased income to purchase extra leisure as shown

a straight hourly wage rate produces income I_2 for the worker and a surplus $I_1 - I_2$ accrues to the firm. This may induce the firm to try to hire more workers of the quality of B. One way in which this can be accomplished is by raising the hourly wage rate (this again is an aspect of efficiency wage theory that we shall encounter in Chapter 11), but the success of this strategy depends on attracting more workers of the quality of B than of the quality of A. Equally, the firm would prefer to pay individual A by results for to pay this person a straight time hourly wage would be to overpay him or her. Despite these arguments, employers may still choose to pay straight time hourly rates, set at the market clearing level, to all workers. This may be either, because they are unable to distinguish individual workers' productivities, or because productivity is largely outside the *individual* worker's control, being technologically or group determined.

In circumstances in which output is under the control of the individual and the volume of this output can be measured, piecework schemes can be operated. The introduction of such a scheme might in itself raise the total productivity of the workforce. Realizing that if they worked harder they could earn more might result in an upward shift in the schedule as illustrated in Fig. 3.15(b). But note again that this need not lead to an increase in output produced if individuals cut their hours of work, as with the individual shown here. Our theory enables us to distinguish the most appropriate type of payment system, once we know individuals' preferences but, as before, until we know what these are we cannot determine what the outcome will be.

SUMMARY

In this chapter we have looked at the various ways in which the modern state intervenes in the labor market as a consequence of its need to raise income to finance its activities and its desire to change the distribution of income. We evaluated the labor supply consequences of different income tax and benefit schemes. When raising income the state does so in a way that changes the slope of the wage rays confronting individuals and so sets in motion income and substitution effects, the net result of which may be either to increase or decrease labor supply, we cannot say, *a priori*. When providing income replacement or income maintenance the state has generally provided this in the form of additions to individuals' unearned income and although the rate at which such supplements are withdrawn and hence the disincentives to work have differed between systems, the general result of such schemes has been to reduce labor supply. Part of the costs of the state's redistributive activities has therefore been lower levels of labor supply and hence output, but it has been a cost that most advanced industrial countries have been willing to pay.

We also examined the labor supply consequences of different forms of payment system, distinguishing between the effects of payment-by-results and a straight time hourly wage payment. All of the analysis up to this point had been premised on the assumption that individuals could turn the money income they received from work into the goods and services they desired. We therefore examined the consequences for labor supply of rationing in the goods market as has existed throughout much of Eastern Europe. Such rationing was seen to have substantial adverse consequences for labor supply.

How well does the elementary theory developed above explain the facts of labor supply, and indeed, what are the 'stylized facts' of labor supply? In the next chapter we detail developments in labor supply in recent years in the United Kingdom and the United States, and report the explanations that have been offered for these.

PRINCIPAL CONCEPTS

In this chapter we have developed the following concepts. Students should insure that they have a clear grasp of these before proceeding to the next chapter.

1. A household production function.
2. Income replacement and income maintenance programs.
3. The replacement ratio.
4. Added and discouraged worker effects.
5. A minimum income guarantee.
6. The poverty trap.
7. The tax threshold.
8. The post-tax wage ray.
9. Effective full income.

QUESTIONS FOR DISCUSSION

1. Does the theory of household production and the nature of household decision making modify the results of our theory of individual labor supply?
2. Why do income replacement schemes typically replace only a modest proportion of previous earnings?
3. Discuss the proposition that some individuals may be willing to 'pay' to work and the implications of this for income replacement schemes?
4. Do lump-sum severance payments reduce the supply of hours of work?
5. How does the 'poverty trap' arise; what are its consequences?
6. How do changes in the tax threshold and tax rate affect the supply of labor?
7. Discuss the consequences of a reduction in the basic tax rate for the labor supply of higher rate taxpayers.
8. Discuss the advantages and disadvantages of the negative income tax scheme compared to a 'no welfare' and 'guaranteed income' scheme.
9. Discuss the problems of mounting controlled experiments in the social sciences with specific reference to the NIT experiments in the United States.
10. Explore the consequences of rationing in the goods market for individual labor supply.
11. Illustrate the gain in utility that could result from paying some workers by results.

FURTHER READING

For details of the complex and ever changing tax and benefits system in the United Kingdom the reader is referred to Kay, J.A. and King, M.A. *The British Tax System*, published by Oxford University Press, presently in its fifth edition. Creedy, J. and Disney, R. (1985) *Social Insurance in Transition: An Economic Analysis*, Oxford, Clarendon Press, also provides an informative analysis of the UK system. For the United States the student is referred to the first few chapters in Part 4 of Musgrave, R. and Musgrave, P.B. (1988) *Public Finance in Theory and Practice*, McGraw-Hill.

4

EMPIRICAL EVIDENCE ON LABOR SUPPLY: LONG-TERM TRENDS AND LIFE CYCLE DIMENSIONS

In the two previous chapters we have developed the short-run theory of labor supply. We have shown how individuals vary their labor supply as the opportunities confronting them in the labor market change. Those opportunities can vary substantially between individuals and in Chapters 5 and 6 we shall therefore discuss how individuals can improve, or if they get it wrong, diminish, the opportunities that confront them in the short run. For the moment we look at the empirical evidence on the behavior of labor supply. We distinguish the proportions of men and women in each of the major industrial nations that want to work and look at how these proportions have varied over the years. We distinguish the extent to which the working lives of individuals in each of these countries are of a similar length, and the number of hours people in each country are prepared to work each year. We shall also look in some detail at the marked change in the labor supply of married women, for this represents one of the most substantial changes to have occurred in the labor market this century.[1]

---

1. A note of caution. We shall examine the supply of labor at a number of different moments in time, and we shall interpret the outcomes as reflecting the underlying preferences of individuals with regard to their labor supply. Yet at any particular moment in time some individuals will be in the process of adjusting from one equilibrium to another. The approach adopted in economics is to proceed as if, when taken in the aggregate, the outcomes we observe can be regarded as equilibrium outcomes. Certainly in the long run we should not expect to find levels of employment and hours of work persisting which did not reflect individuals' preferred outcomes. Even though an individual's hours of work and level of economic activity deviate from the optimum in the short run this should be no more than a temporary phenomenon.

We should also bear in mind that when these are equilibrium outcomes, the combinations of hours worked and earnings, we observe are the result of the interaction of the forces of *both* supply and demand. The levels of wages and hours of work represent points on the aggregate labor supply *and* the aggregate labor demand curves given by the point at which they intersect.

TRENDS IN LABOR FORCE PARTICIPATION

The proportion of the population of working age which is in the labor force is known as the *labor force participation rate*. This is also called the *economic activity* rate or simply 'the activity rate'. The labor force comprises all those individuals currently looking for or holding paid employment. It is the total number of employees in employment plus the self-employed and armed services together with the unemployed.

Typically, the population of working age refers to the population between school leaving age and the age at which individuals become eligible for state retirement pension, but on this latter point practice differs for there is no statutory reason why individuals should not continue to work beyond retirement age. Over the years there have also been changes in that part of the population considered to be of working age because countries have raised the school leaving age—the age at which individuals can enter the labor force in a full-time capacity. Some analysts exclude the armed forces from the numerator when calculating the participation rate, dealing only with the civilian labor force; this is a convention adopted in the United States.

Developments this century in the United States and the United Kingdom

Perhaps surprisingly the proportion of the total population beyond school leaving age who are in the labor force seems to have changed little over the last century in either the United States or Britain. In 1980 the labor force participation rate of all those aged 14 and over in the United States was 54.0 percent, in 1970 it was 55.7 percent. In Britain the labor force participation rate of those aged 20 and over was 61.3 percent in 1890 and in 1981 it was 61 percent. This stability of the overall participation rate has been described as 'one of the great ratios in economics'.[2]

The stability of the ratio for the population as a whole hides many and substantial changes. The participation rate for males has been declining and there has been a decline in the participation rates of both the young and the old. Young people have stayed longer at school and more have entered higher education while older workers have retired earlier. Offsetting these developments there has been a marked rise in female participation, particularly among married women.

The rise in female activity rates and decline in male rates is evident from Table 4.1 This reveals that female activity rates have risen steadily in Britain and the United States throughout this century. In contrast, the decline in male rates seems to have occurred in spurts. In Britain it has been concentrated in the years since 1960 while in the United States the decline was concentrated in the years from 1930 to 1940. In addition the decline has been more pronounced in Britain than in the United States. It is noteworthy that although starting from a much lower level, female participation

2. Klein, L.R. and Kosobud, R.F. (1961) 'Some econometrics of growth: great values of economics', *Quarterly Journal of Economics*, **75**(2), 173–98, quoted in Pencavel, J.H. (1986), 'Labor supply of men: a survey' in Ashenfelter, O. and Layard, R. (eds.), *Handbook of Labor Economics*, North-Holland, New York and Oxford.

Table 4.1 Labor force participation rates in Britain and the United States: all males and females 1900/1–1980/81

Years[†]	Females		Males	
	USA[‡]	Great Britain[§]	USA[‡]	Great Britain[§]
1900/1	20.4		87.3	
1910/11	22.8		86.3	
1920/21	23.3	32.3	86.5	
1930/31	24.3	34.2	84.1	90.5
1940/41	25.4	n.a.	79.0	n.a.
1950/51	28.6	34.7	79.0	89.0
1960/61	34.5	37.4	77.4	88.6
1970/71	41.6	42.7	76.8	85.8
1980/81	50.5	45.6	77.9	77.8

Source: Killingsworth, M.R. and Heckman, J.J. (1986) 'Female labor supply: a survey', and Pencavel, J.H. (1986) 'Labor supply of men: a survey,' both in Ashenfelter, O. and Layard P.R.G. (eds.), *Handbook of Labor Economics*, North-Holland, New York and Oxford.
[†] USA 1920, 1930, etc., Britain 1921, 1931, etc.
[‡] Up to and including 1960 all those aged 14 or older, 1970 and 1980 those aged 16 or older.
[§] 1921, those aged 12 or older; 1931, aged 14 or older; 15 or older after 1951. No census conducted in 1941.

is now much higher in the United States than in Britain. In the former the increase in female participation rates has been most pronounced in the period since 1950 while in the latter the rise has been greatest in the rather shorter period since 1960.

Table 4.2 casts a bit more light on developments this century by distinguishing rates for persons aged between 20 and 64. It reveals that the rates among males in this age bracket are much higher than those for all males, reported in Table 4.1, and that while they show some reduction from their levels in 1890 they have, in general, held fairly steady. Those reductions that have occurred are in the 20–24 and 45–64 age groups, a reflection of the changing life cycle pattern of participation among older and younger workers. For males aged 25–44, 'prime-age' males, there has been practically no change in economic activity rates over the 90 years from 1890. In contrast there has been a sharp rise in female participation rates at all ages. In the United States the rates have doubled among those aged 20–24 and quadrupled among those aged between 25 and 64. In Britain the rise has been less dramatic, for in 1890–91 the rate was already almost twice as high as in the United States among all age groups. Since 1891 the rates for women in Britain have risen still further among all age groups although they are now significantly less among 'prime-aged' females than in the United States. Table 4.2 emphasizes once again that the most dramatic changes in participation that have occurred this century have been among females.

The long-run rise in female participation rates in Britain and the United States is examined in Table 4.3 which distinguishes between married, single and widowed/

Table 4.2 Male and female participation rates in the United States and Britain among persons aged 20–64

	Males				Females			
	USA		Britain		USA		Britain	
	1890	1982	1891	1981	1890	1980	1891	1981
20–24	92.0	86.0	98.1	89.2	30.8	67.8	58.4	69.3
25–44	97.6	95.1	97.9	97.5	15.6	64.9	29.5	59.5
45–64	95.2	81.0	93.7	90.2	12.6	50.5	24.6	51.9

Source: Pencavel, J.H. (1986) and Killingsworth M.R. and Heckman J.J. (1986), *op. cit.*

divorced. From this table it is evident that this century there has been a very sharp rise in the labor force participation of married women in the United States and Britain. It reveals that in Britain fewer than 1 in 10 married women were in the labor force in 1921 but that by 1981 almost one in every two was economically active. In the United States again fewer than 1 in 10 was economically active in 1920 but this had risen to 41 percent by 1980/81. In both cases the participation rates of married women have risen faster than those of women in general. Table 4.3 also reveals that the economic activity rates of single and widowed/divorced women have risen in the United States, but that these have fallen in Britain. The rise in female participation rates in the United States is therefore a much more general phenomenon than in Britain, but in both cases the main cause of the sharp rise in female participation rates is the substantial increase in the economic activity rates of married women.

The sharper rise in the participation rates of married women in Britain results from one important feature of the British labor market which distinguishes it from that of the United States. In Britain a majority of married women, 52 percent, work part time. By 1980, almost 42 percent of all working women in Britain were working part time, their numbers having quadrupled in the 30 years since 1950. The OECD records that

Table 4.3 Labor force participation of married women[†]

	Married women		Single women		Widowed/divorced	
	Britain	USA	Britain	USA	Britain	USA
1900/1	—	5.6	—	—	—	37.5
1920/21	8.7	9.0	72.5	—	25.5	—
1930/31	10.1	11.7	74.0	55.2	21.2	34.3
1960/61	30.1	31.8	69.4	50.7	22.8	36.1
1970/71	42.9	38.2	61.5	47.5	23.6	35.0
1980/81	47.2	40.8	60.8	61.5	22.9	44.0

Source: Killingsworth, M.R. and Heckman, J.J. (1986), *op.cit.*,Tables 2.5 and 2.7 therein.
[†] See footnotes to Table 4.1.

in the United States the incidence of part-time working among women is lower than in Britain with only around one-quarter of all women working part-time.[3] Moreover, in the United States, 40 percent of all part-time working is by those aged less than 24 while this same age group accounts for less than 3 percent of all part-time working in Britain. The existence of part-time working opportunities in Britain has facilitated the return to work of women with children of school age. This is reflected in the fact that in Britain the majority, 54 percent, of women part-timers fall in the 25–44 age range.

Part-time working is therefore a rather different phenomenon in the United States than it is in Britain. In the former it is typically carried out by young women among whom, as we shall see from Table 4.10, participation rates have risen sharply in recent years. These are typically young college students 'moonlighting' while in full-time education. In Britain, as we shall see in Chapter 6, many fewer young people attend full-time education and accordingly a much larger proportion are looking for full-time employment. In Britain part-time working has been concentrated among, and has facilitated the return to work of, married women after childbearing. These women are in the 'second phase' of their working lives.

Recent developments in selected industrial nations

Consider these developments in the United Kingdom and the United States in a wider context as detailed in Table 4.4. In contrast to developments in both these countries, participation rates among women in Germany and Japan have actually fallen in the period since 1960. Indeed striking differences emerge in the participation rates of both men and women in different countries since 1960. In 1960 over half of all women aged 16 and over in Japan were in the labor force while only around a third of women in this same age group were economically active in the United States and Australia. However, by 1984 the disparity in the female participation rates in the five countries shown had reduced considerably. The rate rose sharply in the United States and Australia and less rapidly in the United Kingdom so that by 1984 more than half of all women aged 16 and over were in the labor force in the United States and around 45 percent were economically active in the United Kingdom and Australia. In contrast the rates had declined in Japan and Germany to bring Japan more into line with the United States, the United Kingdom and Australia but to reduce Germany to the lowest of all.

Male participation rates have shown a steady decline in all countries. Rates in excess of 80 percent were evident in all countries in 1960, and were at their highest in the United Kingdom. However, the rather sharper decline in the latter meant that by 1984 the rate was little different from that in the United States. The decline was even greater in Germany with the result that by 1984 male participation rates were significantly lower in Germany than in the other countries shown. Indeed, taking males and females

---

3. See Leicester, C. (1980) 'Part-time employment in Great Britain: its natural causes and problems', in Jallade, J. (ed.), *Part-Time Workers in Europe* and 'Part-time employment in OECD countries', *Employment Outlook*, September 1983, Ch. III, pp. 33–42, OECD, Paris.

Table 4.4 (a) Male and female participation rates in selected countries: 1960–84 (population aged 16 and over)

	USA		Australia		Germany		UK		Japan	
	Males	Females	Males	Females	Males	Females	Males	Females	Males	Females
1960	80.4	36.5	84.7	33.3	83.4	41.8	86.8	39.3	84.8	54.5
1973	75.9	43.0	82.5	40.7	76.0	38.6	79.4	42.1	86.4	48.3
1984	74.2	51.9	76.2	44.9	69.7	39.0	74.0	45.9	78.8	48.9

(b) Percentage change in participation rates

	Males	Females	Males	Females	Males	Females	Males	Females	Males	Females
1960–73	– 5.6	17.8	– 2.6	22.2	– 8.8	– 7.7	– 8.5	5.5	1.9	– 11.4
1973–84	– 2.2	20.1	– 7.6	10.3	– 8.3	1.0	– 6.8	9.0	– 8.8	1.2
1960–84	– 7.7	42.2	– 10.0	34.8	– 16.4	– 6.7	– 14.7	15.0	– 7.1	– 10.3

Source: OECD, *Employment Outlook*, various issues, OECD, Paris.

together, Germany stands out among the countries reported here as the country with the least economically active population. The very high rates of male participation make Japan the country with the most economically active population.

Conceptually there are two distinct effects underpinning the aggregate figures above. First, changes in the proportion of the population who were ever in the labor force; second, a change in the pattern of participation over the life cycle of those who have been or are presently in the labor force. An example of the former effect is the rise in the proportion of women who now work at some stage of their lives. An example of the latter is the change in the length of the working lives of men. Both effects constitute a change in life cycle aspects of labor supply and will be explored in more depth later, for the snapshot figures above fail to reveal these dynamic aspects of labor supply.

Participation is of course only one dimension of labor supply. There are others we need to study before we can say what has happened to labor supply in recent years. Consider therefore how hours of work have changed over this century.

HOURS OF WORK

Long-term trends in weekly hours

One of the most striking developments in the labor market this century has been the decline in the number of hours that people work a year. This decline has two quite distinct aspects. First, a decline in hours of work per week and, more recently, a decline in the number of weeks worked per year.

Table 4.5 Average weekly hours of work in manufacturing industry (all production workers)

	USA	UK
1900	55.0	
1906		56.0
1910	52.2	
1920	48.1	
1924		47.0
1930	43.6	47.8
1938		47.8
1940	37.6	
1945		49.4
1950	40.5	47.2
1960	39.7	47.4
1970	39.8	45.3
1980	39.7	41.9
1985	40.5	42.0

Sources: US: Department of Labor, Bureau of Statistics *Handbook of Labor Statistics* and, more recently, *Employment and Training Report to the President.*
UK: *British Labour Statistics, Historical Abstract 1886–1968* and *Year Book*, Department of Employment, HMSO, London.

Information on hours worked is presented in Table 4.5 for the United Kingdom and the United States. For the early part of this century this information is rather patchy and generally available for manual workers in the manufacturing sector of the economy only, but it is clear from Table 4.5 that there has been a substantial fall this century in hours of work per week in both the United Kingdom and the United States. In the former a nine-hour day, six-day week was established around the middle of the nineteenth century and this persisted until the end of the First World War, after which time the standard eight-hour day, five-and-a-half-day week was generalized. There was little change for the next 40 years until the 1960s when the five-day week and eight-hour day was introduced. Subsequently there has been a further slow but steady decline in hours of work per week. It is noteworthy that in the United Kingdom actual hours worked have always exceeded the standard working week by an average of some three to four hours. In 1985 the standard working week was below 40 hours per week; the difference between actual and standard hours is accounted for by overtime working which remains a persistent feature of the UK scene.

In the United States the move to the 40-hour week came much earlier—in the 1930s. Once the 54-hour week had been abandoned in the early years of the twentieth century

Table 4.6 Weekly hours of work of full-time workers

	USA		UK	
	Males	Females	Males	Females
1955–59	42.6	36.4	48.4	41.2
1960–64	42.5	35.3	47.5	39.7
1965–69	42.7	36.2	46.4	38.5
1970–74	41.8	34.2	45.2	37.7
1975–79	41.6	34.2	44.0	37.3
1980–86	40.6	34.1	43.1	38.1

Sources: Pencavel J.H. (1986), *op. cit. Historical Abstract of Labour Statistics* (HMSO, London, (1986), Table 9). Killingsworth M.R. and Heckman J.J. (1986), *op. cit.* Table 2.11 *Department of Employment Gazette* (October Survey) and *Monthly Labour Review*, November 1986.
The US figures refer to all workers; the UK refer to only manual workers. The figures for the US exclude those in agricultural employment.

there was a steady decline in hours worked through to the 1930s but since the eight-hour day, five-day week was achieved there has been no change.

A more recent picture is presented by Table 4.6 in which weekly hours of work are reported in a wider range of industries and services. These reveal that in the United Kingdom and the United States there has been a fall in hours worked by both males and females during the 1970s and 1980s and that in both countries females work fewer hours than men. It is clear from Table 4.6 that the fall in hours worked has been both more continuous and more substantial in the United Kingdom than in the United States. Over these years the typical male in the United Kingdom has experienced a reduction of over five hours in the length of the working week, while females have experienced a reduction of three hours. As a result weekly hours worked in the United Kingdom are now rather closer to those in the United States than they were at the start of the period.

Table 4.5 and that part of Table 4.6 which refers to the United Kingdom detail hours paid for as distinct from hours actually worked. The former include paid holidays and fail to exclude those absent from work due to illness or other unscheduled reasons and those who are on strike.[4] Paid for hours can therefore

4. Hart, R.A. (1987) *Working Time and Employment*, Allen and Unwin, London and Winchester, Mass. identifies four reasons why paid for and actual hours of work may differ. The first is payment for days not worked, vacations and public holidays. The second is payment for hours not worked. A typical day's 'work' in Britain it is apocryphally believed includes time for a tea break, and may include some cleaning-up time, and time off for attendance at union meetings. The third source of payment for hours not worked results from technical constraints, the time required to start up production and conduct necessary maintenance. The final reason is the deliberate underutilization, the hoarding of labor, at various stages of the business cycle. We shall have more to say about this last aspect in Chapter 9.

differ considerably from actual hours worked.[5] We shall be looking at days lost through strikes later in the book (see Chapter 14) but for the moment consider absenteeism and paid holidays, two of the most important reasons why hours actually worked differ from those paid for.

Paid vacations

The importance of adjusting for the number of paid vacations is indicated by Table 4.7. This reveals that alongside the fall in hours of work has gone a fall in the number of weeks worked per year. Paid vacations have risen substantially over the last 30 years in all the countries shown, although they have risen least in the United States. Indeed a sharp contrast emerges between Europe and the United States, for in Europe paid vacations are now generally double those in the United States. There is however no substantial difference in the number of paid public holidays in each of these countries. Of course we should note that not all entitlements to paid vacation are necessarily taken, as any of the more active researchers in an economics faculty will be able to testify. Working during vacation time is reputed to be a marked feature of the Japanese labor market where, not unusually, as little as half the entitlement is actually taken. Furthermore, Japanese holiday entitlement is small compared to all the other main industrial nations.[6]

Annual hours of work

The above figures enable us to calculate the change in the annual hours of work of full-time workers in the United Kingdom and the United States since the 1950s.

In the United States in the early 1950s Table 4.7 indicates production workers received a total of around 3.6 weeks off with pay each year (paid vacation and public holidays) leaving them 48.4 weeks to work in a year. According to Table 4.6 men worked an average of 42.6 hours in each of these remaining 48 weeks and 2 days and full-time women 36.4 hours. So in the late 1950s men in the United States worked around 2062 hours per year (42.6 hours in each of the 48 weeks and 2 days) while full-time women worked 1762 hours per year (36.4 hours in each of the 48 weeks and 2 days). Similar calculations for the United Kingdom (exactly the same weeks per year multiplied by 48.4 hours per week for men and 41.2 for women) suggest many more

5. Kunze, K. (1984) 'A new BLS survey measures the ratio of hours worked to hours paid', *Monthly Labor Review*, June, 3–7, US Department of Labor, Bureau of Labor Statistics, reports that in 1982 hours worked in the United States accounted for about 93 percent of paid for hours in the case of production and non-supervision workers. The 7 percent of 'paid for but not worked' hours included only paid holidays, sick leave and vacations. If all the other items we have identified could be quantified we should discover that employers are paying for many more hours than they fully utilize.
6. See Hart, R.A. *et al.* (1987) *Trends in Non-Wage Labour Costs and their Effects on Employment* p. 25. Commission of the European Communities, Brussels.

Table 4.7 Vacation time in selected countries (production workers)

	Paid vacation (weeks)		Paid public holidays (days)
	1954	1982	1982
USA	1.6	2.4	10
UK	2	4.6	8
West Germany	2.3	5.8	9
Australia	2.4	4	n.a.
France	3	5.6	10
Sweden	3	5.8	11

Source: Green, F. and Potepan, M. (1987) 'Vacation time in the United States and Europe,' mimeo.
Note that 0.2 of a (working) week equals one day.

hours were worked by both men (some 2342 hours) and women (1994 hours) in this country than were worked in the United States at this time.[7]

By the early 1980s annual hours of work in the United States were reduced to 1932 for men and 1623 for full-time women or by some 6 percent and 8 percent respectively. In the United States the fall in annual hours worked by both men and women appears to be accounted for by an additional week's holiday and a shorter working week which, when taken over the year as a whole, is equal to a further two weeks' holiday. In the United Kingdom the fall in annual hours of work is far more substantial. By the early 1980s the number of hours worked per year by male manual workers was down to 1974, a level only a little above that of men in the United States. The hours of full-time women had also fallen sharply to 1745 but were still well above their US counterparts. In the United Kingdom there had been a fall in hours worked per year of some 16 percent for men and 12 percent for women. The reductions in annual hours of work in the United Kingdom comprised an extra 2.6 weeks' paid vacation and a reduction in the length of the average working week which was equivalent to almost an extra 6.5 weeks' holiday a year for men and 4 weeks for women. In the United Kingdom men enjoy longer holidays than men in the United States but this appears to be almost completely offset by the fact that men in the United States enjoy a shorter working week. Women in the United Kingdom also generally enjoy more generous holidays than their US counterparts but because they

7. Table 4.6 provides the most accurate guide to recent trends in hours worked because it calculates the averages for five-year periods and thereby eliminates the effects of the business cycle. It is for this reason that we employ the information contained in Table 4.6 to calculate annual hours of work. Regrettably the vacation time shown in Table 4.7 does not distinguish between men and women. Women's holiday entitlements will be less than those shown in Table 4.7 because extra days of holiday are often awarded by firms on the basis of seniority or length of service. Women have less seniority and shorter tenure than men and so are likely to receive fewer of these discretionary holiday awards. For this reason our calculations probably understate annual hours of work of full-time women in both countries.

Table 4.8 Annual hours worked per person in selected countries 1890–1983 (Whole economy; all workers)

	1890	1979	1983
United Kingdom	2807	1617	1528
United States	2789	1607	1596
Japan	2770	2129	2161
France	2770	1727	1609
Germany	2765	1719	1698

Source: Maddison, A. (1982), *Phases of Capitalist Development,* Oxford University Press, and *OECD Employment Outlook,* September 1985, Table 3. OECD, Paris.

work substantially more hours per week, over the year as a whole those in full-time employment appear to work around 8 percent more hours than women in the United States.

This move in recent years toward similar annual hours of work in the United States and the United Kingdom is reported in Table 4.8. This table reports the annual hours worked per year over the period 1890 to 1983 in a wider selection of countries. The figures here differ from those calculated above for here they include part-time workers; we should expect them to be lower.

Table 4.8 reveals that toward the end of the last century annual hours of work were practically identical in the five major industrial countries shown. However, since that time differences in weekly hours of work and holiday entitlements have resulted in some diversity. Most notably in 1979 the Japanese worked a third more hours than the country with the lowest hours, the United States, and almost 25 percent more than the country with the next highest, France. By 1983 these differences had widened. Annual hours of work had actually increased in Japan while they had continued to fall elsewhere. Now the Japanese worked some 40 percent more hours per year than workers in the United Kingdom and some 25 percent more than the next highest, Germany. Annual hours of work do not appear to differ substantially in the United States, the United Kingdom, France and Germany but in Japan they are substantially longer than in any of these countries.

Absenteeism

Absenteeism also reduces the number of hours actually worked. Little systematic information is available on this issue but what there is available suggests that this is a more substantial problem in the United Kingdom than in other countries. Calculation of the absenteeism rate for the United Kingdom reveals that in the early 1980s this ran at around 8 percent per annum compared to 4.7 percent in the United States. The absenteeism rate is calculated by expressing days lost due to absenteeism as a proportion of total days contracted to be worked. For comparison the rate per annum for Australia was 4.3 percent, for Sweden and Germany 3.0 percent, France 5.9 percent and Japan 2.5 percent.[8]

LIFE CYCLE LABOR SUPPLY

The participation decision and, contingent on working, the number of hours worked both have significant life cycle dimensions. Individuals can choose when to start, stop and interrupt their working lives, and how many hours to work in a given week. Individuals' labor supply varies substantially over the course of their working lives. Here we shall concentrate primarily on these life cycle aspects of the participation decision.

Changing patterns of lifetime labor supply

Underpinning the changing participation rates mapped out in Tables 4.1 to 4.4 were substantiated changes in the pattern of life cycle labor force participation on the part of both men and women. Consider these aspects in more detail.

Women Life cycle patterns of labor force participation have traditionally been quite different for men and women. When we map the participation rates over the life cycle of a cohort of men (a group with a common characteristic, in this case those born at the same time), we find that participation rates rise with age until the early twenties level of well in excess of 90 percent thereafter, and then decline sharply from around the late fifties. In contrast, the pattern for women traditionally displayed a distinct bimodality, with peaks around the early twenties and again in the late thirties. This pattern for women results from the behavior of married women who are numerically by far the single largest group of females. Examples of the traditional patterns of women's life cycle labor force participation are shown in Figs. 4.1 and 4.2 which refer to the United States and Britain respectively. However, in the last two decades there are signs of substantial changes in the behavior of married women in both countries and this pattern is beginning to disappear.

The traditional bimodal pattern for married women reflected the timing of childbearing and rearing. These activities are in general concentrated in the early twenties and in the past women with a young family were much less likely to work than those without. Studies found that in Britain in the early 1970s women with the youngest child under three years old had a participation rate 67 percent lower than

8. These statistics emerge from a study by Klein, B.W. (1986) 'Missed work and lost hours: May 1985', *Monthly Labor Review*, November. For the United Kingdom they were calculated using the *New Earnings Survey*, produced annually by the Department of Employment. This reports the number of employees absent in the survey week.

In 1987 the Confederation of British Industry reported that in 1986 absenteeism in Britain was 11 percent among manual workers and 6 percent among non-manual workers. Sickness was reported as the reason for absence in 90 percent of these cases. They estimated that such absenteeism cost British industry £5000 million annually.

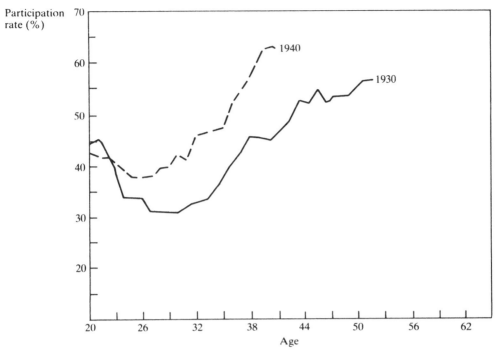

Figure 4.1 Employment to population ratios for the United States for women born in 1930 and 1940. (*Source:* Smith, J.P. and Ward, M. (1984) *Women's wages and work in the twentieth century*, Report R3119 HICHD, The Rand Corporation, Santa Monica, California.) Reproduced with permission of the author

women with no child at home, while data for the United States in 1960 revealed a rather smaller but still significant effect. In the United States the presence of a child under six reduced the female participation rate by around 40 percent.[9]

In recent years, however, family size has fallen in both countries due in no small part to the revolution in contraception. There are also signs that women are postponing the age at which they get married and as a result the proportion of never married women among 25–29-year-olds in the United States rose from 12.2 percent in 1970 to 20.8 percent in 1980. Having married, there is also an increase in the number of years before women start a family.[10]

9. The results for the United Kingdom emerge from the studies of Layard, P.R.G., Pichaud, D. and Stewart, M. (1978) 'The causes of poverty', *Royal Commission on the Distribution of Income and Wealth*, Background Paper No. 5, HMSO, London. The results for the United States are reported in Killingsworth, M.R. and Heckman, J.J. (1986), *op. cit.*
10. See Bloom, D. and Trussell, J. (1984) 'What are the determinants of delayed childbearing and permanent childlessness in the United States?' *Demography*, **21**, Part 4, 591–611 and Rogers, C. and O'Connell, M. (1984) 'Childspacing among birth cohorts of American Women : 1905 to 1959', *Current Population Reports*, Series P 20 number 385.

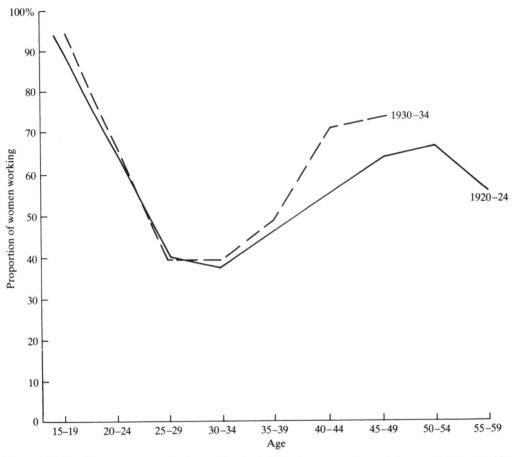

Figure 4.2 Employment to population ratios in Britain for women born between 1930 and 1934 and between 1920 and 1924. (*Source:* Adapted from Martin, J. and Roberts, C. (1984) *Women and Employment: A Lifetime Perspective*, HMSO, London). Reproduced with permission of the publishers

Together these developments have the effect of allowing women to build a career and invest in human capital, both features which substantially increase their chances of securing employment when they return to the labor force after raising a family or which increase the likelihood that they will not leave it in the first place. There is also evidence that in the United Kingdom the interval between children has fallen so that women who have more than one child have been able to resume their careers earlier. Added to all this is the fact that it is now easier for women to raise a family without interrupting their careers. Maternity leave has permitted them to reclaim their jobs on returning after childbearing, and changing attitudes toward and increased facilities to support working mothers have reduced the pressures to quit work. Finally, there is

Table 4.9 Labor force participation rates of older people in Britain and the United States: males and females aged 65 and over

	Females		Males	
	USA	Britain	USA	Britain
1900/1	9.1	13.4	68.3	
1930/31	8.0	8.2	58.3	47.9
1950/51	7.6	5.3	41.6	31.1
1980/81	8.7	3.7	19.1	10.8

Sources: Pencavel, J.H. (1986) *op. cit.* and Killingsworth, M.R. and Heckman, J.J. (1986) *op. cit.*

evidence in the United States that the proportion of women who have never married has been rising sharply among females born since 1935.[11]

For all these reasons, while women's labor force participation continues at a lower level than that of males, it is beginning to exhibit a rather similar pattern over the life cycle.

Older workers Other aspects of the changing pattern of participation over the life cycle are common to men and women. In general, both are retiring earlier as detailed in Table 4.9. In the United States and Britain in 1930/31 around half of all men aged 65 and over were still in the labor force, by 1980/81 this had reduced to fewer than one in five in the United States and one in ten in Britain. Similarly, while one in 12 females aged 65 and over was working in Britain in 1930 this had reduced to fewer than one in 25 by 1980. Only in the United States has the proportion of elderly women still working remained constant over the period, at around one in 12. It is not immediately apparent why this should be so for the trend toward earlier retirement is evident in most Western industrialized nations. Thus in Germany the labor force participation rate of those over 65 has fallen from 16.5 to 10 percent over the period from 1956 to 1975 and it has fallen from 20.7 to 7.1 percent over this same period in France and from 20.5 to 10.9 percent in Sweden.

Young workers At the other end of the age range, reported in Table 4.10, labor force participation rates have also been falling as young people remain longer in full-time education. The fall in the participation rates of the under twenties is most dramatic in Britain where in 1981, 65 percent of males and 56 percent of females were economically active compared to 85 percent and 71 percent respectively in 1930. Though the fall is substantial, these participation rates are still substantially higher than those in the United States where the participation rate for the marginally younger group of 19-year-olds and below is less than 50 percent for both men and women. In the United States in the 1950s the participation rate among young women was little

11. See Schoen, R., Urton, W., Woodrow, K. and Baj, J. (1985) 'Marriage and divorce in 20th century American cohorts', *Demography*, **22**(1), 101–14.

Table 4.10 Labor force participation of younger people in Britain and the United States: males and females

	Females		Males	
	USA	Britain	USA	Britain
Age	14/16–19[†]	<20[§]	14/16–19[†]	<20[§]
Year				
1900	26.8	—	61.1	—
1930/31	22.8	70.5	41.1	84.7
1950/51	22.5	78.9	39.9	83.8
1980/81	45.7	56.4	47.5[‡]	64.6

Sources: Killingsworth, M.R. and Heckman, J.J. (1986), *op. cit.* Tables 2.1 and 2.3; Pencavel, J.H. (1986), *op.cit.* Tables 1.2 and 1.1; and *Employment and Training Report to the President.*
[†] 14–19-year-olds up to and including 1950, 16–19-year-olds 1980.
[‡] Adjusted for comparability with the earlier figures. See Pencavel, J.H. (1986) *op. cit.* footnote to Table 1.1.
[§] 14–19-year-olds in 1931 and 15–19-year-olds in 1951 and 16–19-year-olds in 1981.

over 20 percent but in the following 30 years it rose sharply. In contrast the rate for men was little changed over the 30 years from 1950 to 1980. It appears that at least part of the explanation for the rise in young women's participation rates is the increase in part-time working—'moonlighting'—by those still in full-time education.

The differences between the United States and Britain in life cycle participation are striking. Older people are much more likely to be working in the United States, while younger people and married women are much more likely to be working in Britain. The allocation of time to market work during the lifetime of men in the United States and Britain, which is revealed by the statistics reported above, is brought together and illustrated in Fig. 4.3.

Theoretical considerations

What insights does theory offer into life cycle labor supply issues? The situation can be depicted by adapting the standard figure used in previous chapters to illustrate the determinants of the number of hours of work. In the life cycle context the constraints confronting the individual can now be thought of as, first, the number of years they expect to live; second, the discounted present value of their expected annual earnings, giving an expected annual wage rate; and, third, non-labor income, where non-labor income represents the discounted present value of the total expected annual return on assets. Treating this last as a constraint requires that the individual's consumption expenditure equals his or her income in each period. In a manner analogous to that for the standard figure hypothetical full income could then be depicted as the point of intersection of the annual wage ray and the vertical axis. This is constructed by

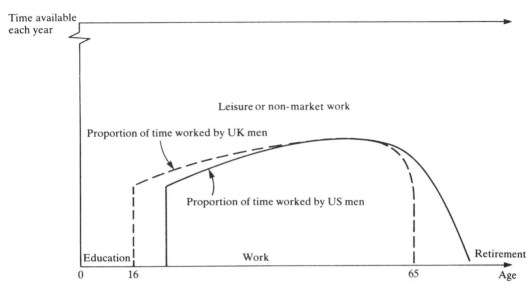

Figure 4.3 Labor supply over the life cycle of men in the United States and the United Kingdom. The profiles show the allocation of time to market work. In the United Kingdom males typically join and leave the labor force earlier than their US counterparts. Total annual hours of work now differ little between the two countries, although the composition of these hours is different. Males in the United Kingdom work longer per week, but this is compensated for by longer annual vacations

assuming that the individual works the maximum number of hours per year in each of the years between leaving school and the expected year of retirement.

Take an individual who expects to live to age 90, there are 74 years available to work after leaving school at age 16. The *lifetime budget constraint* is illustrated in Fig. 4.4. The individual's preferences for years of leisure and goods and services can again be summarized in an indifference map. The point of tangency between these *lifetime indifference curves* and the lifetime budget constraint determines the optimum for the individual and indicates the number of years he or she expects to work during his or her lifetime. Thus the individual depicted in Fig. 4.4 works N out of the 74 years that are available to him or her. As before a rise in unearned income displaces the budget constraint vertically and is likely to result in fewer years of work. An increase in the present value of expected annual earnings pivots the annual wage ray and sets in motion income and substitution effects but again we cannot determine, *a priori*, whether this will lead to more or fewer years being worked.

However, the figure tells us nothing about either the distribution of years of work across the lifetime nor yet about the form in which this leisure is taken. Some of the years not worked could be used to improve subsequent productivity. This is just one way in which the constraints facing the individual are endogenized. Thus if the individual decides to invest in five years' college immediately upon leaving school the

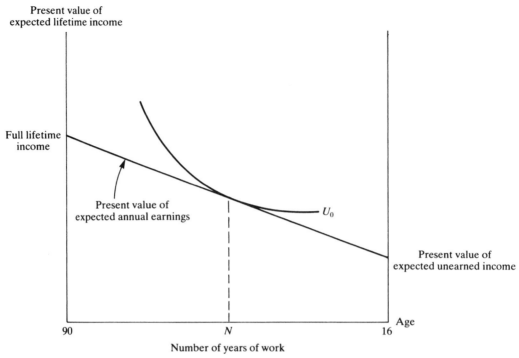

Figure 4.4 The choice of lifetime years of work. The lifetime budget constraint facing individuals is determined by: the number of years they believe are available to them in which to work; the present value of their expected annual earnings in each of these years; and the present value of their expected unearned income. These constraints can be relaxed. By saving, individuals can increase their unearned income, and by investing in human capital they can enhance the quality of their labor and hence their annual earnings

number of years available to the individual during which to work will reduce. This would be depicted in Fig. 4.4 by a shortening of the horizontal axis, to indicate that fewer years were now available in which to work, but there would also be a steepening of the annual wage rate to indicate the higher annual earnings that are expected subsequent to this investment. Relaxing the assumption that the individual's annual consumption of goods and services equals annual income allows him or her to save and endogenizes unearned income. The return individuals would earn on the assets they would acquire would increase the present value of expected unearned income, which could be depicted by displacing the budget constraint in a vertical direction. Under these circumstances we might expect individuals to work fewer years during their lifetime.

The above analysis required that the individual's lifetime preferences be depicted in a single set of indifference curves. One way in which we could construct such lifetime indifference curves would be to aggregate the individual's underlying annual indifference curves under the assumption that the marginal utility of leisure remains constant over the individual's lifetime. However, the value of leisure, or of non-market time, is likely to vary during an individual's lifetime for a number of reasons. First, there may be fixed costs associated with taking leisure. If leisure is better taken in Spain or Florida than in Birmingham or New York, this will give rise to fixed costs associated with commuting between these destinations. Once fixed costs are introduced it becomes rational to consolidate periods of work and periods of leisure in order to reduce these fixed costs. In the limit individuals may choose to work uninterrupted for part of their lives and then retire completely. Second, if work skills are not constantly practiced they may depreciate, and it may be sensible to consolidate working into early years and leisure into later life to minimize the consequences of depreciation.

Against these arguments for bunching one's leisure time and retiring in later life, are considerations of risk and household productive efficiency. Considerations of risk may lead individuals to take leisure early in their lives or to distribute it at regular intervals over their working lives for they might not expect to reach retirement age—the 'live for today' philosophy reflects a pessimistic appraisal of one's own mortality! Individuals may also be disposed to take leisure now rather than postpone taking it until old age for they recognize that their productive efficiency in non-market activities declines with age. Whether they believe this to be due to the passing of the years or to the onset of infirmity, they may conclude that in the latter stages of their life certain of the commodities they value most, such as skiing, windsurfing or playing football, will only be produced by considerably greater expenditure of effort and resources than in earlier life. For all the above reasons the value that individuals place on leisure is likely to vary over their lifetime, and we have no clear guide as to at which points in the life cycle the marginal value of leisure is at its greatest. It will be apparent that the determinants of life cycle labor supply cannot easily be depicted in diagrammatic form.

Consider in greater detail a number of aspects of lifetime labor supply that have changed substantially in recent years and indeed are likely to continue to change.

The move to earlier retirement

Table 4.9 revealed a very sharp fall in the labor force participation of older males. Two developments help to explain this. First, the introduction of and improvement in the level of benefit from government old-age pension programs (social security programs in the United States) and, second, the growing incidence of private pension plans.

In the United States the Social Security Act of 1935 introduced an old-age insurance program. Since that time successive amendments to the Act, most notably in 1939, 1956 and 1965, have extended the coverage of the Act and improved the level of benefits. In 1940, 200 000 individuals in the United States were recipients under the program. This number had risen to 36 million by 1980. In the United Kingdom universal entitlement to old-age pension for males aged 65 and over and females aged 60 and over was introduced in consequence of the Beveridge Report of 1942. Since that time the real value of pensions has increased substantially. What are the labor supply consequences of such programs?

Social security payments are met from general taxation, and the manner in which the tax is levied may have redistributional consequences. The existence of old-age pensions paid for by a progressive tax will reduce the lifetime incomes of higher earners and increase those of low wage earners. This will alter both the position and the slope of the budget constraints affecting both groups. Private pension benefits are not independent of the individual's date of retirement. Annual pension benefits are most frequently linked to years of service or some combination of years of service and recent salary. Simply linking to years of service might, *ceteris paribus*, induce workers to retire later rather than earlier. The same will be true where benefit is linked to recent salary and age-earnings profiles are steep and continuously rising. On the other hand, application of this last formula where salaries decline in later years of life will, *ceteris paribus*, induce earlier retirement.

The issues involved are complex but a number of researchers have attempted to estimate the effects of these provisions on labor supply in the United States. Thus it has been estimated that a doubling of pension or social security benefits would reduce the average age of retirement by one year. While an earlier study had suggested that social security was the cause of the reduction in the labor force participation rates that occurred in the 1950s and 1960s,[12] other studies have suggested that the effect of private pension schemes had been to induce people to leave their jobs earlier than would otherwise have been the case.[13]

In the United Kingdom two further factors explain the uniquely sharp decline in the participation rate of older males during the late 1970s and early 1980s. First, the inability of many older workers to find jobs at this time led them to quit the labor force before reaching retirement age. This 'discouraged worker effect' resulted from the persistently high unemployment among older workers during this period. Second, many older workers were in receipt of redundancy (severance) payments. In Chapter 3 it was shown that this can result in the purchase of more leisure, via a straight income effect, which in this context means early retirement of older workers.

Increased vacation time and the shorter working week

Table 4.7 revealed a substantial increase in vacation time in Europe and there is now pressure in the United States to increase annual vacation entitlements. Why should reductions in lifetime labor supply take this form? If there are fixed costs associated with certain forms of leisure, the costs of driving to the coast, or flying to the sun, these costs are minimized if leisure time is bunched. The more substanital these fixed costs

12. Mitchell, Olivia M. and Fields, Gary S. (1984) 'The economics of retirement behavior', *Journal of Labor Economics*, **2**, 84–105. Boskin, M.J. (1977) 'Social security and retirement decisions', *Economic Enquiry*, **15**, 1–25.
13. Gordon, R.J. and Blinder, A. (1980) 'Market wages, reservation wages and retirement decisions', *Journal of Public Economics*, **14**, 277–308. Gustman, A. and Steinmeier, A. (1982) 'Partial retirement and the analysis of retirement behaviour', NBER Working Paper 1000.

the greater the arguments for bunching leisure into distinct vacation periods. Indivisibilities in certain of the commodities produced by using leisure time may also merit bunching. Thus if the commodity is 'complete relaxation' it may only be possible to relax fully if a vacation lasts at least two weeks.

In Europe recent reductions in the working week have increasingly taken the form of longer weekends. This again may reflect the fixed costs associated with certain of the leisure activities individuals wish to pursue on weekends. Evidently the manner in which individuals choose to take their leisure over their lifetime depends on the nature of the commodities they wish to produce in their leisure time. The evidence, of the form which reductions in annual hours of work have taken, suggests that these are commodities which have high fixed costs.

LIFETIME HOURS OF WORK

When taken together the reduction in lifetime labor force participation rates, in hours worked per week and in weeks worked per year, means that the total number of hours worked per lifetime has fallen substantially in most countries. It has been calculated that the reduction in lifetime participation in the United Kingdom means that the number of years worked per lifetime for a typical male has fallen from 56 to 46 years over the century to 1980.[14] Together with the fall in annual hours of work this reduction in the number of years worked means a reduction of 43 percent in lifetime hours of work in the United Kingdom over the period 1891 to 1981. The fall is most pronounced for men and has occurred most rapidly in the 10 years to 1981, due to a conjunction of earlier retirement, longer periods in full-time education, a reduction in weekly hours of work and increased holiday entitlement.

While the same figures are not available for other countries, it is nonetheless possible to draw some general conclusions. In Japan participation rates among males are the highest of any country reported, as are annual hours of work. It appears indisputable that males in Japan work substantially more hours during their lifetime than do males in any of the other countries shown. In the United States and the United Kingdom males now work a similar number of hours per year (although this is split rather differently between vacations and weekly hours of work) while overall male participation rates are almost identical. The number of hours that males in the United Kingdom and the United States work in a lifetime is, as a result, now almost the same. Finally, in Germany annual hours of work are longer than in the United States or the United Kingdom but participation rates are lower. It is not unlikely therefore that, on average, males in this country now work a similar number of hours during their lifetime as do males in the United States. So Japan stands out as the country in which males have by far the longest working lives.

We saw also that in the United Kingdom and the United States there has been a decline in the annual hours of work of women, although this has been less substantial

14. Armstrong, P.J. (1984) *Technical Change and Reductions in Life Hours*, Technical Change Centre, London.

than that for men. In these same two countries there was however an increase in both the proportion of women working at some stage during their lives and an increase in the number of years typically worked. The relative magnitudes of the decline in hours worked and rise in participation rates suggest that overall lifetime hours of work of women in the United Kingdom and the United States have probably risen. In contrast, participation rates declined among women in Germany and Japan and it therefore seems likely that the lifetime hours of work of women in these two countries have declined. Having said this, we immediately qualify this judgment because of course here we focus on market work only. As Table 2.1 revealed, the household division of labor is such that women perform the majority of non-market work in the United Kingdom and the United States and it is unlikely to be substantially different in these other countries. A change in market work does not in itself indicate that there has been any change in the lifetime hours of work of women, for non-market work might have changed in an offsetting manner. However, improved home technology, and perhaps more help from spouses seems likely to have reduced women's work in the home. A further reason for supposing there has been a reduction in the amount of non-market work performed by women in most of these countries in recent years is the reduction in average family size. It is possible therefore that in both the United States and the United Kingdom, as in Germany and Japan, there has been a fall in the lifetime hours devoted to total market and non-market work by women.

What are the implications of the developments we noted above for labor supply? What do they tell us about the shape and slope of labor supply curves in the different countries? It is evident that many forces have produced the patterns we observed above but to identify the labor supply curve we need to describe the relationship between the quantity of labor supplied and its price—the real wage rate. Only multiple regression analysis or some variant of this can strip away—hold constant—the many influences on labor supply we have discussed above and permit us to distinguish this relationship. So we now turn to consider the empirical results from the many econometric studies in this area.

REGRESSION ANALYSIS[15]

Over the last 20 years there has been a veritable outpouring of empirical work evaluating the determinants of labor supply. In the early, first generation, studies ordinary least squares estimates of the income and substitution effects were obtained from estimating equations of the form:

$$\ln H_i = a_0 + a_1 \ln \frac{W}{P_i} + a_2 \ln \frac{Y}{P_i} + a_3 X_i + e_i \tag{4.1}$$

15. This section relies heavily on the excellent survey articles by Pencavel, J.H. (1986), *op. cit.* and Killingsworth, M.R. and Heckman, J.J. (1986), *op. cit.*

where the variables refer to individual i and remain as defined in earlier chapters while X represents a range of other variables designed to capture differences in tastes. Thus X might include age or sex, for it might be hypothesized that tastes for work differ between age groups and perhaps between the sexes, while e is an error term standing for unobserved tastes for work. This logarithmic specificiation provides a direct estimate of the elasticities. Thus the coefficient a_1 in Eq. (4.1) represents the real wage elasticity of hours of work ε^s, and this in turn can be broken down into the income and substitution effects.[16]

There are several problems with using such an estimating equation to analyze labor supply. In particular it appears to be inappropriate for analyzing the labor supply of women. Large numbers of women do not work, because the market wage W/P does not exceed their reservation wage, W^*/P, and among such females small changes in W/P will therefore produce no change in H. Any change in the wages offered to them will in turn have no effect on the labor supply of their husbands for, if the wife is not working, the husband derives no unearned income from this source. A problem arises because we cannot measure the W^*/P of non-working wives, so we do not know the wages they would need to be paid to induce them to participate in the labor market.

At first glance it might appear that the solution is to fit the equation to data for working women only but to do this is to run into problems of *selectivity bias*, for working women are not then representative of women in general. Indeed they are evidently those with the lowest reservation wages, *ceteris paribus*, for to induce any individual to work W/P must exceed W^*/P. Looked at another way, if all women had the same reservation wage those women who worked would be those who could command the highest wage rates in the labor market. On both counts working women

---

16. Note that in Appendix 2B to Chapter 2 it was shown that the real wage elasticity of hours of work could be broken down into the income and substitution effects. It was shown that $\varepsilon^s = \varepsilon_1 + \varepsilon_2$ where ε^s is the real wage elasticity of hours of work, ε_1 is the income compensated elasticity of hours of work with respect to the real wage and ε_2 is the non-labor income elasticity of hours of work. In Eq. (2B.2) of that appendix it was shown that

$$\varepsilon_1 = \left(\frac{\overline{w}}{H}\right)\left(\frac{\partial H}{\partial w}\right)_{U \text{ - const}}$$

and

$$\varepsilon_2 = -\left(\frac{\overline{w}}{\overline{y}}\right)H\left(\frac{\overline{y}}{H}\right)\left(\frac{\partial H}{\partial y}\right)$$

Now in Eq. (4.1) the coefficient $a_1 = \varepsilon^s$ and therefore $a_1 = \varepsilon_1 + \varepsilon_2$ as shown above. The coefficient a_2 in Eq. (4.1) gives a measure of

$$\left(\frac{\partial H}{\partial y}\right)\left(\frac{\overline{y}}{H}\right)$$

and because we know that

$$a_1 = \left(\frac{\overline{w}}{H}\right)\left(\frac{\partial H}{\partial w}\right)_{U \text{ - const}} - \left(\frac{\overline{w}}{\overline{y}}\right)H\left(\frac{\overline{y}}{H}\right)\left(\frac{\partial H}{\partial y}\right)$$

it follows that the substitution effect (the first term on the right-hand side above), ε_1, is given by $a_1 - a_2$ when $(\overline{w}/\overline{y})H = 1$ or $\overline{w}/H = y$.

will be unrepresentative of the female population in general and therefore ordinary least squares estimates of Eq. (4.1) will suffer from bias. Further problems arise because the effects of the unmeasured reservation wage W^*/P, which will be captured in the error term, e, in Eq. (4.1), may also be correlated with some of the independent variables included in the equation. As an example consider those women who work despite having a high level of unearned income, Y_u/P, *ceteris paribus* they must have a relatively low taste for leisure but in turn their taste for leisure is one of the determinants of their reservation wage. For these reasons equations of the form of (4.1) will provide biased measures of the behavior of women in general and of working women in particular.

The solution to such problems has been to estimate both a labor supply function, which reveals the determinants of hours of work *and* a participation function, which reveals the behavioral determinants of the discrete choice of whether or not to work. Estimates of the real wage elasticity and the income and substitution elasticities of labor supply for men in the United States and Britain are reproduced in Table 4.11.

The studies suggest that the labor supply curve for males is backward sloping in both Britain and the United States. For Britain all of the studies shown in Table 4.11 suggested that the gross wage elasticity of hours of work is negative. A 1 percent rise in the real wage generally results in a reduction in hours of work of between -0.13 and -0.33 percent. In all cases the negative income effect, which seems typically to fall in the range of -0.2 to -0.4 percent, overwhelms the positive substitution effect which appears to fall in the range of 0.1 to 0.2 percent. Similar results emerge for the United States, where the overall wage elasticity of hours of work seems to be slightly smaller than in Britain, typically falling in the range of -0.1 to -0.2 percent. Again this results from an income elasticity, of the order of probably -0.2 to -0.3 percent overwhelming a positive substitution elasticity of around 0.1 percent. Although it has to be noted that in the United States one or two of the studies reported here have produced estimates at considerable variance with these, it seems safe to conclude that the empirical evidence on the labor supply of males suggests that the labor supply curve is backward sloping in both the United States and Britain and that it is rather more negatively sloped in Britain than the United States. A 1 percent rise in the real wage of males in both countries results in a larger reduction in labor supply in Britain than it does in the United States.

At this stage it should be recalled that in Table 3.1 we reported some estimates of labor supply elasticities derived from the negative income tax experiments in the United States. These seemed to point to a positively sloping labor supply curve for males due to the substitution effect overwhelming the income effect. This was largely due to the smaller income effects that emerged from the NIT experiment, since the estimates of the substitution effects were little different. It is not surprising that smaller estimates of the income effect should result from the NIT data, for the experiment was perceived to be temporary and, for all the reasons outlined on page 78 in Chapter 3, such a temporary change is likely to lead to a smaller reduction in hours of work than a change that is perceived to be permanent. It appears that real wage increases that are

Table 4.11 Estimates of elasticities of labor supply for men in Britain and the United States

	Gross wage elasticity (ε^s)	Income elasticity (ε_2)	Substitution elasticity (ε_1)
US males			
Ashenfelter and Heckman (1973)	− 0.16	− 0.27	0.12
Bloch (1973)	0.06	− 0.06	0.12
Boskin (1973)	− 0.29	− 0.41	0.12
DaVanzo, DeTray and Greenberg (1973)	− 0.15	− 0.004	− 0.14
Dickinson (1974)	− 0.11	0.08	− 0.19
Fleisher, Parsons and Porter (1973)	− 0.19	− 0.23	0.04
Greenberg and Kosters (1973)	− 0.09	− 0.29	0.20
Ham (1982)	− 0.16	− 0.11	-0.05
Hausman and Ruud (1984)	− 0.08	0.63	0.55
Kniesner (1967)	− 0.17	− 0.01	− 0.16
Kosters (1966)	− 0.09	− 0.14	0.04
Masters and Garfinkel (1977)	− 0.11	− 0.05	0.06
Wales and Woodland (1979)	0.14	− 0.70	0.84
British males			
Ashworth and Ulph (1981)	− 0.13	− 0.36	0.23
Atkinson and Stern (1980)	− 0.16	− 0.07	− 0.09
Blundell and Walker (1982)	− 0.23	− 0.36	0.13
Blundell and Walker (1983)	− 0.004	− 0.20	0.20
Brown, Levin and Ulph (1976)	− 0.13	− 0.35	0.22
Brown *et al.* (1982–83) single worker	− 0.33	− 0.50	0.17
two workers	− 0.14	− 0.44	0.30
Layard (1978)	− 0.13	− 0.04	− 0.09

Source: Pencavel, J.H. (1986), *op. cit.*, Tables 1.19 and 1.20. See the footnotes that accompany these tables.

perceived to be temporary may result in increased hours of work but those that are perceived to be permanent result in a reduction in hours of work.

Of the large number of studies that have evaluated female labor supply most have focused on the largest group among these—married women. In Table 4.12 the results of some of the most important of the recent studies are reported. These seem to suggest that the labor supply curve of married women is positively sloping. In general a 1 percent rise in the real wage in the United States appears to give rise to an increase in women's labor supply in the region of 0.4 to 0.6 percent, although some estimates suggest the response may be larger. Against this there is now a trickle of evidence suggesting that the labor supply curve for women might not after all be that different from that for men. The study by Nakamura and Nakamura reported here is one example of this. In Britain the estimates are more varied suggesting the gross wage elasticity may be anything from slightly negative, − 0.21, to strongly positive, highly elastic, 2.03, but the most recent studies seem to be producing consistently large and

Table 4.12 Estimates of elasticities of labor supply for married women in Britain and the United States

	Gross wage elasticity (ε_s)	Income elasticity (ε_2)	Substitution elasticity (ε_1)
US women			
Heckman (1976) White wives aged 30–44	1.46	– 0.02	1.48
Schultz (1980) White wives aged 35–44	0.16	– 0.05	0.21
Black wives aged 35–44	0.60	0.26	0.34
Cogan (1981) White wives aged 30–44	0.65	– 0.03	0.68
Yatchew (1985) Wives	0.47	– 0.89	—
Nakamura and			
Nakamura (1981) Wives aged 30–34	– 0.27	– 0.36	0.11
Wives aged 35–39	– 0.31	– 0.19	– 0.12
Wives aged 40–44	– 0.09	– 0.27	0.18
British women			
Zabalza (1983)	1.59	– 0.23	1.82
Ashworth and Ulph (1981)	– 0.09 to	0.02	– 0.04 to
	– 0.21 to	– 0.05	– 0.23
Arrufat and Zabalza (1986)	2.03	– 0.21	—
Blundell and Walker (1982) No children	0.43	– 0.22	0.65
One child	0.10	– 0.22	0.32
Two children	– 0.19	– 0.22	0.03

Source: Killingsworth M.R. and Heckman J.J. (1986), *op.cit.*, Table 2.26. See also the footnotes that accompany this table.

positive elasticities. Of course these estimates vary according to the time period to which the data relate, the population from which the sample is drawn and the estimating techniques employed—to mention just three important aspects. But it is noticeable that the British studies generally agree on the magnitude of the negative income effect. It is the estimates of the size of the compensated wage, the substitution, effect which reveal the greatest dispersion.

Until recently the received wisdom among labor economists was that while the labor supply curve for men was negatively sloped, for permanent changes in the real wage, that for women was positively sloped. While for men the negative income effect dominated, for women the positive substitution effect dominated. It was also generally agreed that the elasticity of labor supply was larger for women than it was for men so that taken together the results suggested that, for the population as a whole, the aggregate labor supply curve was positively sloped in both the United States and Britain. It appeared that the elasticity of aggregate labor supply was probably of the order of 0.2 to 0.3 percent in the United States and that it might be slightly larger in Britain, for in Britain, although there appeared to be a slightly larger negative men's elasticity, the positive women's elasticity was also larger and again dominated this. At least this was the received wisdom up to the mid-1980s. However, recent evidence on the slope of the women's labor supply curve has begun to cast doubts on the slope of the overall labor supply curve. If the women's labor supply is no longer as positively sloped as was once suggested, or is perhaps negatively sloped like that for men, the overall labor supply curve may now be negatively sloping.

FURTHER OBSERVATIONS ON THE LONG-TERM TREND IN WOMEN'S PARTICIPATION

Finally, consider again the general forces that have been at work over the years which have produced the rise in female participation rates at all ages. The regression analysis, of women's labor supply above, suggested that until recently a positive substitution effect dominated the negative income effect.Over the years there has been a rise in the real wages of women which has exceeded that for males and this rise in women's real wages has been a major cause of the rise in participation and hours of work. Empirical work has also revealed a strong positive association between women's educational attainment and participation. This result emerges even after controlling for the women's wage (which will be higher for the more educated), the number of children (which may be fewer) and the husband's wage (which will be higher).[17] These results may reflect the role of education in changing women's tastes toward work and therefore the long-run rise in educational standards may also help to explain the long-run trend in participation.

A further feature of the post-war period, proposed to explain the long-term increase in women's labor supply, has been a change in men's tastes for, that is their attitudes toward, women working. Men's tastes will, where they combine in households, influence women's reservation wages and this change in men's attitudes has likely caused a substantial reduction in women's reservation wages. It has been argued that the two world wars were largely responsible for substantial changes in men's attitudes toward women at work. The wars resulted in a large increase in women's participation as they undertook the work of the men who had gone to the front. Having shown that they were perfectly capable of doing what had previously been regarded as 'men's work' there was now less resistance to women occupying these jobs once the war was finished.

Long-run changes in household productivity will also have affected women's labor supply. Innovations in home technology, as a result of the development of consumer durables (fridges, hoovers, dishwashers, washing machines, freezers, microwaves, food processors), have all substantially increased the productivity of the household. This in turn has increased the amount of time available to women to devote to market activities. However, it is not clear just what the causal relation is. Has the increased presence of women in the labor market created the demand for such technology, or did such technology emerge and facilitate increased women's participation? Does it really matter? Evidently there is now a substantial demand for and hence return from

17. See Killingsworth, M.R. and Heckman, J.J. (1986), *op. cit.*

developing such labor saving devices, which can only enhance women's labor market opportunities in the future.

SUMMARY

In this chapter we have detailed the substantial changes in labor supply that have occurred in the major industrialized nations during the twentieth century. The participation rates of men decreased sharply as they retired earlier and entered the labor force later with the result that the number of years the typical male now works has declined substantially. The weekly hours of work of males have also declined sharply and their holiday entitlements have risen so that by 1980 men in the United Kingdom and the United States were working around one-third fewer hours a year than they were at the start of the century. This decline in the length of the working year, when taken in conjunction with the decline in the number of years of work, means that by 1980 a typical man in the United States and the United Kingdom was spending between 40 and 45 percent less of his life working than was a man at the start of the twentieth century.

The weekly hours of work of full-time women have also declined and they too have benefited from longer holidays, but now there are many more females working than there were at the start of the century and the number of years that the typical woman spends in market work has also risen. In contrast to males therefore women in the United Kingdom and the United States are devoting more of their lives to paid market work than ever before. Offsetting this has probably been a decline in the amount of time women devote to non-market work, but whether on balance they are working more or less is difficult to say.

The explanations for these developments are many and complex and they are not uniquely of an economic nature. Nonetheless it was evident that the rise in women's real wages provided an important part of the explanation of the rise in their economic activity. For women we saw that the labor supply curve was probably, but by no means certainly, positively sloping, while that for men was, almost certainly, negatively sloping. The positive association between wages and women's labor supply might overwhelm the negative association between male wages and male labor supply so that it was possible that in the economies of the United States and the United Kingdom as a whole a positively sloping labor supply curve exists.

PRINCIPAL CONCEPTS

The following concepts have been developed in this chapter. Students should ensure that they have a clear grasp of these before proceeding to the next chapter:

1. The labor force participation rate.
2. Life cycle patterns of labor supply.
3. Lifetime budget constraint.

4. Lifetime hours of work.
5. Selectivity bias.

QUESTIONS FOR DISCUSSION

1. Why have male participation rates fallen in most industrialized countries?
2. How do we explain the trend toward earlier retirement? Will it continue?
3. How do you account for the change in life cycle labor market participation of married females in the United Kingdom and the United States in the last 30 years?
4. How do you explain the substantial rise in labor market activity by females of all ages in the United Kingdom and United States?
5. How might you explain the decline in female activity rates in Germany and Japan while they have risen in Australia, the United Kingdom and the United States?
6. Are labor supply considerations alone sufficient to account for the rise in part-time employment in the United Kingdom in recent years?
7. How might you explain the rise in vacation time and the fall in the length of the working week in the United States and the United Kingdom?
8. Identify the main factors which account for the fall in the lifetime hours of males in the United Kingdom and the United States?
9. What does regression analysis tell us about the magnitude of the income and substitution effects and the shape of the labor supply curves for men and women in the United States and the United Kingdom?

REFERENCES AND FURTHER READING

Throughout the text I have referred to and made considerable use of the excellent surveys by Pencavel and Killingsworth and Heckman in the *Handbook of Labor Economics*. The full references are Pencavel, J.H. (1986) 'Labor supply of men: a survey' and Killingsworth, M.R. and Heckman, J.J. (1986), 'Female labor supply: a survey', in Ashenfelter, O. and Layard, P.R.G. (eds.), *Handbook of Labor Economics*, vol. 1, North-Holland, New York and Oxford pp. 3–102 and 103–204 respectively. I am grateful to these authors and the publisher for permission to reproduce the material used in this text. It is also from these studies and Killingsworth, M.R. (1983), *Labour Supply*, Cambridge University Press, that the reader can obtain the complete references for the many empirical studies referred to in the tables although the interested undergraduate would be well advised to read the Pencavel and Killingsworth and Heckman surveys before dipping into these articles. The volume edited by Layard and Ashenfelter also contains a survey of economic explanations of retirement by Lazear, E.P. entitled 'Retirement from the labor force'.

5

LABOR SUPPLY IN THE LONG RUN: THE SIZE OF THE POPULATION OF WORKING AGE

In this chapter we are concerned with one of the two principal aspects of labor supply in the long run: the size of the population of working age. The second aspect, the skills possessed by that population, will be addressed in the next chapter. In this chapter we are no longer concerned with the number of hours individuals wish to work, or indeed with the proportion of individuals from a given population who wish to work, but with the size of the population itself. We have already seen that the population of working age can be defined in at least two ways: first, as the population beyond the minimum school leaving age but below retirement age; and second, as the total population beyond school leaving age. Although school children can and do work it is conventional to exclude them from the population of working age. Some among the adult population are also not fit to work, due to either mental or physical impairment, and should therefore be excluded from the labor supply. However, these are not the issues we consider in this chapter. Instead we are concerned with the long-run determinants of the size of a country's population for this determines the bounds from which the population of working age, however defined, is drawn.

The principal determinants of the size of a country's population are two. First, demographic factors such as birth and death rates and second, migration. In this chapter we shall be looking in detail at demographic factors and migration, and at the role that economic forces play in shaping these, in order to distinguish the long-run labor supply curve. We shall also look at projections of the size of the labor force in the United Kingdom and the United States over the period to 1995. This involves projecting both the size of the population of working age and participation rates. First, however, we will concentrate on demographic change.

DEMOGRAPHIC CHANGES

Once we have excluded migration, 'entries' to the population of working age, where this is defined as that beyond the minimum school leaving age but below retirement age, are indicated by the number of births 16 years earlier. 'Exits' reflect the death rate among the working population and the number of retirements; in turn, in the UK, reflecting the number of births of females 60 years earlier and males 65 years earlier. Births and deaths are therefore the two key variables setting the upper limit to this aspect of labor supply in the long run.

In Britain in recent years the net effect of migration on labor supply has generally been very small and so there has been only a small difference between the domestic population of working age and the total population of working age. The same cannot be said of the United States for there has been substantial migration into the United States for many years. In the United States as in the United Kingdom, however, the single most important contributor to changes in the population of working age in recent years has been demographic change. Both countries have recently experienced and are projected to continue to experience a reduction in the rate of increase in the population of working age during the late 1980s and 1990s. The cause of this in both cases has been the reduction in birth rates during the late 1970s.

Birth rates reflect both the number of women of childbearing age in the population and the fertility rate (the number of births per woman). In both countries the fertility rate has been falling steadily over the last few decades although the number of women of childbearing age has fluctuated in long cycles, reflecting the post-war 'baby boom' in both countries and the subsequent maturation to childbearing age of these individuals. The previous chapter revealed that the proportion of women ever getting married had fallen steadily since the early 1950s in both the United States and the United Kingdom. Further, it revealed that the average ages at which women married and had their first child were both increasing while the average number of births per marriage had fallen due to the revolution in contraceptive practice. In consequence, while the birth rate in the United States in the mid-1960s was around 20 births per 1000 of the population, by the mid-1970s this had fallen by over a quarter to less than 15. This decline in the birth rate in the mid-1970s will result in a much slower increase in the population of working age in the United States during the early 1990s. In the United Kingdom the birth rate is lower still. It fell from around 18 in the mid-1960s to less than 12 in the mid-1970s at which level it seems to have stabilized. By comparison, death rates among the populations of both countries are projected to be much more stable over this period. It is therefore variations in the birth rate that are the principal determinants of the projected changes in the size of the populations of working age in the United States and the United Kingdom during the late 1980s and 1990s.

The economic determinants of population changes

Economics has much to say about the determinants of population changes. Economists from the time of Thomas Malthus, whose *Essay on Population* was first published in

1798, have considered the role that economic forces play in determining population changes. From Malthus's writings can be deduced a crude theory of labor supply in the long run. Malthus argued that population was determined by the response of both fertility and mortality to changes in income. Although Malthus admitted to one 'voluntary' check on the number of births, which was the age at which people married (the later they marry the fewer the number of births), the essential check on population was the subsistence level of income. Population he predicted would grow quickly if wages grew, because the average person would marry earlier—and for this reason have more children—and deaths would fall. However, the growth of population would always push up against the limit set by the productive capacity of the economy because the rate at which the population could grow (a geometrical progression) exceeded the rate at which the productive capacity of the economy could grow (an arithmetic progression). These arguments are illustrated in Fig. 5.1. Here the subsistence real wage is assumed constant at W/P. Now suppose aggregate labor demand is given by L_1^d, this is just adequate to support a working population of L_1^s and their dependants. Any increase in the number of dependants would reduce *per capita* incomes below subsistence level and result in a rise in the death rates. On the other hand, any increase in aggregate labor demand to L_2^d, would be accompanied by a rise in the real wage

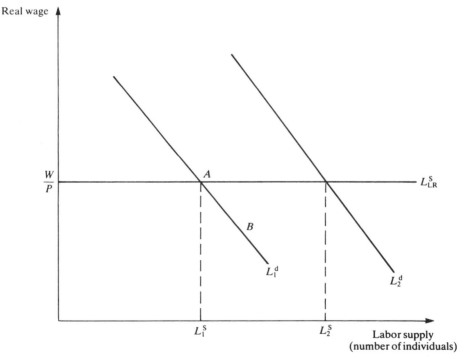

Figure 5.1 Malthusian long-run labor supply curve. The naive Malthusian model of population results in a perfectly elastic long-run labor supply curve. At a fixed and unchanging subsistence wage, W/P, the population is predicted to expand to accommodate any change in labor demand

which would encourage individuals to marry earlier and have more children. As the population grows the labor supply increases and wage rates fall back toward W/P. Thus in the long run labor supply is perfectly elastic as indicated by labor supply curve L^S_{LR} in Fig. 5.1. One implication of this is that in the long run real wages are entirely supply determined; given the minimum subsistence level they are determined quite independently of demand. Only if the minimum subsistence level is steadily rising, will the long run labor supply curve be positively sloping.

It is clear that voluntary checks on population growth have been far more important historically, in accounting for population growth, than the effects of death rates.[1] The experience of all advanced industrial nations in recent years has been contrary to that anticipated by Malthus. The growth of national income has outstripped that of the population and in consequence real incomes have risen substantially. In all these countries there has been a decline in the rate of population growth, despite a reduction in mortality rates, for in all these countries there has been an even larger decline in birth rates. Technological advances in contraception have assisted this decline in birth rates but this decline was in evidence even before these technological innovations. Contrary to Mathus's proposition, that the birth rate was solely determined by biological capacity, there is substantial evidence of the existence of 'voluntary' checks on the number of births. Indeed such evidence was available in Malthus's time for Adam Smith (1776) had already shown that in almost all societies the size of a family was inversely related to relative family income.[2]

At the base of Malthus's 'theory' of population is the view that births result not from the rational maximizing calculus of the individual but are the product of simple biological determinism. Children, he proposed, are produced at constant cost, with the supply of these responding passively to demand. Even ignoring the lags involved in the time between an increase in aggregate demand for labor and the subsequent increase in the population of working age, which will afford the opportunity for at least a transitory increase in real income, such a view of individual behavior is unsatisfactory. Yet we should note that such a view lives on today in the writings of biologists, who talk of the 'population time bomb' and extrapolate present birth rates in the developing world into the future, and predict a global catastrophe.

In the years after Malthus the study of population was, until recently, almost exclusively the province of demographers. The explanations provided by demographers were confined to finding mathematical formulae to represent the process and were therefore essentially descriptive rather than analytic. Only recently have a set of theories based on a view of human behavior and the economic calculus been offered. However, the incursion by economists into this area was not without opposition.[3]

1. See Lee, R.D. (1987) 'Population dynamics of humans and other animals', *Demography,* **24**, November, 443–67.
2. Smith, A. (1776) *The Wealth of Nations* (Cannan edn), The Modern Library, New York, 1937.
3. When editing the seminal volume of papers on the *Economics of the Family* (Chicago University Press) in 1974 Theodore Schultz was driven to comment 'I anticipate that many sensitive, thoughtful people will be offended by these studies of fertility because they may see them as debasing the family and motherhood. These highly personal activities and purposes of parents may be seen to be far beyond the realm of the economic calculus'. But his defense was that the analytical core of these studies rests on the

The economics of fertility

The modern approach to fertility regards children as a consumption good and the demand for children is accordingly analyzed within the framework of consumer demand theory. Within this framework children are considered to be normal goods and thus the demand for children rises as income rises.

Consider a simple model which illustrates how the resources and preferences of the household affect the number of children produced by the household. Thus in quadrant (IV) of Fig. 5.2, the household production function is shown. The household combines expenditures, E, on the necessary inputs (food and clothes being the most obvious examples) together with its own time, T, to produce and rear children, N. Thus $N = N$ (E,T). For simplicity the input of time is assumed fixed, parents devote a constant proportion of their time to rearing their children. Accordingly, if members of the household decide to offer less market work this leaves more time for other non-market activities or leisure. Again this assumes some agreed division of labor within the household. Quadrant (III) identifies the budget constraint facing the household. The slopes of the budget constraint reflect the relative prices of those commodities required as inputs into the production of children and those commodities which result in pure consumption. Mapping through the 45° line in quadrant (II) enables us to describe a convex line in quadrant (I) which details the combinations of consumption goods and children that are available to the household. The preferences of the household are mapped in the usual way in a set of indifference curves, U_0 and U_1, and the point of tangency between the concave function describing the consumption opportunities available to the household and the highest indifference curve, point A, represents the optimum for the household.

Now consider an increase in the income of the household. This is indicated by an outward movement of the budget constraint in quadrant (III) which in turn increases the consumption opportunities open to the household as depicted by the outward movement of the convex line in quadrant (I). The increase in income results in an increase in both the number of children produced and the consumption of other commodities; the move to point B. The same diagrammatic apparatus can also be used to show the effects, on the household's production of children, of a change in relative prices. Such a change is, of course, reflected in a change in the slope of the budget constraint in quadrant (III).

One of the predictions that would appear to arise from the above model is that the number of children is positively associated with income, as was the case in the example shown. (This was also an assumption of Malthus.) However, it turns out that the

economic postulate that the reproductive behavior of parents is in large part a response to the underlying preferences of parents for children. Given the state of the birth control technology and the various classes of uncertainty associated with contraception, infant mortality, the health and fecundity of the parents and the income and wage rates parents expect to realize over their life cycles, these preferences are constrained by the parents' resources and the associated alternative economic opportunities in using their resources. In turn, these resources imply sacrifices, measured in terms of opportunity costs, that parents must be prepared to make in acquiring the future satisfactions and productive source they expect to realize from children' (*op. cit.*, p. 4). There is today no better statement of why economists should study fertility.

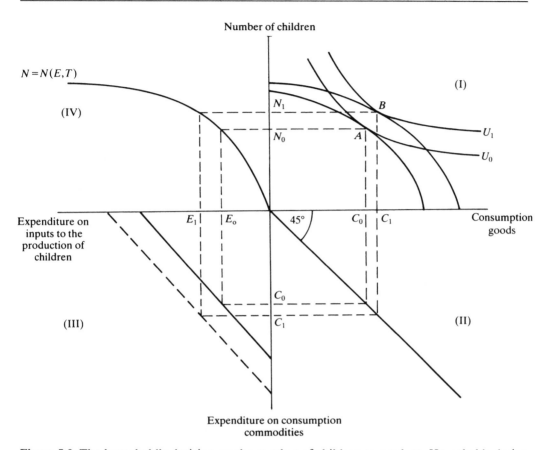

Figure 5.2 The household's decision on the number of children to produce. Households derive utility from the number of children they produce and the commodities they consume. These preferences are mapped in a set of indifference curves in quadrant (I). Children are produced by the household using a fixed amount of its time T and varying amounts of expenditure on the commodities required to produce children. These arguments are reflected in the production function in quadrant (IV). Families face a budget constraint shown in quadrant (III), the position of which is determined by their income and the shape of which reflects the relative prices of inputs to the prodution of children and commodities. The budget constraint in conjunction with the production function determine the opportunities facing the household. The points of tangency between the functions mapping these opportunities and the indifference curves represent the optimum for the household, as shown at A and B in quadrant (I)

opposite is the case. The model above makes one crucial simplifying assumption—that the amount of time devoted to the production of children is fixed. If the time devoted to the production of children is a variable then the wage rate, particularly the female wage rate, serves as a proxy for the price of time devoted to this activity. Now a rise in wage rates raises the opportunity cost of time spent in producing children and the relative magnitude of the income and substitution effects determines whether more or less time is devoted to this activity.

The above model emphasizes that the number of children a household produces is determined by: the efficiency of the household, in combining the inputs of time and commodities to produce children, as reflected in the production function; the resources at the disposal of the household, as reflected in the position of the budget constraint; the relative prices of inputs and consumption commodities, as reflected in the slope of the budget constraint; the tastes of the household, as reflected in the indifference map. These factors determine this aspect of the supply of labor in the long run but there is little clear empirical evidence on these issues and therefore little guide as to the shape of the long-run labor supply curve arising from purely demographic considerations.[4] Consider the other aspect of long-run labor supply.

INTERNATIONAL MIGRATION

For many countries in the world, migration has been an important contributor to changes in labor supply. Indeed for some among them, it has been the single most important contributor to the changes in labor supply that have taken place over the past 40 years. What, then, have been the patterns of migration in recent years and how important have these flows been to both the host and the originating countries? Moreover, what have been the determinants of, and what are the economic consequences of, these flows? First consider the scale of migration in the modern world.

The scale and pattern of migration

As economic and political fortunes ebb and flow so do the patterns of labor migration. The countries of northern Europe, North America and the Australian subcontinent were the principal recipients of migrants during the 1950s and 1960s and, more recently, they have been joined by the oil producing countries of the Middle East. Migrants have flowed to these countries from southern Europe, North Africa, the Indian subcontinent, the Caribbean and Latin America. These flows have not always been monitored with great accuracy for many migrate illegally. Some measure of the scale of legal migration can be gained from the following figures for the number of foreign residents as a percentage of the population of certain European countries. Foreign residents in 1983 comprised 7.6 percent of the population of West Germany, 6.8 percent of France, 3.1 percent of Britain, 4.9 percent of Sweden and 5.0 percent of Switzerland. These were the host countries. In the same year 10 percent of the population of Italy, 6 percent of that of Spain and 40 percent of the population of Portugal lived abroad. Of course these figures substantially understate the true scale of migration, for three reasons. First, as mentioned, they exclude illegal migration. Second, they exclude those migrants who have become naturalized citizens of the host country. If we include these individuals, as can most easily be done in the case of Sweden, they raise the proportion of migrants in the Swedish population, from 4.9 to

4. See Montgomery, M. and Trussell, J. (1986) 'Models of marital status and childbearing', in Ashenfelter, O. and Layard, P.R.G. (eds.), *Handbook of Labor Economics*, North Holland, pp. 205–72.

7.0 percent. The same multiple would not however be appropriate in other countries which often have rather stricter naturalization laws. Third, they reflect only the net flow of migrants. Thus, while net migration to Germany fell substantially in the late 1970s, until it averaged only 14 000 in each of the years 1976 to 1983, this was still the difference between an annual inflow of 444 000 and an outflow of 430 000. Consider first the scale and pattern of gross migratory flows in recent years.

Gross migration The scale of the inflow of migrants to selected European countries, the United States, Canada and Australia over the period since 1970 is depicted in Fig. 5.3. In 1970 the annual inflow to Europe was much greater than to the United States but by the early 1980s the rates were almost equal. The annual inflow to the United States had climbed from around 400 000 to 600 000; that to Europe had fallen from over 1.5 million to under 700 000. This period also saw a change in world migratory patterns. The proportion of migrants to the United States, Canada and Australia that came from Europe declined while the proportion that came from Asia and Oceania climbed sharply. In addition the substantial flow of illegal migrants to the United States consisted mainly of nationals from outside Europe. The changing pattern of international migration is detailed in Table 5.1.

Of couse not all those who migrate to a country stay and some native born citizens of the recipient countries migrate to other countries. In recent years the inflow to Europe has increasingly been matched by an outflow of almost equal magnitude as Table 5.2 reveals. Despite the fact that over the period 1976–83 the annual inflow to Germany exceeded 440 000 this was matched by an almost equal outflow of 430 000. In France the annual average inflow of 105 000 over the period 1975–82 was offset by an outflow of 76 000, so that net migration ran at only 29 000 per annum. Many migrants to these countries, although staying longer than had originally been anticipated, eventually return to their home countries. The rates of return from France and Sweden are lower than from Germany, which in part reflects the rather more

Table 5.1 Inflows of foreign population by region of origin (%)

	Destination					
	United States		Canada		Australia	
	1972	1980	1972	1980	1972	1980
Origin:						
Europe	23.4	13.6	42.0	27.3	70.1	52.7
Asia	31.5	44.5	19.1	38.3	11.9	27.0
Oceania	0.9	0.7	1.8	—	4.0	12.0
America	42.6	38.5	29.6	25.9	9.2	3.7
Africa	1.7	2.6	6.8	8.5	3.9	4.6
TOTAL	100.0	100.0	100.0	100.0	100.0	100.0

Source: OECD *Employment Outlook*, September 1985, Chapter III, Table 23. OECD, Paris.

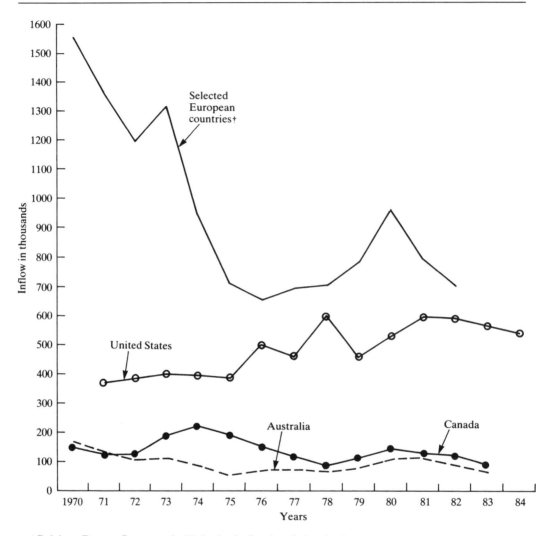

† Belgium, France, Germany, the Netherlands, Sweden, Switzerland

Figure 5.3 Inflows of foreign populations: selected European and non-European countries, 1970–83. (*Source:* OECD *Employment Outlook*) Reproduced with the permission of the OECD

liberal naturalization policies in the former two countries. Changes in nationality among the foreign population ran at 55 000 per annum in France over the period 1975–82, and 21 000 per annum in Sweden between 1976 and 1983, rates of 1.5 and 5.1 percent per annum respectively, compared to 0.8 percent per annum in Germany.

Net migration Despite much higher rates of return migration, net migration to Europe still exceeded that to the United States over the period from 1964 to 1973. As Table

Table 5.2 Annual inflows and outflows of migrants in France, Germany and Sweden: 1968–83

		Inflows ('000)	Outflows ('000)	Net migration ('000)
France	1968–74	231.9	102.0	129.0
	1975–82	105.2	75.8	29.4
Germany	1970–75	753.6	527.2	226.5
	1976–83	444.4	429.8	14.6
Sweden	1970–75	38.8	26.0	12.8
	1976–83	31.5	17.3	14.2

Source: OECD, September 1985, *op. cit.*, Table 19, OECD, Paris.

5.3 indicates, over the 10-year period to 1973 net migration added some 3.9 million to the population of the United States and some 3.2 million to that of Germany. This represented a much more substantial addition to the population of Germany than to that of the United States. On average in each of the 10 years to 1973 the net annual inflow of migrants to Germany was equivalent to an additional 0.5 percent of the population. In comparison, the net inflow to the United States when expressed as a percentage of the population, was only around 0.2 percent per annum.

Table 5.3 Net migration flows for selected countries

	1964–73	1974–83
United States		
Total for period[†]	3890	4690
Annual rate (%)[‡]	0.193	0.210
United Kingdom		
Total for period[†]	– 350	– 260
Annual rate (%)[‡]	– 0.063	– 0.047
Australia		
Total for period[†]	980	700
Annual rate (%)[‡]	0.803	0.483
Germany		
Total for period[†]	3170	390
Annual rate (%)[‡]	0.520	0.064
France		
Total for period[†]	1298	353
Annual rate (%)[‡]	0.260	0.067

Source: OECD, *Labour Force Statistics*, 1964–84. OECD, Paris.
[†] ('000)
[‡] Per hundred population

Of the countries listed Australia stands out as the country with the largest proportional net inflow. Over this period the annual rate was 0.8 percent adding some 8.3 percent to its population over this decade. It is noticeable that net migration to Europe and Australia slowed in the decade after 1973 while that to the United States increased. The United Kingdom is one of the few developed countries which is a net exporter of people.

Permanent and temporary migration In the 1950s and 1960s it seemed appropriate to draw a distinction between, on the one hand, the type of migration to Europe and, on the other, that to North America and Australia. The countries of Europe believed that the vast majority of the migrants they received were temporary while Australia and North America recognized that the majority of their migrants were intent on permanent settlement. The economic consequences of these two forms of migration are potentially quite distinct.

Temporary migrants are typically prime age workers, who leave most of their family, including often their wives and children, at home while they migrate to participate in the labor force of another country. Temporary migrants therefore have very high attachment to the labor force of the host country—the participation rate among foreign nationals living in Germany in the 1960s and 1970s was in excess of 80 percent. Permanent migrants, on the other hand, typically comprise households headed by prime age workers who bring their wives and other members of their immediate, and sometimes their extended, family with them. The average participation rate of the members of the households of permanent migrants is as a result far lower than that for temporary migrants. Temporary migrants remit part of their earnings to the sending country. Indeed, in the extreme case of migrants from Turkey, the scale of their remittances during the early 1970s was equivalent to 65 percent of that country's export earnings. Migrants' remittances were also equivalent to over 40 percent of Portugal's export earnings, 30 percent of Yugoslavia's and 20 percent of Greece's.

More recently the distinction between temporary and permanent migrants has become blurred. A pronounced feature of migration to Europe over the last decade has been an increase in applications for permanent residence on the part of those who were once thought to be temporary migrants to this area. A pattern has now emerged in which the initial migrant is followed in turn by other working members of the migrant's family, to be followed by non-working dependants, wives, children and elderly relatives. In 1968 only around 50 percent of married male migrants to West Germany were accompanied by their wives, by 1980 this proportion had risen to 80 percent. Accordingly, over the years the participation rates of foreign born members of the population have begun to move into line with those of the domestic population as Table 5.4 reveals.

Table 5.4 shows the relative participation rates of foreign born workers and of the total population in France and Germany, the only two major countries for which such statistics are available. It is evident from this that France welcomed many more dependants from the start, and that, by 1981, the foreign born and native born

Table 5.4 Labor force participation rates

	Foreign born population			Total population
	1960	1970	1981	1981
France	62.0	61.5	55.7	55.0
Germany	79.0	86.4	69.7	53.6

Source: OECD, *The Future of Migration*, 1987, p. 52. OECD, Paris.

population had almost the same activity rates. In Germany, the system of the *Gastarbieter,* the guest worker, was most highly developed, but even here although reduced in number, many migrants to Germany have settled permanently and brought in dependants with the result that participation rates have fallen sharply. The essential difference between the nature of migration to Europe and North America and Australia, has been in the length of time between these various stages in the migration chain.

It would be a mistake to believe that all of the migration to the United States and Australia resulted in permanent settlement. Some migrants wish to return to their 'own country' when they retire, as with the return to Greece of many of those who once migrated from that country to Australia. Others return because they become disillusioned with the outcome of migration, as with the 'whingeing poms' who return to the United Kingdom from Australia. It has been estimated that 31 percent of the 15.7 million migrants to the United States between 1908 and 1957 re-migrated while 20 percent of migrants to Australia between 1947 and 1980 re-migrated.[5] In recent years there may also have been a substantial increase in the number of temporary migrants to the United States as a result of illegal migration. It is estimated that there are now between 3.5 and 6 million illegal migrants in the United States, coming mostly from Latin America and the Caribbean.

Skills of migrants There appears to be little evidence about the skills that migrants bring to their host countries although it has generally been supposed that migrants to Europe in the 1950s and 1960s were largely unskilled. Indeed 82 percent of all migrants from the Mediterranean countries to Germany in 1972 fell into this category; by 1980 this proportion had fallen to 74 percent. Immigrants to Australia appear to be of a rather different quality. A recent study[6] reveals that in 1981–82 only 15 percent of immigrants were unskilled, 28 percent were semiskilled, 21 percent skilled, 14 percent clerical and administrative and almost 20 percent professional and technical workers. A large proportion of the unskilled and semiskilled were refugees. Thus among other migrants the skilled manual workers and non-manual workers predominated. Increasingly, in recent years, as more countries have been experiencing a surplus of unskilled labor alongside skill shortages, they have been accepting largely skilled workers as immigrants.

5. Price, C.A., *Australian Immigration*, Australian National University Canberra.
6. Chapman, B.J., Pope, D. and Withers, G. (1985) 'Immigration and the labour market', *Australian National University*, Centre for Economic Policy Research, Discussion Paper 128, September.

Migration increases the labor supply of the host country but depletes that of the sending country. This may matter little if the sending countries are those with a substantial labor surplus but the scale of migration from some countries is such as to outstrip this. Migration can therefore deplete countries of scarce skills. We shall shortly consider the economic consequences of migration for both the host and sending countries but first we analyze the determinants of migration.

The determinants of international migration

Migration is analogous to investment. Like an investment decision it requires an appraisal of the costs and benefits of the proposed course of action and, like the investment decision, it involves incurring costs now for expected benefits some time in the future.[7] The expected benefits of migration result from being able to sell one's labor in a market in which it commands a higher price, in transferring to the market in which the net pecuniary and non-pecuniary returns to one's labor are highest.

Because the benefits of migration accrue in the future they need to be discounted to reflect the lower value we assign to income received in the future. In general, individuals are not indifferent to the distinction between income that accrues in the future and income that accrues today. All other things being equal, individuals prefer present income and consumption to future income and consumption. In consequence, it is necessary to discount in some way to find the present value of future money sums. Deducting the costs from the discounted present value of the benefits enables us to distinguish the net present value of migration (*NPVM*). More formally this may be shown as:

$$NPVM = \sum_{i=1}^{N} \frac{B_i}{(1+r)^i} - C_0 \tag{5.1}$$

where the benefits, *B*, accruing over the year 1 to *N* are discounted at an appropriate rate, probably the interest rate, *r*, and then summed. From this total are then subtracted the costs incurred in the initial period.[8] If the present value of benefits

7. This view of immigration contrasts with that of the Scottish writer Robert Louis Stevenson who, wishing to visit a woman in California who was later to become his wife, to save money traveled steerage as an immigrant aboard the SS *Devonia* which left Glasgow on the 7 August 1879 bound for New York. In the *Amateur Emigrant* (Cassell and Company, London, 1886) he records 'As far as I saw, drink, idleness and imcompetency were the three great causes of emigration: and for all of them, and drink first and foremost, this trick of getting transported overseas appears to me the silliest means of cure'. Elsewhere in the book Stevenson recalls a conversation with 'a kind and happy Scotsman, running to fat and perspiration in the physical'. 'I asked him his hopes in immigrating. They were like those of so many others, vague and unfounded: times were bad at home, they were said to have a turn for the better in the States, and a man could get on anywhere, he thought. That was precisely the weak point of his position; for if he could get on in America, why could he not do the same in Scotland?'
8. If migration is regarded as one among a number of investment opportunities confronting the individual then it is appropriate to discount at the rate of return we might expect on the best alternative investment which, if returns across assets are equalized, will be represented by the interest rate.

exceeds the costs the net present value of migration will be positive and the individual will be disposed to migrate. This elementary framework however requires further elaboration.

First, it should be recognized that there may be substantial impediments to migration and that even though an individual may desire to migrate, it may not be possible to do so. Perhaps, more than any other aspect of the labor market, international migration is heavily regulated by governments. Few governments, with the exception of some in communist countries, place restrictions on the freedom of their citizens to emigrate, but every country places restrictions on the scale of immigration. Quantity or quality controls are imposed. Numbers are limited and/or certain criteria, such as the possession of scarce skills, or having dependants already resident in the country, are established for entry. Economic models have found it difficult to incorporate such arguments, for they are exceedingly difficult to model, and we should therefore not expect that our theory will provide a complete explanation of migration flows. Nonetheless, economic variables play a critical role in the migration decision.

Early models of migration focused on the push of adverse conditions in the sending country and the pull of attractive conditions abroad. However, such a dichotomy between adverse conditions at home and favorable conditions in the potential host country seldom exists. Rather, people decide to migrate as a result of an evaluation of the relative benefits from migrating: the relative wage gains; the relative cost of living; and the relative economic and political conditions in the sending and host countries. The principal considerations that enter individuals' calculations fall into two groups,

1. Pecuniary considerations
   (a) The difference in real wages and fringe benefits between the sending and host countries.
   (b) The probabilities of employment in the sending and host country.
   (c) Differences in the prospects of promotion and advancement in each country.
   (d) The costs of moving.
2. Social considerations
   (a) Social and cultural environment differences.
   (b) Differences in the physical environment.
   (c) The political climate in the sending and host countries.

Individuals will weigh each of these aspects differently depending on their current circumstances and tastes. For those individuals seeking to escape political persecution, as are a large number of migrants even today, the political climate in the sending and host countries will be paramount. For physicians contemplating leaving the United Kingdom for the United States the items listed under (1) are likely to figure more prominently than those listed under (2). However, common to all individuals are two fundamental aspects of the decision to migrate. First, the decision has significant life cycle aspects, neither all of the benefits nor all of the costs will be experienced immediately. Second, individuals cannot know with certainty the precise magnitude of the costs and benefits that will accrue over the years and it is thus the *expected* magnitudes of these that enter the calculations they must make. Accordingly, Eq. (5.1) needs to be modified. The net present value calculations now involve summing the discounted present value of the difference between the expected gross benefits from migration, $E(B^M)$, and the expected gross benefits from staying put, $E(B^s)$, over each of the 1 to N years and deducting from these the cost incurred in the first period. Equation (5.1) is therefore modified to show that:

$$NPVM = \sum_{i=1}^{N} \frac{E(B^M) - E(B^S)}{(1 + r)^i} - C_0$$

(5.2)

Graphically the situation confronting the individual may be depicted as in Fig. 5.4. Associated with the two alternatives facing the individual, which are to migrate or 'stay

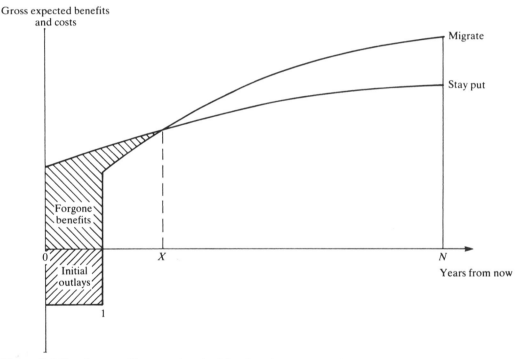

Figure 5.4 Earnings profiles associated with migration and 'staying put'. The lifetime stream of benefits that is expected to arise from migration is compared to the lifetime stream of benefits that is expected to arise from 'staying put'. From the former must be deducted the costs of migrating, then the two streams must be discounted, to discover their present values, and the resulting magnitudes compared. If the net present value of the expected gross benefits from migration, after subtraction of the costs of migration, exceed the net present value of the expected gross benefits of 'staying put' then the individual will find migration an attractive investment

put', is a stream of expected earnings or profits. As depicted the expected total benefits from migration in the period to year X, fail to cover the costs of migrating which take two forms. First, opportunity costs, that is forgone benefits which take both an economic (an initially lower income) and a social form (the costs of breaking existing social ties and establishing new ones). Second, costs are incurred in the form of direct outlays, such as expenditure on moving.

The pecuniary and social considerations listed at (1) and (2) above identify in more detail the arguments that underpin the individual's calculations which were summarized in 'Eq. (5.2). Expected earnings in the host country, together with fringe benefits, represent the principal pecuniary benefits from migration, call these $E(W^M)$, but these then need to be adjusted by the probability, α, that the individual will secure such pecuniary rewards by obtaining a job in the host country. Individuals must also evaluate the expected magnitude of these same factors if they decide to stay put—call these $E(W^s)$ and β respectively. Relative promotion prospects will also enter as determinants of the annual values of $E(W^s)$ and $E(W^M)$ while the expected level of prices, P, in each country will determine the real value of these benefits. Individuals also need to consider their net tax position, T, resulting from the taxes that will be levied on income and expenditure and the magnitude of the welfare provisions that are provided in each country.

Not all the benefits associated with migration are of a pecuniary nature. Individuals migrate to countries with more congenial climates, or to ones offering more agreeable conditions in which to raise a family. Empirically such factors have proved difficult to quantify although a framework for assigning implicit prices to these characteristics now exists within the theory of compensating differences which we shall encounter in Chapter 11.

The cost of migrating will also take both a pecuniary and a non-pecuniary form. At the outset individuals incur initial search costs, S, as they discover the opportunities for and assess the magnitude of the returns from migration.[9] Friends and relatives in potential host countries offer important informal information channels which lower the costs of information acquisition. In addition to search costs there are other direct costs, C, arising from the move itself. The costs of selling and buying houses, the costs of transport and removals are all examples.

In addition to these financial outlays there will also be non-pecuniary costs: the costs of learning a new language and culture, of breaking valued social ties and of interrupting children's schooling. This last set of costs is reduced if individuals migrate to countries which use a language they know. Thus we find that the principal flows of migrants into France are from Morocco, Algeria and Tunisia, where French is an important second language, and into Britain from the Indian subcontinent where English is the second language. Again the existence of friends and relatives in the host country can further help lower the adjustment costs individuals experience after migration. The existence of friends and relatives in particular areas in the host country helps to reduce both the psychic and the informational costs associated with

---

9. See Todaro, M.P. and Maruszko, L. (1987) 'International migration', in *The New Palgrave*, Macmillan.

migration. These are some of the reasons for the existence of *migration chains*. There are well-established migration chains from North Africa to Marseilles, from Puerto Rico to the tri-state area in the United States and from India to Birmingham in England.

Incorporating each of the above arguments into Eq. (5.2) results in:

$$NPVM = \sum_{i=1}^{N} \frac{\left[\left(\alpha \frac{E(W)}{P}\right)^M (1-T)^M - \beta \left(\frac{E(W)}{P}\right)^S (1-T)^S\right]_i}{(1+r)^i} - (S+C) \qquad (5.3)$$

In the above manner the individual may be thought to determine whether the net present value of the expected magnitude of the pecuniary gains from migration, exceeds that of the expected costs. It is easy to see that the decision to migrate involves a complex calculation and that the variables that enter this can never be known with precision. Given this uncertainty, individuals' preferences toward risk will be an important determinant of migration.

One important fact that helps explain the pattern of migration we observe, is that the magnitude of some of the costs identified above varies over an individual's life cycle.[10] It follows that during the years in which costs are high the probabilities of migration are low and vice versa. Thus people are most inclined to migrate at a time when there has been a disruption of existing social relationships, either of an anticipated nature, as when leaving higher education to take up a first job, or of an unanticipated nature, perhaps upon divorce or upon the death of a close relative. Individuals are most inclined to move when their children are young, and not therefore wedded to a particular schooling system, or when they are old and are retiring from the labor force. The costs, and indeed the benefits, vary over the life cycle of individuals and dispose them toward migration at certain stages of the life cycle. In general, the earlier in their life individuals migrate the greater the number of years between 1 and N, over which they can amortize the costs and enjoy the net benefit from their investment. While the younger the migrant the less established will be social ties and hence the lower are the psychic costs of migration.

These life cycle considerations serve to remind us that the decision to migrate is in most cases taken within a household context. In many cases the decision to migrate is a joint decision taken by the senior members of a household. In these circumstances the decision to migrate reflects the attempt to maximize the discounted net present value of household income and can be modeled as before except that into this calculation will now enter the costs and benefits to each member of the household. Not unusually the net benefits of migration for some members of the household are negative while those for other members are positive. For example, a study of the post-migration earnings of wives, who accompanied their husbands when migrating within the United States, found that the wives' earnings fell while those of their husbands rose. It follows that the costs of migration to a household may be lower when

10. Mincer, J. (1978) 'Family migration decisions', *Journal of Political Economy*, **86**(5), 749–73.

only one spouse is working, and accordingly we might expect to find a greater propensity to migrate on the part of such households. Empirical evidence confirms the accuracy of this prediction.[11]

In the previous chapter we reported the rising labor force participation rates of married women, which would seem to suggest that there will be a reduction in the scale of migration from and within the advanced industrial nations in the future. However, in the same chapter we reported the growing number of single person households which would appear to be working in the opposite direction.

Wages rates and employment prospects have been shown to play a central role in individual decisions to migrate. Higher wage rates and lower unemployment rates in the host country are reported as the two most important reasons for migration in a number of studies.[12] Consistent with this there appears to be an inverse relationship between unemployment in the host country and the level of migration. This might simply be due to the lower probability of attaining or retaining a job in the host country when unemployment in that country is high, or, it may be because unemployment in the host country leads governments to introduce quotas which cut the numbers of migrants permitted to enter.[13] Other studies have shown that relative earnings, and changes in earnings differences between countries also play a prominent role in the migration process.[14]

Estimates of the private returns to migrants suggest that, at the outset, the earnings of immigrants are often lower than the earnings of otherwise identical natives. One explanation offered for this finding is that, initially, employers have less information about migrants and they may therefore regard them as more risky. However, it has also been found that over the years the earnings of migrants to the United States grew more rapidly than those of native workers. After 10–15 years the age–earnings profiles of migrants and native workers crossed with the result that after 20 years the earnings of migrants were higher than those of otherwise identical US born workers.[15] These results are in part due to the fact that during the final stages of the life cycle, when earnings are highest, only the most successful migrants remain. Those who had failed 'to make a go of it' have returned home, and these estimates therefore overstate the relative earnings of all migrants. It is not implausible to suggest that immigrants might eventually earn more than natives. Where migration is voluntary, migrants are likely to comprise a self-selecting group of the more able and enterprising individuals from the sending country.[16] However, a recent study has suggested that, in the last 20 years,

11. See Sandell, S. (1977) 'Women and the economics of family migration', *Review of Economics and Statistics*, **59**, and Mincer, J. (1978), *op. cit.*

12. Ulgalde, A.F. (1979) 'International migration from the Dominican Republic', *International Migration Review*, No. 13, 235–54 and Cornelius, W.A. (1978) 'Mexican migration to the United States', *Migration Study Group*, MIT.

13. Chapman, B.J., Pope, D. and Withers, G. (1985), *op. cit.*

14. See Kritz, M.M., Keely, C.B. and Tomasi, S.M. (eds.) (1981), *Global Trends in Migration: Theory and Research on International Population Movements*, Centre for Migration Studies, New York.

15. See Chiswick, B.R. (1978) 'The effect of Americanization on the earnings of foreign born men', *Journal of Political Economy*, **86** (5), 897–921.

16. This view runs counter to firmly held beliefs among Scots that the migration of Scots to England raised the average IQ in both countries.

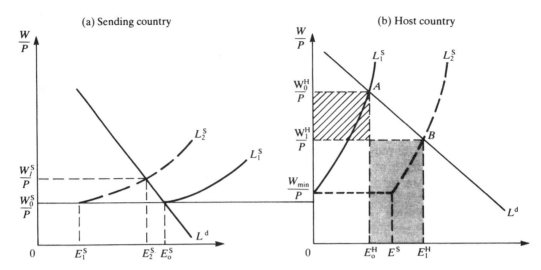

Figure 5.5 Immigration of unskilled workers. The migration of unskilled workers reduces labor supply in the sending country with the result that the wage rises above the subsistence level W_0^S/P to W_1^S/P and a new equilibrium level of employment is established at E_2^S. In the host country the introduction of E^S immigrants shifts the labor supply function outward, with the result that wages fall to W_1^H/P and employment increases to E_1^H. Initially the employment of natives of the host country falls by $E_0^H - (E_1^H - E^S)$. However, the second round effects may well lead to an increase in the demand for native labor

the quality of migrants to the United States and accordingly their relative earnings have declined.[17]

The economic consequences of international migration

International migration will have economic consequences for both the host and the sending countries. The view in the United States and Australia is that the net effects have been favourable for the host country although other countries have taken a rather different view.[18]

The effects will differ according to the type of labor that is migrating and the state of the labor market in the host and sending countries. Consider first the situation depicted in Fig. 5.5.

17. See Borjas, G.J. (1985) 'Assimilation, changes in cohort quality and the earnings of immigrants', *Journal of Labor Economics*, **3**(4), 463–89.
18. The 1986 *Economic Report of The President* states 'For much of the nation's history, US immigration policy has been based on the premise that immigrants have a favourable effect on the overall standard of living and on economic development. Analysis of the effects of recent migrant flows bears out this premise.' United States Government, 1986, p.234. See Withers, G. (1989) 'Immigration and Australian economic growth', in Baker, L. and Miller, P. (eds.), *The Economics of Immigration*, Australian Government Publishing Service, Canberra.

Suppose that the sending country, shown in Fig. 5.5(a), has a large supply of unskilled labor as depicted by the bold line L_1^s and that, given the demand for this type of labor, wages hover just above subsistence level at W_0^s/P. In contrast, in the host country, wages, at W_0^H/P, are high to compensate for the perceived disamenity associated with unskilled work. Now suppose that $E_0^S - E_1^S$ individuals from the sending country are prepared to migrate and they require a wage only slightly above W_0^s/P to defray the costs of migration. This is shown as W_{min}/P in Fig. 15.5(b). Migration on this scale shifts the labor supply curve in the host country outwards and produces a new labor supply curve, L_2^S. If labor demand remains unchanged, wages in the host country fall to W_1^H/P and employment rises to E_1^H. $E_1^H - E^S$ natives of the host country retain their jobs, and $E_0^H - (E_1^H - E^S)$ have lost their jobs so that now fewer natives are employed at lower wages. Back in the sending country the unskilled supply of labor has fallen to L_2^S with the result that wages have risen to W_1^S/P. Migrants appear to be better off at the expense of the employment and wages of natives of the host country. Indeed there are still gains from migration since the difference between the wage rates in the host and sending countries more than covers the costs of migration. We might expect that migration will continue until the gains from such activity have been eliminated; that is until wages in the two countries differ by only the cost of migrating between the two countries. This tendency toward an equalization of wages is one consequence of unrestricted migration. However, this is by no means the end of the story, nor indeed the only one that can be told.

The above captures only the first round effects, it reflects the insights gained as a result of static, rather than dynamic, analysis.[19] Looking at the wider picture it is clear that the fall in wages in the host country reduces the costs of production of the goods and services that were being produced by unskilled labor in that country. If the product market is competitive, this will result in lower prices and an expansion of the demand for these goods and services, assuming that the demand for these products is other than completely inelastic. The second stage will therefore be a shift of the labor demand curve for this type of labor, L^d, in the host country to the right. In consequence wages will again rise and employment expand, and if there is no further immigration, employment among natives will now rise. Whether employment and wages will return to their previous level cannot be predicted without exact knowledge of the elasticities of demand for unskilled labor and the products they cooperate to produce.

If the product market is monopolized the initial fall in labor costs may result in higher profits because final product prices have been held. The outcome now depends on the disposition of these profits. If they are immediately reinvested, to increase the scale of production of these or other products, there will be an increase in demand for labor in the investment goods industries. If, alternatively, profits are distributed as income to the owners of the firm, and this leads them to increase their consumption and investment expenditures, it will again generate additional jobs. In addition there

19. Keynes's view of migration is interesting to note. He suggested 'that it was largely because of migration that the United States economy was always growing rapidly and out-stripping capacity. There was consequently less risk in undertaking investment, and capital formation was larger, more rapid and more confident.' (Quoted in Withers (1989), *op. cit.*) For Keynes the dynamic effects clearly dominated.

is the possibility of increased expenditures by the expanded workforce. The change in the *total* earnings of labor in the host country as a result of immigration is indicated by the gray area minus the hatched area, and will depend on the elasticity of demand for unskilled labor. If this is elastic, the earnings of the unskilled, and with them total expenditures will rise; if inelastic, total earnings and expenditures will fall. Evidently we cannot predict the outcomes of the immigration process, *a priori*, but one thing is clear. To focus on the initial displacement of native workers by migrants is to capture only part of the picture.

In recent years migration by the unskilled has accounted for a diminishing share of world migration, as Europe and Australia have admitted almost exclusively skilled and professional workers. The economic consequences of migration by skilled and professional workers or entrepreneurs can be quite different from those described above. Take as a specific example the migration of professional workers (doctors) to the United Kingdom in the 1960s and 1970s. The labor supply curve for doctors who were trained in Britain is depicted as L_0^S in Fig. 5.6(a). This takes a less familiar shape for it is suggested that below W_1^P/P the labor supply curve is elastic, as more people would be induced to enter medical school as the real wages of doctors rose. However, the number of places in medical school was strictly limited by government so that beyond the point E_0^D supply from domestic resources was completely inelastic. In equilibrium a salary W_2^D/P would therefore have prevailed, but because doctors' salaries were regulated by the state to W_3^D/P, a shortage equal to $E_S^D - E_0^D$ prevailed. Note that one consequence of this situation was that most doctors were paid a wage, in excess of their opportunity wage, W^0/P; those that managed to secure a place in medical school

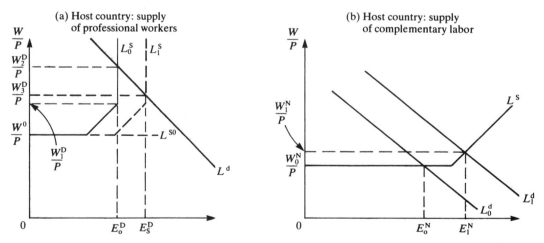

Figure 5.6 Immigration by professional workers. (a) Migration by professional workers equal to $E_S^D - E_0^D$ increases supply to L_1^S and eliminates the shortage prevailing at regulated wage W_3^P/P; (b) The increased supply increases the demand for complementary labor and shifts out the labor demand curve for this complementary labor from L_0^d to L_1^d, increasing both their wages and employment

enjoyed earnings in excess of those they required to remain in this profession: they enjoyed an economic rent.

One policy that could have been adopted was to increase the number of places in medical school to produce $E_S^D - E_0^D$ extra doctors. However, expanding the training facilities takes time. An alternative policy that was adopted was to allow the migration to Britain of doctors from abroad. If a sufficient number were willing to work at the existing rate of pay, W_3^D/P, migration would shift the labor supply curve to the right, to L_1^s. If only numbers sufficient to cure the 'shortage' were permitted to migrate to Britain this would not prejudice the jobs of those trained in British medical schools nor would it remove the rent they earned. If, however, more doctors from overseas were permitted to migrate to Britain, and their labor supply curve were perfectly elastic at a lower wage rate such as (W^0/P) (as depicted by L^{S0}) this would result in a reduction in the wage rates of domestically trained doctors and the removal of the rent.

Consider the implications of this shortage of doctors for the rest of the system. Suppose that, in general, nurses and hospital orderlies had skills that were best regarded as complementary to those of doctors. Although a sufficient number of these may have been trained and available to work, at the prevailing wage rates, the demand for their services would be reduced by the shortage of doctors. The position of nurses is depicted in Fig. 5.6(b), where E_0^N are employed at W_0^N/P. It is easy to see that this situation could be improved by a change in policy.

An increase in the number of doctors employed would increase the demand for complementary factors of production, it would shift out the demand curve for nurses to L_1^d in Fig. 5.6(b). This could reduce their unemployment, raise their wages or some combination of both these effects as depicted. The above example of professional workers is merely one among many in which migration increases the employment of the existing residents of the host country. We might equally have chosen to illustrate this point by reference to the migration of entrepreneurs. It has been claimed that during the 1960s and 1970s Britain suffered from a shortage of entrepreneurial talent, but recent immigration from North America and East Africa, in particular, has gone some way to remedy this. The employment of entrepreneurs increases the demand for complementary factors of production as they create new or expand existing businesses.

Finally, return again to consider the position of the sending countries. If the sending country had an unemployed 'surplus' of skilled professional or entrepreneurial talent then migration to other countries, by individuals possessing these attributes, does not detract from the employment prospects, or welfare, of the remaining residents of the sending country. Where this is not the case the gains in employment in the host country may be offset by reductions in employment in the sending country.[20]

20. The migration of professional workers from the United Kingdom to the United States was the subject of considerable debate in the United Kingdom in the 1960s and again in the mid-1980s. Termed the 'Brain Drain' it has been suggested that about 1000 British scientists and engineers settle permanently in the United States each year—as many as the number from all other Western European countries put together. As we shall see in the next chapter the costs of acquiring a professional qualification in the United Kingdom are considerably lower than in the United States, due to a large element of state subsidy in the former. Accordingly, starting salaries are lower in the United Kingdom than in the United States. It was estimated that in 1985 the starting salary of a physics graduate in the United Kingdom

INTERNAL MIGRATION

The same analytical framework as that developed above can be used to analyze movements within nations. In the United States there has been an outflow from the north eastern and north central states to those states in the south and west of the country. Over the three-year period to 1978 net migration from the north eastern states totaled some 700 000 persons or 235 000 per annum, while from the northern central states it totaled 690 000 or 230 000 per annum. The southern and western states were the recipient areas. Net migration into the southern states was over 1.35 million per annum over this period while the west received around 400 000, or over 100 000 per annum. Again these are net migration flows and therefore understate substantially the magnitude of the gross flows. Over these three years the gross inflow to the south was 2.9 million and to the west 1.9 million. Indeed there were also substantial gross inflows into the northern and north central states of almost 900 000 and 1.5 million respectively. The scale of this intra-national movement is therefore very much greater than the scale of migration into the United States. Intra-US migration exceeds migration to the United States by a factor of at least 6.[21]

One study attempted to assess how many extra jobs result directly from the movement of employed persons from one part of the United States to another.[22] It found that over the period from 1958 to 1975 the in-migration of one employed person into the southern states of the United States was associated with 1.3 additional jobs, or 2.3 jobs if these include in-migrants' jobs. Similarly, each migrant into the western states created 0.4 additional jobs while those into the north eastern and north central states created 0.3 and 0.1 additional jobs respectively. Thus, in general, the processes of internal migration, far from reducing job opportunities for native workers, increased them. Only in the metropolitan areas of Los Angeles was there found to be a substantial displacement of native workers by in-migrants.

The US population also appears to be much more geographically mobile than the UK population. In the United Kingdom the pattern of net migration, in response to differences in relative unemployment rates and wages rates, is from the north of England to the south. Over the five years to 1981 there was a net outflow of half a million individuals from the north of England. However, a prominent feature of migration in the United Kingdom is that much of the longer distance migration that takes place is employer initiated. Over one-third of all those employees who migrated in excess of 80 miles over these five years did not change employer.

was equal to $12 000 per annum (at an exchange rate of £1 = $1.5), compared to $24 000 in the United States. Further, this differential increased so that a physicist with 10–14 years' experience working in US industry would earn an average of $52 000 while his UK counterpart would earn little over $20 000 per annum. Physicists clearly gain substantially from migration, for they realize a much higher financial return on their investment. However, by migrating, physicists remove the opportunity for the government to realize any return on the investment it has made in their education, and it is for this reason that the issue continues to attract public debate.

21. US Bureau of the Census *Current Population Reports*, Series p-20, 'Mobility of the Population in the US'.
22. Greenwood, M.J. and Hunt, G.L. (1984) 'Migration and inter-regional employment redistribution in the United States', *American Economic Review*, **74**(5), 957–69.

One of the explanations offered for the relative immobility of the UK population has been the difficulty of transferring within the state owned housing sector. In the early 1980s one-third of residences in the United Kingdom were owned by the public sector—local government—which was responsible for allocating these houses to the local population. Researchers have found that, while equally willing to move, it is three times as difficult for a tenant in the public housing sector to move as it is for an owner occupier.[23]

THE LONG-RUN LABOR SUPPLY CURVE

The shape of the long-run labor supply curve is likely to vary substantially between countries. Demographic factors and migration rates combine to ensure that the curve is relatively elastic in the United States and Australia, in both of which countries, as we saw in Chapter 1, employment had grown rapidly over the last 25 years. In Europe the position is less clear, migration has slowed and the rate of growth of the native born population has also diminished. In the extreme case of West Germany the population is now in decline. In Europe long-run labor supply curves are in general more steeply inclined than in either the United States or Australia.

THE SIZE OF THE LABOR FORCE IN THE PERIOD TO 1995: LABOR FORCE PROJECTIONS

Finally, in this chapter, we bring together the analysis of the size of the population of working age and the determinants of the participation rate, discussed in earlier chapters, to consider recent and projected changes in the size of the labor force, in Britain and the United States, in the period to 1995.[24]

First consider the projections for the United States. Recent estimates of the size of the civilian, non-institutional, population of working age (the population aged 16 and over as distinct for the population aged 15 and over reported in Table 1.3) in the US project are that this will rise from 176 million in 1984 to 194 million in 1995. These projections reflect the birth rates reported above, together with the assumptions of increasing life expectancy and an unchanged annual level of net immigration at around 400 000. The results are shown in the first row of Table 5.5. From this total the civilian labor force can then be calculated by multiplying through by the relevant participation rate. In the United States participation rates are projected for some 82 age, sex, race or ethnic groups by an extrapolation of past trends for each of these groups. For the

---

23. See Hughes, G.A. and McCormack, B. (1986) 'Migration intentions in the UK: which households want to migrate and which succeed?', *Economic Journal*, **95**, Supplement, 113–23.
24. Such projections are made at regular intervals by the Department of Labor in the United States and Department of Employment in the United Kingdom. The projections are reported in the *Monthly Labor Review*, published by the Bureau of Labor Statistics at the US Department of Labor and in the *Employment Gazette*, published by HMSO for the Department of Employment. These projections are taken from the *Monthly Labor Review* for November 1985 and *Employment Gazette* for March 1988.

Table 5.5 Labor force projections for the United States and Britain

	Actual			Projected	
	1975	1980	1984	1990	1995
USA					
Working population ('000)	153 153	167 745	176 383	186 655	193 817
Participation rate (%)	61.2	63.8	64.4	65.7	66.6
Civilian labor force ('000)	93 775	106 940	113 544	122 653	129 168
(Average annual percentage rate of change in each of previous 5 years)	2.5	2.7	1.5	1.3	1.0
Britain					1991
Working population ('000)	41 163	42 426	43 447	44 530	45 616
Participation rates (%)	61.5	61.8	60.8	62.3	62.8
Civilian labor force ('000)	25 305	26 198	26 428	27 790	28 073
(Average annual percentage rate of change in each of previous 5 years)	0.4	0.5	0.2	0.8	0.2

Sources: USA, *Monthly Labor Review* (November 1985), US Department of Labor, Bureau of Labor Statistics, Washington.
Britain, *Employment Gazette* (March 1988), Department of Employment, HMSO. London.

period shown this results in the prediction of a continued decline in male participation rates, from 77.9 percent in 1975 to 75.3 percent in 1995, and an increase in the participation rates of women, from 46.3 percent in 1975 to 58.9 percent in 1995. Aggregate participation rates are shown in the second row of Table 5.5. Application of these participation rates to the working population leads to the prediction that the labor force in the United States will rise from 107 million in 1980 to around 129 million in 1995, or an increase of 21 percent.

A rather smaller rise in the civilian labor force is projected for Britain over the period to 1995. Similar techniques to those employed in the United States are used, with both countries assuming an unchanged level of labor demand in their projections. In Britain the activity rate among males aged 65–69 is projected to decline further from 13.6 percent in 1984 to 8.7 percent in 1995, resulting in an overall decline in male participation rates from 74.3 percent in 1984 to 73.3 percent in 1995. In contrast that among females rises quite sharply from 48.4 percent in 1984 to 53.0 percent in 1995, but this rise still leaves the rate much lower than that for females in the United States. The application of these participation rates to the population of working age results in a projected increase in the size of the population of working age of almost 3 million, a rise of only 11 percent over the period from 1975 to 1995. As a comparison of the final row in both parts of Table 5.5 indicates, the projected annual rate of increase in the population of working age in Britain is considerably less than that in the United States.

Table 5.6 Annual rates of growth of labor force

	1968–73	1979–86	1986–90	1990–95
Australia	2.7	2.1	2.1	1.8
Germany	0.7	0.6	– 1.1	– 0.9
Japan	1.0	1.2	0.9	0.6
UK	0.2	0.6	0.0	0.0
USA	2.2	1.6	1.0	1.0

Source: OECD, *Employment Outlook,* September 1987. OECD, Paris.

A rather different set of projections for a wider sample of countries have been produced by the OECD and are reported in Table 5.6. Again these largely reflect the extrapolation of past trends. From this table it is evident that of the featured countries, Australia is the one with the highest projected annual rate of growth of the labor force. In all countries the rate of growth is projected to be lower in the 1990s than it was in the 1980s while in Germany the labor force is projected to decline. The principal reason for this slowdown in the growth of the labor force is the slowdown in the growth of the population of working age. This deceleration is more marked in Japan and Europe than in Australia or the United States. In all countries there is a reduction in the inflow of young people into the working age population, itself a reflection of the decline in fertility rates detailed earlier, but in addition in Europe and Japan there is a larger outflow of older people from the working age population. The rates of growth remain higher in the United States and Australia than in the other countries shown, in part because of the higher projected rate of migration to these two countries.

These developments will be accompanied by substantial changes in the demographic composition of the labor forces in each of these countries. Table 5.7 details the smaller

Table 5.7 Projected demographic composition of total labor force

		Males			Females			
		15–24	25–54	55 +	15–24	25–54	55 +	Total
Australia	1984	13.2	40.6	6.7	11.5	25.7	2.3	100
	1995	11.3	40.3	5.9	10.3	30.4	1.8	100
Germany	1986	11.6	42.7	6.7	9.8	25.7	3.5	100
	1995	6.8	48.1	4.4	5.4	32.8	2.5	100
Japan	1986	6.3	42.5	11.4	6.2	26.7	6.9	100
	1995	6.6	40.2	13.2	6.4	25.4	8.2	100
UK	1986	13.5	36.5	7.9	11.3	26.5	4.4	100
	1995	9.3	40.7	7.8	7.6	30.1	4.5	100
USA	1986	11.0	37.9	7.3	9.3	29.4	5.1	100
	1995	9.5	39.6	5.4	7.5	33.8	4.2	100

Source: OECD, September 1987, *op. cit.* OECD, Paris.

share of the labor force that will be accounted for by young people, those aged between 15 and 24 years, by 1995 in all but one of these countries. The proportion of young people decreases most in Germany and the United Kingdom. In all countries, except Japan, the proportion of prime aged workers, those aged between 25 and 54, is projected to increase, as the cohort resulting from the earlier 'baby boom' moves into the prime age group and female participation rates among this age group continue to rise. In Japan things are rather different, the youth population begins to decrease only in the 1990s and as the population ages there is a substantial increase in the proportion of the elderly in the total labor force.

These changes in the composition of the labor force are likely to have several profound implications. First, in contrast to the excess supply of young people, that was a feature of the labor markets in some European countries in the 1970s, there is likely to be an excess demand for young people in the 1990s. This in turn will require that employers traditionallly used to recruiting only young workers to certain jobs will now need to recruit and train from among less traditional groups. This should improve the relative employment prospects of some recently disadvantaged minority groups, and women. If, however, these prove not to be adequate substitutes, youth wages will rise, relative to those of older workers, as employers bid for their services.

If the projections in Tables 5.5 and 5.6 are correct they give some indication of by how much the labor supply curves are expected to shift outwards over the period to 1995, and, if unemployment is not to rise, indicate the likely number of new jobs each economy, except Germany, will need to create over this period. Of course, as we have seen, participation rates are determined by both tastes and opportunities, by economic arguments. If tastes toward work change adversely, if real wage rates rise less (or more) rapidly than assumed, if unearned income changes in an unanticipated manner, the outcome will be different from those we predict. It will be interesting to compare the outcomes in the 1990s with these projections from the late 1980s!

SUMMARY

In this chapter we have looked at one aspect of labor supply in the long run—the size of the population of working age. We have seen how migration flows and demographic changes affect this population and the role that economic forces have played in explaining these. We saw that while birth rates have fallen substantially in the United Kingdom and the United States over the last two decades, the populations of these countries are still projected to grow, although at a slower rate than in the past. Modern microeconomic theories have sought to explain population change as an aspect of consumer behavior within the context of household production. However, while economic factors play a large part in explaining population change, few unambiguous predictions emerged from these theories.

Migration flows to Europe were seen to be much reduced in recent years while those to the United States had grown. Nonetheless, migration has added substantially to the permanent labor supply in both these continents. Differences in the pecuniary returns from work in different goegraphical locations figure prominently in explanations of the patterns of migration, although for substantial numbers of migrants the motives are of a social nature—they are accompanying the principal income earner—or political—they are refugees. Since it is often difficult to distinguish between these groups, it is not surprising that the empirical evidence on the nature of the economic determinants of migration flows is less than conclusive.

Finally, the chapter brought together information on migration flows and demographic changes with that on projected changes in participation rates to construct forecasts of the size of the labor force in the United Kingdom and the United States in the period to the mid-1990s. In both countries the labor force is forecast to continue to grow, although in the United States at a substantially reduced rate compared to the past. Nonetheless, the annual rate of growth in the United States is still projected to add some 1.3 million people to the labor force in each of the years to 1995.

PRINCIPAL CONCEPTS

The following concepts were introduced in this chapter. Students should ensure that they understand these before proceeding to the next chapter.

1. Gross and net migration.
2. Temporary and permanent migration.
3. The net present value of migration.
4. Children as a consumption good.
5. The long-run supply curve of labor.

QUESTIONS FOR DISCUSSION

1. Does Malthus's theory of population have any application in today's world?
2. What insights are offered by economic theories of fertility?
3. How important has the distinction between gross and net migration flows been to the countries in Europe in recent years?
4. How might you account for the convergence in the experience of Europe and the United States with respect to temporary and permanent immigration?
5. Discuss the economic consequences of migration for both the host and sending country.
6. Does economic theory provide a satisfactory theory of international migration?
7. Discuss the probable shape of the long-run labor supply curve in the United States and United Kingdom. Is it more elastic than the labor supply curve in the short run?
8. What factors might account for the projected changes in the size of the labor force in the United Kingdom and the United States?

FURTHER READING

Montgomery, M. and Trussell, J. (1986) 'Models of marital status and childbearing', in Ashenfelter, O. and Layard, P. R. G. (eds.), *Handbook in Labor Economics*, vol. 1, North Holland, pp. 205–71, provides a very useful survey of the contrasting approaches of demographers and economists to the issue of fertility. The collection of papers on *The Economics of the Family: Marriage Children and Human Capital* edited by Theodore W. Schultz in 1974 (University of Chicago Press, Chicago and London) is also essential reading for those wishing to inquire further into this area. Unfortunately no similarly succinct references are available on the topic of migration. For the facts of migration the reader should consult the publications in this area that are regularly produced by the OECD in Paris. Regular labor force projections for the medium term are published by the Department of Employment in *The Employment Gazette*, HMSO, London, and by the Bureau of Labor Statistics at the US Department of Labor, Washington, in the *Monthly Labor Review*.

6

LABOR SUPPLY IN THE LONG RUN: THE SKILLS OF THE LABOR FORCE

In this chapter and the previous one we analyze the determinants of labor supply in the long run. In the previous chapter we analyzed the determinants of the size of the working population; in this chapter we focus on the skills possessed by that workforce. In the last chapter we looked at the determinants of the *quantity* of labor available in the long run, now we analyze the determinants of the *quality* of that labor supply. Like the decision to migrate, the decision to acquire skills is an investment decision. The decision to enhance one's productivity requires the outlay of resources now for returns in the future. We describe the process as that of investment in *human capital,* and the return to investment in human capital is the net addition to lifetime earnings that results from selling skilled as opposed to unskilled or 'raw' labor. Skilled labor will generally command a higher price than raw labor because it is more productive.

Acquisition of skills is only one of several forms of human capital investment that individuals can undertake. Investment in good health may also improve individuals' productivity. Human capital is moreover only one type of investment opportunity that is open to most individuals. Individuals can invest in non-human capital, in plant and machinery, buildings and land or purchase financial securities. Accordingly, before such investment is undertaken, the returns on human capital must compare favorably to those on alternative forms of investment. Today a major part of the investment undertaken each year and a major part of the capital stock of modern economies takes the form of human capital. It has been estimated that between 50 and 90 percent of the total capital stock of the United States takes the form of human capital.[1]

---

1. See Becker, G.S. (1988) 'Family economics and macro behavior', *American Economic Review*, **78,** 1–13 and Jorgenson, D.W. and Frautheni, B.M. (1987) *The Accumulation of Human and Non-Human Capital: 1948–84*, Harvard University Press, Cambridge, Mass.

The human capital that concerns us in this chapter is the part that is acquired through education and training. Human capital investment can be undertaken at the workplace and at educational establishments provided specifically for this purpose. It can be acquired through formal training, with proficiency recognized by the award of certificates, or it can be acquired informally, by 'learning by doing'. In this chapter we are concerned with each of these types of human capital investment. First, however, we consider the theory of human capital.

THE CONCEPT OF HUMAN CAPITAL

The idea that education and training constitute an investment in individuals, which is analogous to investment in machinery, was developed long ago. It was Adam Smith in 1776 who first drew the analogy between education and investment in a machine.[2] Smith argued that differences between the wages of individuals, with different levels of education and training, reflected differences in the returns necessary to defray the costs of acquiring these skills. As with other forms of investment, increasing the stock of human capital necessitates outlays now for returns some time in the future. Smith recognized that the returns from investment in skills must be compared to the returns from investing in physical capital and must be no less than those returns, when all relevant circumstances have been taken into account. Indeed, he suggested that one of these circumstances may not be equal between men and machinery. For in Smith's day, when life expectancy was much shorter than today, the 'uncertain duration of human life' compared unfavorably to the 'more certain duration of the machine'. All other things being equal, the return to human capital would need to be higher than the return to physical capital to warrant such investment.

Yet, while the analogy between investment in a machine (physical capital) and investment in individuals (human capital) may be illuminating, there are important differences between the two. While a firm may own, and thus secure the property rights to, the services of a machine this dimension is missing from human capital. Except in a slave society, or on the rare occasions when an individual legally binds himself to work for a firm for a specified period (as with the armed services), firms cannot own individuals, nor can they acquire the property rights to the labor of individuals. When investing in individuals, firms have fewer guarantees, than they do with machines, that they can secure the continuing use of their services. Individuals, unlike machines, can

2. 'When an expensive machine is erected, the extraordinary work to be performed by it before it is worn out, it must be expected, will replace the capital laid out upon it, with at least its ordinary profits. A man educated at the expense of much labour and time to any of those employments which require extraordinary dexterity and skill may be compared to one of those expensive machines. The work which he learns to perform, it must be expected, over and above the usual wages of common labour, will repay him the whole expense of his education, with at least the ordinary profits of an equally valuable capital. It must do this too in a reasonable time, regard being had to the very uncertain duration of human life in the same manner as to the more certain duration of the machine. The difference between the wages of skilled labour and those of common labour is founded upon this principle.' (*The Wealth of Nations* (1776) Chapter X, Part 1(2), 'Wages vary with the cost of learning the business' (Cannan), The Modern Library, New York, 1937.)

always decide to leave the firm, or they can decide to withdraw their labor, strike, go absent or work badly. The services of individuals, and hence the returns from investing in individuals, are less certain than are those from physical capital. It is partly for this reason that individuals and firms may be reluctant to bear all the costs of investing in human capital.

A large part of the cost of investment in education is borne by the state in most countries. Indeed the laws of most countries require some investment in human capital. Everyone is required by law to stay at school until age 16 in the United States and Britain. This public provision of junior and secondary education increases the supply of certain basic skills to industry, those of literacy and numeracy, and in so doing reduces the premium that industry must pay to acquire these skills. It was not always so, as John Stuart Mill noted in 1848: 'Until lately all employments which required even the humble education of reading and writing could be recruited only from a select class. Since reading and writing have been brought within the reach of a multitude the monopoly price of the lower grade of educated employments has greatly fallen.'[3] At the start of the nineteenth century the human capital embodied in the ability to read and write was not widely possessed.

The motives for such state provision of general education reflect, less a desire to reduce the costs to business, than a recognition that the modern state cannot flourish without certain basic standards of literacy and numeracy. Some forms of investment in human capital offer both private and social benefits but not all human capital investment is of this type.

Theory proposes that individuals will invest in human capital if the private benefits exceed the costs that they incur and that they will invest up to the point at which the marginal return equals the marginal cost. Many fewer individuals choose to invest in advanced education in the United Kingdom and Australia than do so in the United States and many other countries. Does this therefore mean that the returns to this type of human capital investment are lower in the United Kingdom and Australia than in the United States? Before we can answer this question we need to develop the theory in more detail.

THE COSTS AND BENEFITS OF HUMAN CAPITAL INVESTMENT

The private costs of human capital investment

First consider the private costs of human capital investment. The costs borne by the individual can take a psychological, social and monetary form. Psychological costs are those costs experienced by individuals, perhaps the less able, who find learning difficult and experience considerable anguish and anxiety as a result. Social costs take the form of forgone non-market opportunities, the time devoted to investment in human capital

---

3. Mill, John Stuart (1848) *Principles of Political Economy*, vol. 11, XIV 2.

may preclude leisure activities. Monetary costs take the form of both forgone market opportunities and direct financial outlays. Consider the measurable components of the costs.

Forgone opportunities Time devoted to investment in human capital precludes the possibility of devoting that time to other market or non-market activities. These opportunity costs can be quantified for as we saw in previous chapters a monetary value can be assigned to each hour not spent working. The price devoted to human capital investment, and in consequence an hour not spent working, is the wage rate. Opportunity costs generally constitute the major component of the costs of a college education. Thus an individual able to command a wage of $8 an hour in an alternative job in 1988 would, by attending college, forgo full-time earnings of almost $15 500 per year (48 weeks per year, 40 hours each week at $8 an hour). Many individuals replace part of this lost income by working outside college hours but, if such work does not take place during the working day, this may not diminish the scale of forgone earnings for such additional income could also have been generated when holding down a regular job.

There are two determinants of the magnitude of forgone earnings. First, the level of earnings in the next best alternative job to which the individual can reasonably aspire, and second the probability of the individual securing such employment. In the early 1980s there was substantial youth unemployment throughout may industrial nations, and thus the typical school leaver's probability of securing alternative employment was substantially reduced. The unemployment rate in the jobs open to young people provides one indication of the ease with which the college student might have been able to obtain alternative employment. If the relevant unemployment rate equaled 20 percent, the opportunity cost of college education would fall to $(1 - 0.2) = 0.8 \times \$15\ 500 = \$12\ 400$ per year. All other things being equal we should therefore expect investment in human capital among young people to increase at times of high youth unemployment and this is indeed what happened.

Direct financial outlays The direct financial outlays differ according to the type of human capital investment being undertaken. The direct costs of a college education differ substantially between the United Kingdom and the United States. Such direct costs take three forms: (i) the costs of college tuition, these ranged from around $2000 in public colleges to around $10 000 per annum in private schools in the United States in the mid-1980s. In the United Kingdom the state pays tuition fees; (ii) additional living costs, these include the additional costs of accommodation, food and travel beyond those that would have been incurred in the alternative job. In the United Kingdom the state pays the living costs of those involved in full-time education whose parents' incomes fall below a certain level. It also pays a diminishing proportion of these costs for most students with higher parental incomes. This maintenance grant in general more than defrays the additional living costs of attending college and therefore goes some way to replacing the income lost from not working; (iii) books and equipment costs, which although relatively small, may nonetheless, in the age of the word processor and PC, be far from trivial. These are borne by the individual in both countries.

In the United Kingdom the direct financial costs of investing in human capital are substantially less than in the United States and we might therefore expect that, *ceteris paribus*, the demand for post-school investment in college would be greater in the United Kingdom than in the United States. However, this does not appear to be the case. Could the benefits of such investment therefore also be lower in the United Kingdom?

The private benefits of human capital investment

The private benefits which result from human capital investment take both a pecuniary and a non-pecuniary form. The pecuniary benefit is the enhancement of real lifetime earnings. The non-pecuniary benefit is the improvement in the conditions in which the individual works.

Private pecuniary rewards Education and training increase the pecuniary rewards from work because they equip individuals with skills that improve their productivity in the labor market.[4] According to competitive theory it is an individual's productivity that determines his or her real wage. The gross pecuniary benefits from investment in human capital constitute the lifetime income associated with that investment. To illustrate the manner in which investment in human capital enhances lifetime earnings we depict, in Fig. 6.1, an individual aged 16, expecting to retire at age 60, evaluating the gross pecuniary returns expected to derive from two different labor market opportunities.

The first of these opportunities is not to invest, simply to leave school at 16 and enter an unskilled job. The individual's gross lifetime earnings, if this option is chosen, are represented by the area *OHID*—the area beneath the solid horizontal line. The second option is to undertake five years' additional investment which is expected to produce lifetime earnings equal to *GEFD*. These earnings streams constitute the gross benefits and the magnitude of these will be affected by a number of factors that we

---

4. A dissenting note has been struck by a researcher in Britain who has suggested that there are economic rewards for staying away from school. Hibbert, A. (1987) in 'Early adult outcomes of truancy', Social Statistics Research Unit Occasional Paper, found that truants were earning more by their early twenties than their classmates who stayed at their desks. Furthermore, once family background and educational attainment were taken into account the returns to truants increased. There appeared to be a reward for not investing in education. Not surprisingly this result has not gone unchallenged. Other explanations for these findings have been advanced. It is likely that by the age of 23, the age at which these returns were measured, some of those who stayed at their desks have just completed further education and were thus at the start of their earning career. It is not therefore surprising that they would be earning less. Truants may also be in higher paid but less regular employment or in more dangerous or unpleasant work environments. But this study reminds us that many individuals may not regard investment in secondary education as enhancing their earnings. Those that choose to truant may be displaying more enterprise than their colleagues who stay at their desks and the higher earnings may be a reflection of this.

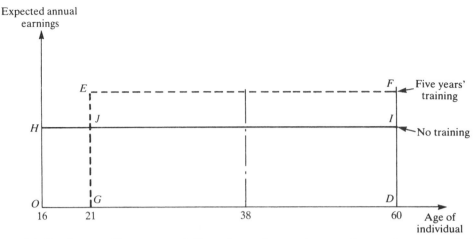

Figure 6.1 Earnings profiles compared. Two alternative earnings profiles confront an individual considering whether or not to invest in human capital. When no training is undertaken expected annual earnings are represented by the line HI. If five years' training is undertaken expected annual earnings beyond age 21 are greater by the area *JEFI* but to achieve this, earnings equal to *OHJG* have been forgone. Training raises an individual's productivity and hence their wage and so produces benefits, but by undertaking training the individual also incurs costs. The decision whether or not to train constitutes an investment decision for present costs must be balanced against future returns

consider below. Because the benefits from education are the higher earnings that accrue in the future, they must be discounted to the present, so we consider this first.

Discounting benefits Individuals are not in general indifferent between income that accrues in the future and income that accrues today. All other things being equal, individuals prefer present income to future income: they prefer present to future consumption. It is therefore necessary to discount in some way the money sums received in the future. The rate at which the individual discounts will be a matter of personal preference, but one appropriate choice is the rate of return that could be earned on alternative investments, that is the interest rate r. Thus in Fig. 6.1 it would be necessary to calculate the present value of the income stream of each of the two lifetime earnings profiles and this could be done by discounting the earnings in each of the *future* periods by the interest rate r.

If PVI_{NT} stands for the present value of the lifetime earnings stream when no training is undertaken, and I_{16} to I_{60} represent the income earned in each of the years from current age 16 to retirement at 60 then:

$$PVI_{NT} = I_{16} + \frac{I_{17}}{(1+r)} + \frac{I_{18}}{(1+r)^2} \cdots \frac{I_{60}}{(1+r)^{60-16}} \tag{6.1}$$

or more concisely

$$PVI_{\text{NT}} = \sum_{i=16}^{60} \frac{I_i}{(1+r)^{i-16}} \tag{6.2}$$

Similarly, the present value of the lifetime earnings streams resulting from five years' training is:

$$PVI_5 = \sum_{i=21}^{60} \frac{I_i}{(1+r)^{i-21}} \tag{6.3}$$

Discounting in this manner attributes least weight to those earnings received furthest into the future, just how much weight depends on an individual's present orientedness.

The consequences of present orientedness The size of the discount rate employed by individuals will reflect their present orientedness. Those individuals with a marked preference for present over future consumption we describe as present oriented, they will apply a high discount rate to future earnings. The higher is the discount rate the less likely it is that *GEFD > OHID* when we calculate the present value of each of the earnings streams shown. The higher the discount rate the less weight is attached to future earnings and it is evident from Fig. 6.1 that the longer the investment period the further into the future are the superior earnings such an investment produces. Accordingly, the greater an individual's present orientedness the smaller will be the perceived pecuniary benefits from human capital investment and the less likely he or she will be to undertake such investment.

The effects of age The lifetime earnings streams depicted above were evaluated over the period from age 16 to age 60. If instead these investment opportunities had been presented at age 38 the lifetime earnings streams associated with each would have been substantially shorter. The 'payback period', over which the original investment could be amortized, would have been shortened to 17 years, if five years' education were undertaken. Because there would now be fewer periods, over which to sum the superior earnings stream associated with such investment, this would reduce the net present value of the benefits from education and make such investment less likely.

The continuity of employment The effects of increased age are analogous to those of an interrupted working career. If a discontinuous working career is anticipated, then fewer years are expected to be available during which a return on investment can be earned. Thus if women anticipate one or more interruptions to their working lives, for purposes of childbearing and rearing, the period during which a return on human capital investment can be earned will be less and the propensity to invest in human capital will accordingly be reduced. Similarly, those who anticipate being unemployed for periods during their working lives anticipate a shorter payback period and this too will dispose them to invest less.

To summarize, the greater an individual's age, or the more interrupted it is anticipated that working life will be, the smaller will be the percived pecuniary benefits from undertaking human capital investment.

Private social benefits The private returns from education may go beyond the private pecuniary rewards detailed above. Education may enhance individuals' understanding of the nature of and opportunities that exist in society. This may in turn increase the satisfactions they derive as a member of that society. It may broaden and inform tastes, both developing those that exist and revealing new ones. Such spiritual and cultural enrichment is a significant benefit deriving from certain forms of education. Education may also enable individuals to lead a longer as well as a more satisfying life. It has been shown that educated people live longer for they know more about the types of behavior that constitute a healthy lifestyle and the types of behavior that promote longevity.[5] The importance of these further benefits from education or training should not be overlooked, although they are difficult to quantify and are not our concern in this book.

The net benefits of human capital investment

The individual evaluating different opportunities for human capital investment is concerned with both costs and benefits, that is with the net benefits associated with an investment. One procedure for discovering which of the opportunities offers the greatest net benefits is to calculate and compare the net present value of each project. An alternative is to calculate the internal rate of return.

The net present value

This is calculated by deducting the discounted present value of the direct costs from the discounted present value of the gross benefits. The resulting magnitudes, representing the net present values of each investment opportunity, are then ranked in descending order of magnitude to determine which one among them offers the highest net return.

The procedure can be illustrated as follows. The present value of the gross benefits of two market opportunities shown in Fig. 6.1 was calculated in Eqs (6.2) and (6.3). The next step is therefore to calculate the present value of the *direct* costs associated with each of these. The present value of the direct costs of five years' training, PVC_5, is found by discounting the annual cost outlays, C_j, in the manner described above to give:

$$PVC_5 = \sum_{j=16}^{21} \frac{C_j}{(1+r)^{j-16}} \tag{6.4}$$

5. See Rose, S. and Taubman, P. (1979) 'Changes in the impact of education and income on mortality in the US', *Statistical Uses of Administrative Records*, US Department of Health, Education and Welfare, Washington.

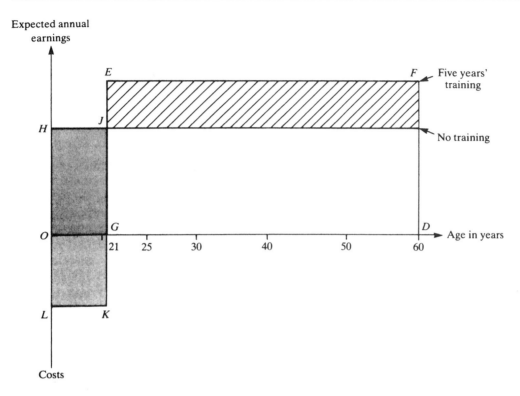

Figure 6.2 The discounted present values of the costs and benefits of human capital investment. The figure illustrates the discounted present values of both the outlays and expected annual earnings associated with human capital investments. If no investment is undertaken, gross discounted earnings equal the area *OHID*. If five years' investment is undertaken gross discounted earnings equal the area *GEFD* while direct costs equal the area *OLKG* and indirect costs equal the area *OHJG*. Does investment in human capial offer earnings superior to those obtained by not investing? The answer is found by comparing the shaded, cost, area to the hatched, additional benefit, area. If the hatched exceeds the shaded area, investment enhances lifetime income

There are, of course, no costs associated with the other labor market opportunity for this was the no training option. The discounted costs can now be deducted from the discounted benefits to determine the net present value of the investment. The situation is now depicted in Fig. 6.2 which is similar to Fig. 6.1, but is now assumed to depict the *discounted present value* of both costs and benefits, while the direct costs associated with the investment are now identified. Thus the gross discounted returns from no training are depicted as equal to *OHID* and in this case these gross returns are equivalent to the net returns for there are no investment outlays. The gross returns from five years' training are depicted as *GEFD*, but after deduction of direct costs equal to area *OGKL*, the present value net of costs, the net present value, is less than before. More formally the net present value is calculated as follows:

$$NPV_5 = PVI_5 - PVC_5 \tag{6.5}$$

or

$$NPV_5 = \sum_{i=21}^{60} \frac{I_i}{(1+r)^{i-21}} - \sum_{j=16}^{21} \frac{C_j}{(1+r)^{j-16}} \tag{6.6}$$

Which of the two opportunities should be taken? Should the individual invest? By ranking and comparing the net present value associated with the two opportunities, the individual can determine which of the two offers the highest return. Note that the process of ranking and comparing the two projects also takes account of the opportunity costs of the investment. The opportunity costs (forgone earnings equal to area *OHJG*) are captured in the net present value of the next best alternative, the no training opportunity. The same result can also be achieved by simply examining the magnitude of the *additional* benefits from investment. In terms of Fig. 6.2 this involves comparing the magnitude of the additional earnings consequent upon human capital investment (the hatched area *JEFI*) to the magnitude of the additional costs (the shaded area *LHJK*). If the discounted present value of the additional earnings exceeds the discounted present value of the additional costs, the investment enhances lifetime earnings. Clearly this last approach is easiest when we are evaluating any two opportunities. The former approach of ranking all opportunities is the more general approach.

The internal rate of return

There is, however, an alternative method of appraising competing opportunities. This is to calculate the *rate of return* associated with each investment opportunity. This involves finding the unique rate of discount which just equates the discounted present value of the earnings stream resulting from an investment to the cost of that investment. The procedure no longer involves discounting the returns at the individual's chosen time rate of discount, represented by *r*, instead it involves solving the equation to find the unique rate of return, *R*, that just equates benefits to costs. Suppose for simplicity that all costs amount to a single annual sum, *C*, incurred in the first year, we then find *R* for the five-year investment opportunity by solving:

$$C = \sum_{i=21}^{60} \frac{I_i}{(1+R)^{i-21}} \tag{6.7}$$

Having calculated *R*, the rate of return on the investment, this is then compared to the rate of return available on alternative investments in order to determine whether investment in human capital is worth while. If the rate of return on an alternative, non-human capital assets, is given by the interest rate, r, the appropriate procedure is to compare the rate of return, R, to the interest rate. If $R > r$ human capital investment offers the highest return and should be undertaken, if $R < r$ the alternative investment opportunities appear superior.

From the above discussion of benefits and costs we may draw a number of conclusions about the determinants of an individual's willingness to invest in human capital. First, individuals' willingness to invest in education or training will be inversely related to their age and present orientedness. Second, the desire to invest will be inversely related to the level of forgone earnings while training, the level of tuition fees and the level of other direct costs. Third, the desire to invest will be positively associated with the difference between the earnings in the trained occupation and the next best occupation on completion of training. Finally, it will be inversely related to differences in the probability of unemployment in the two jobs.

We noted above that in the United Kingdom the direct costs of most types of education are lower than in the United States. In the United Kingdom the government pays tuition fees and a proportion of living expenses for most students. There would therefore appear to be a greater incentive on grounds of lower costs, for individuals to invest in education in the United Kingdom, yet in the United Kingdom the supply of educated individuals is smaller than in the United States. The above analysis suggests a number of reasons why this may be so. One might be that the returns to education, the earnings of skilled labor, are lower in the United Kingdom than in the United States. Alternatively, individuals may be more present oriented in the United Kingdom than in the United States. A further explanation may be that a higher incidence of unemployment in the United Kingdom has lowered the probabilities of enjoying returns from investment in human capital. Yet a further explanation may be that the lower level of household wealth in the United Kingdom constrains those who wish to invest in human capital there.

Any restrictions on the supply of individuals willing to undertake human capital investment in the United Kingdom will, *ceteris paribus*, raise the rate of return to education there. Even so, though the rate of return to investment in human capital could then be higher in the United Kingdom than in the United States, absolute differences in costs and benefits between the two countries will still encourage the migration of individuals trained in the United Kingdom to the United States. For in the United States benefits are greater. If unrestricted, over time the process of migration will tend to equalize the returns and costs in both countries.

THE CASE FOR STATE SUBSIDIES TO EDUCATION AND TRAINING

Wealth constraints

Typically the costs of human capital investment are incurred during the first years while the returns accrue at a later period. Outgoings exceed income during early years while the surplus accrues in later years. Individuals may therefore need to borrow or run down their wealth at the start of the period in order to finance the investment. If individuals possess neither the wealth nor the collateral to support borrowing, human capital investment may not take place.

Wealth and borrowing power are related, for the possession of income-yielding assets is the most acceptable form of collateral. Unlike other forms of investment, prospective returns on human capital investment are often not regarded as suitable collateral on which to raise a loan, for there is a greater prospect that the anticipated returns on human capital investment may not materialize. They may not do so for a number of reasons. First, ill-health or infirmity may preclude working. Second, the individual can choose where and when to sell the human capital acquired and may choose to sell in markets offering only a low price. Third, human capital cannot generally be turned over to new ownership, transferred from one market to another or one firm to another, without the individual's consent. Individuals cannot be compelled to earn the rate of return once envisaged. The risks that are associated with ensuring a return on human capital are often greater than for other assets and this explains why expected future earnings are often not regarded by financial institutions as providing adequate collateral for loans. Where these wealth constraints are severe there may be a deficient supply of human capital.

One answer to this problem has been state subsidies to human capital investment. These subsidies often take the form of free provision of higher education by state funded institutions. An alternative system is to provide students with grants or vouchers which they then use to buy education from private educational establishments. Yet another alternative is for the government to act as the banker and provide guaranteed loans to all those wishing to undertake appropriate forms of human capital investment. The government would in this manner accept future earnings as collateral but it would also bear the risk of default on these loans.

Social benefits

There are further reasons for state subsidies to human capital investment. Certain of the benefits that accrue from such investment are essential to the functioning of a democratic state. A democratic state cannot function without a citizenry that possesses some minimal standard of literacy and numeracy. A capacity, on the part of the vast majority of its citizens, to read and write and perform simple mathematical calculations is a minimal requirement for the operation of the modern state. If certain forms of human capital investment also imbue citizens with notions of citizenship and social responsibility, the state may wish to subsidize these.

THE NUMBERS WHO INVEST IN FURTHER EDUCATION

In most countries children can leave compulsory education at age 16 but many choose to stay on, and invest in human capital after compulsory schooling is finished. Figure

6.3 provides a broad overview of the proportions of men and women who continued in education in selected countries in 1986 while Table 6.1 reports the proportions who stayed on at school for an extra year (17-year-olds) and for an extra two years (18-year-olds) in selected countries in 1980. Table 6.1 also reports the proportions in each country who went on to invest in a university or other further education at age 19. In the United Kingdom, Australia and the United States individuals typically enter university at 18 while in Germany the typical age is 19, thus by 19 in all four countries secondary education is complete and those who stay on are in advanced and non-advanced institutes of further education.

It is noteworthy from Table 6.1 that in 1980, with the exception of the United States, significantly fewer women than men invested in further education. At age 19 more than 40 percent of males were continuing their education in Australia, the United States and Germany, but the proportion of women in further education was some 14 percentage points fewer than that for males in Australia and 5 percent fewer in Germany. The proportion of both sexes who continued into higher education is lower in the United Kingdom than in the other three countries. In the United

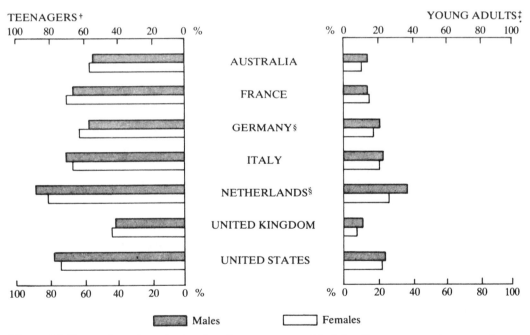

Figure 6.3 Proportion of youths in education as measured in labor force surveys; by age and sex, 1986. Defined as the proportion of youths in each country's labor force survey who indicated that they were following a school or university course either during the reference week of the survey or within the four weeks preceding the survey.[†] The term 'teenagers' generally refers to the 15–19 age group, with some exceptions: the age group is 14–19 in Italy, and 16–19 in the United Kingdom and the United States.[‡] Data refer to persons 20–24 years of age.[§] Data refer to 1985

Source: Employment Outlook (1989) OECD. Reproduced by permission of the OECD.

Table 6.1 The proportion of each age group who invested in additional schooling in selected countries in 1980

		Individuals aged:				
		17	18	19		
		At school		In further education		
				Total	Full-time	University
United States	Male	85.0	53.0	41.0	n/a	37.6
	Female	84.5	51.3	40.5	n/a	37.9
United Kingdom	Male	56.4	44.0	32.8	14.0	8.1
	Female	48.8	30.4	25.0	11.4	5.5
Germany	Male	91.9	74.9	47.6	19.1	2.3
	Female	86.5	65.6	42.6	24.1	4.3
Australia	Male	61.8	51.5	43.5	15.5	7.7
	Female	51.3	34.3	29.3	17.0	6.1

Source: OECD, *Educational Trends in the 1970s: A Quantitative Analysis. OECD*, Paris, 1984.

Kingdom less than one-third of all men and only one-quarter of all women were in higher education in 1980. However, the differences between the United Kingdom and the others narrow when we focus on only those woh enter full-time education. Now some 14 percent of males aged 19 invested in full-time education in the United Kingdom compared to 15.5 percent in Australia and 19.1 percent in Germany (comparable figures are not available for the United States). When we look only at full-time education it also emerges that the proportion of women investing in this form of education is now greater than for men in both Australia and Germany. A corollary of this is that a far smaller proportion of women invest in part-time education in these two countries.

The 19-year-olds reported in Table 6.1 may be in either advanced or non-advanced institutes of further education. In Germany most of the advanced further education takes place in technical institutes and, accordingly, the proportion who enter institutions described as universities is lower than in the other three countries shown. In sharp contrast almost all 19-year-olds who invest in further education in the United States do so in a college or university. The systems of further education are most similar in Australia and the United Kingdom and it is noteworthy that in both these countries a similar proportion of 19-year-olds were at university. However, even allowing for the fact that students are taught to an advanced level outside the university sector, it is evident from Table 6.1 that a much smaller proportion of 19-year-olds proceeded to advanced further education in the United Kingdom than in the United States. In 1979 around 16 percent of 19-year-olds undertook advanced further education in the United Kingdom compared with 37 percent in 1980 in the United States.

GENERAL AND SPECIFIC EDUCATION AND TRAINING

Up to this point the analysis has considered education and training without distinguishing the type of human capital that was acquired or the types of jobs that qualified workers perform. However, it is important to distinguish between the type of human capital investment that raises a worker's marginal product in a range of different firms and the type of human capital investment that raises a worker's marginal product in only a single firm. Where investment raises an individual's productivity across a range of different firms this investment is said to be general, where the human capital investment raises productivity in a single firm, the investment is said to be specific, firm specific. The distinction between general and specific training is crucial to an understanding of the operation of the labor market. Its importance turns on who bears the costs of the two different forms of human capital investment.

First, consider again the magnitude of the costs of human capital investment. Above we saw that these comprised both direct and opportunity costs which in Fig. 6.2 were represented by the shaded area *HJKL*. Consider the situation depicted in Fig. 6.4, in which the worker is confronted with two alternatives: to train, job B; or not to train, job A. The costs of training again involve direct outlays and opportunity costs. The direct outlays comprise the hatched area and the opportunity costs the shaded area. Figure 6.4 differs from Fig. 6.2 in that it is assumed that the marginal product of the individual undertaking training is no longer zero as in Fig. 6.2, instead it rises from *A* at the outset of training to *B* on completion. The existence of the direct costs results in a lower net marginal product while training as indicated by the line *FGB* (line *FGB* is constructed by deducting the hatched area from *AB*). The total costs of training for job B can be depicted as the sum of the opportunity costs, *AXD*, and direct costs indicated by the area *FGBA*. The total costs are therefore depicted by the area *FGBXD*. Having detailed the magnitude of the costs of training the next issue to consider is who should bear these costs.

General training Suppose initially that the training, or education, is general in nature, that is the human capital acquired can be readily employed in a range of firms with the same resulting effect on output. Training enhances the workers' marginal productivity in a large number of firms. If the firm bore the total costs of training this would require paying the worker a wage equal to the wage the worker could have earned elsewhere while undergoing training as well as bearing the direct costs. The opportunity wage of the worker is indicated by the line *DG* and the direct costs by the hatched area. If the firm bore all the costs it would bear costs equal to *FGBXD*. In the first part of the training period the costs would comprise wages in excess of marginal product, equal to area *DXA*, plus direct training outlays. But after *X* the workers' marginal product exceeds the opportunity wage and so, if the firm continues paying a wage equal to the opportunity wage of the worker, the excess of the workers' marginal product over this wage will defray an increasing part of the direct costs.

A profit maximizing firm will only bear the costs of an investment in human capital if it can enjoy the return that arises from this investment. In this example the return

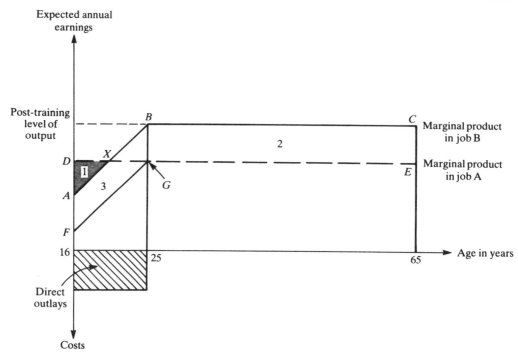

Figure 6.4 Training within the firm. If workers bear the full costs of training, they receive a wage equal to *FG* while training. In this manner they bear the opportunity costs indicated by the area *DXA* and the direct costs indicated by the area *FGBA*. The line *AB* represents their marginal product during training and the line *BC* their marginal product after training. If the workers bear the costs they will expect to enjoy some of the post-training returns indicated by the area *BGEC*. If firms bear the costs of training they will pay the worker a wage equal to their opportunity wage as indicated by line *DE*. They incur direct costs equal to the hatched area and indirect costs equal to the shaded area. They now expect to enjoy some of the post-training benefits indicated by the area *BCEG*. Just who bears the costs and enjoys the benefits turns on whether the training in question is general or specific

is represented by area *BCEG* and the whole of this will accrue to the firm if it is able to pay the worker the same wage after training as it did before: a wage equal to *DGE*. However, general training raises the productivity of the worker in firms other than the firm bearing the cost of training, and it would therefore profit other firms to try to tempt the trained worker to take a job with them. After training, the marginal product of the worker is equal in value to *BC*. Any wage less than *BC* therefore results in excess profits for other firms. Other firms will therefore find it profitable to bid for the trained worker by offering a wage in excess of *GE*. If the worker is free to quit the firm, which paid for the training (there is no transfer fee or penalty payment involved), other firms will find it profitable to go on bidding for the services of this worker up to the point at which they are paying a wage equal to *BC*. Any wage below *BC* results in supernormal profits for those firms that did not bear the cost of training.

The firm that paid for the training is in a less strong position to compete effectively for the services of the worker it has trained. This firm requires a return on its investment which can only be realized by paying a wage less than *BC*. Rationally the firm might reason that bygones are bygones, that training costs are sunk costs, and in the short run, bid up to *BC* to retain the services of the trained worker. However, this will influence the firm's future policy toward training. It will be reluctant to pay for such training again. Therefore, it seems clear that if training provides general skills and the worker is free to quit his employment, it will not pay firms to bear the costs of this training. The costs of general training will be borne by the worker.

Specific skills Now consider the opposite case in which the training the worker acquires raises productivity in only one firm. Such training is called specific training, for it is specific to (unique to) a single firm. Specific training arises where an employer uses a unique production process. The skills a worker acquires are no longer 'portable', and if the worker loses the job the skills acquired cannot be re-employed elsewhere. Should the costs of specific training, like the costs of general training, also be borne by the worker?

Suppose that the workers bear the whole of the costs of specific training and that these are again as depicted in Fig. 6.4. Each worker would receive a wage equal to their net productivity, *FG*, while training and, after training, would expect to receive a wage sufficiently in excess of *GE*, to offer a return on this investment. The area *FGBXD* represents the magnitude of each worker's investment for they have borne both the direct costs and the opportunity costs.

The specific nature of the investment means, however, that the workers can earn a return on their investment only if they remain with the firm, for the skills they have acquired cannot be re-employed elsewhere. If, therefore, the workers are not confident that they will be employed for a sufficiently long period to collect their return they will be reluctant to undertake such investment. Uncertainty about the duration of employment with the firm may arise for a number of reasons. Workers may fear that the firm will go out of business; they may fear that they will be subject to permanent layoff or they may believe that the firm will sack them for other reasons. Any of these will reduce the workers' willingness to bear the total costs of investment in specific human capital.

Alternatively, suppose the firm bore all the costs of specific training, the situation would be as depicted before when discussing general training. The firm bears cost equal to area *FGBXD*. Now the specifically trained workers receive a wage, equal to their opportunity wage but in consequence they have no preference for this firm over others, and therefore no particular incentive to stay with this firm. Were the workers to quit, the firm is denied the opportunity of earning a return on its investment. Although the workers could not do better elsewhere, and have no particular incentive to quit as before, if for any reason the firm believes the workers are likely to quit, it will be reluctant to bear the costs of specific training.

An obvious answer to the problem that emerges above is to split the costs and the returns between the workers and the firm. One way in which this can be accomplished is for the firm to pay the workers a wage equal to their marginal product while training and to pay the direct costs of the training. The wage would rise along AB, and the firm's net outlays would then be equal to the area $ABGF$. The costs borne by the worker would now be equal to the forgone opportunity wage, as indicated by area AXD. The parties would by this method share the costs of specific training. Training yields a positive return if the present value of the area $BCEG$ in Fig. 6.4 exceeds the present value of the costs $FGBXD$. If the parties share the costs of the investment the returns will need to be divided between them in some manner. The sharing of returns leads to a wage after training which is higher than the workers' opportunity wage, but which is lower than their marginal product, BC. We shall discuss the magnitude of these returns and the manner in which they are divided in Chapters 9 and 12. Here we move on to consider the different forms of human capital investment that have been undertaken by the working population and the magnitude of the returns from human capital investment.

THE SKILL COMPOSITION OF THE WORKFORCE

Few jobs today require no human capital investment. Even those we classify as unskilled, such as the refuse collector, embody some skills. The refuse collector, for example, needs to learn the most effective way to lift the garbage can and in what order to work the street to complete the job most quickly. Jobs are therefore distinguished, not by the possession or absence of human capital investment, but by the degree of investment that each job requires. In some, as in the example above, it may be trivial; in others it will be substantial. For convenience we classify as unskilled those jobs embodying a trivial degree of investment.

A feature of the labor market in industrial nations in the twentieth century has been the reduction in the share of employment accounted for by unskilled workers and a corresponding increase in the share of skilled and professional workers, an increasing proportion of whom are self-employed. In part this is reflected in the decreasing share of employment accounted for by manual workers and the accompanying increase in the share of employment accounted for by non-manual workers. These trends are evident in both Britain and the United States and are detailed in Table 6.2. In the period immediately prior to the First World War almost half the labor force in each country was either semi-skilled or unskilled. Today less than one in five of all workers can be similarly classified and their numbers are reducing sharply. In contrast the share of professional workers has risen from around 4 percent in both countries in 1910/11 to 17 percent in the United States by 1982 and to almost 14 percent in Britain by 1981. The share of clerical workers has also been rising steadily in both countries. One notable feature of Table 6.2 is that the occupational composition of employment in the United States and Britain is now rather more similar than it was back in the early part of this century.

Table 6.2 Occupational composition of the employed labor force in Britain and the United States: 1910/11–1981/82

	USA			Britain		
	1910	1970	1982	1911	1971	1981
Professional	4.4	14.2	17.0	4.2	10.6	13.6
Proprietors and managers	23.0	12.7	11.5	10.4	12.3	12.1
Clerical and related	5.2	17.4	18.5	7.3	15.7	16.3
Sales worker	5.0	6.2	6.6	5.7	9.0	10.1
Skilled workers	11.7	12.9	12.3	13.9	15.5	16.1
Service workers	6.8	12.4	14.0	10.4	11.8	12.2
Semi-skilled and unskilled	43.9	24.1	20.1	48.2	25.1	19.6
TOTAL	100.0	100.0	100.0	100.0	100.0	100.0

Sources: Routh, G. (1980) *Occupation and Pay in Great Britain, 1906-1979*, Macmillan, London, Table 1.3, and OECD *Economic Survey United States*, and Office of Population Census and Services, *1981*, Census of Population, Great Britain, Economic Activity Table, HMSO.

Table 6.3 Actual and projected changes in the occupational distribution of civilian employment in the United States and the UK

	Share of employment			
	USA		UK	
	Actual 1986	Projected 2000	Actual 1987	Projected 1995
White Collar				
Executive, administrative and managerial	9.5	10.2	12.8	13.2
Professional	12.1	12.9	22.1	24.5
Technicians and related	3.3	3.9		
Sales and personal service workers	27.0	29.5	19.2	18.8
Clerical and related workers	17.8	16.6	14.5	14.4
Blue Collar				
Precision production, craft and repair	12.5	11.7	13.1	13.2
Operators, fabricators and laborers	14.6	12.6	18.4	15.8
Farming, forestry and fishing	3.2	2.6		
Total employment	100.0	100.0	100.0	100.0

Sources: For USA, *Monthly Labor Review*, Department of Labor, Washington. For UK, *Review of the Economy and Employment: Occupational Update 1988*, Institute for Employment Research, University of Warwick, England.

A more recent picture together with projections as to the occupational composition of the workforce to the year 2000 for the United States and 1995 for the United Kingdom is presented in Table 6.3. The decline in the share of blue collar employment, at all skill levels, is projected to continue and it is projected that for the first time there will be a decline in the share of employment of clerical and related workers. In both countries the share of employment of technical, professional and executive workers is projected to continue to expand. The projections are therefore for a continued decline in the share of blue collar employment and an increasingly service oriented, professional and technical labor force.

It is interesting to note the projected changes in some of the specific occupations that lie behind these aggregate figures for the United States. It is forecast that in the period to the year 2000 the number of computer programmers and systems analysts will increase by around 75 percent, the number of lawyers will increase by 36 percent, the number of nurses by over 44 percent and the number of guards and security men, by 48 percent. Among the fastest declining occupations are projected to be railway workers, farmworkers, statistical clerks and compositors, whose numbers are projected to decline by 40 percent, 28 percent, 26 and 17 percent respectively. Even the number of college and university faculty is predicted to decline by 4 percent.

THE RETURN ON HUMAN CAPITAL

It is evident from the foregoing discussion that different levels of human capital investment begin to explain differences in individual earnings. Figure 6.2 suggested that investment in human capital enhanced individual earnings and if some individuals invest more than others, earning inequalities will emerge. Indeed, differences in individuals' human capital and hence in individuals' productivity are believed, by many economists, to provide the major part of the explanation of the differences in earnings we observe between individuals in most societies. Thus emerges a theory of income distribution based on differences in individuals' marginal productivity which in turn reflects differences in individual human capital investment. How much of the difference in earnings we observe does human capital theory explain?

Earnings functions

Estimates of the rate of return on human capital may be derived by the use of regression analysis. The seminal contribution to this area is the work of Mincer[6] and we follow his approach here. Suppose that in the absence of any further investment in human capital beyond the years of compulsory schooling, individuals would have sold their 'raw' labor for real earnings W/P_i. Theory suggests that the level of these earnings will reflect the influences of a range of variables measuring individual, market, and workplace characteristics. We shall look later at precisely how we might specify each of these factors, but for the moment suppose they are captured by a vector of variables, X_i.

6. Mincer, J. (1974) *Schooling, Experience and Earnings*, NBER, New York, Table 3.3 and pp. 53–5.

Individuals who invest in further human capital will enjoy a return, R (assumed constant for the purposes of simplicity) on the amount they invested. If we further assume for simplicity that the amount invested is equal to the wage, W/P, that they forgo every year they undertake investment (that the costs are only forgone earnings), then a year's investment results in earnings in the second year equal to W/P multiplied by the rate of return that is $W/P(1 + R)$. If such investment is undertaken for each of I years then the earnings of individual i, with I years of investment in additional education in school is given by:

$$W/P_i = W/P_i (1 + R) I_i + X_i + \varepsilon_i \tag{6.8}$$

where ε_i is a random disturbance term which is normally distributed with mean zero. If we now take logs of the first three terms in this expression this gives:

$$\log W/P_i = \log W/P_i + I_i \log (1 + R) + X_i + \varepsilon_i \tag{6.9}$$

then the log of the coefficient, $(1 + R)$, on I measures the rate of return on a year's education, which will be equal to R if R falls in the range of 0.05 to 0.20. This is because the log of $(1 + R)$, the log of $1 + 0.05$ to the log of $1 + 0.2$, is approximately equal to R. Now an estimate of the magnitude of the rate of return to additional years of schooling can be obtained directly by regression analysis. Our estimating equation becomes

$$\log W/P_i = a_1 + a_2 I_i + a_3 X_i + \varepsilon_i \tag{6.10}$$

where a_1 represents the log of earnings when there has been no additional investment in human capital (the first term on the right-hand side in Eq. 6.10 above) and a_2 measures the proportionate effect of an extra year's schooling on earnings, that is it measures R, because $\partial \log W/P_i/\partial I_i = a_2$. Note, however, that the rate of return to schooling may not be constant and it is therefore usual to include in estimating equations of this form a further non-linear term, I^2, to capture this effect. Thus the equation becomes

$$\log W/P_i = a_1 + a_2 I_i + a_3 I_i^2 + a_4 X_i + \varepsilon_i \tag{6.11}$$

In which case $\partial \log W/P_i/\partial I_i$ is equal to $a_2 + 2a_3 I_i$ so that R is no longer simply equal to a_2. If the returns to schooling diminish, $a_2 > 0$ but $a_3 < 0$. The significance of a_3 in our regression analysis will inform us of the appropriateness of including such a term.

So what of the estimates of the return to human capital that have been derived by estimating such equations? A relatively straightforward example of regression analysis using an equation of the form of (6.11) is contained in the seminal study of Mincer. For a sample of white non-farm male workers in the United States in 1959 he obtained:

$$\ln W = 4.78 + 0.424I - 0.010\,5I^2 \qquad R^2 = 0.347$$
$$ (10.0) \qquad (-6.1) \tag{6.12}$$

the t ratios are shown in parentheses. Now the marginal return to schooling is given by $a_2 + 2a_3$, thus the marginal return to graduating from high school after 12 years of school is given by $0.424 - (2 \times 0.0105 \times 12) = 0.172$ or 17.2 percent. While the rate of return to completing the fourth year of college is $0.424 - (2 \times 0.010\ 5 \times 16) = 0.088$ or 8.8 percent. Thus the marginal return to years of schooling is diminishing: although additional years of schooling result in extra earnings, the magnitude of the addition to earnings associated with each extra year of school is declining.

Table 6.4 contains estimates of the returns to different levels of education in different regions of the world in the 1970s and early 1980s. It can be seen from this that the private returns to education are greatest in the least developed countries of Africa, Asia and Latin America and for those in primary and higher education. In all countries the returns to all levels of higher education exceed 12 percent, rates which compare favorably to those earned on other forms of investment. The returns to higher education differ substantially between the advanced industrial nations. The same study reporting the data on which Table 6.4 is based revealed that in the late 1970s the returns varied from a low of 5.3 percent in the United States, through 8.3 percent in Japan and 10.5 percent in Germany to 21.1 percent in Australia and 23.0 percent in the United Kingdom. Again this same study reported that in the early 1970s the rate of return in a sample of 14 countries varied from a high of 13 percent in economics,

Table 6.4 The returns to education by region and level of education

Region or country type	N	Private		
		Primary	Secondary	Higher
Africa	(16)	45	26	32
Asia	(10)	31	15	18
Latin America	(10)	32	23	23
Intermediate	(9)	17	13	13
Advanced	(15)	a	12	12

Region or country type	N	Social		
		Primary	Secondary	Higher
Africa	(16)	26	17	13
Asia	(10)	27	15	13
Latin America	(10)	26	18	16
Intermediate	(9)	13	10	8
Advanced	(15)	a	11	9

Source: Psacharopolous, G. (1985), Tables I and II, in 'Returns to education: a further international update and implications', *Journal of Human Resources*, **XX**(4), Fall.
a Not computable because of a lack of a control group of illiterates
N = number of countries in each group
Primary = primary educational level
Secondary = secondary educational level
Higher = higher educational level

through 12 percent in law and medicine, to a low of 8 percent in science, maths and physics. A more recent study suggested that rates of return have fallen substantially in the United Kingdom. Private returns to a university education over the period 1979–84 ranged from 17 percent in arts subjects to a high of 15 percent in the social sciences.[7] It is also noteworthy that in most countries and at all levels of education the private returns exceed the social returns.

There are however a number of difficulties that researchers encounter in estimating these returns and there are, as a result, reasons for believing that many of the estimates derived to date do not accurately measure the true return to human capital investment.

Difficulties in estimating rates of return

On-the-job training The first problem that researchers encounter, in attempting to derive an accurate measure of the rate of return on human capital, is that investment in human capital often continues for much of an individual's working life. Thus we overstate the returns on the initial human capital investment, such as schooling, if we fail to allow for and distinguish separately the return to subsequent on-the-job (OJT) investment. Where OJT is of a formal nature this can be allowed for by the inclusion of further variables capturing the dimensions of this in the estimating equation (including years of OJT just as we included years of schooling). However, where this is of a less formal nature, that is comprises *learning-by-doing*, it is much more difficult to allow for its effects. It is largely through on-the-job training that individuals acquire specific skills and thus, in attempting to measure the scale of OJT, we are trying to measure the magnitude of specific training. Economists have taken as evidence, of the widespread existence of informal OJT, the fact that earnings profiles are not as depicted earlier in Figs. 6.2 and 6.4. Earnings do not jump to a new level on the completion of training and remain at that level thereafter, rather they rise on completion of training, and then continue to increase gradually for several years as illustrated in Fig. 6.5.

One approach to estimate the returns to general training is to focus the analysis on the period after the completion of formal training but prior to the effect of on-the-job training. In Fig. 6.5 this is obviously the individual's 25th year, in which the individual's earnings overtake those of the person with no training. It is indeed this 'overtaking year' on which Mincer focused in his study reported above. Another approach is to assume that on-the-job-training is proportional to years of job experience after leaving school, or that the part of it which represents tenure in existing job is a measure of specific training. Hence the earnings function, Eq. (6.11) above, is augmented by the inclusion of a variable, J, measuring years of work experience since leaving school, or T, years of tenure in the current job. Again to allow for non-linearities in their effects, further variables J^2 or T^2 are entered much as before.

---

7. Clark, A. and Tarsh, J. (1987) 'How much is a degree worth?', *Audit*, 109–15.

Real earnings

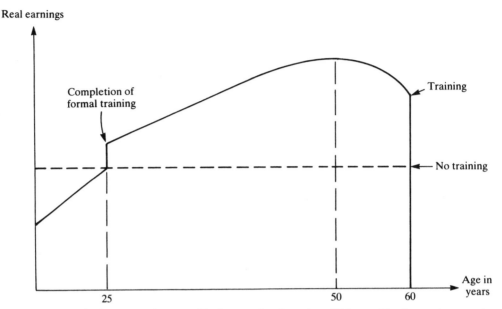

Figure 6.5 A typical age–earnings profile for a trained worker. This profile shows that earnings jump, upon completion of training, and thereafter increase through to late middle age when they decline slowly until retirement. Earnings are positive during training but seldom equal to the opportunity wage. The profile above depicts the profile of lifetime earnings of a typical middle to senior white collar employee

Thus equation (6.11) becomes

$$\log W/P_i = a_1 + a_2 I_i + a_3 I_i^2 + a_4 J_i + a_5 J_i^2 + a_6 X_i + \varepsilon_i \qquad (6.13)$$

where $\partial \log W/P_i/\partial J_i = a_4 + 2a_5 J$ measures the marginal return to on-the-job-training, or specific training if T and T^2 are included instead of J. In the study reported earlier, Mincer reported that

$$\ln W = 6.20 + 0.107 I + 0.081 J - 0.0012 J^2 \qquad R^2 = 0.285 \qquad (6.14)$$
$$ (72.3) \quad (75.5) \quad (-55.8)$$

again t ratios are in parentheses. J is usually assumed = age $I - 5$, for it is assumed the individual started school at age 5 and started work immediately after completing education. Then for a 30-year-old high school graduate, $J = 13$ and $a_4 + 2a_5 J_i = 0.081 - (2 \times 0.001\ 2 \times 13) = 0.049$ or 4.9 percent. A comparision of this result with that derived from Eq. (6.12) reveals that the rate of return on schooling is lower once we allow for the effects of on-the-job training.

There are strong reasons for supposing that total work experience is not an adequate measure of on-the-job training. Indeed one group of researchers claimed to have found an inverse relationship between work experience and workers' performance.[8] They reported that workers with more experience were judged less productive by their supervisors. On the face of it this appears rather implausible but it could well be correct for if performance increases at a rate which differs between individuals it is not unlikely that those who learn fastest will have the shortest experience in the job because they are the most likely to be promoted. Those who have the longest tenure in the job may be less productive than some younger more able workers but these older workers would have been less productive without OJT.

However, this still does not mean that total work experience is an adequate measure of on-the-job training. It remains the case that there are many jobs that require a relatively trivial level of OJT although the individuals who occupy these jobs have done so for a long time. Experience is in these cases a poor proxy for the magnitude of additional skills acquired on the job. Similar arguments suggest that tenure is unlikely to measure exclusively returns to specific training. Indeed one study suggests that the effects of tenure, or time in current job, on earnings are small and that it is general labor market experience which accounts for the major part of the wage growth that individuals enjoy over their careers.[9]

Ability On average people who are more able, more hardworking, energetic and enterprising are more likely to invest in human capital. Further, in the process of matching individuals to jobs employers will seek to fill those jobs which have the greatest on-the-job training requirements with workers of greatest ability.[10] The estimated rates of return to human capital will therefore overstate the true return to schooling and on-the-job training. Those qualities which we summarize as ability, would probably have increased individuals' productivity, and hence their earnings, even if they had not invested in human capital. Unless we can measure ability, the return we attribute to education, or training, will overstate the real return, for it will also capture the return to ability.

In recent years several studies have made an attempt to control for ability, by including IQ scores or measures of mathematical reasoning as well as measures of human capital investment, in earnings equations. The inclusion of measures of ability typically reduces the return to human capital investment, from around 10 to 5–7 percent, suggesting that without allowing for the effect of ability, the return to human capital investment will be overstated. Indeed, one researcher has gone further, and suggested that the major part of what such estimates take to be ability is in fact a reflection of family background and early upbringing, although there is still a significant proportion which is genetically endowed. This particular researcher concluded that 'Education has relatively little influence on earnings except for people

8. Medoff, J. and Abraham, K. (1981) 'Are those paid more really more productive?', *Journal of Human Resources*, **16**, 181–216.
9. See Altonji, J. and Shakotko, R. (1987) 'Do wages rise with job seniority?', *Review of Economic Studies*, **54**(3) July, 437–61.
10. Griliches, Z. (1977) 'Estimating the returns to schooling: some econometric problems', *Econometrica*, **45**, 1–22 and Barron, J.M., Black, D.A. and Lowenstein, M.A. (1989) 'Job matching and on-the-job training', *Journal of Labor Economics*, **7**(1), 1–19.

who obtain a Ph.D., M.D. or LL.B.'[11] However, while indicators such as IQ may predict success at school, they may less accurately measure the ability that matters most in the workplace. In the workplace it is variously one's enterprise, resourcefulness, diligence and dexterity that matter and these may correlate very poorly with IQ and other such indicators. The issue of ability is an aspect of what has come to be known in the literature as the *self-selection problem* for it would seem that those who invest most in human capital are a self-selecting group of the more able. One solution to this problem has been to employ econometric techniques which deal with problems of selectivity bias. We shall return to this issue shortly.

'Old boy networks' The acquisition of information about workers' productive characteristics necessitates expenditure by firms who will therefore seek out methods of obtaining the appropriate information at least cost. 'Old boy networks' represent informal channels for transmitting information, about individuals' productive characteristics, and may offer opportunities for firms to economize on their expenditures on the process of acquiring information about potential employees. If high paying firms use such channels there is now a real return to the individual who gains access to the old boy network. If access to the network is gained by social contacts or attendance at a particular school (the 'old school tie'), the estimated return to human capital will once again be overstated for it will now include a return to the 'old boy' or 'old school tie' network. No independent measures of these effects have yet been devised.

Fringe and non-pecuniary benefits Most studies of the rate of return of human capital estimate the returns from such investment in terms of earnings. Earnings are, of course, the most easily measured reward from working and comprise the major part of an individual's pecuniary returns from work. However, an individual's total compensation comprises both earnings and fringe benefits. Fringe benefits tend to rise as a fraction of total compensation as earnings rise, thus failure to measure these benefits understates the pecuniary returns from human capital investment.

Information acquired during the process of education may also enable some individuals to select the safest and most pleasant jobs, that is those jobs with the greatest non-pecuniary advantages. In Chapter 11 we shall develop the theory of compensating differences which suggests that, in general, a job with inferior non-pecuniary advantages is compensated by a higher wage. In this case failure to include the non-pecuniary aspects of jobs would appear to overstate the true return on human capital. However, such a compensating differential only emerges when individuals are equally knowledgeable about job characteristics. If additional schooling affords some individuals an information advantage, then those with the most schooling may be able to identify the most desirable jobs. In consequence the focus on earnings will

11. Taubman, P. (1976) 'Earnings, education, genetics and environment', *Journal of Human Resources,* **11**(4), 447–61 and (1976) 'The determinants of earnings: genetics, family and other environments: a study of male white men', *American Economic Review,* **66**(5), 858–70.

understate the true return to human capital investment. Individuals with additional schooling will enjoy jobs with superior earnings and superior non-pecuniary characteristics.

Overestimates of costs Each of the above arguments qualified estimates of the rate of return to human capital, for they emphasized the imprecision with which we can measure or attribute the benefits. However, there are also problems with measuring costs. The financial costs, associated with certain forms of human capital investment, may overstate the true level of these costs. If college days really are the 'best days of your life' they offer consumption benefits that are superior to those that would have been gained had the individual been working. The net costs of attending college are therefore lower than the magnitude of forgone earnings and direct costs suggest. If the costs are lower the rate of return for any given income stream will be higher. Our estimates will then understate the real rate of return to education.

Selectivity bias Consider again the proposition that not all individuals have an equal aptitude for all jobs. If the individuals who invested in human capital and became brain surgeons had not done so but instead gone straight into work, perhaps as insurance salespersons, they might have earned less than the average insurance salesperson. Perhaps the reason that they trained as brain surgeons was that they knew they would be no good as insurance salespersons! Reciprocally, individuals who became insurance salespersons may have realized that they had no aptitude for brain surgery and that, had they followed such a career, they might have done less well than the average brain surgeon. In consequence the measured rate of return to the human capital investment of the brain surgeon understates the true return, for this individual would have earned less than the average insurance salesperson had such a career been chosen. Equally the measured rate of return to the insurance salesperson overstates the rate of return for, had the insurance salesperson invested sufficient to become a brain surgeon, this person would still have earned less than the average brain surgeon. The magnitude of these selectivity biases cannot be known with precision for we do not know how these individuals would have prospered 'if they had not done what they did'. We know neither the distribution of these varying aptitudes nor yet how they correspond to the demand for these aptitudes.

The above example highlights the general assumption imbedded in human capital theory, which is that all individuals are equally suited for all jobs. However, individuals differ in ability (only around one-sixth of the population have IQs above 120) and aptitude, and therefore part of the differences in earnings that is observed is attributable to these factors. If certain abilities and aptitudes are in persistent short supply, as in the case of 'unique talents', they will enjoy a higher rate of return in consequence. If ability and aptitude are correlated with human capital investment, estimates will overstate the rate of return to human capital. If, in constrast, ability and aptitude exert an independent yet significant influence on earnings (they are not correlated with human capital), human capital earnings equations will now provide a poor explanation of earnings differences.

Non-competing groups Restrictions on ability, differences in tastes and lack of financial resources may limit the investment opportunities open to some individuals. In 1848 Mill argued that 'employment which required even the humble education of reading and writing could be recruited only from a select class, the majority having no opportunity of acquiring those attainments' and, elsewhere, that 'the really exhausting and the really repulsive labours' are 'performed by those who have no choice'. Mill argued that they had no choice, over the type of occupation they would enter, and were therefore restricted in the type of investment in human capital they could undertake. From this idea of Mills grew the notion of *non-competing* groups developed by Cairnes and Taussig.[12] The existence of non-competing groups means that competition will not bring into equality the rates of return on different forms of human capital investment.

Human capital earnings equations explain some 25–50 percent of the variance in individual earnings. Other as yet unmeasured forces are evidently at work. In the middle of the 1980s real earnings in the United States were approximately twice as high as in Britain and Japan. Although a larger proportion of US workers invest in general training than do British workers, their investment in general training is little different from that in Japan. Moreover, as we shall see in Chapter 10, job tenure, and therefore perhaps specific human capital investment, is much greater in both Japan and Britain than in the United States. If only general and specific training and human capital investment are believed to account for earnings differences between individuals, then Japanese workers would be expected to earn more than either their US or British counterparts. Evidently many other as yet unmeasured forces are at work.

SCREENING AND EDUCATIONAL SIGNALING

Contesting the arguments of human capital theory some economists have suggested that investment in general skills, particularly schooling, does nothing to enhance an individual's labor market productivity. They have argued that all or most of the returns that have been attributed to human capital are really no more than returns to ability. On this view certain individuals would have enjoyed the highest labor market rewards even without additional schooling. However, even though schooling does not impart productive characteristics it still plays a useful role for it testifies to the pre-existence of such characteristics.

The view that schooling merely distinguishes individuals' pre-existing abilities has been labeled the *screening hypothesis* for, on this view, schooling screens individuals and labels them according to their pre-existing ability. It is not surprising that this view has not endeared itself to many who work in the education sector, for they believe themselves to be developing skills that make individuals more productive workers, skills which enable them to get and hold down better jobs when they leave college.

If the screening hypothesis is correct, employers have a strong incentive to adopt alternative and cheaper screening strategies. If firms can identify the most able individuals when they leave secondary education, rather than after screening by

12 Mill, John Stuart (1848), *op. cit.*, vol. III, XIV 2, and XIV 1. Cairnes, J.E. (1874) *Some Leading Principles of Political Economy Newly Expounded.* Taussig, F.W. (1929) *Principles of Economics.*

colleges, they will be able to hire these same workers at reduced rates of pay. However, if they are unable to do so and they recognize that there is a correlation between schooling and productive ability, they will continue to recruit and reward individuals according to their educational qualifications. To the individual it may therefore make little difference whether education is viewed as a screening or productivity enhancing device. For as long as employees use education as a screening device those individuals wishing to enhance their future earnings will have to attend college and acquire the necessary qualifications. Though they may recognize that college itself imparts no productive skills, if this is the only way in which they can acquire the documentation necessary to signal their abilities to employers, they will have little choice but to attend college. Individuals *signal* to employers by their attendance at college and by their educational attainment the extent of their pre-existing ability. On this view education is used by firms and workers as a screening and signaling device, respectively, because each of them can devise no superior alternatives.

If schooling is merely a screening device we might expect to find that the self-employed invest less in college education than do employees in general. The self-employed presumably know their own productive ability and, therefore, do not need to acquire signals that testify to this. This suggests a way of testing the screening hypothesis. There is some evidence that the self-employed do indeed acquire less schooling than employees. The average length of schooling of self-employed workers in the United States at 13.95 years is less than that of salaried workers at 14.55 years.[13]

However, it is far from a perfect test for those who are currently self-employed may not have known, when deciding whether or not to invest in college, that they would be self-employed. Moreover, even if they had known, they might still have regarded such employment as a temporary state of affairs and, therefore, have sought to acquire the signals that enhanced their subsequent mobility. If, in addition, the customers of the self-employed have little appreciation that education is just a screen, they may demand evidence of the acquisition of the necessary certificates as testimony to their competence. For this reason the psychiatrist, orthodontist and physician display their degree certificates and qualifications on the walls of their offices.

It has also been argued that if schooling were merely a screening device employers might initially reward individuals according to their level of schooling, but as evidence accumulated of the employees' abilities in the workplace, years of schooling would become a less important determinant of earnings. Employers would discover by their own experience who among the most highly qualified were the most productive and reward them accordingly. We should then expect to observe a narrowing of the earnings differentials enjoyed by the most highly qualified. Yet we observe a continued growth in the earnings differentials between those with different levels of human capital investment. Does this refute the screening hypothesis? Advocates of the screening hypothesis counter that the continued association between earnings and schooling testifies to the fact that the screening in schools was successful. The

13. Wolpin, K.I. (1977) 'Education and screening', *American Economic Review*, **67**(5), December, 949–58.

conclusion to this debate seems to be that education and ability are related and that earnings are positively associated with both of these.

The screening hypothesis cannot be regarded as a general critique of the theory of human capital investment. It has little applicability to those undertaking vocational training at college, and it makes no sense to suggest that this applies to human capital investment at the workplace. The hypothesis applies to a restricted area of human capital investment, non-vocational general training taking place outside the workplace. Nonetheless, expenditures in this area alone account for a substantial proportion of the estimated 7 percent of GNP spent directly on formal education in the United Kingdom and the United States each year.

The screening hypothesis questions the wisdom of the post-war increases in the school leaving age in the United Kingdom and the United States and of the expansion of higher education in both countries. Sixty years ago in the United Kingdom possession of a secondary school leaving certificate testified to above average ability but it now requires a degree to do the same thing. In the United States it requires a Master's degree to indicate that individuals are in the top decile of the distribution of ability for their age group. In the United Kingdom possession of a Bachelor's degree indicates the same thing.

Estimates suggest that higher education in the United States offered the investor a return of little over 5 percent in the late 1970s. Given that part of this is a return to ability it would appear arguable whether, on purely financial grounds, education at that time represented a good investment when the rate of return is compared to that of other investments. Much of the decline in the rate of return to higher education in the United States in those years was revealed to be accounted for by a decline in the relative earnings of new entrants or recent graduates.[14] However, the situation appears to be changing. It is predicted that the rates of return to human capital investment for those who graduate toward the end of the 1980s and during the first part of the 1990s are set to rise.[15]

DIVERGENCE FROM EQUILIBRIUM: THE CONSEQUENCES OF A LENGTHY TRAINING PERIOD

Finally, consider some of the difficulties that are likely to result from the long lead times required to produce certain types of human capital. It takes in the region of five to six years to produce lawyers, doctors and qualified accountants. Individuals, deciding whether to enter these professions, may base their decisions on their present perceptions of the net advantages of these jobs. However, over the period during which they are training the balance of supply and demand, and hence the rewards offered by

14. Freeman, R.B. (1976) *The Overeducated American*, Academic Press, New York and (1979) 'The effect of demographic factors on the age earnings profile in the US', *Journal of Human Resources*. Welch, F. (1979) 'Effects of cohort size on earnings : the baby boom babies financial bust', *Journal of Political Economy*, **4**.
15. Stapleton, D.C. and Young, D.Y. (1988) 'Educational attainment and cohort size', *Journal of Labor Economics*, **6**(3), 330–61.

the job, may change substantially from what they anticipated. A model which explores the consequences of this is the so-called Cobweb model depicted in Fig. 6.6.

Suppose that, in the absence of other information, individuals believe that the real income of accountants, relative to all the other occupations they have considered for a career, will be the same in six years' time when they emerge fully qualified, as it is when they enter training. Suppose, further, that the market although recently in equilibrium at point A, has experienced an unanticipated increase in demand for the services of accountants which has pushed demand out to L_1^d. Because it takes time to train accountants there is initially no supply response to this increse in demand, and the competition for the services of the existing number of accountants, E_1 increases salaries to W_2/P. We start our analysis at this point.

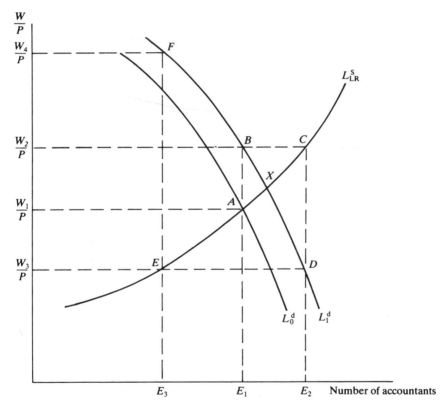

Figure 6.6 The cobweb: the consequences of a lengthy training period. Current labor supply is a function of past wage rates. If L_0^d rises to L_1^d with only E_1 individuals available, wage rates rise to (W_2/P). On the basis of these wage rates labor supply equal to E_2 is forthcoming in the next period but when this arrives on the market, at an unchanged level of demand, wage rates shrink to (W_3/P). In the subsequent period supply therefore falls to E_3. In the period following that wages rise to W_4/P, at an unchanged level of demand, and so the process continues. This process is described as a diverging cobweb. This initial disturbance, the rise in labor demand to L_1^d, gave rise to an increasingly divergent movement from equilibrium

Prospective entrants to the profession base their decisions on the wage rate ruling in the market, W_2/P, and if $E_2 - E_1$ individuals are induced to enter the profession, six years later this number emerges to join the ranks of qualified accountants. However, over this interval the demand for their services has not changed from L_1^d and E_2 will only be employed at real wage rate, W_3/P. Those individuals contemplating a career as an accountant at this time observe the relatively low wage, W_3/P, revise their plans, and train for other professions with the result that six years further on supply is only equal to E_3. At which point if demand has remained at L_1^d there is an excess demand for accountants and so wages rise again to W_4/P; and so the cycle continues. The picture is one of alternating surpluses and shortages.

In this example current supply was a function of lagged wages, $L^s = W_{t-6}$, and in the example chosen as we moved further and further away from the equilibrium point X, the cobweb diverged. This need not always be the case, converging cobwebs also exist. What form the cobweb takes depends on the relative slopes of the long-run labor supply and demand curves. If the absolute value of the slope of the labor demand schedule is less than the absolute value of the labor supply curve the cobweb will converge.

How realistic is such a model? One researcher noted that the supply of new engineers in the United States exhibited a distinct cyclical pattern.[16] It appeared that decisions to enrol in, and complete, engineering training, were substantially influenced by the current starting salaries of engineers and thus a cobweb phenomenon seemed to exist. These large swings in supply emerge because of information imperfections. Each individual, acting rationally in the light of the information he or she possessed, invested in human capital, but then found that because so many other individuals had taken similar action the outcome was very different from that which he or she had anticipated. Individuals reacted to a disequilibrium price without knowing it. However, they could have avoided this outcome if they had acquired additional information and had based their decisions on other than current wages. Individuals have a strong incentive to construct a more fully informed expectation of the wage rate that will rule for their skills in the future, for they are engaging in a substantial investment. We might therefore expect them to devote considerable resources to acquiring appropriate information and eliminating such extreme fluctuations.

SUMMARY

In this chapter we have focused on the supply of skills, the supply of trained and educated manpower, to the modern economy. Economists view the process of acquiring skills as analogous to an investment decision. Like other investment decisions it requires the outlay of resources now for expected returns in the future, and like other investment decisions it is the prospect of these returns that motivates the individual to undertake such investment. Human capital theory gives rise to earnings functions that attempt to explain the observed differences in earnings between

16. Freeman, R.B. (1976) 'A cobweb model of the supply and starting salary of new engineers', *Industrial and Labor Review*, **29**, 236–46.

individuals and such functions have been estimated with some degree of success. Yet although they have been able to explain a substantial part of the observed variations in individual earnings, the estimated coefficients, the estimated rates of return to human capital, have been shown to exhibit substantial bias. One important source of this bias was their inability to control for the separate contributions of experience and ability. In fact the impact of ability and human capital investment on earnings is unlikely to be independent. A high level of ability may be an essential precondition for successful human capital investment. Not just ability but also family background has been revealed to be associated with an individual's capacity to benefit from, and disposition toward, investment in human capital. The high earnings of one generation may lead them to construct a family environment which disposes their offspring to invest in human capital. This may mean that the earnings inequality of one generation produces an echo in the next generation. The opportunities to invest in human capital are not uniformly distributed across the population.

PRINCIPAL CONCEPTS

After reading this chapter students should be familiar with the following concepts:

1. Human capital investment.
2. Net present value.
3. Rate of return.
4. Forgone earnings opportunities.
5. Present orientedness.
6. General and specific training.
7. On-the-job training.
8. Learning-by-doing.
9. Earnings functions.
10. Non-competing groups.
11. Screening and signaling.

QUESTIONS FOR DISCUSSION

1. How complete is the analogy between human and physical capital investment?
2. Can we measure accurately the private costs and benefits of human capital investment?
3. Why do we discount when we evaluate the costs and benefits of human capital investment and what factors affect the rate at which we discount?
4. If an individual's willingness to invest in education or training is positively related to differences in earnings between trained and untrained jobs, and these differences increase with age, why are older workers less willing to invest in human capital investment?
5. How do you account for the relative ease with which many individuals can raise a loan to finance investment in physical capital and the relative difficulty they

experience in seeking loans to finance human capital investment? What are the implications of the difference?

6. Why aren't firms willing to bear the costs of specific training when workers pay for the whole of any investment in general training?

7. Discuss the problems researchers experience when estimating the returns to human capital.

8. What factors might lead us to conclude that most empirical estimates overstate the rate of return to human capital?

9. What are the implications for human capital theory of the notion of non-competing groups?

10. Does education enhance individuals' labor market productivity or screen for pre-existing productive characteristics?

FURTHER READING

Two economists are responsible for the development of human capital theory. 'Investment in human capital' (1961) *American Economic Review*, **51**, 1–17, by Theodore Schultz, represents the pioneering work in this field, but the most complete initial statement is that by Gary Becker (1964) in his book *Human Capital*, National Bureau of Economic Research, New York. The pioneering empirical work in this field is the book by Jacob Mincer (1974) *Schooling, Experience and Earnings*, National Bureau of Economic Research, New York, referred to in the text. All three remain seminal contributions and should be consulted. The notion of education as screening originates in an article by Kenneth Arrow (1962) 'Higher education as a filter', *Journal of Public Economics*, **2**, 193–216. A recent and informative review of the human capital literature is offered by Robert J. Willis (1986) 'Wage determinants: a survey and interpretation of human capital earnings functions', in Ashenfelter, O. and Layard, P.R.G (eds.), *Handbook of Labor Economics*, North-Holland, New York and Oxford.

7

INSTITUTIONS AND LABOR SUPPLY

In each of the previous chapters labor was assumed to be supplied under competitive conditions. However, on many occasions such an assumption is inappropriate. The most studied exception is where a trade union controls supply and acts as a monopolist. In this chapter we shall look into the factors that determine the amount of labor that is supplied in unionized markets. The trade union's principal impact on labor markets is to change the nature of, and the conditions under which, labor is supplied. In order to understand the manner in which this occurs we shall study in some depth the nature of union preferences and the mechanisms that exist to ensure that trade unions are able to exercise effective control over labor supply.

In studying trade unions we study one of the major institutional constraints on labor supply that exist in a modern economy but the union is by no means the only, or perhaps any longer the most important, qualification to competition in this area. The conditions under which labor is supplied are frequently affected by rules and conventions, social norms, and these too can militate against competitive behavior. These norms can lead individuals to act in concert, one with another, and, although not intended as such, they have the effect that the individuals concerned effectively act like monopoly suppliers of labor. In this chapter we assess each of these possibilities, in order to distinguish further the institutional constraints on competitive labor supply that characterize the labor markets in most economies. We should note further that the forces of competition are muted, if not almost entirely shut, in further circumstances that we shall discuss in Chapter 12. This occurs where individuals possess a unique skill or talent: leading sportsmen, artists and musicians, successful entrepreneurs and managers are also examples of this. A more mundane, but far more frequent, example is where the magnitude of hiring and firing costs precludes competition for jobs and again we shall discuss this in Chapter 12.

LABOR SUPPLY UNDER TRADE UNIONS

The labor supply curve tells us how much labor is supplied at different wage rates. For the individual this is discovered by identifying the individual's preferences and the changing opportunities that confront him or her in the labor market. Similarly, to describe a labor supply curve for a trade union we need to identify the preferences of the union and the constraints that confront it. However, in the static theory of labor supply the constraints were determined exogenously, but the same cannot be said for the trade union. One of the avenues by which a trade union achieves its objectives is by altering the labor market constraints that confront it. Unions seek to alter both the slope and the position of the labor demand curve which faces them, an issue we shall explore in detail in the next chapter. For the moment we are concerned with analyzing the manner in which a trade union affects labor supply and we start by analyzing union preferences.

Union government: the formation of union preferences

In detailing the preferences of the trade union there are at least two distinct steps to the analysis. A trade union constitutes a collection of individuals who construct and implement a common policy. We therefore need to consider both the nature of the preferences of the individuals who compose the union, and the degree to which these preferences are reflected in the preferences, or policies, of the union. If the union is democratic, its policies will reflect the wishes of its membership: which part of the membership will depend on the type of electoral system the union operates. If the union is run along autocratic lines its policies may reflect the wishes of a small group of individuals who run the union in their interests. In this case we are less concerned with the preferences of individual union members for they count less in the construction of union policy. The issue of union government takes us into the realms of political theory, an area usually avoided by economists, but it is important if we are to construct an appropriate model of a trade union.

One prominent view of union government[1] proposed that the increasing bureaucratization of representative institutions had reduced their degree of democracy. This view proposed that unions do not respond to the preferences of their membership but reflect the interests of a small group of individuals who control the union.[2] The essence

1. Almost 80 years ago the view was articulated, by Michels, R. (1911) *Political Parties*, Free Press, that 'who says organisation says oligarchy'. In the words of other reasearchers 'at the head of most private organisations stands a small group of men most of whom have held high office in the organisations' government for a long time and whose tenure and control is rarely threatened by a serious organised internal oppositions'. Lipset, S.M., Trow, M. and Coleman, J. (1956) *Union Democracy: The Internal Politics of the International Typographical Union*, Free Press.
2. Ross, A. (1948) *Trade Union Wage Policy*, University of California Press, Berkeley, argued that unions were essentially political rather than economic entities and that their aims were to ensure the long-run

of this criticism of union democracy was that power, within the union, was not distributed uniformly across all members and that the preferences of some members, the office holders, counted for more than those of others. It is not difficult to see why power may be heavily weighted in favor of the incumbent office holders. The union leadership may be able to manipulate both the agenda on which members vote and the information that is available to members. In so doing the leadership can sharpen or blur the focus of members' discontent. Incumbents also often enjoy the power of patronage, and are sometimes able to determine the timing of elections. It is, moreover, difficult, given the resources available to individual members, for them to organize and remove incumbents from office. In the United Kingdom the periodic re-election of union leaders and voting by secret ballot were requirements of legislation introduced in the 1980s for they were argued to be essential devices for ensuring membership control over union leaders and shop stewards.

The mechanism, by which union members induce their representatives to behave in a manner which realizes the members' objectives, is considered by the *economic theory of agency*. Typically the trade union leader, the agent, has to choose a course of action, from among a number of alternative possibilities, and the action chosen affects both the agent's and the membership's, the principal's, welfare. Problems arise, in this type of relationship, because the agents have an information advantage and their actions cannot be fully observed by the membership. The issue, therefore, is how to construct an incentive structure to insure that the leadership behaves in the manner desired by the membership. Complex and contingent schedules of monetary rewards are clearly one device, but the transaction costs associated with these are prohibitive. Continuous monitoring of the agent's behavior is also ruled out for the same reasons. The solution now most widely practiced is to construct a restricted set of rewards and penalities. The rewards often take a social and non-monetary form; the penalties take the form of non-re-election. For this last to be an effective sanction the elections must be fair and open. If this is the case and the union is run along democratic lines, to whom, from among a diverse union membership, is the agent most likely to be responsive? Whose preferences, from among all those who comprise the membership, are most likely to be reflected in union policy? This is the issue addressed by the following model.

The median voter model

One view of the manner in which union preferences are formed is offered by the median voter model. Suppose that a union with n members comprises two homogeneous groups, j, containing $1 \dots m$ members, and k, comprising $m + 1 \dots n$ members. If officials are elected by majority voting and $j > k$ union wage policy is determined by the preferences of individuals in j, and conversely if $k > j$. However, it

---

survival and stability of the union. Of course such political aims cannot be entirely divorced from, nor are they incompatible with, economic objections for such an aim is an essential precondition for the realization of the unions' economic aims in the longer run. The distinguishing feature of such a view is that aims are ascribed to the union as institution and no attempt is made to justify this by reference back to the underlying preferences of individual union members.

is unlikely that the preferences of union members can be divided in quite this way. It is more likely that they ranged along a spectrum on most issues. The *median voter model* proposes that, where the preferences of the membership and the distribution of power are diverse, and union policy is decided by representatives elected on a simple majority vote, union policy will reflect the preferences of the median voter. Take as an example the preferences for leisure and goods and services of the five individuals A,B,C,D and E represented in Fig. 7.1(a).

Confronted with wage W_1/P they would all choose to work quite different hours. However, suppose that only one of these combinations, of the wage and hours, will be offered to them all. Which option will they vote for? Individual A would prefer W_1/P and H_1^A and after that the combination preferred by B,C,D and E in that order. Equally E would most prefer the combination W_1/P and H_1^E and after that in descending order of preference those offered by D,C,B and finally A. Similarly, B would prefer that of C or A to that of D and certainly E while D would prefer that of E and C to that of B and A, and so on. If the issue is resolved by pairwise voting, H_1^C is the option that will win, for it would beat all others in pairwise voting, it is described as the Condorcet winner. No other combination of hours of work and goods and services would beat this in a run-off, a seemingly satisfactory result.

Individuals' preferences are seldom so uniformly distributed. More typically they peak around certain options in the manner depicted in either of the two distributions in Fig. 7.1(b). Even though only two candidates may stand for election, the platform they eventually adopt will again be one that reflects the preferences of the median voter. To show this suppose that individual union members' preferences with regard to hours of work are reflected in distribution A in Fig. 7.1(b) and there are two candidates for union office, X proposing everyone work H_1 hours and Y proposing everyone work H_2 hours. Everyone to the left of S, the mid-point of the distances XY, will vote for X while everyone to the right of S will vote for Y. Everyone votes for the candidate closest to his or her own position but, in this case, because there are more than 50 percent of voters to the right of S (the median lies to the right of S), candidate Y wins. Of course candidate X can increase his or her share of the vote by moving toward Y's position, thereby shifting S to the right. Similarly Y can increase his or her share of the vote by moving toward the median point of the distribution. Accordingly both candidates are propelled toward the position of the median voter, the voter whose preferences fall at the mid-point of the distribution of preferred hours. Thus, with diversity of opinion and majority voting, union policy reflects the preferences of the median voter. Who the median voters are and what their preferences are therefore matter if we are to use such a model to predict the outcome.

If preferences centre around a single peak as shown for either distribution A or B in Fig. 7.1(b) the median voter outcome will be observed. Where preferences are not distributed along such a continuum, perhaps the distribution of preferred hours of work exhibits multiple peaks, the outcome will be less clear. In fact the constituencies that most unions represent, in both the United Kingdom and United States, are often quite diverse and we might anticipate that such single peaked distributions will be

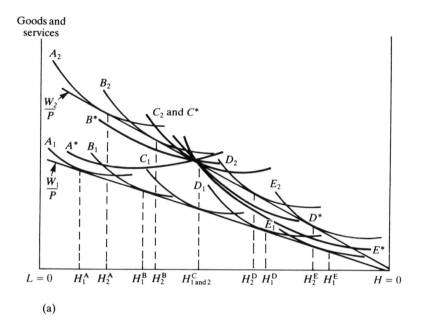

(a)

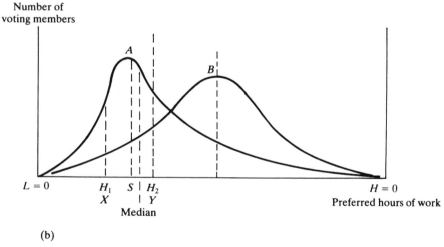

(b)

Figure 7.1 The median voter model (a) Preferences and power are widely dispersed. If the individuals shown have to select only one of the five preferred combinations of hours of work and goods at W_1/P which they then all work, H_1^c will be the hours of work selected. Pairwise voting will result in H_1^c beating all other combinations (b) The preferences shown in distribution A are less evenly distributed than in part (a) and the distribution exhibits a distinct peak. The preferences of the median voters, the voters in the middle of the distribution, will again be those whose preferences are adopted

relatively rare. Most unions in the United Kingdom represent workers across a wide and diverse range of industries, distinguished only in that they tend to organize in either the public or the private sectors of the economy. In the United States industrial unions are more typical, but they in turn organize across a wide range of different occupations and levels of skill. These observations qualify the generality of the median voter model.

Figure 7.1(a) also enables us to provide at least one answer to a further question that arises in discussions of unions and labor supply which is why should individuals belong to a union? Why should they compromise on their preferred outcome and vote for a policy that does not coincide entirely with their preferences? Consider Fig. 7.1(a). If individuals believe that by combining they can secure a wage rise, from W_1/P to W_2/P, which is greater than would otherwise occur, despite working different hours than they would optimally choose, they may still be better off, as indicated by the higher, bold, starred indifference curves in each case. As with any cartel Fig. 7.1(a) also reveals the considerable gains that can be made by cheating on the agreed terms. Thus, individual A could enjoy a substantial improvement in real income, by offering H_2^A at W_2/P, and B could gain by working H_2^B hours at wage W_2/P. Of course, by so doing they undermine the restriction on labor supply that raised the wage rate in the first place, for the belief that the union exercised sufficient control over labor supply persuaded the employer to buy labor on union negotiated terms in the first place. The union, either by means of the closed shop, or by reducing labor supply by a strike or go slow, will seek to demonstrate to the employer that it exercises sufficient control over labor supply. Part of this demonstration involves penalizing individuals, who supply labor against the union's wishes, as occurs when sanctions are imposed on blacklegs during a strike.

Any restriction on labor supply which results in a higher wage will generally mean less employment and this might be thought to dampen union members' enthusiasm for such a policy. Where unemployment is determined by a random draw, and all union members stand an equal chance of being unemployed, we should expect this fact to have some influence upon union wage policy.[3] However, it does not follow that the higher wage need mean fewer jobs for union members. The nature of union government may be such, that rules are devised to insure that union members do not each stand an equal chance of unemployment. Those with the biggest influence on union policy may devise rules which ensure that they have the least chance of unemployment. Thus a rule for layoffs or redundancies may be that they occur in reverse order of seniority; according to the convention of 'last in, first out'. Such practices help insulate senior workers from the unemployment consequences of union wage claims, and may result in a rather lower weight being given to unemployment in the unions' policies.

---

3. Random assignment of union jobs still occurs in some industries. These are industries in which hiring is through a union hiring hall, as in the construction industry in some countires. See Quinn, M.D., (1980) 'Construction', in Sommers, G. (ed.), *Collective Bargaining: Contemporary American Experience*, Industrial Relations Association, Madison, Wisconsin.

The renewed emphasis on the micro foundations of economics has meant that much of the discussion of unions has focused on individual union members' preferences. However, prior to this the typical approach to the issue of union objectives was to specify goals for the union, and to ask only as a secondary consideration, to what extent these reflected the preferences of members. This idea of a union preference function, constructed without reference to individual union members' preferences, still features prominently in the literature on trade unions. It is appropriate where the union objectives reflect those of a small group within the union such as the leadership. Perhaps in the same way as the goals of the firm can be viewed as those of its management, the unions' goals can be viewed as those of its leadership.[4]

The nature of union preferences

If union leaders have considerable discretion with respect to how they serve their members it may be sufficient to talk of the goals of union leaders and to seek to distinguish these. In the past several such goals have been identified and, in a similar way to that in which we use indifference maps to illustrate individual preferences, union indifference or preference curves have been drawn to illustrate unions' preferences.[5] Thus unions concerned only to maximize the wage rate will have a set of horizontal preference curves, U_0, U_1, U_2 etc. when drawn in wage/employment space while a union concerned to maximize only employment would have a set of vertical 'curves'. Such preference curves are illustrated in Figs 7.2(a) and (b) respectively, in which the MRP_L curve describes the labor demand curve.

A union concerned to maximize the wage rate, would push the wage rate up to the maximum compatible with the firm just covering its wage costs, so that employment level L_1 resulted. Although such a situation is not compatible with the firm remaining in business in the long run such tactics have been adopted by some unions. Aware that the firm has little intention of remaining in this line of business in the long run, the union sets out to secure for itself the profits that would otherwise constitute the return to capital. Pushing the wage up to the point at which it is just equal to average revenue means that the firm is just able to cover its variable costs and this provides sufficient incentive for it to remain in business in the short run. Such a strategy has been termed an 'end game' and has been claimed to have operated in the US steel industry in the early 1980s.[6] In this case due to substantial excess capacity several producers had no intention of remaining in this business in the long run. Unions, therefore, set out to capture for their members that part of the revenues which would otherwise have comprised the firm's profits and the means of renewing the capacity in that industry. However, such examples are rare, for typically unions are also concerned about employment.

4. This is the view taken by Pencavel, J.H. See Chapter 3 of *The Labor Market under Trade Unionism* (1990 forthcoming).
5. Fellner, W.J. (1951) *Competition Among the Few*, New York, Alfred A. Knopf, pp. 252–76. Cartter, A.M. (1959) *Theory of Wages and Employment*, Richard D. Irwin, Homewood, Illinois, Chs. 7 and 8.
6. Lawrence, C. and Lawrence, R. (1985) 'Manufacturing wage dispersion: an end game interpretation', *Brookings Papers on Economic Activity*, pp. 47–106.

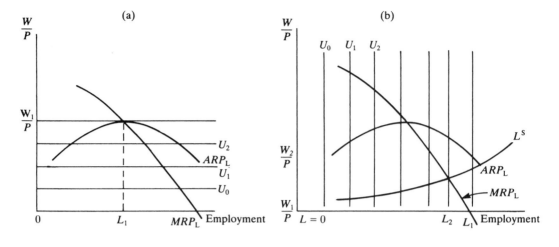

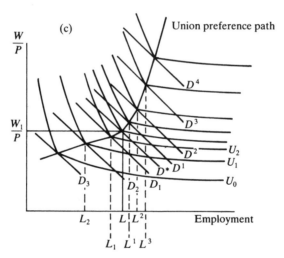

Figure 7.2 Union preference functions. (a) An all powerful union concerned to maximize the wage rate pushes this to W_1/P at which point average revenue, ARP_L is just equal to average cost, W_1/P. The firm earns no return to other factors, merely covering labor costs in the short run, with employment, equal to L_1. (b) A union concerned to maximize only employment, ought to negotiate a wage of zero for at this level maximum employment, L_1, is assured. Clearly this is unlikely for the lower limit to the wage is set by competitive supply L^s. (c) If the level of labor demand departs from its existing level, D*, in a downward direction the union resists a fall in the wage rate and employment accordingly falls sharply. If, on the other hand, demand rises from the existing level it prefers to take this in the form of a wage rise rather than as an increase in employment. These arguments give rise to the 'union preference path' depicted above

If the union were concerned only about employment the situation would be as depicted in Fig. 7.2(b). The union could increase employment by negotiating successive reductions in the wage rate; in the limit if it pushed the wage to zero, employment would be L_1. Of course this would not be permitted, for the lower limit to the wage would be set by the competitive supply curve that would exist in the absence of the trade union. Suppose this were as represented by L^s, then L_2 would be the maximum to which employment could be expanded.

More probably the union is concerned about both wages and employment as illustrated in Fig. 7.2(c). Union preferences are kinked at the ruling wage W_1/P. A reduction in the wage rate consequent upon a reduction in demand from D^* to D_1 or D_2 is resisted by the union and the burden of adjustment therefore falls on employment which falls to L_1 and L_2 respectively. On the other hand an increase in demand to D^1, D^2 or D^3 is largely used to increase wages resulting in a relatively small increase in employment to L^1, L^2 and L^3. These propositions about union preferences originally arose from the observation that wages are sticky in a downward direction. It was conjectured that in the face of a decline in demand, unions would rather take a cut in employment than see wages reduced. On the other hand faced with an increase in labor demand they would prefer to see wages rather than employment increase. How do such conjectures about union preferences stands up in the face of recent theories of union government?

A union may be able to hold the wage in the face of falling employment if those who become unemployed are either unlikely to be union members, or, though union members, count for little in union decision making. Yet there is evidence that, in the United States at least, the unionized unemployed feature prominently in unions' decision making. In the United States, unions covering around a quarter of all unionized workers, augment state unemployment payments with benefits negotiated as part of the collective bargaining agreement. Again, during the recessions of the early 1970s and early 1980s many US unions made substantial 'wage concessions' to enable former workers, then on layoff, to return to their jobs.

'Last in first out' redundancy criterion is one example of a rule that appears to insulate senior union members from the consequences of unemployment. Seniority, or rather the lack of it, frequently counts as a criterion in determining redundancy. But this does not mean that senior workers are protected from the consequences of job loss. Again, in the United States, layoff of the least senior workers usually results in a reallocation of work among the remaining workforce. In turn this results in some senior workers being retained in lower ranked jobs at lower wages. This practice of senior workers 'bumping' junior workers is much more prominent in the United States than in Europe, but in both continents the criteria governing who loses their job is likely to be the outcome of negotiations and therefore managerial requirements will intrude. For this reason senior workers in both continents may have good reason to be concerned about even moderate reductions in employment.

In general, therefore, unions' objective functions would seem to embrace both employment and wages. However, the weights that are assigned to each of these will differ between unions, and between countries. The practices of US unions suggest that they weight employment more heavily than do many European unions, and certainly most UK unions. Moreover, if the unions' objective function is the leadership's

Table 7.1 Recent levels of union density in selected countries

	1970 %	1979 %	1984/5 %
Australia	52	58	57
Germany	37	42	42
Japan	35	32	29
UK	51	58	52
USA	31	25	18
Denmark	66	86	98
Sweden	79	89	95

Source: Freeman, R. (1988) 'Contraction and expansion: the divergence of private sector and public sector unionism in the United States,' *Journal of Economic Perspectives,* **2**(2), 63–88.

function then this is also likely to include union membership as an argument. For a larger membership endows the leadership with more prestige and influence and may even enhance their wealth. Finally, the wage rates of workers in other jobs, comparison wages, are also likely, for reasons to be developed later in this chapter, to feature in the unions' objective function. This suggests a union utility function of the general form

$$U = U(W,E,W^C,M) \tag{7.1}$$

where W and E are as before, while W^C represents comparison wages and M union membership. Union utility is an increasing function of W,E and M, but a decreasing function of W^C. The above represents a general statement of union objectives, the exact weights that attach to each of these arguments are likely to differ between countries and even within countries between unions.[7] We shall return to the issue of union objectives and consider how they affect wage determination under trade unions in Chapter 14.

Union control over labor supply

Unions will only exert an influence on wage and employment outcomes if they have sufficient power to realize their objectives. The source of union power is control over labor supply or the ability to convince employers that they exercise effective control over labor supply. In these circumstances firms can only buy labor on terms acceptable to the union. Unions appear to exert control over labor supply in many countries.

One measure of the control unions exercise over labor supply is union density, the proportion of the eligible labor force who are union members. Table 7.1 shows that in recent years union density has been on the decline in the United States, United Kingdom and Japan while in Australia and Germany it has held steady. In contrast, in Scandinavia it has continued to grow so that now almost the complete workforce is

7. The general issue of union objectives is discussed in detail in a forthcoming book by Pencavel, J.H. (1990), *op. cit.* I was fortunate to have the opportunity to read the manuscript of this book while preparing the final draft of this section and this is reflected in the facts and arguments above.

unionized. The decline in the United Kingdom occurred in the 1980s but it occurred earlier in the United States. In the United States density levels are now no higher than they were in the 1940s while in the United Kingdom they are now back to the levels of the late 1960s (see Table 7.2).

A wide variety of explanations has been offered to explain the recent reductions in union density in both countries among which are: structural shifts in the composition of the workforce, notably the decline in the heavily unionized manufacturing sector and rise of the less heavily unionized service sector; anti-union policies on the part of government as exemplified by changes in the law in the United Kingdom and the handling of the air traffic controllers strike in the United States; a more militant anti-union stance by many managements; and finally, the high levels of unemployment experienced by both countries in the early 1980s.[8]

But what do such figures mean, how many employers were confronted with unions as the sole sellers of labor and how did this vary in the short and long run? In the short run an employer seeking to employ a particular class of labor may have no option but to buy from and negotiate with a union, if all labor of the type required is unionized. Such circumstances occur in the case of pre-entry closed shops, called closed shops in the United States, but they are relatively rare. A UK example was printworkers on the London newspapers in the period up to the mid-1980s, after which time such practices were declared illegal. In the United States the closed shop has been illegal for far longer under the Taft–Hartley Act of 1948, but notwithstanding this many employments still effectively operate like closed shops. A rather less substantial control over supply exists in the case of the post-entry closed shop, referred to as the union shop in the United States. In this case employers are free to recruit whom they want and how many employees they wish, but on employment the individuals recruited have to become union members. It is then their labor supply subsequent to employment, that is their hours of works, which is controlled by the union.

How important are these two forms in Britain and the United States? In 1980 and again in 1984 surveys of the industrial relations practices of establishments in Britain were conducted. These surveys revealed that in 1980 23 percent of all establishments had some workers covered by some form of closed shop arrangement, pre- or post-entry, but that this had fallen to 18 percent by 1984. Taken together both types of closed shop covered approximately 20 percent of all employees, or between 3.5 and 3.7 million employees in 1984. This compared to between 4.7 and 4.9 million in 1980. Since earlier estimates had put the figure at at least 5.2 million in 1978, the closed shop appears to have been in steady decline in the United Kingdom since the late 1970s.[9] Only a quarter of those employed in closed shops in Britain are in the pre-entry variety, so that less than 1 million workers were covered by these arrangements. Thus employers would seem, in general, to have considerable discretion over where they buy their labor.

8. See the 'Symposium on public and private unionism', in the *Journal of Economic Perspectives*, **2**(2) spring 1988, 59–110, for a summary of these issues and a guide to the relevant literature.
9. See Millward, N. and Stevens, M. (1986) *British Workplace Industrial Relations 1980–84*, Gower Press.

Table 7.2 Trade union density 1900–86

	United Kingdom[†] %	United States of America[‡] %
1900	12.7	3.0
1910	14.6	5.9
1920	45.2	12.0
1930	25.4	7.5
1940	33.1	14.6
1950	44.1	22.1
1960	44.4	22.3
1970	49.4	25.4
1980	56.0	19.6
1981	55.0	19.0
1982	53.8	17.8
1983	53.0	16.6
1984	51.4	16.1
1985	49.5	—
1986	48.8	—

Source: For the US, Reder, M.W. (1988), 'The rise and fall of unions : the public sector and the private,' *Journal of Economic Perspectives*, **2**(2), 89–110; for the UK, Metcalf, D. (1988), 'Water notes dry up', *Centre for Labour Economics, Discussion Paper*,
[†] Union membership as a percentage of employees in employment, i.e. the employed labor force minus the armed services and self-employed.
[‡] Union membership as a percentage of the total labor force.

Union control over labor supply extends beyond that indicated by figures on the closed shop. Some employers grant *de facto* control over labor supply to the union by hiring labor only on terms negotiated by the union. Firms might adopt such practices because they believe that, despite only organizing a minority of employees, the union has the capacity to mount an effective picket or boycott of the firm. Others, without a union presence, may do so to remove any incentive to unionization. Still, other employers may extend union negotiated terms and conditions to all the workforce believing these to be 'fair' wages. In each case this practice grants effective control over the price of labor to the union.

We have no way of estimating precisely the degree of such informal control but some hint is given for Britain by the following figures. In 1984 73 percent of all establishments in Britain had some union presence as Table 7.3(a) indicates; non-union establishments were in a relatively small minority. However, not all the establishments in which there was a union presence recognized a union for purposes of bargaining hence figures on union presence overstate unions' control over labor supply. Table 7.3(b) indicates unions were bargaining on behalf of at least some manual workers in 62 percent of all establishments in 1984 and on behalf of

Table 7.3 (a) Proportion of establishments with a union presence in Britain in 1984

	Manual union	Non-manual union	Any union
Non-union	29	40	27
Union presence	68	58	73

(b) Proportion of establishments recognizing at least one union for purposes of bargaining

	Manual union	Non-manual union	Any union
1980	55	47	64
1984	62	54	66

(c) Proportion of workforce covered by the terms and conditions negotiated by unions

	Manual	Non-manual
1984	58.9	49.7

Source: Millward, N. and Stevens, M. (1986) *British Workplace Industrial Relations 1980–1984*, Gower Press.

non-manual workers in 54 percent of establishments in the same year. Trade unions therefore played at least some part in negotiating pay in two-thirds of all establishments in Britain in 1984. What proportion of the workforce did these establishments in which unions bargained cover?

The 1984 survey suggests that almost 59 percent of all manual workers in Britain effectively had their pay and conditions of work settled by union negotiation.[10] Similarly almost 50 percent of the total non-manual workforce of Britian effectively had their pay and conditions determined by union negotiations as indicated by Table 7.3(c). Unions therefore negotiated the pay and conditions of well over half the British workforce in 1984 at a time when union density was about 50 percent.

For the United States similarly detailed information is not available. Nonetheless, in a country in which as we have seen union density is substantially lower than in the United Kingdom, it has been estimated that around half of all private sector non-farm employment is in establishments in which a majority of either production or

---

10 From the 1984 survey, it emerges that where firms recognized at least one manual union for purposes of bargaining they typically extended the union negotiated terms and conditions to all their manual workforce. The survey revealed that while in those establishments employing manual workers *and* recognizing a manual union, trade union density among manual workers was 83 percent in 1984, union negotiated terms and conditions were extended to 95 percent of all manual workers in these establishments. Again, where a non-manual worker union was recognized for purposes of bargaining the terms and conditions the unions negotiated were extended to 92 percent of the non-manual workforce of such establishments. See Millward, N. and Stevens, M. (1986), *op. cit.*

3non-production employees are unionized.[11] In addition to these there will always be small groups of union members at some other establishments. However, it is union recognition not union membership that is of principal concern because it is in these circumstances that unions have the potential to influence pay and conditions. This same study suggests that 50 percent of the US workforce works for companies that have some dealings with unions.

Thus for many classes of labor the union is the single seller of labor to the employer, either because it has secured control over labor supply or because it has been granted this, *de facto*, by the employer. Can we therefore draw an analogy between the trade union as the single seller of labor and the monopoly firm as the single seller of a product? On this point economists differ. Some noting that 'unlike the monopoly firm that sets prices to maximize profits unions rarely set wages; they *bargain* over wages with employers. Unless one believes that the process of bargaining is a sham the wages obtained by unions must be viewed as the joint responsibility of management and labor.'[12] Against this view it should be noted that the situation described is no different from the joint responsibility for prices that emerges in commodity markets in which a monopoly seller confronts a single large buyer. This does not alter the fact that the supply side of the market is controlled by a single seller.

Unions are on occasion seen to set the wage unilaterally and in Chapter 14 we shall examine wage determination under trade unions in some detail. For the moment we confine our analysis to a description of their impact on labor supply. The description of the trade union as a monopolist, as the single seller of labor, refers to its effective control over labor supply and to the absence of alternative sources of labor in the short run. If the employer believes that there is no alternative but to buy labor at a price agreed with the union, this confers on the union the status of monopoly supplier of labor. A possible difference between the monopolistic firm and the trade union lies in the goals that they pursue. In economics it is widely assumed that the goal of the monopoly firm is to maximize profits; the goal of the union is a matter of debate. A profit maximizing firm is indifferent to the amount it has to sell to achieve this objective. The union is likely to be concerned about both price and quantity, that is wages and employment.

Competition can still exist even where labor supply is effectively controlled by trade unions. In Great Britain and to a smaller degree in the United States in recent years there has been increasing competition between trade unions to supply labor to newly establishing firms, and to represent workers in established areas of white collar employment. In the past, such competition for membership among unions was often prohibited by conventions that delineated the constituency from which each union could recruit. However, in the 1980s these conventions have come under increasing pressure so that over the long run there is now a small degree of competition between trade unions. This competition is largely confined to the long run because once a union has agreed to represent a group of employees, once it has been recognized by an

11. See the 'Symposium on public and private unionism', *op. cit.*
12. Freeman, R.B. and Medoff, J.L. (1984) *What do Unions Do?*, Basic Books, New York.

employer, there is no further competition: the union's 'contract' with the firm to represent the workers does not come up for renewal.

Union labor 'supply' curves

Does the existence of a trade union alter the shape and position of the labor supply curve when compared to that which would exist under competition? The answer is certainly yes. But can the objectives of unions in turn be depicted in terms of labor supply curves and if so how? This is not quite so clear. As a monopoly seller of labor the trade union negotiates or sets a price, the wage, for the labor it is selling: the wage is therefore endogenous. In contrast, when we describe a competitive labor supply curve, we detail the number of workers or hours supplied at given, exogenous wage rates.

In unionized markets union labor is supplied at the established wage and it is generally up to the firm to decide how much to buy. If, subsequently, the union does not like the employment consequences of the wage it has established it may try to re-open the bargaining process or set a new wage. The union will have in mind a set of preferred wage and employment combinations, each corresponding to a given level of labor demand. These combinations can be described as a set of points in price/quantity space which can be depicted as a union 'supply' curve. The shape that this 'supply' curve will take will again depend on union preferences.

Figure 7.3 contrasts the union 'supply' curve with that which would exist were labor supply competitive. The union supply curve, L_U^s, is depicted as kinked at the ruling, union negotiated, real wage W_U/P in the manner described by the union preference paths in Fig. 7.2. In general unions would appear to resist substantial reductions in the wage, in the face of a fall in demand, but withhold additional labor supply in the face of a rise in labor demand. These arguments are illustrated in the labor supply curve L_u^s. Where labor supply is competitive, more workers would have been willing to work at each of the union negotiated wage rates. The difference between labor supply under the two conditions is greatest at the highest wage rates. The competitive labor supply curve L_c^s in Fig. 7.3 is therefore suggested to be substantially more elastic at higher wage rates. Of course, without knowing the exact preferences of individuals in the absence of a union, we cannot say exactly how these two curves should be drawn but the above appear to be reasonable conjectures about the shape of the supply curve under the two conditions.

SOCIAL CONSTRAINTS ON LABOR SUPPLY

Individuals' tastes and preferences, together with the opportunities that confront them in the labor market, determine the amount of labor that they are willing to supply. However, these tastes and preferences are not formed in a vacuum. The competitive theory of labor markets is predicated on both a diversity of tastes, and opportunities, and consequent upon the former, the inability of individuals to act in concert. Yet

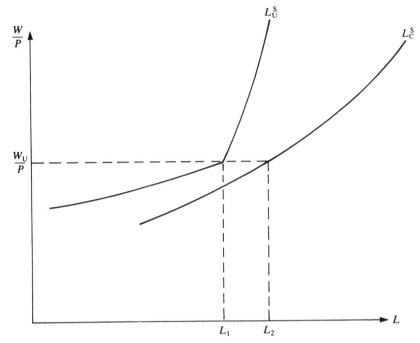

Figure 7.3 Competitive labor supply and labor supply under a trade union. The labor 'supply' curve in the presence of a union, L_U^S may be less elastic than the competitive labor supply curve, L_C^S, at wage rates above the existing wage rate W_U/P if unions restrict labor supply to enforce higher wages. However, it may be more elastic below the existing wage if unions seek again to protect wages at the expense of employment

there are powerful forces in society, social conventions and customs, that push individuals toward conformity, toward the adoption of common attitudes and common norms of behavior. Such forces can have a powerful effect; they can lead individuals to develop a common set of tastes and through their resulting actions, to substantially restrict competition in labor supply.

Pressures to adopt modes of behavior that are common to a group of individuals, to adopt group norms, are more important in some societies than in others. Thus Scandinavian societies are often described as relatively homogeneous, and are said to exhibit powerful pressures to conform, while the societies of the United States and the United Kingdom are frequently described as individualistic. 'Socialization' pressures have long been recognized by sociologists, but they have generally been given short shrift by economists. In two areas economic theory has however considered the role of social pressures in shaping individuals' tastes: concern over relative wages and concern about relative levels of consumption. Individuals' labor supply may be a function of their relative rather than their real wages as previously assumed. Why this should be so is not generally understood, but perhaps the most common explanation for concern over relative wages is that it reflects individuals' notions of fairness.

Fairness

The notion of fairness seems to exert a powerful influence over individuals. Individuals can be heard to comment on the fairness of their wages, and rewards in the labor market are evaluated according to whether or not they are fair. The call for a 'fair day's work for a fair day's pay' is often voiced. On the face of it therefore fairness would seem to be an important influence on labor supply. Less clear is what people regard as fair. Moreover the competitive outcome may be regarded as fair according to one interpretation of the notion. In competitive equilibrium equals, those with identical productive characteristics and tastes who supply labor under the same conditions, are rewarded equally. Conversely, where any of these aspects is different, a competitive equilibrium will result in unequal rewards—it will treat unequals, unequally. Yet, the notion of fairness is constantly contrasted with market outcomes and it is therefore evident that some individuals have other ideas in mind when they talk of fairness.

In a recent study two psychologists and an economist set out to discover community standards of fairness.[13] They confronted a sample of individuals with a number of hypothetical situations and analyzed their replies. They discovered that individuals consider transactions, such as an employer fixing a wage, to be fair or unfair, by reference either to another transaction occurring at the same time elsewhere or to previous transactions conducted between the same parties. Such *'reference transactions'* served as a precedent for judging the fairness of a transaction and gave rise to the belief that individuals had an entitlement to be treated no less well than occurred in the reference transaction. Importantly this was not because they regarded the reference transaction itself as fair but because they regarded the reference transaction as normal. What is normal of course changes as circumstances change so that the standard by which present actions were judged fair changed over time. This meant that the gap between outcomes regarded as fair and market outcomes diminished through time.

One consequence, of framing behavior with regard to the reference transaction, was that people's judgments about the fairness of situations changed only slowly. Individuals' attitudes, and with it their behavior, adapted slowly with the result that adaptation to short-term fluctuations in labor supply and demand was resisted, and the market cleared only slowly. It emerged that changes, in external circumstances which were unrelated to an individual's own enterprise and efforts, were not regarded as appropriate criteria for changing the treatment of individuals with regard to either wages or employment. An excess supply of labor would not be an appropriate reason for cutting wages.

Underpinning individuals' conceptions of fairness were certain features attested to in the psychological literature. When the costs resulting from a particular action were experienced as losses the outcomes were judged to be less fair, than when the costs were experienced in terms of forgone gains, in terms of opportunity costs. Economic theory makes no such distinction between costs but evidently individuals do. In this we can see support for the proposition that it is easier to gain acceptance of real wage

13. See Kahneman, D., Knetsch, J.L. and Thaler, R. (1986) 'Fairness as a constraint on profit seeking', *American Economic Review*, **76**(4), 728–41.

cuts if this results from prices rising in excess of money wages, rather than by cutting money wages. This psychological principle, that 'losses evoke greater aversion than objectively equivalent forgone gains' emerges as the most important from their studies. Less surprisingly it also emerged that outcomes were judged more or less fair according to the capacity of individuals to absorb any change. For example, it might be regarded as unfair to dismiss an older unskilled worker with few alternative job prospects although it might not be considered unfair to dismiss a younger skilled worker for whom finding another job would be no problem. Notions of fairness appeared to strongly influence market outcomes, largely by affecting the willingness of individuals to supply labor in particular market conditions. Individuals' notions of fairness affected their economic behavior.

How and why do individuals select the reference transactions that play such a pivotal role in their economic behavior? Psychological studies suggest that any stable state of affairs eventually comes to be accepted, if for no other reason than that alternatives to it no longer spring readily to mind. Persistence, and enforcement through repetition therefore become important determinants of the reference transaction. Even in the absence of these aspects individuals may still make use of reference transactions because of the existence of *bounded rationality*.[14] The notion of bounded rationality proposes that while individuals behave rationally, in the sense that the ordering of their preferences is complete, consistent and transitive, their ability to obtain and process information is bounded—it is limited by the computational capacity of the human mind. Research has shown that as tasks become more complicated individuals adopt simplifying decision-making strategies. The use of simplifying rules and heuristics becomes more common the more complex is the task.[15] Thus the reference transaction may serve as a summary outcome of a set of complicated interactions and its emulation acts as a useful guide to appropriate action. One such reference transaction may be the wages of other groups of workers or one's own wage in the past. We shall consider the consequences of such reference transactions for individuals' labor supply later in this chapter. First, consider another consequence of the notion of 'bounded rationality' which may affect labor market outcomes—the adoption by individuals of formal or informal rules of behavior.

Rules

Rules exist in all societies and play an important part in determining individuals' behavior and hence their labor supply. Some types of rules, which we shall call

14. This notion was first developed by Simon, H.A. (1957) *Models of Man: Social and Rational Mathematical Essays on Rational Human Behaviour in a Social Setting*, John Wiley, New York and 'Rationality as process and as product of thought', *American Economic Review*, **68**(2) May 1978, 1–16. Also see Williamson, O.E., Wachter, M.L. and Harris, J.E. (1975) 'Understanding the employment relation: the analysis of idiosyncratic exchange', *Bell Journal of Economics*, **6**, spring, 250–78, for an application of this idea.
15. See Russo, J.E. and Dasher, B. (1983), 'Strategies for multi-attribute choice', *Journal of Experimental Psychology: Memory, Learning and Cognition*, **9**, 676–96.

regulations, originate with government. Others are unwritten and take the form of social conventions; in the labor market they are often referred to as custom and practice. A rule offers a guide to behavior, in an economic context a guide to allocating scarce commodities, between competing ends. Rules assist in the process of choice, sometimes by prescribing certain choices. 'Rules-of-thumb' indicate ways of behaving, either in the context of less than perfect information, in consequence of the substantial costs associated with the collection and processing of information, or as a result of bounded rationality. Rules can be seen as ways of economizing on the resources required to reach a decision and, therefore, represent an alternative device to the market for allocating scarce commodities.

However, rules also impinge on market allocations. Social conventions may determine the amount of labor that individuals are willing to supply in particular circumstances. Thus orthodox Jews will not work on the Sabbath nor will members of the Free Church of Scotland work on Sunday. Religious beliefs and the rules of behavior they establish constitute a halfway house between the spontaneous social conventions that emerge in a society and the web of statutes and laws that control our behavior. An example of a social convention may be the British 'habit' that leads them to queue for buses. Other examples might be the conventions that proscribe women from certain jobs in coalmines or as public executioners and which until recently in Britain, also included the occupations of bus driver or bricklayer.

Such social conventions may initially have been founded in an objective appraisal of the facts, i.e. that coalmining constituted heavy manual labor that was beyond most women, and out of this grew a 'rule-of-thumb' which both women and coal-owners chose to adopt when choosing a career or hiring labor. However, as conditions change the objective facts that gave rise to these rules may cease to exist. Thus, mechanization has removed most of the heavy manual element from coalmining so that women could now, if they were not before, be equally productive as men. However, it is in the nature of social conventions that they live on beyond the change in objective circumstances. Rules will therefore continue to influence labor supply in conditions in which they are no longer appropriate. Social conventions are extremely important determinants of both the choice of careers and the number of hours that individuals are prepared to offer in any job. Where they prevent individuals from pursuing certain occupations they reduce the potential labor supply to that occupation. Where they set ceilings on hours they also reduce labor supply.

Rules of behavior, trade unions and notions of fairness combine. A trade union can be viewed as a powerful vehicle for implementing notions of fairness and for codifying these in a set of formal and informal rules. Trade unions may insure that notions of fairness become enshrined in custom and a network of informal rules which sometimes continue to operate after the initial rationale for them is past. An example is that trade unions promote the idea of a 'common rate for the job', of 'taking wages out of competition'. Trade unions emphasize relativities, that is they set the wage rate for one job by reference to the rate for a similar type of labor in other firms, regardless of the differing economic circumstances of the firms or the state of the product markets in which the firms operate.[16] Trade unions thus codify and institutionalize the reference transaction in a set of rules that influence labor market behavior.

Relative income and wages

The 'reference transaction' may be the wages of other groups of workers. Relative wages, relative income and relative consumption standards have all been proposed as of greater concern to individuals than the absolute levels of any of these. In consumer theory the relative income hypothesis argued that it was individuals' relative income and their relative consumption standards that determined their utility,[17] while others emphasized the importance of the individuals' relative position in the income distribution.[18]

Individual notions of poverty or of the minimum necessary subsistence income have also been shown to be defined in relative terms. Thus, asked 'what is the smallest amount of money a family of four needs to get along in this community?', respondents in the United States have over the years increased the required amount at roughly the same rate as the rise in national income. The average amount rose from $50 a week in 1950 to $177 a week in 1976. Expressed as a proportion, of the average disposable income for a family of four in the United States, it was 42.7 percent in 1950 and 42 percent in 1976![19] The relative nature of individual real income aspirations has naturally led researchers to question whether it might not be relative rather than real wages that determine individuals' labor supply. The outcomes of the collective bargaining process in many countries, which we shall analyze in Chapter 14, suggest substantial support for this proposition.

The possible form that such relative concerns take is described by *equity theory*. This proposes that in inter-personal exchange, individuals are concerned with the ratio of the perceived value of outcomes to inputs, and that they consider themselves to be fairly treated when this ratio is the same in their job as they perceive it to be elsewhere. If the outcome is the wage and the input labor supply, individuals will act to insure that this ratio is brought into line with that they perceive to hold in other jobs. Thus, if wages rise elsewhere and their own do not, they will reduce their labor input to re-establish the previous ratio and bring it back into line with that in other jobs.[20]

16. See Burton, J. and Addison, J.T. (1977) 'An institutionalist analysis of wage inflation : a critical survey', *Research in Labor Economics* vol. 1, pp. 333–76 and Elliott, R.F. (1976) 'The national wage round in the United Kingdom: a sceptical view', *Oxford Bulletin of Economics and Statistics*, **38**(3), 179–201 for a review of the evidence on wage patterns and wage rounds in the United States and the United Kingdom.
17. Duesenberry, J. (1949) *Income Saving and the Theory of Consumer Behavior*, Harvard University Press, Cambridge, Mass.
18. Scitovosky, T. (1976) *The Joyless Economy*, Oxford University Press and Thurow, L. (1975) *Generating Inequality*, Basic Books, New York.
19. Frank, R.H. (1985) *Choosing the Right Pond: Human Behavior and the Quest for Status*, Oxford University Press, New York, and Oxford.
20. See Akerlof, G. and Yellen, J. (1987) The fair wage effort hypothesis and unemployment, mimeo, University of California, Berkeley.

In the conventional model of labor supply the wages of workers in other jobs, which represent the opportunity wage, are the only comparisons that are relevant for the workers. The opportunity wage will be the wage paid in a restricted class of jobs for which the worker is qualified. However, in equity theory it is likely to be wages in a much wider class of jobs that constitute the reference transactions. These will include those jobs for which an individual is qualified but they are also likely to include those of co-workers, who possess different skills, and other highly visible occupations in the market.

How might such considerations be illustrated in a model of individual labor supply? Consider Fig. 7.4, which depicts individuals concerned about their relative income, that is relative weekly wages. Suppose there exists some wage rate, call this W^*, at which an individuals' weekly wage rate, W_i, is equal to that of their reference group, W_a. If they work H^* hours per week this is regarded as the fair wage. If individuals receive a relatively higher wage rate they consider themselves to be treated generously and, if the relative wage falls below the reference wage, they consider they are being unfairly treated.

Individuals' concern over relative weekly wages could result in the following pattern of preferences. Wage rates below W^*, which produce relatively low weekly wages result in sharp reductions in labor supply as individuals believe they are being unfairly treated and seek to restore the balance between inputs, hours of work, and outcomes of the wage. Above W^* individuals are less concerned to improve their relative income and take much of the rise in their relative wage rate in terms of additional leisure. Reactions to wages above and below the reference wage are asymmetric. In this case the indifference map would have the shape identified in Fig. 7.4(a) and the consequence of this is shown in Fig. 7.4(b). The result would be that at all wage rates below $W^* = W_i = W_a$ the labor supply curve would be relatively elastic but beyond that point it would be highly inelastic or even backward bending.

An alternative way of viewing the problem[21] is to suggest that individuals' utility depends on the difference between their present wage, W_i, and an aspiration or reference wage, W^*. Again W^* might be set by reference to the wage of some other group of workers, W_a, and in equilibrium $W_i = W_a$. Again there is an asymmetry in deviations of the individuals' wage from W^*. Thus a fall in W_i below W^* evokes a greater utility loss than an increase in W_i of equal magnitude above W^* evokes gain. The total utility function for an individual might therefore appear as in Fig. 7.5. One consequence of such a total utility function is that marginal utility is discontinuous at W^* and this could give rise to kinked union indifference curves such as shown in Fig. 7.2(c).

The essential difference, between the approaches above and conventional labor supply models, is that the utility of individual i is, in part, a function of the wages of the reference group a. The importance of relative wages in union pay negotiations is evidenced by 'pattern bargaining' and 'wage rounds'. The former was observed in the United States for much of the 1950s and 1960s and represented an attempt by unions

21. For a brief discussion of this notion see Oswald, A.J. (1986) 'Is wage rigidity caused by layoffs by seniority'? in Beckerman, W, (ed.), *Wage Rigidity and Unemployment*, Duckworth, London.

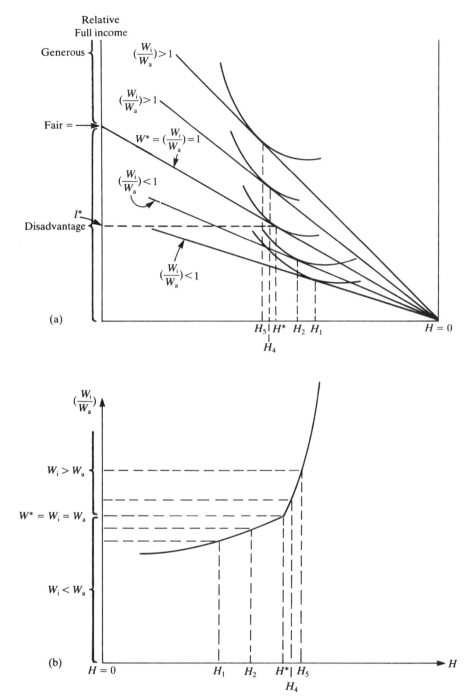

Figure 7.4 Labor supply is a function of the individual's wage relative to that of a comparator group. Relative wages and hours of work are the sources of utility for the individuals shown here. Hourly wage rate W^* is regarded as fair and at this wage the individual chooses to work H^* hours producing I^* income. If the wage rate falls below what individuals regard as fair, they cut back substantially their hours of work as illustrated by H_1 and H_2. At wage rates above W^* they regard themselves as generously paid, but this does not evoke a substantial increase in hours of work. The result is the labor supply curve shown in (b). Behavior is asymmetric with reference to the fair wage

208

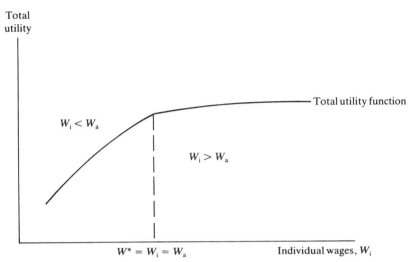

Figure 7.5 An individual's total utility reflects concern over relative wages. Individuals' utility may be a function of the difference between their own wage W_i and the reference wage W_a. If the reference wage W_a comes to be established as the current wage, W^*, subsequent reductions in an individual's wage lead to large reductions in utility. Asymmetric increases in an individual's relative wage, $W_i > W_a$, produce smaller increase in utility

to secure uniform pay levels and working conditions across a wide range of manufacturing industries. The latter was observed in the United Kingdom and was an attempt on the part of a large number of different bargaining groups to secure the same wage increases across a wide range of very different industries. We shall explore more fully the consequences of this behavior in our discussion on incomes policy in Chapter 14.

SUMMARY

In this chapter we have looked at the manner in which competition in the supply of labor is qualified and restricted in many labor markets. The first way in which this occurs, and the most studied case, is where a trade union organizes workers. We analyzed the degree of union control over labor supply in the United States and the United Kingdom and found that this was much more pronounced in the latter than in the former. In order to understand the consequences of this, for labor supply, we need to know something about the preferences and tastes that inform policy and the manner in which union policy is formed. We therefore looked at a variety of different union preference functions and in detail at one model of union government, the median voter model.

A second major qualification to competition in labor supply results from social constraints. Individuals' behavior is governed by notions of fairness. The fairness or otherwise of a situation, or a wage, appeared to be determined by the difference between the current situation, or wage, and an 'aspiration' or 'reference' level of each of these. One explanation for this behavior is that individuals select reference transactions as a way of economizing on the resources they would otherwise have to devote to processing information. Similarly, the rules which govern individuals' labor supply could reflect individuals' desire to economize on the use of the scarce resource time as well as limited cognitive and processing capacity. Such considerations will likely give rise to concern over relative rather than real wages and labor supply curves reflecting such arguments were therefore detailed. It would seem that much labor is supplied under less than competitive conditions in the modern economy. Qualifications to competition in labor supply appear to be substantial.

PRINCIPAL CONCEPTS

In this chapter we have developed the following concepts and notions. Students should insure that they understand their meaning and their application in the context of labor market analysis, before proceeding to the next chapter.

1. The median voter.
2. Principals and agents.
3. Union preference curves.
4. Closed shops and the union shop.
5. Concepts of fairness in the labor market.
6. Reference transactions and aspiration wages.
7. Equity theory.
8. Rules of behavior and 'rules-of-thumb'.
9. Bounded rationality.

QUESTIONS FOR DISCUSSION

1. How adequately does the median voter model identify the manner in which union preferences are formed?
2. Give examples of union policies which might arise when the median voter model represents an appropriate description of the formulation of union policy.
3. Why might a union prefer to take a fall in employment rather than a fall in wages in the face of a reduction in labor demand?
4. How do unions exercise control over labor supply? What is the magnitude of such control in the United Kingdom and the United States?
5. Can we only understand the objectives of unions by reference back to the underlying preferences of individual union members?
6. How might we explain the notions of fairness to which individuals subscribe in labor markets?
7. Why do rules govern individuals' behavior in labor markets?

8. Are workers concerned about relative wages and, if so, what are the consequences of such concern?

9. Give examples of social conventions that restrict competition in labor supply.

FURTHER READING

In this chapter we have touched on areas of fundamental importance, some of which do not normally figure in textbook discussions of labor supply. However, there is a wide and diverse literature which the reader can access.

The notion of bounded rationality originates with Herbert Simon and it is stimulating to read *Models of Man: Social and Rational Mathematical Essays on Rational Human Behavior in a Social Setting*, John Wiley, New York. Arrow, K.J. (1974) *The Limits of Organization*, Norton, New York, provides a general and interesting discussion of the role of the invisible 'institutions' of moral principles in allocating scarce resources between competing uses. The reader might also like to consult Kahneman, D., Slovic, P. and Tversky, A. (1982) *Judgement under Uncertainty: Heuristics and Biases*, Cambridge University Press, London and Hogarth, R.M. and Reder, M.W. (1987) *Rational Choice: The Contrast between Economics and Psychology*, University of Chicago, Chicago, which explore respectively the way in which people judge and react to uncertain events and the assumptions of rationality underlying economic theory. I was fortunate when completing this chapter to have the opportunity to read the manuscript of a forthcoming book, *The Labor Market Under Trade Unionism: Employment, Wages and Work Hours* by John Pencavel. Chapter 3 provides an excellent analysis of trade union objectives and is strongly recommended.

PART 3

LABOR DEMAND

In Part 3 we consider the demand for labor, we focus on the other half of the labor market and consider the determinants of the amount of labor that firms wish to buy. Initially we assume that labor is a variable factor of production and that the price of labor is the wage rate. Firms can simply vary their output by varying the amount of labor they employ. Such an assumption underpins the earliest versions of the neoclassical theory of labor demand and it is this theory on which we focus in Chapter 8. In this chapter we look at the demand for labor in the short and the long run and distinguish the manner in which demand curves differ between the firm and the industry. We develop measures of the elasticity of labor demand and reveal the most important determinants of this.

The last 20 years have seen a substantial increase in the fixed costs of employing labor. Firms, wanting to take on additional labor, are, in many cases, now faced with substantial one-off costs and these fundamentally affect their demand for labor. A consequence is that, in many jobs, labor can no longer be regarded as a variable factor of production. For the firm the decision to employ labor is analogous to an investment decision. It requires an appraisal of the benefits and costs, which now accrue over a number of time periods, to determine whether the firm should expand employment. In many cases it is cheaper for the firm to offer additional payments to its existing workforce, to induce them to work longer or harder, than it is to recruit additional workers. Incumbents and those outside the firm no longer compete on equal terms for many jobs. In Chapter 9 we turn to consider this important dimension of labor demand. We assess the magnitude and explore the consequences of fixed labor costs.

8

THE DEMAND FOR LABOR

In the nineteenth century the theory of the demand for labor was advanced as *the* theory of the determination of wages. It took Marshall to remind his contemporaries that:

> Demand and supply exert co-ordinate influences on wages; neither has a claim to predominance; any more than has either blade of a pair of scissors, or either pier of an arch. (A. Marshall (1890) *Principles of Economics*, p. 442 Macmillan, London.)

The theory we develop here is that underpinning the second blade of the scissors. Together with an appropriate labor supply function the labor demand function will describe the labor market, and the intersection of the two functions will determine the equilibrium level of employment and wages. The central question we address here is what is the shape of the labor demand curve? Does a lower wage rate mean more labor will be employed?

In the following pages we develop at some length the formal theory of the demand for labor, first in the short and then in the long run. The short run is defined as a period in which labor is the only variable factor of production, while the long run is defined as the period during which all factors of production are variable. In both periods we distinguish between the firm and the industry, for the elasticity will be different in each case. It is the elasticity of labor demand and the determinants of this that are of greatest interest, and we shall consider the magnitude of the elasticity when we consider the empirical evidence on labor demand.

215

THE FIRM'S LABOR DEMAND CURVE IN THE SHORT RUN

The demand for labor is a derived demand, a demand derived from that for the final product which labor cooperates to produce. Firms demand labor because it is an input into the production process and they produce in order to make profits. The ultimate reason why firms demand labor is because it is profitable to do so. Precisely how much labor firms demand depends on a number of factors. First, the technical nature of the production process as reflected in the production function; second, the revenue that results from selling the output of labor; and, finally, the prices of the factors of production. We consider each of these aspects in turn, starting with the nature of the production process.

The nature of the production process

The production function is a mapping of the exact relationship between a firm's inputs and its output. Thus, typically,

$$Q_i = f(L_i, K_i, T_i)$$

where Q_i represents the output of firm i and L_i, K_i, and T_i are inputs of labor, capital and the state of technical knowledge, respectively. Assuming, for simplicity, that there are only two inputs, labor and capital, or that any others are fixed, the production function may be illustrated as a family of different isoquants, an isoquant map, as in Fig. 8.1. Quantities of labor and capital are mapped along the horizontal and vertical axes respectively, and each isoquant represents a unique level of output achieved by combining labor and capital in different proportions. Thus in Fig. 8.1(a) at point A we are able to produce output level Q_0 by combining K_1 capital with L_1 labor. This is a relatively capital intensive method of production, for many more units of capital, than units of labor, are used. At B the same output, Q_0 is produced by relatively labor intensive methods, combining K_2 with L_2, and at C the method is even more labor intensive.

The slope of the isoquants is given by dK/dL when Q is constant and where the d's represent infinitesimally small changes in the quantities of labor and capital employed. The isoquants have a negative slope, are convex to the origin, and record successively higher quantities of output as we move to the north-east. The negative slope suggests that K and L are substitutable to some degree. The rate at which one input can be substituted for another is reflected in the slope of the isoquants. The *marginal rate of technical substitution (MRTS)* between the factors of production, tells us, for a given production technology, the rate at which labor must be substituted for capital in order to maintain a constant level of output. It is defined as (the negative of) the slope of the isoquant. Thus:

$$MRTS = -\frac{dK/Q}{dL/Q} \text{ or } -\frac{dK}{dL}\bigg|_{Q \text{ is constant}} \tag{8.1}$$

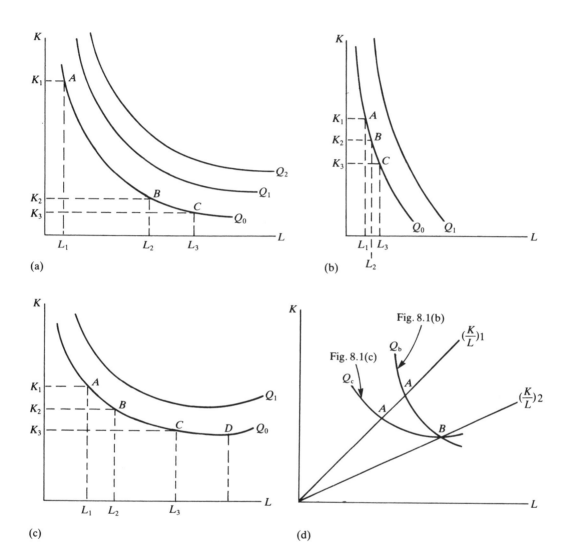

Figure 8.1 Differences in levels of output and in the marginal rate of technical substitution. (a), (b) and (c) show three differently shaped 'families' of isoquants. The different slopes of the isoquants reflect differences in the *MRTS*, the rate at which labor must be substituted for capital in order to maintain a constant level of output. Note that between points *A* and *C* the *MRTS* is greater in (b) than in (c). Capital is more essential to production in (c) than it is in (b), for if we reduce the input of capital from K_2 to K_3 in each case we require a larger increment to labor in (c) if output is to be maintained at level Q_0. (d) Compares the isoquants in (b) and (c). The move from point *A* to point *B* involves the same change in the capital/labor ratio in each case. However, the percentage change in the *MRTS* is different as the different slopes of the isoquants suggest. Accordingly, the elasticity of substitution is smaller in (c) than in (b)

If, for example, output remained constant when we increased our use of labor by one unit and cut our inputs of capital by one unit then the slope of the isoquant would be − 1 and the isoquant would be a straight line of slope − 1 to the L axis reflecting the fact that labor and capital were perfect substitutes. Indeed any straight line isoquant has a constant *MRTS*. This is clearly not the case with the isoquants we have drawn for they are convex, and therefore imply a diminishing marginal rate of technical substitution. They are drawn to reflect the fact that as we move from B to C in Figs. 8.1(a) to (c), further reducing the small amount of capital we had at B, we require a larger input of labor in order to keep output constant.[1] The more labor we already have the less is each additional unit of labor a satisfactory substitute for a unit of capital.[2]

The isoquants shown in Figs. 8.1(b) and (c) are quite different although both exhibit a diminishing *MRTS*. In both cases, as we move from point A to B and then to point C, we require successively larger inputs of labor to compensate for the reduction in the quantity of capital, while insuring that output remains constant. However, in Fig. 8.1(c) we require much larger increases in labor input, for any given reduction in capital input, than we do in Fig. 8.1(b): the *MRTS* is smaller in Fig. 8.1(c) than it is in Fig. 8.1(b). Labor is less productive in Fig. 8.1(c) and capital is more essential to production. Accordingly, the ease with which output can be maintained while substituting labor for capital is less in Fig. 8.1(c) than it is in Fig. 8.1(b). Note also that just beyond point D, in Fig. 8.1(c), further increases in labor input actually detract from output. Additional units of labor have to be combined with *additional* units of

---

1. Note that with the numerator, dK, falling and the denominator, dL, rising the absolute value of the *MRTS* is falling (as we move round the isoquant the *MRTS* falls).
2. This last statement means that the productivity of a unit of labor, the marginal product of labor, MP_L, is falling the more labor we already employ. It can be shown that the MRTS is equal to the ratio of the marginal product of capital, MP_K, to the marginal product of labor. For the more mathematically minded this can be done by setting up the total differential of the production function, which reveals the magnitude of the change in Q consequent upon a change in both L and K where dL and dK respectively measure the magnitude of these changes. Thus

$$dQ = MP_L \times dL + MP_K \times dK$$

Since along any isoquant dQ = 0 (output is constant) then

$$- MP_L \times dL = MP_K \times dK$$

that is the output gain by increasing K is exactly offset by the ouput lost by decreasing L. Upon rearranging this gives

$$\frac{MP_L}{MP_K} = - \frac{dK}{dL}$$

which in turn, from Eq. (8.1), gives

$$- \frac{dK}{dL}\bigg|_{Q \text{ is constant}} = \frac{MP_L}{MP_K} = MRTS$$

It also follows from the above that since both MP_L and MP_K will be positive (no firm would choose to operate where either marginal product was negative) the *MRTS* will also be positive, and because the negative of the *MRTS* is the slope of the isoquant, the slopes of those isoquants we observe must be negative. `

capital if output is to be maintained. No rational firm would operate in this region, known as the non-economic region, and therefore we can ignore it.

A measure of the 'ease' with which labor can be substituted for capital and therefore of the difference between the isoquants in Figs. 8.1(b) and 8.1(c) is the *elasticity of substitution*, σ. It measures the relative responsiveness of the capital/labor ratio to given proportional changes in the *MRTS* and is defined as the percentage change in the capital/labor ratio, K/L, divided by the percentage change in the *MRTS*.

$$\text{Elasticity of substitution} = \sigma = \frac{d(K/L)/(K/L)}{d(MRTS)/MRTS} \tag{8.2}$$

Consider the two isoquants, Q_c and Q_b from Figs. 8.1(c) and 8.1(b) respectively, which are reproduced in Fig. 8.1(d). The K/L ratio at any point is measured by the slope of a line from the origin and the change in the K/L ratio by the move from $(K/L)_1$ to $(K/L)_2$. As we move from point A to point B on each isoquant the change in the K/L ratio, and hence the numerator in Eq. (8.2), is the same for both the isoquants shown. However, it will be clear from our earlier discussion that the percentage change in the *MRTS* is different in each case. The change is relatively greater in the case of the isoquant from Fig. 8.1(c), in which the *MRTS* was smallest, than it is for the isoquant from Fig. 8.1(b). Hence the value of σ is smaller in the case of Fig. 8.1(c) than it is in Fig. 8.1(b), reflecting the greater 'difficulty' of substitution in the former case.[3]

The marginal product of labor

In the short run, with capital fixed, if we wish to increase output we have to increase our use of labor. This is illustrated in Fig. 8.2 in which K^* is the fixed capital stock. In order to move from Q_0 to Q_1 we must increase our use of labor by the proportion OL_1/OL_0 and in order to move to Q_2 from Q_1 we must increase our use of labor by the proportion OL_2/OL_1, etc. As we move along the ray K^* each successive isoquant that we cut has a shallower slope until in the limit we just reach isoquant Q_5. The shallower slope of each successive isoquant means that, *ceteris paribus*, the distance between any two isoquants must be increasing, and hence successively larger increments of labor are required to increase output by equal amounts. However, all other things are not equal. The returns to scale characteristics of the production function can overwhelm this effect over some range. In Fig. 8.2 the production function displays first increasing, then constant and finally decreasing returns to scale. In consequence the returns to—the addition to output consequent upon the use of more—labor, first increase up to Q_2, are then constant and finally decrease somewhere from Q_3 onwards.

The addition to output that results from the employment of one extra unit of labor, is called the marginal product of labor (MP_L).

$$MP_L = dQ/dL \tag{8.3}$$

---

3. Mathematically it can be shown that σ is inversely related to the curvature of the isoquant hence the smaller value of σ in Fig. 8.1(c) reflects the greater curvature of the isoquants here.

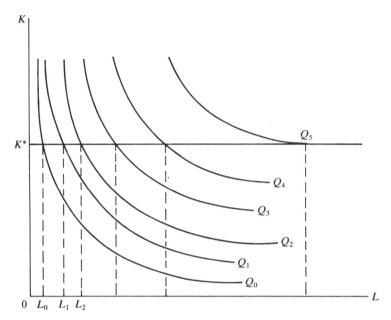

Figure 8.2 A short-run expansion path. Capital K^* is fixed and output can only be increased by increasing labor input, L. Despite the successively shallower slopes of the isoquants, cut by the ray K^*, the increments to output, resulting from employing additional units of labor, may still increase over some range. This will occur where the returns to scale characteristics of the production function overwhelm the effects of the diminishing $MRTS$

In Fig. 8.2 the *total output* produced by adding successive increments of labor to our given capital stock, K^*, first increases at an increasing rate and then increases at a decreasing rate until output reaches a peak at Q_5. This relationship between total output and labor input is shown in Fig. 8.3, in which we reproduce the total product of labor curve (TP_L), the curve that maps out changes in total output resulting from increasing the use of the variable factor, labor.

The slope of the short-run total product curve reflects the returns to scale characteristics of the production function and the $MRTS$; it reflects both the position and the slope of the isoquants. From such a total output curve we can derive the associated marginal and average product of labor curves. The average product of labor $AP_L = Q/L$ and is therefore measured by taking the slope of a ray from the origin to any point on the TP_L curve. At point A, $AP_L = Q_2/L_2$ and at point B, $AP_L = Q_3/L_3$. Note that the slope of any line drawn from the origin to a point on the total product curve is increasing up to point B. Hence up to point B, the AP_L is increasing. At point B, AP_L is at a maximum and after that point the AP_L is declining. This suggests an AP_L curve of the shape shown in Fig. 8.3(b) which is drawn immediately below Fig. 8.3(a) to show the correspondence of the TP_L, AP_L and MP_L curves.

Now consider the marginal product of labor, $MP_L = dQ/dL$ and it is therefore given by the slope of the TP_L line in Fig. 8.3. The MP_L is given by the slope of a line drawn

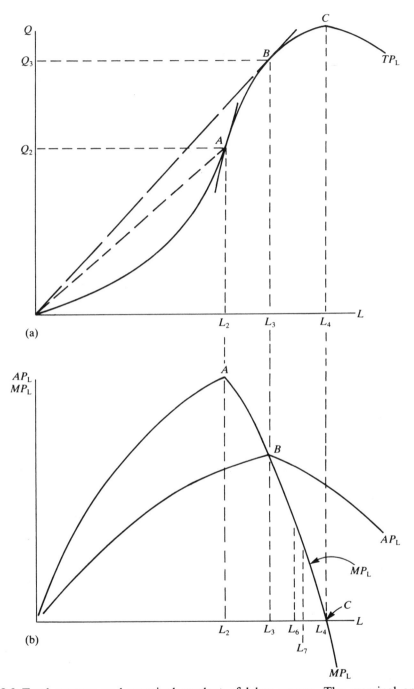

Figure 8.3 Total average and marginal product of labor curves. The marginal and average product of labor curves in (b) corresponds to the total product curve in (a). At the inflection point A, MP_L is at a maximum, thereafter it decreases until at L_4, where total output is at a maximum, $MP_L = 0$. At point B the $MP_L = AP_L$

tangent to any point on the TP_L line. From Fig. 8.3(a) it is evident that the slope of the TP_L line is increasing up to point A, the inflection point, but thereafter up to point C while the slope is still positive it is decreasing in value. At point A a line drawn tangent to the curve has a steeper slope than any line drawn from the origin. Hence at point A the MP_L has a value higher than any attained by the AP_L curve. At point B a line drawn tangent to the TP_L curve has the same value as a ray drawn from the origin so that at B the $AP_L = MP_L$, but beyond B, up to C, any tangent drawn to the TP_L curve has a shallower slope, is of a smaller magnitude, than a ray from the origin, so that in this region the $MP_L < AP_L$. Beyond C the $AP_L > 0$ but $MP_L < 0$ for the TP curve has a negative slope. The AP_L and MP_L curves are drawn in Fig. 8.3(b) to reflect these relationships and correspond directly to the shape of the total product curve in Fig. 8.3(a).

The position of the average and marginal product curves depends on the amount of capital employed. This is illustrated in Fig. 8.4. If the capital stock were K_1 instead of K_0 we should no longer be able to reach Q_0 with labor input L_0 nor Q_1 with L_1, etc. A given quantity of labor is producing a smaller quantity of output and accordingly the total produce curve for K_1 lies below that associated with K_0. Again the average and marginal product of labor curves associated with K_1 would lie inside those associated

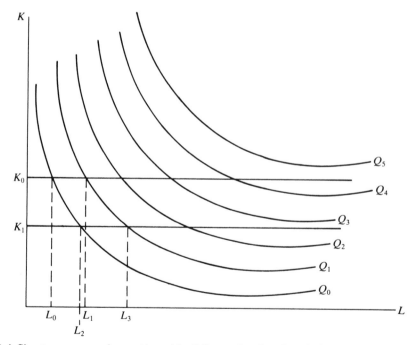

Figure 8.4 Short-run expansion paths with different levels of capital stock. If the capital stock is reduced from K_0 to K_1 more labor will be required to produce any given level of output. For example Q_0 can no longer be produced using L_0 amount of labor, it now takes L_2. Similarly, Q_1 can no longer be produced using L_1, it now requires an input of L_3 units

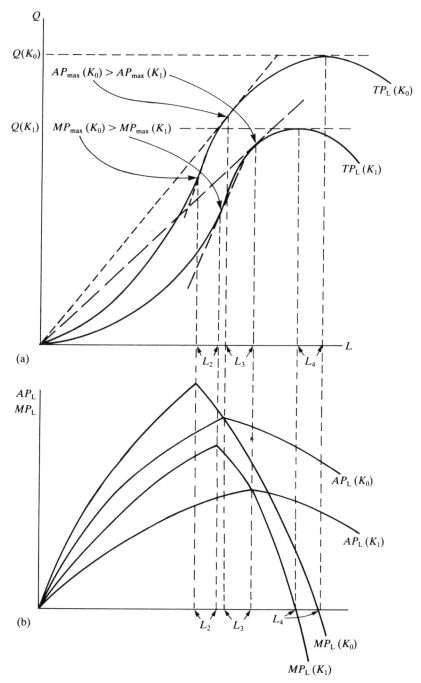

Figure 8.5 The effect of changes in the size of the capital stock on the total, average and marginal product of labor curves. Higher marginal and average product curves are associated with the larger capital stock $K_0 > K_1$. The marginal and average curves are derived in the same way as shown in Figure 8.3

with K_0 as illustrated in Figs. 8.5(a) and (b). At its peak the output produced by K_1 would be lower than that produced by K_0, $Q(K_0) > Q(K_1)$. Since it would take more labor to reach any given level of output the AP curve for K_1 would lie below that for K_0 and would reach its (lower) peak at a higher level of L. Similarly, the MP_L curve for K_1 would lie below that for K_0 and would reach its (lower) peak at a higher level of L. These features of the two curves are detailed in Figs. 8.5(a) and (b). It is evident from these that the marginal product of labor, often referred to as 'the productivity of labor', is lower the lower is the capital stock. The marginal product of labor, as reflected in the position of the MP_L, schedule, is also determined by the size of the capital stock.

A number of important conclusions emerge from this analysis. The MP_L, the amount of output produced by any single additional unit of labor, depends on: first, the nature of the production function, the position and slope of the isoquants; second, the size of the capital stock; and third the number of previous units of labor employed. Thus is Fig. 8.3 the unit of labor L_6 is more productive, has a higher marginal product than L_7 not because L_7 is any less diligent or hardworking than L_6 but because, before L_7 was employed, all the other units of labor employed, up to and including L_6, had more capital at their disposal. The employment of L_7 meant that the available capital was spread more thinly among the workers. In this simple model all workers are assumed to be equally as hard working and diligent but this does not mean they are equally productive. They may add less to output than their predecessors, simply because they have less capital with which to work.

The marginal revenue product of labor

The firm is concerned not just with how much output a worker produces but also with the price obtained for this output when it is sold in the product market. The price the firm obtains will depend on whether the firm is a price taker—a perfectly competitive firm—or a price maker—a monopoly—in the product market. In the former case the firm faces a perfectly elastic demand curve for its product, this means that the price, P, equals the average revenue, AR, which in turn equals the marginal revenue, MR. The firm can sell all it wants at the prevailing price. In contrast, a monopoly has to lower the price of its output if it wants to sell more for the demand curve facing the firm is the market demand curve. In this latter case P does not equal MR, and the schedule describing MR lies below the average revenue schedule.[4] The change in

---

4. The precise relationship between price and MR can be found in the following way. First write the inverse form of the demand function, $P = f(Q)$, where $f'(Q) < 0$. Total revenue PQ is therefore $Qf(Q)$, and

$$MR = d(PQ)/dQ = f(Q) + Qf'(Q) \qquad (8.4a)$$

Now price elasticity of demand, η:

$$\eta = -\frac{dQ}{dP} \times \frac{P}{Q} = -\frac{1}{f'(Q)} \times \frac{P}{Q} = -\frac{P}{f'(Q)Q} \qquad (8.4b)$$

Now since $MR = f(Q) + Qf'(Q)$ and $P = f(Q)$ we can multiply the last term on the right-hand side of Eq. (8.4b) by P/P and then factor out P from the right-hand side to obtain:

$$MR = P\left[1 + \frac{Qf'(Q)}{P}\right] \text{ which gives } MR = P\left[1 + \frac{1}{\eta}\right] \qquad (8.4c)$$

revenue that results from selling the output produced by employing an additional unit of labor will therefore differ between these two market types. In both cases the addition to revenue, resulting from selling the product of the last unit of labor employed, can be found by multiplying MP_L by MR, but only in the competitive case can this also be done by multiplying MP_L by P, for only in this case does $P = MR$. The marginal revenue product of labor is defined as

$$MRP_L = MP_L \times MR \qquad (8.4)$$

We shall use the expression the marginal revenue product to describe the addition to revenue resulting from the sale of the output produced by the last unit of labor employed in both the competitive and monopolistic case. Sometimes, and indeed originally, the term value marginal product, VMP_L, was used for the competitive case with the term MRP_L being reserved for the monopolistic case, but this practice is now less common. The marginal revenue product of labor thus represents the change in the firm's total revenue, consequent upon the sale of the output produced by the last unit of labor employed. MRP_L tells us the revenue that the firm earns from the last worker it employs. Graphically the marginal, average and total revenue product curves can be constructed in the case of a perfectly competitive firm by simply multiplying the marginal, average and total product curves shown in Fig. 8.3 by the price of output, P. Evidently the shape of the resulting TRP_L, ARP_L and MRP_L curves will be the same for we are simply multiplying through by a constant. Thus the shape of the revenue curves is dictated by the shape of the corresponding product curves. In the monopolist's case the revenue curves are derived from the same shaped product curves but they will now differ from those under perfect competition for there is an additional force at work. In the monopolist case the MRP_L curve slopes down to the right, *both* because the MP_L declines as employment is increased *and* because MR declines as output expands. We should therefore expect the MRP_L curve for a monopolistic industry to decline more sharply than would have been the case had the industry product market been competitive.

The labor demand curve

Having detailed the construction of the firm's marginal revenue product of labor curve, MRP_L, we are now in a position to describe the labor demand curve. A profit maximizing firm is concerned to equate marginal cost, MC, to marginal revenue, MR. Assume, for simplicity, that it purchases labor in a perfectly competitive labor market. The firm faces a perfectly elastic supply curve of labor and the marginal cost of employing an extra unit of labor is the wage rate. In this case $MC = W$ and since $MR = MRP_L$ the rule for profit maximization reduces to ensuring that $W = MRP_L$. In Fig. 8.6 we describe an MRP_L curve and a perfectly elastic labor supply curve at W_1.

The above arguments enable us to identify how much labor the firm will wish to employ at each wage rate, that is to identify the firm's labor demand curve. At W_1 the

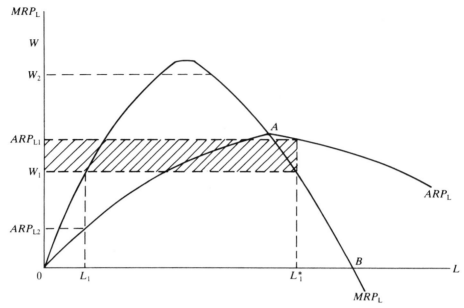

Figure 8.6 The firm's labor demand curve in the short run. The profit maximizing firm will equate *MR* to *MC* subject to *AR* > *AC*. In labor market terms this means that the profit maximizing firm takes employment up to the point at which $MRP_L = W$, subject to the ARP_L > *W*. These conditions are satisfied at W_1 and at all points between *A* and *B* on the MRP_L curve

firm will wish to employ L_1^* units of labour.[5] At this point $W_1 = MRP_L$ and the firm is earning profits equal to the shaded area above W_1 but below ARP_{L1} multiplied by OL_1^* units of labor. The average revenue the firm receives from selling the output of labour OL_1^*, is ARP_{L1} while the average cost it incurs to produce OL_1^* is the wage W_1.

5. This result can be shown by simple maths as follows. The short-run production function takes the form

$$Q = f(L) \tag{8.5a}$$

The marginal product of labor is accordingly $dQ/dL = f'(L)$. The profit function is

$$\pi = TR - TC \tag{8.5b}$$

If the producer operates in perfectly competitive product and labor markets then the market price of output, *P*, and the wage rate, *W*, are given and therefore $TR = PQ$ and $TC = WL$. Incorporating these into Eq. (8.5b) and combining this with Eq. (8.5a) gives

$$\pi = Pf(L) - WL \tag{8.5c}$$

The profit function is at a maximum where $d\pi/dL = 0$ and is therefore found by differentiating Eq (8.5c) with respect to labor input and setting the result equal to 0. That is:

$$\frac{d\pi}{dL} = Pf'(L) - W = 0 \tag{8.5d}$$

which can be rearranged to show that: $Pf'(L) = W$. Therefore profits are maximized where the marginal product of labor is equal to the wage rate.

The above represents the first order, or necessary, condition for a profit maximum. The sufficient condition is found by further differentiating Eq. (8.5d) to give

$$\frac{d^2\pi}{dL^2} = Pf''(L) < 0$$

Hence the total revenue it earns is $OL_1^* \times ARP_{L1}$, the total cost is $OL_1^* \times W_1$ and total profits are therefore $OL_1^* (ARP_{L1} - W_1)$.[6]

The coordinates W_1, L_1^* identify one point on the labor demand curve. Yet another point may be identified by considering that part of the MRP_L which lies above the maximum of the ARP_L curve. At W_2, W may still equal MRP_L but now the wage exceeds the ARP_L, and the firm would be making losses. Clearly firms will not demand labor at wages in excess of the maximum of the ARP_L and therefore the relevant section of the MRP_L curve is that section, below the maximum of the ARP_L curve but above the horizontal axis. The distance A to B in Fig. 8.6 constitutes the firm's short-run demand for labor curve. It identifies the amounts of labor that the firm would like to employ in the short run at different levels of the wage rate.[7]

This conclusion is premised on the assumption that the wage appropriately represents the marginal cost of employing an extra unit of labor. In Chapter 9 we shall argue that such an assumption may no longer be appropriate in many modern contexts. In particular, where the additional units of labor represent additional workers rather than, say, hours, the firm may be confronted by costs additional to the wage every time it takes on another employee. In this case we shall need to modify the analysis of labor demand and we do this in Chapter 9.

6. Note that at wage W_1 employment beyond L_1^* detracts from profits for now, $W > MRP_L$, and each extra unit of labor employed is costing more in wage than it is adding to revenue. At points below L_1^* each additional unit of labor adds more to revenue than it does to costs and so it pays to increase employment. Note that W also equals MRP_L, at L_1 but that at his point W exceeds ARP_L. Were the firm to operate at this point it would make losses equal to the area $OL_1 (W_1 - ARP_{L2})$. Thus while $W = MRP_L$ is a necessary condition for profit maximization it is not sufficient. The sufficient condition requires that $ARP_L > W$. It is more usual to state this sufficient condition in terms of the second derivative of the profit function as shown in the previous footnote.

7. The theory of efficiency wages, which we shall encounter more fully in Chapter 11, suggests that an individual's output is positively related to his or her wage. One approach to conceptualizing this is to imagine that each individual embodies a given number of 'efficiency units' and it is these which are traded in the labor market. Efficiency wage theory proposes that a rise in the wage induces a greater supply of efficiency units over some range. The notion of efficiency wages was first proposed by Alfred Marshall, *Principles of Economics*, Book VI, Chapter III, 'The earnings of labor'. One way of accommodating such a notion into the theory developed here is to relabel the horizontal axis in Fig. 8.6 so that is measures the quantity of labor in terms of efficiency units. Equilibrium then obtains where the marginal cost of the last efficiency unit purchased, the wage per efficiency unit, is equal to the marginal revenue product generated by that efficiency unit. For most purposes, however, this refinement is ignored and theory is constructed under the assumption that, within the classes of homogeneous labor on which we focus our analysis, each individual embodies the same number of efficiency units. In which case since, in equilibrium, there will be no unexploited gains to be made from paying higher wages the marginal revenue product of labor curve will continue to represent the labor demand curve.

It is interesting to note that although developing the notion of 'efficiency wages' Marshall did so to emphasize the equalizing tendencies of competition. 'The tendency then of economic freedom and enterprise (or in more common phrase, of competition) to cause everyone's earnings to find their own level, is a tendency to equality of *efficiency earnings* in the same district' (*op. cit.*, VI, III 2). It was left to Hicks (1932), *Theory of Wages*, to propose that 'higher wages may react favourably on a man's efficiency in several ways' (Ch. 5, Part II).

THE INDUSTRY AND MARKET LABOR DEMAND CURVE IN THE SHORT RUN

The industry demand for labor is found by aggregating the demands of all the firms in an industry. Where a single industry is the sole employer of a particular class of labor this will also constitute the market demand for labor, but where that class of labor is employed in more than one industry the market demand is found by aggregating across all industries that employ that particular type of labor. Policemen and judges are examples of industry-specific skills but the majority of individuals possess skills that are in demand for use in more than one industry. Thus the services of electricians, draughtsmen, clerks, truck drivers, software analysts, finance directors and accountants, to name but a few, are in demand by a large number of industries. For these particular types of labor the market demand stretches beyond a single industry and comprises an aggregation of several different industries.

Moving from the firm to the industry has one important consequence. In the process of aggregating we can no longer assume, even where the product market is perfectly competitive, that changes in output will have no effect on product price. Each industry, as distinct from the firms that comprise the industry, faces a downward sloping demand curve. If all the firms in an industry employ more labor and increase production the consequence will be a fall in product price. These arguments are illustrated in Fig. 8.7.

Figure 8.7 details the MRP_L curve for a representative firm in industry A. Suppose that there are 1000 such firms in this industry and at the outset, with the wage at W_0,

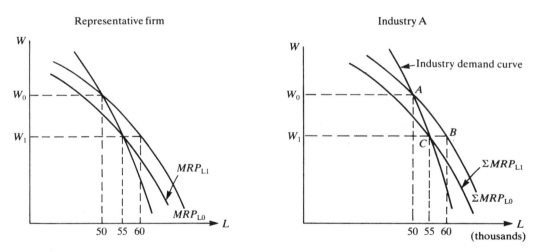

Figure 8.7 The short-run industry demand curve for labor. A competitive industry comprises a large number of identical firms, in this case 1000. Confronted by a fall in the wage rate from W_0 to W_1 each firm in the industry moves to employ more labor and produce more output. However, when this output comes to the market product price falls from P_0 to P_1. This displaces each firm's MRP_L curve to the left, with the result that ΣMRP_{L1} lies to the left of ΣMRP_{L0}. The industry demand curve for labor now comprises the locus of points A and C on these curves

they each demand and employ 50 people, giving a total industry demand of 50 000 people. Now suppose that the wage rate falls to W_1, each firm seeks to expand production and to employ more labor, they move down the existing MRP_L curve, labeled MRP_{L0} and employ, say, 60 people. Thus the industry demand for labor at the new wage, and the existing product price, is for 60 000 people and is illustrated by a move down ΣMRP_{L0} from A to B. Yet, of course, if all firms in an industry employed more labor and produced more output the product price would fall. In the product market the supply curve would shift outwards and the consequent fall in product price would result in a downward displacement of the horizontal (product) demand curve facing each firm in the industry. Now each unit of output produced by labor would sell for a lower price than before and hence the marginal revenue product of labor would fall. This is reflected in a downward shift in the MRP_{L0} curve of our typical firm to MRP_{L1}. Now it employs, say, 55 and not 60 people as it would have done before the price of output fell. There emerges a new ΣMRP_L for the industry, ΣMRP_{L1}, comprising the sum of each of the MRP_{L1} curves and indicating that at W_1 industry labor demand is now for 55 000 units.

It would be wrong to call either this new curve ΣMRP_{L1}, or its predecessor ΣMRP_{L0}, the industry demand curve. Each curve only identified points on the true industry labor demand curve, for each of them was drawn under the assumption that the final product price did not change. While this assumption was appropriate for the individual firm, it was untenable at the level of the industry. The industry labor demand curve is therefore found by joining points A and C on ΣMRP_{L0} and ΣMRP_{L1} respectively, and is evidently steeper than either of the MRP_L curves that underpin it.[8]

If the demand for a particular type of labor extends beyond a single industry, the sum of the several industry labor demand curves that together comprise the market for this category of labor gives us the market demand curve. This is illustrated in Fig. 8.8. For simplicity we assume that the market for this kind of labor comprises only two industries, A and B, and thus, to obtain the market demand for labor at each wage rate, we simply sum the demand curves for each of these industries.

In each case points A and C on the industry demand curves are identified, to remind us that these curves represent the locus of a set of points on the underlying ΣMRP_L curves and that we have, therefore, taken full account of the price changes consequent upon the change in the level of output in each industry.

THE FIRM'S LABOR DEMAND CURVE IN THE LONG RUN

In the long run both labor and capital are variable. The firm no longer has to work with a particular level of capital, increasing output only by adding labor, it can now vary

---

8. The implicit assumption in the foregoing analysis was that the number of firms in the industry, 1000 in our case, was fixed. Yet of course there are two ways in which industry output can expand. First by each of the existing firms producing more output, as illustrated above, and second by more firms entering an industry. We should expect to observe this latter effect only in the long run and so we shall study this aspect in the section that looks at firm and industry behavior in the long run.

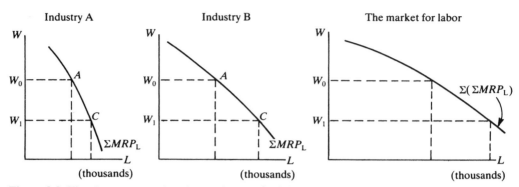

Figure 8.8 The short-run market demand curve for labor. Where the market for a particular class of labor extends beyond a single industry the market demand curve is found by summing the underlying industry demand curves derived in the manner described in Fig. 8.7

the amount of labor and capital it employs. Consider how this wider choice affects the firm's demand for labor.

The constraints on the firm's activities in the long run are two. First, the technical possibilities open to the firm, which are summarized in the isoquant map representing the production function and, second, the financial resources of the firm, summarized in the budget constraint. We have discussed the first of these in detail above, the latter is illustrated in Fig. 8.9.

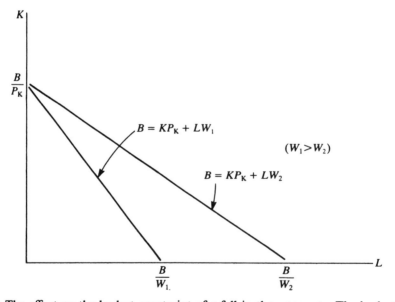

Figure 8.9 The effect on the budget constraint of a fall in the wage rate. The budget constraint B is given by $KP_K + LW_1$ where P_K represents the price of capital and W_1 the wage rate. B/P_K gives the intercept on the vertical axis and $-W/P_K$ gives the slope of the line. A reduction in W, from W_1 to W_2, flattens the line

If the price of capital services is P_K per unit, and the price of labor is W per unit, then the firm could afford B/P_K units of capital if it spent all of its budget, B, on capital, and B/W units of labor if it spent all of its budget on labor. The points B/P_K and B/W therefore give the intercepts on the vertical and horizontal axes, respectively, in Fig. 8.9. If capital is bought in quantity K and labor in quantity L, then if the amount spent on capital, KP_K, and the amount spent on labor, LW, exhaust the budget,

$$B = KP_K + LW \qquad (8.5)$$

Manipulating Eq. (8.5) enables us to show that the intercept on the vertical axis equals B/P_K (since $K = B/P_K - L(W/P_K)$, the first term on the right-hand side reveals the amount of K that can be purchased out of B if $L = 0$) while the term $-W/P_K$ gives the slope of the line. The line joining B/P_K and B/W shows the various combinations of units of capital, K, and labor L, which the firm can afford out of the budget, B. Such a line is termed an *isocost* or *isoexpenditure line* and is analogous to the budget constraint familiar from consumer demand theory. Thus if the total budget were $100 000, the price of a unit, say an hour of labor, were $20 and the price of renting a unit of capital were $40, in the limit the firm could afford 5000 labor hours, or 2500 units of capital. The intercepts on the K and L axes would be 2500 and 5000 respectively, and the slope of the budget constraint, $-W/P_K = -20/40 = -0.5$.

Suppose there was a fall in the price of labor to $10 an hour, the firm would now be able to afford 10 000 units of labor. This would pivot the budget constraint in Fig. 8.9 around point B/P_K and it would now intercept the horizontal axis at a point to the right of the original B/W. The slope of this line would be considerably shallower than before; $-W/P_K$ would now be $= -10/40 = -0.25$. An increase in the size of the budget, B, on the other hand, is illustrated by a parallel outward movement in the isocost line, revealing that more of both K and L could be purchased. Therefore changes in P_K or W affect the slope of the isocost line, while changes in B affect the position of the isocost line.

To find the firm's labor demand curve in the long run recall that a profit maximizing firm is concerned to produce any given level of output at minimum cost. Suppose that Q_1, depicted in Fig. 8.10, is the output which the firm aims to produce and that the technical possibilities for producing this level of output are summarized in the shape of the isoquant Q_1. The different budget outlays which might be available to produce Q_1 are shown as B_0, B_1 and B_2. The firm could not produce Q_1 with a level of expenditure equal to B_0 for it cannot reach Q_1 with this budget. It therefore has a choice between B_1 and B_2. It could produce Q_1 for expenditures B_2, by using either K_1 in conjunction with L_1 or K_2 in conjunction with L_2. However, in both cases the expenditures involved are higher than the minimum necessary to produce Q_1. The optimum is point Z, the position of tangency between Q_1 and the lowest isoexpenditure line, involving a budget outlay of B_1. At Z, K^* units of capital and L^* units of labor are employed and the firm is producing Q_1 at minimum cost, given the relative prices of K and L. K^* is now the size of the capital stock that the firm takes into the short run and which underpins its short run labor demand curves developed earlier.

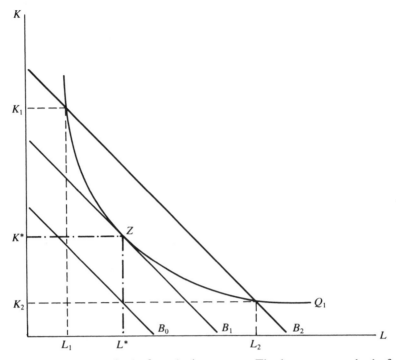

Figure 8.10 The least cost method of producing output. The least cost method of producing a given output in the long run is indicated by the point of tangency between the isoquant and the lowest budget constraint, as shown at point Z. At Z the marginal rate of technical substitution is equal to the factor price ratio. Cost minimization is an essential precondition for profit maximization

At the point of tangency the slopes of the isoquant and isoexpenditure line are equal. The slope of the isoquants is of course the negative of the $MRTS$ and the slope of the isoexpenditure line, $-W/P_K$, is the ratio of the relative prices of labor and capital. Thus at the point of tangency:

$$MRTS = \frac{W}{P_K} \qquad (8.6)$$

the marginal rate of technical substitution equals the factor price ratio. Note also that since the $MRTS = W/P_K$ the elasticity of substitution given at Eq. (8.2) can be defined as the ratio of the proportional change in the capital/labor ratio to the proportional change in the factor price ratio. That is

$$\sigma = \frac{d(K/L)/(K/L)}{d(W/P_K)/(W/P_K)} \qquad (8.7)$$

This gives us a quantitative measure of the degree of substitutability of the factors of production.

Earlier it was shown that the *MRTS* is equal to the ratio of the marginal products of labor and capital (Footnote 2 in this chapter). It therefore follows from Eq. (8.6) above that

$$MRTS = \frac{MP_L}{MP_K} = \frac{W}{P_K}$$ (8.8)

This in turn can be rearranged to show that

$$\frac{MP_L}{W} = \frac{MP_K}{P_K}$$ (8.9)

In equilibrium each factor of production is employed up to the point of equality between the ratio of its marginal physical product to the price of that input. This means that the last \$1 spent on capital was as productive, no more and no less, than the last \$1 spent on labor. This shows the essential conditions for cost minimization, and in turn cost minimization is an essential precondition for maximizing profits.

How does the firm react to changes in the wage rate in the long run? How do we obtain the firm's long-run demand for labor function? To answer this we recognize that a change, say a fall, in the wage rate does two things. First, it changes relative prices, it lowers W relative to P_K and so, as we have seen above, pivots the isoexpenditure line. Second, it makes the firm better off. It reduces the cost of producing a given level of output and therefore either enables the firm to produce the same output for a smaller budget outlay or to produce more output from a given budget.

Figure 8.11 illustrates the pivoting of the isoexpenditure line as a result of the fall in the price of labor. A consequence of this fall in the wage rate is that the firm is now able to produce more output for the same level of expenditure, it moves from Q_1 to Q_2. At this new level of output, Q_2, the firm is using both more labor, labor input rises from L_1 to L_2, and more capital, K_1 to K_2, it has moved from point A to C.

In Fig. 8.11 producing Q_1, at point A involves the use of K_1 capital. If we had taken K_1 as fixed and moved into the short run, we would have been able to build up the associated marginal product of labor, and marginal revenue product of labor curves. By equating the latter to different levels of the wage in the short run, we could then describe the firm's short-run demand for labor schedule as before. In Fig. 8.12, we draw such a curve, corresponding to K_1, tracing only that part of the labor demand curve below the *ARP* curve and above the horizontal axis.

For each level of capital there is a different MP_L and hence MRP_L curve. The greater the volume of capital that labor has to work with the higher is its marginal product and hence the greater is the value of the MRP_L at any given level of labor input. The greater is K, *ceteris paribus*, then the further to the right lie both the MP_L and the MRP_L curves. Accordingly, the MRP_L curve, which would be associated in the short run with K_2, in Fig. 8.11, would lie to the right of that associated with K_1 and this is also illustrated in Fig. 8.12. There exist a family of marginal revenue product curves each associated with a particular level of the capital stock and it is now simply a matter of

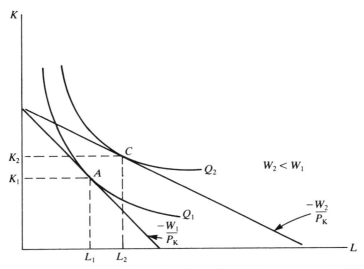

Figure 8.11 The new cost minimizing point after a fall in the wage rate. A fall in the wage rate, from W_1 to W_2, reduces the costs of production and enables the firm to produce more output for a given level of expenditure. The fall in the wage rate pivots the isoexpenditure line and enables the firm to move from isoquant Q_1 to Q_2

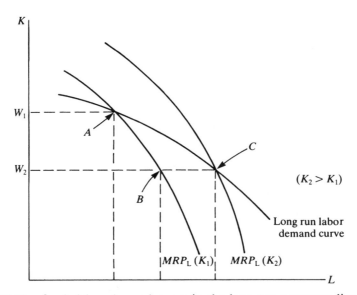

Figure 8.12 The firm's labor demand curve in the long run corresponding to Fig. 8.11. The long-run labor demand curve for the firm comprises the locus of points A and C. As a result of the fall in the wage, the firm chose to increase the size of the capital stock and this gave rise to the new MRP_L curve lying to the right of the original. The locus of the points on each MRP_L curve, at the appropriate wage rate, constitutes the long-run labor demand curve

plotting the appropriate wage rate against each of these to build up the firm's long-run labor demand curve.

Point A in Fig. 8.12 is the point on MRP_L (K_1) at which wage W_1 equals MRP_L. In the short run if the wage rate fell to W_2 this would cause the firm to move from point A to point B down the curve MRP_L (K_1). In terms of Fig. 8.11 this would involve moving along a ray drawn horizontally through point A. In the long run, the firm is free to vary the amount of capital it uses and it might no longer wish to operate with K_1. In the example depicted in Fig. 8.11, the firm chose to buy more capital, to increase the size of the capital stock, from K_1 to K_2. This larger capital stock gave rise to a new MRP_L curve, MRP_L (K_2), and to point C on this associated with the new lower wage W_2. The firm has effectively moved from point A on MRP_L (K_1), to point C on MRP_L (K_2). The long-run labor demand is the locus of points A and C in Fig. 8.12.[9]

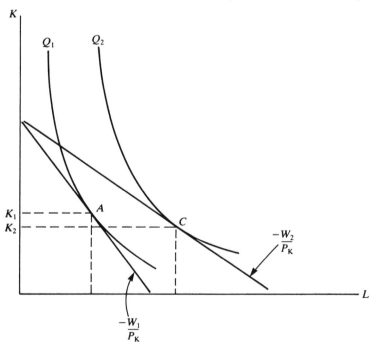

Figure 8.13 Less capital may be used at the new cost minimizing point. The isoquants shown here are more steeply sloped than in Fig. 8.11. As a result a fall in the wage rate leads to a reduction in the amount of capital that is employed. This results in the long-run labor demand curve shown in Figure 8.15

9. It should be noted that there exists a further effect in the long run consequent upon the fall in the wage rate. This effect, known as the *profit maximizing effect*, results from the downward shift in each competitive firm's marginal cost curve due to the fall in the wage rate. This leads all firms to a new and higher level of expenditure and ouput as they try once again to maximize profits. The consequence is a further outward shift of each firm's MRP_L curve and hence for the industry as a whole an outward shift in the ΣMRP_L. In so doing it again exerts a downward pressure on price which partly offsets the outward movement in each MRP_L and the ΣMRP_L. We shall assume that this effect is fully accounted for in the shift in the MRP_L curves as shown.

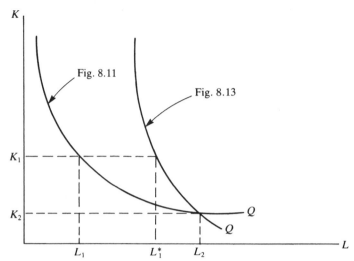

Figure 8.14 Comparing the *MRTS* in Figs. 8.11 and 8.13. The absolute value of the *MRTS* is smaller for the isoquant in Fig. 8.11 than it is for the one in Fig. 8.13

In the example above the long-run labor demand curve was more shallowly sloped than were either of the underlying short-run labor demand curves, but such a result need not always emerge. It depends on the technical possibilities confronting the firm which are summarized in the isoquant map. To illustrate this point suppose that the isoquants look like those drawn in Fig. 8.13. These isoquants are more steeply sloped than those in Fig. 8.11, reflecting a different *MRTS* and a different elasticity of substitution between the two figures. A comparison of the isoquants in Figs. 8.11 and 8.13 is conducted in Fig. 8.14, from which it is evident that a reduction in the amount of capital used, from K_1 to K_2, requires a larger increase in the amount of labor that is used if the isoquants are of the slope shown in Fig. 8.11, than is required if the isoquants take the form of those in Fig. 8.13. The isoquants shown in Fig. 8.11 require an increase in labor from L_1 to L_2 if output is to be held constant while those in Fig. 8.13 require an increase in labor of only L_1^* to L_2. The absolute value of the *MRTS* is smaller in Fig. 8.11 than it is in Fig. 8.13.

Consider what happens when the wage rate falls from W_1 to W_2, as before, but the isoquants are sloped as in Fig. 8.13. A fall in the price of labor of the same magnitude as occurred in Fig. 8.11 now results in the firm using less capital, moving from K_1 to K_2 in Fig. 8.13. This gives rise to a new $MRP_L (K_2)$ curve which lies to the left of the original and this is illustrated in Fig. 8.15. This reveals that the long-run labor demand curve joining points A and C is now steeper than either of the underlying short-run demand curves.

Substitution and scale effects

The outcome differs between Figs. 8.12 and 8.15 because of differences in the *substitution* and *scale* effects of the wage rate change in each case. The substitution

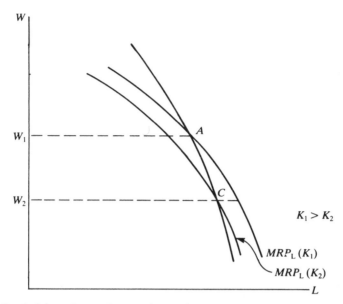

Figure 8.15 The firm's labor demand curve in the long run, corresponding to Fig. 8.13. A fall in the wage rate results in less capital being used. Accordingly, the long-run labor demand curve is steeper than either of the underlying short-run MRP_L curves

effect distinguishes the firm's reaction to the change in the relative price of capital and labor, holding constant the scale of production. The scale or output effect distinguishes the change in the level of output while abstracting from the change in relative prices. To illustrate the differences between the two we redraw the isoquant maps of Figs. 8.11 and 8.13 as Figs. 8.16(a) and (b).

The substitution effect abstracts from the change in the scale of operations and captures only the firm's reaction to the change in relative prices. It is therefore represented as a movement around an isoquant. In contrast, the scale effect reflects the firm's decision to change the scale of its operations (the level of its output) and it is therefore illustrated by a movement between isoquants. First consider the substitution effect. The new set of relative prices resulting from the fall in the wage rate is reflected in the slope of the new shallower isoexpenditure line. The firm's reaction to this new set of relative prices can therefore be captured by drawing a line parallel to the new isoexpenditure line, just tangent to the original isoquant, Q_1. In so doing we have held output constant and abstracted from scale effects. The new points of tangency, B, in each case capture the firm's reactions purely to the new set of relative prices. Confronted with these prices but constrained to produce Q_1 firms would, in both cases, have reduced the amount of capital they used, from K_1 to K_3, and increased the amount of labor they used, from L_1 to L_3. The fall in the wage rate, the relative cheapening of labor, leads firms to substitute out of capital and into labor.

The scale effect reflects the firms' further reactions to the situation produced by the fall in the wage rate. A consequence of this fall is that a given budget now goes further,

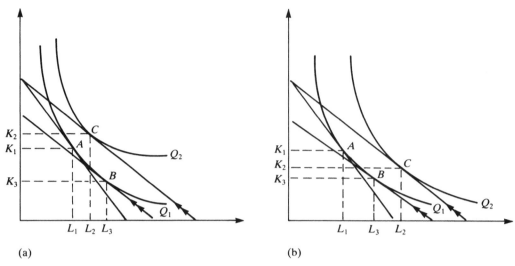

(a)   (b)

Figure 8.16 Scale and substitution effects resulting from a wage change. (a) The scale effect, the move from B to C, exceeds the substitution effect, the move from A to B, so more capital is used after the wage fall. (b) The scale effect, the move from B to C, is less than the substitution effect, the move from A to B, so less capital is used after the wage fall

it can be used to increase the scale of the firms' activities—to produce more output. We should expect the perfectly competitive firm to produce more output for it can sell all it can produce at the prevailing market price, and the fall in the wage rate has increased the profitability of its operations. Q_2 is the highest isoquant that the firms can reach, given the size of their original budget and the increase in the scale of their operations is therefore represented by the move from B to C in each case. In both cases the scale effect leads to the use of more capital, and capital stock increases from K_3 to K_2. But now the reasons for the difference between Figs. 8.16(a) and (b) can be clearly seen. The difference lies in the relative magnitude of substitution and scale effects.

In Fig. 8.16(a) the move from B to C, the scale effect, involved the use of less labor and substantially more capital. In contrast, in Fig. 8.16(b) the scale effect led to a small increase in the use of capital and a substantial further increase in the use of labor. The net outcome, when we combine the substitution and scale effects, is that in Fig. 8.16(a) more labor *and* more capital are used to produce Q_2 at C than were used to produce Q_1 at A. In Fig. 8.16(b) less capital and substantially more labor were used. In Fig. 8.16(b) the increased use of capital due to the scale effect was not sufficient to offset the reduction in the use of capital due to the substitution effect, the net result was that less capital was used. It is therefore the relative magnitude of the substitution and scale effects which produces the quite different outcomes we depicted in Figs. 8.12 and 8.15.

In summary, if (when expressed in terms of the amount of capital employed), the scale effect > substitution effect, more capital will be used and the long-run labor demand curve will be shallower than either of the underlying short-run curves. If the scale effect < substitution effect less capital will be used and the long-run labor demand curve will be steeper.

One final point should be made here. In the case of the competitive firm it is evident that a fall in the price of labor will lead to an increase in output. The firm will take advantage of the potential to increase output that its reduced costs have afforded it, for by this means it can increase profits. In other market forms such as monopoly, where producers have market power, this may not always occur. If the nature of the *product* demand curve is such that an increase in output results in a fall in total revenue, the firm may decide not to increase output and to forgo the opportunities to increase production. In this case the final outcome will be determined purely by the substitution effect, and will involve the use of more labor and less capital. In these circumstances the labor demand curve will be steeper in the long run than in the short run.

THE INDUSTRY AND MARKET LABOR DEMAND CURVE IN THE LONG RUN

As before the move from the firm to the industry means that we can no longer assume that the price of output is given. As all firms in an industry expand their output, the price of the final product will fall just as happened in the short run. In order to describe the *industry* demand curve for labor in the long run, we have to take account of both the change in product price and the change in the use of capital. The fall in the price of final output will result in a move to the left of each firm's MRP_L curve and a shift to the left in the ΣMRP_L curve. This may partially or even completely offset any tendency there may have been for the ΣMRP_L curve to move to the right as firms expanded their use of capital. The inward shift of ΣMRP_L will produce a steeper industry demand curve in the long run.

Examples of this are shown in Figs. 8.17 and 8.18. In Fig. 8.17 the ΣMRP_L shifts outward as a result of each firm using more capital, K_1 to K_2 (Fig. 8.17(a)), but as Fig. 8.17(b) shows this is partially offset as a result of the fall in product price, from P_1 to P_2. The industry demand in the long run is found by joining points A and C. An alternative outcome is shown in Fig. 8.18. Here the curve ΣMRP_L (K_2) lay to the left of ΣMRP_L (K_1) as a result of less capital being used after the change in relative prices. This inward shift is further reinforced by the fall in product prices from P_1 to P_2, with the result that in this case the long-run industry demand curve is still further steepened. Just how steep we do not know, although in both cases point C still lies to the right of A, a point that can be proved mathematically, if rather tediously.[10]

---

10. The curves in Figs. 8.17 and 8.18 were drawn under the assumption that the number of firms in the industry was constant, but this is no longer a valid assumption in a competitive industry in the long run. Now the increased profits as a result of a fall in the wage rate will attract in further producers. This will have two effects. First it will mean we are summing over a greater number of firms and thus the ΣMRP_L will be shifted to the right. However, the entry of new firms, adding to industry output, will further depress product price exerting an influence in the opposite direction. The net outcome of these two effects is difficult to predict.

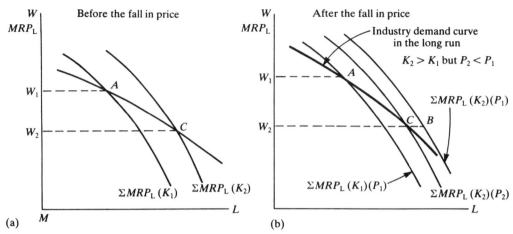

Figure 8.17 Industry demand for labor curves in the long run (when more capital is used). (a) More capital is used by each firm in the industry following a reduction in the wage rate, so that at an unchanged product price, P_1, the new ΣMRP_L (K_2) lies to the right of the original ΣMRP_L (K_1). (b) As the extra output that is produced comes to the market, product price falls and this partially offsets the effects of using more capital. $\Sigma MRP_L(K_2)$ at P_2 is shifted inwards resulting in a steeper industry demand curve for labor

ELASTICITY OF LABOR DEMAND

Up to this point it has merely been established that the demand curve for labor is likely to be downward sloping. However, we need a quantitative measure of the magnitude of the change in labor demand consequent upon any change in the wage rate. The elasticity of labor demand provides this, it measures the magnitude of the proportional change in employment relative to the proportional change in wages. Elasticity tells us two important things about the consequences of any wage change: first, the magnitude of any change is employment, E; second, the consequences of the change in the wage rate for total payments to, and therefore earnings of, labor, $W \times E$. *Own wage elasticity of demand for labor* is defined as:

$$\varepsilon_{ii} = \frac{dE_i/E_i}{dW_i/W_i} = \frac{dE_i}{dW_i} \times \frac{W_i}{E_i} \tag{8.10}$$

where elasticity is denoted by ε and i denotes the category of labor. The own price elasticity of demand measures the proportional change in employment of labor category i, consequent upon a change in the wage rate of i. Sometimes to insure that the elasticity takes a positive value the formula is preceded by a negative sign, for we anticipate that without this the resulting measure of elasticity would take a negative value, since a rise in the wage rate generally brings a fall in employment. However,

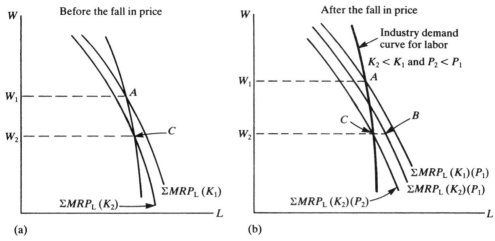

Figure 8.18 Industry demand for labor curves in the long run (when less capital is used). (a) Less capital is used by each firm in the industry following a reduction in the wage rate. $\Sigma MRP_L (K_2)$ lies to the left of $\Sigma MRP_L (K_1$ at original price P_1. (b) The fall in the product price from P_1 to P_2 reinforces the effects of using less capital and results in a yet steeper industry demand curve for labor as shown

there is no necessity for this. Scale and substitution effects are of course the determinants of the magnitude of own wage elasticities.[11]

A *cross-wage elasticity of demand for labor* can similarly be defined as:

$$\varepsilon_{ij} = \frac{dE_i/E_i}{dW_j/W_j} = \frac{dE_i}{dW_j} \times \frac{W_j}{E_i} \tag{8.11}$$

This measures the proportional change in the employment of category i consequent upon a change in the wage rate of category j. Consider each of these concepts in greater detail.

11. Own wage elasticity of labor demand to industry i can therefore be decomposed into

$$\varepsilon_{ii} = \varepsilon_{iiQ} + \varepsilon_{iQ}\eta S \tag{8.10a}$$

where the first term on the right-hand side measures the substitution effect and the second term measures the scale effect. The substitution effect, ε_{iiQ}, measures own wage elasticity as we move around an isoquant (Q held constant). The scale effect, $\varepsilon_{iQ}\eta S$, consists of three different elements: first, the output elasticity of labor demand ε_{iQ}; second, the price elasticity of demand for final output, η; third the share of labor in total costs, S. This is true under perfectly competitive conditions although more generally this last term is the elasticity of product price with respect to the wage rate. If each of these took the following values $S = 0.7$, $\eta = -0.5$, $\varepsilon_{iQ} = 1$ and $\varepsilon_{iiQ} = -0.3$ they would produce $\varepsilon_{ii} = -0.3 + 1(-0.5)(0.7)$ or -0.65. See Fallon, P. and Verry, D. (1988) *The Economics of Labour Markets*, Philip Allan, Oxford and New Jersey, Chapters 3 and 4, for a more detailed discussion of the several different measures of elasticity of demand each defined according to what else is being held constant.

Own wage elasticity

First consider the values that own wage elasticity can take and the consequences of each of these for the total wage bill or the total earnings received by the category of labor:

Value of elasticity	Description	Consequences for the total wage bill
$\varepsilon_{ii} > 1$	Elastic	A fall in the wage rate increases the wage bill, a rise in the wage rate reduces the wage bill
$\varepsilon_{ii} = 1$	Unit elastic	No change in wage bill
$\varepsilon_{ii} < 1$	Inelastic	A fall in the wage rate reduces the wage bill, a rise in the wage rate increases the wage bill

Thus if the demand for labor is elastic, a fall in the wage rate will produce an increase in the amount of labor employed which is sufficiently large to offset the fall in the wage rate of all those previously employed. The result is that there is a rise in the total wage bill because $dE/E > dW/W$. The opposite is the case when the demand for labor is inelastic. Then the earnings of the additional labor that is employed, consequent upon the fall in the wage rate, are insufficient to offset the effects of the fall in the wage rate on the earnings of all those individuals previously employed: $dE/E < dW/W$.

A rise in the wage rate will of course produce opposite effects. Where demand is elastic the total earnings of labor will fall, because at the new higher wage rate the fall in earnings, due to the fall in employment, is greater than the effects of the increase in earnings for all who remained employed. Where demand is inelastic, the opposite holds; total earnings rise because the reduction in employment is not sufficient to offset the rise in earnings of all those who remain employed.[12]

Cross-wage elasticity

The cross-wage elasticity informs us of the effects of a rise in the wage of group j on the employment of group i. In this case we are interested in both the magnitude and the sign of the elasticity so we never precede the formula with a negative sign.

---

12. The relationship between the change in total earnings, dTE, that is marginal earnings, ME, and own wage elasticity, can be shown as follows: $TE_i = W_i \times E_i$ by definition and $ME_i = dTE_i/dE_i$ hence:

$$\frac{dTE_i}{dE_i} = W_i + E_i \left(\frac{dW_i}{dE_i} \right) = W_i \left(1 + \frac{E_i}{W_i} \times \frac{dW_i}{dE_i} \right) \text{ and from Eq. (8.10) this gives}$$

$$= W_i \left(1 - \frac{1}{\varepsilon_{ii}} \right)$$

Where the cross-elasticities are positive, the categories of labor i and j are *gross substitutes*. A rise in the wage rate of category j leads to an increase in the employment of category i, revealing that i is being substituted for j. Where the cross-elasticities are negative i and j are *gross complements*, for as the wage rate of j increases the employment of i falls, alongside the fall in employment in group j.

The relative magnitudes of the substitution and scale, or output, effects determine whether i and j are gross complements or gross substitutes. We shall be able to understand exactly what is happening if we distinguish between gross and *net substitutes*. The term net substitutes is used to refer to the pure substitution effect. Thus suppose that a rise in the wage rate of j leads to substitution out of j and into i so that employment of i rises, then the two categories of labor i and j are net substitutes. However, if the rise in the wage rate of j means that less output can be produced for a given budget, the firm will cut back the scale of its activities. This cut in the scale of activities may lead the firm to cut back on its use of both j and i. If, as a result of reducing the scale of its acitivities, the firm cuts back its use of i by more than the increase due to the net substitution effect, then the overall use of i will fall. The rise in the wage rate for j will then have resulted in an overall fall in the use of i and j and i are described as gross complements. It is clear that the relative size of the scale and the substitution effects determines whether i and j emerge as gross complements (the scale effect > substitution effect) or gross substitutes (the scale effect < substitution effect). The relative sizes of the scale and substitution effects therefore determine both the magnitude and the sign of the cross-elasticities.

The determinants of the elasticity of demand for labor

The principal factors influencing own wage elasticity have been summarized in what are known as the '*Hicks–Marshall Rules of Derived Demand*'. There are four of these and they reflect variously the scale and substitution effects. The rules propose that, *ceteris paribus*, the own wage elasticity of demand for labor will be higher:

1. The higher is the absolute value of the price elasticity of demand for the final product labor produces,
2. the more easily can other factors of production be substituted for labor.
3. The more elastic the supply of other factors of production,
4. the larger is the share of labor in total costs.

Let us take each of these in turn.

Rule 1 states that the own wage elasticity of demand for labor will be higher the higher is the absolute value of the price elasticity of demand for the final product. The easier it is for consumers to substitute into other products, then the greater will be the employment reductions associated with any wage rise. This reminds us that the demand for labor is a derived demand, for this rule focuses on conditions in the product market. It follows that (with the exception of a monopoly) the demand for labor will be more elastic at the level of a single firm than at the level of the industry. Where the product market is competitive each firm faces a highly elastic demand for its products, for consumers can easily substitute the output of one firm for that of others in the industry.

It also follows from this that own wage elasticity is likely to be greater in the long run than in the short run. The price elasticity of product demand may be low in the short run because consumers are locked into a certain technology or because firms are monopolists in the product market. However, over the longer run new investment by consumers will increase the opportunities for substitution, while new technologies are likely to increase substantially competition in product markets. Both will have the effect of increasing the elasticities of product demand and hence the own wage elasticity of the demand for labor.

Rule 2 states that the own wage elasticity of labor demand will be higher the more easily other factors of production can be substituted for labor. The substitution possibilities are summarized in the slopes of the isoquants as measured by the *MRTS*. Again we might expect own wage elasticity to be higher in the long run than in the short run for the technically feasible substitution possibilities are greater over the long run. Indeed the long run is distinguished as a period within which capital is variable and this latter is a precondition for capital–labor substitution. However, there exists an extreme case where there is only one technically feasible way of combining capital and labor, that is where the $MRTS = 0$. This is known as a fixed coefficients production function, and here there are no substitution possibilities.

Rule 3 states that the own wage elasticity of labor demand will be greater the more elastic the supply of other factors of production. Evidently this is contingent on the existence of substitution possibilities discussed under Rule 2 above. This rule emphasizes supply conditions in the markets for substitute factors of production. Suppose, for example, that the supply of capital were highly inelastic, as it will be when the capital goods industry is working at capacity, then an increase in the demand for capital will lead to a rise in the price of capital. In turn, the rise in the price of capital will deter firms which have an elastic demand for their final product from taking advantage of the substitution possibilities. If firms substitute they will need to raise their product prices, but in turn this will result in a fall in product demand. Inelastic supply of competitive factors therefore either precludes or deters the substitution possibilities identified in Rule 2 above.

Rule 4 states that the own wage elasticity of the demand for labor will be greater the larger is the share of labor in total costs. If labor accounts for a large share of total costs, a rise in the wage rate will result in a significant rise in the firm's total costs and it will seek to recoup this by a rise in product prices. If the demand for the final product is completely inelastic, such a rise will have no adverse effect on employment, but in all other circumstances there will be some reduction in employment. The fall in employment will be greater at a given product price elasticity, the greater the share of total costs accounted for by labor. Conversely, it follows from this that at a given product price elasticity any adverse employment effects of a wage rise will be less, the smaller the share of labor in total costs. This had resulted in this fourth rule being termed 'the importance of being unimportant'.

However, it is not always desirable to be unimportant, there is an exception to this rule. This exception occurs when it is easy to substitute other factors of production for labor *and* the price elasticity of demand for the final product is high. For in these circumstances although labor accounts for a large proportion of total costs and although it may be technically feasible to substitute other factors for labor, firms will be deterred from doing so because of the cost implications of such a substitution. The substantial costs of making such a substitution will deter them if they know that when they do try to pass on the rise in costs, in the form of higher prices, there will be a sharp fall in product demand. In this case the elasticity of labor demand will be lower where labor accounts for a large share of total costs. This rule, as did Rule 1, focuses on the scale effects of a rise in own wage rate.

TRADE UNIONS AND LABOR DEMAND

Most of the analysis of trade unions focuses on their effects on labor supply, but the Hicks–Marshall rules provide an appropriate framework for considering the circumstances in which trade unions are likely to be able to negotiate the most favorable outcomes. The rules provide a framework for considering the objective conditions which enhance trade union power on the demand side of the labor market.

If trade unions are concerned about both wages and employment as we have conjectured in Chapter 7, then the own wage elasticity of labor is of vital concern to them. If they can reduce the own wage elasticity of demand for trade union labor they can reduce the adverse employment consequences of any wage rise. By providing a framework for distinguishing the determinants of own price elasticity the Hicks–Marshall rules therefore provide a framework for analyzing this second dimension of union policy. If the first thrust of union policy is aimed at reducing the elasticity of labor supply, the second is aimed at reducing the elasticity of labor demand. Consider, in the context of the Hicks–Marshall rules, how unions seek to achieve this.

Frequently unions devise policies that are designed to reduce competition in product markets. Such policies, if successful, have the effect of reducing the elasticity of demand for the final products of unionized firms. One mechanism for achieving this is to unionize complete industries. If unions fail to achieve this, consumers will be able to substitute the output of non-union labor for that of union labor should the price of the latter rise.

There are a number of notable cases in which there has been a sharp fall in unionized employment, due to the failure of a union to organize the complete industry and thus mitigate the adverse employment consequences of the wage rises it secures. In the 1920s, in the United States, the United Mine Workers experienced a sharp fall in membership as customers switched from high priced union produced coal mined in the northern bituminous coal industry, to cheaper coal produced with non-union labor in the south.[13] More recently the Union of Airline Pilots in the same country was faced with a severe decline in membership as customers switched to non-unionized carriers that gained an increasing share of the market in the 1970s and early 1980s.

Unions frequently advocate the introduction of import controls. Restrictions on imports reduce competition in domestic product markets, and reduce the price elasticity of demand for domestically produced goods. Such policies were for many years advocated by steel and autoworkers' unions in both the United Kingdom and the United States and by the mineworkers in the United Kingdom. In each case unions had successfully organized the domestic industry, but they then saw the elasticity of demand for the products of unionized labor increase steadily through the 1970s and early 1980s as foreign producers gained an increasing share of the domestic markets. For the steel and autoworkers the competition came from Europe and Japan. For mineworkers the competition came from South Africa and Poland.

It could also be argued that it was the desire to reduce competition in product markets that led unions in Britain and continental Europe to become enthusiastic advocates of public ownership, or nationalization. Although there were undoubtedly ideological reasons, there were also simple pragmatic reasons why unions advocated taking certain industries into public ownership. Nationalization of a complete industry, such as occurred with shipbuilding, steel, the railways and the coalmines, to name just a few of the industries nationalized in Britain in the past, effectively reduces and in some cases eliminates competition in the product market and in so doing reduces the elasticity of demand for unionized labor. Perhaps for these reasons the reverse of this policy, 'privatization', has often been opposed by unions, although privatization *per se* need not increase competition in product markets nor, therefore, need it weaken union power. When the emphasis in privatization is on maximizing the revenue secured by the sale of the nationalized industry, a higher price will accrue where the firm's monopoly position is maintained. Policies more likely to have a pronounced impact on the elasticity of demand for unionized labor, and therefore to weaken union bargaining power, are those of deregulation, and relaxation of import controls for these have a direct impact on product market competition.

The second Hicks–Marshall rule helps us understand why unions attempt to reduce the degree to which other factors of production can be substituted for unionized labor. Again, by organizing a complete industry or category of labor, unions may be able to reduce the elasticity of substitution. By so doing they confront firms in the industry with uniform cost conditions, and thereby reduce the desirability of substituting union for non-union labor. It is for this same reason that employers, once organized, have shown a degree of enthusiasm for such union policies. They recognize that the success of these policies prevents 'undercutting' by non-union firms. Unions can also reduce the elasticity of substitution by legislative or bargained restrictions on the substitution possibilities. Bargained manning agreements which stipulate the number of individuals per machine, the number of guards and drivers on a railway train for example, or

13. See Rees, A. (1977) *The Economic Effects of Trade Unions* revised edn, Chicago University Press.

legislative restrictions such as those for the minimum number of crew on an aircraft flight deck, are all examples of this.

Union policy can also be directed at reducing the own wage elasticity of the demand for union labor by reducing the elasticity of supply of substitute factors. Much of the occupational licensing by the medical and legal profession in the United States and in Europe can be regarded in this light.

EMPIRICAL EVIDENCE OF THE DEMAND FOR LABOR

A wide variety of different approaches has been employed to investigate the nature of the elasticity of the demand for labor. Perhaps of greatest interest to researchers have been estimates of the constant output, own wage elasticity of labor demand. At the level of the whole economy or in any major sector of an economy the scale effects will be irrelevant if the economy or sector is, or can reasonably be assumed to be, at full employment. The demand for labor, L, can then be estimated for changes in own wages holding constant the level of output, Q, and other factor prices, P_K. This suggests an estimating equation of the form $L = L(W/P, P_K, Q \ldots)$.

Such a formulation will capture only the substitution effects and it is therefore also appropriate in the case of a single firm where its output is constrained by the level of demand. However, in general an individual firm or a particular industry will be able to expand or contract output as the wage changes, in which case scale effects on employment demand are also relevant. The appropriate model will then be one that allows for these effects and estimates the demand for labor holding constant the price and quantities of other inputs, K. In which case $L = L((W/P), P_K, K \ldots)$.

A recent survey of the 'huge empirical literature' on demand elasticities has concluded that 'in developed economies in the late twentieth century, the aggregate, long-run constant-output, labor demand elasticity lies roughly in the range of -0.15 to -0.50'.[14] Estimates of elasticity are reported in Table 8.1. The elasticity of demand for labor will of course vary between industries and through time due to differences in technology. The reported studies result from a wide range of different specifications and sample periods but they produce a fairly consistent range of estimates.

What happens when output is allowed to vary, when we include a scale effect? This is evidently appropriate when it is believed, for example, that unemployment is substantially above the equilibrium rate. We might then expect the estimates of the aggregate labor demand elasticity to rise and indeed this appears to be the case. It further appears that in general own wage elasticity is smaller the greater is the amount of human capital embodied in the labor. Models involving several types of labor enable us to study the degree of substitutability between different types of labor and other factors of production. A general finding is that non-production and skilled workers are less easily substitutable for physical capital than are unskilled workers. Indeed it has been suggested that skilled workers and physical capital are best regarded as

14. Hamermesh, D.S. (1986) 'The demand for labor in the long run', in Ashenfelter, O. and Layard, P.R. G. (eds.), *Handbook of Labor Economics*, pp. 429–72, North Holland.

Table 8.1 Studies of the aggregate employment–wage elasticity

Author and source	Data and industry cover		Own-wage elasticity
Constant capital stock			
Symons and Layard (1984)	Manufacturing quarterly 1956–82	Germany	– 0.4
		France	– 0.3
		Japan	– 2.4
		USA	– 1.3
		Britain	– 1.8
Layard and Nickell (1985)	Annual (Britain) 1954–83		– 0.9
Constant output			
Hamermesh (1983)	Private non-farm, quarterly based on labor costs, 1955–78 (USA)		– 0.47
Rosen and Quandt (1978)	Private production hours, annual, 1930–73 (USA)		– 0.98
Clark and Freeman (1980)	Manufacturing quarterly, 1950–76 (USA)		
	Employment		– 0.33
	Hours		– 0.51
Nadiri and Rosen (1974)	Manufacturing employment, quarterly, 1948–65 (USA)		
	Production		+ 0.11
	Non-production		– 0.14
Schott (1978)	Annual (Britain)		
	Employment		– 0.82
	Hours		– 0.25
Nickell (1981)	Manufacturing quarterly, 1958–74 (United Kingdom)		– 0.19

Source: Hamermesh, D.S., (1986) *op. cit.*

complements. This capital–skill complementarity hypothesis suggests that policies designed to encourage investment, such as investment subsidies or tax credits, will increase the demand for skilled labor but may reduce that for unskilled labor. It also emerges quite consistently from these studies that women are substitutes for young workers. The rapid growth in female employment in most industrialized countries in the past two decades has therefore led to a decline in the equilibrium wage rate for young workers and appears to have contributed to the high rates of youth unemployment in these countries.

SUMMARY

In this chapter we have developed a simple theory of the demand for labor. We have distinguished between the firm and the industry in the short and the long run. Working under the assumption that labor is a variable factor of production it was shown that either a single marginal revenue product of labor schedule or points on a number of these schedules constituted the labor demand curve. Firms, it was proposed, hired labor up to the point at which the marginal revenue product of labor equalled the wage rate.

Of course, the term wage rate was really just a shorthand for the many elements of labor costs that the firm incurs when it secures the services of labor. The simple theory proposed that the rational firm would take employment up to the point at which the total costs of employing the last unit of labor were just equal to the marginal revenue product generated by that unit. Yet immediately we broaden the definition of labor cost we realize that some among these costs are not encountered on a recurring basis. Some are set-up or fixed costs as, for example, when a firm incurs hiring and training costs and it would therefore seem more appropriate to treat these as investment or fixed costs. The simple theory we have just developed makes no allowance for the distinction between fixed and variable labor costs. Without such a distinction the theory will have limited application to wide areas of most developed economies, for a feature of recent years has been the substantial growth of the fixed element in labor costs. The purpose of the next chapter is therefore to evaluate the demand for labor in circumstances in which there is a substantial fixed element in labor costs.

The concept of greatest importance to emerge from this chapter was that of the elasticity of labor demand. Measures of own and cross-wage elasticity have considerable practical importance for they enable us to estimate the magnitude of the employment and wage bill effects of changes in own or other groups' wages. We saw that the Hicks–Marshall rules provided a framework for distinguishing the principal factors influencing own wage elasticity. In turn they suggested that a range of quite familiar trade union policies could be understood as designed to reduce the wage elasticity of labor demand for trade union labor. Finally, we evaluated the empirical evidence of demand elasticities and found that these lay in the range of -0.15 to -0.50 in most developed countries over the long run—confirming that the labor demand curve had a negative slope in the long run.

PRINCIPAL CONCEPTS

Students should have encountered and understood the following concepts developed in this chapter:

1. The production function.
2. The marginal rate of technical substitution.
3. The elasticity of substitution.
4. The marginal product of labor.
5. The marginal revenue product of labor.
6. Isocost or isoexpenditure lines.
7. Substitution and scale effects.

8. Own wage elasticity of labor demand.
9. Cross-wage elasticity of labor demand.
10. The four Hicks–Marshall rules of derived demand.

QUESTIONS FOR DISCUSSION

1. Discuss the relative effectiveness of policies that have been developed by trade unions to minimize the adverse employment consequences of an own wage rise.
2. Rank in ascending order, according to your estimates of own wage elasticity, the following categories of labor in your country. Give reasons for your ranking: automobile workers, textile workers, judges, airline pilots, economic consultants, nuclear power station operators.
3. Detail the possible effects on labor demand of a substantial fall in youth wages.
4. Distinguish those circumstances in which it is appropriate to ignore the scale effects of a change in own wage rate.

FURTHER READING

An extremely thorough review of the empirical work in this area has been produced by Hamermesh, D.S. (1986) 'The demand for labor in the long run', in Ashenfelter, O. and Layard, P.R.G. (eds.), *Handbook of Labor Economics*, vol. 1, North Holland. Also in this same volume is an excellent discussion of 'Dynamic models of labor demand' by Nickell, S.J. However, the undergraduate reader will find both of these surveys tough going. A more accessible treatment of the topic is to be found in Fallon, P. and Verry, D. (1988). The chapters on labor demand in their book, *The Economics of Labour Markets*, Philip Allen, Oxford, provide a slightly more advanced treatment than offered here and are particularly good at describing the methodologies employed by labor economists to estimate wage elasticities.

9

LABOR AS A FIXED FACTOR

In the previous chapters we have characterized labor as a variable factor of production. This was common practice up to the 1960s when it came to be widely appreciated that there is also a large fixed element in labor costs. Many firms encounter large initial payments each time they take on a new employee. The magnitude of these costs is such that it is inappropriate for the firm to attempt to recoup these costs immediately. It is more sensible to regard these initial payments as an investment in labor, and to seek to recoup such outlays over a number of years. A condition for realizing these returns is that the employee remains with the firm for a period of years, and even beyond this period the firm will still have a preference for retaining the employee in which it has invested. By retaining the employee the firm avoids the additional outlays it would incur if were to recruit replacements.

Firms and individuals have incentives to invest in human capital. In Chapter 6 we looked at individual investment in human capital and distinguished between investment in general and specific skills. In this chapter we look again at this issue and focus in particular on specific skills, the costs of which are likely to be shared between the firm and workers. A consequence of the sharing of costs is that firms and workers become locked together in a mutually advantageous long-term employment contract. Such a relationship has two important consequences: first, in a recession firms will be reluctant to discharge those employees in whom they have invested, for to do so will reduce their chances of earning a return on their investment; second, in the short run, at least, the wage and marginal revenue product of labor no longer stand in the fixed relationship posited in the previous chapter. In consequence there is likely to be considerable discretion in wage setting.

An important initial task is to identify the magnitude of the fixed costs associated with different types of labor. These emerge as significant for certain types of labor in all countries in recent years. We then consider more formally the consequences for labor demand of fixed labor costs and the discretion that their existence imparts to wage and employment fixing.

THE DISTINCTION BETWEEN FIXED AND VARIABLE LABOR COSTS

The costs that the employer incurs to acquire the services of labor fall into two categories. First, there are *fixed labor costs*, these take two forms: (i) once-over, set-up costs that the firm incurs each time it takes on a new worker; and (ii) those costs that the firm incurs on a regular recurring basis, so long as it continues to employ that worker, but which do not vary with the number of hours or with the intensity with which an employee works. The essence of fixed labor costs is that they are costs that are independent of the number of hours or the intensity with which an employee works. Second, there are variable costs. These are the costs that vary according to the number of hours, or the intensity with which an employee works. The fact that most forms of employment combine elements of both of these has led to the description of labor as a *quasi-fixed* factor of production.[1]

Non-recurring fixed costs

The initial training of a worker is perhaps the classic example of a once-over fixed cost, although the increasing emphasis on retraining employees means that training, taken as a whole, is now most appropriately viewed as a recurring fixed cost. The example of training costs serves to remind us that these fixed costs need not involve direct money outlays. The largest part of the costs of training is opportunity costs. To the employer these take the form of the lost output both of the person being trained and of the person supervising the trainee. To the employee these opportunity costs take the form of the wage forgone while training. Additional once-over fixed costs are the hiring and screening costs the firm encounters each time it tries to fill a vacancy. These are the costs of advertising the vacancy, securing applicants and selecting one from among these.

There is a finite probability that the firm will at some stage wish to dispense with the services of any worker it hires. The firm thus incurs a further set of once-over fixed costs each time it hires a worker—the potential firing costs. In Britain and continental Europe these can be substantial due to the existence of job security policies. Throughout Europe a variety of policies has been implemented in order to promote job security. European labor law restricts employers' discretion in dismissing workers, and reflects the different rights and obligations of employers in Europe from the United States. Infringement of these can mean action before the courts, before an industrial

1. See Oi, W. (1962) 'Labor as a quasi-fixed factor', *Journal of Political Economy*, December, 538–55 and Becker, G.S. 'Investment in human beings', *Journal of Political Economy*, **70**, October, 9–49.

tribunal. In the United Kingdom there are some 35 000 such cases each year and it has been suggested that the average compensation and legal fees resulting from such cases amount to around four months' pay for each case.[2] Again, in most countries firms incur substantial costs if they wish to declare redundancies, for most make severance payments.

Recurring fixed costs

All the above are one-off non-recurring fixed costs. There also exist fixed costs which the employer must pay on a recurring basis no matter for how many hours or how intensively the individual works. Employers' contributions to unemployment insurance funds, to health insurance and pension funds are paid on a recurring basis and the level of such payments can be independent of how long or hard the employee works. Such contributions are usually subject to an upper ceiling and for all those employees earning above the upper ceiling the contributions to such funds are largely independent of the amount they earn. More usual examples of recurring but fixed costs are certain fringe benefits (canteen facilities, company cars), the clerical and administrative costs associated with employing labor and those parts of the personnel and welfare offices that devote themselves to helping existing employees. Most important of all is payment for days not worked. Holiday pay, both statutory (public holidays) and negotiated, and sickness pay constitute the most important of these.

THE MAGNITUDE OF FIXED LABOR COSTS

Identifying the fixed elements of labor costs is no simple matter, but substantial progress has been made in this area in recent years.[3] The direct costs of training, the costs of supervisory time but not output forgone, have been quantified. The evidence shows that direct outlays on training accounted for no more than 2.0 percent of total labor costs in the United Kingdom in 1981 and 0.2 and 0.5 percent in the United States and Japan, respectively, in the same year. Benefits in kind, housing allowances, subsidized mortgages, subsidized sports facilities, restaurants/canteens and cars constitute largely fixed costs. Together these accounted for only around 0.2 to 0.4 percent of average total labor costs in the United Kingdom and the United States in 1981 but were around 2.0 percent in Japan. Payments for days not worked, payments while on public and other holidays, paid sick leave and redundancy pay are by far the largest element of fixed labor costs. By 1981 they accounted for over 10 percent of total labor costs in the United Kingdom, having risen from 8 percent in 1972. At 9 percent of total labor costs they were unchanged in the United States over this period. In contrast, Japanese holidays payments are small, they appear to be around only 2 percent and constant over the period. Not all of these payments for days not worked

2. Nickell, S.J. (1986) 'Dynamic models of labor demand', in Ashenfelter, O. and Layard, P.R.G. (eds.), *Handbook of Labor Economics*, vol. 1, pp. 473–524, North Holland.
3. See Hart, R.A. (1984) *The Economics of Non-Wage Labour Costs*, Allen and Unwin, London.

are appropriately regarded as fixed costs in their entirety because redundancy pay and sick pay are often linked to earnings and hence to hours of work.

Old-age pensions, sickness benefit, unemployment benefit and industrial injury benefit constitute the main items of social welfare and in most countries firms are required to contribute to these funds via a payroll tax levied as a proportion of earnings. On the face of it, these contributions vary with the number of hours the employee works and should be regarded as a variable cost. However, the levy is generally subject to some ceiling beyond which increased earnings do not lead to increased contributions, and therefore beyond this point these payments are appropriately regarded as a fixed cost. In this case they represent a fixed, although recurring, payment that the firm incurs so long as it continues to employ this labor. The ceiling for these payments changes over the years and it is therefore no simple matter to calculate the proportion of total social welfare payments that contribute to fixed costs. In the United Kingdom the ceiling fluctuated around a level equivalent to 1.6 times average annual earnings during the 1970s, while in the United States it fluctuated around a similar level for contributions to old-age and sickness benefit although the threshold was as low as half the average annual wage for contributions to the unemployment benefit fund. Given the dispersion of earnings in both countries it seems probable that around 75 percent of total welfare contributions are best regarded as variable costs, and the remaining 25 percent constitute fixed costs. In 1981 *total* social welfare costs, statutory and voluntary, accounted for 16 percent of the total labor costs in the United Kingdom, 17 percent in the United States and 14 percent in Japan, having grown from 10, 14 and 11 percent, respectively, since 1972.

Comparative estimates of the ratios of fixed to total labor costs are presented in Tables 9.1 and 9.2. Ratio I is the narrowest definition of fixed labor costs and comprises all those elements of non-wage labor costs that do not vary with hours of work, other than paid for holidays. Ratio II includes paid for holidays as a fixed cost, for although this element typically contains both fixed and variable elements it is impossible to separate them. Table 9.1 reports the changes in these ratios over the period from 1973 to 1985 in Japan, the United Kingdom and the United States. In both the latter two countries the ratio of fixed costs to total labor costs is greater than in Japan. This is true of Europe in general and is in part due to the considerably more generous paid for holidays on this continent. In the United Kingdom the ratio had risen above that in the United States by the 1980s: by 1981 it was almost 30 percent in the United Kingdom compared to around 23 percent in the United States and less than 15 percent in Japan. This point emerges again in Table 9.2 which reports a wider range of comparisons which now include France, Germany and Italy for 1981. No simple pattern emerges from this. The ratio of fixed to total labor costs on the widest definition is now highest in the United Kingdom but lowest in Italy. It appears very similar in France, the United Kingdom and the United States and there is no suggestion of any distinction between Europe and the United States and Japan.

The determinants of the ratio of fixed to total labor costs are several. The incidence of specific training in industry will be an important determinant of the magnitude of training costs borne by industry. The heterogeneity of the labor force and rates of

Table 9.1 Fixed labor costs as a proportion of total labor costs in Japan, the United States and the United Kingdom (all industries)

	Ratio	1973	1975[‡]	1978	1981	1985
Japan[†]	Ratio I[§]	—	8.0	13.0	14.0	11.0
	Ratio II[§]	—	11.0	16.0	16.0	13.0
USA	Ratio I	6.5	8.9	—	9.3	9.6
	Ratio II	20.2	23.0	—	22.8	23.0
UK	Ratio I	—		—	—	—
	Ratio II	19.4	22.9	26.8	29.7	—

Source: Hart R.A., Bell D.N.F., Frees R., Kawasaki S., and Woodbury S.A. *Trends in Non-Wage Labour Costs and their Effects on Employment*, 1988, Commission of the European Community, Brussels.
[†] An all industries figure is not available for Japan and in this column the figures are therefore for services.
[‡] For the USA the figures are 1976/7.
[§] See text for definitions

turnover will be determinants of the magnitude of hiring costs. The incidence of job security legislation and negotiated agreements will determine the magnitude of the fixed firing costs. Employees' preferences between different types of non-wage benefits and wages, and the tax systems which influence such preferences, will determine the magnitude of benefits in kind. The level of social security provision and the manner of its financing will determine the magnitude and nature of payments into each of the social welfare funds. Evidently employee preferences, and the degree of state and private provision, of each of the above non-wage labor costs, will differ substantially between nations and accordingly no simple pattern of differences in the ratios of fixed to total labor costs emerges. In all countries fixed costs are a substantial component of total costs and they appear to have increased substantially as a proportion of total labor costs over the period since 1970.

Table 9.2 Fixed costs as a proportion of total labor costs: selected OECD countries (manufacturing industry), 1981

	France	Germany	Italy	Japan	UK	USA
Ratio of fixed to total labor costs (excl. paid holidays)	0.14	0.07	0.03	0.15	0.12	0.13[†]
Ratio of fixed to total labor costs (incl. paid holidays)	0.24	0.21	0.15	0.18	0.26	0.25[†]

Sources: Hart R.A. *et al.* (1988) *op. cit.*
[†] All industries

Japan is an interesting case for a feature unique to the Japanese wage payment system is the role of bonuses. Annual bonuses account for around 20 percent of total labor costs in that country and have shown very little variation over the last 20 years. It has been argued that bonuses represent labor's share of the returns from specific human capital investment in Japan. Bonus payments, it has been argued, constitute the employees' return to their specific human capital investment.[4] If employers enjoy similar returns on their share of specific human capital investments then the magnitude of firm-specific investments in Japan must be considerable. Investments in specific human capital of this order of magnitude suggest substantial recurring fixed labor costs. As we shall see from the next section fixed costs substantially change the nature of the labor demand function in these countries.

THE FIRM'S LABOR INVESTMENT DECISION

In Chapter 8 we saw that the profit maximizing firm will take employment up to the point at which the *current* marginal cost of obtaining the services of the last employee, the wage, is just equal to their *current* marginal revenue product. Labor was regarded as an entirely variable factor of production and the labor demand curve was given by the marginal revenue product of labor curve. The financial outlays the employer had to make to hire the services of labor varied in strict proportion to the number of hours that labor worked. The firm insured that in each period there was equality of the wage and marginal revenue product and this determined how much labor the firm employed in each period. The application of this simple decision rule each period meant that the firm's employment decisions each period were quite *independent*. If for some reason the marginal revenue product of labor fell below the wage, perhaps because of a recession, then the firm would at a given level of wages reduce employment to re-establish the equality of the MRP_L and W. Conversely, if the MRP_L exceeded the wage the firm would increase employment. In this manner employment would vary to ensure equality of the wage and marginal revenue product of labor in each period.

The above simple decision rule is appropriate in circumstances in which the costs of obtaining the services of labor vary in proportion to the number of hours worked. However, where the firm faces large fixed costs when it employs labor, these costs are most appropriately regarded as an investment in labor on the part of the firm and this rule is unlikely to apply. It is likely that most of the fixed costs, the non-recurring fixed costs, will be encountered during the initial periods of employment, while the greatest returns from employing labor are likely to be enjoyed during the later periods. Thus, the profile of outlays and receipts will differ substantially and we have to discount future revenues to allow for this. Now the rule for the firm is to take employment up to the point at which the discounted present value of the revenue from the marginal employee is just equal to the discounted present value of the investment and wage

4. Hashimoto, M. (1979) 'Bonus payments, on-the-job training and lifetime employment in Japan', *Journal of Political Economy*, **87**, 1086–104 and Hashimoto M. and Raisian J. (1988) 'The structure and short-run adaptability of labor markets in Japan and the United States', in Hart, R.A. (ed.) *Employment, Unemployment and Labour Utilization*, Unwin Hyman, London and Boston, pp. 314–40.

costs of the marginal employee. In calculating the marginal benefit from taking on each employee the firm has to adopt a longer planning horizon than in the absence of fixed costs.

Suppose for simplicity that the firm's planning horizon stretches to three periods. The firm is then concerned to calculate the *present value* of the marginal revenue product of each potential employee, $PVMRP_L$, over the three periods and the present value of the costs of employing each person over the complete period, $PVMC_L$. The firm maximizes profits if it takes employment up to the point at which the last person hired, the marginal employee, adds as much in present value terms to revenue as he or she does to costs. At the margin employment is determined by the condition that

$$PVMRP_L = PVMC_L \qquad (9.1)$$

Consider each of these terms more fully. The present value of the marginal revenue product of labor is equal to the sum of the discounted present values of the marginal revenue product in each of the three periods, Thus,

$$PVMRP_L = MRP_{L0} + \frac{MRP_{L1}}{(1+r)} + \frac{MRP_{L2}}{(1+r)^2} \qquad (9.2)$$

or

$$PVMRP_L = \sum_{i=0}^{2} \frac{MRP_{Li}}{(1+r)^i} \qquad (9.3)$$

If we assume for simplicity that all fixed costs are encountered in the first period, then the present value of the marginal cost of hiring an additional employee comprises the fixed costs of labor, F_0, and the wage costs incurred in each of the periods. Thus,

$$PVMC_L = F_0 + W_0 + \frac{W_1}{(1+r)} + \frac{W_2}{(1+r)^2} \qquad (9.4)$$

$$= F_0 + \sum_{i=0}^{2} \frac{W_i}{(1+r)^i} \qquad (9.5)$$

by substituting Eqs. (9.2) and (9.4) into Eq. (9.1) we obtain

$$MRP_{L0} + \frac{MRP_{L1}}{(1+r)} + \frac{MRP_{L2}}{(1+r)^2} = F_0 + W_0 \frac{W_1}{(1+r)} + \frac{W_2}{(1+r)^2} \qquad (9.6)$$

From which it can be seen that, if, in the base period

$$F_0 + W_0 - MRP_{L0} > 0 \qquad (9.7)$$

then in the remaining periods:

$$\frac{W_1}{(1+r)} + \frac{W_2}{(1+r)^2} - \left(\frac{MRP_{L1}}{(1+r)} + \frac{MRP_{L2}}{(1+r)^2} \right) < 0 \qquad (9.8)$$

Equations (9.7) and (9.8) can also be combined to show that for the marginal employee

$$\frac{W_1}{(1+r)} + \frac{W_2}{(1+r)^2} - \frac{MRP_{L1}}{(1+r)} + \frac{MRP_{L2}}{(1+r)^2} = F_0 + W_0 - MRP_{L0} \qquad (9.9)$$

Equations (9.9) tells us that the net present value of the surplus earned in the second and third periods must be equal to the net present value of the deficit incurred in the first period.

A visual presentation of these relationships is presented in Fig. 9.1 from which it will be evident that the analysis here is similar to that in Chapter 6. Consider Fig. 9.1 in more detail. Suppose the fixed costs take the form of non-recurring recruitment and training costs. These fixed costs, F_0, together with the discounted present values of the wage and marginal revenue product, are mapped on the vertical axis while the horizontal axis shows the three time periods. The sum of the wage, W_0, and the

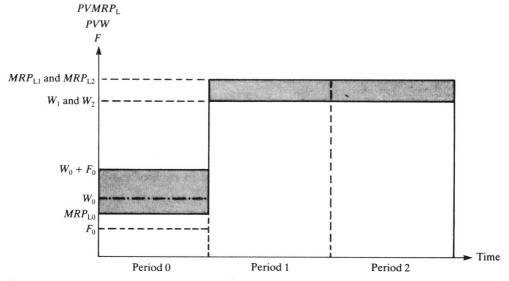

Figure 9.1 Discounting the costs and benefits of an additional employee in the presence of fixed labor costs. We depict the discounted costs and benefits of an extra employee when fixed training costs are incurred each time a new employee is taken on. In this example the discounted present value of the costs of the employee is given by:

$$PVMC_L = F_0 + W_0 + \frac{W_1}{(1+r)} + \frac{W_2}{(1+r)^2}$$

while the discounted present value of the benefits received from employing this person are:

$$PVMRP_L = MRP_{L0} + \frac{MRP_{L1}}{(1+r)} + \frac{MRP_{L2}}{(1=r)^2}$$

Above, F_0 represents the training costs incurred in the first period while all other variables are labeled as before. In this example, the net investment in period 0 is equal to the net surplus in periods 1 and 2, as illustrated by the equality of the shaded areas above

training and recruitment costs, F_0, paid out in the first period, represents the firm's gross outgoings in this period. Partly offsetting these is the marginal revenue product produced by this person, MRP_{L0}. However, it is evident from the diagram that $W_0 + F_0 > MRP_{L0}$ by the shaded area shown. In this period $W_0 + F_0 - MRP_{L0} > 0$. In the following period, after the training is completed, the MRP jumps dramatically to MRP_{L1} and now exceeds the wage paid this perioid, W_1, by the shaded area. Again in the final period MRP_{L2} exceeds the wage paid, W_2. For the marginal employee, the last person employed, the sum of the shaded areas in periods 1 and 2 equals the shaded area in period 0.

We could draw a similar diagram to illustrate the calculations involved for each of the individuals the firm might be willing to employ. In each case, except that of the marginal employee, the $PVMRP_L > PVMC_L$ as a result of the assumption of the diminishing marginal product of labor. We can therefore draw a demand curve for labor which shows individuals ranked in descending order of their $PVMRP_L$. If the fixed costs and wages are the same for each potential employee we can also draw the associated marginal cost curve, $PVMC_L$. $PVMC_L$ represents the effective labor supply curve to the firm in the presence of fixed labor costs, and it is evident that in the example this is assumed to be perfectly elastic. $PVMC_L$ and $PVMRP_L$ are shown in Fig. 9.2. Taken together these show the optimal level of employment for the firm. This is given by point A, for at this point the conditions identified in Eq. (9.1) are satisfied.

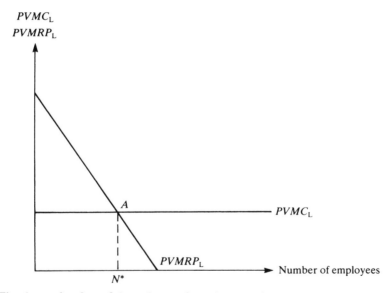

Figure 9.2 The determination of the volume of employment in the presence of fixed labor costs. Under the assumption of a diminishing marginal product of labor we can describe a downward sloping labor demand curve. Underpinning this is the $PVMRP_L$ of each potential employee ranked in descending order. The $PVMC_L$ of each employee is assumed constant and employment is taken to be the point at which $PVMC_L = PVMRP_L$

More realistically the marginal cost of an extra worker is likely to rise. Suppose the costs of hiring represent the only fixed costs and these comprise the costs of advertising and screening applicants. We might anticipate that the greater the number of workers hired, the deeper the firm will have to dip into the applicant pool, and the more resources will have to be devoted to distinguishing suitable employees. In which case the marginal hiring cost schedule is likely to be positively sloped and to diverge increasingly from the wage as depicted in Fig. 9.3. Employment will again be determined by the point of intersection $PVMC_L$ and $PVMRP_L$ but will be lower than in the absence of rising fixed costs.

In Figs. 9.2 and 9.3 the demand curve, the $PVMRP_L$ curve, and supply curve of labor, the $PVMC_L$ curve, are fundamentally different from those developed in the previous chapter. However, they tell us nothing about the relationship between the MRP_L and W in each period, only that for the last employee hired the discounted present value, of the sum of the marginal revenue accruing from selling the output of this employee, will be equal to the discounted present value of the sum of the marginal

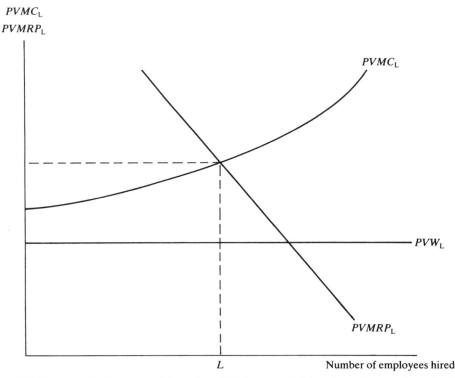

Figure 9.3 The marginal costs and benefits of hiring an additional employee when fixed costs rise with the volume of hiring. If the fixed costs associated with hiring each additional employee are rising, then the schedule reflecting the present value of the marginal costs of each employee will be positively sloping, and will diverge increasingly from the wage schedule. The level of employment will be determined by the intersection of $PVMC_L$ and $PVMRP_L$

cost of employing that person when considered over all periods of the proposed labor contract. A wedge has therefore been driven between the wage and the marginal revenue product of labor in each period and there can now be a substantial difference between the wage and MRP_L in any particular period without this having any effect on employment.

To understand the significance of this point consider what happens when we now move forward to the start of the second period and look forward over the remaining two periods. If the fixed labor costs were incurred in the first period, by the second period these initial investment outlays represent sunk costs. If the firm envisages paying the same wage in each of the two remaining periods then $PVMC_L$ is given by:

$$PVMC_L^2 = W_1 + \frac{W_2}{1+r} \text{ or } \sum_{i=1}^{2} \frac{W_i}{(1+r)^i} \qquad (9.10)$$

Again the present value of the marginal revenue product $PVMRP_L$ is given by:

$$PVMRP_L^2 = MRP_{L1} + \frac{MRP_{L2}}{1+r} \text{ or } PVMRP_L^2 = \sum_{i=1}^{2} \frac{MRP_{L1}}{(1+r)^i} \qquad (9.11)$$

The situation can again be depicted with the aid of Fig. 9.1.

For the marginal employee depicted in Fig. 9.1 the $PVMRP_L^2 > PVMC_L^2$ over the two remaining periods. Although this surplus was required by the firm to enable it to recoup its initial investment outlays, by the start of the second period these outlays represent sunk costs. Two important consequences flow from this. First, because $PVMRP_L^2$ exceeds $PVMC_L^2$ the firm will no longer automatically reduce employment in the second period if there is a fall in the marginal revenue product of labor below $PVMRP_L^2$. While $PVMRP_L^2$ continues to exceed $PVMC_L^2$ the firm earns a surplus over its variable costs, the wage. The MRP_L would now have to fall below W_1 and W_2 in both periods before the firm would consider discharging this employee. Although the firm may no longer be earning a return on its original investment, while $PVMRP_L^2$ exceeds the discounted sum of the wages paid in each period it is doing the best it can under the circumstances for it is covering its variable costs.

Moreover the firm will only consider reducing employment if the reduction in demand is regarded as permanent. If the firm believes that the level of demand, and with it $PVMRP_L$, will recover, it might be wise to retain its existing workforce. If it dismisses them during the downturn they may be unavailable for re-employment when demand recovers. Whether or not labor that is discharged now is available for rehire in the future depends on the nature of the recession. If the recession is specific to the firm the firm may regard the chances of dismissed employees gaining employment elsewhere as high and the chances that they will be available for rehire as correspondingly low. If the recession is general then the chances that discharged employees will find a job elsewhere may be small and the firm's chances of re-employing the workers correspondingly higher. All other things being equal, firms would prefer to lay off the workers and save on wages but they will only do so if this does not prejudice the possibility of earning a return on their prior investments. The firm will, therefore, retain its existing employees provided the present value of $MRP_{L1} + MRP_{L2}$ does not fall below the present value of $W_1 + W_2$ by a magnitude greater than the expected costs of identifying, recruiting and training the replacement labor required at some time in the future.

A firm's speculations as to whether or not to dismiss its employees in the recession will be different where the employee has a stake in the firm, as occurs when the employee has borne part of the costs of specific investment. In Chapter 6 we suggested that where the human capital investment took the form of specific training, workers and firms would share the costs. Under these circumstances the employee's marginal product, and hence wage, is higher with the firm in which he or she was trained than with other firms and hence if dismissed or laid off an employee might still make himself or herself available for re-employment. A worker who shares the investment in firm-specific human capital might be viewed as purchasing stock in the firm for he or she has a stake in the firm which those who have not invested do not. Knowing this could either reduce or perhaps increase the firm's reluctance to lay off such employees.

The firm is now no longer indifferent between its existing workforce and the external labor supply to the firm. The external labor supply either does not possess the skills the firm requires, and/or it is costly to recruit. The firm will therefore prefer to retain its existing employees rather than recruit new employees to do the work it requires. The firm is locked in to its existing labor force, and the consequence of this is that the firm is likely to be more 'receptive' to claims by its workforce for wage rises. Consider how far the marginal employee, depicted in Fig. 9.1, could raise his or her wage before the firm dispensed with this employee's services. Clearly the employee could push the wage up to MRP_{L1} and MRP_{L2} that is secure the whole of the surplus that would otherwise accrue to the firm, in the second and third periods. This surplus in the second and third periods represents a periodic rent and the worker could attempt to obtain all of this. This is an issue we shall return to in Chapter 12.

Firm-specific labor investment in Europe, Japan and the United States

In general where there is a fixed element to labor costs employment is likely to exhibit greater stability over the business cycle than would otherwise occur. It has been suggested that those firms, or indeed countries, that invest heavily in specific training are likely to exhibit the greatest employment stability. Such an argument has been advanced to explain the much more substantial variations in employment over the business cycle which are evident in the United States when it is compared to either Europe or Japan. Evidence certainly exists which is consistent with the view that there is greater investment in specific human capital in Japan than in the United States. First, the job tenure of male workers in Japan is much longer than that of their US counterparts. By the time a typical male worker reaches the age of 65 he will have held approximately five jobs in Japan but 11 jobs in the United States. Moreover this longer job tenure does not appear to reflect any fundamental historical difference between the societies, for it appears to be a recent, post-Second World War, phenomenon in Japan.[5] Second, as noted above, bonus payments account for around 20 percent of total labor costs in Japan and these have been suggested to represent a return to firm-specific investments. Finally, wage profiles are far steeper in Japan than in the United States and seem to reflect firm-specific investments rather than general labor market experience. Hence after 20 years' employment most of which, 85 percent, is firm specific, a typical Japanese school leaver can expect to see an earnings increase of 214 percent. A comparable US worker can expect to see an earnings growth of only 93 percent.[6]

These features of the Japanese labor market are consistent with the existence of substantial firm-specific human capital but they do not constitute irrefutable evidence of its existence and, even if this interpretation is correct, it is an open question as to which came first, firm-specific human capital or long job tenure.

Japanese firms also appear to invest in other forms of specific human capital; namely building long-term relationships. This has the effect of lowering the transaction costs of business by lowering the information costs associated with employing and deploying labor.[7] Japanese employers and employees, it would appear, devote more resources to keeping each other fully informed of their intentions and to insuring that firms' and workers' objectives coincide. Whether the amount that they invest fully explains the earnings profiles and job stability we observe remains to be seen. But, as we shall see later, the industrial harmony that ought to be a product of such arrangements is certainly a feature of the Japanese industrial relations system. No doubt this plays no small part in the productivity advantage that so many Japanese firms enjoy over their US and European competitors.

LABOR UTILIZATION: WORKERS AND HOURS

The analysis above focused on the non-recurring fixed labor costs that firms incur each time they take on a new employee. While this investment imparted a marked degree of stability to the demand for employees, firms can still vary labor input by varying the number of hours each individual works. If hiring and firing represent long-run adjustment in the presence of fixed labor costs, then varying hours represents one short-run method of adjustment.

Faced with fluctuations in product demand, firms can vary the quantity of labor input either by varying employment or by varying hours per employee. Firms can vary either the stock of employees or their utilization, that is the hours they work. A possible path of adjustment for both hours and employment is shown in Fig. 9.4. Here a permanent one unit increase in sales leads to a permanent increase in labor demand. Initially 60 percent of the increased labor demand is satisfied by increasing hours of work and only 40 percent by increased employment, but thereafter employment

5. Hashimoto, M. and Yu, B.T. (1980) 'Specific capital, employment contracts and wage rigidity', *Bell Journal of Economics*, **11**, 536–49.
6. Hashimoto, M. and Raisian, J. (1988) in Hart, R.A. (ed.), *op. cit.*
7. Hashimoto, M. and Raisian, J. (1988) in Hart, R.A. (ed.), *op. cit.*

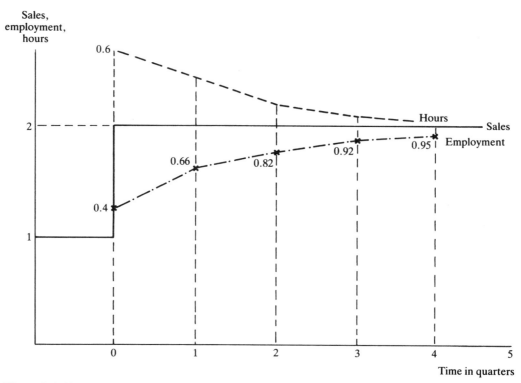

Figure 9.4 Short-run adjustment of hours and employment to an increase in sales. A permanent one unit increase in sales leads to a permanent increase in labor demand. At the outset 60 percent of this increase in labor demand is satisfied by extra hours and 40 percent by increased employment. In subsequent periods an increasing proportion of labor demand is satisfied by increased employment and extra hours worked are correspondingly reduced. The precise path of adjustment, to changes that are perceived to be permanent, will depend on the relative cost of adjusting employment and hours.

continues to rise while hours of work fall back to their trend level. Thus at the end of the first period two-thirds of the increased labor demand is satisfied by additional employees and only one-third by additional hours, at the end of the second period over 80 percent is satisfied by additional employees and less than 20 percent by extra hours, and so on. Eventually hours return to the long-run trend and increased employment has satisfied the whole of the addition to labor demand.

In general, extra hours can only be bought at a premium, i.e. overtime rates, and therefore where the change in sales, and hence labor demand, is perceived to be permanent the increase in labor demand may be satisfied at least cost by hiring additional employees. However, over the short run it may prove more expedient to incur overtime costs than to pay the once-over investment costs associated with hiring new employees. Average hours of work therefore act as a buffer to accommodate any shortfall or surplus of employment, and they do this by substantially exceeding or falling below, respectively, their equilibrium values. The precise paths of adjustment followed in any particular firm will reflect the relative costs of adjusting hours and employment.

By the same token, where a decline in demand is believed to be temporary firms and workers have incentives to maintain attachments. Such attachments offer the prospects that returns on past investments will resume when the recovery occurs. Only when the permanency of the downturn is perceived will employment be severed. In most major industrialized nations the beginning of any significant cyclical downturn in economic activity is marked by a reduction in hours of work below the trend established prior to the fall. Thus the oil price shock of 1973/74 was followed immediately by a reduction in hours while firms evaluated the permanence of the reduction in activity. Only in 1975 and 1976 did employment then begin to fall below trend.

It is interesting to contrast the relative volatility of average weekly hours and employment in different countries. Thus, as Table 9.3 reveals, fluctuations in numbers employed are significantly greater in the United States than they are in either the United Kingdom or Japan. Over the whole period 1963 to 1980, variations in employment, as measured by the standard deviation of the percentage rates of change of employment, are, at 4.05, almost twice as large in the United States as in either the United Kingdom, at 2.18, or Japan at 2.03. However, fluctuations in employment differ little between Japan and the United Kingdom. Again, fluctuations in hours of work, at 1.09 are significantly smaller in the United States than in either Japan, at 1.98, or the United Kingdom at 1.74. Thus in the United States adjustments in labor demand are more frequently achieved by varying employment than in either the United Kingdom or Japan, while in these latter two countries adjustment has been achieved by varying hours. Although both hours and employment generally fluctuated less, the same relative picture emerges in the period to 1972—the period prior to the first oil price rise.

Firms that are anxious to retain their labor in the face of a downturn in economic activity, that is believed to be temporary, may fail to reduce either hours or workers. Firms may instead continue to buy the same quantity of labor but use this less intensively. This is the phenomenon known as *labor hoarding*, whereby a gap emerges between paid-for and utilized or effective working hours. The distinction between

Table 9.3 Variations in manufacturing hours and employment in the United Kingdom, United States and Japan

	1963–80			1962–72		
	USA	UK	Japan	USA	UK	Japan
Employment (N)	4.05	2.18	2.03	3.39	1.95	2.15
Average Hours (H)	1.09	1.74	1.98	1.06	1.37	1.17
Total of N and H	4.78	3.22	1.09	4.06	2.70	0.91

Source: Gordon R.J. (1982) 'Why US wage and employment behaviour differs from that in Britain and Japan', *Economic Journal*, **92**, 13–44.

paid-for and effective hours is likely to be a feature of almost all jobs, for firms usually pay for set-up time and some idle time, but labor hoarding involves the deliberate underutilization of labor as a device to retain the services of labor until the anticipated pick-up in demand. Evidence of substantial labor hoarding has been produced for the United States and the United Kingdom.[8] The existence of such a phenomenon is also suggested by the sharp rise in labor productivity that marks the recovery stage of the economic cycle in most industrialized nations. Such a phenomenon appears most pronounced among blue collar workers in the United Kingdom and the United States.

TOPICS IN LABOR DEMAND

Flexible staffing arrangements

Firms operate in an uncertain environment and have to accommodate unexpected variations that occur in product and factor markets. There are a number of ways of doing this: laying off or taking on additional 'permanent' staff; increasing or reducing the hours that individuals work; building up and running down inventories; lengthening and shortening delivery and waiting times. But in recent years a further mechanism has found increasing favour—that of hiring staff on an as-needed basis. These sorts of flexible staffing arrangements have been shown to be an important and growing component of many US employers' short-run adjustment strategies and they are now growing in importance in Europe. Agency hires in particular have grown substantially in Europe in the 1980s.

Employers use flexible staffing arrangements to deal with stochastic elements in both product demand and labor supply. Employers develop different staffing arrangements to cope with the expected and the unexpected components of demand. Permanent staff, hired either on a full- or a part-time basis, will be engaged to cope with any permanent increase in demand. Expected permanent variations in labor supply may also result in the engagement of extra permanent staff. Deliberate overstaffing is one way of accommodating expected absence due to illness, staff vacations and leave. In contrast, where there is an unexpected increase in demand or an unexpected shortfall in labor supply and where either the fixed costs of taking on permanent staff are high or firms have to pay premium rates to induce existing employees to supply extra hours, then hiring temporary workers may be the least cost solution. The fixed cost of hiring temporary staff may be lower if these staff are not covered by legislation restricting the circumstances under which they can be dismissed or if they are not eligible for certain types of fringe benefits or severance pay.

Hiring staff on an as-needed basis can have disadvantages. They may have less experience with the particular tasks they will be required to perform and are unlikely to possess any of the specific skills that are required. Such flexible staffing arrangements are only appropriate for filling vacancies that require either no skills or general skills.

8. Taylor, J. (1974) *Unemployment and Wage Inflation with Special Reference to Britain and the USA,* Longman.

If temporary workers expect to be on the job for only a short while, they will not be motivated by the expectation of future or deferred rewards that may form an element of a permanent employee's lifetime compensation package. For this reason those hired on an as-needed basis may perform less well. Yet despite these shortcomings it is evident that the net benefits of flexible staffing frequently exceed those of permanent hires for the practice is widespread in the United States.

A 1986 survey of nearly 800 private firms in manufacturing, finance, insurance and health care in the United States revealed that 77 percent of all organizations made some use of agency temporaries, 64 percent made their own short-term hires, and 36 percent had a pool of workers who were on call.[9] In all, 93 percent of the organizations had resort to at least one of these arrangements. Typically, agencies were relied on for the services of accountants, clerical help, laborers, maintenance workers and nurses, all general or unskilled occupations. The typical length of such an assignment was between one and four weeks. Short-term hires were used to deal with rather more predictable but irregular peaks in demand such as those associated with Christmas or the summer vacation. Accordingly, the typical length of such a short-term hire was between one and three months. Finally, the typical duration of employment of a worker on call, such as laborers hired through union hiring halls, or retirees recalled occasionally, was shortest of all at less than one week.

Those organizations which made most use of flexible staffing arrangements had low levels of unionization, on average less than 10 percent. Unions typically oppose the use of such flexible staffing arrangements and thus raise the costs associated with this method of adjustment in unionized firms. Organizations reporting either a highly variable or highly seasonal product demand also made greatest use of flexible arrangments. But the survey also found that there was no distinction between large and small firms in their use of flexible staffing arrangements.

Flexible staffing arrangements may also serve another purpose: they may act as a screening device. Employers are often better able to judge the potential productivity of employees when they observe them at work. Such temporary employment arrangements may also suit those individuals wishing to acquire more information about the characteristics of different jobs. A large number of respondents to the 1986 survey said that they occasionally or frequently hired the flexible staffers into permanent jobs.

Workweek reductions

So far we have focused on hours and employment as quantities that adjust to varying degrees in the short and longer run to achieve the desired changes in labor demand. The choices that confront the firm with respect to combinations of employees and hours can be depicted as in Fig. 9.5. For a given expenditure on labor the firm can employ various combinations of workers and hours—these combinations are depicted by the isocost line $L_c L_c$. If the firm chooses to buy fewer hours from each worker it

---

9. See Abraham, K.G. (1988) 'Flexible staffing arrangements and employers' short-term adjustment strategies', in Hart, R.A. (ed.), *op. cit.*, pp. 288–311.

can employ more of them, or it can employ fewer workers and induce each of them to work longer by paying overtime premiums. The extent to which it can trade off hours for workers is reflected in the slope of the line L_cL_c. If workers work more than a standard working week the firm must pay an overtime premium. It is for this reason that the labor cost line L_cL_c is kinked at N_1 and slopes downwards more steeply beyond the 40-hour standard week. The slope of the isocost line L_cL_c reflects the relative price of workers and hours.[10] In general it is steeper the more expensive are hours relative to workers and shallower the greater are the fixed costs of labor relative to the hourly wage. The intercept of the isocost line on the vertical axis is, at any given level of expenditure, determined by the magnitude of the fixed costs of employing more workers. As these increase the isocost line shifts downwards and we shall discuss an example of a change in fixed costs shortly.

A family of isoquants reflecting different levels of output produced by various combinations of hours and workers can also be drawn. The slope of these isoquants reflects the relative productivity of hours and workers. Why should productivity differ? If we hire an extra worker the hours we obtain may contain some devoted to set-up time which are not directly productive. While if we buy only hours these may all be productive. Of course, workers could become fatigued if they work long hours and under certain circumstances it may be more productive to hire additional workers. The steeper the isoquant the more workers must be substituted for a unit decrease in hours, therefore the greater the relative productivity of hours. Equilibrium is determined as illustrated by a point of tangency between an isoquant and labor cost line. At the point of tangency the ratios of the marginal costs are equal to the ratios of the marginal products of hours and workers. Such a point is illustrated at Y in Fig. 9.5.

Suppose that the relative efficiency of hours and workers were such that in equilibrium all workers worked some hours overtime as indicated by point Y. Now fewer workers would be employed than if they all worked only the standard working week shown as point X. What would happen if there were a reduction in standard hours of work to 35 per week? After such a reduction has been implemented the ratio of fixed to variable labor costs rises and the slope of the budget constraint beyond the new standard working week of 35 hours becomes more shallow as indicated by the slope of L_c^1. The effect of the reduction in standard hours of work has been to reduce the *relative* price of hours. Accordingly, at the new equilibrium, Z, fewer workers, N_3, are employed and each works relatively more overtime than they did before the reduction in hours. Each worker is working $H_3 - 35$ hours per week compared to $H_2 - 40$ before the cut. Of course, at this new equilibrium, the firm's total outlay on labor has not changed. If, instead, the firm increased its expenditure in order to maintain output Q_1, the new equilibrium would be Z^1. Now more workers would be employed than at Z but each worker would be working a longer workweek than before the hours cut because they would each be working substantially more overtime. Nonetheless, some increase in employment would have occurred.

10. Hart shows that the isocost lines are in fact also convex to the origin, but for simplicity of diagrammatic exposition we depict the isocost line as a kinked straight line in Figs. 9.6 and 9.7. See Hart, R.A. (1987) *Working Time and Employment*, Allen and Unwin, London and Boston.

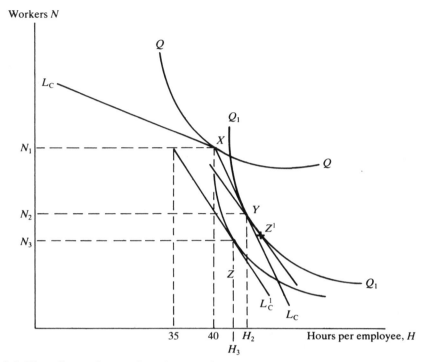

Figure 9.5 The effects of a workweek reduction on employment of hours and workers. The isocost line L_cL_c is kinked at $H = 40$ because hours worked in excess of this are paid at premium rates. Each isoquant maps the various combinations of hours per employee, and workers that can be used to produce a given level of output. Equilibrium is indicated by the point of tangency between an isoquant and isocost line. Two such equilibria are indicated: X at which all employees work the standard 40-hour week and Y at which all work some overtime. Starting from Y suppose there was a reduction in the standard workweek, this will: (i) flatten and shift inwards the labor cost line to L_c^1 if the firm spends the same on labor services before and after the workweek reduction. Scale and substitution effects will reduce employment and increase overtime hours. Equilibrium will reduce from Y to Z; (ii) flatten the labor cost line if the firm increases its expenditure on labor services in order to continue producing Q_1. Only the substitution effect will operate reducing employment and increasing overtime hours. The equilibrium point shifts from Y to Z^1

The above result is of considerable policy interest. The high unemployment which Europe and the United States experienced in the early 1980s led, in Europe, to proposals for *worksharing*. Such proposals seemed to suggest that there existed a fixed amount of work which should be redistributed and, chief among the proposals to reduce unemployment, was one to reduce the standard working week. We have seen above that such a policy will raise the ratio of fixed to variable costs and therefore raise the relative price of workers. This is because at given overtime rates a lower proportion of total hours per worker are now compensated at the cheaper standard rate. This results in a substitution effect out of workers and into hours. Fewer workers will be employed and, provided that workers are prepared to work overtime, each worker will work longer hours. The exception is where the firm increases its expenditure on labor.

However, where the firm is constrained in its expenditures there will be a reduction in the scale of its activities. The negative scale effect, the move from Z^1 to Z, will then reinforce the substitution effect, the move from Y to Z^1.

Estimates of the impact of reductions in standard weekly hours or overtime hours have confirmed that such a reduction leads to a rise in overtime hours to compensate. Long-run estimates for the United Kingdom reveal that a reduction in standard hours results in a reduction in total hours of only two-thirds this size.[11] Again, cross-section estimates for the United Kingdom suggested that in 1980, when the average annual hours worked per operative in industry were 1850, a reduction of 10 percent, 185 hours worked, resulted in a rise in overtime hours of 125 per annum in those enterprises working overtime.[12]

On the other hand, simulation exercises using large-scale macroeconomic models tend to find positive employment responses to reductions in the workweek. A 10 percent reduction in the workweek has been suggested to produce a 3.7 percent rise in employment in the United Kingdom,[13] and 6 to 8 percent in the cases of France[14] and West Germany.[15] Such macro models have the advantage that they set the issue in a general equilibrium context. They variously, although certainly not always, allow for inflation, balance of payments, monetary, fiscal and investment effects. However, the highest estimates are produced by assuming that the increase in wages is fully compensated by a productivity increase and that the government accommodates these changes through reducing taxation—both highly questionable assumptions. There are still further reasons for being skeptical about these results for none of the models adequately distinguishes between fixed and variable labor costs which, as we have seen, are a crucial determinant of the choice between workers and hours.

Temporary layoffs

A feature of the US labor market is the extent to which firms resort to temporary layoffs to accommodate cyclical fluctuations in economic activity. They discharge their employees with the declared intention of re-engaging them when economic activity picks up. This is part of the explanation of the much greater variation in employment in the United States recorded in Table 9.3. Yet the analysis earlier in this chapter suggested that resort to layoffs represents a risky strategy where the workers laid off embody significant levels of firm-specific human capital. Temporary layoffs increase the probability of permanent separation and thus prejudice the resumption of returns

11. Neale, A.J. and Wilson, R.A. (1985) 'Average weekly hours of work in the UK, 1948–1980: a disaggregated analysis', University of Warwick.
12. Hart, R.A. and Wilson, N. (1988) 'The demand for workers and hours: micro evidence from the UK metal working industry', in Hart, R.A. (ed.), *op. cit.* pp. 162–79.
13. Whitely, J.D. and Wilson, R.A. (1986) 'The impact on employment of a reduction in the length of the working week', *Cambridge Journal of Economics*, **10**, 43–59.
14. Oudiz, G., Roul, E., and Sterdyniak, H. (1979) 'Reduce induree du travaille: quelles consequences?', *Economie et Statistique*, May, 3–17.
15. Henize, J. (1981) 'Can a shorter work week reduce unemployment? A German simulation study', *Simulation*, La Jolla, California, pp. 145–56.

on prior investments when economic activity recovers. Why therefore do US firms employ this adjustment device and why is it so little used in Europe?

One suggestion is that the unemployment system in the United States effectively subsidizes layoffs. Contributions to unemployment insurance schemes are not fully related to the use of the scheme and benefits are not taxed as ordinary income. The lack of experience rating in contributions effectively subsidizes high layoff firms, for the shorter average tenure of their workforce does not result in higher unemployment insurance contributions from such firms. Thus it has been calculated that in the State of Michigan a firm with an average layoff rate of 3 percent per annum receives a subsidy of 0.3 percent of its labor costs. In contrast, a firm with layoff rate of 15 percent receives a subsidy of 7.5 percent of labor costs.[16]

But although firms may find layoffs an attractive strategy, we should still expect to find them taking steps to minimize the probabilities of permanent separations. They will therefore lay off workers with the greatest stake in the firm: those with the strongest interest in returning. Workers who enjoy privileges of substantial non-transferable fringe benefits, as a result of their seniority, or workers with wages above the market clearing rate are likely to have a strong interest in returning to the same firm. All these are characteristics of unionized workers and indeed it has been confirmed that unionized firms have a much higher propensity than non-unionized firms to use lay-offs to achieve labor reductions. Non-unionized firms appear to make more use of quits and rehires than of layoffs and recalls.[17]

Yet a puzzle emerges. Why are temporary layoffs so uncommon in Europe and Japan? Here the conditions which we have identified above as those which should encourage layoffs are more prevalent than in the United States. In Europe no attempt is made to link contributions to firms' layoff experience, thus the gross subsidy from low to high layoff firms should be more pronounced. In addition, the incidence of unionization is greater in Europe than in the United States and the level of unemployment benefits is more generous. So why no layoffs? One explanation advanced is that there are more institutional barriers to layoffs in Europe where statutory provision protects against unfair or arbitrary dismissal, but in fact such statutes usually specifically permit temporary layoffs. An alternative explanantion is that the low earnings threshold on contributions to the unemployment insurance fund in the United States effectively means that increases in such contributions constitute an increase in fixed labor costs.[18] In Europe the high earnings ceilings for contributions result in an increase in contributions adding to variable costs. An increase in fixed relative to variable costs, such as will result from a contribution increase in the United States, induces a substitution out of workers and into longer hours of work. Equally an increase in contributions in Europe will add to variable costs and induce reductions in hours rather than workers. Thus it has been proposed that the distinction between

16. Topel, R.H. and Welch, F. (1980) 'Unemployment insurance: survey and extensions', *Economica*, **47**, 301–22.
17. Medoff, J.L. (1979) 'Layoffs and alternatives under trade unions in US manufacturing', *American Economic Review*, **69**, 380–95.
18. See Fitzroy, F.R. and Hart, R.A. (1985) 'Hours, layoffs and unemployment insurance funding: theory and practice in an international setting', *Economic Journal*, **95**, 700–13.

fixed and variable costs and the manner in which they change might provide an explanation of the preference for hours reduction in Europe and Japan and temporary layoffs in the United States.[19]

Marginal employment subsidies

On various occasions in the recent past both the United States and United Kingdom have experimented with marginal employment subsidies. The New Jobs Tax Credit operated in the United States and the Temporary Employment Subsidy and Small Firms Employment Subsidy operated between 1975 and 1979 in the United Kingdom. These schemes were introduced to improve the employment prospect of particular groups. The general form of such policies is that they are of limited duration and they have therefore been designed to aid recruitment and not to provide a permanent subsidy to employment. Typically they are targeted on individuals who would be unemployed in the absence of the subsidy.

The intended effects of a marginal employment subsidy can be illustrated using Fig. 9.6. The subsidy might take one of two forms. First, a subsidy to the variable costs of employing the target group, an hourly wage subsidy; second, a subsidy to the fixed costs, some form of lump sum payment. The former of these will flatten the lower section of the labor services curve below N_1, since a given budget will now buy more hours, the latter will steepen the section of the labor services curve above N_1 since a subsidy to fixed costs, or per worker, will permit more workers to be employed. These effects are illustrated by the broken lines in Fig. 9.6. The nature of the labor services that will subsequently be purchased depends on both the initial equilibrium position and the nature of isoquants. If the firm were initially at Z_0 a subsidy to hourly wage costs would result in a new equilibrium, Z_1, which would likely involve the purchase of more workers, $N_3 - N_2$, and more hours per employee, $H_3 - H_2$. The full effect of such a subsidy will not be translated exclusively into additional employment. If the initial equilibrium were at Y_0, where the firm's employees were working no overtime, a subsidy per worker would result in a new equilibrium involving a reduction in hours per employee and a substantial addition to employment as indicated by Y_1. Both scale and substitution effects have produced the outcomes shown here and they suggest that if the practical problems associated with constructing such a policy can be overcome, marginal employment subsidies can improve the demand for the labor services of the targeted group. However, the practical problems can be substantial.

First they are likely to lead to *displacement*: an increase in employment of the target group at the expense of other groups. Thus if young people are the target group they are likely to be substituted for women, for as we have seen before there is empirical evidence suggesting that women and young people are reasonably close substitutes. The subsidy will also, likely, be paid on all new jobs created for the targeted group for it is virtually impossible to distinguish and subsidize only those new jobs that result from the existence of the subsidy. This may limit the cost effectiveness of such a measure.

19. See Hart (1987), *op. cit.*

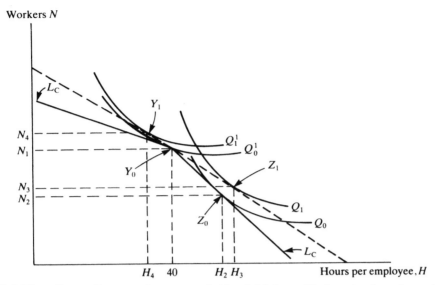

Figure 9.6 The effects of an employment subsidy. Initial equilibrium is given by points of tangency between the isocost line $L_c L_c$ and the isoquant, Q_0^1. A lump sum subsidy to the fixed costs of employing the targeted group steepens the labor cost line above N_1. A subsidy to the variable costs of employing the targeted group, an hourly wage subsidy, flattens the labor cost line below N_1. The outcome of each of these policies depends on the initial equilibrium and nature of the isoquants. Starting from an initial equilibrium Y_0 at which employees work only a standard workweek, a subsidy per worker increases employment from N_1 to N_4. Starting from Z_0, at which point all employees work some overtime, an hourly wage subsidy leads to an increase in employment from N_2 to N_3, and an increase in hours from H_2 to H_3

Finally, such policies are most likely to be introduced when there is a downturn in economic activity. At such times labor hoarding may be substantial and firms may not be realizing any return on their previous investments in firm-specific human capital. Under these circumstances the prospect of reduced labor costs at the margin is unlikely to prove a sufficient inducement to increase employment.

Part-time working

One of the most striking features of the labor markets in most countries has been the growth of part-time employment. As Table 9.4 reveals, by the late 1980s almost one in two females in Sweden and the United Kingdom and around one-third of females in Australia, Germany and Japan were employed in a part-time capacity. One-fifth of the total working populations in Australia and the United Kingdom and a quarter of the workforce in Sweden were employed in a part-time capacity.

Why has there been this substantial growth in part-time employment? Explanations have typically focused on the supply side of the labor market, emphasizing the increasing willingness to work of married women with children, of the preferences for a gradual move into retirement, via part-time work, on the part of older workers and,

Table 9.4 The share of the working population in part-time employment in various countries[†]

	All persons	All males	All females
Australia	20.0	7.4	39.2
France	11.8	3.4	23.2
Germany	12.9	2.1	29.8
Japan	16.6	7.3	30.5
Sweden	25.2	6.7	45.1
United Kingdom	21.6	4.6	45.0
United States	17.3	10.2	26.1

Source: OECD *Employment Outlook*, September 1988, Table 1.4
[†] The data refer to 1986 for France, Germany and the UK and to 1987 for the remaining countries.

as we have seen in the United States, the propensity of students to work part time to help finance their education. However, the demand side has not been totally neglected for it has also been suggested that the changing industrial composition of employment, as a result of the growth in service sector employment, has led to a substantial increase in the demand for part-time workers.

In much of Europe, the growth in part-time employment contrasted with a decline in full-time jobs, although in Japan there has been a growth in both full-time and part-time employment. However, the European experience suggests that we should look in more detail at developments on the demand side and in particular at the role played by relative costs. Economic theory would suggest that, *ceteris paribus*, part-time employment will expand relative to full-time employment if the hourly labor costs of part-time workers fall, relative to those of full-time workers, or if the fixed and quasi-fixed costs of part-time employment fall relative to those of full-time workers. In both Europe and the United States the total labor costs of part-time workers are substantially below those of full-time workers. This is due to a variety of reasons. Part-time hourly wages and fringe benefits are frequently lower than those of full-time workers, even after controlling for the differential incidence of unionization across the two groups. In addition, part-time workers are sometimes not eligible for employer-financed social welfare programs or for redundancy payments.

These points are illustrated in Fig. 9.7 in which, as before, a labor cost line is drawn to identify the number of hours of work that are secured at a given level of expenditure by various combinations of part-time and full-time labor. If part-time labor is relatively cheaper than full-time labor the line will have a shallow slope as indicated. The particular combination of full- and part-time workers chosen will depend on both the relative cost of full- and part-time hours and on their relative productivity. The relative productivity of full- and part-time hours is reflected in the isoquants, Q_0 and Q_1, drawn in Fig. 9.7. The hours of full-time and part-time workers might differ in productivity for a number of reasons. Full-time workers may prove less productive than part-timers at some jobs due to the effects of fatigue. Full-timers might be less

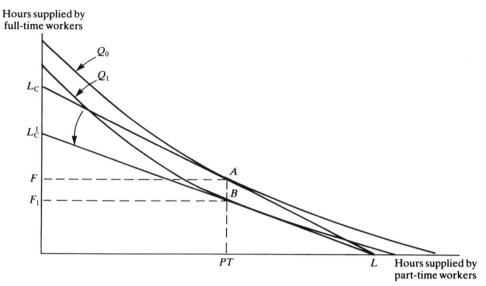

Figure 9.7 The impact of a change in relative labor costs on the shares of full-time and part-time employment. As the costs of full-time labor rise relative to those of part-time labor, the labor cost line L_c flattens to L_c^1. We move away from the old equilibrium A and a new equilibrium is established at point B. In this example the relative cheapening of part-time labor results in a fall in the demand for full-time labor, while that for part-time labor remains unchanged. The substitution effect in the above example resulted in a move out of full-time and into part-time labor. This was partially offset by the scale effect which reduced the demand for both full- and part-time labor. The relative share of part-time employment has risen

productive in jobs that require short concentrated bursts of attention. Again full-timers will be less productive where the pattern of product demand is subject to marked peaks and troughs, as in many personnel service industries, and they therefore spend periods doing little. On the other hand, part-timers will be less productive in those jobs that require sustained periods of application and continuity of decision making.

Equilibrium occurs where the labor cost line is just tangent to the highest isoquant attainable as shown at A. At this point the familiar conditions are realized. The ratio of the marginal costs of full- and part-time work is just equal to the ratio of the marginal products of full- and part-time labor. Now it is easy to illustrate that a rise in the hourly wage of full-time workers—part-time workers' wages remaining unchanged—will flatten the labor cost line to L_c^1, and result in a reduction in the amount of full-time employment.

In Fig. 9.7 the new equilibrium is shown as point B and in this example full-time employment falls from F to F_1 but part-time employment remains unchanged. Clearly, in this example, the share of part-time employment has increased due to the fall in its relative price. The exact outcome will of course depend on the magnitude of the substitution and the scale effects. The substitution effect will lead to a move out of full-time hours and into part-time hours when the relative price of the former increases. The scale effects may either reinforce or offset this development, we cannot say *a priori*.

The above would provide an explanation of developments in both the United States and Europe. It proposes that the relative cost advantage of part-time labor must have increased in recent years and that this development has been most pronounced in Europe. Is there empirical evidence to support this contention? To date few studies have investigated the issue from this perspective but for the United States there seems to be some support for this hypothesis.[20] In Europe the evidence is scarce and inconclusive.[21] However, it seems clear that both the level and the timing of the growth in part-time employment cannot be explained by factors on the supply side of the labor market alone. Relative costs and, in particular, relative fixed and variable costs are likely to be an important part of the explanation of the trends we have observed.

SUMMARY

How important are fixed labor costs? Those that are measurable appear to amount to at most 25 percent of total labor costs in some countries. This may not seem large enough to warrant the special attention we have devoted to this issue here. However, while a quarter of labor costs is not an insubstantial magnitude it must be recognized that the methods of calculating these are very much in the development stage. A typical firm's expenditures on labor contain a large fixed element for which no measure has yet been devised. This element is training costs, the major component of which is the opportunity cost of the forgone output of the trainee and supervisor.

The existence of substantial fixed costs means that the decision to take on extra workers is frequently an investment decision. For this reason an increase in product demand will seldom lead to an immediate increase in employment. Employment will increase with a lag as the permanancy of the new level of product demand comes to be appreciated. Similarly, employment is unlikely to be cut immediately there is a downturn in product demand. Indeed if the downturn is believed to be temporary firms may not reduce employment at all. They will wish to insure that they can re-engage the services of the workers in whom they have invested once economic activity picks up, for only in this way can the returns on their investment resume. Prominent among the fixed, often non-recurring, investments undertaken by firms is specific training. The existence of specific training, in particular, provides an explanation for one of the pronounced features of modern labor markets. The attachment of workers to a single firm for long periods of time and the reluctance of that firm to allow employment to fluctuate in line with output. This may be the

---

20. See Ehrenberg, R.G., Rosenberg, P. and Li, J. (1988) 'Part-time employment in the United States', in R.A. Hart (ed.) *op. cit.*, pp. 256–81.
21. Among the few studies are Disney, R. and Szyszesak, E. (1984) 'Protective legislation and part-time employment in Britain', *British Journal of Industrial Relations*, **22**, 78–100 for the United Kingdom and Buchteman, C.F. (1988) 'Entwicklungstendenzen det Teilzeitebeschaftigung and Gerinfugiigkeitsgrenze', *Wissenschaftszentrum Berlin Fur Sozialforschung*, for Germany.

explanation for the quite different pattern of variations in employment and hours of work that we observe in the United States, Japan and Europe.

The magnitude of fixed labor costs is also an important determinant of the effectiveness of some of the policies that were proposed in the 1970s and 1980s to combat unemployment. Worksharing was a policy frequently advocated in Europe and there were several variants of this. Cuts in the standard working week were advocated in the belief that, in order to secure the same input of labor services, firms would have to recruit more workers. Job splitting, two part-timers instead of one full-timer, was another proposal. In the face of substantial fixed labor costs both policies are likely to prove unsuccessful. Cuts in the workweek will lead to a substitution out of workers and into overtime hours. Promoting part-time employment may be unnecessary where part-timers enjoy a relative cost advantage, but where there are substantial fixed costs associated with both full- and part-time employment, job splitting will raise the costs of production and, via scale effects, reduce the volume of employment. Marginal wage subsidies could be more successful although the exact outcome would depend on whether the subsidy were to fixed or variable labor costs. The problems with marginal wage subsidies are those of insuring that improved employment for the targeted group is not at the expense of other workers.

PRINCIPAL CONCEPTS

Students should understand the following ideas and concepts that have been introduced in this chapter.

1. Fixed labor costs.
2. Non-recurring and recurring fixed costs.
3. A quasi-fixed factor of production.
4. The present value of the marginal revenue product and marginal costs.
5. Labor utilization and labor hoarding.
6. Temporary layoffs.
7. Marginal employment subsidies.

QUESTIONS FOR DISCUSSION

1. Why is equality of the wage or total variable labor costs, and the marginal revenue product of labor no longer the rule determining the level of employment in most firms?
2. Why does firm-specific training above all other elements of fixed labor costs explain worker and firm attachment?
3. What would be the labor market consequences of the introduction of a scheme under which workers post bonds to cover the costs the firm encounters when hiring and training labor?
4. Do we know how important specific training is in the major industrialized nations?

5. Contrast the effects on employment of a cut in the workweek without loss of pay with a cut in pay in line with the cut in hours.
6. What are the necessary conditions for the success of worksharing arrangements in reducing unemployment?
7. What are the advantages, if any, of subsidizing net additions to the firm's workforce compared to a general labor subsidy encompassing the total workforce?
8. What are the implications of the extensions of job security policies for firms' workers/hours decisions?
9. Why are temporary layoffs so rare in Europe and Japan?
10. Can developments on the demand side of the labor market contribute to our understanding of the recent growth in the share of part-time employment?

FURTHER READING

This chapter has been strongly influenced by the writings of Arthur Okun and Bob Hart. Okun, A. (1981) *Prices and Quantities: A Macroeconomic Analysis*, Blackwell, Oxford, argues persuasively for the role of fixed labor costs, in explaining both firm and worker attachment and the persistent growth of prices in the face of apparent excess supply. For Europeans familiar with the experience of stagflation in the early 1980s this book makes compelling reading. The student is recommended to read the early chapters of this book.

Hart has, for several years now, stressed and investigated the role of fixed labor costs in determining labor market outcomes. His early contribution *The Economics of Non-Wage Labour Costs*, Allen and Unwin, London, 1984, and more recent *Working Time and Employment*, Allen and Unwin, London and Winchester, Mass, 1987, offer more advanced treatments of the topics treated here. The more adventurous student is also recommended to read his most recent contribution *Employment, Unemployment and Labour Utilization*, Unwin Hyman, London and Boston, 1988.

PART 4

THE LABOR MARKET

In Part 4 we bring together the previous analysis of labor demand and supply and examine a number of aspects of the market for labor as a whole. In Chapter 10 we examine the mechanisms by which the market adjusts, recognizing that competition is but one of the two principal mechanisms by which labor market adjustment occurs. In the previous chapter it was shown that the scale of fixed labor costs frequently locked employers and workers together in long-term employment relationships, and that, as a result, labor markets fail to clear in the simple manner proposed by the competitive paradigm. Here it will be shown that other aspects of transaction costs, in this case the substantial costs of collecting and processing information, provide further explanations as to why the role of competition in allocating labor may be reduced. Institutions play an important allocative role in labor markets and, in this chapter, we shall examine those that are used to collate and process the information essential for matching workers and firms. The institutions of the labor market, that process and collect information, are many and varied yet their dynamics and impact are still far from well understood.

In Chapter 11 we look at the distribution of labor market rewards which might be expected to emerge if the labor market is competitive. The theory of equalizing differences, which is perhaps the most important proposition in labor economics, will be examined. However, we shall see that not all the predictions of this theory are realized and, accordingly, we shall examine a recent development, which tries to account for certain of the remaining unexplained differences in labor market rewards—efficiency wage theory. This theory attempts to provide a further competitive explanation for some of the observed phenomena.

In Chapter 12 we focus attention on the market for labor within the firm. Known as the internal labor market it is here that we find those labor markets that have been called career markets. In many circumstances the external market provides little guide to the appropriate levels of pay, and for this reason the internal market in many firms is far from a mirror image of the external market in the skills the firm employs. The magnitude of transaction costs is such as to shut out the forces of competition over a wide range of different jobs, and in consequence pay is determined by bargaining and rules. A distinctive feature of the internal market is the role that rules play in allocation. The internal labor market has quite distinct characteristics and dynamics of its own and the reasons for this will be discussed. Analysis of the consequences, for labor market behavior of the widespread existence of internal labor markets, is still in the early stages of development but is potentially one of the most important areas in labor economics.

Finally, in Chapter 13 we look at the persistent differences that exist, between the pay of men and women, and, between white and black workers, in the majority of advanced industrial nations. We review the competing explanations for discrimination in labor markets and the empirical evidence to support these theories. In the last part of this chapter we turn to look at the government policies, which have been designed to remove discrimination, and at the success they have encountered.

10

LABOR MARKET CLEARING: COMPETITION AND INSTITUTIONS

In previous chapters we have conducted a detailed, but separate, analysis of both the supply and the demand sides of the labor market. In all subsequent chapters we bring the two sides together and consider the market for labor as a whole. First, we consider the dimensions of the labor markets we are to study: the way in which we delineate one labor market from another. We look at what our definitions of a market mean in practice. We then move on to discuss the different mechanisms by which labor markets clear. A recurring theme, in many of the subsequent chapters, is that the forces of competition are shut out over wide areas of employment, and that very different mechanisms have to be relied upon to clear the market. The explanation for this is that the transaction costs associated with changing jobs are high. One of the reasons for this is that information in labor markets is very far from perfect. Another is that the fixed costs of taking on new employees are high. Firms and workers have to deploy considerable resources to collect and process information about labor market opportunities, and in order to do this they frequently rely on institutional rather than market mechanisms. In this chapter we look at the channels by which individuals collect information and at some of the institutions they construct to assist them in the process.

THE BOUNDARIES OF THE LABOR MARKET

The labor market is an analytical construct, distinguishing the area in which the buyers and sellers, of a particular type of labor, come together to complete transactions involving the exchange of labor services. This exchange involves the provision of a certain quantity of labor at an agreed price, the wage rate, and although the terms on which it takes place can be settled without the particular parties to the exchange meeting, when the time comes for delivery of the labor services, those providing them have to do so in person. Individuals have to travel to a place of work to deliver their labor services and the geographical distance over which such journeys take place is one determinant of the boundaries of the labor market.

Most frequently analysis focuses on *local labor markets*. These have been defined in terms of the frictions that inhibit labor mobility. Workers, it is proposed, seek to maximize the utility associated with their place of residence and achieve this, for any given level of expected benefit, by minimizing the pecuniary and psychic costs associated with both the daily journey to work and the search costs associated with distinguishing alternative employment opportunities. This in turn suggests that when defining a local market we shall need to take account of: (i) the travel-to-work costs; (ii) the employment opportunities; (iii) the composition of the labor force; and (iv) the availability of information on wage and job vacancies which exists within each geographical area.[1] Thus a local labor market is defined to be a spatially delineated area which, simultaneously, fulfils the following requirements:

1. An insignificant proportion of daily travel-to-work journeys are made across the boundary.
2. Employment opportunities within the market do not discriminate significantly, in terms of the pecuniary or psychic daily travel costs, between suppliers of labor from different places within the boundary.
3. Each supplier of labor has (almost) complete information concerning the wage and employment opportunities within the boundary.
4. Firms obtain the major proportion of their labor supply within their own boundary.

At a higher level of aggregation a *regional labor market* may be defined as a collection of local markets but with the following additional characteristics:

1. The psychic and pecuniary costs of migration within any region are significantly less than those associated with migration between regions.
2. Information on wage and employment opportunities within a region, while far from perfect, is still significantly less imperfect than is information between regions. It should follow from the above that the level of intra-regional migration is significantly higher than is the level of inter-regional migration.

Both local and regional labor markets are therefore defined with respect to the 'frictions' that inhibit labor mobility. Areas are distinguished by reference to discontinuities that appear to exist when we consider the sources of such frictions in

---

1. Hart, R.A. (1981) 'Regional wage change transmission and the structure of regional wages and unemployment', in Martin, R.L. (ed.), *Regional Wage Inflation and Unemployment*, Pion, Methuen Inc., pp. 17–45.

a geographical setting. Sometimes, the boundaries are not as rigid as we imply and are best regarded as bands, which identify different levels of resistance, where the boundaries of one or several local and regional markets overlay those of others. Sometimes labor markets are geographically distinct due to their geographical remoteness or because they are separated by the existing structure of road and rail links. As a result distinct travel-to-work patterns emerge and it is these that are used to distinguish different labor markets in empirical work. The labor market is accordingly delineated by the geographical dimensions of the underlying labor supply and labor demand schedules.

LABOR MARKET ADJUSTMENT

In the standard competitive model of the labor market the equilibrium wage and associated level of employment are determined by the intersection of the labor supply and demand schedules. Their intersection produces a market clearing wage, at which level there are no frustrated buyers or sellers of labor, with the result that the quantity of labor willingly supplied, at that wage, exactly equals the quantity of labor willingly demanded. How is this equilibrium achieved? Two alternative mechanisms for achieving the desired outcome may be identified. These may be thought of as, in one case voting with one's feet, and, in the other, giving voice to one's grievances. The two mechanisms correspond respectively to the attainment of equilibrium through competition and through an institutional mechanism. We shall refer to the former mechanism as 'exit' and the latter as 'voice'.[2] Together they describe the two mechanisms by which human society adjusts to changing circumstances, and they correspond, respectively, to adjustment as an economic process and adjustment as a political process.

To illuminate this distinction consider the following, frequently remarked, situation of a couple in a restaurant with an unwelcome source of protein in their soup, a fly. Two distinct avenues for adjusting to this unwelcome situation are open to them. They may either voice their discontent, call over the waiter and demand that the situation be rectified, or simply register their dissatisfaction by walking out of the restaurant. Evidently the method chosen will depend on the costs and benefits of each channel. To get up and leave the restaurant will be the most costly option if the couple were looking forward, with pleasurable anticipation, to the main course; if this happens to be a rare lapse on the part of their favorite restaurant; or if, quite simply, they wouldn't 'get another table at a decent restaurant at this time of night'. When the transaction costs, associated with switching to another supplier, are perceived to be prohibitively high the voice mechanism will be the preferred avenue of adjustment. In contrast, if the costs of going elsewhere are perceived to be low, perhaps it was a fastfood joint and it was a marginal decision to go there anyway since there was another down the street, or perhaps the waiter is strangely absent, voting with one's feet, as proposed in the competitive paradigm, may be the preferred method of adjustment. These two

2. See Hirschman, A.O. (1970) *Exit, Voice and Loyalty*, Harvard University Press, Cambridge, Mass.

mechanisms describe the alternative ways in which individuals adjust to changing conditions. Consider the precise form they take in the labor market.

Competition—exit

A competitive market is characterized by many buyers and many sellers of a particular type of labor. The market clears, that is a wage emerges at which supply equals demand, because individuals are both willing and able to respond to the changes in market conditions they perceive. The nature of this adjustment process is described in Fig. 10.1 in which labor supply L_1^s is a positive function of the real wage and labor demand L^d exhibits diminishing returns. The point of intersection of the two schedules identifies the level of employment L_1 and real wage W_1/P, at which the labor market is in equilibrium.

Now suppose that there is a change, say a deterioration in the conditions of employment in this labor market. The advantages of employment in this labor market have deteriorated at the prevailing real wage W_1/P so that now fewer people are willing to work in this industry at that real wage rate. If $L_1 - L_2$ fewer people are willing to work at W_1/P then the labor supply curve shifts back to L_2^s. For this reduction in labor supply to occur employees must perceive the change that has occurred and, some

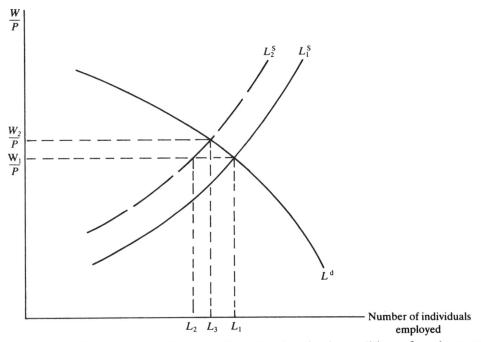

Figure 10.1 Equilibrium restored through quits. A deterioration in conditions of employment in this industry leads to a reduction in effective supply from L_1^s to L_2^s. Quits rise and firms counter by raising the wage rate from W_1 to W_2 to restore equilibrium

among them, those least attached to this industry (those earning the smallest rent), must decide that it is no longer worth remaining in this industry and, as a result, quit this job to search for new employment. Employment initially falls to L_2 but this is not the end of the story, for the firm reacts to the increased quit rate by raising the wage it pays employees. It thus attracts some individuals back into its employment or, if the offer is instantaneous, induces some to reconsider their position and stay on. Equilibrium is re-established at W_2/P and L_3. At this new equilibrium a higher wage is now being offered to compensate workers for the increased disamenity resulting from the change in the nature of the job.

The necessary conditions for the establishment of this new equilibrium were: first, that the existing labor force perceived that a deterioration in their working conditions had indeed occurred; second, that the deterioration was of a sufficient order of magnitude to lead to a desire to quit; and, third, that there were no substantial obstacles to their quitting. In addition, the model implied that there was no communication between workers and employers, for the only way that the workers' dissatisfaction was brought to the firm's attention was when they quit its employment. For these workers the benefits from quitting, the wage and the change in the conditions of work they would enjoy as a result of taking another job, exceeded the costs of quitting. The mechanism through which adjustment was secured, in this case, was that of 'exit' for the new equilibrium was established by workers 'voting with their feet'.

Implicit in this mechanism is a world in which information is conveyed by the behavior of individuals, in which preferences were not revealed until the workers quit. Indeed, even after the workers have left, their reasons for doing so may still not be understood by the firm. Employers took action because an unusually large number of workers began to quit their jobs. Increased quits served as a signal to increase wages, they signaled to employers that something was wrong, but they did not inform employers what was wrong.

Where the individuals who quit embody specific human capital investment, part of which has been paid for by the firm, the firm loses the opportunity of securing further returns on its investment. Moreover, the cost to the firm of quits will vary between individuals because not all workers are equally well suited for all positions. In general those jobs which require the most training are best filled by the more able individuals[3] and in order to identify workers of higher ability firms will have to engage in more extensive screeening.[4]

Individuals who quit also experience costs. These costs may take the form of lower earnings and the loss of returns on any prior specific human capital investment. Those who quit will also incur the costs of searching for jobs and screening out unsuitable ones and the costs of any further investment in human capital that may be required. The costs to the individual of quitting to seek or take a new job are likely to vary

3. See Topel, R. (1986) 'Job mobility, search and earnings growth', *Research in Labor Economics*, **8**, 199–233.
4. See Barron, J.M., Black, D.A., and Lowenstein, M.A. (1989) 'Job matching and on-the-job training', *Journal of Labor Economics*, 7(1), 1–19.

substantially between workers. Those individuals, with only a few years left before they quit the labor market, will be reluctant to quit one job and invest in another for they have only a limited period left during which to earn a return on any new investment. Similarly, those individuals who have invested in specific human capital, will be reluctant to quit for by so doing they forgo the opportunity of earning further returns on their investment. We might therefore expect to find a lower incidence of job changing among workers who have invested in specific human capital and among older workers and those workers, predominantly women, who intend to leave the labor market for non-market work at some point in the future.

Individuals may bear additional costs when they quit to change jobs. Job changing will, in somes cases, necessitate a change of location and residence. As we saw in Chapter 5, such migration decisions have important life cycle and family dimensions. The costs of quits which entail migration are likely to be greatest for those with working dependants or dependants in education. The mechanism of quits will therefore be used more frequently by some groups than by others. We might reasonably deduce that it will be younger workers, unmarried workers and those with the least specific human capital who will be the most likely to vote with their feet, and that it will be older workers and married workers who may stay put despite a deterioration in their working conditions.

While the competitive model requires that all workers are equally perceptive and are all equally prepared to quit (if they were not the employer would perceive that the workforce was no longer homogeneous and start to offer different contracts to each worker), it is not desirable that all workers behave in the same way. If, in consequence of a deterioration in working conditions, all workers had decided to quit (i.e. if the labor supply had been perfectly elastic) the firms in this industry would have had to shut down until they were able to recruit another workforce. Quits penalize the firm for inappropriate behavior, with regard to its own employees, but the penalty levied in this case would seem to be excessive. If the penalties are not to be too severe it is desirable that a firm's workforce contains a mixture of mobile and immobile workers. It may moreover be desirable that the less mobile are also the less perceptive workers. For if some workers perceive the deterioration in conditions, but are unable to quit in response to this, their morale and performance may be adversely affected. Alert and mobile workers provide firms with the necessary signals, that some change in relative pay and conditions is required, while the immobile provide them with the opportunity to remedy the situation while it is still retrievable. The competitive outcome, while emphasizing that the check on firms' behavior is that their workforce can always 'vote with their feet', in practice requires that only some workers behave in this way.

Table 10.1 provides some measure of the propensity of workers of different ages in Britain to 'vote with their feet', to change jobs in response to changing labor market opportunities. If, as seems likely, there is no substantial difference in the degree to which there were unexpected changes in the conditions of work or in the ability of different age groups to discern these, the differences in Table 10.1 reflect the much greater readiness to quit of younger workers and females. It is also evident from the

Table 10.1 (a) Percentage of full-time workers in Britain who had two or more employers in the last 12 months in 1984

Age	Men	Women
16–17	19	33
18–24	16	18
25–34	8	11
35–44	4	7
45–54	4	5
55–59	2	1
60–64	1	2

(b) Percentage of full-time workers in Britain who had two or more employers in the last 12 months over the period 1973–84

	1973	1976	1981	1984
Men	14	9	6	7
Women	18	12	9	11

Source: General Household Survey (1984), Table 6.39, London.

lower part of this table that the propensity to change jobs has varied over the years. In 1973, at the peak of the business cycle, the proportion changing jobs was highest for both males and females while 1981 was a year in which unemployment grew sharply and quits were at their lowest.

Rather different figures are available for the United States. Table 10.2 shows the proportion of workers who have been with their current employer for less than 12 months. The figures differ from those for Britain because they include new entrants and re-entrants to the labor force. Thus we should expect them to be rather higher than the figures reported above. However, we know that new entrants of both sexes are concentrated in the 16–24 age group, and that the vast majority of re-entrants are married women returning to work after childbearing. The figures for males aged 25 and over should therefore be roughly comparable to those reported in Table 10.1. As in the case of Britain they suggest that job changing declines with age and the figures again suggest that females change jobs more often than males; although we cannot be completely confident of this latest result for the female figures include re-entrants that swell these proportions.

Comparison of Tables 10.1 and 10.2 suggests that US workers at all ages are at least twice as likely as their British counterparts to change their jobs. US workers appear to have a greater propensity to vote with their feet than do British workers.

Table 10.2 Percentage of workers in the United States who had been with their current employer less than 12 months in 1983

Age	Men	Women
16–24	56.1	56.7
25–34	27.6	33.1
35–44	16.8	24.3
45–54	11.1	15.5
55–65	8.9	10.8

Source: Sehgal, E. (1984), 'Occupational mobility and job tenure in 1983', *Monthly Labor Review*, October, 18–23, US Department of Labor, Bureau of Labor Statistics.

These figures alone tell us nothing about the incidence of job changing within the working population. A succession of annual figures, recording that 10 percent of employees have been with their current employer less than 12 months, could mean either that a different 10 percent change employers each year, with the result that each employee changes jobs once every 10 years, or that the same 10 percent change their jobs every year. Job changing could be concentrated among a relatively small part of the population with the majority never or seldom changing jobs. In order to examine the truth of this statement we need to look at the other side of the coin: at information on job tenure; at information on the typical length of a job in the United States and Britain.

This information is reported in Table 10.3 from which it clearly emerges that many workers in both countries seldom if ever change jobs. Thus in 1979 almost 40 percent of males in Britain had already been with their current employer for more than 10 years while almost two-thirds had been with their current employer more than five years. The proportions are again much lower in the United States where 45 percent of males had been with their current employer more than five years, compared to 62 percent in Britain. Again, in the United States only 33 percent of females had been with their employers for more than five years compared to 45 percent in Britain for this same period. It is interesting to compare these figures for Britain and the United States to those for Japan. In Japan 54 percent of males had already been with their current employer more than 10 years and a substantial 80 percent had been with their current employer more than five years. No figures are available for females in Japan. It is apparent from these figures that workers are much more ready to 'vote with their feet' in the United States than they are in Britain and that in Britain they are much more ready to 'vote with their feet' then they are in Japan. The differences between the United States and Japan are therefore substantial.

It has been estimated that fewer than one-third of the jobs of full-time males, that were in progress in Britain in 1968, would end within 10 years; 56 percent would end

Table 10.3 The length of a job in Britain, Japan and the United States—years of tenure with current employer

Years	USA 1983 (aged 16 and over)		Japan 1979[†] (aged 21 and over)	Britain 1979 (aged 18 and over)	
	Males	Females	Males	Males	Females
1 or less	24.7	30.5	8.0	9.9	14.6
2 to 5	30.2	36.7	12.0	28.1	40.3
6 to 9	12.2	12.6	25.0	23.1	25.1
10 to 14	11.7	10.0	19.0	13.8	10.3
15 to 19	7.5	5.0	36.0	8.5	4.2
20 or more	13.7	5.2		16.6	5.3
TOTAL	100	100	100	100	100

Sources: Main, B.G. (1982), 'The length of a job in Great Britain', *Economica*, **45**, 329–33. Sehgal, E. (1984), *op. cit.* Hashimoto, M. and Raisian, J. (1985), 'Employment tenure and earnings profiles in Japan and the United States', *American Economic Review*, **75**(4), September, 721–35.
[†] These figures are read from Figure 2 in the Hasimoto and Raisian article and are not therefore as precise as those for the USA and Britain. Note also that the three final categories are 5–10 years, 10–15 and 15 + .

within 20 years; while 44 percent would last for more than 20 years.[5] Evidently in Britain most workers remain with the same firm for long periods of time. Indeed a substantial proportion remain with the same firm for the majority of their working lives. Workers in the United States have a higher propensity to change jobs but even here there is substantial stability. Thus it has been calculated 'that among workers aged 30 and above about 40 percent are working in jobs which will eventually last twenty years or more'.[6]

It is evident that even in the United States a substantial part of the workforce come to a stage in their working lives where they cease to 'vote with their feet'. How then do they adjust to changing conditions of work? How do they realize their objectives if not by changing jobs? Consider the alternative 'voice' mechanism.

Institutional mechanisms—voice

The transaction costs, which are associated with the process of labor turnover, explain why many workers are reluctant to quit. These transaction costs principally comprise the forgone returns on prior human capital investment, the costs of searching for a further job and the costs of further training. However, in addition to the magnitude of these transaction costs, reasons of risk aversion and uncertainty, due to incomplete information, may make workers reluctant to quit their jobs. The empirical evidence suggests that many workers seldom, if ever, quit even though they may no longer be

5. Main, B.G. (1982) 'The length of a job in Great Britain', *Economica*, **45**, 329–33.
6. Hall, R.E. (1982) 'The importance of lifetime jobs in the US economy', *American Economic Review*, **72**(4), 716–24.

completely satisfied with their present job. It is therefore hard to escape the conclusion that the competitive paradigm does not accurately describe the adjustment process throughout a significant part of modern labor markets.

What then happens to those that are tied to a firm, those who are immobile due to the substantial costs associated with quitting? Consider an extreme example in which all workers are tied to the firm in the short run, with the result that the short-run labor supply curve confronting the firms in this industry is perfectly inelastic. This is shown as SRL^s in Fig. 10.2. Over the longer run the number of individuals willing to work in this industry is an increasing function of the real wage as described by L^s. Now suppose there is a deterioration in the conditions of employment in this industry. Unlike the situation described above there will be no reduction in employment in this industry, employment will remain at L_1. If workers perceive the deterioration in their conditions of work but are unable to quit, their morale and with it their performance will deteriorate. The fall in productivity will lead firms to demand less labor at existing wage rates. The magnitude of the fall in labor demand is depicted by the inwards move of L_1^d to L_2^d. If firms are constrained to employ L_1 they will wish to pay each of the L_1

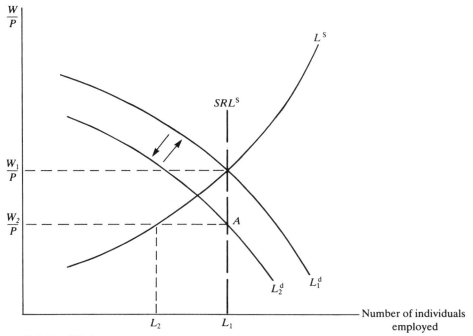

Figure 10.2 Equilibrium restored through 'voice'. Individuals are tied to the firm in the short run, the labor supply curve is inelastic above L_1. A deterioration in the conditions of employment in this industry leads to a reduction in morale and productivity, reflected in a downward shift in the labor demand curve from L_1^d to L_2^d, but if the firm cuts the wage in line with the deterioration in productivity this will result in a further fall in productivity. The solution is to create institutions informing the firm of the reasons for the deterioration in morale, thereby enabling it to take action to remedy the situation; to shift L_2^d to L_1^d again

individuals a lower wage W_2/P that is commensurate with their productivity. The new 'equilibrium' point is depicted at point A. However, if morale depends on wages this may not be an equilibrium. A cut in pay from W_1/P to W_2/P could lead to a further deterioration in morale, and hence in productivity, necessitating a further wage cut and so wage cuts are not the appropriate strategy in this situation.

In the above two examples detailed in Figs. 10.1 and 10.2 a deterioration in working conditions led, in the first case, to a rise in quits and, in the second, to a deterioration of morale. Common to both was an absence of communication between the parties, between the firm and its workers. In the absence of substantial transaction costs associated with quits this may not matter. However, where the costs are substantial the firm will wish to take steps to minimize these and one remedy open to the firm is to improve information flows. The firm must devise mechanisms, to construct institutions, which articulate and bring to the firm's attention the sources of employee dissatisfaction. Where the costs of quits are high, where the transaction costs associated with labor turnover are high, it is rational for either or both employers and employees to construct institutions that articulate and resolve employees' grievances.

What form might such institutions take? Trade unions constitute the most prominent of the labor market institutions constructed by workers. Works committees, employee representative councils and consultative committees are those most often initiated by firms. All can be viewed as mechanisms designed to articulate employees' grievances and to inform management about employees' preferences: they constitute mechanisms that promote adjustment and restore equilibrium. These institutional mechanisms have been described as the mechanism of 'voice', evidently since in this case employees give voice to their grievances; employees articulate their concerns through appropriate institutions.

Voice is a highly personal mechanism: it requires communication and interpersonal contact between employer and employee. In contrast 'exit' is entirely impersonal, it is the 'invisible hand' of Adam Smith and requires no communication between the parties. For some, the appeal of 'exit' is that it avoids the 'cumbrous political channels' associated with the alternative mechanism.[7] Yet in many circumstances there is no alternative to the cumbrous political channels.

Which of the two mechanisms is chosen will depend on the relative costs and benefits of each. We have already identified the costs of quits, but there are also costs associated with the voice mechanism. It can be slow and cumbersome. The institutions created may assume a degree of permanency and pursue objectives beyond those originally intended. The direct costs of establishing and administering such institutions can be substantial and, where they place demands on employees' time, there will also be opportunity costs, in terms of forgone output. It might seem that the costs associated with the voice mechanism are so substantial as to preclude the use of this mechanism. However, it appears that the extensive use of just such a mechanism goes some way toward explaining the industrial success of Japan. Mechanisms for improving information flows between workers and employers are an integral part of

7. Friedman, M. (1962) *Capitalism and Freedom*, Chicago University Press, Chicago, Ch. 6.

the organization in Japanese enterprises.[8] It has been argued that these substantially reduce the transaction costs associated with the employment of labor in Japan.[9]

One of the principal reasons for the existence of labor market institutions is to improve information flows in labor markets. Institutions are a feature of all markets, even those that are most competitive, for no markets rely exclusively on one or the other mechanism. All markets suffer from imperfections in information and exhibit differing degrees of immobility of labor. None is as frictionless as is proposed in simple competitive theory. In some cases these imperfections exist to a trivial degree, and it is therefore appropriate to assume them away for reasons of expositional clarity; in others they cannot be ignored. The predictions of competitive theory are powerful and it is not therefore difficult to see why this view of the world has had a powerful influence over economists' minds. Yet in those markets in which imperfections are paramount we must look to alternative models to understand behavior. In the following pages the markets we study will embody aspects of, and we shall see evidence for the existence of, both these mechanisms. First consider the particular institutional channels, which firms and individuals respectively have constructed, to acquire the information on which they base their hiring and joining decisions. These constitute the first steps in the job matching process.

THE JOB MATCHING PROCESS

Job matching constitutes the process whereby heterogeneous workers are matched to heterogeneous jobs. The first step in this process is discovering appropriate individuals and persuading them to join the firm. The second step may be providing the worker with specific skills. We have already looked at this second stage in Chapters 6 and 9 so here we concentrate on the first stage.

The analysis of information in labor markets started as an attempt to understand the procedure by which workers search for jobs and the consequences of this for unemployment. The early work in this field of job search focused on the search by employees for a suitable job and evaluated the efficiency of different rules of search.[10] In such models, it was assumed, firms were able to distinguish the productive potential of those they recruited from a pool of applicants who were homogeneous with respect to productivity. These early models abstracted from the complexities of the information gathering and job matching process and ignored problems of asymmetric information, which lead employers and workers to construct elaborate devices to distinguish workers and firms of a suitable quality. Asymmetric information is the term used to describe a situation in which the parties have unequal access to the same

8. See Dore, R. (1973) *British Factory—Japanese Factory*, George Allen and Unwin, London. In which he contrasts British management style and industrial relations practices with those of the Japanese enterprise.

9. See Hashimoto, M. and Raisian, J. (1988) 'The structure and adaptability of short run labor markets in Japan and the United States', in Hart, R.A. (ed.), *Employment, Unemployment and Labor Utilization*, Unwin-Hyman, Boston and London.

10. Stigler, G.J. (1962) 'Information in the labor market', *Journal of Political Economy*, **70** (Supplement), October.

information. Early theories took little account of the complex nature of the information firms and workers require for successful job matching. Firms develop methods and procedures to elicit information, where one party has an informational advantage and to economize on the resources devoted to the task of distinguishing the productivity of applicants. They create institutions, to economize on the substantial costs of information collection and processing, and the study of these institutions represents an important and expanding area of labor market inquiry. Before we turn to evaluate these theories we first consider the types of information which both workers and firms require and the procedures that each adopt to acquire information. The complicated and detailed nature of the information that is required will, as a result, become evident and this helps us to understand why firms develop the institutional structures we discuss subsequently.

Procedures used to acquire information for job matching

When assessing applicants for jobs the firm wishes to know two things: first, how productive they will be (i.e. what will their marginal product be); and, second, what compensation will they require? Reciprocally, applicants wish to know how much labor they will be required to provide and what the reward for supplying this labor will be. The determinants of an individual's productivity are several and frequently difficult to distinguish, while the total pecuniary and non-pecuniary rewards offered by a firm are often equally difficult for potential employees to discern. Some information on each of these aspects can be gained by scrutinizing the published information made available by each party, but other information is by its nature difficult to obtain. There are three principal procedures by which information about workers and jobs is conveyed: first, by examination; second, by recommendation; and, third, by experience. Consider each of these in turn from the perspective of the firm and the worker.

Examination Some aspects of the rewards associated with a particular job are relatively easily discovered by workers. Firms will generally publicize the wages that are on offer, the hours of work required, the type of pension arrangements provided, the annual holiday entitlement, and even the existence of such fringe benefits as company cars, subsidized meals, medical insurance and low interest loans. Typically they do so in the information package they provide to prospective employees or they are stated in a newspaper or trade journal advertisement. Applicants are able to process and evaluate such information relatively easily and the truth of these statements can, in general, be easily confirmed by checking with the existing workforce. There are therefore relatively few ambiguities or difficulties associated with interpreting this information. Accordingly, information of this type is easily conveyed through the formal channels identified.

Equally the employer has little difficulty in discovering the applicant's qualifications, age, sex and, perhaps, previous training and experience. Such information is conveyed to the employer in the letter of application, in the accompanying curriculum vitae, or résumé, in the completed application form or again at interview. The authenticity of these claims can be easily checked. The information is relatively 'hard' and is easily obtained: it can generally be readily verified and it can be processed using established procedures.

Recommendation There exists a further range of information, which both firms and applicants require, which is less easily conveyed along the above channels and which is considerably more difficult to authenticate. Firms will frequently be concerned with the reliability and trustworthiness of applicants, with their motivation and competence, with their punctuality and application, and with their capacity for independent thinking and innovation. It is tempting for applicants for a job to overstate their capacities in each of these areas. Equally, applicants are concerned with the general nature of the work environment, its pleasantness and safety, the extent and nature of supervision, the conviviality or hostility of their co-workers, and with their prospects for promotion and advancement. It is tempting for the firm to suggest that the workplace is pleasant, the atmosphere convivial, promotion rapid, etc.

Each party has an incentive to provide less than accurate information about themselves. For this reason declarations by firms and applicants as to the nature of each of the above may, quite simply, not be believed by the other party. Each party has an incentive to exaggerate the attractive aspects and to withhold information on unfavorable aspects; to reveal only that information which suits their purpose.

The problems associated with such behavior can be overcome where there exist third parties who have an incentive to provide true information. Thus the applicant may seek the advice of friends who work in the firm to which the individual has applied. Friends have an incentive, the desire for a continuation of that friendship, to provide true information when they are in possession of it. Moreover, since friends, as members of the same social group, are likely to have similar tastes the information will be processed in a similar manner and for this reason information obtained via this channel is likely to prove more 'reliable' than that which could be obtained elsewhere. Assessments by friends will therefore carry considerable weight.

In a similar manner firms may use their existing employees to provide them with references for applicants whom they know. If existing employees wish to retain the goodwill of their employers, they may believe that this will be forfeited if they are responsible for the hire of an unproductive worker. Recommendations by existing employees will therefore weigh heavily in employers' decisions as to whom to recruit. Equally, references by a third party, the college professor, or an individual of some standing in the local community, may be used to attest to the possession of desirable characteristics. Third parties, appropriately chosen, have a stake in providing true information.

In each of the above cases the *reputation* of a third party, an employee, friend or the representative of an institution, was at stake. The third party had an incentive to provide accurate information. Yet even these two channels may not be sufficient to convey all the information required.

Experience Experience may be the most effective way to gain some of the information that is required. Experience may be the manner in which the firm learns of the productivity of the individual or the manner in which the worker learns of the complete range of non-pecuniary advantages and disadvantages of a particular job. Recognizing that certain dimensions of the productivity of a worker will not be fully appreciated, until a period has been spent in the job, some firms place workers on probation, while for similar reasons workers give firms a 'trial period'. One study, in particular, has emphasized that workers begin many jobs with less than perfect information about the job.[11] They update this information on the job and revise their reservation wages accordingly. If the position becomes particularly unattractive they quit the job. Workers are suggested to be engaged in a continuous process of experimentation.

Examination and recommendation represent the gathering of information by the firm and worker before hiring, *ex ante*, while experience represents the gathering of informations, *ex post*. In some jobs the *ex ante* and *ex post* gathering of information may be regarded as substitutes. The firm may, on the basis of little prior information, 'give the guy a job and if it doesn't work out, fire him'. In other jobs the cost of hiring an employee who 'fouls up' may be prohibitive and the information will be gathered *ex ante*. The more general the nature of the task and hence the easier it is for the firm to hire replacements, or for the individual to obtain another job, the smaller the costs of any mistake, then the more likely it is that firms and workers will employ probationary or trial periods. The greater the initial investment in the job by the firm and employee, the more specific the nature of the job task, the greater the costs of a mistake, then the less likely it will be that such trial or probationary periods will be used.

The effectiveness of information gathering procedures

The various procedures adopted by firms and individuals to match individuals, with varying skills and attributes, to the diverse range of jobs on offer have been represented above. Which of these procedures are most frequently adopted in the first stage of job matching and what do we know of the effectiveness of each of these? Studies show that workers make considerable use of friends and relatives to search for jobs. Thus a survey of unemployed youth in the United States in 1981 reported that 85 percent of those who reported searching for work used 'friends and relatives' while only 53 percent used a state employment agency and 58 percent a newspaper.[12] This same study revealed that 'friends and relatives' was one of the two channels which resulted in the most job offers, the other source of substantial job offers being direct applications.

11. Viscusi, W.K. and C.J. O'Connor (1984) 'Adaptive responses to chemical labelling: are workers Bayesian decision makers?', *American Economic Review*, **74**(5), December 942–56.
12. Holzer, H. (1988) 'Search methods used by unemployed youth', *Journal of Labor Economics*, **6**(1), January, 1–20.

The prominence of direct applications may be explained by the fact that employers believe that use of such a channel testifies to a worker's enterprise and initiative in seeking out job vacancies on their own. Alternatively, it may simply be that direct applicants have been hunting round and get to the jobs first. More important than mere job offers are job acceptances. The successful marrying of applicants and firms is evidence of the successful conclusion of a job search. Again, it is revealed that the use of friends and relatives resulted in the highest rate of job acceptance of any channel of job search.[13]

Similar but not identical results emerge for the United Kingdom. In the United Kingdom the nationwide network of public employment agencies, job centres, is far larger than in the United States and it has been estimated that these agencies are notified of twice the proportion of total vacancies of their US counterparts. Yet, despite this, only about 15 percent of all those who obtained employment in the United Kingdom in 1981–82 heard about the vacancy from a job centre—a rate half that of those who heard about the vacancy from friends and relatives.[14] Firms also make extensive use of employee contacts. Indeed there is some evidence that the higher paying the firm the more likely it is to recruit manual workers by employee contacts.[15]

These figures for the United Kingdom refer to the previously employed and to the unemployed for it is not only the unemployed who search for jobs. However, when we pick out the unemployed alone the results are quite different. In the United Kingdom the unemployed appear to rely on those channels that are least likely to produce job offers. Periodic surveys in the United Kingdom consistently report that when searching for a job over one-third of the unemployed use job centres while 20 percent rely on newspaper advertisements and only 10 percent on personal contacts.[16] Undue reliance on job centres by the unemployed may be explained partly by the pronounced occupational and geographical concentration of unemployment in the United Kingdom. This concentration means that unemployment among the 'friends and relatives' of the unemployed is also high and, without a job of their own, 'friends and relatives' are in no position to inform other unemployed individuals of job vacancies.

Job acceptance is only one criterion by which to judge the efficiency of a channel of job search. The successful marrying of worker to firm is only the first stage in the process of job matching. Final assessment depends on whether workers' and firms' expectations are realized and they stay together for the period originally intended. We generally have no way of knowing exactly what this intended period was but some insight into the relative efficiency of different channels may be provided by evidence of the association between job tenure and method of job search. Those channels

13. Holzer, H. (1988), *op. cit.*
14. General Household Survey, 1984, HMSO, London.
15. See Gasteen, A., Newlands, D. and Yannopoulos, A. (1989) in Elliott, R.F. and Speight, A.E.H. (eds.), *Unemployment and Labour Market Efficiency: A Study of the Aberdeen and Grampian Experience*, Aberdeen University Press, pp. 25–42.
16. See Green, A.E. *et al.* (1986) 'What contribution can labor migration make to reducing unemployment?' CURDS Discussion Paper 73, University of Newcastle upon Tyne.

producing the longest tenure are presumed most efficient. Thus in the United Kingdom those manual and lower white collar workers finding a job as a result of a newspaper advertisement or through job centres quit their jobs sooner than do those relying on relatives and friends. Those finding jobs using friends and relatives seemed more likely to find 'the right job' and, unless the costs of this method of search substantially exceed those of the others, friends and relatives would therefore seem to be one of the most efficient channels of job search.

The role of the institutions of the labor market

Many of the institutions we observe in labor markets assist in the process of job matching. They represent an attempt to devise rules and alternative processes, to deal with deficiencies of information that arise when more direct procedures are precluded. It is now recognized that a wide range of the institutions that we observe in labor markets have been constructed, in large part, to minimize the substantial costs associated with the collection and processing of scarce information. Consider, briefly therefore, how the existence of imperfect and/or asymmetric information in labor markets can be used to explain the existence of a variety of institutions that exist in labor markets.

Screening Screening is a general description of the process by which firms evaluate information as to the productive potential of job applicants. In Chapter 6 we examined an aspect of this, the screening hypothesis, which suggested that formal education may be regarded as a device for sorting and labeling individuals according to their productive potential. On this view education did not enhance individuals' productive potential but merely attested to those pre-existing abilities. Education provided the credentials which enabled firms to distinguish between more and less productive individuals. Firms then screened individual job applicants in order to discover those in possession of the credentials they required. On this view the formal educational system assumes the role of an institution designed to provide information to firms. Earlier we elaborated the screening hypothesis, and evaluated the evidence to support it, so we shall not repeat it here but it is important to note that the screening hypothesis suggests that educational establishments are institutions which help employers to identify the most productive workers.

Old boy networks An 'old boy network' is the name given to a device sometimes used for acquiring information by recommendation. Not all the information, which is required about a potential recruit, can be as easily certified and as readily conveyed as the screening hypothesis suggests. Evaluations of individuals' drive and motivation, of their general attitudes, loyalty and trustworthiness may all be required. Old boy networks represent one device for eliciting such opinions. Thus attendance at the right school, membership of the right club, recommendation by the 'right chap', or even possession of the right genes (nepotism) may all be regarded as important criteria for selection. Some jobs, for example the British Secret Service, place considerable weight on such networks with recruitment focusing on individuals with particular social and educational backgrounds. However, as the experience with the spies Burgess, Philby, MacLean and Blunt recruited in this manner only too clearly demonstrates, such information channels may have important deficiencies. They are not by their nature open to external scrutiny and they are susceptible to corruption and incorrect labeling.

Reputation: a version of efficiency wage theory On occasion firms have very little idea of the productive potential of applicants. What then is to be their recruitment strategy? One version of efficiency wage theory addresses this issue.

If firms cannot distinguish the productive or productivity related characteristics of individuals they will have no option but to hire at random from the applicant pool. They can then adopt one of two strategies: either adopt a policy of hire, try out, and then fire if unsatisfactory or attract a high quality applicant pool. One version of efficiency wage theory suggests that it may pay a firm to offer high wages, to establish a *reputation* as a higher payer, for in this manner it will attract a high quality applicant pool. The conditions for the success of this strategy are that applicants are able to assess their *relative* productive potential and that this is positively correlated with their reservation wages. Under these circumstances higher quality workers will have higher reservation wages and a larger number of these will be attracted into the applicant pool of firms paying high wages. By paying high wages the firm increases the proportion of high productivity workers in its applicant pool, and thereby the probabilities that, if it hires at random, it will obtain a larger number of high quality workers. In practice many large firms appear to be concerned with their reputation as employers, while others establish and maintain reputations as 'high payers'.

Career labor markets Career labor markets represent an alternative mechanism to recruiting outsiders to fill senior posts. Career labor markets are distinguished by 'job ladders', by a hierarchy of rewards, in the form of discretionary increments and promotions within the firm and we shall study them in more detail in Chapter 12. These rewards reflect the fact that it is easier for firms to monitor the performance of their existing employees, and to assess their suitability for filling more senior posts, than it is to assess the suitability of outsiders. Career labor markets represent a device which enables firms to collect information about their existing employees.

Career labor markets have further information advantages. They constitute a mechanism which induces individuals to employ the specific information they possess to enhance productivity within the firm. If work tasks require the application of a considerable amount of firm-specific information, then existing employees must be encouraged to employ this to best effect. Discretionary payments and promotions represent ways of encouraging existing employees to reveal and apply the specific knowledge they possess. Thus, taking an example from the engineering industry, the machine-minder must be encouraged, by an appropriate reward system, to employ his or her knowledge as to the right speed and length of time at which to run the machine, the right interval to change the drill bit, the correct amount of coolant to spray on the metal, etc. No amount of reading the accompanying manual will reveal the machine's idiosyncrasies; only experience will tell the operator of the machine's likes and dislikes, as any car owner will testify.

Rules and norms and behavior The nature of many employment contracts is that they require substantial investment by both employer and employee and this leads to what has been termed *asset specificity*. Assets cannot be readily or costlessly redeployed, with the result that employers and employees are reluctant to sever the employment contract. Transactions costs, like those we have analyzed in this chapter and in Chapter 9, are significant in many different types of employment. One consequence is that long-term employment relations emerge in which firms and workers enjoy particular information advantages; each party possesses information that is not possessed by either an outsider or often the other party: information is asymmetric. A corollary of this is that unless appropriately constrained, either or both parties may seek to exploit this information advantage. They may seek to disclose only that information which acts to their advantage and this may result in a lower level of efficiency. This has been described as 'self-seeking with guile' and it is in order to obviate such behavior that in certain institutions in the labor market, rules and norms of behavior have emerged.[17]

Social rules, norms of behavior, govern relationships and behavior at the workplace. A social institution has been described as a regularity of social behavior that is agreed to by all members of society.[18] It specifies behavior in specific, recurrent, situations and it is either self-policed or policed by some external authority. The emergence of such norms of behavior is a feature of all societies and has been observed to emerge in experimental 'supergames'. These are games played again and again in which players develop rules to guide their behavior, and although social rules have been found to be inferior in any single game they pay off, that is they work, in the long run. It is noteworthy that the rules that are devised are often of a cooperative, rather than a competitive, form. Such rules emerge it is suggested to mitigate the inefficiencies associated with 'self-seeking with guile'.[19] Social and behavioral norms induce employees to behave in a responsible and productive manner, and set limits to the extent to which individuals will ruthlessly exploit their informational advantage.

The above are all strands to what has generically been titled the new *institutional economics*.[20] They have in common the argument that information is not acquired costlessly or even immediately as assumed in the simple competitive paradigm. These theories recognize that information is acquired through time, by experience, by the

17. Williamson, O.E. (1975) *Markets and Hierarchies: Analysis and Antitrust Implications*, The Free Press, New York. The author is principally responsible for this interesting theoretical development and for the terminology associated with this.
18. See Schotter, A. (1981) *The Economic Theory of Social Institutions*, Cambridge University Press, New York, p. 11.
19. See Axelrod, R. (1984) 'Effective choice in the prisoner's dilemma', *Journal of Conflict Resolution*, **24**, 3–25, 379–402 and *The Evolution of Co-operation*, Basic Books, New York.
20. See Langlois, R. (ed.) (1986) *Economics as a Process: Essays in the New Institutional Economics*, Cambridge University Press; Williamson, O.E. (1975), *op. cit.*; and 'The economics of governance', in Langlois, R. (ed.) (1986) *op. cit.*

process of learning-by-doing. It is worth contrasting the views that underpin the new institutional economics with those that underpin the competitive paradigm. The new institutional economics recognizes the existence of 'self-seeking with guile', in contrast, the competitive market emphasizes 'self-seeking with candid disclosure'. In the competitive model the position of individuals is fully and candidly disclosed before trade takes place, there are no surprises. In contrast, under conditions of less than perfect competition and particularly where the outcome is determined by bargaining, the parties may have an incentive to conceal their true intentions. In the new institutional economics information is quite deliberately less than perfect. The new institutional economics is founded on long-term employment relationships arising from asset specificity and its focus is firmly on market clearing via the 'voice' rather than the 'exit' mechanism.

The institutions of the labor market also constitute devices for economizing on the use of resources devoted to gathering and processing information. The concept of bounded rationality, developed in Chapter 7, emphasized the cognitive limits of human beings in relation to the complexity of the problems and information that confront them. Individuals have been described as 'intendedly rational but only limitedly so':[21] they are rational but up to the limit of their capacity to receive and process information. It is thus not merely a question of deficiencies of information that determine market outcomes but of deficiencies in the human capacity to process that information. Individuals' rationality is 'bounded' by their processing capacities and, in turn, this leads them either to develop norms of behavior, 'rules-of-thumb', or to adhere to social conventions. Both represent ways of economizing on the resources devoted to processing any new information.

Above we evaluated a range of labor market institutions each of which plays a prominent role in the process of job matching. We saw further that some were also designed to encourage productive behavior by a firm's employees. Common to all was the view that institutions constituted mechanisms for improving the flow of information in labor markets. It is as yet a relatively new area of research and as such there is little empirical evidence to bear on this, however, it represents a substantial advance in our understanding of why labor market institutions exist.

TWO STUDIES IN MARKET CLEARING

Finally in this chapter we turn from theory to two topics in labor market analysis that continue to attract considerable attention: the issues of the general flexibility of labor markets and the minimum wage. We put aside the question of how the labor market clears, and the extent to which different mechanisms emerge to cope with problems of processing and obtaining information, and instead analyze market outcomes. However, it is noteworthy that the debate on the minimum wage is largely predicated on the view that the labor market is competitive, that is it clears by means of the exit mechanism. How we view the issue of labor market flexibility, how appropriate we

21. Simon, H.A. (1982) *Models of Bounded Rationality*, 2 volumes, MIT Press, Cambridge, Mass.

judge the degree of flexibility or inflexibility we observe in labor markets to be will again depend on our views as to how labor markets clear.

Minimum wages[22]

The fascination of economists with the minimum wage is such that it features in almost every introductory textbook in economics. The fascination stems from the widespread agreement among economists of all types as to the predicted effects of a minimum wage, while for labor economists it holds the added attraction of enabling us to study the effects of an exogenous increase in the price of labor.

In the United States the Fair Labor Standards Act of 1938 introduced a national minimum wage. Set at $0.25 an hour the rate was equivalent to 40 percent of the hourly wage in manufacturing and covered roughly 43 percent of all blue and junior white collar workers. In the United Kingdom comparable legislation was introduced as the Trade Boards Act of 1909. This legislation established a number of Wages Councils which set effective but different minimum rates of pay in a range of service industries now accounting for only 6 percent of the workforce.[23]

In both countries the coverage of the minimum wage increased steadily thereafter to a peak in the late 1960s in the United Kingdom and in the 1970s in the United States. At its peak in 1977 coverage in the United States extended to almost 87 percent of all junior white collar and manual workers, although in the United Kingdom coverage has rarely exceeded 10 percent of all employees. Recently the coverage of the minima has fallen substantially in the United States and the United Kingdom. In the United States an increase in the minimum wage, which had been set at a level of $3.35 an hour in January 1981, was only agreed at the end of 1989. In the United Kingdom the minima established by the Wages Councils are uprated each year but these minima constitute the effective rates of pay for only a proportion of those covered by the legislation.[24] In both countries therefore the importance of minimum wages is diminishing.

What are the predicted effects of the introduction of a minimum wage? First consider the impact of the introduction of effective minima that covered *all* workers. Such a situation is depicted in Fig. 10.3. Suppose that prior to the introduction of the minimum wage the labor market for unskilled labor was in equilibrium at wage W_0/P. At this wage there is only frictional unemployment, caused by the normal process of job turnover and search in labor markets, the magnitude of this is indicated by the distance between L^F and L^S, that is $L_1 - L_0$. The curve L^F details the number of

22. See Brown, C. (1988) 'Minimum wage laws: are they overrated?', *Journal of Economic Perspectives*, **2**(3), summer, 133–48, for a useful summary of this issue.
23. In the United Kingdom it has been estimated that no more than 6 percent of establishments employing manual workers and 4 percent of those employing non-manual workers are affected by Wages Councils. See Daniel, W. and Millward, N. (1983) *Workplace Industrial Relations in Britain*, Table VIII. 1, Heinemann, London.
24. Elliott, R.F. and Murphy, P.D. (1990) 'National wage agreements', in Thomson, A.W. and Gregory, M. (eds.), *A Portrait of Pay: Pay Developments in the 1970s*, Oxford University Press, estimated that in 1982 53 percent of all workers in Wages Councils had hourly rates of pay no greater than 10 percent of the statutory minima.

individuals who wish to work at each wage rate and its shape reflects the fact that the participation rate is a rising function of the wage rate. However, at any one time only a certain proportion of this number of individuals will be in a position to accept jobs, only a certain proportion will constitute the effective labor supply to firms, this is indicated by L^S.

The imposition of a minimum wage equal to W_{min}/P results in firms moving back along their labor demand curves to a position such as A, at which point the marginal revenue product of labor and the new minimum wage are now equal. The demand for unskilled labor falls from L_0 to L_2, with the result that in addition to frictional unemployment, now equal to $L_4 - L_3$, there is further unemployment equal to $L_3 - L_2$ due to the imposition of the minimum wage. How substantial will be the reduction in employment? The change in employment is simply calculated as the product of the elasticity of labor demand multiplied by the proportional rise in the wage. Note that quite plausibly we show the frictional component of unemployment, as now smaller than before, for with higher unemployment labor turnover and 'voluntary' search unemployment reduces.

Some turnover, nonetheless, remains and, since this is generally quite high, in unskilled jobs this may well be the mechanism by which firms reduce employment. They may simply not fill the posts that become vacant as a result of normal attrition. For this reason it is unlikely that the introduction of a minimum wage will be accompanied by a 'wave of sackings' as casual analysis might suggest. The introduction of such legislation could have the effect of shortening the number of weeks per year that many unskilled individuals are likely to work at the new higher rate, rather than confining one section of the population permanently to unemployment.

The simple predictions of the model are therefore that the imposition of an effective minimum wage with uniform coverage will result in an increase in unemployment. Of course, such a prediction assumes that all other things remain equal. They may not. If the economy is expanding, causing all labor demand curves to shift outwards, such effects may overwhelm those of the new minima. Thus if the labor demand curve for unskilled labor shifted outwards to intersect L^S at point B, there would be no increase in unemployment. The minimum wage would merely have anticipated what would anyway have been the new market clearing wage, in which case the passage of such legislation would then have been unnecessary. That all other things do not remain equal is surprisingly frequently ignored in debates about the effects of a minimum wage as scrutiny of the US Congressional debates on this issue shows.[25]

In neither the United States nor the United Kingdom do statutory minimum rates of pay apply to all workers. In the United States the uncovered sector consists for the most part of small retailers and service industries. Thus we need to extend the above analysis to consider the likely outcome where we have a covered and uncovered sector. Suppose that Fig. 10.3 now represents the position in the covered sector while Fig. 10.4 depicts that in the uncovered sector. Initially both are in equilibrium at W_0/P but the introduction of W_{min}/P in the covered sector reduces labor demand in that sector

25. See Brown, C. (1988), *op. cit.*

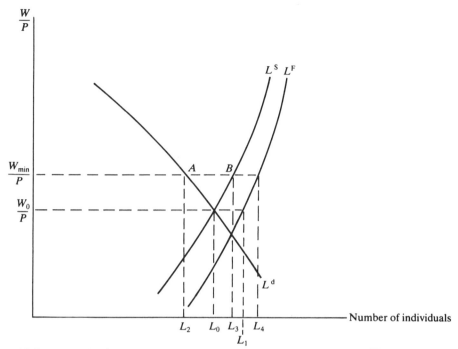

Figure 10.3 A model of the minimum wage with complete coverage. L^F measures the labor force, L^S represents the effective supply of labor. Prior to the introduction of the minimum wage, the labor market is in equilibrium at W_0/P with a natural rate of unemployment equal to $L_1 - L_0$. The introduction of an effective minimum wage, W_{min}/P with complete coverage, reduces labor demand to L_2 resulting in $L_3 - L_2$ unemployment in addition to the natural rate $L_4 - L_3$

and employment falls from L_0 to L_2. $L_0 - L_2$ workers who previously had jobs in what has become the covered sector now, provided their reservation wages do not preclude this, seek work in the uncovered sector. These displaced workers will only find jobs in the uncovered sector if wages fall sufficiently in that sector, in which case a new equilibrium wage of W_1/P emerges in the uncovered sector.

However, note the efficiency loss that results from such a policy. Employment in each sector is taken to the point at which the marginal cost of labor, the wage, equals the marginal revenue product of labor and, it is clear from Figs. 10.3 and 10.4, that the marginal product of labor of the last individual employed in the covered sector is greater than that of the last individual employed in the uncovered sector. Were the last individual employed in the uncovered sector now to be transferred back to the covered sector, his or her marginal product would rise by an amount equal to the distance W_{min}/P (in Fig. 10.3) – W_1/P (in Fig. 10.4). Similar transfers of $L_2 - L_0$ individuals now employed in the uncovered sector would raise each of their marginal products and so total output would rise. Such transfers would occur naturally in the absence of a minimum wage, but are precluded in the presence of a minimum wage. The minimum wage therefore results in an efficiency loss, and

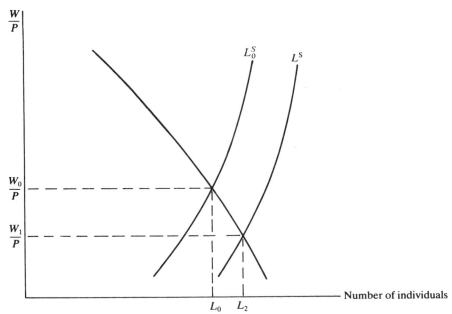

Figure 10.4 The impact of a minimum wage on the uncovered sector. Figure 10.3 now represents the covered sector and Fig. 10.4 the uncovered sector. Introduction of a minimum wage of W_{min}/P in the sector represented by Fig. 10.3, displaces $L_0 - L_2$ workers from the covered to the uncovered sector, effectively increasing labor supply to the uncovered sector, and driving wages down from W_0/P to W_1/P. This will not occur, however, if the wage in the uncovered sector is less than the reservation wages of displaced workers, or if displaced workers choose to wait for a job in the covered sector. In the latter case unemployment will rise

associated with this are adverse distributional effects as a wage gap opens between the covered and uncovered sectors.

Workers' reservation wages may, of course, be set at such a level that they are not prepared to work at the wages now on offer in the uncovered sector, in which case the introduction of a minimum wage will result in a reduction in the participation rate. Alternatively, workers may prefer to queue for those jobs in the covered sector, which fall vacant due to natural turnover. They have some probability, P, that they will obtain a job. P will be less than 1 and is given by the ratio of employment, E, to labor force participants, LF, in the covered sector, $P = E/LF$. Now they remain in the covered sector provided $P \times (W_{min}/P) > W_U/P$, where W_U/P is the wage they can expect in the uncovered sector. In this case the introduction of a minimum wage is associated with a rise in recorded unemployment, where this unemployment constitutes a queue for covered sector jobs.

One qualification to the above predictions of the effects of a minimum wage is the case of monopsony. As the single buyers of labor, monopsonists are conscious that any attempt on their part to buy more labor will result in a general increase in the level of wages in the labor market they dominate. Hence monopsonists are aware that they face an upward sloping marginal cost of labor curve, MC_L, which lies to the left of the labor supply curve for that market. Such a situation is depicted in Fig. 10.5. Profit maximizing monopsonists take employment to the point at which the marginal cost of labor equals the marginal revenue product of labor, as indicated by point A, but pays a wage equal to W_1/P.

Under these circumstances a skillfully set minimum wage can increase the total earnings of labor. The introduction of a minimum wage in excess of W_1/P changes the marginal cost of labor to the firm and therefore effectively flattens the MC schedule. Thus a minimum wage of W_{min}/P produces the marginal cost schedule BAC, while a minimum wage of W^1_{min}/P produces a marginal cost schedule of DFE. In the former case wages are increased by $(W_{min} - W_1)/P$ without loss of employment. In the latter case wages rise from W_1/P to W^1_{min}/P and employment increases from L_1 to L_2. In both cases the total earnings of labor have increased without adverse employment consequences. Such an outcome could only be sustained if the firm in question were previously making supernormal profits and the rise in its labor costs were accommodated by these. Had the firm in question been operating in a competitive product market and realizing only normal profits, a substantial rise in its labor costs would drive it out of business. Appealing as such an outcome is to the advocates of minimum wage legislation it has to be said that this theoretical

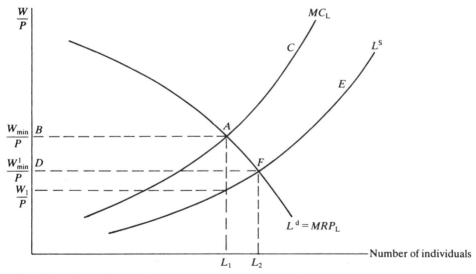

Figure 10.5 The effect of a minimum wage on a monopsonist. In the absence of the minimum wage the monopsonist equates MC_L to MRP_L at point A and pays a wage of W_1/P with employment at L_1. A skilfully set minimum wage of W_{min}/P would increase wages, by $(W_{min} - W_1/P)$ with no reduction in employment. Alternatively, a minimum wage such as W^1_{min}/P could increase wages and employment. The imposition of a minimum wage effectively changes the marginal cost of labor confronting the monopsonist: it flattens the MC_1 schedule to BAC in the case of W_{min}/P and to DFE in the case of W^1_{min}/P

possibility is seldom encountered in practice. The 'company town' is seldom the context in which the minimum wage operates.

Finally what does the empirical evidence tell us about the effects of a minimum wage? Little is known about the employment consequence of the UK Wages Council legislation but in the United States there has been substantial work into the effects of the Fair Labor Standards Act. The results of some two dozen studies suggest that a 10 percent increase in the minimum wage in the United States reduces teenage employment by between 1 and 3 percent and that this can translate into an increase in the teenage unemployment rate of up to 3 percentage points.[26]

There is also evidence that minimum wages increase the proportion of teenagers employed part-time and, complementary to this, that they increase school enrollment,[27] for by reducing the employment prospects for these groups minimum wages reduce the opportunity costs of continuing in education.

Labor market flexibility

In the 1980s Japan, and to a lesser extent the United States, generally experienced lower levels of unemployment than Europe and Australasia. This was suggested to be due to the greater rigidity or inflexibility of the labor markets in these latter continents. Some elements of rigidity will be a feature of most labor markets for, as we have seen, long-term attachments arise for efficiency reasons where workers embody specific human capital or where for other reasons transactions' costs are high. However, unexpected supply shocks, such as those resulting from the sharp rise in oil prices toward the middle and at the end of the 1970s, may require a permanent change in labor market arrangements. It is therefore important to know how long it takes to break through the short-run stickiness of wages and prices.

Four broad aspects of labor market flexibility have typically been distinguished:

1. Flexibility of the general level of real labor costs.
2. The relative flexibility of real labor costs between industries.
3. Labor mobility.
4. The degree of flexibility in working time and work schedules.

Here we consider in detail only the first of these since the remaining three are discussed elsewhere in the book.

Flexibility in the general level of real labor costs The term 'real wage gap' is used to describe the divergence of real wages, or more properly real labor costs, from the level required to maintain full employment. Thus an inflationary external price shock, such

26. Brown, C., Gilroy, C. and Kohen, A. (1982) 'The effect of the minimum wage on employment and unemployment', *Journal of Economic Literature*, **20**, 487–528.
27. Matilla, J.P. (1981) 'The impact of minimum wages on teenage schooling and on the part-time/full-time employment of youths', in Rottenberg, S. (ed.), *The Economics of a Legal Minimum Wage*, American Enterprise Institute, Washington, DC., pp. 61–87.

as the oil price hikes or a trend decline in factor productivity, requires a downward adjustment in real wages. Circumstances also arise which require some degree of flexibility in nominal labor costs, chief among these will be those variations in inflation and productivity which occur in the course of the business cycle.

An inflationary external price shock, such as a rise in oil prices, typically translates into a rise in domestic prices (since in the short run there are limited factor substitution possibilities), a fall in output and a rise in unemployment. The consequences of such developments for production costs therefore depend in part on the reaction of money wages to both inflation and the rise in unemployment. One way of measuring flexibility in the short run is to divide the short-run elasticity of money wages with respect to consumer prices by the elasticity of money wages with respect to the unemployment rate. Low values for the nominal wage/consumer price elasticity and high values for the nominal wage/unemployment elasticity signify real wage flexibility. Expressing these two elasticities as a ratio, the former over the latter, provides a measure of real wage flexibility. This flexibility being greater the lower is the ratio. From such an exercise it emerges that over the period from 1975 to 1982 there was a high degree of short-run real wage flexibility in the United States, Canada and Japan but that the ratio was generally higher in Europe, most notably in the United Kingdom. Figure 10.6 combines this ratio with the rise in the unemployment rate in each country over this period.[28] A very strong positive correlation emerges with the United Kingdom appearing to exhibit some of the highest short-run real wage rigidity over this period and the United States and Japan some of the least.

An alternative approach is to calculate 'warranted' real labor costs, that is the level of labor costs that would be required to maintain unemployment at some previous level.[29] The difference between actual and 'warranted' real labor costs then provides some measure of real wage flexibility. A similar approach is to estimate the growth in the productivity of labor and to use this to construct an index of the growth in the real wage that would be required to maintain full employment.[30] The difference between this index and the actual real wage is then another measure of the wage gap. Both measures point to a much greater degree of real wage flexibility in the United States than in Europe, with the United Kingdom over the period to the early 1980s having the largest real wage gap, the least flexible real wage structure, of any of the major OECD countries.

One feature, noted in the previous chapter, which may go some way toward explaining labor cost inflexibility is the growth in non-wage labor costs. In many instances such costs are not proportional to wages and thus they constitute fixed and quasi-fixed labor costs. The effective indexation by·statute and prior commitment of many of the elements of non-labor costs imparts a rigidity to this element of costs. Although this may be pronounced in the United Kingdom and continental Europe, it

28. See Klau, F. and Mittelstadt, A. (1986) 'Labor market flexibility', *OECD Economic Studies*, No. 6, spring, 8–46, OECD, Paris.
29. Bruno, M.N. and Sachs, J.D. (1985) *Economics of Worldwide Stagflation*, Basil Blackwell, Oxford.
30. Sachs, J.D. (1983) 'Real wages and unemployment in the OECD countries', *Brookings Papers on Economic Activity*, No. 1.

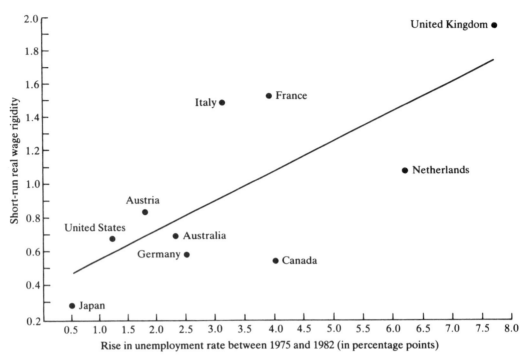

Figure 10.6 Short-run real wage rigidity and unemployment. *Source:* Klau, F. and Mittelstadt, A. (1986) 'Labour Market Flexibility', in OECD *Economic Studies*, vol. 6, pp. 7–44. Reproduced with permission of the OECD.

is unlikely to explain the substantial difference between these areas. The explanation is likely to lie in the different behavior of money wages, which has resulted in a greater degree of real wage flexibility, in the United States and Japan. In the United States this has frequently been attributed to the comparatively low degree of unionization, the decentralized nature of the union bargaining and, most significantly, the rapid inflow to the labor force of young persons, women and immigrants, all willing to accept employment at low wages. In Japan flexibility in money wages is secured by the system of annual bonus, for a large part of workers' earnings is tied to the profitability of the enterprise.

Other dimensions of flexibility The above discussion focused on the flexibility of the general level of wages in different countries, but a further dimension of labor market flexibility is the extent to which relative wages adjust to changes in patterns of labor supply and demand, across different industries, in the short run. The degree of flexibility in this respect will reflect the characteristics of the wage bargaining process, its coverage and degree of centralization, the relative level of unemployment insurance benefits which determine reservation wages, and the degree of labor mobility. Each of these aspects is discussed at various stages throughout the book.

Table 10.4 Indicators of labor market flexibility (1970s and early 1980s)

	US	Japan	Germany	France	UK
1. Short-run real wage rigidity	Low	Low	Low	High	High
2. Inter-industry wage differentials[‡]	High	High	Low	Low	Low
3. Unemployment replacement rates[§]	Low	Low	High	High	Low
4. Change in part-time employment relative to full-time employment	Small increase	Small increase	Strong rise	Strong rise	Small increase
5. Change in annual hours worked per employed person	Small fall	Small rise	Average fall	Strong decline	Strong decline

Source: Klau, F. and Mittelstadt, A. (1986) 'Labor market flexibility', *OECD Economics Studies*, **6**, spring, 41.
[‡] Coefficient of variation of inter-industry hourly wage differentials (pay for time worked).
[§] Unemployment benefits per unemployed person as a percentage of net income of average production worker.

If wages fail to adjust then quantities must, but how flexible is employment in the different countries? The degree of flexibility of working time and working arrangements has as yet been imperfectly measured. One dimension of flexibility is the flexible staffing arrangements identified in Chapter 9, but to date attention has largely focused on the growth of part-time employment. Why does 'part time' mean more flexible employment? One reason is that in some countries certain forms of job protection legislation and some types of non-wage labor costs do not apply to part-time workers. However, it is also assumed implicity, in most of the studies that focus on this dimension, that part-time working accommodates, more readily than does full-time employment, the variable elements of labor supply and demand. This is because part-time workers exhibit a higher rate of turnover than do full-time employees and because there often exists greater scope for increasing the hours of part-time workers to meet short-run contingencies.

The various dimensions of labor market flexibility identified above are summarized in Table 10.4. No weighting is given to each of these factors, but each is likely to be an important contributor to the degree of aggregate real wage flexibility. While we have some way to go in refining our measures of labor market flexibility, it must nonetheless be clear from the foregoing that in the period up to the early 1980s the labor market in the United Kingdom exhibited a marked degree of inflexibility relative to that of most of its competitors, particularly the United States and Japan.

SUMMARY

In this chapter the different mechanisms by which the labor market moves toward equilibrium have been examined. The mechanisms of exit and voice were detailed and it was suggested that market clearing was accomplished by some combination of each of these in most labor markets. Underlying the competitive mode of adjustment was the propensity of workers to quit. Yet, as we saw, such a course of action would be less readily employed by older or married workers, by those who enjoyed some seniority in their job, or by those who had invested in firm-specific human capital. Moreover, we saw that at all ages there was a marked difference in the propensities of US and British workers to quit. Where the transaction costs of quitting or engaging replacements are high the voice mechanism will be the mechanism emphasized. The voice mechanism represents adjustment through an institutional process, as opposed to a market process.

Institutions feature prominently in all labor markets. Some of those we observe constitute mechanisms for conveying and processing information. Asymmetric information is a prominent feature of most labor markets and a wide range of mechanisms have been designed to deal with this problem. Screening, old boy networks, and reputations represent institutions primarily designed to assist in the process of job matching. Career labor markets also perform this function, although they address a wider range of informational problems. These are issues in the new institutional economics which is an important and emerging area of research.

At the end of the chapter we looked at two different aspects of labor market clearing. Minimum wage legislation and the degree of flexibility exhibited by the labor markets of different countries. Although we examined a theoretical case in which a minimum wage could increase both wages and employment, empirical evidence seemed in general to suggest that minimum wage legislation had an adverse effect on employment. Studies of labor market flexibility indicated that up to the early 1980s the market in Britain was much less flexible than that in the United States and Japan in particular. This was not simply a product of long job tenure, for in both Britain and Japan workers remain in the same job much longer than in the United States. Rather it appeared to reflect the different institutional mechanisms that Britain had constructed. Part of the inflexibility of wages, in Britain when compared to the United States, may be due to the higher incidence of unionism.

PRINCIPAL CONCEPTS

Students should be familiar with the following concepts introduced in this chapter:

1. The local labor market.
2. The distinction between 'exit' and 'voice'.
3. Job matching.
4. The role of reputations in the labor market.
5. Asymmetric information.

6. The *ex ante* and *ex post* gathering of information when hiring.

QUESTIONS FOR DISCUSSION

1. How easily can we distinguish the boundaries of local and regional labor markets?
2. What are the origins of the transaction costs that preclude labor market adjustment via a competitive process?
3. What are the principal procedures adopted by both firms and workers to distinguish the characteristics essential to job matching? Distinguish the characteristics of workers and jobs which are likely to determine the particular procedures employed.
4. At some stage you are likely to ask your professor to write you a letter of recommendation, a reference, for a prospective employer. Why do employers use this mechanism? Discuss the costs and benefits associated with it.
5. Certain institutions of the labor market may be viewed as mechanisms for the efficient collection and processing of information. What are these institutions and is this their only, or indeed principal, role?
6. How does the existence of social rules mitigate problems of asymmetric information?
7. Are minimum wage laws overrated?
8. Is the much greater propensity of workers in the United States to quit the explanation for the greater degree of wage flexibility we observe in the United States compared to Britain?

FURTHER READING

Most of the seminal contributions to this area already appear as footnotes to the text but the reader is particularly encouraged to read: Arrow, K.J. (1974) *The Limits of Organization*, Norton, New York; Langlois, R. (ed) (1975) *Economics as a Process: Essays in the New Institutional Economics*, Cambridge University Press, England; and Williamson, O.E. (1975) *Markets and Hierarchies: Analysis and Antitrust Implications*, The Free Press, New York.

11

WAGE DIFFERENCES IN COMPETITIVE LABOR MARKETS: THE EQUALIZATION OF THE NET ADVANTAGES OF DIFFERENT JOBS

In this chapter we look at the explanation of wage differences which is offered by competitive theory. We have already encountered (Chapter 6) one competitive explanation of wage differences, that offered by human capital theory. The theory of human capital is an element of the theory of equalizing differences which we shall develop here. According to this theory individuals are offered a total compensation package that is equal to their marginal revenue product in the long run. However, the elements of this package take both a pecuniary and a non-pecuniary form and differ substantially between different jobs.

Until recently an increasingly important constituent of the compensation package was fringe benefits. We shall, therefore, examine the form that these take and some of the explanations that have been offered for the growth in this element of compensation. It has become clear in recent years that firms often choose to pay above what appears to be the market clearing rate. The competitive explanation of this behavior focuses on the heterogeneity of labor, and the trade-offs that exist between the different elements of total labor costs that confront the firm. The competitive explanations have recently been brought together under the heading efficiency wage theory and we shall examine this theory here.

THE THEORY OF EQUALIZING DIFFERENCES

The theory of equalizing differences has been suggested to be '*the* fundamental (long-run) market equilibrium construct in labor economics',[1] yet it finds its earliest and still most authoritative statement in the writings of Adam Smith over 200 years ago:

> The whole of the advantages and disadvantages of different employments of labour and stock must, in the same neighbourhood, be either perfectly equal or continually tending to equality. If in the same neighbourhood there was any employment either evidently more or less advantageous than the rest, so many people would crowd into it in the one case, and so many would desert it in the other, that its advantages would soon return to the level of other employments. This at least would be the case in a society where things were left to follow their rational course, where there was perfect liberty and where everyman was perfectly free both to choose what occupation he thought proper, and to change it as often as he thought proper. Everyman's interest would prompt him to seek the advantageous and shun the disadvantageous employment. (Adam Smith, 1776, *The Wealth of Nations*, Book 1, Ch. X)

Today this remains the classic statement of the equalizing tendencies of competition in the labor market. It emphasizes that such equalization is conditional on perfect mobility 'free . . . to change it as often as he thought proper', and on perfect knowledge, jobs are '*evidently* more or less advantageous'. According to Smith, each person, seeking his own advantage, would move into the most desirable and vacate the least desirable jobs. Competition for the most desirable jobs would reduce their advantages, principally the wages they paid, while exit from the least desirable jobs would require employers to raise the wage in order to retain labor. In this manner the whole of the advantages and disadvantages of different jobs would be brought into equality.

Smith argued that the advantages of different jobs comprised much more than the wage associated with the job. Smith observed that 'pecuniary wages . . . are everywhere in Europe extremely different according to the different employments of labor', and suggested that this was due to 'certain circumstances', of which he identified five principal ones, 'in the employment themselves' (op. cit., Book X, Part 1). Thus was born the theory of net advantages, the idea that competition equalizes the whole of the pecuniary and non-pecuniary advantages and disadvantages of different employments within a local labor market, and indeed over the longer run over wider geographical areas within which there is labor mobility.

Competition will only equalize *wages* between jobs in which *all* other conditions of work are the same. It follows that on the many occasions on which labor economists talk of competitive forces equalizing wages they have implicitly controlled for all other differences between the jobs in question. When this is clearly not the case they must then be talking of net advantages and using the wage to proxy this. It will be clear from what follows that the two, the wage and net advantages, can only be used interchangeably under very special circumstances. In what follows we shall initially assume that information is perfect or that its acquisition is trivially costless and

---

1. See the survey by Rosen, S. (1986) 'The theory of equalizing differences', in Ashenfelter, O. and Layard, P.R.G. (eds.), *Handbook of Labor Economics*, vol.1, pp. 641–92, North Holland.

therefore immediate. This assumption of perfect information on the part of workers and employers underpins the theory of net advantages, or as it is now more commonly known 'the theory of equalizing differences'.

Adam Smith's theory of net advantages

Smith identified five principal reasons why wages will differ between jobs. The first of these he termed '*the agreeableness of the job*', by which he meant the nature of the working environment. Many factors determine this, but the safety and cleanliness of the workplace, the friendliness of one's workmates and perhaps the intrinsic satisfactions gained from the job itself, are likely to be the most important. We would expect an unskilled worker in a coalmine to receive higher pay than an unskilled worker acting as a cleaner in a hospital. The former is recognized to be a dangerous and dirty job, while the latter is relatively safe and clean. Moreover, to the extent that the relative dangers of working in mines increases, we would expect the difference in wages between these two categories of labor to increase; conversely, if, as coalmining becomes mechanized, it also becomes cleaner and safer, the differential should reduce. Again, we should expect to find that those who are working with hazardous chemical processes are paid higher wages than comparable workers in a less hazardous environment. Part of the relatively high earnings of steel erectors, steeple jacks, deep sea fishermen, policemen and coalminers is accounted for by the dangers associated with these jobs.[2] When we test this proposition empirically, we need to take account of other differences between the jobs being analyzed. Having done so we should expect there to be a positive association between the wage received by an individual and the unpleasantness of the job, as perhaps measured by the risk of death or injury associated with the job.

The second explanation of earnings differences identified by Smith he termed the '*cost of learning the business*', by which he meant the cost of acquiring the training and education essential for the job. We have already looked in detail at the theory of human capital, and seen that wages will be greater the greater is the education and training required to perform a job, as indeed Smith predicted, so this need not detain us further here.

Third, Smith drew attention to the '*constancy of employment*', by which he meant the extent to which a job is subject to predictable interruptions. Jobs in which production, or demand, is seasonal, or which are subject to regular layoffs or short-time working will, all other things being equal, require a higher rate of pay than more stable jobs. In the past the demand for automobiles exhibited a marked cycle of about five years' duration. This could be partly met by building up and running down inventories, but it also gave rise to periodic layoffs. If, under these circumstances, car makers were to attract employees of a quality comparable to those working elsewhere

---

2. An example of compensating wage differentials comes from the British nuclear energy industry. An article in *The Independent* on 17 November 1988 under the headline 'Pay for Radiation Offer' reported that 'British Nuclear Fuels may offer workers at its Sellafield plant more money for work which exposes them to higher doses of radiation'. A spokesman for BNF said that people might want to work in the first generation nuclear reactors, where exposure to radiation is highest, if they were paid more money in a manner analogous to the way 'that steeplejacks get paid more than people who walk around on the ground'.

they would have to pay a wage which was higher than that paid in jobs which offered more constant employment. The wage they offered would have to be sufficiently high so that when averaged over the periods when individuals were out of work as well as in employment, it provided a level of real income comparable to that offered in the more stable jobs. In that way it would fully compensate the workers for the wages they lost during the time they were laid off.[3] By the same token, if car workers are eligible for unemployment pay when laid off, the wage that is required to produce an equivalent real income is reduced.

Finally, Smith suggested two characteristics of jobs which today receive less emphasis. The first of these was the '*trust to be reposed*' and the second was '*the probability of success*'. The former of these proposes that those in trustworthy positions, such as the physician whom we trust with our life, the lawyer whom we trust with our reputation and/or fortune, the nanny whom we trust with our children and the member of MI5 whom we trust with our national security should, *ceteris paribus*, be offered higher wages than they would obtain if they employed their talents in less trustworthy jobs. However, it is not immediately evident why this should be so. Underpinning Smith's argument is the proposition that if we pay individuals more, this will induce them to behave in a trustworthy manner. Smith defends his argument by citing the case of the physician and the lawyer. Smith suggests that we would have no confidence 'in people of a very mean or low condition', and there is some empirical support for this as evidenced by the dress and deportment of the confidence trickster who persuades the old lady to part with her money, or the dress of the average insurance salesman. Conversely, it could be argued that we might regard the particularly ' well heeled' lawyer or physician with some misgivings, and that we would therefore be unwilling to trust such individuals with our lives, still less our fortunes. Essentially Smith advances a psychological postulate for which there is no unambiguous support.

The case for paying members of the secret service a compensatingly higher wage is different. Often they are both the producers of and the protectors of state secrets. It could be argued that the value of the marginal product of such individuals is equal to the price they could obtain from selling their secrets to the highest bidder and we should therefore pay our security services a wage equal to this. However, far from such a practice producing a market price for trust, such a system would suffer from problems of moral hazard. Agents possess an information advantage over co-workers, and they might be inclined to overstate the price they have been offered, indeed they might be tempted to offer free samples to attract buyers! An alternative approach is therefore to raise the costs of revealing state secrets, simply put, to shoot traitors. Another approach would be to develop social rules and conventions which dispose individuals to act in a loyal and trustworthy manner. Trustworthiness may be a product of either social background or innate characteristics and may be a commodity

3. Strictly, if individuals derive some utility from the time they are laid off, if they derive utility from time not spent working, then a wage which, when averaged over periods in and out of work, was exactly equal to the wage in the job with constant employment, would overcompensate the worker. It would make the worker better off, because such a wage provides an equivalent income to the job with constant employment, together with more hours of leisure.

in short supply, in which case if it is bid for in the market place the differential reward for this facility represents a rent earned by those in possession of this scare commodity.

The compensating differential related to the 'probability of success' results from individuals' immodesty. Smith suggested that the average wages of jobs requiring a similar level of skill, and for which all other conditions of employment were the same, varied inversely with the probability that some, from among all those working in the job, would achieve success; that some would achieve very high wages. Jobs in which some workers achieved very high earnings, such as popstars, would have a lower average wage than those in which the distribution was very narrow as with, say, typists. Consider Fig. 11.1 which details the wage distribution of two jobs requiring comparable levels of skill—waiters and jugglers to illustrate this point.

If all the individuals, who consider entering these jobs, correctly calculate the odds of emerging as one of the few very highly paid jugglers in the lottery that determines which jugglers succeed, the mean earnings of jugglers and waiters will be no different; average wages will be equal in the two jobs. If, however, as in the case illustrated here, individuals systematically *overestimate* their own chances of success, their chances of becoming one of the few very highly paid jugglers, this will attract more people into juggling than into waiting and compete down the mean wage for jugglers. Smith suggested that due to individuals' lack of modesty, jobs which display a wide dispersion of wages, in which there are a few very high earners, will exhibit a lower average wage than those jobs displaying a narrow dispersion of pay. Again Smith advances a psychological postulate.

Smith's theory of net advantages focuses on the non-pecuniary advantages and disadvantages of different jobs and in so doing advances a theory to explain the

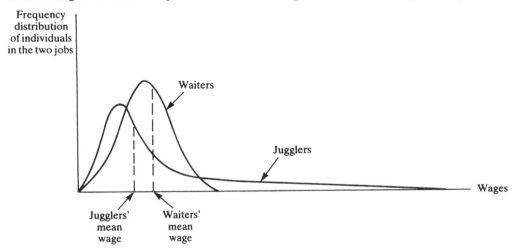

Figure 11.1 The average wage is inversely related to the dispersion of wages. The jobs of waiters and jugglers require comparable levels of skill and are in all other respects equal. However, individuals systematically overestimate their chances of becoming one of the few highly successful jugglers and of earning high wages. Accordingly, more people choose to become jugglers and this depresses the mean wage in this job

differences in wages between jobs. Despite the question marks that exist against the last two of his propositions, this remains the best statement of the theory of equalizing differences or compensating differentials that exists.

A formal model

The arguments advanced by Adam Smith can be developed more formally with the help of indifference curves and isoprofit lines. They enable us to develop the modern theory of equalizing differences into which Smith's original hypothesis has now been transformed. We first analyze the behavior of a single individual and firm, then generalize this to the many individuals and firms who populate any single labor market.

The shadow price Implicit in Smith's approach is the notion of a set of shadow prices for each of the non-pecuniary aspects of jobs. To illustrate, suppose that an individual's preferences can be simply defined in terms of two commodities, one a desirable market commodity, C, and the second an undesirable commodity, J, which is a characteristic of certain jobs. This results in the utility function, $U = U(C,J)$. Suppose also that both commodities are infinitely divisible and can therefore be defined as continuous variables, and the $U = U(C,J)$ is quasi-concave. Individuals' preferences can now be represented by a set of convex indifference curves drawn in CJ space, an example of which is shown in Fig. 11.2.

The preference direction is to the north-west. Higher levels of utility result from consumption of more of the desirable commodity and less of the undesirable characteristic. Individuals are willing to work in the unpleasant jobs, and to experience correspondingly higher levels of the undesirable characteristic, only if they are compensated by larger amounts of the desirable commodity. If this desirable commodity can be purchased in commodity markets an individual will only be willing to experience a level of the undesirable characteristic J_0 if compensated by an addition to the wage of ΔW.

Suppose that the competitively determined wage for jobs involving exposure to level of disamenity J_1 is W_1, and that the competitive wage for jobs involving exposure to the next lowest level of the disamenity J_0, is W_0, then $W_1 - W_0$ represents the implicit price that is paid in the labor market for exposure to an additional amount of the disamenity equal to $J_1 - J_0$. $W_1 - W_0$ is the 'shadow price' of the further increment $J_1 - J_0$ to the disamenity, from level J_0. Note that in this particular case the increment to the wage, $W_1 - W_0$, exceeds the increment to consumption goods, ΔC, which is required by the individual to compensate for the increased disamenity. The individual would thus be willing to work in the job with disamenity level J_1 for all $\Delta W > \Delta C$. Conversely, if $\Delta W < \Delta C$, the 'price' would be too low, and the individual would not be prepared to undertake the job involving exposure to disamenity level J_1.

Differences in individual tastes Take an extreme example of two individuals, A and B, who are currently contenders for a potentially dangerous job. Both workers'

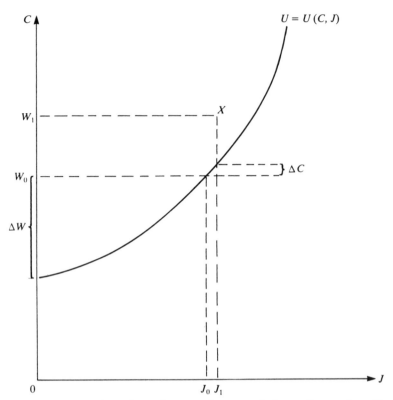

Figure 11.2 The shadow price of an increase in a workplace disamenity. C represents a commodity, greater amounts of which afford positive increments to utility. J represents a disamenity, more of which detracts from utility. The individual requires an increment to the wage equal to ΔW if they are to experience level J_0 of the disamenity and be no worse off than they were before, at zero level of J

preferences can be represented by a utility function $U = U(C,D)$, where C is as before, and D is now the danger associated with this job. Suppose they differ in their aversion to danger as suggested in Fig. 11.3. Individual A's preferences result in indifference curves of the shape shown in Fig. 11.2. Individual A dislikes danger, and demands a higher wage the greater the exposure to danger. Indeed, the greater the level of danger already experienced the larger the increase in the wage demanded if individual A is to be exposed to still more danger. Looked at another way individual A is willing to pay, that is willing to experience a lower wage, in order to be exposed to less danger. On the other hand, individual B likes a certain amount of danger, and, up to D_1, would be willing to accept a lower wage in order to experience the thrills associated with additional danger. Thus B's indifference curve is negatively sloped, up to D_1.

The disamenity–wage trade-off Now consider the determinants of the degree of danger at the workplace. The danger itself is a function of the particular commodity being

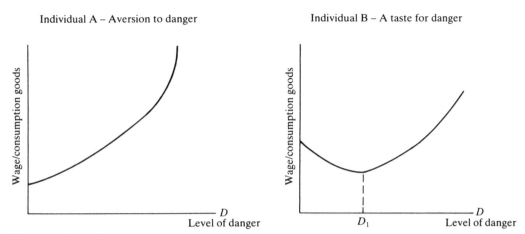

Figure 11.3 Individuals' preferences for danger. Individuals differ in their tastes for danger. Individual A is willing to pay to minimize exposure to danger while individual B is willing to pay to increase exposure to danger up to the level D_1

produced and the range of production technologies currently available with which to produce it. While there may be only one basic technology, this can often be modified or the workers' routines and practices can often be amended to minimize the danger. These methods of reducing danger have in common that they require either the use of additional resources or they reduce workers' output. In each case it is costly to reduce danger. Accordingly, if the firm is to reduce danger but still secure a given level of profit, it must pay a correspondingly lower wage. At any given level of profit, as indicated by a single isoprofit curve, such as π_0 in Fig. 11.4, the firm faces a trade-off between the wage it can pay and the level of danger at the workplace. Each isoprofit line is concave because it becomes increasingly costly to reduce danger and, as a result, the firm can only secure a given level of profits by larger reductions in the wage. Of course at any given level of danger, say D_1, the lower the wage the higher the profit. This is indicated by the increase in profits as we move from π_0 to π_1 and π_2 with the wage reduced from first W_0 to W_1 then to W_2.

Equilibrium of the individual and firm Now consider workers' preferences and the firm's profit opportunities taken together. Equilibrium occurs when the preferences of the worker coincide with the profit opportunities of the firm, as represented by a point of tangency between an isoprofit line and an indifference curve. In Fig. 11.5 level of profit π_0 can be secured by employing individual A at a wage of W_0 and exposing that person to level of danger D_1. To provide any lower level of danger for this individual would necessitate the payment of a lower wage, if the same level of profit π_0 were to be earned, but in turn this would place individual A on a lower indifference curve. Equally, exposure to a higher level of danger, accompanied by payment of the higher wage the individual would require to experience such danger, would reduce the profits of the

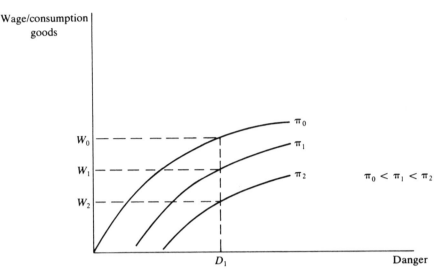

Figure 11.4 The technological trade-off between wages and danger. π_0, π_1 and π_2 represent a family of isoprofit lines. The shape of each isoprofit line reflects the fact that it is costly to reduce the level of danger at the workplace. Accordingly, the lower the level of danger the lower will be the wage the firm will pay, while sustaining a given level of profit. Profits increase as we move from π_0 to π_1 to π_2

firm. Neither of these last two positions is one of tangency and therefore neither will be an equilibrium.

Faced with a choice between the two individuals shown in Fig. 11.3, individual A with the aversion to danger and individual B with the taste for danger, the firm would not employ A. It can secure a higher level of profit, π_1, at wage W_0 by employing individual B and exposing that person to associated level of danger D_0. Alternatively, at level of danger D_1, it could secure profit level π_1 by employing individual B at wage W_1, although of course this does not represent an equilibrium, and would not be sustainable. In Fig. 11.5 equilibrium is realized by employing individual B at wage W_0 and danger level D_0. At this point the firm reaches the highest attainable isoprofit line, and the individual employed his or her highest indifference curve. Unusually in this last example, due to the differences in individual tastes, there is *no* compensating differential for the increment to danger $D_0 - D_1$: no increment to the wage is offered to individual B to experience the additional danger $D_0 - D_1$. However, it would be unwise to generalize from this example. More typical will be individuals with tastes like those of A. In the case of individual A a compensating wage differential equal to $W_2 - W_0$ would have to be paid in order to induce this person to experience the additional danger $D_0 - D_1$.

There was no compensating differential for the increment to danger $D_0 - D_1$ when B was employed because of the difference in tastes between individuals A and B. However, this result will only hold at the aggregate level if a second condition is met, that is, that the number of individuals with tastes for the disamenity in question, in

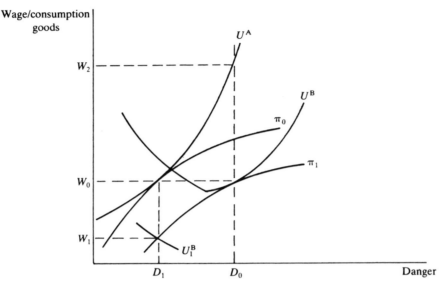

Figure 11.5 The profitability of employing the individual with the least aversion to danger. Equilibrium is described by the points of tangency between workers' indifference curves and firms' isoprofit curves. Where individuals differ in their tastes, firms will find it more profitable to employ those individuals, such as B above, with a smaller aversion to the disamenity. By employing B at wage W_0 and exposing that person to level of danger D_0 the firm enjoys a level of profits equal to π_1, compared to the π_0 that would result from employing A at this wage

this case danger, is exactly equal to the demand for people to occupy jobs with these characteristics. Any imbalance, any excess demand by firms for people to work in dangerous jobs, will lead employers to bid for the services of those who like danger and the consequent rise in the wage will lead to the re-emergence of a compensating wage differential. Although this may now be smaller than where all individuals have the same aversion to dangerous jobs, a positive wage difference will still emerge in dangerous jobs. Conversely, an excess supply of people with such tastes will lead to a negative compensating differential in these jobs.

The compensation required to experience particular levels of workplace disamenity will differ according to the individuals' tastes. A corollary of this is that, if we could measure precisely the degrees of disamenity associated with particular jobs, and could control for *all* other characteristics for jobs, we would then be able to measure differences in individual tastes for a particular disamenity. Equally should we fail to control for all other aspects of the job, we would run the danger of attributing to differences in tastes the consequences of measurement error.

The market clearing price for a disamenity When we aggregate across the large number of individuals who occupy any single labor market we generally encounter a diversity of tastes. Tastes are located along a spectrum revealing differences in the degree of aversion to most disamenities. Where individuals differ in their degree of aversion to dangerous jobs, their indifference maps will not coincide and their preferences may be illustrated in a set of indifference curves such as those shown in Fig. 11.6 for individuals A, B and C. In this example A is the most averse to danger for this person demands the largest increment to the wage, to compensate for an increase in danger from D_0 to D_1. Individual A requires an increment to the wage equal to W_0 to W_1 while individual B requires an increase of only W_0 to W_2. Of the three individual C is the least averse to danger. Figure 11.6 illustrates individuals with differing degrees of aversion to danger or, put another way, who are willing to pay different prices to work in safe conditions. Individual A would be willing to pay $W_1 - W_0$ to work in the safer environment D_0, while individual B would be willing to pay only $W_2 - W_0$ for the same reduction in danger, from D_1 to D_0.

What of the supply of jobs with different degrees of danger? The existence of danger is a consequence of the demand for labor by firms which are producing output using technologies which expose workers to a degree of danger. Because firms employ different technologies they are likely to face different costs of reducing danger by a given amount and they will, therefore, differ in the degree to which they need to reduce the wage they pay, in order to maintain a particular level of profits.

The above arguments are illustrated in Fig. 11.7 by drawing the isoprofit lines for firms 1, 2 and 3 when each firm is making normal profits. Each of these firms has to cut wages if they are to find the money they need to reduce danger, but firm 1 finds

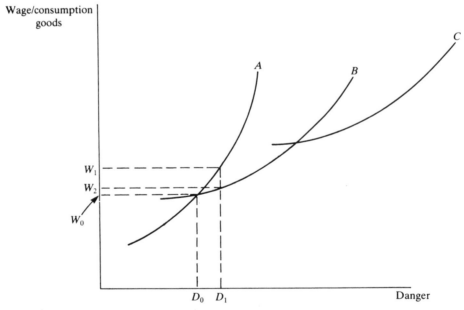

Figure 11.6 Differences in workers' tastes for danger. Individuals differ in their degree of aversion to danger. Individual A is most averse, C the least. A requires an increase in the wage equal to $W_1 - W_0$ in order to experience an increase in danger from D_0 to D_1 while individual B requires an increase in the wage equal to only $W_2 - W_0$ to experience the same increase in danger.

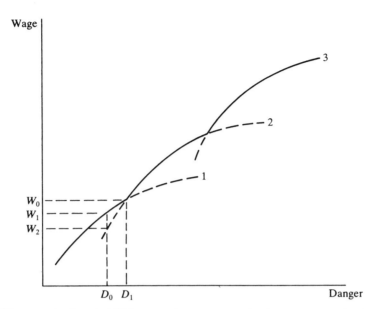

Figure 11.7 Differences in firms' abilities to reduce danger. The figure shows a family of isoprofit curves for three firms, each of which is making normal profits. These firms differ in their abilities to reduce danger. Firm 1 can reduce danger levels from D_1 to D_0 at a cost equal to a reduction in the wage of $W_0 - W_1$ while firm 2 must reduce the wage from W_0 to W_2. Firm 2 finds it more costly to produce low levels of danger than firm 1. The bold sections of the isoprofit lines represent the best combinations of levels of wages and danger that are on offer in the labor market while firms continue to earn normal profits.

it easier, less costly, to reduce danger from D_1 to D_0 than does firm 2. Firm 2 has to cut wages from W_0 to W_2, to reduce danger from D_1 to D_0 while firm 1 need only cut wages from W_0 to W_1. In general firm 1 is able to produce lower levels of danger than either firm 2 or firm 3, but note this is achieved at the cost of a generally lower level of wages. We might think of firm 1 as having bought more modern but also more expensive machinery.

The figure illustrates once again the proposition that you cannot get something for nothing. Reducing danger costs money, and therefore normal profits can only be achieved by paying lower wages. The bold sections of the three isoprofit lines in Fig. 11.7 represent the best set of wages on offer in this market when firms earn normal profits. Clearly individuals would not accept a job at danger level D_0 with firm 2 when firm 1 can offer W_1 for exposure to the same level of danger. The bold segment in Fig. 11.7 is called the *offer curve*.

Equilibrium in the market for dangerous jobs is now found at the points of tangency between the offer curve and the individuals' indifference curves as illustrated in Fig. 11.8. The locus of these points of tangency describes the *market equilibrium curve*, E. In equilibrium individual A works for firm 1 at wage W_A experiencing danger D_A, individual B for firm 2 at W_B and D_B, individual C for firm 3 at W_C and D_C. A set

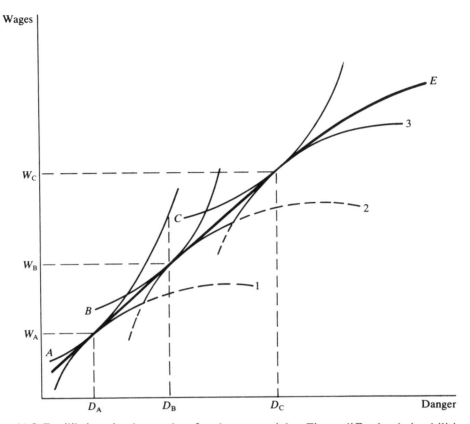

Figure 11.8 Equilibrium in the market for dangerous jobs. Firms differ in their abilities to reduce danger and individuals differ in their tastes for danger. Equilibrium occurs at the points of tangency between workers' indifference curves and the bold sections of the isoprofit lines. The market equilibrium curve E describes the locus of such points and reveals a positive association between the level of wages and workplace danger. Higher levels of danger are compensated by higher wages

of compensating differentials emerges. Evidently there is a tendency toward 'assortive matching' with firms which face the largest costs of reducing danger offering the highest wages and employing those individuals with the least aversion to danger.

Such a situation differs from that in which individuals are identical with respect to tastes and firms are identical with respect to technology. This situation would be illustrated by a single 'representative' indifference curve tangent to a single isoprofit curve. Similarly, if firms were not identical but workers' preferences were homogeneous, firms that could not satisfy these would be driven out of business. For if workers' preferences were homogeneous and could be described by indifference curve A in Fig. 11.8, firms 2 and 3 could not offer an equal level of utility to that of firm 1 while continuing to earn normal profits.

The theory of equalizing differences is predicated on certain assumptions. It is appropriate to remind ourselves just what they are. The first assumption is that workers are fully informed about all the relevant characteristics of the job. All the relevant characteristics can be discovered by examination or recommendation; there are no non-trivial characteristics of jobs that can only be discovered by experience. However, as we saw in the previous chapter there is evidence that in many cases substantial additional information is only gained on the job.[4] Second, it is assumed that once in possession of full information, workers correctly process it and move in response to changing labor market opportunities, thereby indicating to firms something of the nature of their preferences. Again, as we have shown in the previous chapter and in Chapter 5, individuals differ in the degree of mobility that they are willing or able to undertake. The transactions' costs associated with changing jobs mean that a move is frequently best regarded as an investment decision on the part of the worker and such investment is more readily contemplated at certain stages of the inidividual's life. Accordingly, in the short run the 'true' compensating differentials the equilibrium values, may not emerge. Over the long run differentials are more likely to reflect the valuations of the marginal, the more mobile, workers and they may therefore tell us little about the valuations of the rest of the population.

Implicit in the theory of equalizing differences is the idea that there exist certain 'commodities', which can only be consumed at the workplace. The firm is therefore engaged in joint production: it produces commodities for sale to consumers, its main activity, and as a by-product of this, also produces commodities for sale to its workforce. The former are sold in markets at explicit prices, the latter at implicit prices by paying a wage different from the workers' marginal product.

The notion that characteristics of the workplace, such as safety and cleanliness, are best regarded as commodities produced by the firm, has one important corollary. If such commodities are normal goods, expenditure on these will rise with income. Those facing the highest wage rates will therefore purchase more of these commodities. This leads to the prediction that high productivity workers, workers enjoying high earnings, are likely to be found in the most pleasant and the safest and cleanest jobs, while workers of low productivity will fill the 'worst' jobs. Thus it explains what at first glance might appear to be an empirical refutation of the theory of net advantages—low wages in the worst jobs. Once we have controlled for worker ability and productivity, this apparent paradox is resolved.

Frank's theory of status[5]

A recent development within the framework of the theory of net advantages proposes that we should treat status as one of those commodities produced at the workplace for which individuals are willing to pay a price. To illustrate this point, suppose that

4. The study by Viscusi, W.K. and O'Connor, C.J. (1984) 'Adaptive responses to chemical labelling: are workers Bayesian decision makers?', *American Economic Review*, **74**(5), 942–56, shows that workers begin jobs with imperfect information and quit, if the position becomes relatively unattractive, as they learn about the risks associated with jobs.
5. Frank, R.H. (1985) *Choosing the Right Pond: Human Behavior and the Quest for Status*, Oxford University Press, New York and Oxford.

individuals differ in productivity and that those with the highest productivity earn the highest income. This relationship is illustrated in Fig. 11.9(a). Individual F has the highest marginal product and enjoys the highest wage, individuals D and E have the next highest marginal product and enjoy the next highest wages, and so on.

Suppose that individuals are concerned both with the status they derive from their position in the income distribution and with the relative level of consumption that their income affords. Suppose further that individuals differ in their tastes for status, that A, C and E have a weak taste for status while B and D and F have a strong taste for status. These differing tastes for status can be satisfied by establishing a number of local markets for status in which status can be bought and sold. Thus if individual B can persuade another individual to join him or her in a firm and to occupy a position of lower status this will satisfy individual B's demand for high status. Status is, after all, a relative concept and individual B's high status is contingent upon the perception of others. Individual B might be able to satisfy his or her demand for high status by bribing someone into assuming low status within the same firm. Looked at another way individual B is prepared to pay a price for high status. Such deals can only be struck with individuals of lower productivity; evidently B cannot conclude such an arrangement with C, even if individual C displays a weak taste for status, since payment of any monies by B to C would raise C's income and status above that of B's. If individual B is to pay any individual to occupy a low status position, then it has to be individual A of all those shown. B could compensate A for low status and still leave B with enough additional income to be the top earner in group 1. In this manner a series of compensating payments emerge in which individuals, with a desire for high status, join workgroups with a lower average level of productivity, and hence wages, and compensate some among that number for occupying low status positions. The price those who seek high status pay is a wage less than their marginal products; the compensation to low status workers is a wage above their marginal product. The results of these compensating payments are shown in Fig. 11.9(b). In Fig. 11.9(b) wages now differ from marginal product. Firms offer workers a combination of status and wages and workers choose accordingly. In Frank's language workers choose the size of pond that meets their requirements. They decide whether they wish to be a big fish (or frog) in a small pond, or a small fish in a big pond. Choosing the right pond is the name of the game.

In Frank's theory status is a commodity which commands a price and can be traded in the market place. All individuals exhibits a taste for status, they simply differ in the strength of this taste. Those willing to pay a high price, redistribute part of the remuneration they would otherwise earn to the individuals willing to occupy the lower positions in the group. Without the presence of the low productivity individuals the high productivity workers would have no co-workers to admire them. In support of this theory Frank produces an array of evidence revealing that wage-marginal product profiles are relatively flat as suggested in Fig. 11.9(b).

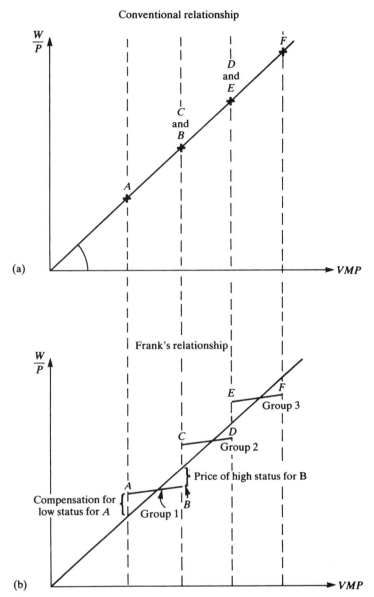

Figure 11.9 The relationship between pay and value marginal product when individuals buy status. (a) Each worker is paid a wage equal to his or her marginal product; (b) Individuals with a taste for high status such as B, D and F join with those of lower productivity and a smaller taste for status to form different groups which satisfy their demands. Those wishing to buy high status compensate those of low productivity, who are willing to occupy low status positions, by paying them a wage in excess of their marginal product

EMPIRICAL EVIDENCE OF EQUALIZING DIFFERENCES

What is the evidence to support the idea that the market behaves in the manner described by the theory of equalizing differences? Several studies have addressed this question both in order to test the theory and in order to estimate the magnitude of the implicit prices of particular non-wage characteristics. The prices that are estimated are typically those for relatively large groups and in practice there may be considerable variations around these means. To understand this consider again Fig. 11.8. Equilibrium in the implicit market for safety was illustrated by the locus of points of tangency between the employers' isoprofit lines and the individuals' indifference curves. The line depicting this set of points, E, and its slope, $\partial W/\partial D$, indicate the value that workers place on the amenity in question. It is evident from Fig. 11.8 that the line does not have a constant slope, and therefore that the price that individuals are willing to pay for safety differs according to the particular level of D chosen. The measured differential $W_B - W_A$ in Fig. 11.8 would provide a considerable *underestimate* of the wage differences that individuals such as A would demand to experience this higher level of danger, as indicated by the slope of A's indifference curve at the point at which it cuts D_B. Not surprisingly most of the empirical work has focused on estimating the average level of the compensating difference for all those individuals experiencing a particular workplace amenity or disamenity. However, Fig. 11.8 reminds us that around such a mean estimate there is likely to be very wide dispersion. We should therefore exercise considerable caution before we assign such values to particular subgroups of the population.

How then do researchers calculate the average price of a safe work environment? How do they calculate the price that individuals are willing to pay to work in a safer environment? This can be done by adapting the human capital earnings function we detailed in Chapter 6. Suppose that S_i measures the incidence of serious accidents at individual i's workplace. In the earnings equation reported in Chapter 6, S_i would be an element of the vector of variables X_i, which capture the non-wage advantages and disadvantages of different jobs. Now we are specifically interested in the coefficient on S_i so that Eq. (6.11) may be rewritten as:

$$\log W/P_i = a_1 + a_2 I_i + a_3 I_i^2 + a_4 S_i + a_5 X_i + \varepsilon_i \qquad (11.1)$$

where as before a_1 represents the log of earnings when there has been no additional human capital investment, a_2 measures the rate of return on a year's education, a_3 captures non-linear effects of education on earnings; X_i is a vector of variables measuring all other non-wage advantages and disadvantages of the job except a_4 which measures the price individuals are willing to pay to work in a safer environment. In this equation I_i and I_i^2 represent control variables. The methodology therefore involves the application of the same general form of earnings function used to examine the returns to human capital. Some among the relevant variables determining earnings such as motivation, determination, application, call these P_i, will remain unobserved and/or unmeasured. Incorporating these Eq. (11.1) becomes:

$$\log W_i/P_i = a_1 + a_2 I_i + a_3 I_i^2 + a_4 S_i + a_5 X_i + a_6 P_i + \varepsilon_i \qquad (11.2)$$

One of the problems with such an earnings equation is that the elements of P_i cannot be observed while those in both I and X are often measured with a considerable degree of error due to problems of extracting, processing and matching data. The estimation of Eq. (11.2) therefore faces problems of omitted variables and measurement error which may bias the estimates of the parameter on S_i. This omitted variable problem raises particular difficulties for those studies that have used cross-section data for the omitted variables are individual specific. They cannot be controlled for by aggregating them into a single term, that is by the usual procedure of dummy variables, for this would require that there now be one such variable for each observation. Recently researchers have therefore advocated the use of longitudinal data to calculate changes in measured characteristics and this means that the intercept dummies now control for those individual characteristics that do not change over time.[6]

Yet even this procedure, while evidently offering advantages over cross-section analysis, introduces its own problem, that of autocorrelation, and this reduces the efficiency of the estimates, although it does not bias the parameters. Some worker characteristics, such as experience, marital status and formal job training, as well as tastes for working in particular types of environment, say smoky environments, change over time, with the result that the market equilibrium curve, E, will shift or perhaps change slope, in an unknown manner this will again reduce the confidence we can place in the resulting estimates. Evidently, research in this area faces a number of difficulties. Yet, despite this, a number of important findings emerge.

One study estimated a version of Eq. (11.2) using longitudinal data with the variables specified as changes over the period 1968–74 for a sample of male employees in Sweden. Table 11.1 reports the results of this exercise. Thus we find that exposure to noise or exposure to smoke or gas in the working environment resulted in wage premiums of almost 4 and 3 percent respectively (the coefficients are 0.038 and 0.031 respectively), while mentally demanding work attracted a premium of almost 5 percent. Most of the control variables have the expected sign and are significant, but there is still no evidence of a compensating differential for hard physical work, and for some of the variables measuring constraints on hours. Such results attest to the considerable difficulty of controlling for the many influences on wages, and indeed, the overall explanation of wage change that is offered by this equation, an R^2 of 0.16, is rather poor.[7] If the researchers had been able to measure and thereby include variables indicating motivation, application, diligence, etc., it is possible they might have reversed the sign and/or changed the significance of several of these variables.

6. See Brown, C. (1980) 'Equalizing differences in the labor market', *Quarterly Journal of Economics*, **94**, February 113–34.
7. See Duncan, G. and Holmlund, B. (1983) 'Was Adam Smith right after all : another test of compensating wage differentials', *Journal of Labor Economics*, **1**, 366–79.

Table 11.1 Empirical estimates of compensating differentials

	Dependent variable (ln 1974 wage – ln 1968 wage)			
Hours			– 0.006	(0.008)
Inflexible hours	0.002	(0.017)		
The use of punch clock is required	0.020	(0.018)		
Difficult to run errands	– 0.036	(0.015)		
Hard physical work			– 0.007	(0.008)
Job involves heavy lifting	0.010	(0.017)		
Physically demanding other than heavy lifting	– 0.014	(0.016)		
Work causes sweating	– 0.012	(0.018)		
Dangerous work			0.002	(0.007)
Work is very noisy	0.038	(0.017)		
Sometimes or always exposed to smoke or gas	0.031	(0.017)		
Exposed to vibrations	0.010	(0.022)		
Exposed to poisons, acids or explosives	0.002	(0.017)		
Stressful work			0.034	(0.010)
Mentally demanding	0.046	(0.016)		
Hectic	0.020	(0.015)		
Control variables				
Education	0.020	(0.006)		
Experience	0.018	(0.006)		
Experience^2/1000	– 0.409	(0.068)		
Married	0.091	(0.021)		
Handicapped	– 0.002	(0.013)		
Supervisory capacity	0.020	(0.008)		
Unemployment 1969–74	0.013	(0.026)		
Job change 1964–79	0.076	(0.019)		
Intercept	0.525	(0.032)		
R^2	0.160			
MSE	0.081			

(Standard errors in parentheses)
Source: Duncan, G. and Holmlund, B. (1983), *op. cit.* Reproduced with permission of the publisher.

Earlier studies are not without interest and have also provided evidence of equalizing differences. It has been found that repetitive work attracts a positive compensating differential, and that bad working conditions, such as extreme temperatures and hazardous conditions, also commanded a differential.[8] In the United States 5 percent of the workforce experience at least one day of lost working time due to injury on the job each year and in the United States a positive differential emerges to compensate for the duration of injury.[9] A negative compensating differential has also been found for jobs which permit individuals to control hours worked, have a safe working environment and offer employment and income stability.[10] Another study found a positive wage differential for risk of layoff.[11] All this is as the theory suggests, and yet each of these studies and others in the area throw up unexpected signs on several variables. Jobs requiring physical strength command lower wages,[12] and there is scant evidence of compensating differentials for non-fatal injuries.[13] This leads one researcher to conclude that there are 'an uncomfortable number of exceptions' to the theory[14] but this is more likely evidence of the difficulties that confront reesearchers when trying to measure all the important worker and job characteristics rather than evidence with which to reject the theory itself.

The most persuasive evidence is that regarding workers' willingness to pay for a reduction in the risk of death while at work. Such risks can be objectively measured on a cardinal scale, deaths per 1000 workers, and this allows the construction of an independent variable which displays greater variance than those measuring other job characteristics which are generally of a dichotomous nature. The results of some of these studies are reported in Table 11.2 in which it is revealed that, in the 1970s, workers in the United States were willing to forgo between $400 and $2000 per annum in wages, in advance, to reduce the risk of death at work by one in 1000. More recently a figure of around $4000 per annum has been suggested. These figures suggest that, collectively, US workers were willing to pay between $1 million and $4 million in 1982 prices to avoid one death at work. By 1986 this figure had risen to just over $5 million. These values should be contrasted with those calculated for the United Kingdom in the late 1970s. A UK study reported that workers place a value on a life of between £800 000 and £1.25 million.

It is noteworthy that these estimates, resulting from the behavior and therefore the (implicit) preferences of the marginal individuals, as registered in the market place, result in a much higher valuation of life than is often admitted for public policy purposes. The procedures adopted by the UK regulatory body, the Health and Safety

---

8. See Lucas, R.E.B. (1977) 'Hedonic wage equations and psychic wages in the returns to schooling', *American Economic Review*, **67**, 549–58.
9. See Hammermesh, D.S. and Wolfe, J. (1988) 'Compensating differentials and the duration of wage loss', *Journal of Labor Economics*, **6**(2),
10. See Duncan, G. (1976) 'Earnings functions and non-pecuniary benefits', *Journal of Human Resources*, **11**, 462–83.
11. See Hutchens, R. (1983) 'Layoffs and labor supply', *International Economic Review*, **24**, 37–55.
12. Lucas, R.E.B. (1977), *op. cit.*, 549–58.
13. Smith, R.S. (1979) 'Compensating wage differentials and public policy: a review', *Industrial and Labor Relations Review*, **32**, 339–52.
14. Brown, C. (1980) *op. cit.* 118.

Table 11.2 Compensating differentials for risk of death at work

Investigator	Willingness to pay for a 1/1000 reduction in the risk of death per annum
USA	*(Current $)*
Brown (1980)	400–600
Smith (1979)	2000
Smith (1976)	1500
Moore and Viscusi (1988)	4333
UK	*(£s)*
Veljanovski (1978)	800–1125
	Implicit value of a life
USA	(1982 $s)
Viscusi (1979)	2.9–3.9 million
Brown (1980)	1–1.5 million

Sources: Brown, C. (1980), 'Equalizing differences in the labor market', *Quarterly Journal of Economics*, **94**, 113–34.

Smith, R.S. (1979), 'Compensating wage differentials and public policy: a review', *Industrial and Labor Relations Review*, **32**, 339–52.

Smith, R.S. (1976), *The Occupational Safety and Health Act: Its Goals and its Achievements*, The American Enterprise Institute for Public Policy Research, Washington, DC.

Veljanovski, C.G. (1978). *The Economics of Job Safety Regulation: Theory and Evidence: Part I—The Market and Common Law* Oxford Centre For Socio–Legal Studies, Wolfson College, September.

Moore, M.J. and Viscusi, W.K. (1988), 'Doubling the estimated value of life: results using new occupational family data', *Journal of Public Policy Analysis and Management*, **7**(3), 476–90.

Executive, to value a life, involve adding the economic value of what an individual can produce to some notional allowance for the fact that society, by providing social welfare payments, is evidently prepared to pay something to allow the individual to subsist even though he or she may not be productive. Such a procedure results in an average valuation of life of around £200 000 in 1984 prices.[15] Evidently private valuations considerably exceed those used to construct public policy in the labor market, and this therefore raises a question mark against the public policies resting on such valuations.

Indeed, if anything, such estimates probably understate the price that individuals would be willing to pay to minimize their exposure to certain unpleasant aspects of work. The compensating differentials emerged as a result of the measured behavior of workers in the labor market. If these estimates are to provide an accurate measure of the sums involved, they must represent equilibrium values, and for this to occur, the labor market must be functioning perfectly. When the labor market is in equilibrium the role of government in formulating life saving or risk reducing programs is

15. See Heywood, J. (1984) *Employment Gazette*.

appropriately confined to those situations in which the risks are largely unknown or misperceived. It is therefore interesting to note that much of the work of the US Occupational Safety and Health Administration (OSHA) and UK Health and Safety Executive (HSE) is concerned with job-related diseases which take a considerable amount of time to reveal their full effects, the carcinogenic effects of absestos-related diseases being a case in point.

If information is imperfect, or for other reasons the market fails to clear, the differentials that emerge will under- or overstate the equilibrium values of the differentials. There is, as we have already seen, evidence that the full characteristics of a job are only learned by experience on the job. One study found that one group of workers who perceived a risk in their current jobs received a compensating differential but also exhibited a higher than average quit rate.[16] This suggested that workers may only become acquainted with the full risks of the job through experience on the job. The higher quit rate is also evidence that the existing differentials did not fully compensate for the eventually perceived risks, and thus they were not at their equilibrium values. Again it was found that positive compensating differentials emerge where workers were required to handle dangerous chemicals, but that exposure to extreme levels of hazard also resulted in increased quits and regrets at having accepted the job in the first place. The findings were, it was suggested, consistent with a model of 'try outs' by workers, necessitated by imperfect information. It was concluded that chemical labeling, which simply informs individuals of the risk level involved (in a more familiar context government warnings that 'smoking can damage your health', or 'smoking can kill'), is inadequate. One alternative to labeling is that government should provide sufficient information to enable individuals to evaluate the relative risks involved.[17]

FRINGE BENEFITS

A major part of the net advantage of most jobs today are the non-wage pecuniary benefits that workers enjoy. Over the last 20 years the structure of workers' compensation has changed substantially. A far smaller part of total compensation is now accounted for by the wage and salary element, while payments-in-kind and deferred compensation, together titled fringe benefits, have assumed increasing significance.

Wage and non-wage compensation

Table 11.3 reveals that over the 20 years since the early 1960s the proportion of total compensation that workers receive in wages has fallen from around 95 percent to 90 percent in United States and Britain. These calculations reflect non-statutory fringe benefits—those provided as a result of agreement between firms and workers. If we add in the payments that employers are required to make into statutory health, social

16. Viscusi, W.K. (1979) *Employment Hazards: An Investigation of Market Performance*, Harvard University Press.
17. Viscusi, W.K. and O'Connor, C.J. (1984), *op. cit.*, 942–56.

Table 11.3 Wage and non-wage compensation

	USA		Britain	
	Wage	Non-wage[†]	Wage	Non-wage[‡]
1966	95.1	4.9	—	—
1968	—	—	94.8	5.2
1970	94.0	6.0	—	—
1972	93.2	6.8	—	—
1975	—	—	93.8	6.2
1976	90.8	9.2	—	—
1978	—	—	90.1	9.9
1980	88.2	11.8	—	—
1984	—	—	90.2	9.8

Source: US Department of Labor, Bureau of Labor Statistics quoted in Woodbury's (1983), 'Substitution between wage and non-wage benefits', *American Economic Review*, **73**, 166–82. Britain—Department of Employment, *Survey of Labour Costs.*
[†] Excludes legally required payments, e.g. social security, workers' compensation and unemployment insurance contributions.
[‡] Excludes legally required payments, national insurance contributions and training costs.

security and unemployment insurance schemes, as detailed in Table 11.4, the share of the total expenditure on labor compensation by employers that takes the form of wages has fallen to only just above 70 percent in both countries. Evidently fringe benefits are a major element in workers' compensation in both countries today.

The range of fringe benefits available in both countries is now extensive. In the United Kingdom they range from subsidized loans to bank employees, provision of a car, payment of the premiums for private health insurance schemes, through to an allowance of several bottles of scotch per year for each employee in the Scottish whisky distilleries. In the United States payment of health insurance, discounts on merchandise and subsidized loans are again important. In both countries by far the most general fringe benefit is paid vacations, although, as we noted earlier, they are far less generous in the United States than in the United Kingdom. Membership of a profit sharing scheme and day-care facilities for children are among those benefits to show the most rapid growth in recent years in both countries. In the last few years, however, there have been signs, in both countries, that the share of fringes in total compensation is beginning to fall back.

The same detail is not available for many countries but as Tables 11.5 and 11.6 reveal non-wage labor costs now account for a very substantial proportion of total labor costs in most countries. They are particularly large in Germany, France, Italy and Sweden, in each of which they account for over 40 percent of total labor costs. In each of these countries statutory social welfare payments (compulsory employee contributions to pensions, health and insurance schemes, unemployment and in some cases short time working and training schemes) account for the major component as Table 11.6 reveals. Payment for days not worked, that is payment for statutory and

Table 11.4 The composition of expenditures by employers on labor compensation in the United States and the United Kingdom

(All employees)	USA 1980 Larger manufacturing firms	UK 1981 Manufacturing, construction and utilities
Pay for working time	72.4	71.9
Pay for leave time	9.5	9.7
(vacations, holidays, sick leave, etc.)		
US pension, life and health insurance, contributions to social security for unemployment insurance, etc.	16.5	
UK statutory national insurance and superannuation and other benefits		16.5
Other—subsidized services	1.6	1.9
meals, cars, etc.		
TOTAL	100	100

Sources: USA Chamber of Commerce, 1980; *Fringe Benefits and Employer Benefits* United Kingdom Department of Employment, *Survey of Labour Costs.*

non-statutory vacation time and sick leave, is also important. In all of these countries the emphasis is on statutory rather than voluntary social welfare.

In the United States the emphasis is on voluntary social welfare provision, and vacation provision is far less than in continental Europe. In the United Kingdom the emphasis is again on statutory welfare provision but the level of provision is far less than in continental Europe. In both these countries non-wage labor costs account for a similar proportion of total labor costs. In Japan paid holidays are least generous of all the countries shown while bonuses are included in wage costs. These features,

Table 11.5 Main non-wage labor cost items as proportions of total labor costs in selected OECD countries (manufacturing industry), 1981

	France	Germany	Italy	Japan	UK	USA
Payment for days not worked	8.3	11.5	10.4	2.2	10.9	8.7[†]
Statutory Social Security	18.9	16.1	21.9	7.2	9.4	7.8[†]
Voluntary Social Security	6.8	3.6	1.5	6.7	6.3	8.9[†]

Sources: Hart R.A. *et. al.* (1988). *Trends in Non-Wage Labour Costs and their Effects on Employment*, Commission of the European Community Brussels.
[†] All industries.

Table 11.6 Non-wage labor costs as a percentage of total labor costs

	1965	1975	1983	Annual rate of growth[†] 1965–83
France	40.2	43.8	44.4[‡]	0.56
Germany	29.7	39.2	44.4	2.25
Italy	44.9	51.4	46.3	0.17
Japan[§]	—	13.9	15.5	0.44[¶]
Norway	22.2	29.9	33.0	2.22
Sweden	19.0	32.2	40.6	4.32
United Kingdom	13.7	19.6	26.5	3.74
United States	17.1	24.0	26.7	2.51
Average (unweighted)[‖]	26.9	31.1	34.7	
Coefficient of variation (%)	39.1	37.7	31.1	

Source: Swedish Employers' Confederation, *Wages and Total Labour Costs for Workers, International Survey.* As reported in Hart, R.A. *et al.* (1988), *op. cit.*

[†] Growth rate is for the proportion of NWLCS to total labor costs.

[‡] Data do not include the extra week of vacation.

[§] Data refer to all employees. Irregular bonuses and payments for days not worked are included in wages for time worked. NWLCs for Japan are thus significantly underestimated in comparison to other countries (see discussion in the text).

[¶] 1970 to 1983.

[‖] Average and coefficient of variation are calculated for all countries, except Japan.

together with far fewer statutory welfare payments by the employer, account for the small proportion of non-wage labor costs in total labor costs in Japan.

Historically, payments-in-kind emerged for a variety of reasons. The 'truck' system emerged in Britain in the mining industry in the nineteenth century partly as an attempt to influence miners' consumption patterns. Payment-in-kind, the provision of food, was in part an attempt to reduce miners' spending on beer. In modern Britain the provision of luncheon vouchers, purportedly to encourage employees to take adequate nourishment during their lunch break, may work in a different direction, for in most London pubs they can readily be exchanged for beer.

What then are the reasons for the growth in fringe benefits in both countries? In order to answer this question we have first to consider employees' preferences for different forms of compensation and then to assess the relative costs of providing the different forms that confront the employer.

A model of benefit provision

First consider employees' preferences with regard to the form in which they receive their remuneration. *Ceteris paribus*, it is reasonable to assume that employees prefer $1 worth of wages to fringe benefits to the value of $1. The latter constrains the individuals' consumption to the type of benefit being offered, while receipt of $1 in wages enables employees to choose from among all commodities available. Thus the employees' indifference curves, with regard to fringes and wages, will be shallowly sloped reflecting the fact that a $1 reduction in wages has to be replaced by more than $1's worth of benefits if the employee is not to be made worse off. Both fringes and wages may appropriately be considered 'goods'. These arguments are detailed in Fig. 11.10.

Suppose that initially the costs to the employer of providing employees with fringe benefits to the value of $1 are exactly the same as the costs of providing $1 in wages: the administrative costs of both forms of compensation are the same, and the employer derives no productive advantage from offering fringe benefits rather than wages. The employer is accordingly prepared to offer a range of different combinations of fringes and wages from which employees can choose. The employer's only concern is with the level, not the composition, of compensation. We can therefore draw a set of isoprofit lines each of which is associated with a different level of compensation and hence profits. The slope of each line reflects the rate at which the firm is willing to substitute fringes for wages and one of these is illustrated in Fig. 11.11. The line shown is the one associated with normal profits. At higher levels of total compensation, represented by lines to the north-east, profits are lower, while lines to the south-west represent lower levels of total compensation and accordingly higher levels of profits. In contrast to the earlier isoprofit curves, these are straight lines indicating that fringes and wages are perfect substitutes. In competitive markets the composition of the wage–fringe benefits package will be determined by the point of tangency between the highest indifference curve, and the isoprofit line associated with normal profits. In Fig. 11.12 point Z giving W_A, F_A is the wage–fringe benefit package selected.

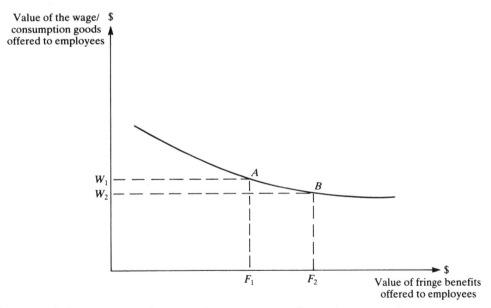

Figure 11.10 Employees' preferences with regard to the form of compensation. A reduction in the wage paid from W_1 to W_2 requires an increase in the value of fringe benefits from F_1 to F_2 if employees are to be no worse off in position B than they were in position A

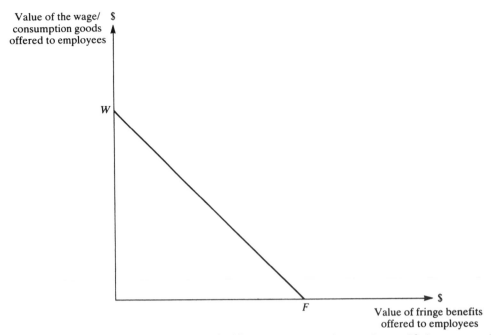

Figure 11.11 The offer by an employer of different compensation packages. If the cost to the employer of providing fringes worth $1 to the employee is the same as the cost of providing a wage of $1 the intercept W and the intercept F are of equal distances from the origin. Wages and fringes are perfect substitutes and the isoprofit line has a slope $= -1$

It can be shown that unilateral provision of fringes by employers results in a lower level of employee utility than could have been achieved had they been offered a free choice between wages and fringes. Thus, if in Fig. 11.12, the firm, starting out from initial equilibrium Z, at wage W_A, and fringe benefits F_A, decides to provide level of fringe benefits F_1 to all employees, this has the effect of displacing the line AB in a parallel direction to the right as shown by $A'B'$. We might imagine that this shift resulted from the introduction of a free health insurance scheme and the withdrawal of the existing benefits package. As a result the budget constraint facing the employee becomes $AA'B'$. Now the new equilibrium is given by point A' at the point where U_2 is just tangent to the new isoprofit line. A higher level of utility could, however, have been achieved had the employee been permitted a choice as to the composition of the compensation package at this new level of expenditure. Given a completely free choice this individual would have chosen to consume rather less of the fringe benefit in question in exchange for a higher wage, and moved to point X on the broken extension line to the new budget constraint.

Typically the employer is not indifferent between providing compensation in the form of a wage or benefits. In the United States and the United Kingdom there are economics of scale in the provision of certain fringe benefits. Large companies can

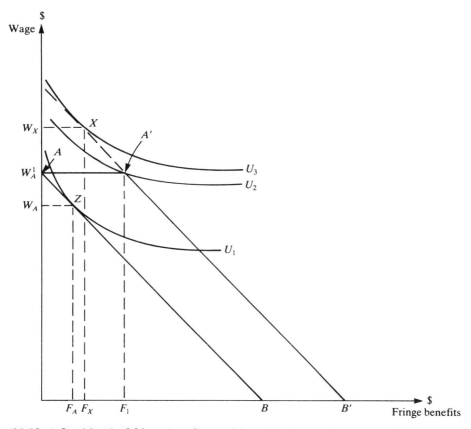

Figure 11.12 A fixed level of fringe benefit provision. The firm replaces the original package of benefits on offer, as reflected in isoprofit line AB, by a fixed level of provision F_1. This shifts the isoprofit line to $AA'B'$ and, while placing the worker on a higher indifference curve, as indicated by U_2, nonetheless reduces welfare below the level that could have been realized if the worker had been permitted a free choice. Had this free choice been permitted, combination W_X, F_X would have been chosen instead of W'_A, F_1.

provide their employees with more of certain types of fringe benefits, such as health insurance, than the employees could secure by taking the money, the firm spent on their behalf, and purchasing the benefit themselves. The reason for this is that the firm is able to purchase such provision cheaply due to the large order it places. Thus a $1 outlay by the firm on the provision of fringe benefits provides more then $1 worth of fringes to the individual. This has the effect of flattening the line AB in Fig. 11.12, as shown in Fig. 11.13. What is the outcome of such a change in the cost of provision? A flattening of the isoprofit line reduces the relative price of fringes, and induces the normal substitution effect into the good whose price has fallen, a substitution into fringes. Normal consumer demand theory tells us that unless fringes are such inferior goods that the negative income effect overwhelms the positive substitution effect, more fringes will be consumed. In Fig. 11.13 the composition of the total compensation package has shifted in favour of fringes. Equal shares of fringes and wages in total compensation are indicated by the 45° line drawn from the origin. In this example the new equilibrium point falls closer to this line than did the old.

Again, if the wages paid out by employers are surcharged or other taxes are levied on the employer (higher wages mean higher social security taxes in the United States, or higher national insurance contributions in the United Kingdom and both are levied as a proportion of the wage) while fringe benefits are not, this will raise the cost to the employer of offering $1 in wages as opposed to $1 in fringe benefits. It will also have the effect of flattening the line AB and produce results similar to those detailed above.

The above arguments focus on the employer's side, on the relative cost of providing $1 worth of fringes as opposed to $1 in wages. As such they determined the slope of the isoprofit line, otherwise known as the employer's 'offer line'. However, taxes are

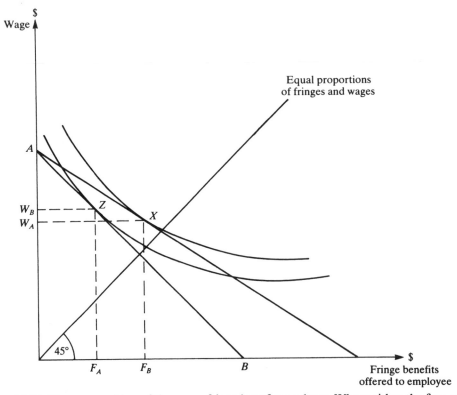

Figure 11.13 The composition of the wage–fringe benefits package. Where either the firm enjoys economies of scale in the provision of fringe benefits, or the wages paid by employers are subject to a proportional tax (as with national insurance payments in the United Kingdom and social security in the United States) this will flatten the budget constraint, AB, confronting the employee. Here we illustrate 'economies of scale' in the provision of fringes, and suggest that this leads the individual to 'purchase' more fringes, changing the composition of the total compensation package toward fringe benefits, as indicated by the move, from Z to X, toward the 45° line.

also levied directly on the compensation received by employees and will therefore affect their preferences. Frequently income tax is levied on employees' gross wages, but not on fringe benefits. This means that the after tax value, to the employee, of a given level of wages, is often smaller than the after tax value of an equivalent outlay on fringes by the employer. This has the effect of changing employee preferences for wages and fringes, and hence the shape of the indifference curve. In order to sustain a given level of utility, any reduction in fringes now requires a larger increment to wages. Such non-neutrality in the tax system has the effect of steepening the employees' indifference curves.

Consider the consequences of both the above developments taken together. First, the effect of levying a tax on the wages paid by employers but not on the value of fringes they offer has the effect of flattening the isoprofit line. This is likely to lead to more fringes being chosen. Second, a tax on the wages the employee receives results in a steepening of the individual's indifference curves, reflecting a change in preferences away from wages and toward fringes. Both developments seem likely to work in the same direction, toward a larger share of total compensation taking the form of fringes and a smaller proportion in wages. These effects are illustrated in Fig. 11.14 in which,

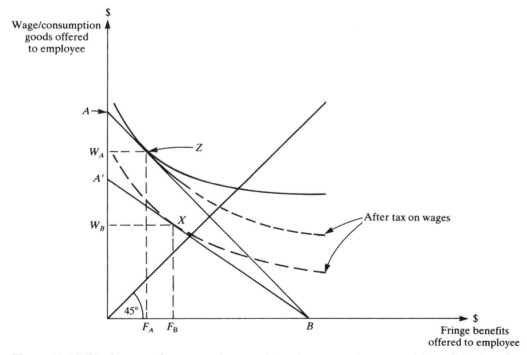

Figure 11.14 The impact of taxes on firms and employees on the composition of the benefits package. The effect of levying social security taxes on the wage provided by employers while exempting certain fringe benefits is to flatten the line *AB* as shown in *A'B*. In turn, taxing the wages received by employees while exempting fringe benefits from tax steepens the indifference curves. The combined effect of these taxes is likely to be a considerable reduction in the wage component of total compensation, as indicated by the move from initial equilibrium *Z* to *X*.

starting from initial position Z, at W_A, F_A in which the tax regime on both employers and employees is entirely neutral, a statutory levy is imposed on employers' wage payments, and only employees' wages are subject to income tax. The result is the new equilibrium at a point such as X lying to the right of Z and nearer to a 45° line drawn from the origin. The share of fringes in total compensation is evidently $F_B/(W_B + F_B)$ which is now greater than the original share given by $F_A/(W_A + F_A)$.

One answer to our question, why has there been such a substantial growth in the provision of fringes in most countries?, is therefore that the tax system is far from neutral with regard to wages and fringes. Statutory payments levied as a proportion of the payroll have in the past made it more expensive for the employer to pay out wages than to provide fringes, while the further taxation of wages received by the employee, and the exemption of many fringe benefits, disposed employees toward fringes rather than wages.[18] However, things may be changing for two reasons. First, increasingly tax authorities are beginning to impute money values to the fringe benefits received by employees, and to levy taxes accordingly. Such reforms of the tax system occurred in the 1980s in the United Kingdom and Australia. Second, in the United Kingdom at least, there has been some move to reduce the magnitude of the statutory additions to the wage bills paid by employers by reducing the size of employers' national insurance contributions. In a number of countries, since the mid-1980s, there has been a flattening of employees' indifference curves, and a steepening of the isoprofit lines. On the basis of these developments it seems reasonable to predict that the share of fringe benefits in total compensation will begin to fall in these countries.

However, it is not just the effects of the tax system which account for the rising share of fringe benefits over the period to the early 1980s. Paying fringe benefits often allows firms to structure the remuneration package in a way that distinguishes between different types of workers. Fringe benefits enable employers to engage in a limited degree of 'wage discrimination'. Suppose that a firm wishes to reduce its labor turnover, one approach is to increase the general level of wages. Alternatively, if it knows that married men with families have lower quit rates than average, it may set about designing a benefits package that appeals specifically to married men. It may offer assistance with children's education fees or pay the premiums on family medical and dental plans. This is one reason why firms may prefer to offer fringes rather than wages. Again, it has been suggested that in periods of statutory incomes restraint, as with the wage–price guidelines of the early 1970s in the United States, the numerous policies of the 1960s and 1970s in the United Kingdom, and the 'Accord' of the 1980s in Australia, employers and employees can circumvent such controls on compensation by payment of additional fringes. By their nature fringes are difficult to detect and quantify, and thus difficult to regulate.

There is empirical support for each of the above propositions. Thus it has been found that larger establishments, which presumably enjoy economies of scale in the provision of fringe benefits, pay out a smaller proportion of total compensation in the form of wages. In the United States the rise in marginal tax rates together with changes

18. In reality the isoprofit lines confronting most firms are rather more complicated than those shown here. Employers' contributions to statutory social welfare programs are subject to ceilings and this has the effect of introducing kinks into the isoprofit lines.

in workers' pre-tax income were found to account for two-thirds of the fall in the share of wages in total compensation.[19] Again, it has been suggested that fringe benefit provision increased during periods of incomes restraint in the United Kingdom in the 1960s and 1970s.[20]

It has been noted that provision of fringe benefits is associated with the incidence of trade unions. Trade unions might negotiate a higher level of fringe benefits because, as we saw in Chapter 7, trade union policies often reflect the preferences of the median voter—typically older, longer tenured workers—who often prefer the security offered by such fringes as health insurance schemes and pension plans. Yet these benefits are often non-transferrable, and a consequence of their provision is that they in turn serve to reduce turnover. In so doing, fringes increase the average length of tenure and therefore produce those conditions that most favour unionism. It is therefore possible that the direction of causality may not run from the existence of unions to superior fringe benefits, but from fringes to unionism. However, there are reasons why trade unions might exhibit a particular preference for fringes. Negotiation of a superior fringe benefits package may appeal to union leaders because this is often the principal way in which trade unions differentiate the product they offer to members. There is, as we shall later see, considerable imitation of union-established wages by non-union employers, and one distinguishing feature of the compensation packages which unions offer is the fringe benefit element.

Does it follow from the above that countries with a very strong union presence enjoy the highest levels of fringe benefit provision? Certainly the more highly unionized European countries have superior vacation entitlements, sick leave and holiday entitlements compared to the less highly unionized United States. However, it is difficult to draw many firm conclusions from this observation. The difficulty we face is that of controlling for the very different tax regimes that exist in the various countries, for as we have seen the structure of company and personal taxation is the single largest factor accounting for the growth of fringes. To date, no studies have been able to control adequately for these different effects and offer an explanation of differences in the incidence of fringes between nations.

INDUSTRY WAGE DIFFERENCES

In this chapter we have outlined the theory of 'equalizing differences', the fundamental long-run proposition emerging from the competitive theory of labor markets. The theory of equalizing differences, and within this the theory of human capital, provides the competitive explanation of differences between the earnings of individuals. Yet, as outlined, this theory has failed to explain one persistent feature of labor markets, namely that the pay of individuals appears to differ according to the industry in which they work. Some industries pay high wages to all classes of labor, while others pay low wages—a finding which appears incompatible with the theories of human capital and

19. Woodbury, S. (1983) 'Substitution between wage and non-wage benefits', *American Economic Review*, **73**, 166–82.
20. Kitchen, D. and Curnow, B. (1981) 'Incomes policy and the higher paid', in Chater, R.E., Dean, A.J.H. and Elliott, R.F. (eds.), *Incomes Policy*, Oxford University Press.

net advantages, or is it? Recent developments in competitive theory have offered an explanation of this fact.

Consider first the gross hourly wages of what is at first glance a fairly homogeneous class of labor, unskilled male workers, in different industries in Great Britain in 1982 as shown in Table 11.7. Hourly rates of pay ranged from £3.53p in the highest paying industry to £2.12p in the lowest. The top rate was some two-thirds greater than the lowest, and the coefficient of variation, a measure of the dispersion around the mean, was 27 percent. This is a large difference when we consider that by choosing unskilled workers we have already standardized for differences in human capital. According to competitive theory the differences that remain ought, in equilibrium, to reflect only differences due to remaining net advantages of these jobs and the balance of supply and demand in each of the submarkets that constitute Great Britain. But even when we standardize for these differences between the industries, differences in wages remain. Consider this issue further.

The theory of equalizing differences proposes that average wages differ between industries as a result of differences in the skill mix of the industries' workforce, in the conditions of employment and in the composition of the benefits package. In order to determine the existence of high and low paying industries we need to construct a model that incorporates each of these agreements. This can be done by adapting the human capital earnings fuction we employed earlier in this chapter. Thus Eq. (11.1) can again be modified so that

$$\log W/P_i = a_1 + a_2 I_i + a_3 I_i^2 + a_4 X_i + a_5 Z_i + \varepsilon_i \qquad (11.3)$$

where as before a_1 represents the log of earnings when there has been no additional human capital investment, a_2 measures the rate of return on a year's education, a_3

Table 11.7 Industry hourly rates of pay for unskilled manual male workers in Britain in 1982

Industry	£ per hour
Agriculture, forestry and fishing	2.12
Energy	3.53
Mineral extraction	2.86
Metal goods, engineering	2.66
Other manufacturing	2.67
Construction	2.60
Distribution, hotels, catering	2.27
Transport and communications	2.73
Banking and finance	2.38
Other services	2.32
All industry mean	2.58
Standard deviation	0.70

Source: Department of Employment, *New Earnings Survey*, 1982.

captures non-linear effects of education on earnings, and X_1 is again a vector of variables measuring all other non-wage advantages and disadvantages of the job including S. Z_i, on the other hand, represents a vector of mutually exclusive industry dummies with the result that the above equation incorporates human capital, equalizing difference and now industry effects to explain earnings differences.

The total explanation of differences in individual earnings that the variables I, X and Z (called the covariates) provide is indicated by the R^2. This approach however has problems, chief among which is that the variables in I and X are likely to be collinear with those in Z, the industry dummies. For example, the technology employed by a particular industry will determine the occupations employed in that industry and hence the human capital mix of the industry. Technology, which is often unique to an industry, is also likely to affect working conditions.

However, we can get round this problem and obtain some idea of the contribution of industry effects to an explanation of differences in individual earnings by the following procedure. First, construct a simple model to explain the variance of individual earnings, $\log W_i$, using only the industry dummies. That is

$$\log W/P_i = a_i + a_5 Z_i + \varepsilon_i \qquad (11.4)$$

and call the R^2 resulting from estimating such an equation A. A clearly provides an upper bound on the size of the industry effects, for the dummies capture all those industry-specific elements which in Eq. (11.3) were captured by I and X.

A lower bound to the size of the industry effects can also be estimated. This is done in two stages. First by estimating Eq. (11.3) without the industry dummies, Z, so that I and X capture all of the industry fixed effects that they have in common with Z: the proportion of the variance of earnings explained by this equation (the R^2) call B. Second re-estimate Eq. (11.3) in full, that is including the industry dummies, Z. The R^2 that results from this estimation then indicates the improvement that results from the addition of dummies which capture industry-specific effects that are independent of I and X. The R^2 resulting from this estimation call C. The procedure is then to compare the two R^2's B and C, specifically subtract B (the R^2 estimated without the industry dummies) from C (the one estimated using the industry dummies) and thereby obtain a lower bound on the importance of industry fixed effects. The R^2, A and the difference between the R^2's B and C then provide, respectively, upper and lower estimates of the role that industry 'fixed' effects play, in accounting for differences in individual earnings.

Researchers who have adopted this approach found that industry fixed effects accounted for between 7 and 30 percent of the variation of non-union wage rates and 10 to 29 percent of the variation of union wage rates in the United States in 1983.[21] The broad range of these estimates testifies to the substantial multicollinearity that exists between I, X and Z. Other researchers have used estimating equations of the general form of Eq. (11.3) to estimate industry effects for the United States in 1977 and have found that the size of industry fixed effects ranged from -10 percent in

21. Dickens, W.T. and Katz, L.F. (1987) 'Inter-industry wage differences and industry characteristics', in Lang, K. and Leonard, J.S. (eds.), *Unemployment and the Structure of Labor Markets*, Blackwell, pp. 48–89.

services to $+23$ percent in mining.[22] The studies found that pronounced industry effects emerged even after controlling for the effects of such non-competitive aspects of labor markets as unionism and discrimination, of which we shall have more to say later. The results confirm those of earlier studies, which revealed the significance of what are typically industry-specific variables, such as profitability and concentration.[23] These ought to play no part in competitive explanations of earnings differences. In Britain similar results emerge, although the nature of the available databases has been such that it has to date been difficult to control for the impact of human capital and workplace characteristics on earnings.

Of course it may be that these estimates of industry effects are erroneous. They might after all merely reflect human capital and equalizing differences agreements which we have as yet been unable to measure. Indeed, as we refine our measures of working conditions and human capital, we should expect the explanation offered by industry to diminish. Yet in the United States and the United Kingdom there is a widespread belief that the industry in which an individual works is in itself an important determinant of earnings. What explanations can competitive theory offer for the persistence of these industry fixed effects? The theory of efficiency wages has recently been advanced as an explanation of this aspect of labor markets.

EFFICIENCY WAGE THEORY

Efficiency wage theory proposes that firms and industries may find it profitable to pay wages in excess of those that clear the labor market because the wage, or more generally the total compensation, that a worker receives affects productivity. Thus a rise in the wage rate that a firm pays (illustrated as the increase from W_0 to W_1 in Fig. 11.15) results in an improvement in worker productivity (represented by the outward shift of the marginal revenue product curve in Fig. 11.15). The impact of the change in the marginal product on the firm's revenue depends on the nature of the product market in which the firm operates, but if the firm is a price taker the increase in marginal product will be reflected in an equivalent proportional increase in the revenue received. As Fig. 11.15 suggests, the rise in MRP_L largely validates the wage rise and as a result employment falls by a far smaller amount than would have otherwise occurred. In the limit, if the rise in revenue productivity is exactly equal to the rise in the wage, there need be no fall in employment. It is apparent that under these circumstances employment is far less elastic with respect to the real wage and that even in the short run the labor demand curve can no longer be represented by a single MRP_L curve. The labor demand curve now comprises the locus of points such as A and B in Fig. 11.15.

22. Kruger, A.B. and Summers, L.H. (1988) 'Efficiency wages and the inter-industry wage structure', *Econometrica*, **56**(2), March, 259–93.
23. See Pugel, T. (1980) 'Profitability, concentration and the inter-industry variation of earnings', *Review of Economics and Statistics*, **62**, 248–53 and Weiss, L. (1966) 'Concentration and labor earnings', *American Economic Review*, **56**, 96–117.

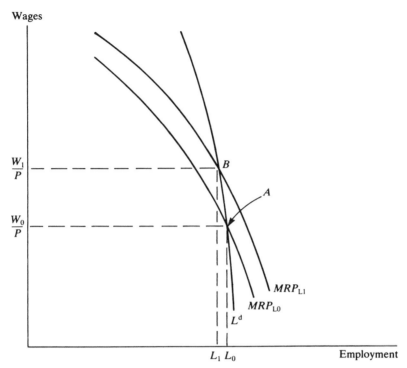

Figure 11.15 The economy of high wages: efficiency wages (marginal product and wages are interdependent). A rise in the real wage from W_0 to W_1 at unchanged prices results in improved worker performance shifting the marginal product curve out from MRP_{L0} to MRP_{L1}. The resulting labor demand curve, the locus of points A and B, is less elastic than the underlying marginal product curves.

One way of viewing the arguments of efficiency wage theory is to imagine that each worker embodies a given number of efficiency units and that the number delivered is a positive function of the wage the worker is offered for each of these. This is illustrated in Fig. 11.16 in which the supply of efficiency units assumes the same pattern as the supply of productive hours depicted in Fig. 3.15 in Chapter 3. In Fig. 11.16 the firm pays a wage W^*, just sufficient to insure delivery of the optimal number of efficiency units. The optimal number is of course determined by the usual marginal conditions, at which the marginal cost, the additional wage expenditure, is equal to the marginal benefit, the additional efficiency units delivered per dollar of wage expenditure. If the firm reduces the wage from the level shown, this reduces the supply of efficiency units and hence detracts from output and profits. One consequence of the fact that firms now purchase efficiency units rather than hours or workers, is that when we express payments in terms of wages per worker the level of payments made to any single worker or group of workers may be greater than the current supply price of labor, in which case we shall observe an excess labor supply and unemployment.

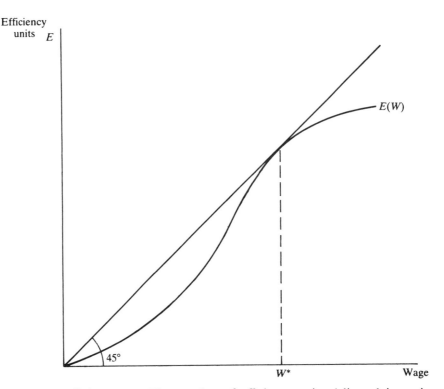

Figure 11.16 The efficient wage. The number of efficiency units delivered is an increasing function of the level of the wage. Initially efficiency units are delivered at an increasing rate, so that output per individual increases at an increasing rate (in the manner detailed in Fig. 3.15). After some point the rate of increase diminishes, and output per person increases at a decreasing rate. The efficient wage is that at which the marginal returns from the last efficiency unit purchased equal the wage rate. This is shown as point $W*$

These arguments although dressed up in new cloths are not new. In the 1950s the idea was proposed that individuals' productivity was positively associated with the wage they were paid. Known as 'the economy of high wages', it proposed that in developing countries higher wages would improve health and nutrition standards, and thereby enable workers to perform more productively.[24] More recently a similar relationship was also proposed for the advanced industrial nations, in which it is claimed high wages improve morale, and with it performance.[25]

An early example of the economy of high wages was the introduction, in 1914, by the Ford Motor Company of the $5 day. This represented a substantial hike in wage rates, for the rate of pay in other companies at that time was between $2 and $3 a day. Why did Ford do this? Contemporary observers provide plausible reasons to refute suggestions that this was either to avert the threat of unionization, or to enable them to get the pick of mechanics in the Detroit area. Rather they suggest that this high wage

24. See Leibenstein, H. (1957) 'The theory of underemployment in backward economies', *Journal of Political Economy*, **65**, 91–103.
25. See Solow, R. (1979) 'Another possible source of wage stickiness', *Journal of Macroeconomics*, **1**, 79–82.

policy produced a substantial leap in productivity as absenteeism fell, obedience to management and discipline increased, and morale improved. It has been estimated that following the introduction of the policy, productivity rose by 51 percent in 1914 alone.[26]

Why should higher wages mean higher productivity as a result of the delivery of more efficiency units? A number of different versions of the theory have been proposed and these are discussed below.

The shirking model This proposes that firms could find it profitable to raise wages above the opportunity wages of their workforce in order to penalize workers for poor performance, that is in order to dissuade them from shirking. In a world of homogeneous workers in which they are all paid their opportunity wage and in which there is full employment, as would occur in competitive labor markets with no transaction and search costs, there would be no penalty for poor performance. In such a world, if workers were fired, they would immediately find a new job at the same wage. It therefore pays each firm to raise its wage, and by so doing, to raise the opportunity cost of losing a job. Of course when all firms raise wages, the wages paid by any single firm will again no longer exceed workers' opportunity wages, provided they can obtain another job. But if all firms raise wages then the current market wage exceeds the market clearing wage and unemployment emerges, so that jobs are now scarce. If workers are dismissed it is now no longer clear that they will be able to obtain another job. A 'reserve army of the unemployed' emerges, not with the purpose of competing down wages as suggested by competitive theory, but as a mechanism by which to penalize shirkers. The penalty for losing a job is the reduced probability that the opportunity wage can be realized, because there are now others who are unemployed queuing for the job. On this view unemployment serves as a disciplining device.[27]

The turnover model A rather more simple notion is that firms may pay higher wages to discourage labor turnover. Labor turnover will be most costly when the costs of hiring and specifically training workers are high. Where there are high once-over fixed labor costs of this type firms will take steps to minimize labor turnover, and paying high wages is one way of achieving this for it has been shown that turnover is inversely related to wage level.[28] However, there is nothing novel about this version of the theory. Firms experience high levels of labor turnover because the net advantages of the jobs they offer are unacceptable to workers. The higher wages which reduce labor turnover therefore constitute no more than compensating wage payments as proposed

26. See Bulow, J.I. and Summers, L.H. (1986) 'A theory of dual labor markets with application to industrial policy, discrimination and Keynesian unemployment', *Journal of Labor Economics*, **4**(3), July, 376–414.
27. This is the version of the theory proposed by Shapiro, C. and Stiglitz, J.E. (1984) 'Equilibrium unemployment as a worker discipline device', *American Economic Review*, **74**, 433–44; see also Stiglitz, J.E. (1985) 'Equilibrium wage distributions', *Economic Journal*, **95**, 595–618.
28. Pencavel, J.H. (1970), 'An analysis of the quit rate in American manufacturing industry', Princeton: Industrial Relations Section, Princeton University and Viscusi, K. (1980) 'Sex differences—worker quitting', *Review of Economics and Statistics*, **62**, 388–98, have attested to the inverse relationship between wages and labor turnover.

by the theory of equalizing differences. The novelty of this version of efficiency wage theory appears to lie with the idea that all firms, or a very large number of firms, offer such compensating payments. However, if all firms begin to behave in this manner the relative advantages of such a strategy to any single firm begin to disappear. Moreover, paying high wages is by no means the only device for reducing turnover. Non-transferrable fringe benefits, seniority payments and incremental payment systems are other devices. For these reasons this version of efficiency wage theory provides no more than a rather limited explanation of why some firms may choose to pay high wages.

The 'superior' job applicant pool A further version of efficiency wage theory emphasizes the difficulties of distinguishing the potential productivity of job applicants which firms experience. This version proposes that payment of higher wages represents a strategy for dealing with imperfections of information and we have discussed this in Chapter 10. Where firms are unable to distinguish workers' potential productivity, where they are unable to screen applicants for jobs in a way which distinguishes the most productive among them, a strategy of paying high wages may be adopted. By paying high wages firms attract a superior pool of applicants and even though they hire at random from this pool, they recruit a more productive workforce.

Some firms certainly establish reputations as high payers, however, they appear to do so for at least two reasons. First, high wages are in some degree a substitute for advertising costs. High paying firms can rely on informal and less costly channels to advertise their jobs because information about high paying jobs is more likely to be transmitted by friends and relatives. However, this is not the argument favored by efficiency wage theorists who argue that by paying high wages firms will, independently of the manner in which information is dispersed, attract more high quality applicants. Thus it is not uncommon to hear remarked, 'that firm X has a reputation for hiring only the best workers!' Payment of high wages is one strategy for establishing a reputation in the labor market. The success of such a strategy, however, depends crucially on the individual workers' perceptions of their own productive potential, and on a positive association between this productivity and their reservation wage. Only if workers can accurately assess their productive potential and more productive workers have higher reservation wages will firms attract high quality workers by paying high wages.

Fair wages A final version of efficiency wage theory proposes that workers are likely to be most productive when they believe they are being treated fairly. A worker's effort will be governed by norms of behavior which are shared with co-workers. These norms emphasize considerations of fairness and therefore workers' morale, and associated with this their productivity is at its highest when they believe they are being treated fairly. Workers believe they are being treated fairly when they are being paid wages above the market clearing level. It has been suggested that the 'gift' of higher wages is reciprocated by a 'gift' of higher productivity.[29] Higher wages satisfy individual

29. This is the theory advanced by Akerlof in a series of articles. Akerlof, G.A. (1982) 'Labor contracts as

demands for equitable and fair treatment, and produce correspondingly superior performance in return.

That workers are concerned with considerations of fairness is not in doubt. Precisely what form these notions take and whether the firm can sufficiently identify these and employ them to its advantage is less clear. Moreover, if workers believe they are being treated unfairly this may well show up in a high turnover rate, so that the turnover and fair wage versions of efficiency wage theory are unlikely to be independent. Appealing as this version of the theory may be, it is by no means clear why the gift of high wages should be reciprocated if firms and workers hold different notions of what is fair. This is a difficult hypothesis to test but to date the evidence to support this view is rather scarce.

The theory of efficiency wages suggests the existence of productive characteristics beyond those normally identified in the theories of human capital and equalizing differences. The theory sets out to explain wages established in excess of the market clearing wage, where the market clearing wage reflects differences in human capital and net advantages. These missing productive characteristics may be summarized in the term 'motivation', for efficiency wage theory is concerned with constructing mechanisms to induce workers to work at their most efficient, to deliver the optimal number of efficiency units. The theory rests on the existence of unmeasured and/or unobservable characteristics which are associated with enhanced productive performance and empirically these characteristics have been captured in a set of industry dummies. It could therefore be argued that efficiency wage theory is merely identifying further aspects of the net advantages of different jobs, which crucially differ between firms or industries but for which we have as yet developed no adequate measures. If this is true the theory represents a development of, rather than an alternative to, the theory of equalizing differences.

Yet there remain factors which have been found to affect the level of an individual's wages but which have no role in competitive wage theory. The degree of concentration of an industry and the level of industry profits have been shown to be positively associated with wages. If these variables are collinear with the industry dummies incorporated in Eq. (11.3) the dummies will then be capturing these effects,[30] but neither concentration nor profits should determine wages according to competitive theory. When we come to Chapter 14 we shall look at wage determination under trade unionism and this may go some way to explaining these results.

Augmented human capital models, augmented to include equalizing differences and efficiency wage arguments, seldom account for much more than half the variance in individual earnings and, surprisingly, the explanation offered by augmented human

partial gift exchange', *Quarterly Journal of Economics*, **96**, 543–69 and Akerlof, G.A. (1984) 'Gift exchange and efficiency wages: four views', *American Economic Review*, **74**, 79–83.

30. Carruth, A.A. and Oswald, A.J. (1987) 'Wage inflexibility in Britain', *Oxford Bulletin of Economics and Statistics*, **49**, 59–78 and Blanchflower, D.G., Oswald, A.J. and Garrett, M.D. (1987) 'Insider power in wage determination, Part II', *Centre for Labor Economics Mimeo*, June, find a positive association between wages and profits in Britain. While Heywood, J.S. (1986) 'Labor quality and the concentration-earnings hypothesis', *Review of Economics and Statistics*, **68**, May, 342–6 and Blanchflower, D.G. (1986) 'Wages and concentration in British manufacturing', *Applied Economics*, **18**, 1025–38 report a positive association between concentrated industries and pay in the United States and Britain respectively.

capital models is not markedly different in the union and non-union sector. There would appear to be further influences on earnings, which we have yet to discover. In the next chapter we shall develop a theory which suggests that there are artificial barriers to mobility in the labor market and that these barriers prevent individuals enjoying the full returns on their human capital. This might be the reason why augmented human capital models, of the type described in this chapter, do not yet provide a complete explanation of the variance of earnings.

SUMMARY

In this chapter we have evaluated the theory of equalizing differences. First proposed by Adam Smith over 200 years ago, this represents the fundamental long-run market equilibrium construct in labor economics. It is an encompassing theory for the theory of equalizing differences incorporates human capital theory and certainly some aspects of efficiency wage theory. Of course human capital theory merits separate analysis for it constitutes the single most important source of the variance in earnings, but it was first suggested in Smith's theory of net advantages.

The evidence suggests that there is support for Smith's contention that the whole of the advantages and disadvantages of different jobs tend to equality. Dangerous and unpleasant jobs attract higher pay, jobs with superior pension and health insurance arrangements receive lower pay. However, these equalizing tendencies are not fully realized, for individuals seldom possess the information required to evaluate fully the relative attributes of different jobs. Many of the characteristics of jobs can only be discovered by experience, and the substantial transaction costs associated with changing jobs means that individuals cannot easily gain access to that information which is only acquired by experience.

Together the equalizing differences and human capital theory explain part, but often only a minority, of the variance of individual earnings. Characteristics unique to industries, among which might be the degree of concentration and the profitability of the industry, also appear to explain a part of earnings. Recent attempts to explain these industry effects have focused on efficiency wage theory. This has the appeal that it attempts to explain why wage rates may be established and remain above the market clearing level. Some of the variants of efficiency wage theory are merely 'old wine in new bottles'. More novel are the versions that emphasize considerations of morale and fairness. These notions are by their very nature difficult to investigate empirically and, it has to be admitted that, at this time there is little empirical support for these versions of the theory. Such a remark is not meant to pour cold water on these ideas for they represent one of the more important developments in labor economics in recent years. However, until we resolve some of the measurement difficulties standing in the way of empirical evaluation of these theories, our appreciation of the importance of these issues is likely to be severely curtailed.

PRINCIPAL CONCEPTS

The following concepts have been developed in this chapter. Students should insure that they fully understand these before moving on to the next chapter.

1. Pecuniary and non-pecuniary advantages of a job.
2. The net advantages of different jobs.
3. The shadow price of a workplace disamenity.
4. The procedure for estimating the price of a disamenity.
5. The market equilibrium curve.
6. The price of status.
7. The offer curve and offer line.

QUESTIONS FOR DISCUSSION

1. Detail the five principal 'circumstances' of jobs, identified by Adam Smith in his theory of net advantages, which account for differences in wages. Which of these are still of importance?
2. Show how compensating differentials emerge in the market for labor.
3. Why are the whole of the advantages and disadvantages only *tending* towards equality? Why are full equilibrium prices unlikely to be realized in practice?
4. Why might individuals be concerned to 'choose the right pond'?
5. What are the principal problems that confront empirical research into the theory of equalizing differences?
6. Why did more of the net advantages of jobs in the United Kingdom and the United States take the form of fringe benefits in the two decades to the end of the 1970s?
7. How have the system of income and social security taxes in the United States and the United Kingdom affected the composition of compensation?
8. What are the procedures for estimating industry fixed effects?
9. Does efficiency wage theory provide a convincing explanation of non-market clearing wages?
10. How adequately does competitive wage theory explain the variance of individual earnings?

FURTHER READING

The student is fortunate that there exist several excellent surveys of the theoretical and empirical literature on the theory of equalizing differences. The most recent of these and the first to read is that by Rosen, S. (1986) 'The theory of equalizing differences', in Ashenfelter, O. and Layard, P.R.G. (eds.), *Handbook of Labor Economics*, vol. 1, pp. 641–92, North-Holland, New York. However, the student is also recommended to read the earlier and rather more accessible surveys by Smith, R.S. (1979) 'Compensating wage differentials and public policy: a review', *Industrial and Labor Relations,*

32, 339–52 and Brown, C. (1980) 'Equalizing differences in the labor market', *Quarterly Journal of Economics*, **94**, 113–34.

The pioneering work in the area of fringe benefits is that by Woodbury, S. (1983) 'Substitution between wage and non-wage benefits', *American Economic Review*, **73**, 166–82. On the broader issue of non-wage labor costs, of which fringe benefits are an element, the book by Hart, R.A. (1984) *The Economics of Non-Wage Labour Costs*, Allen and Unwin, London, mentioned in Chapter 9, should be consulted.

Efficiency wage theory is a fast expanding area of research. It is, as a result, difficult to recommend a single source. However, see Stiglitz, J.E. (1987) 'The causes and consequences of the dependence of quality on price', *Journal of Economic Literature*, **XXV**(1), 1–48. See too the chapter by Dickens, W.T. and Katz, L.F. (1987) 'Inter-industry wage differences and industry characteristics', in Lang, K. and Leonard, J.S. (eds.), *Unemployment and the Structure of Labour Markets*, Blackwell, Oxford and Kruger, A.B. and Summers, L.H. (1988) 'Efficiency wages and the inter-industry wage structure', *Econometrica*, **56**(2), 259–93.

12

WAGE DIFFERENCES IN INTERNAL OR CAREER LABOR MARKETS AND DUAL LABOR MARKETS

In previous chapters we analyzed in considerable detail the determinants of differences in individual earnings. The theory of equalizing differences provided us with a framework for analyzing the differences in pay we observe between individuals performing different jobs, however, we have not yet considered how the rates of pay for particular jobs might relate, one to another, within a particular organization. We have not looked at the market for labor within a particular firm or the structure of pay that emerges as a result. These are the issues we consider in this chapter.

Competitive theory predicts that the forces of supply and demand in the market as a whole will determine the rates of pay within each firm. The relative pay of any two occupations within a single firm will be the mirror image of the relative pay of the same two occupations in the market as a whole. Similarly, the structure of wages across the complete range of occupations we observe within a firm will be the mirror image of the pay structure for these same occupations in the complete market. The pay structure within a firm will accordingly contract or widen as the relative balance of supply and demand for these jobs in the market as a whole changes.

Yet in many firms the structure of wages does not appear to behave in the manner predicted by competitive theory. Analysts have noted that the structure appears fixed and that it changes far less frequently than would be predicted on the evidence of the changing balance of supply and demand in the external labor market. Analysts have noted that many firms increase their employees' rates of pay at regular predetermined intervals irrespective of general market conditions and reward long service *per se*. It has further been observed that some firms seem to display a marked preference for filling senior posts by promotion from within the organization rather than by advertising externally and recruiting outsiders. In short, the market for labor within a firm, the internal labor market, seems to be cut off from the wider forces of competition in the external market and, accordingly, behaves in quite a different manner from that predicted by competitive theory. A separate analysis of internal labor markets is therefore required.

The analytical framework essential for an understanding of internal labor markets has already been developed. In Chapter 6 and again in Chapter 9 we distinguished between general and specific skills. We saw that the cost of specific training was one element of the substantial fixed costs of employing labor in many jobs, and that hiring and screening costs were other elements. We saw in Chapter 10 how these factors led to the distinction between competitive and institutional labor markets, between markets that adjusted by the exit mechanism and markets that cleared by the voice mechanism. Where there were substantial transaction costs associated with employing labor firms placed greater reliance on the voice mechanism. It is the practices and conventions that emerge in the face of substantial transaction costs which account for the distinctive behavior of internal labor markets. In this chapter we consider in detail explanations for the existence of and the nature of internal labor markets.

It will become apparent as our analysis proceeds that jobs in internal labor markets have many desirable characteristics; they have often been described as 'good jobs'. The idea that the labor market can be divided into one sector that comprises 'good' jobs and another that provides 'bad' jobs lies at the heart of dual labor market and segmented labor market theory. These theories developed as an attempt to explain the inequality of opportunity and persistence of poverty that remain as prominent features of most modern economies. The forces of competition, it was argued, have done little to eliminate these and accordingly an explanation for their persistence was sought. The focus of these theories is on jobs and thereby switches attention away from the individual who is the focus of competitive theory. In dual labor market theory it is the characteristics of jobs that matter, in competitive theory it is the characteristics of individuals.

Yet by focusing on jobs rather than individuals dual and segmented theories may obscure the underlying causes of the phenomenon they seek to explain. A more important distinction, than that between 'good' and 'bad' jobs, is likely to be that between 'good' and 'bad' careers. The reason why some working individuals remain in poverty is that they have poor careers, they find they are unable to move from 'poor' jobs to 'good' jobs. The existence of 'poor' jobs is a necessary condition for 'poor' careers but it is not sufficient. It is the combination of 'poor' jobs and immobility which is likely to account for the persistence of poverty. Segmented and dual labor market theory can be viewed as a logical extension of internal labor market theory. It is therefore appropriate that we first turn our attention to internal labor market theory.

INTERNAL OR CAREER LABOR MARKETS

The market for labor within many firms, the internal labor market, displays a number of distinguishing features. These are:

1. The relative unresponsiveness of the rates of pay of some workers inside the firm to the balance of supply and demand for apparently similar labor in the external market. Payment appears to be determined by alternative criteria among which rules figure prominently.
2. An emphasis on promotions from among existing staff to fill senior vacancies and consequent upon this the creation of, what have been termed, job ladders.
3. The emergence of long-term relationships between employers and employees. In Chapter 10 it was revealed that 40 percent of males aged 30 and over in the United States were working in jobs that would last 20 years or more, while in the United Kingdom 44 percent of all males were in jobs that would last 20 years or more.
4. A positive association between wages and length of service as manifest in incremental payment systems which related advances in pay to the age and seniority of employees.

These features of internal labor markets have led to the description of labor markets within firms displaying these characteristics as career labor markets. A single firm now offers its employees the prospect of building a career while remaining in its employment. Such arrangements were always understood to exist in Japan in the post-war period, but it is now recognized that they are also prominent in the United States and Europe, and indeed that they may have become increasingly so in recent years.

The development of internal labor market theory

Internal labor market theory developed as an attempt to explain a number of empirical aspects of labor markets that attracted attention in the 1960s and 1970s. Studies of pay structure in local labor markets in the United Kingdom found that the internal wage structure showed such considerable variation from one plant to the next that it was extremely difficult to establish any general rules to explain this. Studies of local labor markets in the United States reported substantial variation in the rates of pay for particular types of labor. This led researchers to suggest that firms exercised some degree of discretion as to where they established the rate of pay for any particular job, giving rise over the market as a whole to a wide range of differentials.[1] The studies

---

1. Douty, H.M. (1961) 'Sources of occupational wage and salary rate dispersion within labor markets', *Industrial and Labor Relations Review*, **15** and Lester, R.A. (1952) 'A range theory of wage differentials', *Industrial and Labor Relations Review*, **5**, 483–500 for the United States. For the United Kingdom, Mackay, D.I. *et al.* (1971) *Labor Markets under Different Employment Conditions*, George Allen and Unwin, London and Robinson, D. (ed.) (1970) *Local Labor Markets and Wage Structures*, Gower. All these studies report that measures of excess demand in the external labor market appear to have little influence on the internal wage structure of firms. Firms were reported as having considerable discretion over rates of pay. Douty and MacKay *et al.* report that the main influences on earnings within an establishment are characteristics of the establishment itself.

concluded that the forces of competition were to a considerable degree muted or shut out, in the short run at least, and had little impact on the firms' wage structure.

At this time researchers were also reporting that in many firms employment did not fluctuate in line with changes in output. Output fell more than employment during the downswing of the cycle and rose faster during the upswing of the cycle. Nor were wages reduced in line with this decline in labor productivity so that the relationship between the wage and the marginal product of labor varied over the stages of the business cycle.[2] It appeared that employers were hanging on to labor during the recession, that is 'hoarding' labor.

Internal labor market theory developed as an attempt to explain these facts. Internal labor markets were generated it was suggested by three key factors not envisioned in conventional economic theory. First, skill specificity. This resulted both from the requirements of technology, the uniqueness of the technology employed in many firms, and the uniqueness of the jobs that individuals performed. Second, information imperfections, the substantial costs associated with obtaining and processing information about potential employees' productive potential. Third, on-the-job training. Training largely of an informal nature which took the form of learning-by-doing. One consequence of this method of training is that the distinction between different jobs becomes blurred.

A distinctive feature of the internal market is that the allocation of labor and the structure of pay are largely shaped by an unwritten set of rules: allocation is by rules not by price. Contact with the external labor market is severely limited and is confined to what have been described as 'ports of entry'. These are entry-level jobs, for it is at these points that firms recruit the general skills that they need to replenish their stock of labor.[3]

A theoretical framework

The theory of transaction costs provides the analytical framework with which to understand the existence and behavior of, internal labor markets. Those transaction costs, which result in the distinction between the internal and the external labor market, can take two principal forms: first, the costs associated with specific training; and, second, the costs associated with the acquisition and processing of information about the productivity of existing and potential employees.

Specific skills Even in those markets producing a fairly homogeneous product, firms

---

2. The relationship between wages and productivity has long been a matter of dispute. According to Keynes, (1937) *The General Theory of Employment, Interest and Money*, Macmillan, London, both labor productivity and real wages should move counter cyclically but Dunlop, J.T. (1938) 'The movement of real and money wage rates', *Economic Journal*, **48**, 413–34 and others contested this view. The existing consensus is that there is no detectable pattern for real wage rates but that labor productivity exhibits a distinct pro-cyclical pattern. See Fair, R.C. (1960) *The Short-Run Demand for Workers and Hours*, Contributions to Economic Analysis 59, North Holland; and Michie, J. (1987) *Wages in the Business Cycle*, Francis Pinter.
3. See Doeringer, P.B. and Piore, M.J. (1971) *Internal Labor Markets and Manpower Adjustment*, D C, Heath & Co., Lexington, Mass, for the pioneering work in this field.

will employ different technologies or have their own way of doing things. The differences in technology may be trivial, as for example in the market for hamburgers, where some burgers are 'char broiled' while others are simply 'broiled', or they may be more substantial, as in automobile production, where some firms use production line technology while others work in quality circles. Seldom do two firms employ the same technology and even where firms employ the same technology they employ this in a slightly different manner. Firms modify or adapt the machines and workers are responsible for changes to what was once a standard technology. Each machine can have its own idiosyncracies, and is subjecct to minor modifications by its operator to improve its efficiency. As a result, there will only be some among the workforce with sufficient knowledge of these idiosyncrasies and consequently in a position to operate these machines efficiently. Firms will also have different ways of organizing production—they will have their own ways of doing things. Stated formally the production function, the manner in which inputs are combined to produce output, differs almost everywhere between firms. Either the technology or the way of organizing production is firm specific and one consequence of the specificity of the production function is a demand for specific skills.

Information The costs of acquiring information differ substantially for different types of workers. An internal labor market may develop as a response to the high costs associated with acquiring information about workers' productive potential. It may be seen as an essential mechanism in the job matching process. The earlier analysis of information in labor markets in Chapter 10 emphasized that information can be acquired by examination, recommendation and experience. In the internal labor market firms can acquire information by experience, which they could not obtain by either recommendation or examination, and firms can acquire a knowledge about the productive potential of existing employees which they cannot obtain about those outside the firm. There is an information asymmetry and this can have two consequences. First, in order to retain the services of existing employees of known productivity the firm will need to offer them inducements to remain with the firm. Second, it may also lead the firm to fill senior posts by promoting existing employees, for the firm is better able to monitor the performance of and assess the productivity of its existing employees. It is in this manner that distinctive career opportunities begin to emerge within a firm.

These information asymmetries and the existence of specific skills are linked, for the difficulties associated with, and therefore the costs of obtaining, the appropriate information about employees are a function of the specificity of the technology the firm employs. If the production process used by the firm is standard, it is used by many firms, a pool of generally skilled labor will exist outside the firm and the firm can recruit from this. If the firm makes a mistake when hiring a worker, if its prior information proves to be less than accurate, it can always fire the worker and hire a replacement. In contrast, where the skill is specific there will by definition be no pool of appropriately skilled labor outside the firm and where, in particular, the firm bears some of the cost of producing that skill it will no longer wish to fire and hire. Firing and hiring is in these circumstances a costly activity and the firm will therefore try to ensure that it has hired the 'right' workers in the first place. Where a firm employs a specific technology it is likely to place greater emphasis on acquiring information about the potential employees at the hiring stage.

The above arguments may be cast in the framework we have already developed in Chapters 6 and 9. In these chapters we described a situation in which firms and workers shared the costs of investment in specific training and/or information acquisition. Figure 12.1 reproduces a diagram similar to that which we used to analyze the situation in these chapters. In Fig. 12.1 the employer pays the direct costs of training in the initial period, and pays a wage, equal to the workers' marginal product during training, which rises from W_0 to W_1. The employer's gross outgoings in the initial period are therefore the sum of the wage paid and the training costs, here represented by the broken line AB. The employer's net outgoings are accordingly equal to AB minus the area below W_0G, a sum equal to the direct costs alone. The

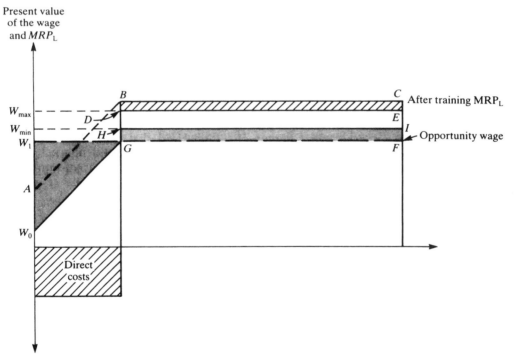

Figure 12.1 Employers and firms share the costs and benefits of specific training. The relative magnitude of the costs and benefits from training determine the magnitude of the surplus that remains to be allocated after training. The costs are represented by the direct costs and the opportunity wage relative to the workers' marginal product while training, the benefits by the enhancement of the workers' marginal product after training. The return to the firm's investment is represented by the hatched area $BCDE$, the return to the worker by the shaded area $HIGF$. The area $DEHI$ is the unallocated area of surplus. No matter who bears the costs, the magnitude of the surplus will be the same. Bargaining or rules will determine the allocation of the surplus when a monopoly seller of labor confronts a monopsonistic purchaser of labor

employees' investment in the job takes the form of the opportunity wage which they forgo while training. Thus the employees' outlay is equal to the area $W_1 W_0 G$.

Upon completion of training both sides expect a return that at least covers their initial costs. The firm wishes to pay a wage sufficiently below the workers' post-training marginal revenue product, represented by the line BC, to insure that it recoups its initial outlays. If we assume that all the costs and revenues identified in Fig. 12.1 are stated in present value terms and that the hatched area $BCDE$ is exactly equal to the hatched area representing the direct costs of training, the firm recoups its outlays provided it concedes a wage *no higher* than DE. The employees also wish to recoup their intial outlays. They need to secure a wage after training sufficiently above the opportunity wage to insure a return on their investment. If we assume that the shaded area $HIGF$ is exactly equal to the shaded area $W_1 W_0 G$, the line HI represents the minimum wage employees demand in the post-training period, in order to recoup their initial outlays. The minimum wage the employees demand in the post-training period is thus W_{min} and the maximum the employer will wish to concede is W_{max}. These values set the upper and lower limits to the wage.

In Fig. 12.1 there remains a surplus to be allocated after distinguishing W_{min} and W_{max}. The magnitude of this area, bounded by $DEHI$, depends on the values of three variables: first, the magnitude of the initial training costs; second, the value of the workers' marginal revenue product in the pre- and post-training period; third, the workers' productivity in other jobs as reflected in the opportunity wage. *Ceteris paribus*, the larger the initial training costs or the lower the post-training productivity, the lower will be the maximum wage the firm is willing to concede upon completion of training and hence the smaller the area of surplus for any given opportunity wage. Conversely, the higher is the workers' marginal product upon completion of training, for a given level of training costs, the larger will be the surplus and the higher will be the wage the firm is willing to concede after training. The value of the opportunity wage also determines the magnitude of the area of surplus. The greater the opportunity wage, relative to the wage the workers receive while undergoing training, the greater will be the workers' net costs and hence the higher will be the minimum wage they will demand post-training. The smaller will therefore be the area of surplus for any given marginal revenue product after training. How does this framework enable us to explain the emergence of those distinctive features of internal labor markets we noted earlier?

The determination of pay

First consider the manner in which the surplus might be allocated. If the training is specific to a single individual, that individual becomes a monopoly seller of labor to the firm. In turn, the firm is the single purchaser of this worker's skill and so the firm becomes a monopsonist. The situation that emerges is therefore one of bilateral monopoly. This will be equally true of a group of specifically trained workers, if they can combine to act as a monopoly seller of labor.

The situation that emerges *after* training is the familiar bilateral monopoly situation which is illustrated in Fig. 12.2. Here the individual who is a monopoly seller of labor

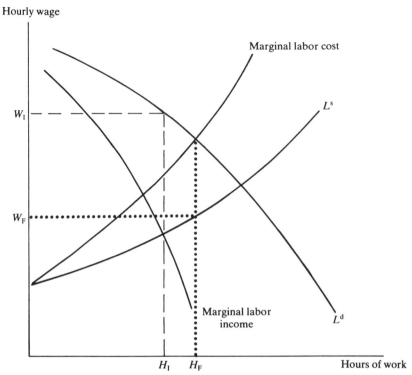

Figure 12.2 Bilateral monopoly. The firm is the sole purchaser of the specific skills of a worker. In consequence, the firm will only purchase more hours at a lower hourly wage, and recognizing this, the worker equates the marginal cost of supplying extra hours given by L^s to the marginal labor income schedule. The worker proposes selling H_I hours at hourly wage W_I. The firm recognizes that it will have to pay a higher hourly wage if it wishes to purchase more hours because the worker is the sole supplier of the labour it wishes to purchase. The firm equates marginal cost, as represented by the marginal labor cost curve confronting it, to marginal revenue, as represented by its demand curve for labor, and proposes to purchases H_F at hourly wage W_F. The model offers no determinate solution for the wage rate and level of employment. It identifies only the upper and lower bounds to these. The wage can settle anywhere between W_I and W_F, and employment can accordingly settle between H_I and H_F

is conscious of facing a downward sloping demand curve for the hours of work he or she is able to supply; the lower the wage asked, the greater the hours the firm will wish to purchase. The lower hourly wage however applies not just to the last hour bought but to all previous hours bought, since the worker is paid a uniform hourly rate. In consequence, the worker recognizes that he or she faces a marginal labor income curve, which bisects the area below the demand curve, for labor services (such a curve corresponds to the marginal revenue curve that lies below the product demand curve of the monopolist). The individual's labor supply curve represents the marginal cost to the individual of each hour of labor that is supplied. The individual will therefore equate marginal cost and marginal labor income and propose supplying H_I hours.

Knowledge of the wage that the firm is willing to pay for each hour supplied leads the individual seller to demand W_I for H_I hours.

In rather similar fashion the firm which is the sole purchaser of the particular skills of this worker, recognizes that the greater the number of hours it buys from the worker the higher will be the hourly wage it must pay. Moreover, the firm recognizes that the higher wage will have to be paid on all the hours purchased from this worker, since it pays a uniform hourly wage. The firm recognizes that it faces a marginal labor cost schedule that lies above the individual's labor supply curve. The firm equates this marginal labor cost schedule to the marginal revenue product of labor schedule, the labor demand curve, and proposes purchasing H_F hours at a wage equal to what it knows to be the supply price of these hours, W_F.

Thus the firm wishes to purchase H_F at W_F and the worker to sell H_I at W_I. A range of indeterminancy exists; there is no determinant wage or employment solution, for as is apparent the model describes only a range within which the wage can settle. In terms of Fig. 12.1 the wage falls within the area distinguished by *DEHI*. There are two principal ways in which the indeterminancy described by Figs. 12.1 and 12.2 can be resolved: bargaining and rules. Bargaining between employers and employees with the outcome determined by the relative strengths of each party or rules that establish conventions and norms of social behavior and which enable the parties to identify an appropriate wage. Consider each of these in turn.

Bargaining If the wage is established as a result of bargaining the level at which it is established will reflect the relative bargaining strength of each party. The magnitude of the area *DEHI* determines the scale of the returns from bargaining. Where these returns are substantial and the skills are specific to the firm but not to a single worker, they offer encouragement to workers to combine to strengthen their hand in bargaining.

Bargaining strength has both a subjective and objective element. Subjectively, workers' bargaining strength depends on the firm's assessment of their willingness to withdraw their labor. This depends in large part on the degree of harmony or discord that characterizes industrial relations in the firm. Objectively, bargaining strength depends on the magnitude of the costs one party can impose on the other. Workers can be said to possess bargaining strength if, by withdrawing their labor, they are able to reduce the output of the firm, and thus diminish the firm's profits. The degree of this strength will be determined by the elasticity of substitution and by the elasticity of supply of substitute factors of production. If workers can be easily replaced by machines or other factors, any interruption to output may be small and temporary. Bargaining strength will also depend on the elasticity of demand for final output. Each of these arguments was evaluated in Chapter 8 when we analyzed labor demand, while bargaining under trade unions is considered in more detail in Chapter 14.

Employees may combine for purposes of bargaining but this is neither easy nor cost free. The benefits from combining to achieve the higher wage are likely to be enjoyed equally by all workers but the costs of combining will be borne by only some workers. The formation and maintenance of a viable bargaining group and the process of bargaining will consume the time and resources of some individuals more than others. If no mechanism is devised for compensating individuals in relation to the degree to which they bear the costs, bargaining coalitions may fail to emerge.

Bargaining may also fail to emerge simply because the total benefits from bargaining are less than the costs associated with it. Bargaining consumes resources both directly, because it involves outlays on research, travel and documentation and indirectly, because of the opportunity cost of the time devoted to bargaining. Bargained outcomes will give rise to labor contracts which specify the contingencies under which the agreement holds and, where revision of labor contracts is generally achieved by bargaining, this may encourage the adoption of inflexible postures to be subsequently conceded in bargaining in exchange for concessions by the other party. In this manner bargaining may encourage a degree of inflexibility on the part of the workforce. Where there is formal bargaining, there is also always the chance that the parties might disagree and resort to sanctions in an attempt to persuade the other party to concede to their terms. For all the above reasons bargaining may be associated with substantial transaction costs and therefore fail to emerge. In the absence of bargaining how will the wage be fixed?

Workplace rules In order to minimize the costs of bargaining it has been suggested that parties will observe certain conventions or rules of behavior.[4] These rules, which are largely unwritten, take the form of custom and practice and are therefore rules in which precedent and convention play a large part in determining outcomes. Unwritten rules of behavior mitigate the excessive costs of continual bargaining and remove the uncertainty that would otherwise characterize these situations. Workplace rules emerge to minimize the costs and resolve the indeterminancy of the bargaining associated with bilateral monopoly. Rules can be viewed as devices consciously erected to minimize the resource outlays on bargaining and can therefore be given an efficient interpretation. A distinguishing characteristic of the internal labor market is that rules are very frequently substituted for market processes. In the internal market it is rules which govern the allocation and pricing of labor within the firm.

What form might such rules take? One general principle that rules might observe is that outcomes should be judged to be fair by both employers and employees. In Chapter 7 we discussed the degree to which considerations of fairness governed labor supply. The indeterminancy that can characterize the internal market provides particular scope for such considerations. Those rules which govern the advance of pay may focus on the pay of other groups. Comparability, the objective of securing a pay increase, comparable to that of similar workers elsewhere, may feature prominently in the rules to establish wages. As a result the rates of pay of several groups in the internal market may be linked together by custom in what have been called *job clusters*. The rates of pay of each occupation within the cluster are then tied to a *key rate* and this key rate, in turn is linked to that of others. Often the key rates relate to jobs that constitute ports of entry to the internal market and hence they provide linkages to the

---

4. Williamson, O.E., Wachter, M.L., and Harris, J.E. (1975) 'Understanding the employment relation: the analysis of idiosyncratic exchange', *The Bell Journal of Economics*, **6**, spring, 250–80.

external market.[5] Movements in these key rates will be prime determinants of changes in the internal wage structure of the firm.

The internal labor market provides a context within which notions of fairness are likely to exert a powerful influence over wages, indeed it is one of the principal contexts in which considerations of fairness influence labor market outcomes. These notions of fairness are likely to translate themselves into implicit agreements, between employers and workers, into implicit contracts. These implicit contracts are sometimes contingent in nature and they can take a number of forms.[6] They may, for example, guarantee the real value of workers' wages, or they may specify that wages grow in line with worker productivity. Alternatively, the understanding may be that pay will grow in line with that of similar workers elsewhere. The form that the implicit contract takes will depend on the particular notion of fairness that influences behavior.

Long-term employment relationships

A second feature of internal labor markets is long-term employment relationships. One consequence of the existence of specific skills is that if it wishes to maintain its current level of production the firm has little choice but to maintain its current workforce: in the short run its present employees are indispensable. The firms' current workforce cannot be replaced by workers from outside the firm because they do not possess the necessary skills. If the firm sacked its existing employees and hired replacements, it would have to write off the investment it had made in the initial period. It would also take time for new workers to become fully trained, and hiring replacements means incurring a further set of investment costs. In the short run, there are no ready substitutes for the firm's existing workforce.

Similar arguments hold for workers. Where they have borne part of the costs of specific training they will have to write off their initial investment outlays if they quit after completing that training. Moreover, if they wish to secure a high wage in the future they will have to consider investing in some form of training with another firm. This new training would involve a further set of investment outlays and for these reasons specifically trained workers will not lightly quit their existing employment.

Taken together these arguments suggest that many firms are no longer indifferent between their existing employees and workers outside the firm while workers are no longer indifferent between their current job and other jobs. The atomistic labor market of elementary competitive theory has disappeared. Workers and firms perceive a mutual interdependence, they are bound together in some form of longer term employment and career relationship.

5. See pp. 16–20 of Dunlop, J.T. (1957) 'The task of contemporary wage theory', in Dunlop (ed), *The Theory of Wage Determination*, Macmillan, London and New York.
6. Hashimoto has suggested that because transaction costs are substantially lower in Japan than in the United States implicit contracts are contingent in nature in Japan and that this gives rise to greater wage flexibility. See Hashimoto, M. (1988) 'Transaction costs and labour market institutions in Japan: a comparative perspective with the United States', paper delivered to a Conference in Corsendonk, Belgium, and also Dore, R. (1973) *British Factory—Japanese Factory*, George Allen and Unwin, London.

The association between wages and tenure

A feature of internal labor markets is that the earnings of workers rise with length of service. As workers' time with the firm increases so do their earnings giving rise to smooth but concave lifetime earnings profiles in which there is no longer the discrete jump in productivity depicted in the earlier figures. This positive association between earnings and tenure with the firm reflects the effect of increased payments over the years for those who remain in a particular job and the effect of promotions. Within the framework of transaction cost theory there are three different explanations of why firms find it profitable to reward their employees in this way.

Investment in job-specific human capital Some components of firm-specific training may be learned in a classroom but others can only be learned on the job. Large group off-the-job teaching can instill only the general principles common to a number of tasks, the more specific elements must be acquired on the job. Skills and expertise, and hence productivity, may slowly build up as individuals learn by experience in their current job.

Productivity data on individuals are seldom available and it is therefore difficult to test the proposition that individuals' productivity increases with experience in their current job but a recent study suggests that this plays a substantial part in explaining differences in individual earnings.[7] In particular it has been argued that the steep earnings–tenure profiles that are observed in Japan are largely explained by on-the-job training. Job tenure is far longer in Japan than in the United States and the difference between starting and peak earnings is greater in Japan and the United Kingdom than in the United States. The evidence shows that workers in small firms enjoy peak earnings some 236 percent greater than starting earnings in Japan while peak earnings are only 140 percent greater than starting earnings in the United States. In large firms in the two countries the figures are respectively 243 percent and 110 percent.

It has been suggested that a very much larger part of the growth in earnings in Japan is due to firm-specific tenure.[8] In small firms in Japan a worker reaches peak earnings in the 24th year, at which time 150 percentage points of the 236 percent growth in earnings are due to firm-specific tenure. The US worker in a small firm reaches peak earnings a year later, after 25 years' experience, but of the 140 percent growth in earnings only 57.9 percentage points are due to firm-specific tenure. In larger firms peak earnings are reached after 27 and 30 years' experience in Japan and the United States respectively, while 205 of the 243 and 53 of the 110 percentage points growth in earnings in Japan and the United States respectively, are accounted for by firm-specific tenure.[9] So while workers in both countries arrive at peak earnings after

7. Kostiuk, P.F. and Follmann, I. (1989) 'Learning curves, personal characteristics and job performance', *Journal of labor Economics*, 7(2), 129–46.
8. See Mincer, J. and Higuchi, Y. (1989) 'Wage structures and labour turnover in the United States and Japan', *Journal of the Japanese and International Economies*.
9. Hashimoto, M. and Raisian, J. (1985) 'Employment tenure and earnings profiles in Japan and the United States', *American Economic Review*, 75, 721–35.

roughly the same number of years in the labor market, earnings profiles are much steeper in Japan than in the United States.

The authors of this study attribute the steeper earnings profiles to the much larger element of firm-specific tenure in Japan and suggest that this in turn reflects the much larger investments in specific human capital in Japan. However, this interpretation should be treated with some caution. Small firms have a higher failure rate than large firms and we should therefore expect workers in smaller firms to be less willing to invest in firm-specific human capital than those in large firms. We should therefore expect workers in small firms to have lower peak earnings than workers in large firms. Although the study reveals that in small firms a smaller proportion, only 64 percent, of peak earnings are accounted for by firm-specific tenure compared to 84 percent in large firms, in both large and small firms peak earnings are around 240 percent greater than starting rates. Earnings growth is therefore almost identical although firm-specific tenure is very different. This suggests that there are other explanations for the steep earnings profiles in Japan that have not yet been discovered.

The job matching hypothesis This constitutes a second explanation for the positive association between earnings and tenure. This hypothesis proposes that workers' productivity is greatest when they are matched to the right job and focuses on the processes by which this matching occurs. According to this hypothesis, the observed association between the growth in earnings and tenure occurs simply as a consequence of sample selection bias. On average, observed wage rates increase with tenure, because it is the good matches, the more productive, which are more likely to survive. This effect is independent of the amount of training the employee receives.[10]

Quite apart from the effects of sample selection bias it has been suggested that the process of job matching explains the positive association between tenure and earnings for at least two further reasons: first, with the passage of time a firm learns more about the productivity of its workforce and it chooses to reward the most productive of these by higher earnings in their current jobs; second, for similar reasons of information, it is likely to fill senior posts from among its own employees. Within the context of this job-matching hypothesis the internal labor market is therefore again viewed as a device for screening to find suitable employees for senior posts.

However, the job-matching and on-the-job training hypotheses can no longer be viewed as distinct. Employers recognize that not all workers are equally well suited for all positions and wish to locate only the more able individuals for on-the-job training. Firms will therefore expend greater resources in screening applicants for those jobs requiring most on-the-job training.[11] Employers filling senior positions, which require training, can also be expected to increase the intensity of their screening on the job. It is now difficult to isolate the independent effects of ability and training for, as the

10. See Topel R. (1986) 'Job mobility and earnings growth: a reinterpretation of human capital earnings functions', in Ehrenberg, R.G. (ed.) *Research in Labor Economics*, vol. **8**, JAI Press, pp. 199–233 and Altonji, J. and Shakotko, R. (1987) 'Do wages rise with job seniority?', *Review of Economic Studies*, **54**, 437–59.
11. See Barron, J.M., Black, D.A. and Lowenstein, M.A. (1989) 'Job matching and on-the-job training', *Journal of Labor Economics*, **7**, 1–19.

above argument implies, they are complementary and it may therefore be impossible to distinguish between observed wage growth on the job, which is a consequence of on-the-job training, and that which is due to the workings of the job matching process. Because firms are likely to select the more able individuals for on-the-job training, it is now also difficult 'to test the prediction of the theory of specific human capital investment that workers pay for their on-the-job training in the firm by receiving a lower starting wage. We need to compare the starting wage of workers of the same ability but who have different amounts of on-the-job training. But where ability is no longer randomly matched to jobs requiring different amounts of training, it will be impossible to disentangle the separate effects of training and ability on the starting wage.[12]

Resolution of the agency problem[13] A third explanation of the association between tenure and earnings emerges from the theory of agency. The economic theory of agency focuses on those forms of payment with which one party, termed the principal, seeks to motivate the other, the agent, to behave in a way which is of advantage to the principal. Problems occur because the agent's behavior may not be fully revealed to the principal although the outcome will be affected by the agent's behavior. In the context of the present analysis of internal labor markets, the firm is the principal and the worker is the agent. Once we depart from the homogeneity of skills assumed in competitive markets and move to a world of specific skills it becomes likely that on many occasions the principal, the firm, no longer knows best the appropriate procedures for maximum efficiency. Asymmetric information gives employees the opportunity to work at less than their most efficient, or to use the information they possess to their advantage in bargaining.

The positive association between earnings and tenure may be viewed as a devise to resolve this problem. Consider Fig. 12.3 in which, to distinguish this explanation from the former two, it is assumed that an employee's marginal product remains unchanged throughout his or her working life. Lifetime earnings still equal lifetime marginal product but the firm now proposes to pay rather less than the MRP_L in the early years of employment and more than the MRP_L in later years so that the shaded area above the MRP_L line beyond T^* equals the shaded area below the MRP_L. Such a compensation scheme is proposed to have two effects: first, to reduce quits, workers wish to stay on to enjoy higher future earnings; second, to reduce shirking, workers wish to work diligently to reduce the chances of being discharged. For both these reasons productivity in such a firm is likely to be higher than in firms not offering such deferred compensation, and for this reason we show the opportunity wage below the workers' MRP_L in this firm.

Resolution of the agency problem in this manner suggests that rising earnings profiles raise lifetime productivity and earnings. However, such an arrangement is not without risks. Employees will not collect on their investment if they are fired during

---

12. Barron *et al.* (1989), *op. cit.*
13. See Arrow, K.J. (1985) 'Agency and the market', in Arrow, K.J. and Intriligator, M.D. (eds.), *Handbook of Mathematical Economics*, vol.III, 1986, Elsevier–North Holland.

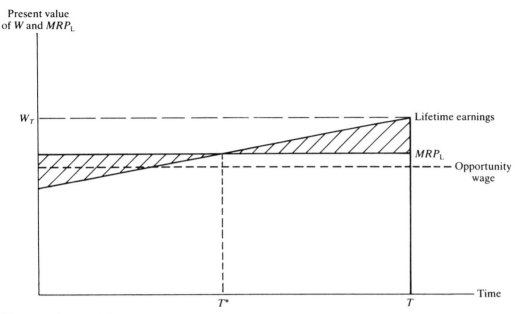

Figure 12.3 A positive association between earnings and tenure as a device to reduce shirking and quits. Deferred payment raises productivity by reducing quits and shirking. Deferred payment results in a positive association between earnings and tenure. Workers now wish to remain in the firm's employ to enjoy higher subsequent earnings and retire at time T by prior agreement with the firm. The firm indicates its willingness to retain the services of workers over the years to time T by instituting last in first out layoff procedures. However, workers may feel more secure if firms bear some of the costs of specific training. This will further steepen the lifetime earnings profile

the period, and as shown in Fig. 12.3, there is a strong incentive for firms to fire workers at time T^*. Nor will firms wish employees to stay on beyond time T by which time annual earnings, W_T, are substantially in excess of either their opportunity wage or MRP_L. One way to solve this last problem is to agree on a mandatory retirement age and to hire workers back at lower wages if they wish to carry on working.[14] Such practice was until recently common in Japan where up to the late 1980s mandatory retirement typically occurred between ages 55 and 60, but workers carried on working well beyond that age.

Older employees may still require some reassurance that they will not be discharged between time T^* and T. This can be achieved by the existence of *seniority* rights in labor contracts: last in, first out clauses or implicit agreements that state that older, and more senior workers will be the last to be laid off or discharged. Of course an alternative protection against arbitrary discharge occurs where employers bear all or part of the transaction costs of hiring and training workers, for we have identified

14. See Lazear, E.P. (1979) 'Why is there mandatory retirement?', *Journal of Political Economy*, **87**, December, 1261–84 for a full exposition of this theory.

above the many conditions under which employers operating internal labor markets will be reluctant to discharge workers. The agency explanation therefore suggests that rising earnings profiles can exist in the absence of the rising marginal productivity schedule associated with internal labor markets. It also follows that, if firms which engage in specific training also construct such deferred compensation schemes to discourage shirking, we shall observe very steep earnings profiles indeed.

However, there exist other devices to resolve the agency problem. In Chapter 10 and earlier in this chapter we recognized that unwritten workplace rules, custom and practice, and indeed wider social conventions can all be interpreted as mechanisms for inducing appropriate and efficient behavior by employees under conditions of asymmetric information. Workplace customs and conventions, inducing a sense of responsibility toward co-workers, can act to discourage shirking and reduce the opportunistic use of information advantages. The internal labor market, with its web of rules can be viewed as an efficient solution to the problems of asymmetric information.[15]

The role of trade unions

The existence of internal labor markets diminishes the role of exit as a mechanism for securing labor market adjustment and the voice mechanism is therefore prominent in this context. We should therefore expect to find those institutions of the labor market associated with use of the voice mechanism represented here. Trade unions and other employees' associations represent one vehicle for conveying to employers information about the preferences of workers and we should expect to find trade unions or similar organizations playing a prominent part in internal labor markets. The combination of the returns from bargaining, as a consequence of bilateral monopoly, and the requirement for an institutional mechanism to convey information between the parties provides strong reasons for the prominence of trade unions in internal labor markets.

Summary

The existence of substantial transaction costs, which take the form of hiring and specific training costs, has resulted in the emergence of a distinct internal market for labor in many firms. Firms offer employees inducements to remain with them in the form of opportunities for promotion and advancement in earnings. Such internal labor markets may therefore be described as career labor markets. The analysis of internal labor markets helps explain some of the most important developments in labor markets in advanced industrial countries in recent years. These features have been long-term employment relations, substantial wage rigidity, the positive association of earnings and tenure and the preference of firms for promoting their existing employees.

However, the theory provides few determinant outcomes, for allocation and pricing ultimately depend on a process of bargaining or on a set of workplace rules the nature of which is less than perfectly understood. Notions of justice and fairness play an

15. This is the view developed by Williamson, O.E., Wachter, M.L. and Harris, J.E. (1975), *op. cit.*, 250–78.

important role in determining outcomes but there is no consensus as to just what form these take. While this remains the case our theory can offer us only a guide to a range of possible outcomes. It cannot predict with accuracy what the wage and employment outcome will be in such labor markets.

We do not have accurate estimates as to just how widespread such internal labor market arrangements are in Europe and the United States. Their incidence depends on how widespread and substantial are the transaction costs on which the theory rests. It has been suggested that they are predominant in France and Italy and have grown in the United Kingdom and Germany in recent years.[16] They would also appear prominent in Japan, however in the United States the picture is less than clear.

DUAL AND SEGMENTED LABOR MARKET THEORY

In Chapters 6 and 11 we have discussed the theories of human capital and equalizing differences. Human capital theory alone provides a significant explanation of the variance of individual earnings and this explanation is improved if we allow for the characteristics of jobs as suggested by the theory of equalizing differences. However, while these 'augmented human capital' models explain a substantial proportion of differences in individual earnings, there remains a large unexplained residual. Part of this residual constitutes a return to the industry in which the individual works and efficiency wage theory sought to account for this. Yet even after allowing for these effects, as much as 42 percent of the variance in non-union wages and 52 percent of union wages in the United States remains to be explained.[17]

It is clear that in the labor market the rewards to any given level of human capital differ between firms: all firms do not reward equal productive characteristics equally. It has been proposed that in most advanced industrial nations the labor market can be divided into a sector in which human capital is well rewarded and one in which it is poorly rewarded. The labor market is segmented into a primary sector and a secondary sector and the return to a given stock of, or increment to, human capital is greater in the primary than in the secondary sector. The primary sector is characterized by 'good' jobs and the secondary by 'bad' jobs.

Not surprisingly internal labor markets have been suggested to be a prominent feature of the primary sector. Internal labor markets offer stability of employment and prospects of both wage growth and career advancement within the firm. In internal labor markets individuals no longer need to change firms to build a career as they can do this within the internal labor market. The existence of internal labor markets results in the existence of good jobs. However, there are also good jobs outwith internal labor markets. Jobs which require general skills and serve as recruitment grades for internal labor markets function within competitive labor markets and they too can enjoy good wages. It is true that they do not necessarily share some of the characteristics of jobs

16. See Marsden, D. and Ryan, P. (1989) 'Employment and training of young people', *Employment and Training UK*, 47–53, *Policy Journals*, London.
17. See Dickens, W.T. and Katz, L.F. (1987) 'Inter-industry wage differences and industry characteristics', in Lang, K. and Leonard, J.S. (eds.), *Unemployment and the Structure of Labour Markets*, Blackwell, pp. 48–89.

within internal labor markets, namely regular wage growth and prospects of advancement, but the careers of generally skilled workers certainly do not exclude these features. Continuity of employment is no longer achieved by staying with a single firm but is realized by appropriate moves between firms. A career is built by moving on to more senior jobs in different firms. Examples of generally skilled workers who build careers in this way are highly trained engineers, computer programmers, accountants and lawyers. Good jobs are not therefore exclusively a feature of internal labor markets. Competitive labor markets generate good jobs as well.

In all economies there exist some less desirable jobs: jobs with low pay, jobs which are of short duration, and those which offer few prospects of advancement or real pay growth. These 'bad' jobs seem almost exclusively to be in the competitive sector for the nature of the internal labor market, its origins and rationale, largely precludes the existence of bad jobs. Bad jobs may be found within firms operating an internal labor market, but such jobs lie outside the internal market and merely provide evidence that some 'firms operate internal *and* competitive labor markets.[18] The distinction between good and bad jobs is central to the notion of dual labor markets although the reasons why such differences emerge is still the subject of considerable debate.

The development of dual and segmented labor market theory

The idea that the labor market does not behave in the manner described by simple competitive labor market theory is not new. Adam Smith detailed the equalizing tendencies within competitive labor markets, but in the nineteenth century John Stuart Mill and J.E. Cairnes expressed their substantial reservations about the theory and proposed what we now label dual labor market theory.[19]

John Stuart Mill (1848), while endorsing most of Smith's arguments, emphasized that 'the really exhausting and really repulsive labors instead of being paid better than others are almost invariably paid the worst of all because performed by those who have no choice'. Labor was segmented into 'castes' according to Mill, who suggested 'so strongly marked is the line of demarcation between the different grades of labourers as to be almost equivalent to a hereditary distinction of caste'. According to Cairnes 'certain industrial circles or groups exist, the workmen composing each of which, while competing among themselves, are from social circumstances excluded from effective competition with the workmen of different groups'. Cairnes described these as 'non-competing groups'. Competition on this view was restricted to within rather than between groups and, as a result, considerable disparities in individuals' total pecuniary

---

18. See, for example, Easterman, P. (1982) 'Employment structures within firms', *British Journal of Industrial Relations*, **XX**(3), 349–61. He notes that certain employees in insurance and banking enjoy stable jobs with high pay and promotion prospects, while others are in poorly paid clerical jobs which exhibit high turnover and offer few career prospects.

19. Mill, J.S. (1848) *Principles of Political Economy with some of their Applications to Social Philosophy*, see edition published in 1909 by Longmans, London, England and Cairnes, J.E. (1874) *Some Leading Principles of Political Economy Newly Expounded*, London, Macmillan.

and non-pecuniary rewards would emerge. Rewards in the labor market would not be equalized in the manner suggested by Adam Smith.[20]

The difference between the predictions of competitive theory and a strict dual labor market can perhaps best be illustrated by considering the distribution of individual earnings that might emerge in each case. The dispersion of earnings, for any homogeneous category of labor in a competitive market, results from transaction and information costs and the resulting distribution of earnings is (log) normal as shown in Fig. 12.4(a). In contrast, dual labor market theory suggests a bimodal distribution of earnings, Fig. 12.4(b), with those in the secondary market effectively constituting a queue for the good jobs in the primary sector. The primary sector offers both greater returns to any given stock of human capital and greater returns to any given increment to human capital. Earnings in the primary sector are almost everywhere superior to those in the secondary sector and are no longer a consequence of the characteristics of workers. Instead they result from the characteristics of jobs.

Dual labor market theory does not suggest that there will be equality of human capital endowment in the two sectors. Some inequality must in fact inevitably arise where part of the individual's human capital is acquired on the job, for it is likely to be only jobs in the primary sector which offer this facility. Access to primary sector jobs therefore becomes a prerequisite for enhancing human capital in this way. Differences in educational attainment may also arise between the two sectors because some groups, e.g. blacks and women, may expect to earn a lower return on their investment in human capital and are therefore more reluctant to undertake such investment in the first place. Competitive analysis takes tastes for education and acquiring productive characteristics as exogenous but dual labor market theory proposes that in these respects tastes are endogenous. Those who expect to be consigned to the secondary sector will be discouraged from investing in human capital. As a result part of the difference in human capital that we observe in the labor market is itself a consequence of the existence of a dual market. Dual labor market theory therefore offers an explanation of the inequalities in educational attainment that exist.

For any homogeneous category of labour competitive forces should equalize rewards between the two sectors. In the secondary segment of the dual labor market shown in Fig. 12.4 some individuals are being paid wages which appear to provide an inadequate return to their human capital. This suggests the existence of unexploited profitable opportunities. Existing employers could step into the secondary market and recruit labor which was equally productive to that in the primary sector but for which they need only pay lower wages. By so doing, they could increase their profits. Even though existing firms might be reluctant to employ such labor, perhaps because it might mean that they would have to discharge their existing labor force, new firms could set up and employ this secondary labor and compete them out of business. As

20. These early writers suggested more than the simple bifurcation of the labor market proposed by dual labor market theory. Writing many years after Mill and Cairnes this early view was endorsed by a leading exponent of the institutional school of labor economists in the United States who described the labor market as 'Balkanized'. See Kerr C. (1954) 'The Balkanization of labor markets' in Wright-Bakke E. *et al.* (eds.) *Labor Mobility and Economic Opportunity*, MIT Press, Cambridge, Mass.

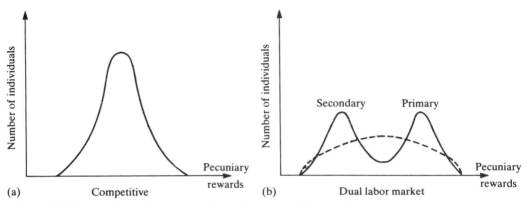

Figure 12.4 The distribution of earnings in competitive and dual labor markets. (a) In a competitive market the dispersion of earnings for any homogeneous category of labor is determined by information and transaction costs; (b) In the dual labor market similar dispersion occurs around the mean earnings in each of two sectors

firms seized such opportunities this would bid up wages in the secondary sector and depress those in the primary sectors, eventually resulting in a unimodal earnings distribution. Such would be the consequences of the forces of competition working in an unimpeded manner. Of course, it may be that the unimodal distribution that emerges displays a substantial degree of dispersion as depicted by the dotted line in Fig. 12.4(b). It might then be appropriate to classify jobs towards the tail of the distribution as comprising the secondary sector, for these are the 'worst' jobs, and describe the rest as comprising the primary sector.

If there is a bimodal distribution of earnings there must be barriers to the operation of competitive forces. Specifically there must be restrictions on the availability of good jobs for there are not sufficient of these on offer to mop up the supply of suitably qualified workers. What are the mechanisms by which good jobs are rationed? Two candidates suggest themselves: discrimination and technology.

1. *Discrimination* Some individuals, minority groups and women, may not be offered jobs in the primary sector, because they possess certain characteristics that are discriminated against in the labor market. Firms may have no desire to recruit individuals with particular characteristics or may be prevented from so doing by those among their existing labor force. Just why they might behave in this way is the subject of the next chapter; for the moment we note that discriminatory practices are one explanation of dual labor markets.
2. *Technology* The supply of good jobs may be inadequate due to the nature of technology; the state of technology may be such that there are simply not enough good jobs to go round. One explanation of why this might occur is that there are barriers to entry in product markets, these prevent the entry of new firms and the expansion of output and employment in those sectors which currently offer good jobs. This is an explanation preferred by some dual labor market analysts. However, it does not explain why existing producers do not avail themselves of cheaper labor

by switching to a more labor intensive technology which can utilize the abundant labor in the secondary market. Thus alongside restrictions on the expansion of output due to barriers to entry in product markets must also go some form of 'technological determinism' which suggests that there are limited substitution possibilities between labor and capital. If there is only one way, or a very few ways, of producing any particular product, the substitution opportunities will also be few.

Implications for public policy

The prescriptions for public policy that arise from dual labor market analysis are very different from those suggested by orthodox competitive theory. If there is concern over the distribution or the level of wages produced by competitive markets the role of public policy is to improve and to equalize educational opportunities. Public policy is directed to equalizing access to the facilities that enable individuals to enhance their human capital and in this manner it may produce more equal earnings opportunities. In contrast, the dual labor market view emphasizes that such a policy will prove inadequate because equalizing educational opportunities and even equalizing human capital endowments may merely lengthen the queue for primary jobs and do nothing to remove the unequal rewards in the two sectors.

If jobs are rationed for technological reasons the relevant question for public policy is how are these scarce jobs allocated? If they are allocated by a random drawing from the whole of the working population, such that all individuals stand an equal chance of obtaining a good job, there need be no role for public policy, for this process results in a 'fair' distribution of the available opportunities. However, if the opportunities are allocated as a result of nepotism, of unions persuading employers to hire only union members, or of discriminatory hiring practices, the distribution of good jobs might become a matter of public concern. Public policy will now be aimed at equalizing access to good jobs by outlawing discriminatory hiring practices, removing trade union restrictions on recruitment and/or by reducing nepotism. In the longer term public policy might also aim to encourage the creation of a larger number of better jobs, perhaps by removing barriers to entry in product markets.

A feature of dual labor market theory is the proposition that some individuals are permanently consigned to bad jobs. Were this not so, those currently occupying secondary jobs should be encouraged to invest in human capital for they could expect to move on at some time and realize a return on their investment. Thus the college student, presently employed as a waiter or cleaner, is not discouraged from investing in human capital for he or she expects eventually to obtain a good job and realize the return on investment. Such an example further serves to remind us why we may find equal levels of human capital unequally rewarded in the two sectors, because quite simply the human capital acquired by the student is not relevant to the job that is currently occupied. All forms of human capital investment are not equally relevant to all jobs; they do not enhance productivity equally in any job. In our example possession of a university degree does little to enhance waiting or cleaning skills and thus the job offers no return on this investment.

Critics of dual labor market theory suggest that the essential distinction is not between good and bad jobs. The essential distinction is between those individuals who experience a temporarily lower return to a given investment in human capital, such as we observe here, and those who experience a permanently lower return, such as occurs when people get stuck in the secondary market. On this view it is not clear why we should be concerned with poor jobs *per se*, some jobs will always be low paying in that they require little human capital, and hence do not reward such investment.[21] The focus of attention should be on those individuals who get stuck in low paying jobs for it is the existence of low wage jobs, together with the inability of some individuals who start in these to subsequently obtain high paying jobs, that is of policy concern. The inability of individuals to move out of low paying into high paying jobs either because they are immobile or because high paying jobs are rationed, is the central policy issue.

On this alternative view the essential distinction is not between primary and secondary labor markets or between good and bad jobs but between good and bad careers. Bad jobs are a necessary condition for the existence of bad careers but they are not a sufficient condition. The sufficient condition is that individuals are permanently consigned to poor jobs.

Empirical evidence

The early empirical work on dual labor markets took two forms. The first approach classified occupations or industries into the primary and secondary sectors on the basis of the judgments of the researchers, then estimated separate human capital earnings equations of the form of Eq. (6.11) for the two sectors and tested for differences in the determinants of earnings in the two sectors. The second approach used statistical techniques, such as factor analysis, to discover whether the characteristics of workers and jobs were sufficiently distinct to enable them to be allocated to two or more distinct sectors.

The first of these two approaches will reveal differences in the returns to human capital in the two sectors. If the returns to education in the secondary sector are smaller than in the primary sector the regression line describing the relationship between human capital and earnings, as depicted in Fig. 12.5, will have a shallower slope in the secondary sector than in the primary sector. The increment to earnings for any given increment to human capital will be significantly less in the secondary sector and a test will then reveal significant differences between the wage equations for the two sectors. If the scatter diagram does not assume the nice tidy pattern suggested in Fig. 12.5 the question then becomes do two wage equations fit the data better than one and do these equations have characteristics which are consistent with the dual labor market hypothesis?

Having identified two or more sectors, a common procedure in such studies has been to relocate, statistically, individuals from the secondary to the primary sector and,

21. In the words of Hicks 'Casual labour is often badly paid, not because it gets less than it is worth, but because it is worth so appallingly little', Hicks, J.R. (1963) *The Theory of Wages*, 2nd ed, p. 82, Macmillan, London, New York.

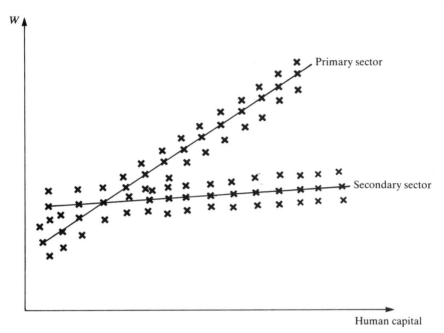

Figure 12.5 Wage equations for the secondary and primary sector. Regression equations describing the relationship between earnings and measures of human capital have a shallower slope in the secondary than in the primary sector. In the secondary sector an increment to human capital is rewarded by a lower increment to earnings than occurs in the primary sector

having done so, to estimate the subsequent increase in their earnings. Effectively, this amounts to estimating the change in the earnings of individuals presently employed in the secondary sector which would occur if their present human capital endowments were rewarded at the rates available in the primary sector. This is a technique we shall explore in more detail in the next chapter, in which we consider the subject of discrimination, for it has in general been more widely employed in that context. The effect of relocating a male manual worker of average quality, from the least advantaged to the most advantaged sector, in the United States in the 1960s and 1970s, was to raise their average earnings by between 25 and 40 percent.[22] The results of a similar exercise for Britain in the mid-1970s raised the earnings of a typical male worker by more than 30 percent.[23]

Researchers estimating earnings equations for the different sectors have found that, in the United States, neither education nor experience contributed significantly to the explanation of earnings in the secondary sector while in the primary sector both these

22. See Wachtel, H. and Betsey, C. (1972) 'Employment at low wages', *Review of Economics and Statistics*, **54**, 121–9.
23. McNabb, R. (1987) 'Testing for labour market segmentation in Britain', *Manchester School*, **55**(3), September, 257–73.

variables were significant.[24] Other researchers, using a similar procedure, found that human capital was largely unrewarded in the US secondary sector[25] but in contrast to these findings, in Britain some researchers found that education had a significant effect on earnings in both the primary and secondary sectors.[26] Of course, as we have already seen in Chapter 6, the incidence of higher education at all levels of attainment is far lower in Britain than in the United States and this difference was even more pronounced in the period before 1970 studied by these researchers. In Britain it is possible that at this time there was no queue of highly qualified applicants for the primary sector as the theory proposes, and there was not therefore a pool of highly qualified labor in the secondary sector.

However, the results of these studies are far from conclusive for the approach suffers from a number of deficiencies. By dividing, or truncating, the sample to create two or more subsamples, researchers may violate the assumptions about the distribution of the error term in the estimated equations and bias downwards the absolute values of the coefficients on age and schooling.[27] The assumption underpinning estimation is that the independent variables included in any equation are independent of the error term but this assumption will be violated if talents, which may later be rewarded in the market place, are presently captured by the error term. Workers in the secondary sector may receive lower returns to human capital variables because the full returns on such investment are only fully realized once they move out of these jobs. There is also the danger of sample selection bias since workers' unmeasured characteristics are likely to be correlated with their choice of occupation or industry.

Most of the studies allocated occupations or industries to the primary sector, according to the judgment of the researchers as to what constitutes good and bad jobs. This is clearly unsatisfactory and indeed most researchers are evidently uncomfortable with this procedure. An alternative approach has been to use statistical techniques to identify different sectors on the basis of their distinctive characteristics. Thus it was found that a distinctive grouping of industries could be distinguished in the United States on the basis of firm size, product market concentrations, unionization, and capital per worker. Each of these factors was suggested to be more pronounced in the primary sector.[28] Again, concentration, plant size and capital intensity were found to distinguish a primary sector in Britain.[29] Similar statistical techniques have been used to allocate individuals to the two sectors on the basis of their individual characteristics. However, the theory proposes that it is the characteristics of jobs which distinguish the two sectors not the characteristics of individuals. Such a procedure does not in itself

24. Osterman, P. (1975) 'An empirical study of labor market segmentation', *Industrial and Labor Relations Review*, **28**, 508–23.
25. Carnoy, C. and Rumberger, M. (1980) 'Segmentation in the US labour market: its effects on the mobility and earnings of whites and blacks', *Cambridge Journal of Economics*, **4**, 117–32.
26. Mayhew, K. and Rosewell, B. (1979) 'Labour market segmentation in Britain', *Oxford Bulletin of Economics and Statistics*, **41**, 81–116.
27. See Cain, G.G. (1976) 'The challenge of segmented labor market theories to orthodox theory: a survey, *Journal of Economic Literature*, **14**, 1215–57.
28. See Oster, G. (1979) 'A factor analytic test of the theory of the dual economy', *Review of Economics and Statistics*, **61**(1), 33–9.
29. See MacNabb, R. and Ryan, P. (1989), 'Segmented labour markets', in Tzannotos, Z. and Sapsford, D. (eds.), *Current Issues in Labour Economics*, Macmillan, London. pp. 151–77.

attest to the existence of different wage setting mechanisms in the two sectors, tests for these have to follow the allocation of individuals to the two sectors.

In fact neither the existence of two distinct wage setting mechanisms nor the existence of two sectors is incompatible with human capital theory in the short run. Although neoclassical analysis generally assumes that a wide range of technical substitution possibilities confront firms, were technology to become sharply discontinuous this could result in two distinct labor markets. Competitive theory would then hypothesize that individuals would choose to join the sector which maximized the expected present value of their lifetime income. However, such differences could not be sustained in the long run. Over the long run, if these choices resulted in widely different real labor earnings for individuals in the two sectors and this gave rise to wide differences in profit rates, the differences in real income would be competed away as more firms moved to adopt the more profitable technology.

In fact the existence of two distinct wage setting mechanisms does not constitute a refutation of human capital theory if individuals are free to choose between sectors and can move from one to another. The issue of mobility is central to the issue of labor market segmentation. Researchers have noted that there is far less upward occupational mobility for blacks than for whites in the United States but there is still substantial movement.[30] For example, one study found that typically half or more of male workers who were inner city residents and held menial jobs moved into primary employment. Schooling and work experience both played a part in assisting such mobility.[31] Two-fifths of young men working in the lowest five occupational categories in the United States in 1966 had moved into the primary sector three years later.[32] Research into the first 10 years in the working lives of those in the labor force in Great Britain, before 1958, found that of those individuals who were in the top part of the primary market at the end of the 10 years less than half had started there.[33] Over 40 percent came from the lower tier of the primary sector and over 10 percent from the secondary sector. A quarter of those occupying the lower tier of the primary sector started out in the secondary sector. Although this 10-year 'snapshot' does not measure lifetime mobility, it does tell us something about the degree of mobility between the sectors at the time of their lives when individuals are in general most likely to change jobs. The results suggest that even in the United Kingdom a not insignificant minority, around one-third, 'escape' from the secondary to the lower and upper tiers of the primary sector. The other side of the coin is that after 10 years two-thirds have made no such change: two-thirds have been stuck in the secondary sector. As in the United States so in Britain, the movement from the secondary to the primary sector is associated with levels of human capital. In both countries human capital is rewarded by both higher earnings in each of the two sectors and it is a principal factor assisting mobility between the two sectors.

30. Carnoy, C. and Rumberger, M. (1980), *op. cit.*
31. Rosenberg, S. (1980) 'Male occupational standing and the dual labor market', *Industrial Relations*, **19**(1), 34–49.
32. See MacNabb, R. and Ryan, P. (1989), *op. cit.*
33. Mayhew, K. and Rosewell, B. (1979), *op. cit.*

More recently an amalgamation of the above two approaches has been employed.[34] Researchers have estimated simultaneously separate wage equations for the two sectors and a third equation which predicts, on the basis of observable characteristics, the sector to which the worker will be attached. The evidence produced by these researchers distinguishes workers in the secondary sector with characteristics appropriate to gain entry into the primary sector and then attributes this states of affairs to discrimination. It was found that the fact that black males in the United States were consigned disproportionately to the secondary sector accounts for 40 percent of the difference in wages between black and white workers. These researchers suggest that discriminatory hiring practices exclude black workers from some of the higher paying jobs, and so confirm the restrictions on mobility reported by other researchers.

There are weaknesses with this approach. While discriminatory hiring practices might be a reasonable interpretation of the evidence in the case of black workers, it is difficult to use discrimination to explain any similar queue of white workers. Moreover, the approach again assigns workers to each sector according to individual characteristics when the theory suggests it is the characteristics of jobs that distinguish the two sectors. Furthermore, the researchers assume that workers will choose employment in one of the two sectors at the beginning of their careers and stay in that sector for their entire working life, that is they maximize an unchanging utility function. By so doing, they rule out the outcome of greatest interest, the degree of mobility *between* the two sectors, and ignore the fundamental explanation proposed for the lack of this by dual labor market theory—negative feedback effects. Dual labor market theory suggests that individuals maximize a changing utility function; it suggests that early labor market experience is an important determinant of workers' later productive characteristics. Workers in the secondary sector could start out with the same human capital as primary workers but they are moulded by the subsequent labor market experience. 'Bad jobs create low quality workers'.[35]

Finally, we should recall that efficiency wage theory proposed a number of reasons why workers in possession of equal human capital might be paid different wages and why in consequence high and low wage sectors might emerge.[36] One aspect of this theory emphasized the role that high wages play in eliciting effort from workers and suggested that some firms pay more than the going rate to avoid shirking. It was also argued that some firms pay high wages to improve morale, and with it productivity, while others pay high wages to reduce turnover. Efficiency wage theory therefore suggests reasons why there may emerge a set of firms willing to pay more than the 'going rate' and as a result create a dual market. However, it does not tell us which firms will do this, nor why, perceiving the advantages from such a move, all firms do not do this thereby establishing a new higher but uniform going rate, and eliminating the two markets.

34. Dickens, W.T. and Lang, K. (1985) 'A test of dual labor market theory', *American Economic Review*, **75**(4), 792–805.
35. Ryan, P. (1981) 'Segmentation, duality and the internal labour market', in Wilkinson, F. (ed.), *The Dynamics of Labour Market Segmentation*, Academic Press, London.
36. See Bulow, J.I. and Summers, L.H. (1986) 'A theory of dual labor markets with application to industrial policy', *Journal of Labor Economics*, **4**, 376–414 and Dickens, W.T. and Lang, K. (1988) 'The re-emergence of segmented labor market theory', *American Economic Review*, Papers and proceedings, May, 129–34.

SUMMARY

In this chapter we have developed the theories of internal and dual labor markets. We have seen that internal labor markets result from the existence of specific skills and 'imperfections' in information which raise substantially the transaction costs of employing outsiders to fill vacancies. These transaction costs, which lead firms to prefer their present employees to outsiders, also afford their employees some monopoly power. In particular, the heterogeneous nature of many firms' production functions means that many workers became the sole sellers of labor to the firm. As a result, many of the devices that we observe in the internal labor market can be viewed as mechanisms for minimizing the conflict that might otherwise characterize the bargaining situation. Others reflect the mechanisms that firms construct to motivate and appraise their employees when the discipline of competition is absent. Employees in internal labor markets seem to enjoy considerably greater employment and wage stability than do employees in more competitive labor markets and the theoretical framework provided by transaction costs helps us explain why.

The analysis of internal labor markets also helps explain why there might exist a primary and a secondary sector in the labor market of most advanced industrial nations. The characteristics of jobs in internal labor markets conform to those of the good jobs we find in the primary sector but internal labor markets are not the sole generators of good jobs. Good jobs can also be found in competitive labor markets. Indeed we concluded that the essential distinction is not that between good and bad jobs but that between good and bad careers. Both competitive and internal labor markets offer good careers, but the majority of bad careers seem to the found in the competitive sector. Bad jobs together with immobility, the fact that some individuals get stuck in bad jobs, make for bad careers. The focus of policy should perhaps be on increasing mobility rather than on trying to eliminate bad jobs.

PRINCIPAL CONCEPTS

Before leaving this chapter students should ensure that they are familiar with the following concepts which have been developed in this chapter:

1. Ports of entry and jobs clusters.
2. The agency problem.
3. Bilateral monopoly.
4. Learning-by-doing.
5. Bimodal earnings distribution.
6. 'Good' and 'bad' jobs.

QUESTIONS FOR DISCUSSION

1. What are the distinguishing characteristics of internal labor markets?
2. Does internal labor market theory help us understand the way the labor market works?

3. Are successful careers only built in internal labor markets?
4. Does the nature of transaction costs in labor markets help to explain the existence and characteristics of internal labor markets?
5. Are internal labor markets likely to exhibit greater wage and employment stability than competitive labor markets?
6. Why can workplace rules be interpreted as a mechanism for minimizing the costs associated with the indeterminacy inherent in internal labor markets?
7. Is the positive association between earnings and tenure explained by the existence of on-the-job training?
8. What are the mechanisms by which good jobs might be rationed?
9. Why might the average level of human capital possessed by individuals in the secondary labor market be lower than the average level possessed by individuals in the primary sector?
10. The imposition of a sufficiently high minimum wage could eliminate bad, i.e. low paying, jobs. Would this be sufficient to eliminate the secondary market?
11. What are the methodological problems that are encountered by economists testing for the existence of a dual labor market?
12. In what manner does dual labor market theory endogenize tastes?

FURTHER READING

The earliest and still one of the most informative discussions of dual labor markets is Doeringer, P.B. and Piore, M.J. (1971) *Internal Labor Markets and Manpower Analysis*, Lexington, Mass, D.C. Heath and Co., but excellent and earlier discussions of these ideas are to be found in Dunlop, J.T. (ed.) (1957) *The Theory of Wage Determination*, Macmillan, London; St Martin's press, New York and Clark Kerr (1954) 'The balkanization of labor markets', in Wright-Bakke, E. *et al.* (eds.), *Labor Mobility and Economic Opportunity*, MIT, Cambridge, Mass, pp. 92–110. More recently the surveys by Cain, G.G. and Taubman, P. and Wachter, M.L. in Ashenfelter, O. and Layard, P.R.G. (eds), *Handbook in Labor Economics*, 1986, North Holland, provided an excellent overview as does the survey by MacNabb, R. and Ryan, P. (1989) in Tzannatos, Z. and Sapsford, D. (eds.), *Current Issues in Labour Economics*, Macmillan, London. The survey by Cain follows his article, 'The challenge of segmented labor market theories to orthodox theory: a survey', in the *Journal of Economic Literature*, **14**, 1215–57, in 1976. Some of the most important insights into the transaction costs literature have been offered by O. Williamson, who together with Wachter, M.L. and Harris, J.E. (1975) 'Understanding the employment relationship: the analysis of idiosyncratic exchange', *Bell Journal of Economics*, **6**, Spring, 250–80, provided a seminal insight into internal labor markets. Okun, A.M. (1981) *Prices and Quantities: A Macroeconomic Analysis*, has also provided an important analysis of the employment and wage consequences of the existence of substantial transaction costs in labor markets in Chapters 1–3 of this book. All the above provide interesting and important insights into the issues discussed in this chapter and should be consulted.

13

DISCRIMINATION IN LABOR MARKETS

In this chapter we are concerned with differences in individual earnings and labor market opportunities that result from discrimination. The normal operation of a competitive market will result in differences in individual earnings but the size of the differences that emerge in the labor markets of most countries appears to be greater than can be explained by competitive theory. They appear to result in part from distinguishing between individuals using criteria that have little or no bearing on their performance in the labor market. Why do characteristics which appear to have little to do with effective performance in the labor market influence earnings and why do the equalizing tendencies of competition, we have identified in Chapter 11, not eliminate such practices?

One explanation might be that those individual characteristics, which are the object of discrimination, are after all related in some way to productive performance. Characteristics we assumed to be irrelevant are relevant. This is the thrust of competitive theories of discrimination. The alternative explanation is that competition is effectively shut out from areas of the labor market. This explanation takes us back to the theories of internal and segmented labor markets which we examined in the previous chapter.

In this chapter we examine a number of theories which try to explain why discrimination persists in the labor markets of so many countries. We also look at the results of econometric studies which have attempted to measure the degree of discrimination that exists and, since this is an area of considerable policy concern, we shall finally examine both the innovations in legislation that have occurred in this area and the success which they have met in eliminating discriminatory practices.

DEFINING DISCRIMINATION

Discrimination takes many forms in modern society. Taken literally, the word means 'to distinguish between according to criteria that are appropriate to the choice' as such it is a task in which individuals ought frequently to be engaged. However, the term has come to assume a different meaning. In particular, it has come to mean distinguishing between individuals and acting to their detriment according to criteria that are not relevant. Characteristics that should have no bearing on the issue at hand are used as criteria for distinguishing between people, with the result that people who are identical in the relevant characteristics are treated dissimilarly. Equals are treated unequally.

Discrimination can take many forms other than a difference in wages. In the labor market it may take the form of excluding certain groups from opportunities for advancement and promotion or of confining them to certain jobs. Outside the labor market it may occur by excluding certain groups from particular educational or housing opportunites, precluding them from membership of particular institutions, or forbidding access to certain facilities. Prejudice is a precondition for the existence of discriminatory practices; discrimination is the behavioural realization or expression of such prejudice. Not all prejudice will give rise to discrimination, prejudicial feelings, desires to discriminate may remain unfulfilled. The means for their expression may not exist, perhaps because they have been prohibited by statute.

In this chapter we are concerned with labor market discrimination–with the measurable outcomes of prejudice in the labor market. In the past this has often been defined as the failure to reward equally productive workers equally. In previous chapters we have seen that there are many different ways to compensate workers of equal productivity and therefore the absence of equal wages for equally productive workers cannot be taken as *a priori* evidence of discrimination. Similarly, we have seen that there are many reasons why wages will depart from marginal product and a wage less than marginal product is therefore no longer *a priori* evidence of discrimination as was once thought. Defining discrimination as 'failure to reward workers of equal productivity equally' is moreover to focus only on the demand side of the labor market and to ignore differing supply conditions. For operational purposes this may be an appropriate procedure where it is known that supply conditions do not differ between the groups studied but it will not be appropriate in all circumstances. The most complete definition of labor market discrimination is that offered by Arrow, 'The valuation in the market place of personal characteristics of the worker that are unrelated to productivity',[1] for it incorporates both demand and supply side considerations.

Race, sex and handicap are perhaps the three characteristics that are most often singled out for differential treatment in modern labor markets, although age, religion and sexual preferences have also been the target of discriminatory treatment in some circumstances. In the following pages we focus on discrimination in the labor market on the measurable labor market outcomes of the exercise of prejudice. This is not to

---

1. Arrow, K.J. (1973) 'The theory of discrimination' in Ashenfelter, O. and Rees, A. (eds.), *Discrimination in Labor Markets*, Princeton University Press, New Jersey.

belittle the importance of discriminatory practices in other walks of life. Indeed, we have already discussed negative feedback effects in our discussion of dual labor markets in the previous chapter. This concept emphasized the way in which expected discrimination can feed back into the pre-market behavior of individuals and affect the skills and human capital that they bring to the market. Individuals might also bring different levels of human capital to the labor market because of discrimination in schooling, health or housing, because of pre-market discrimination. It is not the purpose of this chapter to explain why such pre-market differences exist, important though they undoubtedly are.

THE RELATIVE PAY OF WOMEN AND MINORITY GROUPS

First consider the relative improvement in women's earnings that has occurred in the United States over the last 170 years. From Table 13.1 it is clear that over the very long run there has been a distinct narrowing of the gap between men's and women's earnings. In 1820 women's earnings in manufacturing in the United States were in the region of 30 to 37 percent of those of men. By 1850 they had risen to around 50 percent and by 1900 to around 56 percent. The largest increase in relative earnings therefore occurred during the early stages of industrialization as the increasing use of machinery reduced the rewards to physical strength and as women's relative labor market efficiency improved with the increased division of labor. From the late nineteenth century onwards the ratio of women's to men's pay stabilized in the manufacturing sector. It has been suggested that this stabilization was because from this period onwards manufacturing sought to employ only the least skilled women. However, in this century manufacturing has employed no more than one-third of all women employees so that, although the wage gap remained constant in manufacturing

Table 13.1 Male and female earnings in the United States over the very long run

	Ratio of female to male gross earnings	
	Manufacturing	All occupations
1820	0.30–0.37	—
1850	0.46–0.50	—
1890	0.539	0.463
1900	0.56	—
1925	0.536	0.592
1950	0.537	—
1955	—	0.639

Source: Goldin, C. (1986) 'The earnings gap between male and female workers: an historical perspective', *National Bureau for Economic Research, Working Paper No. 1888.*

after 1890, the ratio of women's to men's pay in the whole economy rose from around 46 percent in 1890 to over 60 percent by 1940. It has remained there since.

The occupational distribution of both male and female employment changed during the first half of the twentieth century but the narrowing in the whole economy does not appear to have been due to this. Instead, it appears to have been due to an improvement in the relative earnings of females within occupations. This occurred as a consequence of advances in the labor market experience of women, increases in the returns to education and in the levels of educational attainment of women, and decreases in the returns to physical strength. These factors it has been suggested may have accounted for around 85 percent of the narrowing of the gap between 1890 and 1940.[2] We shall see that it is these same factors, and above all levels of human capital investment, which have been the focus of attention when explaining relative pay in the period since 1950.

Women's pay: an international perspective

In all of the advanced industrial nations women's earnings are lower than those of men. The ratio of average female earnings to average male earnings in a selection of industrialized nations is shown in Table 13.2. It is evident from Table 13.2 that there are substantial differences in the degree of inequality between countries. By 1980 women's earnings were 90 percent of those men in Sweden and over 70 percent in the remaining European countries and the USSR. However, they were little over half that of men in Japan and only around two-thirds in North America. It is clear from Table 13.2 that there were substantial advances in women's earnings relative to those of men over the 20 years to 1980 in all the countries shown save the USSR and the United States. This advance was greatest in Sweden, Australia and Britain.

Recent advances in women's pay in the United States and Britain

A notable feature of Table 13.2 is the fact that the gap between male and female earnings in the United States was unchanged over the 20 years to 1980, indeed there has been no reduction in the wage gap over the last 50 years in the United States. One reason for the stability of this gap seems to have been compositional changes. There have been two counterveiling tendencies at work in the United States. First, over the period shown, women have, typically, stayed longer in the labor market and this has facilitated advancement into higher occupations and helped raise women's relative earnings. Counteracting this has been the rapid growth in women's labor force participation which has meant many new entrants and re-entrants to the labor force. These have predominantly been women with lower than average education and fewer years of work experience than the average. Their entry has therefore acted to reduce the average years of experience and education of the total stock, and thus depress

2. See Goldin, C. (1986) 'The earnings gap between male and female workers: an historical perspective', *National Bureau for Economic Research Working Paper No. 1888*, for a full discussion of these issues.

Table 13.2 Ratio of average female earnings to average male earnings in various industrialized countries in 1960 and 1980†

	1960	1980
Sweden	0.72	0.90
France	0.64	0.71
Australia	0.59	0.75
Germany	0.65	0.72
Britain	0.61	0.79
United States	0.66	0.66
Canada	0.59	0.64
Japan	0.46	0.54
USSR	0.70	0.70

Source: Table 1 of Gunderson, M. (1989), 'Male–female wage differentials and policy responses', *Journal of Economic Literature*, **XXVII**, March, 46–72. Adapted from Mincer, J. (1985), 'Intercountry comparisons of labor force trends and of related developments: an overview', *Journal of Labor Economics*, **3**(1), January, Supplement, S1–32
† Hourly wage rates of all workers except for: Australia, weekly full-time workers; Britain, hourly manual workers; France, annual full-time workers; Sweden, hourly manufacturing.

relative earnings.[3] However, since 1980 there is evidence that in the United States the gap is beginning to narrow again. This advance in relative pay seems to have been largely confined to white women and appears to be the result of a substantial increase in the demand for this type of labor.

The position of women in Britain was remarkably similar to that in the United States prior to 1970 but since then there has been a substantial improvement in relative pay. Most of this occurred in the period to 1975, during which time both the Equal Pay Act and Sex Discrimination (Equal Opportunities) Act came into effect. Could the introduction of this legislation have produced the improvement in women's relative earnings? It is tempting to conclude that it did until we note that similar legislation, the Equal Pay Act of 1963 and Title VII of the Civil Rights Act of 1964, which prohibited all forms of discrimination in employment, had been passed a decade earlier in the United States and that these were accompanied by no improvement in women's relative earnings. These issues clearly require rather more investigation which we shall undertake later in this chapter.

3. See Smith, James P. and Ward, Michael (1989) 'Women in the labor market and in the family', *Journal of Economic Perspectives*, **3**(1), winter, 9–23.

Table 13.3 Minority group/white earnings ratios in the United States

	1939	1955–66	1967–74	1975–82
Black/White				
Men	0.45	0.62	0.68	0.73
Women	0.38	0.65	0.83	0.94
Hispanic/White				
Men	—	—	—	0.72
Women	—	—	—	0.86

Source: Cain, G.G. (1986), 'The economic analysis of labor market discrimination: a survey', in *Handbook of Labor Economics*, vol. 1, Ashenfelter, O. and Layard, P.R.G. (eds.), North Holland.

The relative pay of minority groups

Table 13.3 shows that there have been substantial advances in the relative pay of black workers in the United States since 1939. Black women's pay relative to that of white women has advanced from 0.38 in 1939 to 0.94 over the period of 1975–82. There has also been an advance in black males' pay relative to their white counterparts but this is far less substantial than for females. Over the period since 1939 it rose from 0.45 of white male rates to 0.73 over the period 1975–82. This sharp improvement in the relative pay of black women has meant a more substantial advance in the pay of black women relative to black men, than was achieved by white women relative to white men. As Table 13.4 reveals the relative pay of white women relative to white men was unchanged at 0.61 over the complete period shown. In contrast that of black women advanced from around 0.51 of black males rates in 1939 to 0.78 in 1979. It has been suggested[4] that this is due in no small part to the massive shift in the occupational distribution of black women, which occurred over this period as they moved out of domestic service. Table 13.4 reveals that this advancement was most rapid among black women who were not married. By 1979 they received some 86 percent of the pay of black males.

The relative increase in the earnings of black workers in the United States seems initially to have been due to the exodus of blacks from low income jobs in the rural South. More recently this reflects relative gains in educational attainment and perhaps health, together with access to better paid jobs. In the United Kingdom, in contrast, we have little understanding of how the relative pay of minority groups has changed over the years. One source suggests that in 1983 unskilled Asian workers earned 91 percent of their unskilled white counterparts, while the relative earnings of unskilled West Indians were 84.9 percent of whites.[5]

Ethnic minorities comprised around 4.5 percent of the population of Great Britain in 1985. Predominant among the minority groups were those of Indian, Pakistani or

4. Fuchs, V. (1986) 'His and hers: gender differences in work and income 1959–79', *Journal of Labor Economics*, **4**(3), Part 2, July.
5. McCormick, B. (1986) 'Evidence about the comparative earnings of Asian and West Indian workers in Great Britain', *Scottish Journal of Political Economy*, **33**(2), 97–110.

Table 13.4 Women's/men's earnings ratios in the
United States (hourly earnings)

	1939	1959	1969	1979
All workers				
White	0.61	0.64	0.61	0.61
Black	0.51	0.68	0.75	0.78
Married				
White	—	0.61	0.57	0.57
Black	—	0.69	0.76	0.76
Not-married				
White	—	0.81	0.77	0.75
Black	—	0.69	0.80	0.86

Source: Cain, G.G. (1986) *op. cit.* Table 13.5 and Fuchs, V.
(1986) 'His and hers: gender differences in work and income,
1959–79', *Journal of Labor Economics* **4**(3), Part 2, July.

Bangladeshi origin, who numbered over 1 million, with those of West Indian and
Guianese origin accounting for over half a million. Members of ethnic minorities
together accounted for 3.6 percent of total male employment and 3.2 percent of total
female employment in 1985. These figures should be contrasted with those for the
United States where blacks account for 8.5 percent of all recorded male employment
while Hispanics account for 5.3 percent. In the United States black women account for
10.4 percent of all female employment while Hispanics account for 4.6 percent.
However, these figures for the United States exclude illegal immigrants and are
therefore likely to substantially understate the share of Hispanics in the workforce.

ECONOMIC THEORIES OF DISCRIMINATION

How then do we account for the differences in earnings that we observe? The fact that
different individuals earn different wages should not be surprising. We have already
identified many reasons why this will occur. The theory of compensating differences
suggests that some individuals may earn more than others because they have more
education or training; because they have more experience; because they work in a less
pleasant or more hazardous environment; because they receive fewer fringe benefits;
because they have more responsibility, and so on. To date we have identified a whole
range of different influences on individuals' earnings which reflect differences in their
productivity and in their willingness to 'buy' certain commodities produced at the
workplace. One of the commodities associated with the work environment is the
company of co-workers. Where employers require some of their employees to work
alongside workers for whom they have an aversion, the employer will be required to
offer higher pay to compensate employees for this disamenity and a wage gap will
emerge. The theory of compensating differences therefore provides one possible
framework for explaining why wage discrimination may emerge in labor markets.

However, it is by no means the only one. Economic theories of labor market discrimination explore the consequences of discriminatory behavior on the part of the three major actors in the labor market: workers, employers, and those that ultimately purchase the output of labor, the customers. Below we explore theories that spell out the consequences of discriminatory behavior by each of these three groups. We start by examining the consequences of discrimination by workers.

Worker discrimination

A theoretical framework for exploring the consequences of worker discrimination is provided by the theory of equalizing differences. If employers hire groups of workers for whom existing employees have an aversion, this would constitute a deterioration in the perceived net advantages of employment for the existing workforce. A compensating wage payment would now be required by the existing workforce to insure they were no worse off and, as a result, a pay differential would emerge between existing and new workers. If the existing workers were men and the new hires women, the rates of pay for women would now be lower than those for equally productive, equally skilled men. Under these conditions higher wages will emerge if employers have no way of segregating their workforce *and* they act to retain the services of prejudiced workers.

Suppose, for example, that certain men resent 'taking orders from a woman', and when required to do so by the firm decide to quit. If the firm wishes to retain the services of these men and is unable to segregate its workforce, to avoid women supervising men, the firm may resort to paying men a higher wage than they would otherwise receive. One reason why firms might wish to retain the services of prejudiced male workers is because of the existence of transaction costs; because of the hiring and training costs, associated with finding replacements. Where transaction costs are trivial and there are equally suitable, equally qualified, female workers, who do not mind being supervised by a woman, the firm may simply let the men go and hire women in their place. The corollary of this is that if all men are similarly prejudiced we shall end up with completely segregated workplaces. Firms will employ either all men or all women but there need now be no pay differences between men and women. Provided the labor supply curves are perfectly elastic, there will be sufficient female replacements for the prejudiced men and competition will eliminate the wage gap.

The above argument proposes that pay differences only emerge between equally productive workers when some among them are prejudiced against others *and* when transaction costs are high. How important is such an explanation of discrimination? Some economists have tried to test this. One prediction that seems to emerge from the above is that if white workers are prejudiced against black workers, the wage differential which white workers will demand will be greater the more integrated the workplace. The chances that some workplaces will be integrated might reasonably be thought to be higher in those states of the United States in which there are a large number of black workers. If plants differ in degree of integration it seems to follow that the dispersion of wages among whites will be greater, once we have standardized for labor quality, in states with a large number of black workers. Some support has indeed been found for this proposition.[6]

If the underlying hypothesis, about white male tastes, on which this theory rests is correct a dispersion in white wage rates will only emerge where the costs to the firm of accommodating the white workforce's tastes for discrimination are less than the costs of discharging them and hiring a black replacement workforce. In fact firms may be able to find ways of accommodating white workers' prejudice without needing to pay a premium. They may, for example, operate a shift system, where the shifts comprise workers of only one race or they may form subgroups or teams. These alternative ways of accommodating prejudice mean that a differential may fail to emerge. However, it also follows that the absence of a correlation between wage dispersion and the incidence of black workers in the population cannot be taken as evidence of the absence of prejudice on the part or white workers.

The emergence of the wage differential above resulted from the scale of transaction costs, which made it difficult to replace the existing workforce. Similarly, either where workers possess unique skills, as occurs in internal labor markets, or where the elasticity of substitution is reduced because workers form a labor union or otherwise act in concert, discrimination in wages is more likely to exist. Necessary conditions for wage discrimination are that some employees are prejudiced and that they possess some degree of monopoly power. Monopoly power is conferred either by the possession of a unique skill, by membership of a trade union, or by transaction costs. In the absence of this monopoly power, in competitive markets, in which workers are wage takers, the theory of equalizing differences predicts that prejudiced workers will find themselves paying for the 'privilege' of working in a segregated workplace; they will received a *lower* wage than equally productive unprejudiced workers.

Customer discrimination

Are the tastes of customers likely to lead to lower wages for certain groups? If consumers express a preference for commodities produced by workers of a particular race or sex then workers from other groups would have to accept lower wages if they are to gain employment in such jobs. Alternatively, they might crowd into the remaining jobs, which would depress their wages. Historical examples are the preference of certain whites in some of the southern states of the United States for service by whites. Where such customer preferences exist, they have the effect of lowering the marginal revenue product of labor of minority workers in jobs where customer contact exists and whites are preferred. However, many jobs do not involve customer contact; this is generally true of most areas of manufacturing industry but is also true of much of the service industry. Thus the individual working as a foreign-exchange dealer, or in the head office of the insurance firm does not meet his customers. According to this theory, the marginal product of minority workers in these

6. Chiswick, B.R. (1973) 'Racial discrimination in the labour market: a test of alternative hypothesis', *Journal of Political Economy*, **81**, 1330–52.

jobs will be no lower than that of majority workers. We might expect therefore that minority workers would specialize in such jobs and avoid competing for jobs for which majority workers are preferred. If they did so in sufficient numbers they might depress wages in these non-customer contact jobs, but in fact they are few relative to the large number of jobs not requiring contacts. Note again, however, that the outcome predicted is for a degree of job segregation but not necessarily a wage premium.

It has been suggested that some evidence in support of this hypothesis is the fact that even in government departments in which we might expect the employer to indulge customer prejudice least, minority employment is concentrated in those agencies that most service minority groups.[7] Thus in the US Department of Agriculture, serving mostly white farmers, only 10 percent of the workforce are members of minorities, while the Department of Housing and Urban Development, more frequently servicing minority groups, is 27 percent minority. In the United Kingdom, the Ministry of Defence employs relatively fewer minority workers than the Department of Health and Social Security. But does this reflect the lower marginal product of minority groups when they attempt to service the white majority, or the higher marginal product of minority groups when they service the minority? It is difficult to see quite how customer prejudices will be translated into the employment practices of government departments in a modern democracy. On the other hand, it is easy to imagine how minority groups might be more productive than the majoirty in certain jobs in government departments. One example may be where minority groups comprise recent immigrants who have not mastered the majority language. Members of the same ethnic group are more likely to be able to communicate successfully with them.

Employer discrimination

The above two theories have in common that the source of discrimination is the willingness of economic agents to pay to avoid contact with members of a specific group. The same ideas have been advanced to explain employer discrimination. In this case employers have to pay, in the form of forgone profits, to indulge their taste for discrimination. However, if the product market is competitive and firms are only earning normal profits, firms are not now in a position to indulge their tastes for discrimination. Those that do will earn below normal profits and cannot stay in business in the long run. The prediction seems to emerge that a competitive market environment drives discriminating firms out of business, that is, competition eliminates discrimination. If true this is an important conclusion, indeed it carries with it an important policy prescription: to eliminate discrimination increase competition in product markets. Evidently we need to consider this theory in some more detail.

Suppose that an employer is prejudiced against black workers or, put another way, in favor of white workers. W_W in Fig. 13.1 represents the white male wage which is equal to their marginal revenue product, $W_W = MRP_{LW}$, and W_B represents the wage they are prepared to pay to blacks. Black males are as productive as white,

7. Borjas, G.J. (1982) 'The politics of employment discrimination in the federal bureaucracy', *The Journal of Law and Economics*, **25**, 251–300.

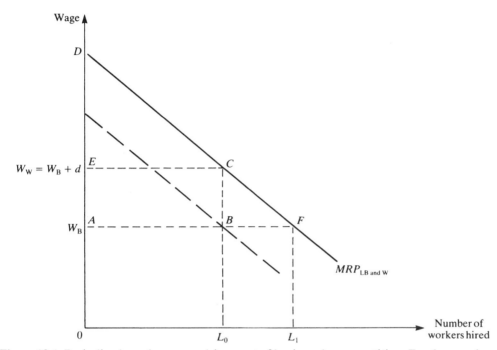

Figure 13.1 Prejudiced employers are driven out of business by competition. Employers who are prejudiced against black workers are only prepared to pay wage W_B if they employ L_0 black workers. The additional profit, represented by area $ABCE$ represents the price they would be prepared to pay to use only white workers. However, other less prejudiced firms faced with the same MRP_L curve will hire black workers up to point L_1, thereby gaining additional profits equal to area BFC. The entry of non-prejudiced firms, the consequent expansion of output and fall in product price would reduce MRP_L until it coincides with the broken line at which point all prejudiced firms have been driven out of business

$MRP_{LB} = MRP_{LW}$, but their productivity is valued less by firms who require higher profits if they are to be employed. The employer faced with a wage rate of W_B for black worker hires L_0 for at that point the marginal product of black workers will be just equal to $W_B + d$, where d represents the price that employers are willing to pay to indulge their taste for discrimination. But note the consequences of this discriminatory behavior. Employing only L_0 workers at wage W_B produces additional profits equal to the area $ABCE$ (total profits = total revenue, the area OL_0CD, minus total cost, the area OL_0BA) where the area $ABCE$ represents the extra profit they require to compensate them for hiring black workers. Alternatively, they could have hired L_0 white workers at W_W, the area of profit $ABCE$ would then be forgone, and would represent the opportunity cost, the price they paid to indulge their taste for discrimination.

However, note what happens if not all employers are equally prejudiced. Suppose that there are some who are not prejudiced at all. Now they can profit by hiring L_1 black workers at wage W_B and earn additional profits equal to area BFC. There is obviously an incentive to non-discriminatory behavior and indeed we should expect to find non-prejudiced employers entering the industry attracted in by the prospect of supernormal profits. The expansion of output in the industry would cause product prices to fall and hence reduce the profits of discriminatory firms below those they required to remain in the business. Eventually only non-discriminatory firms will remain: the discriminators would have been driven out of business.

The same results emerge if we drop the assumption that there is a uniform degree of prejudice on the part of firms and admit more realistically that the degree of prejudice, the price firms are willing to pay to indulge their taste for discrimination, d, is likely to vary. Under these circumstances the aggregate discrimination coefficient measuring the wage differential between black and white workers in the market as a whole, D, will be determined by the employers with the lowest d. Those employers with the largest taste for discrimination, paying the lowest wage to black workers of a given productivity, are not in a position to compete for black workers' services. The employer with the lowest value of d should, in the long run, determine the value of D because, as above, such employers can earn extra profits by hiring black workers at prevailing wages and, by expanding output and lowering prices, they can drive all others with a greater taste for discrimination out of business. It appears that 'only the least discriminatory firms survive.'[8] Competitive market forces compel D towards zero.

From our review of the empirical evidence it will emerge that the prediction, that competition will eliminate discriminatory wage payments, is not borne out by the facts. Substantial pay differences between blacks and whites and between men and women, who appear equal in all the relevant characteristics, still persist. How can this be? The likely explanation is that there are barriers to entry in product markets which mitigate against effective competition. For example, entrepreneurial skills, which are a cooperating factor of production, could be in inelastic supply in the long run. Alternatively, the firm may be a monopoly in the product market by reason of ownership of a unique technology. Monopolists enjoy supernormal profits and can afford to pay for discrimination. Of course, they pay for discrimination by forgoing profits and they could therefore be bought out by other firms, the owners of which do not enjoy or do not have the same taste for discrimination. Again, monopolies tend to be large firms, concerned with their reputation and for this reason they may be perhaps less likely to indulge in discriminatory practices than are other less visible firms. Theory certainly suggests that monopolies are more likely to be in a position to indulge a taste for discrimination but there are 'reasons for doubting that monopoly is a major source of marketwide discrimination'.[9]

The above theories have in common that they attribute discrimination to the 'tastes' of the workers, employers or customers. They have given the abstract concept 'prejudice' the operational definition of a taste for discrimination. Customers, workers or employers exhibiting a taste for discrimination should expect to pay a price for exercising their prejudice.

8. Arrow, K.J. (1973), *op. cit.*
9. Cain, G.G. (1976) 'The challenge of segmented labor market theories to orthodox theories: a survey', *Journal of Economic Literature*, **14**, 1215–57.

Yet the aggregate discrimination coefficient, D, is evidently not the only price of discrimination. This measure pays no attention to the pain or disutility of the victim. As one researcher emphasizes, the black insurance salesperson, who offered the same insurance policy as a white salesperson but sold and earned less because of customer prejudice, might feel worse than if he or she received less because the policy offered less coverage or smaller settlements.[10] The pay of the black worker would be lower in both cases but the utility associated with these lower earnings would also be less in the former case.

Supply side differences

Discrimination in each of the above theories arose because of factors on the demand side of the labor market. Discrimination reflected the willingness of economic agents to pay to avoid contact with members of a specific group. In each case the wages of the minority group differed from the value that a non-discriminatory or objective evaluation of their marginal product would warrant. A more general theory, which again suggests that workers are paid less than their marginal products, has been utilized by some economists to explain male/female earnings differences. More properly described as a theory of '*exploitation*' rather than a theory of discrimination it explains earnings differences by reference to differences on the supply side of the labor market. Specifically, in an attempt to explain earnings differences between males and females, it proposes that the labor supply curve of women is more inelastic than that of men with the result that, confronted by a single buyer of labor—a monopsonist—women are paid less than men. Monopsony can arise either because there is only one buyer of labor or because several employers collude to act in this manner.

Consider this situation which is illustrated in Fig. 13.2. The single buyer of labor confronted by the upward sloping supply curve for male labor in this labor market, S_M, is concious that the marginal cost of employing additional men, exceeds the wage paid to the marginal man, as indicated by the supply curve, for now the same wage must be generalized to all existing employees. Accordingly, the buyer of labor perceives that a marginal labor cost schedule MLC_M bisects the area above the male labor supply curve. A profit maximizing monopsonist employing only men would equate MC to MR, that is equate the marginal labor cost MLC_M to the marginal revenue product of labor, MRP_L but only pay a wage equal to labor's supply price. (Such a point is not shown in Fig. 13.2, but may easily be found.) Under these circumstances the wage paid is lower than that which would occur under competitive conditions. In a monopsonistic market such as this employees are paid a wage which is less than their marginal revenue product, hence the origin of the notion that labor is being exploited.

Now suppose that the elasticity of labor supply for women differs from that for men, specifically that the labor supply curve for women, S_W, is less elastic than that for men. Associated with the female supply schedule is a differently sloped marginal labor cost schedule, MLC_W, again shown in Fig. 13.2. Now a profit maximizing monopsonist employing both men and women will ensure that $MLC_M = MLC_W = MRP_L$, where

---

10. Cain, G.G. (1976), *op. cit.*

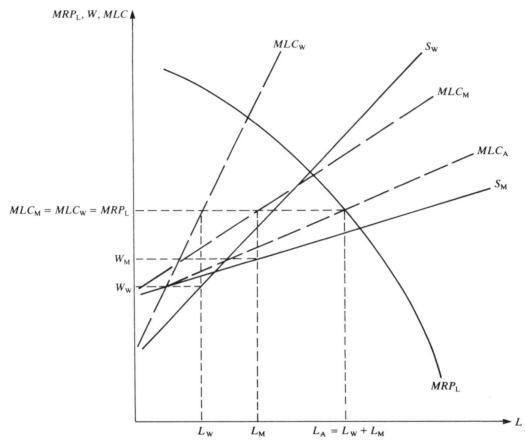

Figure 13.2 Differing supply elasticities result in different wages where the firm is a monopsonist. A monopsonist is confronted by two groups of workers, men and women, with different supply elasticities. The monopsonist recognizes that it is therefore confronted with two quite differently sloped marginal labor costs, MLC, schedules. For profit maximization it takes employment up to the point at which $MLC_M = MLC_W = MRP_L$ as shown by the point at which MRP_L and MLC_A (the marginal labor cost schedule for all workers) intersect. Application of this rule results in L_W women and L_M men being employed but, because the firm pays each group of workers a wage only equal to their supply price, it pays W_W to women, and W_M to men. Because women's labor supply is less elastic than that of men they receive a lower wage. A wage differential $W_M - W_W$ emerges if monopsonists exploit their monopsonistic power

both men and women are equally productive. This is shown in Fig. 13.2 by the point at which the combined marginal wage cost schedule, MLC_A, in Fig. 13.2 cuts the MRP_L curve. Since $MLC_M = MLC_W$, L_W women and L_M men are employed resulting in L_A employment in total. But, of course, each group is only paid its supply price and therefore women are paid wage W_W and men the higher wage W_M. Thus under conditions of monopsony, differing supply elasticities for men and women, or indeed for white and black workers, can give rise to a wage differential. In order to explain the empirical observation that blacks and women are paid less than white males this explanation requires that the supply elasticities of the former two groups are less than that of the latter.

How convincing is this as an explanation of wage discrimination? There is some evidence to suggest that female labor supply is less elastic than that of males reflecting their rather more restricted mobility,[11] but this relative immobility seldom combines with a market dominated by a single buyer of labor. Indeed, as transport facilities have in general improved, the extent to which single employers can be said to dominate particular labor markets has generally decreased. Women's labor supply may be relatively less elastic than men's but they are still able to search beyond the boundaries of areas dominated by single employers. Only in the public sector does there appear to be any exercise of substantial monopsonistic power. In the United Kingdom the government is the sole buyer of police officers' and firemen's skills, and until recently of nurses' and physicians' skills. They were thus in a position to exercise a degree of monopsonistic power. However, a restriction was placed on the exercise of this monopsony power early on for the public sector awarded equal pay to men and women. In the United States the labor markets, in which the government or a single firm is the sole purchaser of a single class of labor, are extremely rare. Save in certain specialist skills required in the armed forces, nuclear submarine operators and astronauts, there are few examples. For these reasons monopsony is unlikely to be an important source of pay discrimination.

Statistical theories of discrimination[12]

Discrimination may derive from imperfections of information in the labor market. In all of the above examples of discrimination, as opposed to exploitation, we suggested that unequal pay arose because of differences in taste as a result of the expression of prejudice on the part of either co-workers, customers or firms. It has also been suggested that discrimination might arise as a consequence of the procedures adopted by firms to assess the productivity of potential employees in a world of imperfect information. These have been called statistical theories of discrimination.

In all of the above examples the true productivity of workers was known to the firm. Suppose, however, that only the average productivity, $\bar{\alpha}$, of a group is known and that the true productivity of individual members of this group, g, is normally distributed around this mean value so that for any individual $g_i = \bar{\alpha} + u_i$ where u_i represents a normally distributed error term with expected mean $E(u) = 0$ and variance $V(u) = \sigma^2$. Under these circumstances each worker will be paid wages equal to the mean value of productivity, $W = \bar{\alpha}$, for the group as a whole with the result that some will be underpaid and others overpaid. However, on average, wages will equal marginal

11. Reagan, R.B. (1978) 'Two supply curves for economists? Implications of mobility and career attachment of women', *American Economic Review*, **65**, 100–7.
12. This section follows the approach of Aigner, D. and Cain, G.G. (1977) 'Statistical theories of discrimination in labor markets', *Industrial and Labor Relations Review*, **30**, 175–87 who develop the approach of Phelps, E.S. (1972) 'The statistical theory of racism and sexism', *American Economic Review*, **62**, 659–61.

product. In a world of imperfect information employers may well judge workers by group rather than individual characteristics. It may be too costly to distinguish exactly the precise productive characteristics of each individual.

Now suppose the wages of two groups are each related to $\bar{\alpha}$ but that on average the productivity of the majority, called whites, is greater than that of the minority of black workers $\bar{\alpha}_W > \bar{\alpha}_B$, then $W_W = \bar{\alpha}_W$ and $W_B = \bar{\alpha}_B$ and $W_W > W_B$. There is no group discrimination because in each case $E(W) = 0$, but there is individual discrimination, because in each group $g_i = \bar{\alpha} + u_i$. If the distributions of productivity are sufficiently close that they overlap, as illustrated in Fig. 13.3, equally productive workers are paid unequally. Black workers of productivity level g_i receive lower wages than white workers of equal productivity. Indeed all those black workers in the shaded upper tail of the distribution receive lower wages than some equally productive whites in the lower tail of the white distribution.

This form of statistical discrimination arises for two reasons. First, a difference in the average levels of productivity $\bar{\alpha}$ and hence in the levels of pay for the groups in question. It is obvious from Fig. 13.3 that if the means and variances of the distributions of productivity for blacks and whites were identical there would be no group discrimination. Individual discrimination would still exist but it would not differ in degree between blacks and whites, for some members of both groups would not be paid a wage equal to their marginal product. Second, statistical discrimination depends on the variance of individual productivity. Thus, suppose that the dispersion of productive ability were much greater among blacks than among whites, so that the

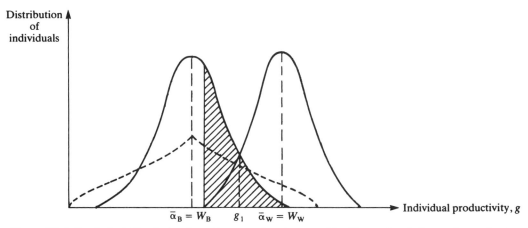

Figure 13.3 Statistical discrimination. Suppose that in a world of imperfect information only the average productivity, $\bar{\alpha}$, of each of the two groups of workers, blacks, B, and whites, W, is known and that $\bar{\alpha}_W > \bar{\alpha}_B$. Suppose further that productive ability is normally distributed around each of these two means as shown in the figure. If each member of the group is paid a wage equal to mean productivity for that group, $W_W > W_B$, those workers in the shaded upper tail of the lower distribution receive lower wages than some equally productive workers in the lower tail of the upper distribution

distribution was as shown by the broken line in Fig 13.3, now a larger proportion of blacks would have productivity at least equal to some whites but still receive lower pay.

There is in addition to the above a third source of statistical discrimination—differences in the reliability with which the productivity of individual members of this group, g, is measured. In the above examples g_i was equal to $\overline{\alpha} + u_i$ but suppose that in addition to basing g on $\overline{\alpha}$, g is also estimated, $E(g)_i$, by the individual's performance in some test, Y. The degree to which performance in this test accurately distinguishes the individual's true productivity, g, is called β. β may be thought of as the coefficient of determination, the R^2, between g and Y. If $\beta = 1$, Y is a thoroughly reliable test and we would expect employers to place all the weight on this test and none on $\overline{\alpha}$, in which case $W_i = g_i = Y$ and pay would advance in line with Y up the 45° line in Fig. 13.4(a). In the more probable case where $0 < \beta < 1$ we should expect them to place some weight on individual test scores and some on the mean productivity of the group as a whole when estimating individual productivity. Thus where $0 < \beta < 1$

$$W_i = E(g)_i = (1 - \beta)\overline{\alpha} + \beta Y_i + u_i \tag{13.1}$$

If, as postulated above, $\overline{\alpha}_W > \overline{\alpha}_B$ the situation will be as depicted in Fig. 13.4(b) but again there is no group discrimination if the test has the same degree of accuracy for both groups, that is if $\beta_W = \beta_B$, and pay advances with Y at the same pace in both groups.

However, consider what happens if the reliability with which Y measures g differs between the two groups. The more reliable the test the more individuals' productivity and pay is determined by Y; the less reliable it is the more weight is given to the average productivity of the group as a whole, $\overline{\alpha}$. Suppose now that the variance of true individual productivity is the same for both the majority and minority groups but that the test is *more* unreliable for the minority group, then $\beta_W > \beta_B$ and it follows that

$$W_W - W_B = (Y - \overline{\alpha})(\beta_W - \beta_B) \tag{13.2}$$

For a given Y score, majority white workers will now receive a higher wage than minority black workers for Y scores above the mean, $\overline{\alpha}$, but they will also receive lower wages for Y scores below the mean. This is illustrated in Fig. 13.4(c) in the steeper slope of the function for whites. Note, however, that group discrimination, defined as an $E(W_W - W_B) > 0$, is still not present. For every member of the minority group who is underpaid there are an equal number who are overpaid and this is equally true of the majority group.

As an example suppose that an employer discriminates between men and women according to the employer's current expectations of the lifetime labor force participation of both groups. On the basis of this expectation the employer decides to train members of one group and not the other, because it is anticipated that the firm is less likely to recoup its investment from the group with the lowest participation. If the mean productivity, $\overline{\alpha}$, differs between the two groups, different wages will be paid to members of each group to reflect this. However, some among the women are likely to exhibit greater lifetime labor force attachment and greater productivity than some men and will thus be underpaid, but equally, some women may exhibit far less attachment than was expected and will accordingly be overpaid, as indeed will some men.

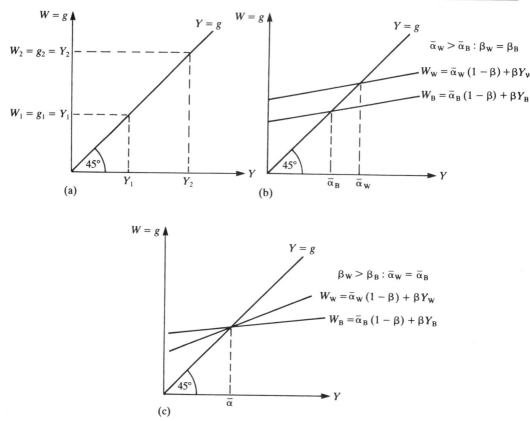

Figure 13.4 Individual wage discrimination results from imperfect measurement of productivity. Statistical theories of discrimination provide an explanation of individual wage discrimination but not of group wage discrimination. (a) If Y provides a measure of individual productivity, g, wages will advance in line with Y only if a test accurately distinguishes individuals' true productivity. (b) The accuracy of the test, β, is < 1 but $\beta_W = \beta_B$ so that while Y measures productivity, g, inaccurately, it does so with the same degree of inaccuracy for both groups. The resulting difference in mean earnings reflects the difference in perceived group productivity, $\bar{\alpha}_W > \bar{\alpha}_B$, but there is no group discrimination, only individual discrimination. (c) If $\beta_W > \beta_B$ but there is no perceived difference in group productivity, $\bar{\alpha}_B = \bar{\alpha}_W$. There will again be differences in individual pay, but in this case not in average pay. Note that in both (b) and (c) as many of each group were paid wages above the group mean as were paid wages below.

Provided the wage accurately reflects the average productivity of the group as a whole there is no group discrimination only individual discrimination.

The model can, however offer an explanation for group discrimination. This occurs when the reliability of the indicator, β, affects the average wage. Suppose that the more unreliable the indicator the lower the perceived mean productivity, $\bar{\alpha}$, and the lower the wage. In Fig. 13.4(c) this would mean that as β reduces, becomes more unreliable, $\bar{\alpha}$ shifts down. Then the functions W_W and W_B would no longer intersect at the same point on the 45° line. Now workers are being rewarded both for their productivity and for the reliability with which they signal this to employers: workers are being rewarded for providing better information. Such a situation is unlikely to persist in the long run, since some productive workers are not being hired only because they have failed to provide employers with accurate information about their productivity. Employees now have an incentive to devise new and more efficient methods of signaling their productivity. Indeed the state might also take a hand in certifying workers to ensure that they transmit more accurate signals, while individuals could offer trial periods to employers during which time they could demonstrate their true productivity.

Statistical theories of discrimination therefore explain individual discrimination but are unlikely to explain group discrimination. If, in general, women are paid less than men it will not be due to statistical discrimination. Statistical discrimination explains why, when there is a dispersion of productivity around the mean, individuals of equal productivity will be paid differently. Essential to an explanation of group discrimination is an explanation of why employers believe mean productivity differs and hence pay different wages. It may indeed be that 'true' productivity differs, in which case the elimination of wage differences requires the elimination of these productivity differences, whether they arise because of differences in pre- or in-market behavior. A more likely explanation is that, in spite of evidence to the contrary, employers behave as if they believe there is a difference in productivity. We are, in other words, back to employer prejudice. Competition restricts the degree to which this can be exercised and, in the limit, eliminates it entirely, but an absence of competition facilitates it.

METHODOLOGICAL PROBLEMS

How much of the difference in earnings that we observe between the different races and sexes is accounted for by discrimination? This is the question that several studies have set out to explain. The starting point for most of these is the human capital earnings function we detailed in Chapter 6, Eq. (6.11), where:

$$\log W/P_1 = a_1 + a_2 I_i + a_3 I_i^2 + a_4 X_i + \varepsilon_i \tag{13.3}$$

where a_1 represents the log of earnings when there has been no additional investment in human capital, I the years of investment in human capital, most simply captured by years of schooling, I^2 captures non-linearities in these effects and X_i represents a range of additional variables measuring individual productive characteristics and the pecuniary and non-pecuniary aspects of the workplace. How can such an equation be adapted to measure discrimination?

The most obvious and straightforward approach is to add a dummy variable, $Z = 1$, to indicate membership of the minority group so that Eq. (13.1) becomes:

$$\log W/P_i = a_1 Z + a_2 I_i + a_3 I_i^2 + a_4 X_i + \varepsilon_i \tag{13.4}$$

Such a technique has the effect of changing, in this case it is presumed to shift down, the intercept term for the minority groups. Thus, a_1 on Z indicates whether membership of the minority group, in the absence of any investment in human capital and holding all other individual and workplace characteristics constant, results in lower earnings. A coefficient $a_1 > 0$ would be taken to be evidence of discrimination and $a_1 = 0$ to indicate its absence. However, this approach is too simple for it does not allow for interactions between membership of a minority group and the other human capital, individual and workplace characteristics for which we are controlling. Minority groups, for example, may well receive lower returns to any given increment to human capital, lower returns to experience, or to danger at the workplace. In this case the coefficients on some of the other variables will also differ for the minority group. Accordingly, the general approach has been to estimate separate human capital earnings functions for each of the different groups and to evaluate both the differences in coefficients and the intercepts for each group. Thus if we take separate earnings equations for whites and blacks so that:

$$\log W/P_W = a_{1W} + a_{2W}C_W + \varepsilon_W \tag{13.5}$$

$$\log W/P_B = a_{1B} + a_{2B}C_B + \varepsilon_B \tag{13.6}$$

where, for simplicity, the range of various human capital and additional individual productivity enhancing and workplace characteristics are summarized by C, and W/P_W and W/P_B represent the mean wages for whites and blacks, respectively, this facilitates a decomposition of the difference in mean wages between the two groups into: (i) the unexplained element represented by differences in the intercept terms; (ii) differences in either the type or level of human capital endowments and individual and workplace characteristics; and (iii) differences due to differing rewards for each of the measured endowments and characteristics. This can be accomplished by adding the term $a_{2W}C_B$ to both Eqs. (13.5) and (13.6) and subtracting Eq. (13.6) from Eq. (13.5) to obtain

$$\log W/P_W - W/P_B = (a_{1W} - a_{1B}) + a_{2W}(C_W - C_B) + C_B(a_{2W} - a_{2B}) \dots \tag{13.7}$$

The terms in Eq. (13.7) can then be interpreted as follows and are illustrated in Fig. 13.5. First, the term $a_{2W}(C_W - C_B)$ in Eq. (13.7) measures the differences in the mean values of all the variables in C when these are valued at whites' prices (a_{2W}), that is according to the rewards that are secured by whites who possess or experience these. This term captures that part of the difference in earnings that is due to differences between the two groups in human capital endowments and other measurably different productive characteristics and to differences in work environments $(C_W - C_B)$, and it values each of these at the prices received for them by whites a_{2W}. Second, the term $C_B(a_{2W} - a_{2B})$ measures the higher prices $(a_{2W} - a_{2B})$, that whites receive, for any of these measured characteristics (reflected in the steeper slope of the earnings function in Fig. 13.5) and thus provides a measure of the proximate sources of discrimination. Finally, the term $(a_{1W} - a_{1B})$, the intercept term in Fig. 13.5, represents a measure of our ignorance: it is the unexplained part of the difference in earnings. Discrimination, D, is then normally measured as $D_1 = (a_{1W} - a_{1B}) + C_B(a_{2W} - a_{2B})$, the sum of the explained and unexplained elements.

The interpretation of the term $a_{2W}(C_W - C_B)$ is by no means unambiguous. The reason why the groups exhibit different workplace or individual characteristics may itself be due to pre-market discrimination. Nor does this decomposition provide a unique measure of discrimination. We could equally have added $a_{2B}C_W$ to both equations which would have enabled us to evaluate each of the characteristics $(C_W - C_B)$ at the prices received by blacks. As is clearly illustrated in Fig. 13.5 this would give us a lower estimate, $a_{2B}(C_W - C_B)$, of the difference in earnings attributable

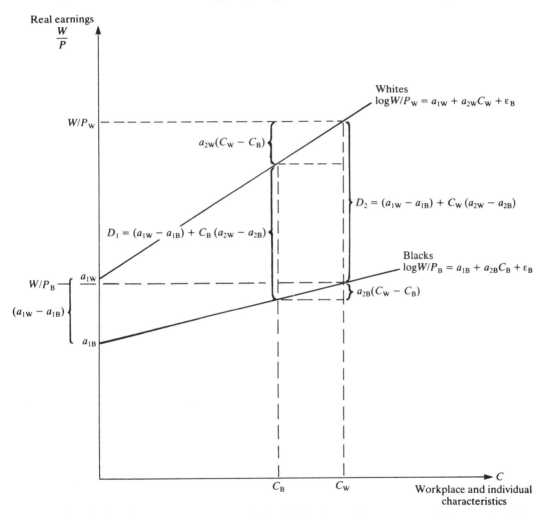

Figure 13.5 Estimating the magnitude of discrimination using augmented human capital earnings functions. The difference in earnings between blacks and whites is due to: (i) the difference in measured productive characteristics $(C_W - C_B)$; (ii) the difference in the intercept $(a_{1W} - a_{1B})$; and (iii) the higher prices that the whites receive for any given characteristic $(a_{2W} - a_{2B})$. The measure of discrimination, D, which is equal to $(a_{1W} - a_{1B}) + C(a_{2W} - a_{2B})$, will differ according to whether we evaluate the differences in characteristics at black or white prices. If these prices are the same, if $a_{2W} = a_{2B}$, discrimination is measured by $(a_{1W} - a_{1B})$ and the source of this is unknown

to the difference in characteristics and because the intercept term $(a_{1W} - a_{1B})$, the unexplained element, would remain unchanged, there would be a correspondingly larger element attributed to the difference in prices, that is to $C_W(a_{2W} - a_{2B})$ as is clear from Fig. 13.5. Accordingly, this second estimate of discrimination, D_2, would be greater than in the first case. Evidently it matters whether we estimate the magnitude of discrimination using the first or second approach, for if the whites' earnings function lies above that of blacks and the slope of the whites' function exceeds that of blacks the second approach will always produce a larger estimate of discrimination than will the first. For this reason many investigators provide estimates of the magnitude of discrimination using both approaches.

One way of tackling the problem, of which prices to use, is to evaluate the differences in the C's at some average of black and white prices. But there is no right answer for we have touched upon the familiar index-number problem which we encounter whenever we sum heterogeneous characteristics (C's) with different sets of prices ($a_{2'}s$). Of course, if there were no difference in prices, if $a_{2W} = a_{2B}$, then the source of discrimination would be unknown for it would reduce to $(a_{1W} - a_{1B})$, the difference in the intercept terms.

Whichever approach is adopted, if we are to have confidence in the resulting estimates of the magnitude of discrimination, it is essential that each of the measured human capital, productivity and workplace characteristics be exogenous. Otherwise the values that they take for each group might themselves reflect the outcome of discrimination and the difference in the coefficients will then no longer provide an accurate measure of the degree of discrimination.

EMPIRICAL ESTIMATES OF LABOR MARKET DISCRIMINATION

What does the empirical evidence reveal about the causes of the lower pay of minority groups and women in various countries? Consider first the explanation for earnings differences offered by the human capital model. If minority groups and women have a relatively lower level of educational attainment or training than white men, we would expect this to result in lower relative earnings. In turn this might reflect either a lower demand by such individuals for these productivity enhancing characteristics or a reduced capacity to undertake such investment. Women or minority groups might undertake less human capital investment because they expect to remain in the labor market for a shorter period than white males or because they anticipate experiencing discrimination.

Historically the market-working life of women has been shorter than that of men, accordingly they have a shorter period over which to amortize the costs of any human capital investment, and thus a smaller incentive to undertake such investment. Thus in 1970 the expected working life of women in the United States was 22.9 years compared with 40.2 for men. It is important to note, however, that expected working life can well diverge from actual. Thus in the United States in 1968 a sample of young women, aged 14 to 24, were asked whether they believed they would be in the labor force at age 35. Only 29 percent of whites and 59 percent of black women thought they would. By the mid-1980s more than half of this group had reached 35 and their labor force participation by then exceeded 60 percent. Their estimates of their labor force participation provided when they were young were in line with the labor force participation rates of their mothers. This emphasizes the role that older generations play in shaping the expectations, socializing, of the young. Evidently their expectations were well below their eventual labor force participation but it is their expectations that will have influenced the amount of human capital investment they undertook. However, there is evidence that things are changing, for a similar question asked of young women some five years later produced answers which more accurately predicted their actual labor market participation.

The role of expectations in explaining the different human capital endowments of women and minority groups is critical. There is evidence that US blacks invest less in education because they expect to be discriminated against in hiring. In the early 1970s in the United States the average years of education were 12.9 years for white males but were only 11.8 years for blacks.[13] It is also, on the face of it, surprising to find that single women are only earning 65 percent of the average for men, when we consider that they are not raising children, work as many hours as men and exhibit equal levels of labor force attachment. However, if these women expected to marry and have children, or for other reasons expected to participate less, this will have influenced their human capital investment decisions. In the past, it has been suggested that, because most young women expected to be mothers they were less willing to experience the long hours and rigorous apprenticeships in medicine, law, business and other financially rewarding occupations. If either through informed choice, social pressure or compulsion women or blacks are channeled into certain careers, this could give rise to the crowding of women and blacks into certain jobs with a consequent depression of the wage rate.[14] Moreover, there is evidence of dissatisfaction with these outcomes for there is a feedback from low wages to decisions to quit the labor force.[15] Again there is evidence that the difference between men and women in these respects is narrowing. More women plan to remain childless, smaller families are planned and fewer hours are expected to be devoted to raising the family.[16] Also, certain types of legislation have been designed to alter the expectations of minority groups and women by positively discriminating in their favor.

Differences in the human capital endowments that individuals bring to the labor market may be a product of differences in expectations and pre-market discrimination. Discrimination in housing allocation or in educational opportunity, if experienced by blacks or single parent families, may mean that the products of such families enter the labor market substantially less well placed than their white or

13. Corcoran, M. and Duncan, G.J. (1979) 'Work history, labour force attachment and earnings differences between races and sexes', *The Journal of Human Resources*, **4**, 320.
14. Fuchs, Victor R. (1989) argues that there are 'powerful forces rooted in biology and culture' that explain the occupational segregation of women. Socialization 'affects occupational segregation through the choice of subjects in school, the patterns of extracurricular activities and the goals one sets'. See 'Women's quest for economic equality', *Journal of Economic Perspective*, **3**(1), winter, 25–41.
15. Gronau, R. (1988) 'Sex related wage differentials and women's interrupted labor careers—the chicken or the egg?', *Journal of Labor Economics*, **6**(3), 277–301.
16. Fuchs, Victor R. (1989), *op. cit.*

two-parent counterparts. Past discrimination in the labor market and consequent lower earnings may also result in such families being less able to support their children through school. Cycles of discrimination and deprivation may emerge and the importance of these aspects has been demonstrated in the United States.[17] Educational attainment and post-school educational investment are strongly correlated with socioeconomic group (SEG), the lower the SEG the lower the educational attainment. Largely for this reason substituting indicators of black socioeconomic background into human capital equations explaining the earnings of whites has been shown to account for up to three-quarters of inter-racial differences in lifetime earnings. Whatever the reasons for differences in human capital endowments the human capital model predicts that these differences in endowments will lead to differences in earnings.

If fewer women and minority groups have invested in human capital in the past, the rates of return to human capital for women and minority groups in the United States and the United Kingdom may be higher than those for males. Indeed, one study has suggested this.[18] However, other studies have suggested that the returns are lower. One study suggested that in the United States each unit of college training produced earnings for women that were 15 percent less than those for males with equivalent training. The same study also suggested that the returns from education enjoyed by women were lower than those of men in Australia and Britain, but that the returns were only 9 percent lower in Australia and a mere 4 percent in Britain.[19]

However, if investment in human capital is measured simply by years of schooling there are no significant differences between men and women in the United States,[20] while in the United Kingdom the years of schooling of minority groups exceed those of white males.[21] For this reason the recent focus has been on the quality of education received by the various groups and on the choice of subjects studied.[22] Women, it has been argued, 'have traditionally chosen majors such as education, arts and humanities which have lower pecuniary returns than subjects such as business and services',[23] while minority groups receive inferior education. Evidence for this has been lower educational expenditure per pupil but this may be a very poor indicator of educational quality.

Women and minority groups may also receive less on-the-job training and accumulate less experience. If women expect to remain in the labor market for a

17. King, A.G. and Knapp, C.B. (1978) 'Race and determinants of lifetime earnings', *Industrial and Labor Relations*, **31**, 347–56.
18. Gwartney, J.D. and Long, J.E. (1978) 'The relative earnings of blacks and other minorities', *Industrial and Labor Relations Review*, **3**, 336–46 and Greenhalgh, C. (1980) 'Male–female wage differentials in Great Britain: is marriage an equal opportunity?', *Economic Journal*, **90**, 751–75.
19. Gregory, R.A. and Ho, V. (1986) 'Equal pay and comparable worth: what can the US learn from the Australian experience?', Australian National University, Discussion Paper No. 123.
20. Corcoran, M. and Duncan, G.J. (1979), *op. cit.*
21. MacNabb, R. and Psacharopolous, G. (1981) 'Racial earnings differentials in the UK', *Oxford Economic Papers*, **33** 413–25.
22. Welch, F. (1973) 'Black–white wage differences in the returns to schooling', *American Economic Review*, **63**, 192–5.
23. O'Neil, J. (1983) 'The trend in sex differentials in wages', Conference on Trends in Women's Work, Education and Family Building, Urban Institute, Washington DC.

shorter period than males, they might undertake less on-the-job investment than males.[24] Of course, the corollary of this, as our model of specific training in Chapters 6 and 9 illustrates, is that we should then expect to observe higher earnings on the part of females at the time when males were investing in specific skills. Young women's rates of pay ought, *ceteris paribus*, to be higher than those of young males but again there is no evidence for this. Yet, there are distinct differences between the years of on-the-job training and years of experience possessed by females and minority groups on the one hand, and white males on the other, in both the United Kingdom and the United States. Researchers in both countries have suggested that these differences explain an important part of the differences in earnings between these groups.[25]

Differential acquisition of on-the-job training and employment experience may in itself reflect the outcome of discrimination if employers are more reluctant to bear their part of the costs of training women and minority workers or they operate a last in, first out practice. The job matching literature, which we referred to in the previous chapter, lays emphasis on the search by firms for individuals suitable for training. If firms and not workers are the central decision making agents, when it comes to investing in on-the-job training, this may act to the disadvantage of women and minority groups.

One further strand to the human capital argument remains to be examined. Childbearing, exclusively, and childrearing, predominantly, have traditionally been considered to be the responsibility of women. This raises the question—could the human capital acquired by women deteriorate during their absence from the labor market and, if so, might women not choose occupations in which these effects were least marked? Initial research seemed to confirm that this depreciation occurred[26] but other research in the United Kingdom and the United States suggests that the effects may be slight.[27] However, it is not just total time out of the labor market which affects earnings, both the timing and frequency of these spells influence earnings and occupational choice.[28] In the United Kingdom the frequency of these spells is reducing as family size decreases, also women's age, at the time of the first withdrawal from the labor force and at the birth of the first child, is rising. The result is more continuous labor market attachment and a larger initial period in the labor market in which to invest in human capital. Nonetheless, in the United Kingdom the effects of family formation still manifest themselves in a career break and reduced participation upon return to work. Upon return many women secure only part-time employment and experience downward occupational mobility. It has been estimated that these two

24. This argument was first advanced in the seminal study by Mincer, J. and Polachek, S. (1974) 'Family investments in human capital: Earnings of women', *Journal of Political Economy*, **82**(2), Pt 2, S76–S108.
25. Duncan, G.J. and Hoffman, S. (1979) 'On-the-job training and earnings differences by race and sex', *Review of Economics and Statistics*, **61**, 594–603 and MacNabb, and Psacharopolous (1981), *op. cit.* and Greenhalgh, C. (1980), *op. cit.*
26. Mincer, J. and Polachek, S. (1974), *op. cit.*
27. Turnbull, P. and Williams, G. (1974) 'Sex differences in teachers' pay', *Journal of the Royal Statistical Society Series A*, **37**, 245–58 for the United Kingdom and Corcoran, M. and Duncan, G.J. (1979), *op. cit.* for the United States.
28. Polachek, S. (1981) 'Occupational self-selection: a human capital approach to sex differences in occupational structure', *Review of Economics and Statistics*, **63**, 60–9.

effects depress women's lifetime earnings, on average, by between 25 and 50 percent.[29] Similar effects are evident in the United States, but here the labor force attachment of black women is superior to that of white women, not least because of the low earnings of black men.

The dual responsibilities of married women in the labor market and at home appear to play an important part in explaining the earnings differences between men and women. It has, for example, been suggested that married women spend less energy on each hour of market work, than do married men working the same hours, and this results in lower wages.[30] The traditional division of labor in the household, means that women working in the labor market may be less flexible than men because of the considerably greater demands on their time. They may be able to offer fewer hours of work than men, less able to stay late at the office or work a weekend and less able to undertake travel associated with work. They may look for jobs nearer to home or jobs that offer hours that coincide with work in the family. These are factors that have been offered to explain the rapid growth of part-time employment in Britain. The hours of such jobs frequently coincide with hours during which children are in school.

A further determinant of the nature of women's labor supply is the fact that they are rarely the principal income earners in the family. In 1980 only 7 percent of wives earned more than their husbands in Britain. Those earning a higher hourly rate were considerably more numerous, 15 percent, because in Britain many women work part-time. By comparison 22 percent of wives earned more than their husbands per hour in the United States in 1979 and there is only a small fall to 18.9 percent when we compare the total income of husbands and wives in the United States.[31] These figures do not take into account lifetime labor force participation and do not therefore reflect relative lifetime earnings. On this measure an even smaller proportion of wives would earn an income which exceeded that of their husbands. It is perhaps for this reason that the labor markets in which the family members operate generally reflect the husband's career decisions. The labor market in which the woman finds herself, and which constrains her job choices, has usually been determined by the career decisions of her husband. Women are therefore left to optimize within the restricted set of opportunities that the husband's job location has determined.

Implicit in the human capital approach is the notion that years of schooling or experience will be rewarded in all jobs. But although women and minority groups may have less human capital investment this need not be relevant to some jobs. Absence of human capital may explain why minority workers occupy some jobs, say hamburger flippers or garbage collectors, but it need not place them at an earnings disadvantage relative to white workers in these jobs. The usual regression procedure in which years of schooling or labor market experience are entered to explain earnings, will assign a

29. See Joshi, H. (1984) *Women's Participation in Paid Work*, Department of Employment, London and Cain, G.G. (1984) 'Lifetime measures of labor supply of men and women', Discussion Paper 749–84, Institute for Research on Poverty, University of Wisconsin-Maddison.
30. Becker, G.S. (1985) 'Human capital, effort and the sexual division of labor', *Journal of Labor Economics*, **3**, (Supplement), January S33–S58.
31. See Table 6, Fuchs, V. (1986) 'His and hers: gender differences in work and income, 1959–79', *Journal of Labor Economics*, **4(3)**, Part 2, July, for the United States and Martin, J. and Roberts, C. (1984) *Women and Employment: A Lifetime Perspective*, p. 99 for Britain.

lower predicted wage to minority workers in these unskilled jobs. However, this only serves to mask actual discrimination, for in these jobs years of schooling and labor market attachment are unlikely to be valid proxies for productivity.

PUBLIC POLICY

In the United States the *Equal Pay Act of 1963*, passed as an amendment to the Fair Labor Standards Act, outlawed separate pay scales for men and women employing similar skills and working under similar conditions. Over a decade later a similar Act, the *Equal Pay Act*, came into full effect in the United Kingdom. Passed into law in 1970, the UK Act allowed a five-year transitional period during which time female rates of pay were to be brought into line with those of males.

Without accommodating changes elsewhere in the labor market such legislation alone would have proved inadequate, for by raising the price of female labor, relative to that of men, it might have restricted women's access to jobs. Accordingly, the legislation was soon accompanied by further statutes designed to produce equal opportunities for women. In the US *Title VII of the Civil Rights Act of 1964*, effective 1 July 1965, made it unlawful for an employer 'to refuse to hire or to discharge any individual or otherwise discriminate against with respect to his compensation terms, conditions or privileges of employment because of such individual's race, color, sex, religion or national origin'. It was enforced by the Equal Employment Opportunity Commission, EEOC, which from 1972 could bring suits itself while individual plaintiffs could expand their suits into 'class actions'. In the United Kingdom the *Sex Discrimination Act*, effective in 1975, also provided for equality of labor market opportunity. Administered by the Equal Opportunities Commission (EOC), it made it unlawful to discriminate on grounds of sex against a person in relation to employment and other fields. At this time the *Employment Protection Act* (1975) gave statutory maternity pay and job reinstatement rights to women in the United Kingdom who met certain qualifying conditions. The consequence of this legislation in the United Kingdom and the United States was to rule out differences in supply elasticities as a reason for different rates of pay.

The improvement in black/white earnings differences in the United States has been most marked in the case of black females and this has been attributed, at least in part, to the passage and subsequent strengthening of the Civil Rights Act and particularly to the introduction of *Affirmative Action*.[32] Introduced in the United States in 1965, the Office of Federal Contract Compliance Programs (OFCC) required contractors above a certain size, supplying goods or services to the federal government, to develop plans to increase their utilization of women and minority labor and to set targets for the employment of these groups. Such plans related to both hiring and promotion practices and were enforced by the threat of cancellation of federal contracts. The existence of affirmative action quotas for minority workers worked to the benefit

---

32. See Leonard, J.S. (1984) 'The impact of affirmative action on employment', *Journal of Labor Economics*, 1(4), 439–63 and Brown, C. (1982) 'The federal attack on labor market discrimination: the mouse that roared' in Ehrenberg, R.G. (ed.), *Research in Labor Economics*, JAI Puss vol. 5, pp. 33–68.

of black women in particular, for hiring black women 'killed two birds with one stone'.[33]

In the decade between those developments in the United States and the United Kingdom Australia introduced equal pay for equal work. The Australian case is particularly interesting due to the different system of minimum wage determination in that country and the substantial rise in females' relative rates of pay that resulted from the change. In Australia minimum wages are determined for each occupation by a network of state and federal tribunals. They determine the wage to be paid according to what is considered necessary to support 'a man and his wife and children living in a civilized community'. Prior to the introduction of equal pay, occupations were categorized into male and female according to whether they were filled predominantly by males or females. Those determined to be female were awarded a wage deliberately marked down from what it would have been had men been doing these jobs. From 1950 to 1969 the mark-down was to 75 percent of the rate a male would have received. Taken together with the occupational distribution of women's employment, this resulted in an aggregate ratio of female to male earnings of 60 percent. In 1969 'equal pay for equal work' was introduced by the Federal Tribunal and in 1972 this was amended to 'equal pay for work of equal value'.

What has been the effect of this legislation? Over the period of the implementation of the Equal Pay Act in the United Kingdom, female pay rose relative to that of men but in the United States no such change occurred. In the United States black rates of pay improved relative to those of whites, but they were improving before and have continued to improve since the passage of the Civil Rights Act. In Australia the ratio of female to male earnings rose from around 59 percent in 1960 to 75 percent by 1980. How much of this is due to the legislation?

Controversy surrounds the impact of legislation in the United Kingdom for it was implemented at the same time as a number of flat rate incomes policies were in operation. These policies, about which we shall have more to say in Chapter 14, awarded equal money increases to most workers and therefore improved the relative position of low paid workers among whom women predominate. Regardless, one study suggests that the legislation increased the relative earnings of females in Britain by 19 percent.[34]

A much smaller effect is detected for the United States, where it is suggested that the influx of women, with less than average experience, offsets the rise resulting from the implementation of the legislation.[35] In Australia it has been suggested that the effect of the policies was greatest of all. It has been estimated that the decisions of the tribunals increased the pay of women relative to that of men by between 25 and 30 percent.[36]

33. See Butler, R. and Heckman, J.J. (1977) 'The government's impact on the labor market status of black Americans: a critical review,' *Equal Rights and Industrial Relations*, Wisconsin–Madison.

34. Zabalza, A. and Tzannatos, P. (1985) 'The effects of Britain's anti-discriminatory legislation on relative pay and employment', *Economic Journal*, **95**, 679–9.

35. Smith, J.P. and Ward, M.P. (1984) 'Women's wages and work in the twentieth century', Report R-3119-NICHD, The Rand Corporation, Santa Monica, California.

36. Gregory, R.A. and Duncan, R.G. (1981) 'Segmented labour market theories and the Australian experience of equal pay for women', *Journal of Post Keynesian Economics*, **1**, 403–28.

Of course, raising rates of pay will have consequences for employment. If equal pay provisions raise females' pay above the rates that prevailed before, and these previous levels were equilibrium levels, we should expect an accompanying reduction in employment. In fact there was a substantial rise in the employment of women in the United Kingdom and Australia when the relative rates of pay improved. In the United Kingdom the total number of hours worked by women rose by 17.6 percent between 1970 and 1980,[37] although during this period there were two quite different regimes. From 1970 to 1975 the annual growth rate was 2.7 percent, while after the legislation came into full effect, from 1975 to 1980, it was a mere 0.6 percent.

In the United States affirmative action is suggested to have increased the growth of employment by 2.8 percent over the period 1974 to 1980 for white females and by 12.3 percent for black females over this same period. Minority groups increased their share of employment in federal contractors over the period 1970 to 1980.[38] However, this does not translate into large effects for the US economy as a whole since relatively few firms were subject to affirmative action.[39]

In the United States and Australia, as reported in Chapter 1, there was a substantial rise in employment during the 1970s. In general therefore these legislative initiatives have taken place against the favorable background of a substantial expansion in the demand for female labor. The demand curve for female labor was shifting out due to changes in technology and changes in the structure of industry.[40] In the United Kingdom, where the labor supply curve of females is less elastic than in the United States, it is probable that females' relative rates of pay would have increased anyway. The legislation might have altered the precise timing of these improvements in relative pay, but is likely better regarded as the proximate rather than the fundamental cause of this relative improvement.

COMPARABLE WORTH

The persistence of differences between the rates of pay of white males and those of minority groups and women led to an extension of legislation in many countries in the late 1970s. In Europe an *Equal Pay Directive*, issued by the European Commission in 1975 and subsequently confirmed by the European Court of Justice, requires 'equal pay for work of equal value'. This concept was introduced in Australia in 1972 and in the United States a number of states (25 in 1984) had legislation relating to a similar concept called 'comparable worth'.

The idea of comparable worth or equal pay for work of equal value resulted from

37. Zabalza, A. and Tzannatos, P. (1985), *op.cit.*, whose findings are supported by Joshi, H. and Newell, A. (1986) *Pay Differentials and Parenthood: Analysis of Men and Women Born in 1946*, Report to Department of Employment, London.
38. Leonard, J.S. (1984) *op. cit.* and Smith, J. and Welch, F. (1984) 'Affirmative action and labor markets', *Journal of Labor Economics*, **2**, April, 269–301.
39. Gunderson, M. (1989) 'Male–female wage differentials and policy responses', *Journal of Economic Literature*, **XXVII**, March, 46–72.
40. Barooah, V.K. and Lee, K.C. (1986) 'The effects of changes in Britain's industrial structure on female relative pay and employment, 1960–1980', Department of Applied Economics, University of Cambridge, October 1986.

increasing awareness of the fact that the earlier legislation did nothing to address the problem of women who are disproportionately represented in, crowded into, certain occupations. One consequence of this, it has been argued, is that the rates of pay in these jobs are relatively low.[41] The few men that occupy these jobs and the majority of females are paid equally, but equal pay legislation does not resolve the problem of low rates of pay for everyone in what are 'women's jobs'. It has been estimated that in the United States and Great Britain around 15 percent of the earnings gap is accounted for by this occupational segregation. The solution proposed was to pay women, according to the intrinsic value of their jobs. This could be established by observing the pay of equally qualified males in other, similar, jobs and paying women their comparable worth. In situations in which it has been applied it has involved raising wages in predominantly female jobs by 10–20 percent.

Various procedures have been suggested to measure the size of the adjustment to female rates of pay that would be required to implement comparable worth. One method is to augment the traditional earnings equations to include a variable measuring the percentage of an occupation that is female.[42] Thus Eq. (13.3) becomes:

$$\log W/P_i = a_1 + a_2 I_i + a_3 I_i^2 + a_4 X_i + a_5 F_i + \varepsilon_i \tag{13.8}$$

where F_i represents the proportion of an occupation that are females. This procedure eliminates the depressing effects on pay of occupational segregation, by standardizing for the effects of the sex composition of the occupation and in so doing produces suitably adjusted coefficients on a_1 to a_4.

An alternative procedure is to estimate a separate equation of the Form of Eq. (13.3) for males and then to use coefficients representing the returns to males from each of the personal and workplace characteristics, together with the measures of these characteristics for females, to predict the salaries of females. This procedure is illustrated in Fig. 13.6. Here the returns estimated from the male equation derived in Fig. 13.6(a) are applied to female characteristics with the consequence that this predicts a higher wage for individuals with the characteristics in question than they actually receive. In the absence of discrimination any inaccuracies that result from using male coefficients, together with female characteristics, to predict female salaries will be entirely random. On the other hand, any systematic differences that emerge will indicate the presence of discrimination. The difference between actual and predicted earnings, as indicated in Fig. 13.6(b), will provide a measure of the 'comparable worth gap'. This procedure is most appropriate where job characteristics are measured according to some 'objective' scale of measurement such as are developed under job evaluation schemes.

41. See Aldrich, M. and Buchele, R. (1986) *The Economics of Comparable Worth*, Ballinger Pub. Co., Cambridge, Mass. and Miller, P.W. (1987) 'The wage effect of the occupational segregation of women in Britain', *Economic Journal*, **97**, 885–96.
42. See Ehrenberg, R.S. and Smith, R. (1984) 'Comparable worth in the public sector', National Bureau of Economic Research, Working Paper.

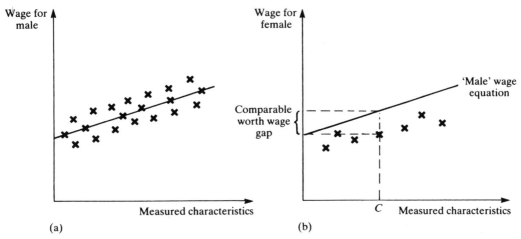

Figure 13.6 A procedure for estimating comparable worth. One approach to estimating the comparable worth gap is first to estimate a separate earnings equation for males as in (a), then to use the coefficients representing the returns to males in conjunction with the measured characteristics of females to predict the salaries of females. This is shown in (b) as the 'male' equation. The difference between actual and predicted earnings provides a measure of the comparable worth gap

A third procedure, recently advocated, is the so-called *reverse regression*.[43] If we ignore other characteristics and focus only on individual human capital characteristics, I_i, Eq. (13.3) becomes

$$\log W/P_i = a_1 + a_2 I_i + a_3 S_i + \varepsilon_i \qquad (13.9)$$

where S_i refers to the individual's minority or majority group status. The reverse regression procedure than requires, as the name implies, that the regression is reversed so that

$$I_i = a_1 + a_2 \log W/P_i + a_3 S_i + \varepsilon_i \qquad (13.10)$$

Now, instead of asking whether the minority group is paid less than the majority group, holding human capital constant, we are asking whether when we hold wages constant the majority possess less human capital than the minority? Such a procedure should enable us to distinguish 'differential overqualification'. Such a term has been used to describe the situation in which females, who enjoy equal pay to males in certain jobs, are nonetheless better qualified than males. This might emerge as a result of the constrained labor market participation of females, which emerges from the

43. See Goldberger, A.S. (1984) 'Reverse regression and salary discrimination', *Journal of Human Resources*, 307–19 for an interesting yet technical evaluation of this technique and Cain, G.G. (1986) 'The economic analysis of labor market discrimination: a survey', in Ashenfelter, O. and Layard, P.R.G. (eds), *Handbook of Labor Economics*, North Holland for a highly informative discussion which draws on Goldberger's analysis.

process of family income maximization discussed earlier.[44] However, this procedure does not provide substantial support for the notion of discrimination and this appears in large part to be due to the fact that it biases downwards estimates of discrimination. It is not surprising therefore that this approach has had some appeal to defendants in discrimination suits.[45]

SUMMARY

In this chapter we have looked at the issue of labor market discrimination. The fact that certain groups of workers—women and minorities—generally have lower earnings than others—white males, is beyond dispute and appears to be a feature of all industrial countries. However, the reasons for this are many and various and their significance is a matter of dispute. We have distinguished two broad sets of reasons why, according to conventional competitive theory, such differences will emerge. First, pre-market differences in the behavior of men and women in the majority and minority groups. Historically, women and minority groups came to the labor market less well endowed with those characteristics that are rewarded in the labor market. Second, we noted further differences in behavior between these groups once they were in the labor market. Either because of the social conventions governing the household division of labor, perhaps because of expectations of discrimination or because of a discontinuous attachment to the labor market, women's behavior and that of minority groups has been different from that of white males. Where such differences can be measured human capital theory can go some way toward explaining the earnings differences that we have observed. Yet we also saw that there were substantial methodological problems associated with the measurement of discrimination. Econometric methodology has therefore come to the fore in the debate on the magnitude of discrimination and most recently in measurement of the comparable worth wage gap.

Economic theories attribute the existence of discrimination to tastes, or put more simply prejudice—on the part of co-workers, customers and employers. To combat the effects of such prejudice the early legislation that was introduced in most countries raised the price of female labor and restricted discrimination in hiring. Yet one conclusion to emerge from neoclassical analysis was that such legislation would have been unnecessary had markets been competitive. Neoclassical analysis would suggest that, if necessary, legislation should be aimed at promoting competition, for the theories we surveyed suggested that competition will effectively limit and should eventually remove discrimination. Discriminatory practices can only be sustained where the practitioners are supported by market power and one important role for legislation is therefore to reduce market power to promote competition.

However, legislation has taken a quite different form. Comparable worth is now on the agenda in Europe and has been implemented in varying degrees in the United States and Australia. This relatively recent development is due to the perception that

44. Frank, R.H. (1978) 'Why women earn less: the theory and estimation of differential overqualification', *American Economic Review*, **68**(3), 360–73.
45. See Goldberger A.S. (1984), *op. cit.*

the earlier equal pay and equal opportunities legislation has not produced all that was intended. Disputes about the appropriateness and effectiveness of this legislation will continue, as will concern over discriminatory behavior. Neoclassical analysis has helped clarify the explanation of differences in earnings and has as a result helped identify some of the root causes of the problem. However, it has also suggested that the causes of the differences in earnings are more deeply imbedded in the fabric of our society than many of the proponents of the original legislation had recognized. It may for this reason prove far more difficult to equalize earnings than had first been thought.

PRINCIPAL CONCEPTS

Students should now be familiar with the following concepts and ideas, which have been discussed and developed in this chapter.

1. Labor market discrimination.
2. Individual and group discrimination.
3. Pre-market differences.
4. Labor market exploitation.
5. Statistical discrimination.
6. Affirmative action.
7. Comparable worth.
8. Differential overqualification.
9. A reverse regression.

QUESTIONS FOR DISCUSSION

1. Identify the main pieces of legislation which have been designed to combat discrimination in the labor markets of either the United States or the United Kingdom. How successful has the legislation been in the country you chose?
2. Why did the pay of women relative to men remain unchanged in the United States in the 20 years to 1980 while it increased significantly in other industrial nations?
3. What were the reasons for the introduction of comparable worth legislation in several major industrial nations in recent years?
4. Detail the various procedures that exist for estimating the comparable worth earnings gap.
5. What procedures have been adopted to estimate the magnitude of earnings discrimination?
6. Can we distinguish the separate contributions of pre-market and in-market differences in behavior to differences in the pay of men and women?
7. What role do expectations play in explaining differences in earnings between males and females?
8. Explain why the most effective way to eliminate labor market discrimination might be to develop an effective anti-monopoly policy.
9. What policy prescriptions emerge from statistical theories of discrimination?

10. Do statistical theories of discrimination provide a satisfactory explanation of group discrimination?
11. Discuss the proposition that economic theories of discrimination tell us no more than that discrimination results from prejudice.
12. Are the average earnings of all females likely to equal those of all males in the foreseeable future?

FURTHER READING

Throughout this chapter reference is made to the substantial body of empirical work that exists in this area. In addition, two very useful and comprehensive surveys on this subject have been produced in recent years. The first by Sloane, P.J. (1987) 'Discrimination in the labor market', in Carline *et al.* (eds.) *Labour Economics*, Longman, London, pp. 78–158 provides a particularly comprehensive survey of the empirical literature in the period to the mid-1980s. The second, written at a more advanced level, by Cain G.G. (1986) entitled 'The economic analysis of labor market discrimination: a survey', in Ashenfelter, O. and Layard P.R.G. (eds.) *Handbook of Labor Economics*, North Holland provides a particularly interesting and informative review of the methodological problems associated with measuring discrimination. Both of these excellent surveys have had an important influence on the writing of this chapter.

PART 5

WAGE INFLATION AND UNEMPLOYMENT

Unions play an important role in wage setting in most industrialized countries. Although their influence declined in many countries during the 1980s, they are still key actors in the wage determination process throughout most of Europe. Despite their prominence the objectives of unions are still poorly understood and attempts to construct rigorous models of union behavior, in which the union maximizes a well-defined objective function, have met with only limited success. In the first part of Chapter 14 we shall review a number of models that have been offered to describe unions' behavior.

Despite the lack of consensus over an appropriate model of union behavior (if indeed their behavior can be encompassed in a single model), one outcome is generally agreed; unions raise the relative pay of unionized workers, by something of the order of 10 percent. We review the different methods by which estimates of the size of this union wage gap have been produced and the manner in which this varies between different sections of the workforce. We also review the arguments that suggest that the size of this gap is overstated because, alongside raising wages, unions also raise worker productivity. Where union wage rises are not fully offset by productivity increases, real wage gaps will emerge. In Chapter 14 we outline a model of aggregate wage setting in unionized labor markets and discuss the economic consequences of the emergence of aggregate wage gaps.

In Chapter 14 we also look at other aspects of union wage bargaining. In particular we focus on the strikes that occur when the parties to wage bargaining fail to agree. We look at different measures of the scale of strikes and we evaluate economic theories of the determinants of strike duration and settlement size. The models of trade union bargaining and aggregate wage setting developed in Chapter 14, and returned to in Chapter 15, reveal that bargainers are insulated to some degree from the forces of competition in labor markets. Apparent excess supply, as manifest in substantial unemployment, may no longer produce wage moderation, in consequence incomes policies, in a variety of forms, have been proposed, from time to time, to moderate the rate of growth of nominal wages. The forms that have been suggested and the success of those policies that have been implemented in the United Kingdom are evaluated in Chapter 14. The United Kingdom has been foremost among the larger western European nations in introducing statutory incomes policies but the rather limited success of such policies' has led to a search for alternatives. Corporatism has been operated in other European countries and has been suggested as an alternative for the United Kingdom. This type of policy is therefore evaluated in Chapter 14.

One of the central objectives of incomes policies has been to mitigate the adverse employment consequences of wage bargaining behavior. Following the analysis of incomes policies in Chapter 14 comes a detailed discussion of the nature and causes of unemployment in Chapter 15. Unemployment was *the* policy concern of the last half of the 1970s and first part of the 1980s. Theories of the causes of unemployment can be split into two broad categories. The first, the Keynesian view, attributes unemployment to a deficiency of aggregate demand; the second, the neoclassical view, attributes unemployment to the existence of too high real wages. In Chapter 15 we review both of these explanations in some detail before returning to reconsider the links that exist between unemployment and wage changes. We evaluate the degree to which excess supply in labor markets leads to moderation in the rate of growth of money wages and we review the range of explanations offered for the sharp rise in the natural, or equilibrium, rate of unemployment, which occurred in most countries during the 1980s.

14

WAGE SETTING UNDER TRADE UNIONS

The analysis up to this point has had little to say about wage setting trade unions. Although we have analyzed the objectives of trade unions and discussed the manner in which unions attempt to realize these objectives, we have not discussed either the general consequences of union wage setting behavior or the specific impact of unions on the general level of wages.

While the process of competition is an important determinant of the general level of wages, it is by no means the only mechanism or indeed, in some economies, the most important one. We have already seen that due to the fixed costs of employing labor, the price of labor can diverge from labor's marginal product in the short run. The existence of substantial hiring and information costs or of specific skills can shut out competitive forces and impart a degree of monopoly power to workers in the short run. Under these circumstances bargaining and rules will determine the price of labor; bargaining can be either between firms and trade unions or between firms and individual workers. Individual negotiations are an important feature of pay determination in professional labor markets, but by far the most important form of bargaining that occurs in blue collar and lower white collar labor markets in most developed countries is that between employers and trade unions.

In chapter 7 we established that trade unions negotiated pay and conditions for probably a majority of employees in Europe. In the United Kingdom, at the start of the 1980s, union density was just over 50 percent and unions negotiated pay and conditions for around 55 percent of all employees. Although since that time union density has fallen, it still seems likely that at the end of the 1980s around 50 percent of all employees in the United Kingdom were covered by union negotiated pay and conditions of work. At the end of the 1980s unionization rates were slightly higher in Australia than in the United Kingdom, while they stood at around 40 percent in Germany and 30 percent in Japan. In contrast, in the United States density was only around 15 percent by the end of the 1980s while at the other end of the spectrum density was 95 percent in Sweden. In Europe coverage of union negotiated pay and conditions is generally much more extensive than indicated by union density figures. Unions evidently play a central role in determining the pay and conditions of work in most but not all of the industrial nations of the West.

Unions achieve their desired objectives by altering both the labor supply and the labor demand conditions that confront a firm. Trade unions attempt to reduce the elasticity of demand for the services of their members, and to control the supply of labor to the firm, that is to become the monopoly supplier of labor to the firm. How are wages and associated employment determined where the firm, or a number of firms, has to 'buy' labor from a trade union? In this chapter we turn our attention to the issue of wage setting under trade unions.

WAGE BARGAINING UNDER TRADE UNIONS[1]

In the union sector of the economy wages are generally the outcome of a bargaining process between employers and trade unions, but one approach to the issue of wage determination under trade unions has been to sidestep the bargaining issue altogether. This is the approach of the monopoly union model, which suggests that the union is able to fix wages unilaterally, leaving the firms to set employment. This is merely the first of four models we shall consider in this section.

The monopoly model

Where a single union is confronted by a large number of small firms, and these firms fail to combine for purposes of bargaining, the union might fix the wage unilaterally. This is likely to occur where the benefits of combination by employers, chief among which is the lower wage that might be set, are less than the transaction costs the firms would experience if they joined together for bargaining. The size of these transaction costs will therefore place an upper ceiling on the magnitude by which the union established wage can exceed the competitive wage. If forming a coalition for purposes of bargaining is prohibitively costly to firms, this then leaves the unions with considerable scope for fixing the wage. The union having set the wage, it is left to firms to set employment. The union acts in a manner analogous to the monopolistic firm operating in a product market.

To illustrate the likely outcome recall that in Chapter 11 it was suggested that the labor demand curve represents the locus of a set of points on the firm's isoprofit curve.

1. The issues discussed here are usefully surveyed in Oswald, A.J. (1985) 'The economic theory of trade unions, an introductory survey' and Pencavel, J.H. (1985) 'Wages and employment under trade unionism: microeconomic models and macroeconomic applications', both in *The Scandinavian Journal of Economics*, **87** (2), 160–93 and 197–225 respectively.

This relationship is shown more explicitly in Fig. 14.1 in which it is shown that points such as A, B, C and D on successive isoprofit lines, constitute the labor demand curve. Thus, confronted by employment level L_1 the firm could increase profits by reducing wages from W_0/P to W_1/P, or confronted by wage W_1/P the employer could raise profits from π_0 to π_1 by reducing labor from L_0 to L_1. As we move down the labor demand curve with wages falling and employment rising, profits increase. In Chapter 7 we discussed the nature of union preferences and suggested that unions were most likely concerned about employment and wages. This proposition gave rise to a set of union indifference curves. These indifference curves, together with the labor demand curve, enable us to illustrate the monopoly model.

Consider a situation such as depicted by point B in Fig. 14.2. In the absence of a union, employment in firm A is determined by the point of intersection of the demand curve and the perfectly elastic supply curve, resulting in competitive wage, W_c/P.

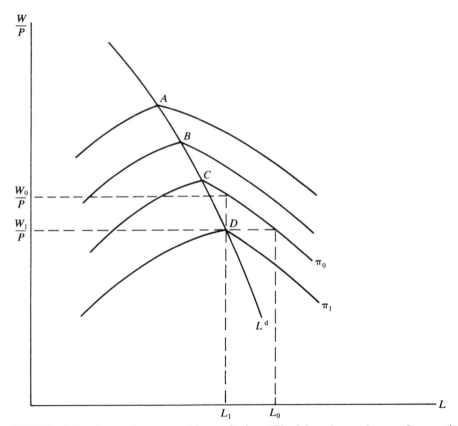

Figure 14.1 The labor demand curve and isoprofit lines. The labor demand curve L_d constitutes the locus of those wage and employment combinations which represent the maximum profits that can be earned for any given wage rate. Confronted by employment level L_1 the firm could increase profits by reducing the wage from W_0/P to W_1/P. Alternatively, confronted by W_1/P it could increase profits by reducing employment from L_0 to L_1

Suppose now that the industry, to which this firm belongs, becomes unionized and that the workforce imposes the higher wage W_m/P. The higher wage at existing employment levels results in an increase in union utility as depicted by the new point C on U_1. However, this new point does not constitute an equilibrium for the firm since it is not a point on the labor demand curve. While firms in this industry are free to determine employment, they can do better by moving back to a point on the labor demand curve for this represents a higher level of profits. Such a point is shown as point A in Fig. 14.2. At this point the ratio of the marginal utility of the real wage to employment, as captured by the slope of the union indifference curve, is equal to the amount by which employers will reduce employment as a result of a small change in the real wage rate. Such a position will be one of tangency between the indifference curve and labor demand curve.

The bargained solution

While the above model may appropriately describe behavior in labor markets in which a single union confronts a large number of unorganized employees, it is of limited

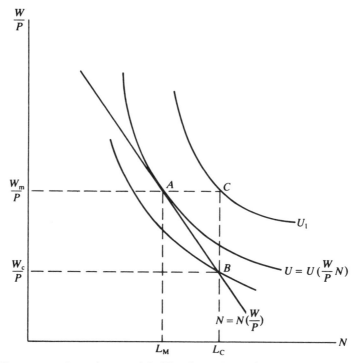

Figure 14.2 The monopoly union model. If unions determine the wage, firms optimize by adjusting employment so that they remain on their labor demand curve as at point A. Such a situation might arise where a single union confronts a large number of small firms that do not cooperate or bargain with the union. In this monopoly model the union sets the wage and firms set employment accordingly

application for it ignores the role of bargaining. In the above example firms accepted the wage imposed by the union and then optimized by adjusting employment. However, it seems more likely that, as a general rule, firms will be active participants in the process of establishing wages; either individually or collectively, firms will try to influence the wage outcome. Where a single union or cohesive group of unions confronts a single employer, as in plant and company bargaining, or a collection of employers, as in national or industry-wide bargaining, a situation of bilateral monopoly pertains and economic rents emerge. Of course, as we saw earlier, the presence of substantial transaction costs is also associated with the existence of economic rents. In both cases there will be bargaining over the division of these, and it is therefore to bargaining theories that we turn to provide a determinant wage and/or employment outcome to these situations. There are numerous different bargaining models to be found in the literature of labor economics, and one of these is described in Appendix 14A to this chapter, but it is not proposed to review them all here.

Common to all bargaining problems is the use of threats and argument by the two parties involved to try to achieve their goals. In particular, strikes, or the threat of a strike, are a prominent feature of the collective bargaining process in many countries. The attitudes of each party to the wage bargain will be determined by what each perceives to be the costs of agreeing to the other party's wage offer or wage claim, weighed against the costs perceived to be attached to the party's disagreeing to the claim or offer. Accordingly, we identify each party's 'bargaining attitude' by the balance of the costs of agreeing relative to the costs of disagreeing and these can be represented as follows:

$$\text{The TU's bargaining atitude} = \frac{\text{Costs of disagreeing with employer}}{\text{Costs of agreeing on employer's terms}}$$

From which it follows that when the costs and benefits are quantified and the ratio emerges as less than 1, the union will not be inclined to settle.

A similar attitude can be described for the employer:

$$\text{Employer's bargaining attitude} = \frac{\text{Costs to employer of disagreeing with union}}{\text{Costs of agreeing on the union's terms}}$$

Where again, if the ratio is less than 1, the employer will not be disposed to settle. These costs cannot by their nature be known or estimated with precision and therefore these calculations take the form of expected values.

Consider first the union evaluating a particular wage offer tabled by the employer. The costs of disagreeing with the employer over this wage offer may be the expected loss of income, and even loss of jobs, for its members if disagreement results in a strike. Or, since most failures to agree simply mean a continuation of the wage and employment conditions presently governing, failure to agree to the employer's last wage offer will be the difference between the offered and the current wage adjusted by the expected employment levels associated with each. The costs of agreeing, on the other hand, will be the addition to the wage that the union believes it might have obtained had it held out. From the employer's perspective, the costs of disagreeing with the last claim lodged by the union could be the loss of profits, both now and in the future, which could result from a strike, or the costs of continuing to pay 'excess' wages if there is reversion to the *status quo*. For their part the costs of agreeing will be the difference between the costs of conceding this wage claim as opposed to the lower wage they believe they might get the union to accept if only they hold out.

Although we can formalize the bargaining process in this manner, the subsequent process of bargaining is not described by this model. The task confronting each party is to maintain and sustain its own bargaining posture while reducing the opposition's will to resist. This can be achieved by convincing the opposition that the costs of disagreeing are greater than they might initially have understood them to be. In essence each party tries to raise the ratio, so that it exceeds 1, by persuading the other party that the costs of their agreeing are less than the costs of disagreeing: effectively they reduce the other party's will to resist.

Although the above is highly abstract, it provides a general framework for considering the process of bargaining. Where exactly, within the range set by the employer's first offer and the union's initial claim, the wage will eventually settle will depend on the relative power of the parties as manifest in their ability, either by argument or threat, to convince the other party that the costs of their disagreeing are too large for them to contemplate. In empirical investigations of the bargaining process, this has meant the search for variables that are likely to influence or proxy those that determine the costs to each party to the bargaining. Thus, in an empirical bargaining model, unemployment might enter as a determinant of the wage, since the higher the level of unemployment the greater would be the costs to the union of disagreeing. If disagreement resulted in a reduction in employment, the level of unemployment would be one determinant of the ease with which dismissed males could obtain jobs. On the other hand, a rise in unemployment benefit might strengthen the union's position since this will lower the cost to the union of any unemployment consequent on failure to agree. Setting the problem up in this way helps us identify the sort of variables that could feature in empirical work on bargaining.

The 'right-to-manage' model

A bargained solution is a central feature of a second model called the 'right-to-manage' model. This represents a modification of the monopoly model and produces a more plausible model of wage determination. This model proposes that either employers acting in concert, or a single firm bargain with the union to set the wage rate and that, having done this, employers are then left to adjust employment unilaterally. This might be an appropriate description of the collective bargaining process in some industries and countries, for bargaining often seems to focus exclusively on the 'price' of labor. However, it seems odd that leaving the firm with a choice of the number of individuals that should be employed attracts the label 'right to manage', for determining employment levels is only one area in which management would wish to exercise choice if it had the right to manage. During the 1980s it was argued that British management secured the 'right to manage', by which it was not meant that managers had won the right to determine how many should be employed, but rather that they had regained the authority to determine the level of employment, the deployment of labor and the intensity with which labor worked. They had in most areas always had the right to determine levels of employment, but they now gained additional powers. The model is therefore rather inappropriately titled.

The model again proposes that bargaining establishes the wage but that the eventual equilibrium is again represented by a point on the labor demand curve. This occurs because once the wage has been established, employers are once again free to adjust employment as occurred in Fig. 14.2 above. However, in this case, as Fig. 14.3 reveals, the eventual outcome is unlikely to be a point of tangency between the labor demand curve and a union indifference curve and it is for this reason we have, in truth, not described an equilibrium. This is shown in Fig. 14.3 in which the monopoly wage point, W_m/P, and the competitive wage, W_c/P, are shown. The latter is the minimum wage necessary to attract labor to the firm, while the former is the maximum wage the firm can concede while earning the normal profits compatible with its remaining in this line of business. However, it is the relative bargaining strengths of the two parties which determine where, within this range, the two parties settle and, save in the special

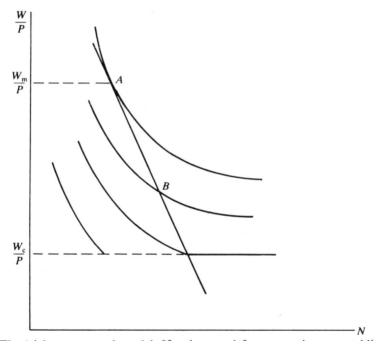

Figure 14.3 The 'right-to-manage' model. If unions and firms negotiate to establish the wage, and then firms are left to set employment, firms will locate at a point on the labor demand curve. However, save in the special case where unions possess all the bargaining power and enforce the monopoly wage, W_m/P, the wage/employment point will not be a point of tangency between the labor demand curve and a union indifference curve. The outcome of the bargain will be described by a point such as B but this will not be an equilibrium

case shown as *A* in Fig. 14.3, where the union possesses all the bargaining power and can enforce the monopoly wage, this will not be a point of tangency between a union indifference curve and the labor demand curve. Where both parties possess some degree of power the outcome of bargaining may be described by a point such as *B* lying somewhere below *A*. Of course, this is not an equilibrium so this model produces no more than a temporary solution to the bargaining problem.

Efficient bargains

One of the central problems with the 'monopoly union' and the 'right-to-manage' models is that the resulting 'equilibrium' is inefficient: both parties could do better. Both parties seem to pass up opportunities for a mutually profitable trade.

To illustrate this consider the family of isoprofit curves and associated labor demand curve, together with a set of union indifference curves U_0, U_1 as illustrated in Fig. 14.4. Point *A*, the point of tangency between the highest union indifference curve, U_0, and the labor demand curve is the monopoly wage, W_m/P, depicted in Figs. 14.2 and 14.3. Point *B* illustrates the competitive wage, W_c/P, which is set by the employees' reservation wage, itself influenced by the levels of welfare support. The 'right-to-manage' model proposed that bargaining would establish a wage within the range between *A* and *B*, on this labor demand curve, and that where exactly in this range would be determined by the relative bargaining strength of the two parties.

Suppose that as a result of negotiations wage W_0/P was established as shown at point *C*. As we noted above this is not an equilibrium for it is not a point of tangency between the labor demand curve and a union indifference curve, and it is therefore apparent that both parties could do better. They could do better if they negotiated a rather lower wage and a higher level of employment as depicted at point *D* in Fig. 14.4. At this point the employer is on a higher isoprofit curve, π_1, than was the case at point *C* where the employer was on π_0, while the union is on the higher indifference curve, I_1 rather than I_0. Point *D* represents one point on the *contract curve* which is given by the locus of points of tangency between the set of isoprofit curves representing firms' profit opportunities and union indifference curves representing union preferences. At these tangency points neither party can be made better off without making the other party worse off and accordingly these contracts are Pareto optimal. From the perspective of the two parties to the wage bargain these are efficient contracts and therefore the contract curve is the locus of all points that represent efficient contracts.

The lowest point on the contract curve is point *B*, the lowest wage union members will accept while continuing to supply labor. The highest point is point *E*, the isoprofit line indicating the lowest level of profits the firm must secure to remain in business, the isoprofit line representing normal profits. The efficient bargain actually struck could lie anywhere between points *B* and *E*, and the exact location along the curve will again depend on the relative bargaining strengths of the two parties. The greater the bargaining strength of the trade union, the closer the equilibrium will be to point *E*, for as we move toward point *E* both wages and employment are rising and the employer's

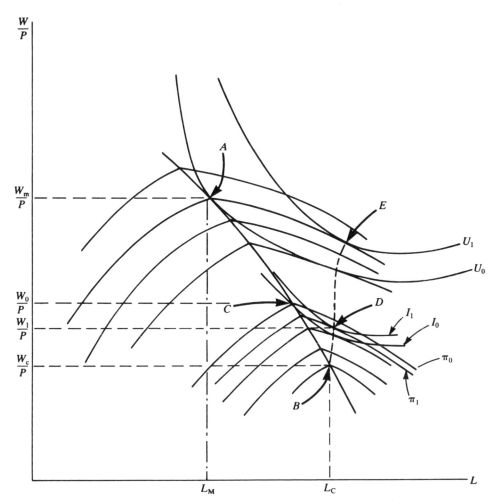

Figure 14.4 The efficient bargaining model. If employers and unions negotiate only about wages the bargains they strike will be inefficient. By moving from a point such as *C* to point *D* both parties could do better. At point *D* firms enjoy higher profits and the union enjoys higher utility than at point *C*. However, in order to reach point *D* they must bargain about wages *and* employment. Points such as *D*, at which no one party can be made better off without the other party being made worse off, lie on the contract curve—the curve describing all such points of tangency between isoprofit and indifference curves

profits are correspondingly less. There are several ways in which the solution may be attained but the most frequently employed in empirical work is the Nash solution detailed in Appendix 14A.

Figure 14.4 shows quite clearly that employment and wages are higher with efficient bargains than they would be in a competitive labor market, and the positively sloping contract curve suggests that the stronger the union the higher may be *both* the level of the wage and employment. Accordingly, there no longer appears to be a trade-off between employment and wages, as summarized by the labor demand curve, for the labor demand curve is no longer the effective constraint. One consequence is that the wage now exceeds the marginal product of labor. This model therefore predicts that unions can increase both wages and employment and represents a refinement of the predictions that emerged from the model of bilateral monopoly considered in Chapter 12.

The model suggests quite a different way of viewing union activity. It suggests that in unionized firms employment may be higher than firms would set voluntarily and that unions therefore produce overemployment; they produce 'overmanning' or 'feather-bedding'. Of course overmanning would drive firms in a competitive industry out of business. So a corollary of this model must be that firms enjoy supernormal profits. Firms will be able to earn supernormal profits over the long run when the product market in which they operate is not open to competition, as in the case of monopolies or some nationalized industries. In the absence of such barriers to entry in product markets the model may therefore best be thought of as describing the short run.

Why should unions produce overmanning? Overmanning may be viewed as quite a rational means of insuring union members against unemployment in the presence of imperfect insurance markets. Individuals cannot buy insurance against unemployment due to problems of adverse selection (it is likely that only those with high probabilities of experiencing unemployment would buy insurance) and moral hazard (employees who bought insurance might act in such a way as to force employers to sack them). However, unions can minimize the risk of any single member being declared unemployed, when redundancies are not determined by some prenegotiated formula, by increasing the number of union members employed.

Under efficient contracts employers would appear, at first glance, to have a strong incentive to 'cheat'. Thus having negotiated a wage such as W_1/P in Fig. 14.4, at point D the employer has an incentive to move to a point on the labor demand curve by reducing employment for, as is evident from Fig. 14.4, if the employer broke the agreement on employment in this manner profits would increase. Employers are unlikely to behave in quite this blatantly opportunistic manner for they have to return to the bargaining table, to meet the union again, in the future. Such opportunistic behavior would not engender trust. However, in a world of information asymmetries in which the firm has an information advantage over the workforce, disguised behavior of this type cannot by ruled out.

An obvious problem with the efficient contract model is that it seems to require rather more complicated institutional arrangements than the monopoly model. For an efficient bargain unions and employers need to negotiate about employment and wages and, while it is understood that trade unions and employers negotiate over wages, it is less generally acknowledged that they negotiate over employment as well. It has been argued that the institutional arrangements necessary to negotiate efficient bargains simply do not exist.[2] However, even where there is no explicit bargaining over employment, there is plenty of evidence of indirect provisions and agreements between unions and firms which go a long way toward determining the level of employment.[3]

A survey of UK union leaders' views about the preferences of their organizations revealed considerable diversity of preferences with a few unions placing a large weight on employment.[4] In certain industries in Britain, the public railways system and the newspaper printing industry up to the mid-1980s were examples, unions and employers negotiated explicity about wages and employment. In the United States longshore industry minimum crew sizes and handling requirements were specified. It is in fact not unusual in either the United Kingdom or the United States to find unions negotiating about employment levels by negotiating manning levels and work rules. In other industries there will be implicit understandings between employers and trade unions about employment levels. When firms are concerned about their reputations they will be reluctant to break such implicit understandings. Therefore, although it remains the case that in general the explicit content of many union-employer negotiations focuses on wages and not on employment,[5] an understanding, at least, about the level of employment serves as a backdrop to most negotiations. Employment is therefore a feature of negotiations and, although not fully efficient, the outcome of bargaining might most appropriately be described as a point to the right of the labor demand curve but to the left of the contract curve.

The seniority model

In the extreme circumstances in which unions are entirely unconcerned about employment, union preferences may be represented in a set of horizontal union indifference curves. Although union indifference curves may nowhere be flat throughout their complete range, they may be flat in the vicinity of the current wage employment coordinates: they may by locally flat.[6] Such a situation may arise because the typical union member, or the member/s whose preferences are reflected in union policy, is insulated from involuntary redundancy. If the median voter determines union policy and redundancy is on a last in, first out basis, such a member will be halfway down the ordering for layoffs. Points of tangency between a series of union indifference curves of this type and a set of isoprofit·curves, as shown in Fig. 14.5, will in these circumstances give rise to a set of efficient bargains. However, now we are back

2. Oswald, A.J. and Turnbull, P. (1985) 'Pay and employment, determination in Britain, what are labour contracts really like?', *Oxford Review of Economic Policy,* Summer, 80–97.
3. See Part 5.2 of Pencavel, J.H. (1990) *The Labor Market Under Trade Unionism: Employment, Wages and Hours of Work* (forthcoming)
4. Clark, A. and Oswald, A. J. (1989) 'An empirical study of union preferences', Centre for Labour Economics, London School of Economics, Discussion Paper No. 352, p. 20
5. See Farber, H.S. (1986) 'The analysis of union behaviour', in Ashenfelter, O. and Layard, P.R.G. (eds.), *Handbook of Labor Economics*, vol. 2, North Holland.
6. See Blanchflower, D., Oswald, A.J. and Garrett, M.D. (1988) 'Insider power in wage determination', Centre for Labour Economics, London School of Economics, Discussion Paper No. 319, August, p. 45

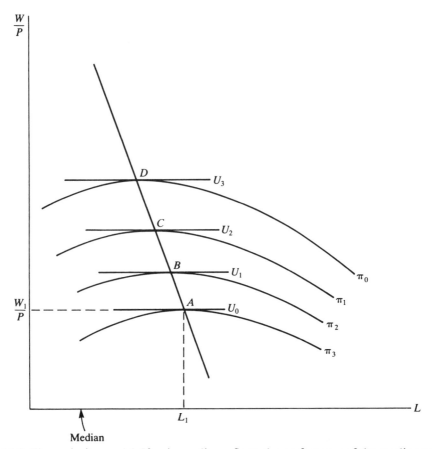

Figure 14.5 The seniority model. If union policy reflects the preferences of the median voter and this individual is unaffected by the prospect of layoff, because redundancies are on a last in, first out basis, union indifference curves will be (locally) flat. Efficient bargains are now represented by points such as A, B, C and D on the labor demand curve. A rise in wages now results in a reduction in employment

on the labor demand curve and higher wages are once again accompanied by lower employment. This model is likely to be a more appropriate description of some union behavior in Europe, particularly in the United Kingdom, than in the United States. It has been shown that in the United States relatively senior workers are indeed concerned about involuntary redundancies among more junior workers, not least because a reduction in the size of the workforce entails the reallocation of the remaining workload and this can adversely affect the earnings of some workers.[7]

7. See Pencavel (1990), *op. cit.* Part 3.3.

Empirical tests of models of union behavior

Which of the above models is best is an empirical question, but it is not one that is easily resolved. Econometric analysis frequently involves a joint test of the structure of the production or demand function and the form of the union utility function, but a number of researchers have recently tried to estimate models of union behavior in which the union maximizes a well-defined objective function. Such an approach enables us to distinguish whether the monopoly union or the efficient wage bargaining model better explains union behavior. However, in these studies the researchers have generally assumed that the union can impose whatever settlement it wishes on the firm, so that the observed wage outcome represents the one most preferred by the union. This approach admits no role for employer resistance or bargaining, although the outcomes may tell us more about the employer's ability to resist than they do about union preferences. The studies differ in the manner in which union preferences are derived and in the industries studied.

Several studies have focused on the printing industry in the United States. One concludes that an efficient bargaining model 'comes closest to providing a satisfactory explanation'[8] although another study suggests that contracts between this union, the International Typographical Union, and employers in this industry are not efficient.[9] Studies of the UK coal and steel industry have rejected the idea that the union placed all of the weight on the goal of high pay for union members[10] as did a study of the US coal industry.[11] There are substantial differences in the degree of emphasis given to the two objectives in the two countries. Again, a study of the US airline industry suggested that union behavior lies somewhere between the monopoly union and efficient bargaining models.[12] There therefore seems to be evidence to suggest that unions are concerned about both pay and employment but that different unions weight each of these factors differently. This seems the most plausible result. Unions, depending in part on the legal and cultural environment in which they operate, attach different weight to employment and pay. Those in the United Kingdom generally attach rather less weight to employment than do those in the United States, but within each country there is considerable diversity.[13]

8. MacCurdy, T.E. and Pencavel, J.H. (1986) 'Testing between competing models of wage and employment determination in unionized markets', *Journal of Political Economy*, **94**, Supplement, S3–39

9. Brown, J.N. and Ashenfelter, O. (1986) 'Testing the efficiency of employment contracts', *Journal of Political Economy*, **94**, S40–S87.

10. See Carruth, A.A., Oswald, A.J. and Findlay, L. (1986) 'A test of a model of union behaviour: the coal and steel industries in Britain', *Oxford Bulletin of Economics and Statistics*, **48**, 1–18; and Carruth, A.A. and Oswald, A.J. (1985) 'Miners' wages in post war Britain: an application of a model of trade union behaviour', *Economic Journal*, **95**, 1003–1020.

11. Farber, H.S. (1978) 'Individual preferences and union wage determination: the case of the united mineworkers', *Journal of Political Economy*, **86**, 923–42.

12. Card, D. (1986) 'Efficienct contracts with costly adjustment: short-run employment determination for airline mechanics', *American Economic Review*, December, 1045–71.

13. The empirical evidence on union preferences is most thoroughly evaluated in Chapter 3 of the book by Pencavel, J.H. (1990), *op. cit.*

UNION RELATIVE WAGES

That unions bargain for higher wages appears indisputable, whether they secure them or not is another matter. Unions may succeed in raising wages but if this in turn results in a rise in productivity, the new wage level will be legitimated and the independent effects of unions disappear. We shall evaluate one hypothesis which suggests that this is indeed what happens shortly. Where there are no offsetting productivity gains and where employment has not also been negotiated, employers will respond to higher union wages by moving up the labor demand curve and employment will consequently fall. The gains of one group, those who remain employed, will be offset by the losses of another, those who lose or fail to gain jobs, and if over the longer run the elasticity of labor demand is unity there will be no change in total wage payments. Such a result is consistent with the observation that over the long run labor's share of national income has been constant.

Two broad approaches, based on micro- and macroeconomic models, have been employed to estimate the impact of unions on relative wages.

Microeconomic models

One approach to estimating the wage gap has been to estimate earnings equations, of the type we have encountered in previous chapters augmented to include an indicator of union status. Such equations have been fitted to cross-section data, which incorporate details of individual and workplace characteristics, to control for human capital differences and the net advantages of different jobs. The approach adopted has frequently been similar to that we encountered in the previous chapter when estimating the magnitude of discrimination. Thus a single equation of the form detailed in Eq. (13.4) might be estimated in which the dummy variable now indicates union status (for Z in Eq. (13.4) substitute U where $U = 1$ if unionized and $U = 0$ if non-union) or two separate equations similar to Eqs. (13.5) and (13.6) can be estimated for union and non-union members respectively. (For subscript w in Eq. (13.5) substitute u to indicate union membership and for subscript B in Eq. (13.6) substitute n to indicate non-union status.) Thereafter a similar procedure can be adopted to facilitate a decomposition which enables us to distinguish: (i) the unexplained element represented by differences in the intercept term; (ii) differences in the type and level of individual and workplace characteristics of unionized and non-unionized workers; and (iii) differences in the measured rewards to union and non-union workers for each of the characteristics.

Most of the fitted equations are encompassed by Eq. (14.1):

$$\log W = a_n + a_{nx}X + U[(a_u - a_n) + (a_{ux} - a_{nx})X] + \varepsilon \qquad (14.1)$$

where X represents the usual vector of variables measuring human capital and workplace characteristics, U is a variable indicating union status equal to 1 if a union member and zero otherwise (where the subscripts u and n indicate union and non-union status respectively) and the a's are the estimated coefficients of the equation. If we measure accurately all the other influences on earnings, the above procedure will enable us to estimate the difference in earnings between a union and non-union worker who are in every other respect identical. Such a measure has sometimes been called the *adjusted wage gap*, for it adjusts for all of the other differences between the workers.

The wage gap should be distinguished from the *wage gain*. The latter refers to the difference between the wages paid to unionized workers and the wages these same workers would have received in the complete absence of unions. The wage gap may be smaller than the true wage gain due to the existence of *threat effects* or larger, due to the existence of *spillover effects*; the wage gap may under- or overestimate the 'true' effects of unionism. The spillover effect suggests that the successful negotiation of a higher wage by unions will cause employers in the union sector to reduce employment, as will occur if either the demand for labor in the union sector is not perfectly inelastic or if unions do not negotiate efficient contracts. The labor displaced from the union sector may now enter the non-union sector and, subject to the floor imposed by the welfare or social minimum, compete down wages in that sector.[14] These arguments are illustrated in Fig. 14.6.

Imagine an economy with two sectors A and B producing two different goods which are sold at parametric prices. The labor demand curves for these two sectors, L_N^d and L_U^d, are detailed and the length of the horizontal axis measures aggregate labor supply in this economy. If the labor market is competitive a single wage $W*/P$ will rule and labor supply will be fully employed. Now imagine the formation of a union in sector A, so that L_U^d now represents the demand for labor in the unionized sector of the economy. The negotiation of a union wage W^U/P, reflecting union preferences as represented by U_0, results in a reduction in employment in the unionized sector, an increase in labor supply to the non-unionized sector and a corresponding fall in the wage rate in that sector. The wage rate in the non-union sector will fall to W^N/P (in the absence of a floor to wages in the non-unionized sector which is in excess of W^N/P). Now OX workers will be employed in the union sector and XL workers in the non-union sector. The estimated wage gap that emerges $(W^U - W^N)/W^N$, adjusted or otherwise, will overstate the union wage gain $(W^U - W*)/W*$. The difference between the wages of unionized and non-unionized workers will be greater than the excess of union wages over the competitive wage. Wages in the union sector will have risen and those in the non-union sector will have been depressed.

The threat effect suggests that employers emulate the union wage. They may, for a variety of reasons, try to match union wages even though their labor force is non-unionized. Non-union firms may match union wages in tight labor submarkets to enable them to continue to recruit labor. They may also be required by law to extend union negotiated wage increases to certain non-union employees.[15] However, perhaps they are most likely to pay union wages in order to prevent or pre-empt unionization.

14. Gramlich, E. (1976) 'Impact of minimum wages on other wages, employment and family incomes', *Brookings Papers on Economic Activity*, **2**, pp. 409–51.
15. Ichniowski, C., Freeman, R.B. and Lauer, H. (1989) 'Collective bargaining laws, threat effects and the determination of police compensation', *Journal of Labor Economics*, 7(2), 191–209, illustrate how models that do not allow for threat effects can overestimate the total effects of unions on total compensation in certain legal environments.

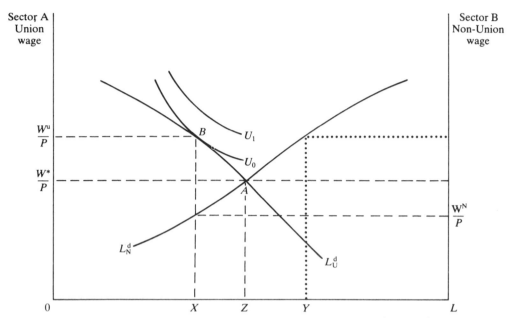

Figure 14.6 Spillover and threat effects. The labor demand curves L_u^d and L_N^d correspond to sectors A and B, while the length of the horizontal axis OL measures aggregate labor supply. Where the labor and product markets are competitive, a single wage W^*/P clears the market. Introduction of a union into sector A results in a rise in wages to W_u/P and a reduction in employment in the union sector to OX. This results in either: (i) a spillover of workers from sector A to the non-unionized sector so that labor supply to this sector is XL and the non-union wage falls to W^N/P. A wage gap $(W^u - W^N)/W^N$ emerges; or (ii) a matching rise in wages in the non-union sector due to the threat of unionization. OX are employed in the union sector and YL in the non-union sector with the result that XY are unemployed. (*Source*: Oswald, A.J. (1982) 'Trade unions, wages and unemployment: what can simple models tell us?', *Oxford Economic Papers*, 526–45) Reproduced with the permission of the author

If firms believe that unionization will impose additional costs, as for example when the union prevents them from operating due to a strike, or reduces the ease with which management can deploy labor, firms may try to prevent unionization. Removing the financial incentives for workers to join a union is one way of achieving this.[16] If firms respond to the threat effect of unionization by matching union wages, then no wage gap emerges and the wage gains from unionization, which accrue to those union and non-union workers who remain in employment, are underestimated. Again this can be illustrated with the help of Fig. 14.6. Now if wages in the non-union sector rise to match those in the union sector, W^U/P becomes the ruling wage and no wage gap emerges. However, it is also clear from Fig. 14.6 that XY workers are now unemployed

16. Dickens, W.T. (1985) 'Wages, employment, and the threat of collective action by workers', University of California, Berkeley has argued that part of the different industry wage premiums we observed in Chapter 11 reflect the differential costs of union avoidance across sectors of the US economy.

as a result of the general rise in wages. Estimates of union relative wage effects therefore need to allow for the possibility of spillover and/or threat effects.

Further difficulties confront researchers in this area. The division of the working population into union and non-union sectors is not determined at random. As a result there are likely to be differences in the quality of workers performing the same jobs in the union and non-union sectors. One source of these differences will be a consequence of the behavior of employers who, confronted by higher union wages, try to regain some advantage by recruiting higher quality workers to fill unionized jobs. Such differences would not matter if it were possible to measure or proxy all the relevant differences in worker quality but, as was seen before in the discussion of the returns to human capital, this is not yet possible. In our regressions therefore we shall be attributing to the union wage gap part of what constitutes a return to superior-worker characteristics in the union sector. Although one result of unionism is to reduce the cost of recruiting workers with superior characteristics to the union sector, such workers would not have been chosen by firms in the absence of the union wage. Although the recruitment of higher quality workers represents the firm's attempts to minimize the adverse cost implications of conceding higher union wages, it does not eliminate it entirely and the firm now employs a higher quality labor force than it would otherwise wish. To this extent unionism promotes overqualification, it leads the employer to recruit workers with qualifications in excess of those required to perform the job at least cost.

A further source of differences in worker quality between the union and non-union sectors is a consequence of the behavior of workers. If unionized jobs pay higher wages or offer a different type of compensation package than non-union jobs, certain types of workers may be attracted to these jobs. If we can identify the characteristics of workers, which dispose them to join a union or accept a unionized job, and these characteristics are independent of those that explain the union wage gap, it would be appropriate to construct a simultaneous equation model consisting of an equation determining union status together with a distinct wage equation. The probability that an individual with measured characteristics will be a union member is then calculated, and this predicted value entered as a variable on the right-hand side of a separate wage equation. However, while admiring the ingenuity shown in developing just such procedures, one of the leading authorities in this field has commented that these 'techniques are not working'. Estimates that have been produced to date have varied substantially and have been suggested to be 'considerably less reliable than their OLS counterparts'.[17] This is because independent explanations of union status have yet to be found and the equations estimated to date have not been very rebust.

An alternative approach has been to use longitudinal data which trace individuals' work histories and compare the wages of individuals as they move in and out of union jobs. The data appropriate for such studies are available at present only in the United States, but even there it appears that a very large fraction of those that reported union status reported no change in status over the period analyzed. Indeed, it appears that

17. Lewis, G.H. (1986) 'Union relative wage effects', Ch. 20, in Ashenfelter, O. and Layard, P.R.G. (eds.), *Handbook of Labor Economics*, p. 1114, North Holland.

inaccuracies in reporting go a long way toward explaining the lower estimates of the wage gap that emerge from longitudinal, as compared to the cross-section, estimates.

Finally, it should be noted that data on individuals' union status are not the appropriate indicator of whether or not an individual is in receipt of a union negotiated wage rate. Many union members are in firms in which they are in such a small minority that the union is not recognized for purposes of bargaining, and so they are not covered by union wage rates. On the other hand, as the threat effect emphasized, there will be many non-unionized workers covered by union negotiated agreements. It is for this reason that some researchers in the United Kingdom have suggested that it is more appropriate to work with data identifying those individuals covered by union negotiated wage rates rather than data on those who are members of a union. This is also true in much of continental Europe. However, such coverage data are generally only available at a reasonably aggregate or macro level.

Macroeconomic models

Macro wage equations measure the union mark-up across a complete industry or occupation. In such equations the incidence of unionism, union density or the coverage of union negotiated wages in an industry, area or occupation is included on the right-hand side of the estimating equation. This procedure starts with the identity

$$\ln W_i = \ln W_i^u \alpha + \ln W_i^n (1 - \alpha) \tag{14.2}$$

Where $\ln W_i$, the average wage in industry W_i, is the weighted average of the wage of unionized workers in that industry, W_i^u, and non-unionized workers, W_i^n, and where α is the fraction of workers unionized. In turn this can be written as

$$\ln W_i = \ln W_i^u \alpha + \ln W_i^n - \ln W_i^n \alpha \tag{14.3}$$

which is equal to

$$\ln W_i = \ln W_i^n + (\ln W^u - \ln W^n)_i \alpha \tag{14.4}$$

This can also be expressed as

$$\ln W_i = \ln W_i^n + \lambda_i \alpha \text{ where } \lambda_i = (\ln W^u - \ln W^n)_i \tag{14.5}$$

here λ equals the average union/non-union wage differential in industry i. Letting $\ln W_i^n = \beta X_i$ we can then construct an estimating equation of the form

$$\ln W_i = a_1 + a_2 \beta X_i + a_3 \lambda_i \alpha + \varepsilon \tag{14.6}$$

where X_i represents a vector of the characteristics of the industry which determine wages in the absence of unions. We then estimate Eq. (14.6) and solve for λ. Macro studies of this type will again suffer from the problem of omitted variables in the vector X_i, and it has been suggested that these problems are more pronounced at this level. It is largely because the omitted variable and measurement error problems are thought to be less at the micro level that most recent estimates have been derived using individual data. However, given the disadvantages that attach to both the micro and the macro approaches, it is clear that there is as yet no right way to estimate union effects on wages.

The size of the wage gap

Estimates of the size of the wage gap vary substantially according to the industry, occupation and characteristics of the worker. Thus, while in the United States the overall wage gap is little different for men and women, it is larger for black workers than for white and for blue collar than for white collar workers: in both cases it is larger by some 10 percentage points. The wage gap is on the other hand smaller, at perhaps 7 percentage points, in manufacturing but it is higher in construction than in other industries. It is again larger for private than for public employees and the wage gap declines as years of schooling, seniority, and firm or establishment size increase. The gap also varies substantially between different states in the United States. Part of the positive association between the wage gap and firm and establishment size is accounted for by worker characteristics, for large plants recruit superior quality workers to compensate for higher wages. The gap becomes larger by some 3 percent once account is taken of fringe benefits, which are generally superior in unionized establishments, but it is lower once account is taken of the longer hours worked by union workers.[18] These and other detailed adjustments have led to the estimates of the upper bounds of the overall mean wage gap for the period 1967 to 1979 in the United States, shown in Table 14.1.

In Britain the aggregate differential has been suggested, rather implausibly, to have risen from 17 percent to around 34 percent in the early 1980s, as shown in Table 14.1. Rather less detail has been available until recently for Britain, where the

Table 14.1 Estimates of the size of the overall union wage gap in the United States and Britain (%)

	USA	Britain		USA	Britain		USA	Britain
1967	11	17	1974	14	22	1981	—	34
1968	11	20	1975	16	33	1982	—	34
1969	11	21	1976	18	29	1983	—	31
1970	12	26	1977	17	26	1984	—	32
1971	15	28	1978	17	28	1985	—	24
1972	12	31	1979	13	19	1986	—	19
1973	15	30	1980	—	28	1987	—	22

Source: USA, Lewis, G.H. (1986), 'Union relative wage effects', in Ashenfelter O. and Layard, P.R.G. (eds.), *Handbook of Labor Economics*, North Holland, Ch. 20. Britain, 1967–83, Layard, P.R.G. and Nickell, S.J. (1987), 'The performance of the British labor market', in *The Performance of the British Economy*, Dornbusch, R. and Layard, R. (eds.), Oxford University Press. The more recent estimates were kindly supplied by these authors.

18. These results are reported in detail in Lewis, G.H. (1986), *op. cit.*

coverage of union negotiated agreements is often quite different from the incidence of union membership and where, accordingly, estimates at the individual level, which do not adjust for differences in coverage, may prove quite misleading. The most authoritative estimates for Britain suggest that semiskilled male manual trade unionists enjoy a wage differential over non-unionists of about 8 percent, but that this reduces to only around 3 percent for skilled workers.[19] It has also been found that the differential is larger in the presence of plant and company bargaining,[20] and that workers in the 3 percent of establishments covered by a pre-entry closed shop in Britain may have enjoyed a premium of 25 percent above the wages of comparable non-union members.[21] However, it has been shown that unless there is also a high incidence of unionization among the other firms in a competitive industry a closed shop in itself is not sufficient to secure a wage premium for unionized workers. Closed shops only produce wage premiums when either the rest of the industry is highly unionized or firms possess a significant degree of market power.[22] Researchers have also confirmed that union membership confers larger fringe benefits. Compared to non-unionists, union members are more likely to receive occupational pensions and sick pay and they enjoy a longer holiday entitlement.[23]

Although we now know quite a lot about the union wage premiums enjoyed by broad groups of unionized workers, these results must still be interpreted with caution. It has to be borne in mind that none of these studies has taken explicit account of the often quite different wage and employment preferences of different unions which, in the previous section, we suggested existed. These general estimates are therefore the outcome of the preferences of different unions and their abilities to realize their goals in the conditions governing at the time.[24]

It appears that in the United States and Britain the union wage gap grew during the mid-1970s, a time when unemployment was rising. It has also been suggested that there was a rise in the wage gap during the recession of the 1930s in the United States and, more recently, a sharp rise during the recession of the early 1980s in Britain. One obvious explanation of such findings is that this reflects the relative rigidity of union wage levels, or rates of growth of wages. If in the recession non-union wage rates decline and union rates remain fixed, then the wage gap will widen. The rigidity of union rates has been attributed to the predominance of long-term (three-year) contracts in the union sector. Certainly union negotiated wage rates appear to be less flexible than non-union rates at times of inflation, when, with the exception of those unions which have negotiated cost-of-living escalator clauses (COLAs), union wages rise more slowly than those elsewhere and the wage gap accordingly narrows. However, this is

19. Stewart, M. (1983) 'Relative earnings and individual union membership in the United Kingdom', *Economica*, **50**, 111–26; and Stewart, M. (1987) 'Collective bargaining arrangements, closed shops and relative pay', *Economic Journal*, **97**, 140–56.
20. Pencavel, J.H. (1974) 'Relative wages and trade unions in the United Kingdom', *Economica*, **41**, 194–210.
21. Blanchflower, D.G. and Oswald, A.J. (1988) 'The economic effects of Britain's trade unions', Employment Institute.
22. See Stewart, M. (1989) 'Union wage differentials, product market influences and the division of rents', paper presented to the European Association of Labour Economists, 1989.
23. Freeman, R.B. and Medoff, J.L. (1984) *What Do Unions Do?* Basic Books, New York.
24. See Pencavel, J.H. (1990), *op. cit.* Part 2.2 for a critical and highly informative review of these estimates.

unlikely to provide the full explanation of the reported behavior of the union wage premium over the business cycles, because union contracts generally contain clauses enabling them to be renegotiated should conditions change. Indeed, in Britain, the duration of contracts is seldom more than one year. A more likely explanation of the relative rigidity of union wages, and hence of variations in the wage gap, is that union contracts overlap; they start and finish at different times.[25]

Given this institutional feature of the wage bargaining process, together with the concern of union negotiators to strike deals no worse than those they see currently in operation, overlapping *and* emulation may together impart the rigidity we observe. One consequence of overlapping contracts, which has been frequently remarked in Britain, is that they may make it more difficult for wage negotiators to break with the past and to adjust the level of nominal wage change downwards when required. It has been noted that in those countries in which the start and finish of contracts are synchronized, as in Japan where the 'spring offensive' marks a new round of negotiations throughout the union sector, and in Germany where 'concerted action' means that all new contracts start around the same time, nominal wages are far less rigid than in the United Kingdom, as we saw in Chapter 10.

However, the evidence that the union wage premium varies countercyclically is far from conclusive.[26] In the recession of the early 1980s, the union–non-union differential barely changed in the United States. The much publicized 'concession bargaining' in the union sector appears to have been matched by an almost comparable reduction in average wages in the non-union sector. Collective agreements in the United States stipulate a variety of responses to a cyclical downtown. Some require worksharing, some specify the order of layoffs, others remain silent on these matters. As a result, it is not surprising that responses in the union sector vary substantially between firms and industries, to such a degree that it has been suggested that naive union–non-union differences miss the critical variations.[27]

Unions and pay inequality

The presence of unions narrows the dispersion of pay. From the earliest time unions have had as a policy objective the application of a standard rate of pay for the job. Inter-country comparisons confirm that those countries with the highest union density, namely the Scandinavian countries, have the lowest dispersion of aggregate pay, while in those countries where the workforce is more evenly divided between the union and non-union sectors, such as the United Kingdom, the unionized sector reveals the narrower dispersion of earnings.[28] The application of uniform rates provides less scope for rewarding individual performance. In the United Kingdom managers are far more

25. See Taylor, J. (1980) 'Aggregate dynamics and staggered contracts', *Journal of Political Economy*, **88**, 1–23.
26. Raisian, J. (1983) 'Contracts, job experience and cyclical labor market adjustments', *Journal of Labor Economics*, **1**(2), 152–70.
27. See Pencavel, J.H. (1990), *op. cit.*, Part 2.5.
28. See Metcalf, D. (1989) 'Trade unions and economic performance: the British evidence', in Dell'Arriga, C. and Burnetta, R. (eds.), *Markets, Institutions and Co-operation: Labour Relations and Economic Performance*, Macmillan, London.

likely to reward individual performance and merit in non-union establishments than they are in union establishments.[29] Again, the union mark-up is higher for women than for men, is greater for blacks than for whites, for unskilled than for the skilled, and for disabled than for the able-bodied.[30] The otherwise least well paid do better as union members and the effect is once again to narrow the dispersion of earnings.

UNIONS AND PRODUCTIVITY

Where unions raise wages above the level that would otherwise exist they will raise the costs of unionized firms. In a monopolistic industry the rise in costs will lead to a rise in prices and perhaps to a reduction in profits, but the survival of the firm is unlikely to be threatened. In a competitive industry, in which only some firms are unionized, it will be a different matter. A rise in labor costs, which is reflected in prices, will reduce the competitiveness of unionized firms and in the long run drive them out of business. How might these effects be mitigated?

The cost implications of the rise in wages will be reduced if unions raise both productivity and wages.[31] If the proportional rise in real wages is the same as the proportional rise in productivity (if $(\delta W/\delta P)PQ^{-1} = (\delta^2 Q/\delta L^2)QL^{-1}$) then costs per unit of output, $(W/P)LQ^{-1}$, unit labor costs, will not rise. If the rise in the wage is compensated by a sufficient upward shift in the marginal product curve this will validate the higher wage at the existing level of employment.

In what manner might unions raise productivity? Earlier we identified two basic mechanisms by which adjustment occurs in labor markets: these mechanisms were those of exit and voice. The less perfect is information and the more specific are skills, the larger are the transaction costs of changing jobs and therefore the less likely it is that adjustment will take the form of exit. Older, more senior, and more specifically skilled workers, will have less resort to exit as a means of adjustment and thus seem more likely to erect, or participate in, institutional structures that incorporate the voice mechanisms.

Where voice is the most efficient way of securing adjustment some form of collective rather than individual voice may emerge. But even though the concerns of an individual may be identical to those of the rest of the group, each individual acting alone may be reluctant to voice his or her concerns, either for fear of victimization, or because for other reasons the private costs of voicing discontent exceed the private benefits. Even though the benefits to the group as a whole of expressing concerns may be large, at the level of each individual the benefits may be small relative to the transaction costs that are encountered when the individual acts alone, with the result

29. See Blanchflower, D. and Oswald, A.J. (1988) 'Internal and external influences on pay settlements', *British Journal of Industrial Relations*, **XXVI**, 363–70.
30. Metcalf, D. (1989), *op. cit.*
31. Termed the 'new view' the idea that unions increase productivity was most recently revived by Freeman, R.B. and Medoff, J.L. (1984), *What Do Unions Do?*, Basic Books, New York. For a detailed but critical review of this provocative book see the symposium in the *Industrial and Labor Relations Review*, **38**(2) (1985). In fact this view is far from new for it has been pointed out to me by John Pencavel, that this view was widely held in late nineteenth-century Britian and is proposed in a chapter of Marshall's *Principles*.

that these concerns will not be articulated and effective action to resolve them will not be undertaken. This situation could exist because the workplace has many of the characteristics of a public good. Many of the aspects of the workplace are non-excludable and non-rival in consumption. Noise, heating, light, the speed of the production line, the attitude of the supervisor all have the characteristics of a public good. However, where the benefits to at least some individuals of forming a collective voice exceed the costs, then just such a voice may emerge.

The above are arguments in favor of a collective voice. They explain why the presence of such an organization can reduce workers' dissatisfaction and, by raising morale, can reduce turnover and increase worker productivity. However, these are arguments for a collective voice that need not necessarily be a union. Worker representatives on the company board, or a system of worker committees, might prove easily as effective as a trade union. However, the trade union appears to have one unique advantage, it is likely to be perceived by the workforce to be independent of the firm. Because it enjoys financial independence from the firm, a union is in a stronger position to take action, where this action appears to clash with the interests of the firm.

It has also been argued that trade unions, by emphasizing the collective interest, minimize competition between workers and foster a cooperative atmosphere which is more conducive to productive behavior. The desirability of such attitudes and behavior will, of course, depend on the technology employed and the product produced and is evidently more essential in some workplaces than others. Cooperation between workers is essential to productive performance in the coalmining industry at the coalface and among a team of economists producing forecasts of economic activity. It may be less essential, indeed undesirable, among professional golfers, secondhand car dealers, and authors of novels.

Trade unions may also increase productivity by reducing turnover. This they do by negotiating firm-specific remuneration packages. Fringe benefits are higher in unionized firms, because fringe benefits represent one of the ways in which unions can differentiate their product in an attempt to attract union members. If these benefits, such as pension rights or social facilities, are non-transferable they will reduce turnover. Finally, it has been argued that by confronting them with new, higher, union negotiated wages management is shocked into the use of more efficient productive techniques. This is a variant of the efficiency wage theory we encountered in Chapter 11 and is premised on the notion that firms are not operating at the efficiency frontier. However, it is only in the absence of effective competition that such non-profit maximizing behavior could previously have occurred and thus this effect will be confined to only some firms.

A burgeoning literature has addressed the issue of union effects on productivity but to date there is little empirical support for the idea that unions significantly raise productivity. Evidence that any rise in productivity, which might occur, fails to offset union wage effects is provided by the finding that in the United States unionism is associated with lower profitability.[32] Studies have also revealed an inverse relationship

32. The evidence on the effects of unions on productivity and profits is surveyed by Addison, J.T. and

between stockholders' wealth, the value of common stock, and unexpected changes in collectively bargained labor costs.[33] Others have found that when unions win representation elections, the market value of the firms is reduced by almost 4 percent.[34] Again, in the United Kingdom, those industries with the poorest financial performance have been found to be those in which unions run a closed shop.[35]

Over the longer run lower profits are likely to lead to lower investment and lower research and development expenditures which will further reduce the efficiency of the enterprise. In the United States there appears to be evidence of lower investment and reduced innovative activity in unionized firms.[36] Unions also have wider effects on firm efficiency. Unions may negotiate manning levels that restrict the right of management to deploy labor efficiently. Furthermore, if they successfully promote protectionist trade legislation, they reduce the spur to efficient behavior that results from overseas competition. When they advocate restrictive labor legislation, such as legal immunity for the closed shop as occurred in Britain, they again reduce efficiency if successful.

At the end of the 1980s the issue of union effects on productivity growth was again the centre of considerable research activity in the United Kingdom. This research appears to show that there was significantly greater productivity growth in unionized than in non-unionized firms in the United Kingdom in the first half of the 1980s, a time when there was a very sharp rise in productivity in certain sectors of British industry. However, the association between unionization and productivity growth does not appear to be due to the productivity enhancing effects of unionism but rather to the relaxation of restrictive work practices that were only possible in unionized firms,[37] together with, perhaps in consequence of, much greater investment in unionized firms.[38] The result is that the sharp rise in productivity in UK manufacturing in the early 1980s is almost entirely accounted for by conventional factors: the rise in productivity in the upswing of the cycle and increased capital investment.[39]

Hirsch, B.T. (1989) 'Union effects on productivity, profits and growth: has the long run arrived?', *Journal of Labor Economics*, 7(1), 72–105.

33. Abowd, J.M. (1989) 'The effect of wage bargains on the stock market value of the firm', *American Economic Review*, 79(4), 774–800.

34. See Ruback, R. and Zimmerman, M.C. (1984) 'Unionization and profitability: evidence from the capital market', *Journal of Political Economy*, 92, 1134–57.

35. Blanchflower, D.G. and Oswald, A.J. (1988) 'Profit related pay: prose discovered', *Economic Journal*, 98, 720–36.

36. Addison, J.T. and Hirsch, B.T. (1989), *op. cit.*

37. Nickell, S., Wadhwani, S. and Wall, M. (1989) 'Unions and productivity growth in Britain, 1974–86: evidence from UK company accounts data', Centre for Labour Economics, London School of Economics, Discussion Paper No. 353, pp. 48. Wadhwani, W. (1989) 'The effects of unions on productivity growth, investment and employment: a report on some recent work', Centre for Labour Economics, London School of Economics, Discussion Paper No. 356.

38. Machin, S. and Wadhwani, S. (1989) 'The effects of unions on organisational change, investment and employment: evidence from WIRS' Centre for Labour Economics, London School of Economics, Discussion Paper No. 355, pp. 57.

39. Wren-Lewis, S. and Darby, J. (1989) 'Manufacturing Investment and Labour Productivity', *National Institute of Economic and Social Research*.

STRIKES

The models discussed so far provide no explicit role for strikes, this may be partly because although strikes attract considerable publicity they are relatively rare. Furthermore, in the United States and Great Britain in recent years the number of days lost through strikes has declined sharply. Yet strikes appear to be one feature of the wage bargaining process and there therefore exists a class of models which attempt to provide a determinate solution to the bargaining problem which admit the possibility that in the process of negotiation a strike may occur.

Models of strikes

The earliest and still one of the most widely employed models of strikes was developed by Hicks.[40] Its appeal lies in the fact that it seems to describe the process by which concessions are wrought from each party in order to reach agreement. Thus Hicks describes *a union resistance curve*, which identifies 'the length of time that [workers] would be willing to stand out rather than allow their remuneration to fall below the corresponding wage', and an *employer's 'concession curve'* as the locus of a set of points at which 'the expected costs of the stoppage and the expected cost of the concession just balance'. The trade union's resistance curve is shown in Fig. 14.7(a). It slopes downwards because rather than experience the costs associated with the duration of a strike shown on the horizontal axis, the union would be willing to accept a wage lower than originally claimed. If it expected a strike of T weeks it would be willing to settle for a rise of only ΔW_1 to *avoid* this.

The employer's concession curve is shown in Fig. 14.7(b). The employer recognizes that concessions must be offered in the form of a larger wage rise to avoid the costs associated with a strike of the expected duration shown. To avoid the costs of a strike expected to last for T weeks the employer would be willing to concede a wage rise of ΔW_1 per week. The employer balances the costs of conceding the wage rise, ΔW_1, against the costs of experiencing a strike of T weeks, and it is the locus of the points reflecting the equality of these two which describes the employer's concession curve.

The schedules therefore appear to describe the process of concessions that will be made by the two parties as they move toward an agreement. Superimposing one curve on another to describe the position of both parties, as is done in Fig. 14.7(c), appears to lead to predictions about the length of strike and the size of eventual wage settlement. But why should a strike now occur? If the parties got together and communicated their willingness to offer or concede wage rises of particular magnitudes, contingent on an expected duration of strike, it would immediately become obvious there was a wage rise on which they could both agree, as shown by the point at which their curves crossed. They could then agree to settle on such a rise now and avoid the costs of the strike. If the duration of a strike and the expected settlement size can be predicted beforehand why should there be a strike? Strikes seem to require that one party has information that is not conveyed to the other party. Strikes would seem to result from information asymmetries.

40. Hicks, J. (1932) *The Theory of Wages*, Macmillan, London.

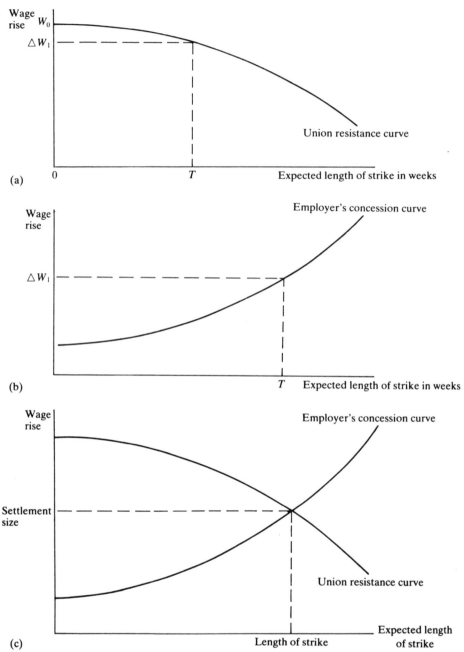

Figure 14.7 Hicks' model of strike duration. (a) A union resistance curve identifies the length of time that workers would be prepared to strike rather than allow the wage rise to fall below the level shown. (b) An employer's concession curve details the wage rise the employer will be willing to concede rather than experience the costs associated with a strike of the lengths shown. (c) The schedules therefore describe the process of concessions that will be made by the two parties as they move toward agreement. The predicted length of strike is shown by the point at which the two schedules intersect

444

The dominant approach in the most recent literature views the problem of strikes in the context of constrained maximization. The firm maximizes the present discounted value of its profits subject to a constraint represented by the union's concession curve. Such models are often viewed as a logical reformulation of Hicks's model and an example of this approach is discussed below.[41] In this model a union's concession curve details the minimum wage acceptable to the union after the duration of a strike of a particular length. It is downward sloping, as in Fig. 14.7, and reflects the union's willingness to modify its position as the strike goes on. Such a concession curve is shown in Fig. 14.8. The principle underpinning the concesssion curve is that experiencing the costs, loss of income, associated with a strike, will make workers willing to settle for a lower wage. Initially they have an exaggerated view of the wage

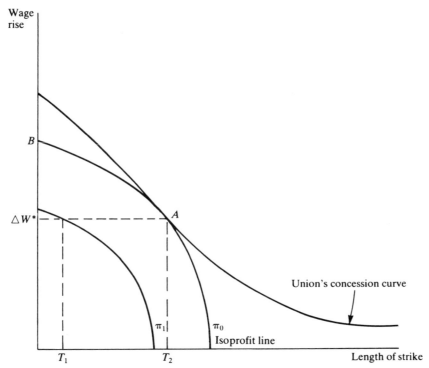

Figure 14.8 A model of the length of a strike. The union's concession curve details the minimum wage acceptable to the union after the duration of a strike of the length shown. Also shown are the firm's isoprofit lines. The union's concession curve acts as a constraint on employer behavior. The employer equates the marginal cost of continuing a strike to the marginal benefit. The marginal cost is represented by the slope of the isoprofit lines and the marginal benefit by the slope of the union's concession curve. Equilibrium obtains at a point of tangency between the two curves as at A above, where a strike of T_2 weeks leads to a rise in wages of ΔW^*.

---

41. This model was suggested by Ashenfelter, O. and Johnson, G.E. (1969) 'Bargaining theory, trade unions and industrial strike activity', *American Economic Review*, **59**, 35–49. See also Hirsch, B.T. and Addison, J.T. (1986) *The Economic Analysis of Unions*, Allen and Unwin, Boston and London.

increase they can obtain but, as the shape of the concession curve reveals, the union soon learns and as a result, in the initial stages, is prepared to concede a considerable amount to reduce the length of strike.

The union concession curve becomes the constraint confronting the employer. Given this constraint the employer determines the optimal length of strike by equating the marginal cost of continuing the strike to the marginal benefit of continuing the strike. The marginal cost is represented by the loss of profits as the strike proceeds and is indicated by the slope of the isoprofit line in Fig. 14.8. The slope of each isoprofit curve indicates that a given level of profits can only be maintained if the wage increase awarded falls to compensate for an increase in the length of the strike. Isoprofit lines further from the origin represent lower levels of profits for at ΔW^* profits will evidently be lower, at π_0 rather than π_1, if the firm has to suffer a strike of duration T_2 rather than T_1. To the employer the marginal benefit of continuing the strike is represented by the slope of the union's concession curve since this tells the employer the length of strike that must be endured if the employer wishes to secure a particular (lower) wage increase. Equilibrium, and therefore the length of strike and size of settlement, is given by the point of tangency of the union's concession curve and the firm's highest isoprofit line as indicated at point A in Fig. 14.8. Thus the length of strike is T_2 and the wage rise is ΔW^*.

The highest conceivable wage the firm can concede will be that which is consistent with normal profits, if the firm operates in competitive markets, and is shown by the intercept of the isoprofit line on the vertical axis at point B. Anything that increases the maximum wage that can be conceded, such as increased firm profitability, reduces the probability of a strike. Anything that increases the minimum wage the union will accept, as shown by the point at which the union's concession curve becomes horizontal, increases the probability of a strike.

In this model the employer is confronted with a trade-off between the size of wage increase and length of strike as reflected in the unions concession curve. One explanation for the shape of this curve is that it arises because of information asymmetries between the union leadership and its members. These result in the union membership persuading the leadership to pitch its claim at an unrealistic level. The union then acts in the naive, mechanistic and entirely predictable way suggested by the shape of the concession curve because the experience of a strike is the way in which the leadership educates its membership about the employer's will to resist. In this model the information asymmetry is between the union leadership and its members. However, the union leaders might do better if they adopted a less passive attitude and instead convinced the employer that the trade-off was other than depicted here. They would do best in the long run if they convinced the employer that the concession curve was a horizontal straight line with an origin at B. While encompassing more plausible behavior on the part of the employer, this model falls down because of its naive views on trade union behavior.

The above model only resolves Hicks's paradox by postulating naive behavior on the part of the trade union. However, by emphasizing that strikes arise due to private information it introduces a notion that has characterized more recent models.[42] Alternative explanations of strikes have also been offered. Strikes, it has been suggested, represent an investment: it might be necessary to strike occasionally to convince an employer that his or her expectations about the union's will to resist were well founded, or strikes may be political in nature, designed to bring about changes in the political and economic structure of a country and, therefore, not wholly explicable with reference to the particular circumstances of the firm being struck.

Measures of strikes

Strikes have a number of dimensions which attract the attention of analysts. The number of strikes, the number of workers involved in strikes and the number of working days lost (strikes x workers involved) have all been used to measure the strike proneness of different countries at different times. *Ceteris paribus*, any one of these measures will be larger the larger the size of the working population. Thus, it is conventional to standardize each measure by expressing the number per 1000 workers; that is to standardize according to the size of the working population. Which indicator is preferred will depend on the purposes for which it is being used. For example, it has frequently been argued that although the number of working days lost per 1000 workers was similar in the United States and Great Britain during the 1960s, Britain had a more severe strike problem than the United States. At that time strikes in the United States were large, infrequent and predictable. They were predictable because they typically occurred at the times when new long-term contracts were being negotiated. Thus, while they frequently involved a large number of workers and a large number of days were lost, their predictability meant employers could minimize the costs of these. They could build up inventories as contracts drew to a close and continue to meet orders when production was interrupted by running these down. In contrast, the British figures resulted from a large number of small, short, unofficial strikes. They were largely unpredictable and for this reason more disruptive. On these arguments the number of strikes, if all were recorded, would be a better indication of Britain's more severe strike problem, at this time, than the number of days lost. Interestingly, this example begs the question as to why US unions permitted firms to build up inventories for this could only have weakened the union's bargaining position, by reducing the costs of strikes to the firm.

The costs of strikes

In most countries in any year by far the most working days lost to strikes are as a result of disputes over pay. Pay issues typically account for a majority of large strikes and strikes over pay therefore account for a majority of all days lost. Disputes over the other issues such as manning, dismissal, redundancy and working conditions frequently give rise to short stoppages, while disputes over pay are typically more protracted.

42. See Pencavel, J.H. (1990), *op. cit.*, Part 5.3.

The principal immediate costs to the worker of going on strike are the loss of income they experience while on strike. The costs of a strike to the firm are the loss of profits. The loss of income to the workers will be greater the smaller are the welfare payments they receive while on strike. In certain states in the United States workers are able to collect unemployment insurance if the strike lasts beyond a certain duration. In Britain striking workers are eligible for means tested welfare benefits. There is some support for the proposition that where workers are eligible for these benefits they prolong the duration of strikes, but in general the eligibility rules are such as to preclude most workers who are on strike and the existence of such payments does not therefore provide a major explanation of days lost.[43]

Commentaries on the costs of strikes seldom focus on the costs to the worker, rather they focus on the costs to firms and the economy in general. Not unusually the costs of a strike are reported in terms of output lost, rather than profits forgone, which is clearly the more appropriate measure. Profits are determined by the difference between the revenue generated by any output sold and the cost of all the inputs that continue to be purchased. If the firm is able to run down inventories the losses may be less. In most circumstances the calculations will be more complicated by the fact that failure to service existing customers may lead to a permanent loss of business, only some employees may have been struck while others remain on the payroll but are unable to produce. Therefore, calculating the costs to firms is both difficult and often uncertain.

At the level of the whole economy the costs of strikes are yet again different. Where product markets are competitive, the loss of sales by the struck firms will be compensated by either an increase in revenue or an increase in sales by other firms, the exact division between price and quantity adjustment will be determined by the elasticity of supply in competitor firms. Strikes will only result in costs to the nation where the competitors are overseas producers and there is concern about the consequences for either or both of the exchange rate and balance of payments account of the country. The cost of a strike to a country is an opportunity cost; it is the net output forgone. Where production is switched to other domestic producers no such costs will be incurred.

Empirical evidence on strikes

The incidence of strikes could be interpreted as a measure of union bargaining power, for only strong unions will have frequent resort to the strike as a means of wringing concessions from the opposition. On the other hand, if strong unions are confronted by weak firms there may be no strikes, for such firms will not wish to incur the costs of strikes they know they will lose. The relationship between strikes and union power is therefore complex. At least until the severe recession of the early 1980s there appeared to be convincing evidence from a range of different sources and periods of

43. See Kennan, J. (1980) 'The effect of unemployment insurance payments on strike duration', in *Unemployment Compensation: Studies and Research*, National Commission on Unemployment Compensation, vol. 2, Washington, USA, and Durcan, J.W., McCarthy, W.E.J. and Redman, G.P. (1983) *Strikes in Post War Britian: A Study of Stoppages of Work Due to Industrial Disputes, 1946–73*, Allen and Unwin, London.

history that the number of strikes varied in a pro-cyclical manner. Pigou conjectured that this was because prosperity 'stimulates workpeople to try to force a rise of wages more strongly than depression stimulates employers to try to force a fall'.[44] Others have conjectured that declining unemployment strengthens the bargaining power of unions although it is not obvious why this fact alone should result in strikes.

The 'stylized facts' of strikes include the observation that the number of strikes is positively associated with firm profitability and establishment size and inversely related to the level of unemployment, while female and part-time workforces strike less than male workforces.[45] Large establishments may be more strike prone than small establishments for a number of reasons which are difficult to disentangle. The more extended channels of information may mean that communications break down and misunderstandings occur more in large plants. Such plants may be more bureaucratically managed, producing a lower level of worker commitment to the firm than occurs in small plants. The fragmentation of tasks and remoteness from ownership that are evident in large plants may also result in greater alienation of the workforce. Increased firm profitability might make unions more ready to push for improved terms and conditions of employment and, if it does nothing to change the firm's willingness to resist a strike, this would explain the positive association between strikes and profitability. However, increased profits might increase a firm's ability to resist or willingness to concede and, if the latter, this makes strikes less likely when profits are high. Evidently the interpretations of the relationships we observe are several and we are still far from a complete understanding of the determinants of strikes.

International comparisons of strikes

Methodology The conventions used to compile strike statistics differ substantially between countries, for this reason international comparisons must be approached with caution. Some countries include workers indirectly involved in the stoppage (those unable to work because others at their workplace are on strike), the United Kingdom and the United States are examples, but other countries, Japan, France and Germany, exclude them. Some countries, the United Kingdom, United States and France, exclude political strikes but again others, Sweden and Germany, include them while France excludes public sector strikes from its statistics. Perhaps of greatest importance is the fact that the minimum criteria for recording strikes differ substantially between countries. When, in 1981, the United States revised its series on industrial disputes to include only those involving more than 1000 workers, it was estimated that this change in convention reduced the recorded number of working days lost by between 30 and 40 percent.[46] The principal differences in the methodology used to compile strike statistics in the major OECD countries are detailed in Table 14.2.

44. See Kennan, J. (1986) 'The economics of strikes', in Ashenfelter, O. and Layard, P.R.G. (eds.), *Handbook of Labor Economics*, North Holland.
45. See Pencavel, J.H. (1970) 'An investigation into industrial strike activity in Britain', *Economica*, **37**, 245–52 and Ashenfelter, O. and Johnson, G.E. (1969), *op. cit.*, 35–49.
46. See 'International comparisons of industrial stoppages in 1986', *Department of Employment Gazette*, **96**, (June 1988) 335–8.

Table 14.2 Industrial disputes: comparisons of coverage and methodology

	Minimum criteria for inclusion in statistics	Are political stoppages included?	Are indirectly affected workers included?	Sources and notes
Australia	10 or more days lost	Yes	Yes	Information from arbitrators, employers and unions.
France	No restrictions on size. However, public sector and agricultural employees are excluded from statistics	No	No	Labor inspectors' reports.
Germany	More than 10 workers involved and more than one day's duration unless 100 or more working days lost	Yes	No	Compulsory notification• by employers to labor offices.
Japan	More than half a day's duration	No	No	Interviews by prefectorial labor policy section or local labor policy office of employers and employees.
Sweden	More than one hour's duration	Yes	No	Press reports compiled by State Conciliation Service are checked by employers' organizations and sent to Central Statistical Office.
UK	Same as Germany	No	Yes	Local unemployment benefit offices make reports to Department of Employment HQ, which also checks press, unions and large employers.
US	More than one day or one shift's duration and more than 1000 workers involved	No	Yes	Reports from press, employers, unions and agencies, followed up by questionnaires.

Source: Department of Employment Gazette (1988) Department of Employment, London, June.

Comparison of working days lost Statistics detailing the number of working days lost per 1000 employees are the most readily available in most countries. A comparison of these reveals striking differences between countries in the experience of industrial disputes which cannot be accounted for simply by the different conventions used to compile the statistics. Table 14.3 reports the number of working days lost per 1000 employees in each of the major OECD countries in the 10 years to the end of 1986. It reveals that a negligible number of working days are lost in Japan, while those lost in Austria and Switzerland are so few that they appear scarcely worth reporting. At the other extreme it is clear that Italy and, in the first half of the period, Canada lost in excess of 750 days per 1000 employees over each of these 10 years. In between these two extremes, stand the majority of countries. Sweden, France and the United States lost between 100 and 200 days per 1000 employees over the period and Australia and the United Kingdom were in the 400–500 range. However, it is noteworthy that in general during the 1980s the trend is downwards. The series shows greatest variation in the United Kingdom and Sweden although they fluctuate substantially in most countries. In the United Kingdom they range from a low of 90 in 1986 to a high of 1280 in 1984 and in Sweden from a low of 10 in four of the recorded years to 1150 in 1980. Large scale, 'one-off' industrial disputes account for the peak years in each of these countries; a typical year is far lower.

Part of the United Kingdom's past reputation as the 'sick man of Europe' resulted from its strike record. With the exception of 1984, when there was a protracted and bitter dispute in the coal industry which spilled over into 1985, the number of days lost has shown a sharp fall since 1982. Other countries too have shown a sharp reduction in the number of days. In general the picture that emerges is one of a convergence in the strike rate in the various countries shown.

THE GENERAL WAGE LEVEL IN A UNIONIZED ECONOMY

In an economy in which unions organize either the majority or a substantial minority of the workforce, unions will have a substantial impact on the general wage level. One approach to evaluating the role of unions in aggregate wage setting in such an economy is to construct models of, and estimate the effects of, union wage setting in each of the submarkets that comprise the aggregate economy. An alternative is to construct aggregate functions, which summarize the behavior of wage bargainers. This latter approach has a long history, as reflected in the development and estimation of the Phillips curve which we shall consider in the next chapter. Also it has recently been adopted by two British researchers who have developed a model that appears to enjoy substantial empirical support.[47]

This, the Nickell–Layard model, assumes that firms and workers have some degree of market power. Prices are set by firms as a mark-up on wage costs and this mark-up tends to rise as output and hence employment rises and, falls when inflation is greater than expected. The former effect may be due to firms' attempts to raise profitability as

---

47. See Layard, P.R.G. and Nickell, S.J. (1987) 'Unemployment in Britain', in Bean, C., Layard, R. and Nickell, S.J. (eds.), *The Rise in Unemployment*, Blackwell, Oxford, and Layard, P.R.G. and Nickell, S.J. (1987) 'The labour market', Chapter 5 in Dornbusch, R. and Layard, P.R.G. (eds.), *The Performance of the British Economy*, Clarendon Press, Oxford.

Table 14.3 Industrial disputes: working days lost per 1000 employees[§] in all industries and services 1977–86

	1977–81	Average[¶] 1982–86	1977–86
Australia	590	280	430
Austria	—[‡]	—[‡]	—[‡]
Canada	780	490	630
France	140	80	110
Germany	50	(70)[†]	(50)[†]
Italy	1140	700	920
Japan	30	10	20
Sweden	250	60	160
Switzerland	—[‡]	—[‡]	—[‡]
UK	580	420	500
USA[‖]	230	110	170

Sources: Department of Employment *Gazette*.
Working days lost: International Labor Office (ILO) Year-book of Labor Statistics 1980 and 1986 (Geneva: 1980; 1987)
Employees in employment: ILO and OECD publications.
[†] Brackets indicate average based on incomplete data.
[‡] Less than five days lost per 1000 employees.
[§] Employees in employment: some figures have been estimated.
[¶] Annual averages for those years within each period for which data are available, weighted by employment.
[‖] Figures for all years reflect the threshold of more than 1000 workers involved which was introduced in 1981.

output expands and the latter will be due to price surprises exerting a downward pressure. Wages in turn are set as a mark-up on expected prices. This wage mark-up increases as employment rises and unemployment falls—as labor markets tighten—but once again falls if inflation is greater than expected—as price surprises erode real wages. These price setting and wage setting equations evidently do not arise from the profit and utility maximizing behavior of firms and workers, respectively, in competitive markets and they are therefore of a quite different nature from the theories we have considered before. The motivations and constraints of firms and workers are not spelt out and the choices that they exercise are accordingly unclear. However, the model produces interesting results.

The behavior of the model can be illustrated by mapping the price setting and wage setting equations in real wage and employment space as in Fig. 14.9. The relationships can be expressed (in log linear form) as follows:

Price setting

$$P - W = a_0 + a_1(P - P^e) + a_2(N - L) + a_3(K - L)$$ (14.7)

where $a_1 < 0$; $a_2 \geq 0$ and $a_3 < 0$ and

Wage setting

$$W - P = b_0 + b_1(P - P^e) + b_2(N - L) + b_3(K - L) + Z$$ (14.8)

where $b_1 < 0$; $b_2 > 0$ and $b_3 > 0$ and W and P are as before, L is the labor force, N is employment and therefore $L - N$ gives U. K is the capital stock and Z is a measure of the determinants of wage pressure, such as the degree of structural mismatch between labor supply and demand, the benefit earnings ratio and determinants of union power.

The price setting equation has a negative slope indicating that real wages fall as employment rises because the higher mark-up in the price setting equation, at any given level of wages, produces falling real wages. The wage setting equation has a positive slope because the mark-up of wages over prices, the real wage, rises as unemployment falls and employment rises. Figure 14.9 reveals that the intersection of

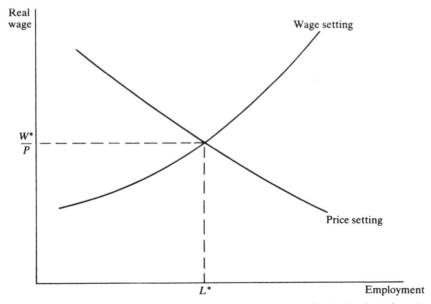

Figure 14.9 The real wage in a unionized economy. The wage setting behavior of trade unions results in a target real wage which is a rising function of the level of employment. This is because the mark-up of wages over expected prices rises as employment rises. The price setting behavior of firms results in a falling real wage as employment rises, because firms raise the mark-up of prices over wages as employment rises. Equilibrium occurs at the point of equality of the wage setting and price setting functions

these curves establishes the equilibrium real wage W^*/P and level of employment L^* in the unionized economy. In the long run the level of employment and the real wage are determined by equality of the feasible real wage, which is the term used for the price setting equation, and the target real wage, the term used for the wage setting equation. Thus a rise in the union mark-up at any given level of employment, such as might occur through increased union militancy, would be reflected in a backward shift in the wage setting equation, and result in a higher real wage and lower level of employment. Factors that increase union power, or exacerbate the degree of structural mismatch in the economy, through the effects of Z in Eq. (14.8) shift the wage setting equation up to the left. It has been suggested that a conjunction of such factors caused real wages to rise in the United Kingdom during the early part of the 1980s and that, more generally, similar developments explain the real wage gaps that emerged in a number of countries in the 1980s. Although we now turn to discuss the issue of real wage gaps, we shall return to this model of the labor market in the next chapter.

AGGREGATE REAL WAGE GAPS

One consequence of an increase in the target real wage, in an economy characterized by union wage bargaining, may be the emergence of real wage gaps. The real wage gap is a measure of the magnitude to which aggregate real wages exceed the market clearing level: it is the difference between the current real wage and the value of the real wage that would be required to insure that the demand for labor was consistent with full employment. In a competitive equilibrium the value of the real wage is given by $W/P = MRP_L$. The real wage gap can then be measured by taking the current real wage and calculating the difference between this and the marginal product of labor: the real wage gap is measured as $(W/P) - MP_L$. Considerable attention has focused on an emerging real wage gap as an explanation of the unemployment experienced by many countries in the 1980s.

In countries in which the labor supply curve is positively sloped, a positive real wage gap will increase labor supply, and thus the effects of wages on unemployment will be greater than their effects on employment. One study suggested that the real gap in the six major OECD countries grew from 0.4 percent in 1965 to 10.4 percent in 1981.[48] The gap increased steadily throughout the 1970s and into the 1980s, a time of rising unemployment, and it is thus tempting to attribute the unemployment of the 1970s and 1980s to too high real wages. The appeal of this explanation increases further when it is realized that during the mid- to late 1970s, when unemployment continued to rise in the United Kingdom but was falling in the United States, the wage gap had been eliminated in the United States but was still growing in the United Kingdom.

The more rigid are real wages the more difficult it will be to eliminate any real wage gap. In Chapter 10 it was shown that in the period to the early 1980s real wages were substantially more rigid in the United Kingdom than in the United States. Undoubtedly the greater incidence of unionism in the former country is a proximate explanation of these differences. However, of greater importance will be the practice

48. Bruno, M.N. and Sachs, J. (1985) *Economics of Worldwide Stagflation*, Blackwell, Oxford.

of union wage negotiators in the United Kingdom, where, although seldom stated formally in collective agreements, wages are effectively indexed by the practice of bargainers. In addition, the absence of synchronization of settlement dates and the role that comparability plays in determining the acceptable or 'going rate', make it extremely difficult to de-escalate the level of pay settlements. It is for this reason that policy makers in the United Kingdom have frequently turned to incomes policy as a means of reducing the level of pay settlements.

INCOMES POLICY

One consequence of union wage bargaining can be that wages are established above the market clearing rate. To counter this, governments have on occasion implemented specific policies, known as incomes policies, which were designed to place a ceiling on wage growth. Such policies were used in the United States and, more extensively, in the United Kingdom in the 1970s, and they were still in operation in a variety of continental European countries and in Australia in the 1980s. These policies take the presence of unions as a datum and seek to mitigate the adverse effects of union bargaining power. However, more recently some European governments have sought a more direct approach and have sought to weaken union bargaining power.

Implicit in the use of incomes policies is the notion that real wages are established above the market clearing level for non-efficiency reasons. Such as outcome was illustrated in Fig. 14.6 as a result of a combination of union wage bargaining and the threat effect. Firms felt compelled to pay wages above the level compatible with normal profits, thus over the longer term there were too few jobs for full employment. The essential argument for incomes policies is that they prevent trade unions exploiting their monopoly power. They do so either by increasing the employer's will to resist, or by penalizing trade unions if they push for high wages.

The success of an incomes policy is likely to depend on the motives which lead trade unions to exploit their monopoly power. One motive may be their concern over members' relative pay. The goal of each trade union may be to match the wage rises achieved by other bargaining groups. Thus if one group secures a high wage settlement and this is subsequently imitated, the rate of nominal wage growth can be set at a rate above that warranted by productivity growth. In the absence of sufficient growth in aggregate demand, this will result in falling employment. In these circumstances incomes policies can take on the characteristics of a public good. They may award equal wage settlements to all groups and thus satisfy trade union aspirations for comparable wage increases, but achieve this at a level of nominal wage growth which is consistent with that warranted by the rate of productivity growth. An incomes policy can thus achieve the desired set of relativities without either the unemployment or the inflation associated with the wage outcomes that might have emerged in an unconstrained bargaining context.

Such a defence of incomes policy will not be appropriate in all circumstances. It will depend on the circumstances which led freely negotiated wage settlements to be established at a non-market clearing level in the first place. Productivity will differ between firms, and if those firms which set the pattern for the subsequent round of wage rises were the most productive, the level of settlements that results will be appropriate for some firms but not for others. Where the productivity performances of industries differ, they no longer warrant a uniform level of wage settlements, and an incomes policy which enforces such a structure is no longer desirable.

How is the ceiling on wage rises imposed? There exist two principal forms of statutory incomes policy: policies designed to penalize the firm if it awards wages in excess of the maximum; and policies which offer incentives to workers to moderate their wage settlements.

Penalties on firms

This form of policy has been the most widely used of the statutory policies. Firms are penalized, their profits are reduced further if they concede wages above the stipulated maximum. By proposing this further reduction in firms' profits, by introducing a further threat to their viability, the penalty serves to strengthen firms' resistance. Such a model might be most effective in an economy in which most firms have some degree of market power for the penalty now diminishes their excess profits. A simple model evaluating the consequence of an incomes policy of this type is detailed in Appendix 14B. Another way in which firms might be penalized for breaking the policy guidelines is to levy an additional tax on the profits of those firms breaking the policy. Typically, these tax-based incomes policies (TIPS) propose levying a fine or tax that is proportional to the extent to which the wage settlement exceeds the stipulated norm. Thus if the normal rate of corporate tax is C, then the new rate of tax, T, under the incomes policy is:

$$T = C + \lambda(W - W_{max}) \qquad (14.9)$$

where λ represents the penal tax rate. Thus if $W = W_{max}$, $T = C$ and there is no change in the firm's corporate tax liability. If $W > W_{max}$ then $T > C$ by a magnitude determined by λ and the degree of non-compliance, the extent to which $W > W_{max}$. If $W < W_{max}$ then the reverse holds, now because $(W - W_{max})$ is negative $C > T$ and the firm's corporate tax liability falls. Thus this policy combines both stick and carrot; it rewards those who comply and penalizes those who fail to comply.[49]

Such 'stick' and 'carrot' policies raise interesting questions of both a practical and theoretical nature. First, the practical. What happens to small firms that comply with the policy but whose profits do not exceed the minimum necessary for corporation tax? How are they to be rewarded? Second, how are non-wage forms of compensation to be handled? Ideally these should be fully costed and the monetary value of such fringes treated in just the same way as a wage rise. In practice this is difficult to do, for it is much easier to monitor highly publicized wage settlements, than to monitor and then

49. Such a policy has been described as a counter inflation tax. It penalizes firms by levying a penal tax rate but, in order to ensure that the *total* burden of taxes placed on firms as a whole is not increased, the general rate of tax levied on all firms is cut by an amount equal to the proceeds of the tax. Thus the relative magnitude of the penalty for non-compliance would be maintained but the tax burden on firms would be unchanged. See Layard, P.R.G. (1986) *How to Beat Unemployment*, Oxford University Press.

cost the money value to workers of improved pension arrangements. It may also be difficult to stop firms with significant market power seeking to recoup profits by raising prices. Finally, consider the theoretical problem of adverse selection. The government will find itself rewarding those whom the incentives induced to comply *and* those who would have complied with the policy anyway. The reward of lower corporate tax payments will be indiscriminately distributed to all those awarding wage settlements below the ceiling, regardless of their reasons for doing so.

Incentives for workers

An alternative approach is to induce workers to comply by minimizing the risks associated with their doing so. One problem inherent in incomes policies is the 'free rider' problem. Individuals will suffer a decline in their real wage if they comply with the incomes policy norm but everyone else, or at least a substantial number of workers, do not. The failure of others to comply will result in higher prices for all and those who exercise restraint will therefore be penalized. Only if all workers comply, will lower price rises result and low nominal wage rises not translate into real wage reductions. One way of resolving this problem is to shift the risk from the individual to the government. This can be done by promising each individual that complies with the policy, or each member of the bargaining group that complies with the policy, a tax credit if the price index rises above some pre-specified level. In this manner those that comply are insured against the possibility that others might break the policy. If prices rise above the threshold they receive a reduction in their personal tax rate. Thus if t is the individual's personal tax rate

$$t = t_1 - (\Delta P - X) \qquad (14.10)$$

where t_1 is the initial basic rate of tax, ΔP is the experienced change in retail prices over some pre-specified period, and X is the threshold rate of price increase. Now if $\Delta P > X$ the individual's personal tax rate, t, is reduced by lowering his or her initial basic rate of tax.

Such a policy was proposed in the United States in the 1970s. X was to be set equal to 7 percent, so that if $\Delta P = 10$ and t_1 was standing at 25 percent then t was reduced by 3 percent to 22 percent.[50] Such policies face problems of adverse selection, reduced tax rates will be awarded to individuals who would have complied with the policy anyway. A more substantial practical objection to such a policy is that in periods of rapid price inflation, the cost to the government of the tax reductions it will have to offer could be quite substantial.

The experience of incomes policies in the United Kingdom

Incomes policies have occasionally been introduced in the United States but they were a common feature of macroeconomic policy in the United Kingdom in the period up

---

50. For an interesting summary and analysis of the US experience with incomes policies see Pencavel, J.H. (1981) 'The American experience with incomes policies', in J.L. Fallick and R.F. Elliott (eds.), *Incomes Policies, Inflation and Relative Pay*, Allen and Unwin, London.

to 1979. However, in the United Kingdom they have met with very mixed success. The consensus now appears to be that such policies frequently arrested the rate of growth of nominal wages while they were in operation, but that once the restrictions were lifted wages rose sharply to make up the ground they had lost. The effects of the policies therefore appear temporary. Further objections have been leveled at these policies. It is argued that by awarding uniform pay increases to all workers, as many of the policies did, they reduced the rewards for ability and skill and thus diminished the incentives to productive performance. It has further been argued that by introducing government as the principal arbiter of the magnitude of nominal wage rises, such policies appeared to diminish the firms' responsibilities for determining the appropriate level of pay. They thus severed any perception of a link between the workers' performance and their pay, while at the same time politicizing the wage bargaining process. This aspect had very substantial and adverse consequences, as manifest in a number of bitter and protracted industrial disputes that occurred in the United Kingdom in the 1970s. These then are the costs but what of the benefits? The major benefit can be simply stated, it is a reduction in the level of unemployment below that which would have otherwise existed.

The performance of money wages in the United Kingdom during periods of incomes policies in the 1970s is detailed in Table 14.4. The form of the policy, the permitted rise in earnings and the actual outcome are detailed and it is clear that the actual outcome always exceeded that permitted. Of course, we need to know what the outcome would have been had such policies not been in operation, for it is possible that increase in money wages would have been even larger had the policies not been in place. However, by the same token, the pay increases that occurred in the policy-off periods might also have been smaller. Several of the policies shown took a flat rate form, they awarded equal money increases to all workers in an attempt to increase their appeal. However, it has been shown that those workers who stood to gain most from such policies were among those who complied least and therefore this aspect of the experiment must be judged a failure. The history of such formal statutory restraints on wage rises is not encouraging. Their history in the United Kingdom, where they have been most widely practiced, suggests they have met with rather limited success.[51]

CORPORATISM

A radically different approach to the issue of real wage restraint has been proposed in a number of countries. Corporatism consists of the creation of institutions which bring together and mediate between the, initially, conflicting interests of the principal interest groups in a society. The creation of tripartite bodies, consisting of representatives of unions, employers and government, to agree the pace of wage increases is an example of a corporatist solution to wage bargaining. The creation of such institutions

51. See Fallick, J.L. and Elliott, R.F. (eds.), (1981) *Incomes Policies, Inflation and Relative Pay*, George Allen and Unwin; Chater, R.E.J., Dean, A. and Elliott, R.F. (eds.) (1981) *Incomes Policy*, Oxford University Press; and Elliott, R.F. and Murphy, P.D. (1989) 'Evasion of incomes policy: a model of non-compliance', *Economic Journal*, **99**, 1054–64.

Table 14.4 Wage growth during periods of incomes policy in the United Kingdom

	Policy[†]	Nominal wage growth			
		Permitted[‡]	Actual[§]	Actual minus permitted	Real wage growth
1970 to Nov. 1972	no limit				
Nov. 1972–Apr. 1973	freeze	0	1.8	1.8	− 2.5
Apr. 1973–Nov. 1973	£1 + 4 percent (£5 max.)	7.5	10.3	2.8	+ 4.3
Nov. 1973–Jul. 1974	£2.25 or 7 percent (£7 max.) + 'threshold'	13.0	14.9	1.9	+ 1.9
Aug. 1974–Aug. 1975	no limit	no limit	25.9	−	0
Aug. 1975–Aug. 1976	£6	10.4	14.3	3.9	+ 0.5
Aug. 1976–Aug. 1977	5 percent (£2.50 min., £4 max.)	4.5	7.3	2.8	− 7.9
Aug. 1977–Aug. 1978	10 percent	10.0	13.9	3.9	+ 5.5
Aug. 1978–Dec. −	no limit				

Source: Ashenfelter, O. and Layard, P.R.G. (1983) 'Incomes policy and wage differentials', *Economica*, **50**, 127–43. Hunter, L.C. (1975) 'British incomes policy, 1972–74', *Industrial and Labor Relations Review*, **29**(1).
[†] It is approximately correct to think of the policies as beginning and ending on the first of the month, while the actual data are recorded at some date during the month.
[‡] *Permitted earnings* 1972–74 (Hunter, 1975); 1975–78 (Ashenfelter and Layard, 1983). These do not allow for the exceptions to incomes policy allowed where women's pay was increased relative to men's during the approach to Equal Pay although they take account of the fact that women's earnings were lower than men's and thus would rise further due to the equal lump sum payments in most policies. For example, between April and November 1973 £1 + 4 percent was expected to raise male earnings by an average 6.7 percent and female earnings by 8.4 percent.
[§] *Actual earnings* There is no monthly series that distinguishes between men and women. The figures therefore relate to both sexes. The data are from Ashenfelter and Layard and relate to full-time *and* part-time workers. They report that for the period April–April they can be compared with the results for full-time workers from the New Earnings Survey and that the results are similar. For the period October–October they can be compared with the results for full-time manual workers from the October Survey and are again similar.

encourages the growth of common interests and goals among the participants in these institutions.

The basic arguments for corporatism rest on the notion that in most industrial countries wages are no longer set with reference to supply and demand in labor markets and that, in consequence, real wages are no longer flexible in the manner supposed by neoclassical theory. In most countries it is argued that the workforce does not approximate the atomistic units required for perfectly competitive markets, instead labor markets have become less competitive and the workforce has acquired considerable power with which to pursue its objectives.[52]

52. For a detailed exposition of these arguments see Schott, K. (1984) *Policy Power and Order: The Persistence of Economic Problems in Capitalist States*, Yale University Press, New York.

In support of the contention that the power of the workforce has increased in most western industrialized societies a number of factors are cited. It is argued there has been a steady rise in the overall levels of union density in most countries over the past three decades. The extension of the franchise, with the result that labor interests are now represented within the legislature of most countries, is also suggested to have increased this power. Finally, it is argued these developments have in turn given rise to an increase in the share of public expenditure in GDP for it is wage earners who demand higher public expenditure. This increase in the power of wage earners poses, it is argued, particular problems for competitive theory, which is based on a pluralist conception of society in which no group is sufficiently large or influential to interfere systematically in economic policy decisions and outcomes.

The argument asserts that the increase in the power of the workforce has resulted in reduced real wage flexibility and enabled the workforce to frustrate the objectives of macroeconomic fiscal and monetary policy. Corporatist arrangements, which accommodate this new balance of power in labor markets and the wider society, enable policy makers to pursue reflationary fiscal and monetary policies without the danger that these will translate into inflationary wage push.

Earlier in this chapter it was shown that if wages and employment could be negotiated, efficient bargains could result. The general absence of such bargains at the micro level reflected the lack of those institutions necessary to negotiate about employment and wages and to monitor subsequent compliance with the terms of agreements struck by the two parties. Corporatism may be interpreted as an attempt to negotiate efficient wage bargains at the macroeconomic level. It represents the deliberate construction of those institutions required to conduct negotiations about wages and employment and to insure subsequent compliance by both firms and unions.

Corporatism has been practiced in a number of countries in which labor has been effectively represented in government over a sustained period. In these countries interest groups are encompassing rather than fragmentary and the two principal interest groups, trade unions and employer organizations, cooperate in areas of economic policy. As a result the state no longer needs to enact authoritarian incomes policies, in an attempt to restrain by legislation the parties to wage bargaining. Their interests are considered and mediated within the corporatist arrangements and such societies are therefore characterized by a low incidence of open conflict. Societies that have been characterized as corporatist are Austria, Norway, Sweden, Japan and Switzerland, and it emerges that these were almost exclusively the nations with the lowest unemployment rates and lowest rates of increase in inflation over the period 1965–81. Since the early 1980s Australia too has attempted to introduce corporatism. In contrast to these countries those with the worst records for increasing inflation and unemployment, Great Britain, Italy, France, the United States, and Australia prior to the 1980s, were believed to display weak forms of corporatism if any at all.

A number of authors have analyzed the performance of corporatist and non-corporatist states. One study, which examined the economic performance of 20 OECD countries, concluded that those that performed best in terms of inflation and growth,

Norway, Germany and Austria, were those societies characterized by a degree of consensus. It also concluded that those whose performance deteriorated most over the two periods 1959–73 and 1974–81, Italy and the United Kingdom among them, were characterized by a lack of consensus.[53] The degree of corporatism and nominal wage responsiveness in a country has also been found to be associated with a more favorable trade-off between inflation and unemployment[54] and with superior economic performance. In corporatist economies wage changes appear more responsive to unemployment and the increase in the level of unemployment over the last two decades has been lower in corporatist than in non-corporatist states.[55] Moreover, it was suggested that during their corporatist 'phases' in recent years Germany, Britain and Japan (there is no consensus on the classification of some countries) were able to achieve a given cut in real wages at the cost of a far smaller increase in unemployment than was possible when they were pursuing non-corporatist policies.[56]

The thrust of the corporatist analysis is that those countries in which corporatism has not emerged have not been able to employ a consensual approach to wage policy. In these countries sectional interests have dominated and the application of (neo-Keynesian) demand management policies has often not had the desired response. Advocates of corporatism therefore suggest that where encompassing groups do not exist, the state should encourage the formation and development of such groups. Not all countries have heeded this message. The 1980s witnessed Great Britain and some other continental European countries dismantle those corporatist arrangements that existed. It has been argued that at the end of the 1980s Britain in some respects appears to be in a rather healthier economic position than at the start of the decade, and it is therefore doubtful that corporatism is the universal panacea its advocates seem to claim.[57]

SUMMARY

In this chapter we have focused on the role of trade unions in the wage setting process. Trade unions play a relatively minor role in wage setting in the United States and, indeed in Japan, but in many European countries they are the principal actors. Despite this prominence considerable uncertainty surrounds the goal of unions and it has therefore proved difficult to construct robust economic models of union behavior. The most we can say is that, in general, the evidence seems to suggest that unions are

53. Hughes, B. (1982) 'Incomes policy the international experience', in Walsh, P. (ed.), *Incomes Policy*, University of Wellington, Victoria.
54. Bruno, M. and Sachs, J. (1985) *The Economics of Worldwide Stagflation*, Harvard University Press, Cambridge, Mass.
55. Bean, C.R., Layard, P.R.G. and Nickell, S.J. (1986) 'The rise in unemployment: a multi-country study', Centre for Labour Economics, London School of Economics, Discussion Paper No. 239.
56. Newell, A. and Symons, J. (1986) 'Corporatism, *laissez-faire* and the rise of unemployment', Centre for Labour Economics, London School of Economics, Discussion Paper No. 260.
57. See Layard, P.R.G. and Nickell, S. (1989) 'The Thatcher miracle?', *American Economic Review, Papers and Proceedings*, **79**(2), 215–19 for an evaluation of the economic record of Britain in the 1980s.

concerned about pay and employment, and that they often bargain with employers about both. However, there appear to be significant differences in the weight that different unions within any one country attach to each of these goals.

The empirical evidence suggests that unions have an important impact on earnings. Union workers enjoy substantial wage premiums although the magnitude of the union wage gap has varied over the years. Despite theoretical arguments, which propose that unions can enhance labor productivity, there is not much convincing empirical evidence to support this contention. Indeed, in the United Kingdom and the United States any favorable productivity effects appear to have been more than offset by union wage effects, for the net effect has been substantially lower profitability.

On occasion, unions threaten strikes to persuade the other party to the wage bargain of the appropriateness of settling on the union's terms. International comparisons show that strikes are far more prevalent in some countries than in others, but the 1980s witnessed a substantial fall in the number of strikes and working days lost in almost all major industrialized nations. Economic theory has found it difficult to construct a plausible theory of strikes and, as a result, recent developments are less than well understood.

Finally, we looked at the policies that have been proposed to deal with the real wage gaps that can emerge in economics in which union wage bargaining establishes the general level of wages. Statutory incomes policies have been tried in several countries, most frequently in the United Kingdom, and they have generally been found lacking. More recently interest has revived in corporatist policies as a result of the economic success of certain corporatist nations and the apparently successful adoption of this policy by Australia in the early 1980s.

PRINCIPAL CONCEPTS

Students should now be familiar with the following concepts developed in this chapter:

1. The contract curve.
2. The union wage gain.
3. The union wage gap.
4. Union threat effects.
5. Union spillover effects.
6. Employer's concession curve.
7. Union resistance curve.
8. The feasible real wage.
9. The target real wage.
10. TIPs.

QUESTIONS FOR DISCUSSION

1. How plausible is the monopoly union model? Can a monopoly union be concerned about wages and employment and if so what does it need to know in order to secure its goals?

2. What are the critical elements of an economic theory of bargaining?
3. Why might it prove difficult for employers and unions to negotiate efficient bargains? Should they try?
4. Does the empirical evidence provide any support for the seniority model of union behavior?
5. What effect do unions have on the distribution of earned income?
6. What are the problems associated with measuring the union wage gap?
7. How might unions increase labor productivity?
8. Can economists explain strikes?
9. What can we learn from an international comparison of strike statistics?
10. Which form of income policy is likely to prove more effective in theory, inducements to workers or penalties on firms?
11. What are the theoretical arguments for corporatism?

FURTHER READING

Despite the much lower profile of unions in the United States, US authors have produced three interesting contributions to the literature in this area. Freeman, R.B. and Medoff, J.L. (1984) *What Do Unions Do?*, Basic Books, New York, provides a challenging view of the impact of unions on productivity, while Addison, J.T. and Hirsch, B.T. (1986) *The Economic Analysis of Unions: New Approaches and Evidence*, George Allen and Unwin, Boston and London provides a very useful summary of the literature on unions up to the early 1980s. More recently John H. Pencavel has produced an excellent survey of this area in *The Labor Market Under Trade Unionism: Employment, Wages and Work Hours* (forthcoming, 1990). This book is highly recommended and I benefited greatly during the later stages of drafting this chapter in having access to the manuscript of this book. Two very useful surveys also appear in the second volume of the *Handbook of Labor Economics*, edited by Ashenfelter, O. and Layard, P.R.G., North Holland, 1986. These are the surveys by Henry S. Farber (Chapter 18) 'An analysis of union behavior' and H. Gregg Lewis (Chapter 20) 'Union relative wage effects'.

APPENDIX 14A   THE NASH SOLUTION TO BARGAINING

An attempt to find a determinate solution to the bargaining process is offered by the Nash solution. In this model the concessions that each party makes lead them to a point where the total gains from the settlement are greatest. The two parties, employers and unions, act so as to maximize the product of their utility gains. The utility gains or utility increments represent the additions to utility that the two parties obtain from reaching an agreement. Suppose that if the parties fail to reach agreement they obtain fallback levels of utility, U_0, and profits, π_0, for the trade union and employer respectively, as depicted by the origin in Fig. 14A.1. For the trade union, this fallback

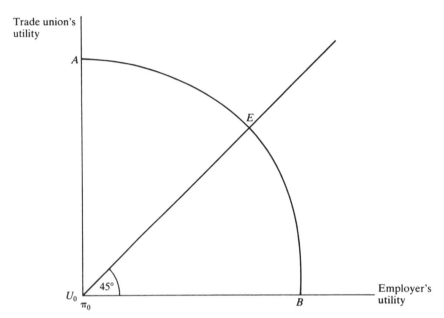

Figure 14A.1 The increments to utility from reaching agreement. The utility increments frontier maps the increments to utility each party enjoys as a result of reaching agreement. The origin represents the fallback levels of utility when they fail to agree, and the intercepts A and B, the gains in utility by the trade union and employer when they, respectively, enjoy the total returns. Points along the frontier represent a division of these gains determined by the relative power of the two parties. E is where they share the gains equally

level might constitute the level of unemployment benefit its members would receive if there were no agreement, $U(B)$, while for the employer there may be some minimum, perhaps even negative, level of profits they obtain if they fail to agree. The coordinate U_0, π_0 is known as the 'threat point', increments to each of these minimum levels enable us to describe a utility increments frontier where the intercepts A *and* B represent receipt of the total gains from reaching agreement by the trade union and employer respectively. The intercepts represent the maximum that each party could gain from reaching agreement, and the concavity of the frontier illustrates that the joint benefits are greater when they result from reaching a settlement. These gains are shared in different proportions except at the point E where the gains are shared equally.

If we represent the utility increments to the trade union above the fallback level as $(U - U_0)$ and to the employer as increments to profits $(\pi - \pi_0)$, the function to be maximized is

$$(U - U_0)(\pi - \pi_0) \tag{14A.1}$$

If the increments to the union's utility are represented by the additions to the wage, $U(W)$, above a fallback level as represented by the position where all union members are unemployed and in receipt of unemployment benefit $U(B)$, then $(U - U_0) = U(W) - U(B)$. Similarly, the increments to the employer's minimum profit level π_0 can be given by total revenue, as a function of employment, $TR(N)$, minus wage costs WN. Thus $(\pi - \pi_0) = TR(N) - WN - \pi_0$ so that Eq. (14A.1), the function we have to maximize, becomes:

$$N([U(W) - U(B)](TR(N) - WN - \pi_0)) \qquad (14A.2)$$

Now if we maximize this function with respect to employment, N, all employees being union members, we find that

$$W = \frac{1}{2}\left[\frac{TR(N)}{N} + \frac{\mathrm{d}TR}{\mathrm{d}N} - \frac{\pi_o}{N}\right] \qquad (14A.3)$$

This tells us that if the final term in brackets, the fallback level of profit $\pi_0 = 0$, then the wage established will be equal to the arithmetic average, of the average revenue products of labor, $TR(N)/N$, and marginal revenue product, $\delta TR/\delta N$. Since the latter term identifies points on the labor demand curve, this schedule evidently lies to the right of the labor demand curve and is in fact a point on the contract curve. The Nash solution therefore identifies an efficient bargain.

APPENDIX 14B   A MODEL OF COMPLIANCE WITH INCOMES POLICY

The firm's profit function is the difference between total revenue and total cost. Total revenue is defined as the product price, P, multiplied by output, Q, where the latter is given by a short-run production function, $f(N)$. Total costs are defined as the product of the wage rate, W, and employment, N. Thus profits $\pi = Pf(N) - WN$. Now the imposition of an incomes policy modifies the profit function, for it imposes a penalty, a fine, on all those firms that are caught contravening the policy, that is, on all those that award wage increases above the specified ceiling. Now the firm's expected profit function is:

$$\pi = (1 - \Theta)(Pf(N) - WN) - \Theta(Pf(N) - WN - F) \qquad (14B.1)$$

Where Θ is the probability that a firm will be caught contravening the policy, in which case its profits are reduced by the size of the fine, F. If firms are responsible for determining the level of employment they will do so with respect to the labor demand function. The next step is to substitute the profit maximizing labor demand function $N = N^*(W,P)$ into Eq. (14B.1) to give the maximum profit function.[B.1]

$$\pi^* = Pf[N^*(W,P)] - WN^*(W,P) - \Theta F \qquad (14B.2)$$

Such a model is not complete without a statement about the union's preferences. Suppose the union's preference function, U, is assumed to be of the following utilitarian form where

$$U = Nu(W) + (M - N)u(B) \qquad (14B.3)$$

B.1. This can be found from

$$\pi^* = (1 - \Theta)[PfN^*(W,P) - WN^*(W,P)] - \Theta[PfN^*(W,P) - WN^*(W,P) - F]$$

where N union members are employed and derive utility $u(W)$ from the wage they receive and $M - N$ of the M members of the union are therefore unemployed and enjoy a level of utility $u = u(B)$ set by the level of unemployment benefit. Then the addition to union utility $U - U_0$, resulting from negotiating wages in excess of the unemployment benefit fallback level of utility, is given by

$$U - U_0 = N^*(W,P)[u(W) - u(B)] \qquad (14B.4)$$

Thus the union gains by negotiating wages in excess of the minimum benefit level but this gain is constrained by the labor demand curve. In a similar manner employers gain by achieving profits in excess of normal profits, π_0, so that a function identifying the increments to employer's profits, $\pi - \pi_0$, can also be identified. The model is finally completed by proposing a solution to the problem of determining the gains to each party, that is a solution to the bargaining problem. This has been set up in the form of the Nash bargaining problem and therefore the solution is found, as before, by maximizing the function

$$\text{Max } Z = (U - U_0)(\pi^* - \pi) \qquad (14B.5)$$

The procedure is then to substitute Eqs. (14B.2) and (14B.4) into Eq. (14B.5) and differentiate the equation with respect to W to yield the first-order conditions for a maximum. An analysis of the comparative statics which result would then show that compliance will increase as the size of the penalty that is levied increases, and the probability of detection, Θ, increases.

15

UNEMPLOYMENT AND WAGES

Economists define unemployment as an excess supply of labor at prevailing wage rates. Unemployment is defined with reference to current wage rates because there will be a level of wages at which almost everyone not currently seeking work, the retired, those engaged in non-market work or higher education, will find it attractive to do so. It is not these people, but only those who are actively seeking work and unable to find employment at existing wage rates that we classify as unemployed.

In the latter half of the 1970s and first half of the 1980s unemployment emerged as the major economic policy issue in almost all Western European nations. By the early 1980s unemployment in these countries had climbed to levels not seen since the great depression of the 1930s. Unemployment also rose in North America and Australia but the rise there was less dramatic than in Western Europe while in Japan it remained at levels little different from those of the 1960s.

What causes unemployment? This is an issue that has long concerned, and divided, macroeconomists. From the time of Keynes, who first fully developed the view that unemployment was caused by a deficiency of aggregate demand, economists have been divided between those who subscribe to Keynes's view and neoclassical economists. The neoclassical view can be summarized in the statement that unemployment is caused by real wages that are too high and, although the causes of the high wages can be many and varied, neoclassical economists generally argue that unregulated markets have a natural tendency to clear and so unemployment would not persist into the long run.[1] Neoclassical economists have subsequently refined their analysis, emphasizing that expectational errors can be one cause of substantial fluctuations in the level of unemployment. Out of neoclassical theory have also come the ideas of the 'natural rate hypothesis' and associated with this a debate about the voluntary and involuntary nature of unemployment. These are some of the issues that will be covered in this chapter.

MEASURING UNEMPLOYMENT

In most European countries the count of the number of unemployed is obtained as the by-product of the process of administering unemployment benefits. For example, in the case of the United Kingdom the 'monthly count of the unemployed', the most widely reported measure of unemployment, reflects the number of individuals claiming either the flat rate unemployment benefit or, when entitlement to this is exhausted, as occurs after 12 months, the number of individuals of working age without jobs who are claiming the means tested income support measure. The advantage of this 'claimant count' is that it is available quickly and cheaply on a regular basis. The disadvantage is that it does not provide an accurate measure of unemployment. Included among its numbers are some individuals who are not available to take a job were one to be offered and others who are claiming benefits but not actively looking for work. For this latter reason the claimant count overstates the number of unemployed. For other reasons this measure understates the number of unemployed. It omits all those individuals who are looking for work but not claiming benefit. The single largest group of these in the United Kingdom is married women. Married women are not eligible for unemployment benefit if they are looking for work immediately following a period of full-time work in the home, and are typically not eligible for means tested income support.

The alternative to counting the number of unemployed, is to conduct a survey of individuals asking whether they had a job or would like to work and in the latter case about the steps they had taken to find work. This is the approach that underpins the most widely used International Labour Organization/Organization for Economic Cooperation and Development (ILO/OECD) measure. On this definition individuals who are without a paid job but are available for work and have either been seeking work in the past four weeks, or are waiting to start a job already obtained are counted as unemployed. This is the definition employed in the United States and available for Britain in one month of each year. Just how this measure compares to the claimant count measure, also used in Britain, is shown in Fig. 15.1. Both measures produced rather similar estimates of the magnitude of unemployment in Britain in 1986 (they

---

1. The most complete statement of the neoclassical theory of unemployment is that of Pigou, A.C. (1933) *The Theory of Unemployment*, Macmillan, London, and it was this that Keynes (1936) attacked in *The General Theory of Employment, Interest and Money*, Macmillan, London. Pigou's response to the publication of the General Theory was decidedly unenthusiastic and his critical review of the General Theory in *Economica* in 1936 resulted in considerable animosity between the two Cambridge colleagues, both once the pupils of Alfred Marshall.

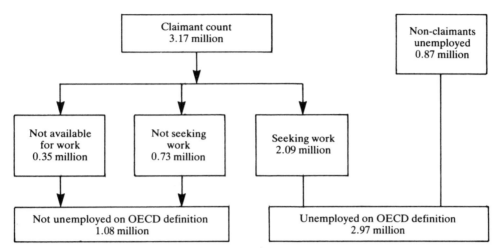

Figure 15.1 Counting the unemployed in Britain in 1986. The OECD definition and claimant count compared

differed by only 200 000 at a time when the level hovered around 3 million) but by quite different routes. In Britain the ILO/OECD measure of unemployment has only been available since 1984.

The unemployment rate

A straight count of the number of people unemployed in a country provides a poor guide to the relative severity of the unemployment problem for, *ceteris paribus*, the number unemployed will be greater the larger the working population. Accordingly, to facilitate comparisons through time and between countries, it is usual to calculate an unemployment rate, which standardizes the number of unemployed by expressing it as a proportion of the total labor force, *LF* (as in the United Kingdom) or the civilian population (as in the United States). Thus in the United Kingdom

$$U = \frac{U}{U + E + S + M} \times 100 = \frac{U}{LF} \times 100$$

where U is the unemployment rate, U is the total number unemployed on either the claimant count or ILO/OECD definition, E is the total number of employees in employment, S is the number of self-employed and M is the number in the armed forces. In the United States the rate is calculated in exactly the same way but using the ILO/OECD definition of unemployment and omitting the US forces from the denominator. How do these unemployment rates compare between different countries?

EMPIRICAL ASPECTS OF UNEMPLOYMENT

An historical perspective

To many observers the sharp rise in unemployment in the United Kingdom in the early 1980s appeared to herald a return to the levels experienced during the great depression of the 1930s. Figure 15.2 reveals that by 1981 the unemployment rate in the United Kingdom was little short of the rate that existed during the depth of the 1930s depression. Comparison of Figs. 15.2 and 15.3 reveals that the contrast between the UK experience and that of the United States is quite marked. Not only was the unemployment rate in the 1980s in the United States far less than in the United Kingdom, but this rate paled into insignificance when compared with the rate which the United States experienced during the great depression. At the height of the depression almost one in four of the labor force was unemployed in the United States, whereas in the 1980s at worst one in ten was unemployed.

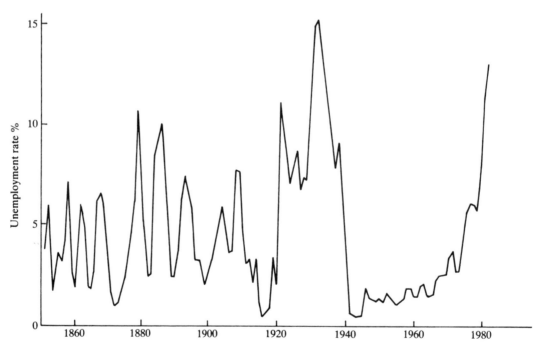

Figure 15.2 The UK unemployment rate. (*Sources:* To 1963: Feinstein, C.H. (1972) *National Income, Expenditure and Output of the United Kingdom 1855–1965*, Cambridge. 1963 onwards: *Department of Employment Gazette.* All figures are adjusted to the basis of unemployment as measured in the 1950s, 1960s and 1970s. 1984 is mid-year. (From Johnson G.E. and Layard P.R.G. (1986) 'The Natural Rate of Unemployment: expectations and policy', in Ashenfelter, O. and Layard, P.R.G. (eds), *Handbook of Labor Economics*, North Holland. Reprinted with permission of the publisher and authors)

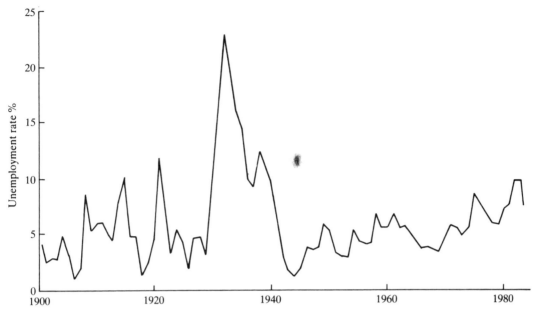

Figure 15.3 The US unemployment rate. (*Source:* 1900–50: The US figures are taken from Lebergott, S. 'Annual estimates of unemployment in the United States 1900–1954', in: Universities-NBER, *The Measurement and Behavior of Unemployment,* Princeton, 1957. Lebergott's rates for 1931–43 have been adjusted for those employed on public works as in Darby, M. *Journal of Political Economy,* 1976. 1950–83: Bureau of Labor Statistics, 1984. Mid-year. (From Johnson G.E. and Layard P.R.G. (1986) *op. cit.* Reprinted with permission of the publisher and authors)

International comparisons of unemployment rates

In almost all industrial countries unemployment was higher in the 1980s than it had been in the 1970s. The mid-1970s had seen an increase in unemployment, after the recession resulting from the first oil price hike in 1973, but the rise in unemployment rates in the early 1980s, following the oil price hike of 1979 was more substantial. This is illustrated in Fig. 15.4. In the intervening period of the late 1970s unemployment rates fell back in most countries but this was everywhere to levels higher than the rates that these countries had experienced in the 1960s and early 1970s. Thus the rise in unemployment in the early 1980s was on top of already high levels of unemployment so that at the peak, in 1983, unemployment reached levels not seen since the 1930s.

More detail on unemployment in the major industrialized nations over the period 1964 to 1988 is reported in Table 15.1. This reveals that unemployment peaked in the mid-1980s, when almost 1 in every 10 of the working age population was without a job in the United Kingdom, France, Italy and Canada and around 1 in 14 in Germany, the United States and Australia. In contrast, only 1 in every 30 was without a job in Sweden and 1 in 40 in Japan.

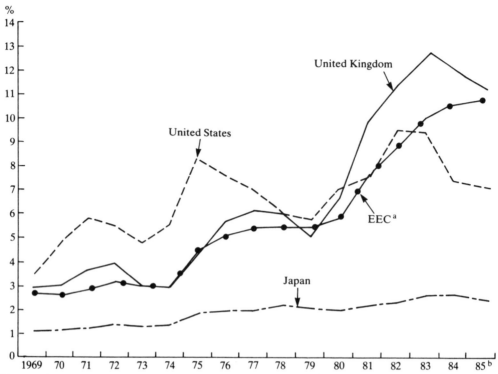

Figure 15.4 Standardized unemployment rates (percent of total labor force). (a) EEC average refers to Belgium, France, Germany, Italy, the Netherlands and the United Kingdom. (b) Average of the first three quarters. (*Source:* OECD estimates.) Reprinted with permission of the OECD

Unemployment rates peaked rather later in Japan and France but in general they began to fall back from the mid-1980s onwards. One of the features of the 1980s was that unemployment rates in the largest European economies, France, Germany and the United Kingdom, caught up with and overtook those of the United States. Prior to the 1980s, as Table 15.1 shows, the United States appeared to be an economy that exhibited a relatively high level of unemployment. It has often been suggested that there is a trade-off between inflation and unemployment (we shall analyze this later) and so it was argued that prior to the 1980s the United States had traded off less inflation for more unemployment when compared with Europe. However, the higher levels of unemployment and inflation in most major European countries during the 1980s gave the lie to this notion, and we shall explore the reasons for this later.

Stocks and flows

Estimates of unemployment are produced once a month in most countries. Those classified as unemployed are those who, on the day of the survey or the count, are without a job and meet the other criteria detailed above. In the interval between these

Table 15.1 Standardized unemployment rates in selected countries

	1964–73	1974–79	1980–85	1985	1986	1987	1988
US	4.5	6.7	8.0	7.1	6.9	6.1	5.2
Japan	1.2	1.9	2.4	2.6	2.8	2.8	2.5
Germany	0.8	3.2	6.0	7.2	6.5	6.5	6.5
France	2.3	4.5	8.3	10.2	10.4	10.6	10.5
UK	2.9	5.0	10.5	11.3	11.2	10.3	8.5
Italy	5.5	6.6	9.2	10.1	10.8	11.6	12.1
Canada	4.8	7.2	9.9	10.4	9.5	8.8	7.5
Australia	—	—	7.1	8.2	8.0	8.1	7.8
Sweden	—	—	2.8	2.8	2.7	1.9	1.7
EC average	2.7	4.9	9.5	11.1	11.3	11.0	10.8

Source: OECD *Economic Progress Report*, Oct. 1987, and Sept. 88 and *Employment Outlook.*

monthly estimates some individuals will have joined and left unemployment, so the count will not include them. Other individuals will be on the register one month but gone the next, so they will feature only briefly while still others will experience long spells of unemployment and so will be recorded month after month. Many more people join and leave the stock of the unemployed during the course of a year than the raw unemployment figures would suggest. Consider the scale of these flows first in Great Britain and then in the United States.

Great Britain During 1986 a total of 4.6 million individuals joined the unemployment register, 2.9 million males and 1.7 million females. Over this same period an almost equivalent number of individuals left the register with the result that the total number unemployed rose by only 100 000 during the year. In a steady state the inflow, I, equals the outflow, O, but any divergence of these will result in changes in the number recorded as unemployed. In a steady state where $I = O$ the unemployment rate $U/LF = (I/LF)/(O/U)$—the inflow into unemployment expressed as a proportion of the labor force divided by the outflow as a proportion of the unemployed. The major flows into and out of unemployment are illustrated in Fig. 15.5. In Britain in 1986 58 percent of the total number of individuals joining unemployment had previously been in work, 42 percent had been out of the labor force. The level of unemployment is the difference between two very large flows; it is the volume of inflows relative to outflows which accounts for changes in unemployment.

Redundancies constitute a major anti-cyclical flow into unemployment. In 1981 there were 532,000 confirmed redundancies in Britain while there had been only 186,000 three years earlier. Other flows into unemployment exhibit a marked pro-cyclical pattern. Voluntary quits fall as the level of unemployment increases when re-entrants to the labor market are also fewer. Individuals perceive that their chances of obtaining a new job, if they quit their existing job or if they seek to transfer from non-market to market work, are reduced. At times of rising unemployment the reduction in voluntary quits and re-entrants can offset any rise in redundancies, so that increased inflows alone may not be the cause of increased unemployment.

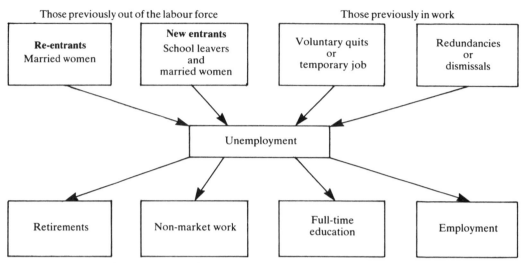

Those previously out of the labour force Those previously in work

Figure 15.5 Flows into and out of unemployment in the UK. (*Source:* 1986 Labour Force Survey)

As Fig. 15.6 illustrates, flows into unemployment in the United Kingdom appear to have exhibited a distinct cycle over the years since the early 1970s. Accompanying this was a pronounced downward trend in outflows throughout the 1970s which was only reversed in the period after 1981. The largest increases in male unemployment in Britain over the period shown in Fig. 15.6, occurred in the years between 1974 and 1976 and between 1979 and 1982 during which times there were substantial increases in inflows but no corresponding increase in outflows. It is clear from this, that in the absence of some compensating rise in outflows, male unemployment was bound to rise. Furthermore, unless the rise in outflows was immediate the average length of time during which an individual remained unemployed was also bound to rise. This rise in unemployment duration in turn further reduced outflows for, as we shall later see when we discuss the notion of hysteresis, the longer individuals remain unemployed the worse their chances of obtaining a job become.

The United States More detailed information on flows into and out of unemployment is available for the United States where the monthly Current Population Survey (CPS) enables us to map the changing labor market status of that part of the population which features in the survey in any two consecutive months. It reveals the previous status of individuals who are entering unemployment and the labor force status of those leaving unemployment. The simple 3×3 matrix reported in Table 15.2 records the gross labor market flows over a typical two-month period in 1984. The diagonal records those whose labor force status did not change between the two months. Thus 100.2 million were in employment in August and remained so in September while 4.1 million remained in unemployment in each of these months. However, by September a further 1.8 million who had been employed in August together with 1.7 million who had been

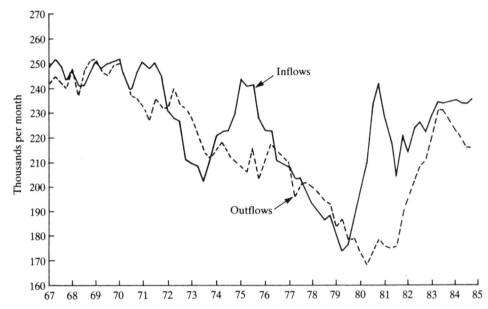

Figure 15.6 Male unemployment inflows and outflows in Great Britain. Note: pre-1982 definition. (*Source:* Figures kindly supplied by Layard, P.R.G. and Nickell, S.J. Some of these are also shown in Dornbusch, R. and Layard, P.R.G. (eds.)(1987) *The Performance of the British Economy*, Oxford University Press)

out of the labor force in August had entered unemployment. The flow into unemployment in September therefore amounted to 3.5 million, equivalent to 46 percent of total unemployment in that month. Yet total unemployment in September was lower than in August by some 300 000: unemployment in September was 7.62 million compared to 7.92 million in August. The outflow from unemployment over the period at 3.8 million therefore exceeded the inflow by 300 000; 2.0 million left unemployment in August for employment in September and 1.8 million left the labor force.

For purposes of comparison it is worth noting that in the United Kingdom inflows into unemployment in the 1980s ran at between 10 and 15 percent of the total

Table 15.2 Gross labor market flows in the United States in 1984 (millions)

Status in August	Status in September		
	Employed	Unemployed	Not in the labor force
Employed	100.2	1.8	4.7
Unemployed	2.0	4.1	1.8
Not in the labor force	3.3	1.7	57.1

Source: Flaim, P.O. and Hogue, C.R. (1985) 'Measuring labor force flows: a conference examines the problems', *Monthly Labor Review*, **108**(7), 7–17.

unemployed per month. In the United States it would therefore appear that the flows both into and out of umemployment are substantially larger than in the United Kingdom; proportionally three times as large. This suggests that there is, on average, far greater turnover and change in labor market status in the United States than exists in the United Kingdom.

Incidence and duration

The large inflows and outflows we reported above have been interpreted by some analysts as indicating that the experience of unemployment is widely dispersed and that while many individuals experience unemployment they each do so for only a short period of time. This is the basis of the so-called 'new-view' of unemployment.[2] An average unemployment rate of 10 percent in a year can either mean that 10 percent of the labor force were unemployed for the whole of the year or that each individual in the labor has been unemployed for 10 percent of the year. The latter could result from the process of job search if everyone in the labor force spent part of the year in unemployment looking for a job, the former quite evidently does not. It is therefore important to know what lies behind the raw unemployment rate, to know just how it is made up if we wish to understand more about unemployment. The average length of a spell of unemployment, the average duration, can be calculated by dividing the unemployment rate by the inflow rate.[3] Such calculations confirm that in both the United States and Britain the average completed duration of a spell of unemployment throughout the 1960s and 1970s is relatively short. It fluctuated between one and two months in the United States and between one and four months in Britain. The averages for Britain and the United States for these periods are reported in Table 15.3.

It is noticeable from this table that once again the British experience is distinct from that of the United States. Above we saw that gross flows into and out of unemployment were typically far larger in the United States than in Britain. Here it emerges that the average completed duration of a spell of unemployment is typically twice as long in Britain as in the United States. It is noteworthy that although the rate of inflow fluctuates sharply, inflows exhibit no distinct trend. Despite this the unemployment rate rose substantially in Britain during the 1980s. This is due to the relative reduction in outflows which resulted in an increase in the average completed duration of a spell of unemployment. The average duration rose from 1.8 months in the period to 1970, to 3.1 months in the period to 1978 and to 7.5 months between 1979 and 1983. The

---

2. This view is associated with Hall, R.E. (1972) 'Turnover in the labour force', *Brookings Papers on Economic Activity*, **3**, 709–56 and Feldstein, M.S. (1973) 'The economics of the new unemployment', *Public Interest*, **33**, 3–42.
3. It was shown above that in a steady state, where the rate of unemployment is unchanged, the unemployment rate u, where $u = U/LF$ was given by the ratio of the inflow, rate i, where $i = I/LF$ to the outflow rate, o, where $o = O/U$. That is $U/LF = (I/LF)/(O/U)$ or $u = i/o$. Now in a steady state, U is also equal to $i \times d$ where d represents the average length of a spell of unemployment, that is $U/LF = (I/LF) \times d$, which gives $d = (U/LF)/(I/LF)$, and $d = u/i$, or $d = U/I$. From the above it also follows that $d = I/(O/U) = U/O$. That is, the average length of a spell of unemployment in a steady state is given by the number of unemployed divided by the number of individuals leaving the register.

Table 15.3 Unemployment flows and duration in Britain and the United States

	United States			Britain (males)		
	Unemployment rate (%)	Inflow rate (%)	Average duration (months)	Unemployment rate (%)	Inflow rate (%)	Average duration (months)
1962–70	4.5	3.7	1.3	2.7	1.5	1.8
1971–78	6.4	3.9	1.6	5.4	1.8	3.1
1979–83	7.8	–	–	13.2	1.5	7.5

Source: Johnson, G.E. and Layard, P.R.G. (1986) 'The natural rate of unemployment: explanation and policy', in Ashenfelter, O. and Layard, P.R.G. (eds.), *Handbook of Labor Economics*, vol. 2, Ch. 16, North Holland.

rise in the duration of unemployment, consequent upon a fall in outflow relative to inflows, appears to account for the rise in unemployment in Britain in the early part of the 1980s. Indeed this fall in outflows relative to inflows appears to be a more generalized European phenomenon. Studies have indicated that the decline in the likelihood of leaving unemployment has been the main source of the secular increase in larger European countries while in Australia, North America and Japan any rise in unemployment has been accounted for by increased inflows as a result of increased quits, layoffs and labor force entry.[4]

The figures for the 1960s and 1970s for Britain and those for the United States for the whole of the period confirm that the typical spell of unemployment in Britain and the United States is of short duration. However, while it is clear that there are a large number of short spells of unemployment and that the average length of all spells is quite short, in neither country do short spells account for the major part of the total weeks or months of unemployment experienced within a year. The reason for this is that alongside the large number of short spells, go a relatively small number of much longer spells and it is these that account for the majority of weeks or months of unemployment in a single year.

In Britain it has been shown that in a single year 47 percent of those unemployed in that year experienced 85 percent of the weeks of unemployment that occurred in that year and 29 percent of the unemployed experienced 66 percent of the total weeks of unemployment. This meant that the burden of unemployment was very unevenly distributed across the labor force. Of the total labor force, 2.6 percent experienced 66 percent of the total weeks of unemployment, and 4.2 percent experienced 85 percent. It is clear that while there are a large number of short spells, because they are so short they do not account for a very large proportion of the total weeks of unemployment in a single year. In Britain the burden of unemployment falls on a very small

---

4. See Flanagan, R.J. (1988) 'Unemployment as a hiring problem', *OECD Economic Studies*, No. 11, autumn, 123–54.

Table 15.4 Long-term unemployment in selected OECD countries

Percentage of currently unemployed who have
been unemployed for 12 months or over

	1979	1987
Australia	18	28
Canada	4	10
France	30	47
Germany	20	32
Sweden	7	8
United Kingdom	24	42
United States	4	8

Source: OECD, *Economic Outlook*, No. 42.

proportion of the labor force, less than 10 percent, who experience either multiple short spells in a single year or one long spell.[5]

In the United States the experience of unemployment appears to be more widespread with between 10 and 20 percent of the labor force experiencing some unemployment. But here again the experience of unemployment is less widespread than the gross flow figures suggest. Around one-third of the unemployed experienced repeated spells of unemployment in a single 12-month period and the majority of the total weeks of unemployment in a single year are accounted for by a minority of those experiencing unemployment.[6] In both countries unemployment experience is very unevenly distributed.

Some indication of the extent to which a minority of the unemployed account for the majority of days lost in all the major industrialized countries is given in Table 15.4. This records the proportion of the currently unemployed who have been without a job for more than 12 months in 1979 and 1987. Again, with the exception of Sweden which has an extensive retraining program for the unemployed, it reveals quite clearly the substantial differences between the experience of North America and Europe. Long-term unemployment has grown in all countries, except Sweden, over these periods regardless of whether unemployment was higher or the same as in 1979. Accepting this, the problem in the United States was trivial compared with Europe.

To summarize, it seems clear that in the United States the experience of unemployment is more widely distributed than in Britain and that flows into unemployment are accordingly much larger. Compensating for this the flows out are

5. See Nolan, B. (1987) *Income Distribution and the Macroeconomy*, Cambridge University Press; Disney, R. (1979) 'Recurrent spells and the concentration of unemployment in Great Britain', *Economic Journal*, **89**, March, 109–19; Flaim, P.O. and Hogue, C.R. (1985) 'Measuring labor force flows: a conference examines the problems', *Monthly Labor Review*, **108** (7), July, 7–17.
6. See 'Moving in and out of unemployment', *OECD Employment Outlook*, OECD, Paris, September 1985; and Clark, K.B. and Summers, L.H. (1979) 'Labour market dynamics and unemployment: a reconsideration', *Brookings Papers of Economic Activity*, **1**, 13–72.

also much larger and typically, of the same order of magnitude as inflows. In Britain inflows and outflows have diverged substantially with the result that the average duration of a spell of unemployment is much longer in Britain than in the United States. All this seems to point to a much more fluid labor market in the United States than in Britain, with proportionately much larger changes in labor market status by individuals in the United States. Having said all this, it remains the case that in both countries a small minority of the labor force experience long duration unemployment and, in doing so, account for a majority of the total weeks of unemployment accumulated each year in both countries.

Characteristics of the unemployed

Above it was emphasized that the incidence of unemployment is far from evenly distributed across the labor force of most countries. Typically the probability of experiencing unemployment is inversely related to the levels of qualification and training of the individual. Unemployment rates are also lower for prime age individuals than for school leavers and those nearing retirement, and for whites than for minority groups. Tables 15.5 to 15.9 spell out the incidence of unemployment across different age, race, sex and occupational groups in Britain and the United States.

From Table 15.5 it emerges that in both countries unemployment rates were lower for women than for men and for married men and women than their non-married counterparts. It has been shown that among unemployed men in Britain the higher unemployment rate of the non-married reflects the much longer duration of unemployment they experience, perhaps because there is less pressure on them to take

Table 15.5 Unemployment rates by sex and marital status in Britain and the United States[†]

	Britain 1986	USA 1983
Men	11.5	9.6
Married men	8.3	6.5
Non-married men	17.8	—
Women	10.6	8.1
Married women	8.9	7.1
Non-married women	14.0	—
All	11.1	—

Source: USA—Becker, E.H. and Bowers, N. (1984) *Monthly Labor Review*, February. Britain 'Measures of unemployment and characteristics of the unemployed', (1988) *Employment Gazette*, HMSO, January.
[†] OECD definitions of unemployment, aged 20 and over in the USA and aged 16 and over in Britain.

Table 15.6 Unemployment rates by occupation in Britain and the United States[†]

	Britain 1986	
	Men	Women
Managerial and professional	3.2	3.9
Clerical and related	5.8	5.0
Other non-manual	6.7	7.3
All non-manual	4.0	5.0
Skilled workers	7.8	9.2
Semi-skilled	10.9	7.7
Unskilled	21.3	17.8
All manual	9.9	8.0

	USA 1983 Men and women
Managerial and professional	2.6
Technical and administrative	5.5
Service occupations	10.2
Precision production, craft and repair	8.2
Operators, fabricators and laborers	12.8
Farming, fishing and forestry	10.6

Source: op. cit., Table 15.5
[†] OECD definition of unemployment aged 20 and over in the USA, aged 16 and over in Britain.

up a job or because prospective employers prefer married men.[7] Table 15.6 reveals that unemployment rates are lowest for the most highly qualified, and among white collar occupations. At the time of the high levels of unemployment in Britain in 1986 almost one in every five unskilled workers was unemployed. Table 15.7 (for which details are available only for Britain) reveals more clearly that unemployment rates decline with level of qualification. Those individuals without any qualifications were over four times more likely to be unemployed than individuals who possessed a degree or equivalent qualification. From Table 15.8 it appears that unemployment rates decline with age. In fact the relationship between age and unemployment incidence exhibits a distinct U shape in both countries. They are highest for men and women among the 16–24 year-olds and decline through to middle age, thereafter they rise again prior to retirement age. Finally, Table 15.9 reveals that those individuals of minority ethnic or racial origin experience substantially greater unemployment rates than the white

7. Nickell, S.J. (1979) 'The effect of unemployment and related benefits on the duration of unemployment', *Economic Journal*, **89**, March, 34–49.

Table 15.7 Unemployment rates by qualifications in
Britain 1986[†]

(All aged 16 and over)	Men	Women
Degree level and above	4.0	5.6
A-level or equivalent	8.0	9.7
O-level or equivalent	10.5	9.8
No qualification	17.3	11.2

Source: op. cit., Table 15.5
[†] OECD definition of unemployment.

Table 15.8 Unemployment rates by age in Britain and the United States
(Britain, 1986; USA, 1985)[†]

	Britain 16–24	USA	Britain 25–44/54	USA	Britain 44 +	USA 54 +
Men	19.0	14.1	9.8	5.6	8.8	4.1
Women	16.6	13.0	10.4	6.2	6.1	4.1

Source: USA; (1986) *Monthly Labor Review* Britain; *op. cit.*, Table 15.5
[†] OECD definition of unemployment.

majority in both countries. Black workers in both countries are more than twice as likely to be unemployed as are white.

These single cross-tabulations reveal little of the more complex explanations lying behind these figures. The higher unemployment rates among those prior to retirement age is in part a reflection of their poor average level of qualifications. The higher rates among minority groups in both countries are in part a reflection of the fact that on average, they tended to be less well qualified and occupy some of the lowest rungs on the occupational job ladder, which in turn is in part a reflection of the discrimination that exists. However, even adjusting for these differences, minorities in both countries experience much higher rates of unemployment than their qualifications, age, sex, etc., would otherwise lead us to expect.

THE COSTS OF UNEMPLOYMENT

Unemployment has profound social and economic costs. The economic costs are represented by the value of the forgone output, the value of the potential marginal products of the unemployed. The social costs are more difficult to quantify but may be many and substantial. Thus it has been suggested that unemployment leads to an increase in mental and physical illness, although the mechanisms by which this occurs are poorly understood. Central to this view is the idea that employment provides both income and a set of relationships contributing toward a structured and meaningful life. Deprived of this, individuals may suffer from stress and anxiety, and in consequence

Table 15.9 Unemployment rates by race and ethnic origin in the United States and Britain in 1985

	USA	Britain
White	6.2	10
Black	15.1	—
West Indian	—	21
Indian	—	17
Pakistani/Bangladeshi	—	31
Hispanic	10.5	—

Source: USA: *Monthly Labor Review;* Britain *Employment Gazette,* January 1987.

of this and perhaps lower income, may adopt unhealthy consumption patterns, ranging from poor diet to drug and alcohol abuse. Empirical work has also focused on associations between unemployment and mortality, suicide, crime, marital breakdown, divorce and child abuse. In each of these areas researchers face considerable difficulties in establishing the directions of causality but the view is widely held that unemployment was a contributory factor to the growth in each of these during the 1980s in most of the advanced industrial nations.[8]

EXPLANATIONS FOR UNEMPLOYMENT

An overview

The essence of the Keynesian explanation for unemployment is that firms demand too little labor because individuals demand too few goods. One of the explanations for this demand deficiency is the existence of unemployment itself. Because of unemployment, individuals have less income and they therefore reduce their consumption expenditure and aggregate demand falls. It follows from this that a policy of reducing wages could further exacerbate the situation, for it would lead to a further fall in income and a consequent reduction in consumption. One answer to this problem is that the government should step in and boost aggregate demand by manipulating the fiscal and monetary instruments under its control, either increasing government expenditure, cutting taxes or raising the money supply.

Against this view classical economists argued that any fall in wages and prices would itself produce an increase in aggregate demand as a result of a 'real balance effect'; the fall in prices would increase the real value of money balances held by the private sector giving rise to increased expenditure. The classical view was that markets had a natural tendency to clear and that the reason that they might not do so was because of

---

8. For a survey of the literature in this area see Sinclair, P.J. (1987) *Unemployment: Economic Theory and Evidence,* Blackwell, pp. 34–7; and Junanker, P.J. (1986) 'Social costs of unemployment', Department of Economics, University of Essex, Discussion Paper No. 292, July.

government regulation or misperceptions by firms and/or workers about prices and wages. The corollary of this view was that unemployment could be eliminated either by removing the government 'distortions' or that unemployment must be voluntary, at least in an *ex ante* sense, because agents formulated these wage and price expectations quite freely. In contrast the corollary of the Keynesian view was that unemployment was involuntary because economic agents acting alone do not have the capacity to boost aggregate demand to the degree required. They were not unemployed as a result of their own freely chosen actions.

In the following pages we develop first the neoclassical explanation for unemployment and then the early Keynesian explanation. This early Keynesian theory has widely come to be regarded as deficient for it contained no detailed microeconomic underpinning. In the subsequent 'reappraisal of Keynes', microfoundations for this theory were provided. Agents were viewed as pursuing the same objectives and operating under the same constraints as in neoclassical theory but, in addition, they now recognized and took account of the possibility of rationing. Rationing arose due to the failure of wages and prices to move to clear markets. However, this in turn highlighted a further weakness of Keynesian theory, namely its failure to provide a theoretical explanation for the existence of rigid wages and prices.

The Phillips curve was initially suggested to provide the microeconomic foundations of Keynesian theory. It suggested the existence of a trade-off between money wage rises and unemployment and provided a theory of sluggish wage adjustment. In so doing it admitted the possibility of protracted periods of unemployment. The neoclassical critique of this theory emphasized that the trade-off proposed by the Phillips curve could emerge only as a result of misperceptions about changes in wages and prices, and this led to the development of the 'expectations augmented' Phillips curve. Yet both the original Phillips curve and the expectations augmented Phillips curve have difficulty accounting for developments during the 1970s and early 1980s in Europe. At that time both wages and unemployment appeared to be rising, a phenomenon that became known as 'stagflation'. It required the development of contract theory and other explanations of sticky wages and prices to illuminate this phenomenon. In the following pages we trace these developments.

The neoclassical theory of unemployment

In a competitive labor market with flexible wages, wages should adjust to clear the market and any unemployment that remains will be voluntary. All those who want work at the prevailing level of wages will have work, and that part of the labor force who are without jobs will be voluntarily unemployed. This situation is depicted in Fig. 15.7, in which we abstract from the heterogeneity of labor and variety of different labor markets and depict *the* market for labor.

The function labelled L^F represents the labor force, and reflects the empirical finding that the participation rate is positively related to the real wage W/P. The function L^S represents the effective labor supply to firms, as before, so that at the real wage W_1/P, $L_1^F - L_1$ individuals are unemployed. In the absence of any form of unemployment benefit this magnitude will reflect the number of individuals who are

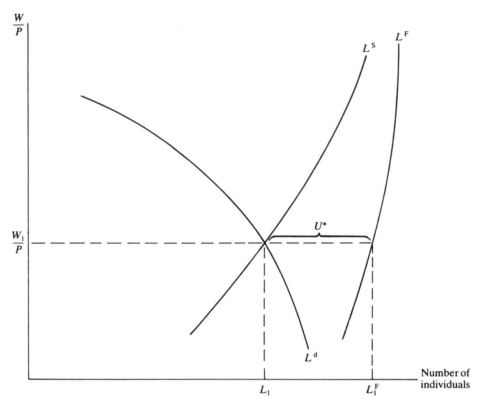

Figure 15.7 The equilibrium level of unemployment. L^F represents the size of the labor force at different real wage rates while L^S represents the effective labor supply at each real wage rate. The differences between L^F and L^S at any real wage rate measure the scale of voluntary unemployment. The figure illustrates that even at the wage W_1/P, which clears the labor market, there will be some unemployment. This is accounted for by individuals experiencing a transitional period of unemployment as they move from one job to another and by new entrants and re-entrants to the labor market who experience a spell of unemployment before they take up jobs. The equilibrium level of unemployment, U^*, is also known as the 'natural rate of unemployment'

moving from an old to a new job and those new and re-entrants who are in the process of taking up a job. It will therefore constitute largely search unemployment and is voluntary in nature. This equilibrium rate of unemployment reflects a given state of technology, individual preferences and endowments, and may be described as the '*natural rate of unemployment*': it is that level of unemployment which prevails at full employment when, given the above arguments, the labor market clears. The notion of the natural rate is more fully explained in the words of Milton Friedman with whom we associate the concept.[9]

9. See Friedman, M. (1968) 'The role of monetary policy', *American Economic Review*, **58**, March. He defines the natural rate thus 'The natural rate of unemployment . . . is the level that would be ground out by the Walrasian system of general equilibrium equations provided there is embedded within them, the actual structural characteristics of the labor and commodity markets, including market imperfections,

For a given labor market structure there will be a unique equilibrium level of unemployment, which emerges from the process of competition. Additonal unemployment could however arise as a transitional phenomenon in such a competitive market as a result of 'distortions'. These could result from the introduction of unemployment benefits, which raise reservation wages, the setting of wages above the market clearing rate either as a result of a statutory minimum or trade union power or information imperfections. Consider each of these in turn.

Too high real wages and benefit-induced unemployment Consider first the general neoclassical explanation for unemployment, a real wage above the market clearing level as illustrated in Fig. 15.8. Suppose for simplicity of exposition that this results from the introduction of a minimum wage W_{min}/P, that exceeds the equilibrium wage,

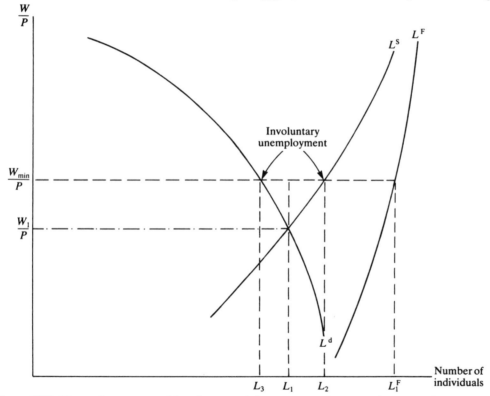

Figure 15.8 Unemployment resulting from a minimum wage. The establishment of a minimum wage, W_{min}/P, above the market clearing level, W_1/P, results in involuntary unemployment, $L_2 - L_3$. This comprises $L_1 - L_3$ individuals previously in employment, and $L_2 - L_1$ additional individuals now wishing to work at the new higher real wage. Note also that at this level the voluntary component of unemployment has reduced as the number of individuals quitting their jobs to search for new ones declines

stochastic variability in demand and supply, the cost of gathering information about job vacancies and labor availability, the costs of mobility and so on.'

W_1/P. This results in the emergence of involuntary unemployment of magnitude $L_2 - L_3$ in excess of the 'natural' rate. Note that the involuntary unemployment comprises both those who have lost jobs due to the rise in the wage above the equilibrium level, $L_1 - L_3$, and the rise in the number of individuals wishing and able to accept a job were one offered at the new higher real wage, $L_2 - L_1$. In contrast, the voluntary component of unemployment, $L_1^F - L_2$ has fallen as the number of individuals quitting jobs to look for new ones diminishes. This idea could also have been illustrated using Fig. 14.6 in which the unemployment experienced by those already in the labor force, as a result of the imposition of a minimum wage above the market clearing level, would have been given by the distance XY. However, the exposition here differs from that in Fig. 14.6 in taking explicit account of the natural rate of unemployment.

It was explained in Chapter 7 that a minimum wage need not always reduce employment. If employers enjoy monopsony power, the imposition of a minimum wage, which prevents the exploitation of that monopsony power, can increase employment. Alternatively, if the coverage of the minimum wage is only partial it may merely reallocate labor from the covered to the uncovered sector in a manner analogous to that depicted in the spillover model in Fig. 14.6. The above is developed to show the general consequences of establishing real wages above the market clearing level.

Trade unions are perhaps the principal institutional mechanism establishing wage rates above the market clearing level. In Fig. 14.6 it was shown that, even in a partially unionized economy, unemployment will result if the union wage rise is emulated by the non-union sector. Again, in Fig. 14.9 increases in the target real wage set by union wage bargainers will displace the wage setting function to the left causing the level of employment to fall and the level of unemployment to rise.

Clearly there is neither perfect nor complete emulation of the union wage for we have empirical evidence of the existence of a union wage gap. If there were no union wage premiums why would individuals join unions? More realistically the wage aspirations, the reservation wages, of those in the non-union sector may be affected by the wages paid in the union sector, they may well rise in line with union wages so that over the longer run a mark-up is retained between union and non-union wages and it is the weighted average of these two which exceeds the market clearing level. In Appendix 15A we show how the level of density and the size of the union mark-up can affect the level of unemployment.

The effects of the introduction of unemployment compensation on the level of unemployment can be illustrated with the aid of Fig. 14.6. This is redrawn as Fig. 15.9. The rise in wages in sector A, consequent upon the formation of the union, results in a spillover of workers from sector A to sector B, from the unionized to the non-unionized sector. However, the introduction of welfare support at the level of B sets a floor as to how far wages will fall in sector B. In consequence X,Y individuals are now unemployed.

Unemployment and job search A further neoclassical explanation of unemployment

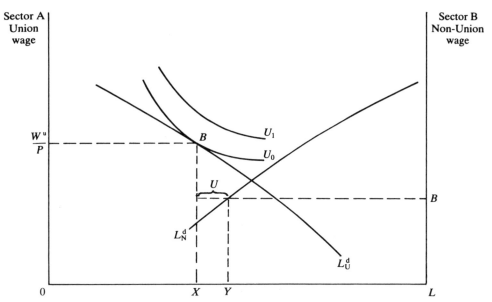

Figure 15.9 Benefit-induced unemployed in a unionized economy. The introduction of the union in sector A results in the negotiation of wage W^U/P and the spillover of workers from the now unionized to the non-unionized sector. However, the existence of a minimum level of welfare support B, sets a floor on the fall in wages in the competitive sector, with the result that XY of the labor force are now unemployed.

emphasizes the consequences of information imperfections in labor markets. Information is no longer supplied immediately and costlessly to individuals, instead they have to devote time and resources to gathering it. Unemployment on this view is a consequence of the process of gathering information about jobs. The essence of the class of models, which explain unemployment as a consequence of the search for jobs by workers, is conveyed in the following simple model.[10] This simple model of employee job search, abstracts from the many characteristics of jobs that concern a worker and instead aggregates all of these into one characteristic we shall call 'the wage'. Here we shall focus on workers of a particular level of skill, and for purposes of simplicity assume they are equally productive. Suppose that workers know the characteristics of the jobs in question and the jobs are identical in all respects, save the wage. Workers are presumed to know the nature of the wage distribution—that is they know the mean, variance and range of wages on offer but they are presumed not to know exactly which firm is offering which wage; it is in this manner that uncertainty arises. Each worker is no longer confronted by a single market wage for his or her skill but by a variety of offers emanating from firms. Without undertaking costly search he or she will be unable to determine which firm is making which wage offer. To consider

10. The approach adopted here follows that of Joll, C., McKenna, C., McNabb, R. and Shorey, J. (1983) *Developments in Labour Market Analysis*, Part 4.2, Allen and Unwin, London and Boston.

the implications of this approach imagine that the distribution of wage offers is as detailed in Table 15.10(a) and that each time a worker inquires about a job, searches the labor market, a constant cost is incurred.

Now the expected wage, $E[M]$, from a random sampling of the above distribution of wage offers is the sum of all the products of each wage W and its probability $P(W)$. That is $(120 \times 0.0129) + (125 \times 0.0452) + \ldots (160 \times 0.0194)$. The maximum expected wage from a random sample of one, a single search is therefore £141.2225. Now what happens to the maximum expected wage, $E[M]$, as the number of searches, n, increases? Suppose that $n = 2$, then this involves the same procedure as before, namely summing the products of the probabilities and the highest wage in each pair selected. In total there are 81 possible pairs from (120,120) to (160,160) with (120,160) (125,155), etc., in between. The probability of drawing £120 and £125 together is given by $[P(W) = 120] \times [P(W) = 125] = 0.0129 \times 0.0452 = 0.0006$, (see Table 15.10(a)), and, since we are interested only in the highest wage in any pair selected, this means £125 $\times 0.0006 = 0.0729$. Now, if we summed the product of all possible pairs, we should arrive at a figure of £146.045 as the expected maximum wage when $n = 2$. That is $E[M \mid n = 2]$. In similar fashion, the worker could calculate the expected maximum wage for all possible values of n. The first four of these are shown in Table 15.10(b).

Table 15.10 (a) Distribution of wage offers

Weekly wage (£)	No. of firms	Probability of obtaining each wage $P(W)$
120	2	2/155 = 0.0129
125	7	7/155 = 0.0452
130	14	14/155 = 0.0903
135	28	28/155 = 0.1806
140	40	40/155 = 0.2581
145	26	26/155 = 0.1677
150	20	20/155 = 0.1290
155	15	15/155 = 0.0968
160	3	3/155 = 0.0194
TOTAL	155	1.0000

(b) Expected maximum wage for some values of n

Sample size n	Maximum expected wage, $E[M \mid n]$ (£)	Total search costs $C(= 2) \times n$ (£)	Expected net benefit $E[NB \mid n] = E[(M \mid n) - Cn]$ (£)
1	141.222	2	139.22
2	146.045	4	142.05
3	148.472	6	142.47
4	150.009	8	142.01

Source: Joll, C., McKenna, C., McNabb, R., Shorey, J. (1983), *Developments in Labour Market Analysis*, George Allen and Unwin, Boston and London. Reproduced with permission of the authors.

So far the worker has calculated only the *gross* benefits from different sized samples, not the net benefit. In order to accomplish this latter the individual needs to deduct search costs. Assume that the cost of *each* search, C, is £2. This gives us the expected net benefits $E[NB]$ from different sized samples in the final column of Table 15.10(b). It is clear from this final column, and would be confirmed if we calculated $E[NB]$ for all n, that 3 is the optimal size of sample for here the expected net gains at £142.47 are at maximum. Thus if this net income represented an improvement on the worker's current weekly income (presently he could either be earning a wage or unemployed) the worker would sample three firms and select that firm with the highest wage from among them.

The situation could be shown diagrammatically (Fig. 15.10(a)) if we approximated the discrete distributions of Table 15.10 with a continuous distribution of wage offers. $E[M|n]$ represents the maximum expected wage, which first rises then eventually levels off as the number of searches increases. Cn represents total search costs, where the marginal cost of search C is fixed at £2. Thus the marginal and average cost of search are the same and Cn is a straight line through the origin. In contrast it is evident that the average and marginal expected wage decline throughout. The marginal curves are detailed in Fig. 15.10(b).

Expected net benefits are maximized where the expected marginal benefit equals the marginal cost of search. That is, where $E[\delta M|\delta n] = C$, at n^* in Fig. 15.10. Having evaluated the expected benefits and costs of job search, and determined that these are equal at the margin after n^* searches, the workers should undertake only n^* searches and take the highest wage offered from among these.

Of course, this is a highly simplified model with a short time period. In reality the worker will remain in the chosen employment for more than the period assumed here so that we really need the present value of the expected maximum wage, over whatever period the worker expects to remain in this employment. However, discounting merely complicates the calculations without changing the basic principles involved, so we shall put this to one side and consider the implications of the simple model. A number of these emerge.

First, if search costs, C, rise, Cn pivots upwards to $C_1 n$ for example in Fig. 15.10(a). The optimal number of searches reduces to n_1 and the expected net benefits $E[M|n_1]$ will be lower. Suppose, that in order to receive a wage offer, a worker has to visit the firms in question, and that he cannot do this while employed, then the time spent searching is also time spent unemployed. Now a reduction in the sample size means a reduction in the time spent visiting firms, viz., a reduction in the duration of unemployment. High search costs, in this model, *ceteris paribus*, reduce the duration and hence the level of unemployment.

Second, and reciprocally, lower search costs will increase the size of sample, and increase the duration of unemployment and the expected wage. The costs of search will be many and varied: transport costs, the opportunity cost of forgone leisure, perhaps even the psychological costs of potential disappointment, to name but some of these. The costs of transport will clearly differ between urban and rural areas, being lower for any given sample size in the urban area where firms are less dispersed. This model

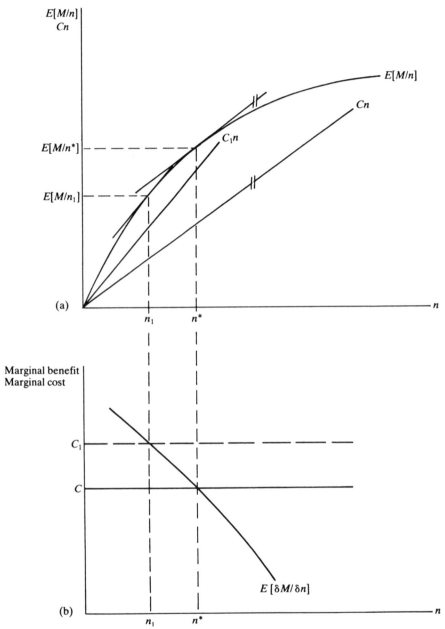

Figure 15.10 A simple model of job search. $E[M|n]$ represents the expected total benefits from different numbers of job search, n. Cn represents the total costs of searching. The associated marginal benefit and marginal costs curves are depicted in (b). The optimal number of searches, n^*, is determined by the point at which the marginal benefit from an additional search equals the marginal cost C. A rise in the costs of search, to C_1, reduces the number of job searches undertaken (*Source:* Joll *et al* (1983). Reproduced with permission of the authors.)

therefore suggests that, *ceteris paribus*, unemployment duration will be greater, and expected wages higher, in the urban area.

A simple model such as the above casts some light on aspects of labor market behavior, but we should be cautious before we draw strong conclusions. The model is most deficient in assuming that, although workers know the exact nature of the wage distribution, they do not known which firms are offering which wages. As we have already seen, some firms quite deliberately set out to establish reputations as high payers in order to attract a pool of high quality applicants. Furthermore, public and private employment agencies record job vacancies and the wage offers of firms, so the search to discover which firms are offering which wage may involve relatively trivial outlays.

A further weakness of the simple model is the assumption of constant marginal search costs. If these are largely transport costs in urban areas, where firms are concentrated geographically, the marginal costs of an additional search might fall rapidly over the first few searches. More importantly, many workers do not need to quit their jobs to search the labor market. They do so in their lunch breaks or when sick. As we saw in Chapter 10 almost as many employed as unemployed workers are looking for jobs at any one time. Having said this, some workers can best acquire information while unemployed so the above model, simple though it is, provides insights into some of the determinants of the natural rate.[11]

Unemployment and efficiency wages In Chapter 11 we detailed a class of models which suggested that profit maximizing firms might in aggregate choose to pay wages above the market clearing level. The result was the coexistence of high wages and unemployment. We outlined four versions of this efficiency wage theory: the labor turnover model, which suggested that firms pay high wages to minimize labor turnover; the superior applicant pool, which suggested that firms pay high wages to attract high quality applicants; a model emphasizing morale effects, the gift of high wages in exchange for the gift of productivity; and last the shirking model. It is this last we analyze further here.

In the shirking model the productivity of the worker hired by firm i, ϕ_i is suggested to be a function of the wage the firm pays and the unemployment rate, U_r.

$$\phi_i = \phi_i(W/P, U_r) \tag{15.1}$$

The firm can be viewed as believing that it is confronted by a supply of effort function in addition to the labor supply function L^s. This function may be described as the no-shirking constraint in this context, or more generally as the 'wage setting function'. It shows the wages that firms *believe* it is necessary to offer to attract a given number of individuals of the right quality and motivation and to dissuade them from shirking. How such a wage setting function will relate to the size of the labor force is a matter of conjecture. If each firm's claims on the labor force are relatively small, they may

---

11. See Mortensen, D.T. (1986) 'Job search and labor market analysis', in Ashenfelter, O. and Layard, P.R.G. (eds.), *Handbook of Labor Economics*, vol. 2, North Holland, for a detailed survey of the many models in this area.

take the labor force as fixed. We shall assume this and draw L^F as a vertical line. Now it is the intersection of the wage setting function and the labor demand function, rather than the labor supply and demand functions, that determines the volume of employment and the real wage. This is illustrated in Fig. 15.11.

From Fig. 15.11 it emerges that a wage is established which exceeds the wage which would prevail in the absence of efficiency wage considerations. If W_2/P is this efficient wage then the natural rate is measured by $L^F - L_3$, and there is also additional unemployment, $L_3 - L_2$, which is involuntary. One view is that this unemployment represents a disciplining device, for now a worker discharged for unsatisfactory performance can no longer automatically secure a job, jobs are scarce. Workers discharged now face a probability greater than 0 that they will fail to obtain another job, because the unemployment that exists is now no longer purely voluntary.

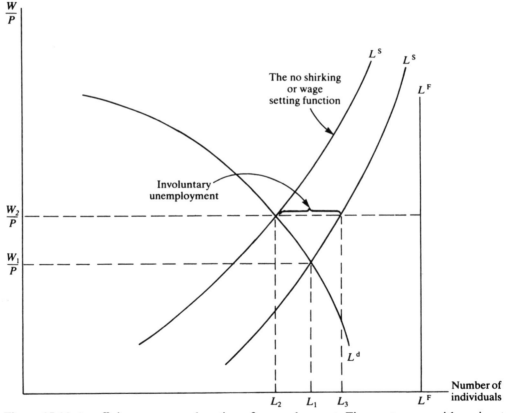

Figure 15.11 An efficiency wage explanation of unemployment. Firms set wages with a view to increasing the efficiency of their labor force. The wage setting function shows the wages firms believe it is necessary to pay to attract a given number of individuals of an appropriate quality and motivation. Now unemployment exceeds the natural rate because $L_3 - L_2$ individuals in excess of those demanded at this wage wish to work and offer themselves for work at the new wage level W_2/P. Jobs are scare and unemployment may be viewed as a disciplining device to encourage worker performance

Whatever the motive for firms paying high wages, in equilibrium all firms pay the same. Were this not the case we should find wage setting firms engaged in a constant leap-frogging process, as each attempted to steal a march on its competitor by raising wages in an attempt to improve still further its productivity. A new equilibrium is established at which the marginal benefit to the firms, in terms of improved worker efficiency, just equals the marginal cost in terms of the premium over the market clearing wage. Such an equilibrium is described at W_2/P in Fig. 15.11.

Each of the neoclassical explanations of unemployment was premised on the notion that wages and prices will move to clear markets when these markets are unregulated. A quite different perspective and explanation for unemployment is offered by Keynesian theory.

Keynesian unemployment

In the above models of the labor market firms could sell all the output they produced, they were never confronted by a deficiency of aggregate demand for their products. The reason for this was that prices were flexible and would fall in the face of deficient demand and rise in the face of excess demand to restore a level of aggregate demand compatible with full employment. However, if prices do not adjust to clear the market, the amount that firms can sell will be determined by the level of aggregate demand. Models which attempt to capture the realities of sluggish price adjustment have been described as 'fix-price' models.

To illustrate such an outcome suppose that product prices are fixed and that the level of aggregate demand in Fig. 15.12 is AD_1 as depicted in Fig. 15.12(b). This results in a level of output, Q_1. The maximum number of workers required to produce Q_1 is L_1 as illustrated in Fig. 15.12(a). Now for wages above W_1/P_1 employment is determined by points on the labor demand curve, and the corresponding unemployment, $L^s - L^d$, constitutes classical unemployment as before. For real wages below W_1/P_1 but above or equal to W_0/P_1, L_1 workers are employed and the level of employment is determined by the quantity constraint Q_1. The distance $L^s - L^d$ 'effective' below W_1/P_1 but above W_0/P_1 identifies unemployment which is Keynesian in nature for it is due to a deficiency of aggregate demand. Finally, note that for real wages below W_0/P_1 employment is given by points on the labor supply curve and we have repressed inflation since there is excess demand in both the labor market and the output markets.

Consider further the consequence of such a constraint. Firms can sell no output beyond the amount Q_1, which is determined by the level of aggregate demand. Hence the output that could be produced by any workers additional to L_1 has no value, and therefore beyond L_1 the effective marginal product of labor is zero. The effective labor demand curve is therefore given by the bold line L^d 'effective'. If we now define equilibrium as the point of intersection of L^s and L^d 'effective' we have no unemployment. The fall in the real wage has discouraged workers from offering their services and the labor market is in equilibrium at the new level L_1 and W_0/P_1. But at any wage rate above W_0/P_1 we have unemployment and, given the fixed price assumptions of the model, there is no reason to choose W_0/P_1 in preference to any

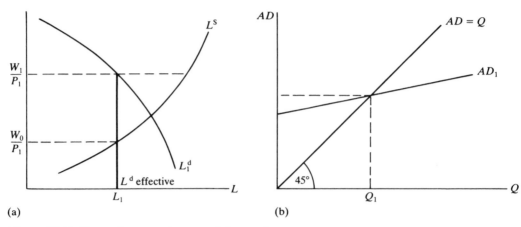

Figure 15.12 Unemployment due to deficiency of aggregate demand. In (b) the equilibrium level of aggregate demand AD_1 determines the level of output Q_1 and the effective demand for labor. The consequences of this particular level of demand for labor, L_1, are shown in (a). The effective demand for labor L^d effective is less than the notional demand L_1^d and at wage rates beyond W_0/P_1 but below W_1/P_1 effective demand is not sufficient to employ all the labor that is willingly supplied. Wages could be established at any level between W_0 and W_1, and at any level above W_0, will be associated with involuntary unemployment equal to $L^s - L^d$ 'effective'. The level of wages no longer determines the volume of employment, employment is determined by AD_1 establishing Q_1 and L_1

other point. The nominal wage could have been established anywhere within the range, W_0 to W_1, including the competitive equilibrium, and at all but W_0/P_1 this will be associated with involuntary unemployment. This simple model illustrates that if the effective level of aggregate demand is inadequate the labor market may fail to clear and unemployment may result.

In the above example, because the market failed to clear, sellers were unable to trade in the quantities they would have liked, in both the product and labor markets. There was excess supply in both the goods and labor markets. At wage levels beyond W_0/P_1 individuals would have wished to supply more labor, and firms would have liked to have supplied more goods. But because individuals were rationed in the amount of labor they could supply, they were also constrained in the amount of goods they could demand. This meant, in turn, that firms were rationed in the amount of goods they could sell. Demand was deficient for both labor and goods. The 'notional' demand by individuals, the amount they would like to buy at the prevailing set of wages and prices, differed from their 'effective' demand, the amount they were able to buy. Equally firms' notional demand for labor exceeded their effective demand for labor.

To consider this further see Fig. 15.13.[12] In the top right-hand quadrant the goods market is depicted. It details the quantity of final goods, Q, demanded at each price level, P, and the quantity of goods firms are willing to sell at each price level. They are,

---

12. See Sinclair, P. (1986) *Unemployment: Economic Theory and Evidence*, Blackwell, for a development of these issues. The approach adopted here follows that in Chapter 2 of this book.

respectively, the aggregate demand and supply curves. The labor market is depicted in the bottom left-hand quadrant, in which the labor demand curve exhibits the usual diminishing returns and, for simplicity, labor supply is assumed fixed. The labor and product markets are linked by the production function in the bottom right-hand quadrant which displays the diminishing returns that are reflected in the labor demand curve. Finally, in the top left-hand quadrant the money wage rate, W^*, is mapped.

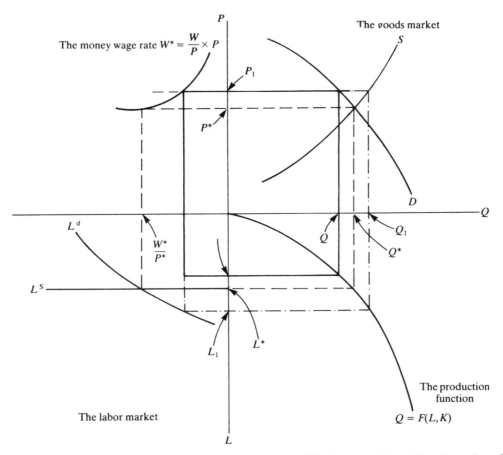

Figure 15.13 Keynesian unemployment. Neoclassical equilibrium is indicated by the point of intersection of the aggregate demand, D, and aggregate supply, S, curves in the goods market. The production function $Q = F(L,K)$ identifies the amount of labor L^* required to produce Q^*. The labor market is in equilibrium at this level of employment at money wage W^* given price level P^*. If prices suddenly rise to P_1 firms are knocked off their supply curves. They produce Q, which requires L amount of labor. But at the initial money wage W^* real wages are lower, since P has increased from P^* to P_1. The lower real wages result in the lower level of aggregate demand at Q. Firms are rationed in the goods market for they would like to supply Q_1, workers are rationed in the labor market for they would like to supply L^*. Keynesian unemployment exists where both the market for goods *and* the market for labor are buyers' markets. (*Source:* Sinclair P.J. (1986) *op. cit.* Reproduced with permission of the author)

This is the product of both the price level and the real wage, $W* = W/P \times P$, the shape of this curve is a rectangle hyperbola.

Consider first the competitive, the neoclassical, equilibrium. This is attained when all markets clear and is indicated by the broken line joining $Q*$, $P*$, $L*$ and $W*/P*$. The attainment of this requires, as previously illustrated, complete flexibility of all wages and prices. Now consider Keynesian unemployment. Suppose initially that there is a rise in the price level to P_1, this lowers the real wage and raises firms' notional demand for labor. At price level, P_1, firms wish to supply Q_1 output, and employ L_1 labor to produce this. But by the same token the higher price level at an unchanged nominal money supply means a fall in individuals' wealth and a reduction in individuals' consumption expenditures. The demand for goods at this new higher price level with an unchanged nominal wage $W*$ is Q. The effective quantity transacted is the lower of demand and supply, and what is described as the *short-side principle* applies. Firms are therefore 'knocked off' their supply curves and to produce Q require only L amount of labor. Unemployment of amount $L* - L$ emerges. Firms are rationed in the goods market and as a result are 'knocked off' both their supply curves and their labor demand curves. The effective marginal product of labor employed beyond L is zero. This Keynesian unemployment 'equilibrium' is illustrated by the bold rectangle in Fig. 15.13.

The above analysis shows that unemployment can result from causes other than too high wage rates. Indeed, if policy were based on the assumption that unemployment were due to too high real wages, it would lead us in entirely the wrong direction. The policy prescription that follows from such a diagnosis is to reduce wage rates but this would further reduce consumption and the level of effective demand, which in turn would reduce the amount of output that could be sold. Production and associated employment would then fall still further. The solution to Keynesian unemployment is not to reduce wage rates but to increase the level of aggregate demand.

Implicit contract theory

The fundamental objection to the above Keynesian arguments is the assumption that is made about fixed prices. If, in the above examples, prices were to fall this would increase the real money supply and increase aggregate demand, for the real money supply is one argument underpinning the position of D in the goods market. The increase in aggregate demand would in turn increase output and employment. There was no theory of the determination of wages and prices in the above model but one proposal to fill this gap is contract theory, aspects of which we have already touched on in earlier chapters.

In the United States the typical duration of explicit union negotiated contracts is three years. If these contracts are negotiated in good times, the real wage growth that results may carry over into the recession, when the duration of these contracts extends into these bad times. For this reason prices may fail to adjust to changing market conditions and the burden of adjustment will be thrown on to output and employment. This is one explanation of wage stickiness but it faces a number of difficulties. It is not, for example, a convincing explanation of wage stickiness in the United Kingdom. In the United Kingdom the duration of labor contracts is seldom specified although typically contracts last for 12 months. On the face of it, therefore, money wages should exhibit greater flexibility in the United Kingdom than in the United States but, as we have seen earlier, this is not so. A supplementary explanation might be that contracts are staggered, they start and end at different times and this enables firms, union negotiators and workers to draw comparisons between the rate of change of their wages and those negotiated in previous contracts. If they then attempt to imitate the wage settlements of other groups and are successful, this will impart a greater degree of rigidity than the duration of contracts alone would suggest. The implicit understandings between workers and firms, the implicit contracts between workers and firms, will embody such notions as comparability and therefore could account for these phenomena. It is, therefore, to examine implicit contracts that we now turn. Implicit contracts also arise for other reasons and there are two quite distinct strands to *implicit contract theory*.

The first of these emphasizes the relative risk aversion of employees.[13] Entrepreneurs being, in the words of one of the founding fathers of the modern Chicago school of economists, Frank Knight, 'confident and venturesome', are willing to relieve the 'doubtful and timid' employees of risk in return for the right to make allocative decisions. Employees are suggested to be more risk averse than employers, because the assets employees possess are held predominantly in the form of human capital while employers hold more diverse portfolios. Employers are also seen as a self-selecting group of those most willing to take risks. They offer a wage–employment package to the employee which, while not guarding against all eventualities, since they cannot obtain assets which allow them to diversify away all risks, minimizes the variability of wages. Employers are viewed as offering workers a contract (one that is implicit rather than explicit), the form of which is determined by their past behavior and declared intentions and the purpose of which is to minimize wage fluctuations.

One way to characterize this is to imagine that the firm pays each employee a wage, W, and retains an insurance premium, IP, which together equal the marginal revenue product, MRP_L. Accordingly, $W = MRP_L - IP$. When conditions are good the $MRP_L > W$ and the employee pays the insurance premium, when conditions are bad the $MRP_L < W$ and the employee is receiving payments from the insurance policy. Note that employees receive no extra income from this arrangement since for the workforce as a whole $W = MRP_L$ over the duration of their contracts. So what is the appeal of this package? Its superiority could lie in the extra leisure employees enjoy when they choose variable hours rather than wages but it is more likely that its appeal lies in the welfare payments the employees receive when out of work. The combination of $W = MRP_L$ in the long run, plus welfare payments when occasionally laid off, increases workers' real incomes.

13. This theoretical development is associated with Aziriadis, C. (1975) 'Implicit contracts and under-employment equilibria', *Journal of Political Economy*, **83**, 1183–202; Baily, M.N. (1974) 'Wages and employment under uncertain demand', *Review of Economic Studies*, **41**, 37–50; Gordon, R.J. (1976) 'Recent developments in the theory of inflation and unemployment', *Journal of Monetary Economics*, **2**, 185–219.

However, there is a fundamental difficulty with such arrangements. It will be difficult to insure that workers stick to their side of the contract. It is always open to the worker to quit when conditions are good, having profited in the earlier period when conditions were bad. We should therefore expect that, in addition to such contracts, employers would offer some inducement to employees to stay on through good and bad times. Such inducements could take the form of seniority payments as discussed in Chapter 12.

The principle alternative explanation for the existence of implicit contracts is one we have already encountered. It emphasizes the heterogeneity of workers as a consequence of specific skills and the accompanying need to construct a set of social institutions and conventions which mitigate the abuse of the monopoly power, that this homogeneity entails.

We saw earlier that where each worker or a group of workers possesses unique skills a situation of bilateral monopoly emerges. Under these circumstances bargaining or rules resolve the indeterminacy that arises. Rules and conventions arise to minimize the transaction costs associated with bargaining. These transaction costs took the form of expenditures of time and resources, and they would be greater still if the parties failed to agree. The rules that arose to minimize these transaction costs constituted an implicit contract offered by the firm to the worker. By the example of their past behavior or by their declared intentions the firm offered a set of terms and conditions which employees found attractive.[14] Rules emerged as an efficient response to the problems of indeterminacy that arose from bilateral monopoly, itself the product of specific skills.

What form do these rules take? At this point our theory can offer little guide. If employees prefer stable wages and less stable employment we must presume that implicit contracts offer such undertakings. Alternatively, if employees prefer variable wages and stable employment they will be offered this. If employees are concerned about issues of fairness and believe that fair treatment requires that their wages grow in line with those of other groups then contracts will have to make overtures to comparability. If, however, they believe that older workers, or those with greater family commitments should be paid more than younger workers or less committed individuals, contracts will presumably reflect this. In short, this version of the theory offers little guide as to the specific form that implicit contracts will take. All we can say is that their specific form will be determined by social attitudes and conventions; wage determination is no longer the outcome of the impersonal play of market forces, rather it is a sociological phenomenon.[15]

Contract theory may offer an explanation of the experience of certain European countries in the early 1980s in which wage growth continued in the face of the unprecedented levels of unemployment. However, it appears less relevant as an

14. The earliest and still most illuminating statement of this interpretation of internal labor markets is provided by Williamson, O.E., Wachter, M.L. and Harris, J.E. (1975), 'Understanding the employment relation: the analysis of idiosyncratic exchange', *Bell Journal of Economics*, **6**, spring, 250–80.
15. The most detailed and perceptive investigation of these issues is contained in Okun, A. (1981) *Prices and Quantities: A Macroeconomic Analysis*, Blackwell, Oxford.

explanation of behavior in the United States. Up to the mid-1980s there had been practically no real wage growth in the United States over the previous decade and real and nominal wage cuts were not unusual as unions engaged in 'concession bargaining', and the non-union sector cut wages. More recently, in Europe, wages began to respond to changing conditions in labor markets during the latter part of the 1980s. In particular, unemployment again began to influence the pace of wage change, and therefore in Europe wages may no longer be as rigid as was once presumed. We now move on to study the link between wages and unemployment together with other determinants of aggregate wage behavior.

AGGREGATE WAGE CHANGE AND UNEMPLOYMENT

In the previous chapter we looked at the impact of unions on wages, and described briefly a model of wage determination in a unionized economy. Now we look in more detail at the responsiveness of aggregate wage change to unemployment in labor markets.

The Phillips curve

First consider the relationship between wage change and unemployment that is likely to occur in competitive labor markets that do not clear instantaneously. Figure 15.14 details the aggregate labor market, the functions L^s, L^d and L^F being as before and positions of excess supply, at W_1/P, and excess demand, at W_2/P, are identified. A proportional measure of the magnitude of the excess demand at W_2/P is given by $(D - S)/S$. In a competitive market in which wages are free to vary we would expect wages to rise toward the equilibrium level W^*/P in the presence of excess demand and fall toward W^*/P in the presence of excess supply. Competition by firms (workers) for workers (jobs) would bid wages upwards (down) toward the market-clearing level. If we assume for the moment that P is fixed then it can be seen that wage change, $\dot{W}$ is some function, α, of excess demand

$$\dot{W} = \alpha \frac{D - S}{S} \tag{15.2}$$

It is evident from Fig. 15.14 that where the labor market is characterized by excess demand as at W_2/P unemployment, measured by the distance $L_1 - D$, is below the rate that would prevail when the labor market cleared, it is below the natural rate. Equally if the real wage settled at W_1/P unemployment, given by the distance $L^F - L^d$, would exceed the natural rate. It emerges that where unemployment is below the natural rate wages will be rising and that where unemployment is above the natural rate wages will be falling.

In Fig. 15.15(a) we illustrate the relationship between wage change, $\dot{W}$, and the level of unemployment measured by deviations from the natural rate. At the origin unemployment is at the natural rate, U^*, and there is no tendency for wages to change. At unemployment levels below the natural rate, points to the left of the origin along

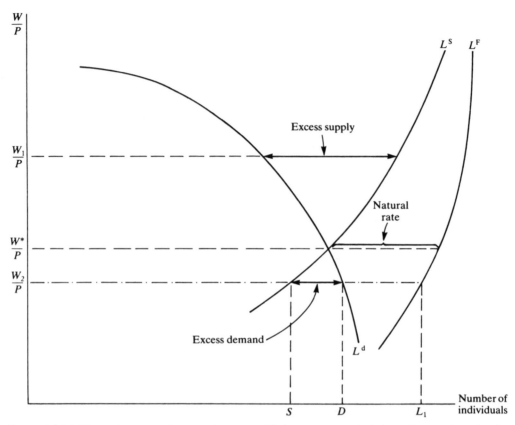

Figure 15.14 Wage change and unemployment. If the wage rate is below the market clearing rate, as at W_2/P, unemployment, measured by the distance between $L^F - L^d$, will be below the natural rate and wages will be rising. If the wage rate is above the market clearing rate as at W_1/P, unemployment, again given by $L^F - L^d$, will be above the natural rate and wages will be falling

the horizontal axis, wage change is positive and hence a line may be drawn in the top left-hand quadrant mapping positive rates of wage change against levels of excess demand for labor. To the right of the origin on the horizontal axis unemployment, U, is above the natural rate, U^*, hence wages are falling, $\dot{W}$ is negative, and we map points in the bottom right-hand quadrant. Therefore we can restate the relationship detailed in Eq. (15.2) in terms of deviations from the natural rate

$$\dot{W} = \alpha(U - U^*) \qquad (15.3)$$

Where $U > U^*$ then $\dot{W} < 0$ and when then $\dot{W} < 0$ $U > U^*$. α therefore indicates the responsiveness of $\dot{W}$ to deviations of $\dot{U}$ from U^* and takes on a *negative* value due to the inverse relationship. Note that, as drawn, the relationship between wage change and unemployment is not symmetric for points above and below the natural rate. It

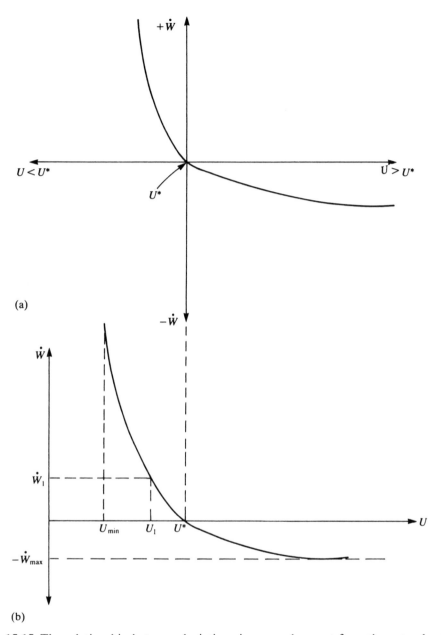

(a)

(b)

Figure 15.15 The relationship between deviations in unemployment from the natural rate and money wage change. The relationship between excess demand and wage change in Fig. 15.14 is translated into the relationship between deviations of unemployment from the natural rate, U^*, and wage change, $\dot{W}$, shown here. Unemployment rates below the natural rate, $U < U^*$, result in positive rates of wage change, while unemployment above the natural rate, $U > U^*$, results in a reduction in nominal wages. The distance from the origin to U^* in (b) indicates the magnitude of the natural rate while $-\dot{W}_{max}$ indicates that no matter how high unemployment is there is a unit to the rate at which nominal wages will be reduced. Similarly U_{min} indicates that unemployment can never fall to zero. No matter how large the increase in wages, there will always be some transitional unemployment.

is suggested that it is easier to bid wages up in the presence of excess demand than to cut wages in the presence of excess supply. Indeed there is a floor to $-\dot{W}$ below which it will not go.

Suppose that we now redraw Fig. 15.15(a), shifting the vertical $\dot{W}$ axis to the left so that the distance from the origin to U^*, as shown in Fig. 15.15(b), indicates the magnitude of the natural rate of unemployment when the labor market is in equilibrium as shown in Fig. 15.14. By redrawing, we emphasize that we never reach a point at which the whole labor force is employed for there will always be some search unemployment no matter how rapid the rate of wage growth. The relationship we depict in Fig. 15.15(b) was first established empirically by a British economist, A.W. Phillips, and the functional relationship was thereafter known as the *Phillips curve*.[16]

The significance of this early empirical work should not be underestimated. It suggested that there existed a trade-off between wage inflation and unemployment and that nations had to choose between low unemployment, at the cost of some wage inflation, or low wage inflation, at the cost of higher unemployment. The Phillips curve presented a 'menu' from which could be chosen the particular combination of unemployment and inflation that the electorate, or politicians, preferred. Throughout the 1950s and 1960s the level of unemployment in the United States was higher than that in Britain. On the other hand, the level of wage inflation in the United States was lower than in Britain. Britain had obviously chosen to go for low unemployment, the United States for low wage inflation. Or so it seemed.

The idea that countries could choose the point on their national Phillips curve at which to locate was based on the belief that countries could manipulate the level of aggregate demand, and hence output and employment, using fiscal and monetary policy. The Phillips curve appeared grounded in a Keynesian view of macroeconomics and indeed the sluggish nature of wage adjustment that would occur if $\alpha < 1$ appeared to provide a theory of the stickiness of wages which underpinned Keynesian macroeconomics.

The rule of the Phillips curve in this form was short lived. No sooner had the relationship been established than it appeared to break down. From the end of the 1960s it became increasingly inappropriate to describe the relationship between wage change and unemployment in terms of a trade-off. Recent estimates reveal that the unemployment elasticity of wages is generally very small. Table 15.11, which summarizes a number of recent estimates, shows that these elasticities fall in a range from -0.1 to -0.3 but centre around -0.1, suggesting a very small unemployment impact on wage change.

Explanations for the 'breakdown' of the Phillips curve focused on the neglect of real wages in this theory. Such a neglect may have been appropriate when prices were rising

16. Phillips, A.W. (1958) 'The relationship between unemployment and the rate of change of money wages rates in the United Kingdom: 1862–1957', *Economica*, **25**, November, 283–99. The underpinnings of this empirical relationship as detailed above were proposed by Lipsey, R. (1960) 'The relationship between unemployment and the rate of change of money wage rates in the United Kingdom: 1862–1957: a further analysis', *Economica*, **27**, 1–31. See also Samuelson, P.A. and Solow, R.A. (1965) 'Our menu of policy choices', in Okun A. (ed.) *The Battle Against Unemployment*, Norton, New York.

Table 15.11 Estimates of the unemployment elasticity of real wages—cross-section and panel data

Study	Data	Notes	Unemployment elasticity
1. Bils (1985)	US NLS Panel, 1970s, 5000 young males	Aggregate annual US unemployment used as independent variable, Few annual observations	−0.12
2. Rayack (1987)	US PSID Panel, 1968–80, 27 000 white males	Aggregate annual US unemployment rates	−0.1 (approx.)
3. Adams (1985)	US PSID Panel, 1970–76, various samples	State and industry unemployment rates	−0.02 to −0.11 (industry rates 0.13 to 0.20 (state rates)
4. Beckerman and Jenkinson (1986)	Panel of 12 OECD countries, 1963–83	National unemployment rates	Approx. zero
5. Beckerman and Jenkinson (1988)	Panel of 14 UK manufacturing industries 1972–86	Unemployment by industry and nationally. Data on 1983–86 constructed by authors	−0.13 (aggregate rates) +0.18 (industry rates)
6. Blanchflower and Oswald (1988)	British BSA, 1983–86, 3800 adult workers	Regional unemployment	−0.12
7. Blackaby and Manning (1987)	British General Household Survey, 1975, 7300 white males	Regional unemployment	−0.16
8. McConnell (1988)	US union contract data, 1970–81, 3000 contracts	State unemployment	Approx. zero
9. Holmlund, and Skedinger (1988)	Panel on Swedish timber industry, 70 regions, 1969–85	Regional and national unemployment	Zero to −0.04
10. Blanchflower, Oswald and Garrett (1988)	British 1984 WIRS, annual workers in 1200 establishments	County unemployment	Zero to −0.14
11. Blanchflower, and Oswald (1988c)	British 1984 and 1980 WIRS. Non-manual workers in 800 establishments	Regional unemployment. Regional wage included as a control	Zero to −0.08
12. Nickell and Wadhwani (1987, 1988)	Panel of 219 UK firms. 1974–82.	Industry and national unemployment	−0.05 (industry) −0.05 (national)
13. Christofides and Oswald (1988)	Canadian union contract data	Provincial unemployment	−0.03 to −0.12
14. Card (1988)	Canadian union contract data, 1293 contracts, 1966–83	Provincial unemployment. National unemployment for some provinces	−0.05 to −0.1
15. Freeman (1988)	US state data. British country data. Changes from 1979–85	State and country unemployment	Zero to −0.1 (approx.)
16. Symons and Walker (1988)	British FES data, 6500 married males, 1979–84. Various samples	Monthly regional unemployment	Zero to −0.2

Source: Blanchflower, D. and Oswald, A. (1989) 'The wage curve', Centre for Labour Economics, *Discussion Paper 340 London School of Economics* and NBER Working Paper No. 3181. Reproduced with permission of the authors.

only slowly, for then the distinction between real and money wages would have been trivial. However, as price inflation took off during the 1960s and 1970s such a distinction could no longer be neglected.

Consider what happens when we bring the rate of price change into the picture. First, we examine the relationship between wage change and price change. Suppose that product prices are determined as a fixed proportional profit mark-up, π, over labor costs. Labor costs in turn are given by wage costs, W, per unit of output, Q. Hence

$$P = \frac{W}{Q} \times \pi \qquad (15.4)$$

From the above it follows that the proportional change in prices, $\dot{P}$, where dots over all the variables indicate percentage rates of change, is given by:

$$\dot{P} = \dot{W} - \dot{Q} + \dot{\pi} \qquad (15.5)$$

$\dot{Q}$ is of course the growth of labor productivity. Thus, given $\dot{\pi}$, prices will be positively related to wage change, at any given rate of change of labor productivity, and inversely related to the rate of change of productivity at any given rate of change of wages. If π is assumed constant, at $\bar{\pi}$, it follows that the rate of growth of prices equals the rate of growth of wages minus the rate of growth of labor productivity and, since the rate of change of wages is a function of the level of unemployment we can rewrite Eq. (15.5) by substituting in Eq. (15.3) to give

$$\dot{P} = \alpha(U - U^*) - \dot{Q} + \bar{\pi} \qquad (15.6)$$

It follows from this that if the profit mark-up is constant while productivity growth is positive, the rate of growth of prices will be less than the rate of growth of wages at any given level of unemployment. Thus if at the level of unemployment U_1 in Fig. 15.15 (b) the rate of growth of money wages $\dot{W}_1$ is positive but is offset by the rate of growth of productivity $\dot{Q}$, so that $\dot{Q} = \dot{W}$, then $\dot{P} = 0$. A feature of both the US and British economies during the late 1960s and 1970s was a slowdown in the rate of growth of productivity, and without a slowdown in the rate of growth of money wages this meant that prices would rise.[17]

The expectations-augmented Phillips curve

A central proposition of neoclassical theory is that workers and employers are concerned with real, rather than nominal, wages: it is real wages that clear the market. If real wages clear the market the Phillips curve, as described above, was misspecified.[18] Expectations of future price changes or demands for compensation for past price changes will also be a determinant of the rate of growth of money wages for this affects the actual or expected growth of real wages. If $\dot{P}^e$ represents expected price

---

17 See Grubb, D., Jackman, R.A. and Layard, P.R.G. (1983) 'Wage rigidity and unemployment in OECD countries', *European Economic Review*, **21**.

18. This was the central contention of Friedman, M. (1968), *op. cit.*, 1–17 and Phelps, E.S. (1967) 'Phillips curves, expectations of inflation and optimal unemployment over time', *Economica*, **34**, August, 254–8.

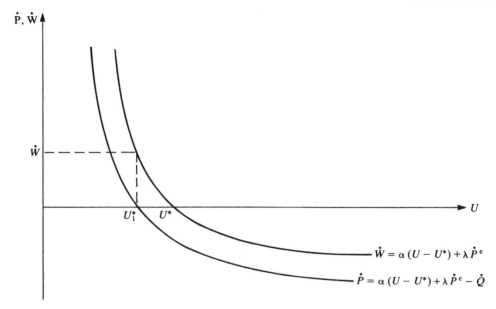

Figure 15.16 The augmented Phillips curve. At any level of unemployment, price change, $\dot{P}$, will be less than wage change, $\dot{W}$, if $\dot{Q}$, the rate of growth of productivity, is positive

changes, Eq. (15.3) should be augmented as follows

$$\dot{W} = \alpha(U - U^*) + \lambda \dot{P}^e \qquad (15.7)$$

where the coefficient λ on expected price changes represents the degree of responsiveness of wage rises to expected price changes. Substituting Eq. (15.7) into Eq. (15.5), holding π constant, gives

$$\dot{P} = \alpha(U - U^*) + \lambda \dot{P}^e - \dot{Q} + \bar{\pi} \qquad (15.8)$$

the equation revealing the determinants of the pace of price change. In Fig. 15.16 we therefore add price expectations as a determinant of the rate of wage change and show how when we deduct the rate of productivity growth and assume that the profit mark-up is constant, as in Eq. (15.8), we are able to draw a function relating price change to deviations in unemployment from the natural rate.

Now consider the possible sequence of events that might occur as a result of an expansion of aggregate demand. This is depicted in Fig. 15.17. Suppose that in the past wage rises have been compensated by productivity growth so that there has been no price inflation. Now suppose that there is an expansion of aggregate demand, perhaps as a result of a monetary expansion, and employers bid for labor pushing unemployment below the natural rate U^*. Competition causes wages to rise and this rise in wages now exceeds the rate of productivity growth and so prices rise. If workers fail to understand fully the mechanism by which current wage change leads to price change, and continue to expect the rate of change of prices to be as in the past, then $\dot{P}^e_1 = 0$ and the current rise in money wages will be perceived as a rise in real wages.

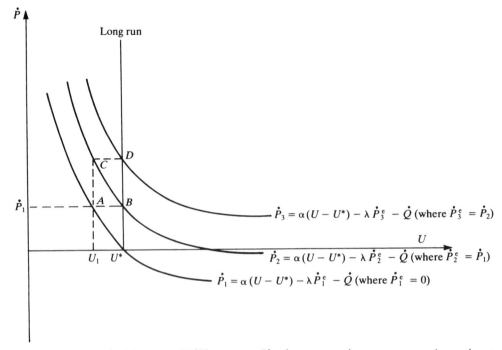

Figure 15.17 A vertical long-run Phillips curve. If price expectations enter as a determinant of wage change, a trade-off will only exist in the short run if actual and expected price changes diverge. To the left of the natural rate actual price change exceeds expected price change. To the left of U^* workers believe real wages are rising faster than is in fact the case and are 'fooled' into accepting employment. As they discover their mistakes, employment falls and unemployment returns to the natural rate at a new higher expected rate of inflation. At all points to the left of the natural rate $\dot{P} > \dot{P}^e$ at points to the right $\dot{P} > \dot{P}^e$ only at U^* does $\dot{P}^e = \dot{P}$.

Workers engaged in the degree of job search underpinning the natural rate will now be confronted by wage offers which they believe exceed their real reservation wages and they will enter employment earlier than would otherwise have occurred. Unemployment will fall below the natural rate and we will move to a point such a A along the Phillips curve at which $\dot{P}_1^e = 0$ as depicted in Fig. 15.17.

The combination of $\dot{P} > 0$ and $U < U^*$ moves us to a point such as A, but when the rise in prices is eventually perceived workers now understand that the rise in real wages was less than they had expected. Those who entered employment, believing that real wages exceeded their reservation wages, might reverse their decisions to take a job and quit to search once again for a job with wages in excess of their reservation wage. In this case unemployment will slip back to U^* but since prices are rising at a positive rate $\dot{P}_1 > 0$, and the experienced rate of price inflation now becomes the expected rate of price inflation, $\dot{P}_2^e = \dot{P}_1$, this will occur at B. Money wages now rise at the rate required to protect real wages at the new higher rate of expected inflation $\dot{P}_2^e$. At the point B, where $(U - U^*) = 0$, the rise in money wage, $\dot{W}$, is equal to the expected price rise, $\dot{P}_2^e$ and point B represents a point on a new curve at all points on which $\dot{P}_2^e =$

$\dot{P}_1$. This new curve lies above the curve corresponding to $\dot{P}_1^e = 0$ for a positive rate of price inflation is now expected.

The sequence of events described above could not be sustained for the rise in prices will erode the rise in the money supply returning it toward its former level. Without further increases in the money supply, it could be argued, the new rate of price inflation cannot be sustained, inflation will fall and the sequence of events be reversed. On the other hand if a further boost to aggregate demand occurs a similar sequence of events, to that described above, will be set in motion but the starting point will now be from $\dot{P}_2^e$ not $\dot{P}_1^e$ as before. We now move up the short-run curve $\dot{P}_2$ from point B to C in Fig. 15.17 and thereafter back to D. Points B and D lie on a vertical line above the natural rate and have in common that at these points $\dot{P} = \dot{P}^e$, the actual rate of inflation equals the expected rate of inflation. When $\dot{Q}$ and $\bar{\pi}$ are fixed and $U = U^*$ this will only be true where $\lambda = 1$, that is wage changes have responded fully to price changes. At all points above the natural rate, therefore, the actual rate of inflation, $\dot{P}$, equals the expected rate of inflation, $\dot{P}^e$, and this could be at any rate of price, and wage, inflation.

It follows from the above that when actual price change is less than the expected price change we are at points to the right of the natural rate of unemployment on the horizontal axis of Fig. 15.17. At such points unemployment will be above the natural rate and inflation will be decelerating: from Eq. (15.8) if $\dot{Q}$ and $\bar{\pi}$ are fixed, if $U > U^*$ $\dot{P} < \dot{P}^e$. Equally at points to the left of the natural rate the actual rate of price change exceeds the expected rate and inflation is accelerating: $U < U^*$ and $\dot{P} > \dot{P}^e$. Only at points vertically above the natural rate is inflation neither accelerating nor decelerating. The natural rate of unemployment (apart from being known as the equilibrium level of unemployment) is therefore also known as the *non-accelerating inflation rate of unemployment* (NAIRU).

This expectations augmented Phillips curve brings to centre stage expectations as a determinant of fluctuations in unemployment. Inaccurate price expectations provide one of the principal neoclassical explanations of deviations in unemployment from the natural rate. Incorrect wage and price expectations cause shifts in the labor supply schedule and the resulting unemployment is therefore deemed voluntary in nature. The greater the deviations between actual and expected prices the greater the deviations of unemployment from the natural rate. However, such deviations are unlikely to persist because the emergence of excess supply or demand will force people to revise their expectations no matter what they initially think.

Expectations play a central role in the above theories of unemployment, and it is therefore important to understand the way in which individuals formulate expectations. The two most widely employed theories of expectations formation are adaptive expectations and rational expectations. Importantly the latter if held in the strong form denies the existence of a trade-off between wage rises and unemployment even in the short run.

Adaptive expectations This assumes that estimates of prices are revised when there are observed differences between the expectations that are currently held and the actual values of the variables.[19]

19. The theory of adaptive expectations proposes that estimates of the rate of price change (inflation),

$$\dot{P}^e_t = \lambda \sum_{n=0}^{\infty} (1 - \lambda)^n \dot{P}_{t-n}$$

(15.9)

The current expected rate of inflation, $\dot{P}^e_t$, is hypothesized to depend on the past rate of inflation, with the weight attached to past rates of inflation $(1 - \lambda)$ getting smaller as time, n, gets larger. Clearly the closer to 1 is λ the more quickly expectations adjust and the more heavily we weight the present. Such a view of expectations formulation could generate a Phillips curve.

Rational expectations The above view of expectations formation has come in for considerable criticism. It has been argued that individuals will take other information, than merely that on past values of inflation, into account when formulating their forecasts of future price rises. If there is other information in the system then individuals will not ignore this. The rational expectations view of expectations formation proposes that individuals use all the information available in order to avoid predictable errors in expectations formation. Thus, most simply stated, in each time period the actual value on inflation $\dot{P}_t$ will equal the expectation of the value of $\dot{P}_t$ that was formed in the previous period, $t - 1$, we call this $\dot{P}^e_{t-1}$, plus an independent random error term, u_t. That is

$$\dot{P}_t = \dot{P}^e_{t-1} + u_t$$

(15.10)

At its simplest the hypothesis proposes that if individuals fail to predict actual inflation in period t this can only be due to random errors. Accordingly, it is only random

---

formulated at time t, denoted $\dot{P}^e_t$ and expected to rule in the next period are revised by some fraction, λ, of the discrepancy between actual inflation at that time $\dot{P}_t$ and the estimate of the rate of inflation at time t which was formulated at time $t - 1$, that is $\dot{P}^e_{t-1}$. This can be shown as follows:

$$\dot{P}^e_t - \dot{P}^e_{t-1} = \lambda(\dot{P}_t - \dot{P}^e_{t-1})$$

Therefore

$$\dot{P}^e_t = \dot{P}^e_{t-1} + \lambda(\dot{P}_t - \dot{P}^e_{t-1})$$

from which

$$\dot{P}^e_t = \dot{P}^e_{t-1} + \lambda\dot{P}_t - \lambda\dot{P}^e_{t-1}$$

and

$$\dot{P}^e_t = (1 - \lambda)\dot{P}^e_{t-1} + \lambda\dot{P}_t$$

Of course for time $t - 1$ we also have

$$\dot{P}^e_{t-1} = (1 - \lambda)\dot{P}^e_{t-2} + \lambda\dot{P}_{t-1}$$

which continues through to

$$\dot{P}^e_{t-n} = (1 - \lambda)\dot{P}^e_{t-n-1} + \lambda\dot{P}_{t-n}$$

so that by iterating backward, substituting in these values of $\dot{P}^e_{t-1}$ to $\dot{P}^e_{t-n}$ into their predecessors we obtain

$$\dot{P}^e_t = \lambda \sum_{n=0}^{\infty} (1 - \lambda)^n \dot{P}_{t-n}$$

for as n approaches ∞, $(1 - \lambda)^n \Rightarrow 0$ and the term $(1 - \lambda)^{n+1}\dot{P}^e_{t-n-1}$ drops out. This tells us that the current expected rate of inflation depends on the past history of inflation.

forecasting errors that present the prospect of a trade-off. In their absence there can be no trade-off in either the short or long run.

Against this view it has been shown that the movement of the unemployment rate through time does not appear to be random.[20] The definition of random, of course, depends on the model being employed and the model in turn depends on the information economic agents possess. It is unlikely that all economic agents either subscribe to or know the properties of the 'appropriate' economic model and it has been suggested therefore that this theory provides few insights into the workings of the labor market.

CHANGES IN THE NAIRU

In the previous chapter an alternative theoretical perspective with which to view the determinants of wage change was suggested. In that chapter a model was detailed in which prices were set as a mark-up over wages and wages as a mark-up on expected prices. The wage setting and price setting schedules we detailed in Fig. 14.9 provide the underpinnings for the target real wage and feasible real wage schedules we detail here. The former schedule reflects the wage aspirations of bargainers, while the feasible real wage represents the level of the real wage warranted by the current output of goods and services; it has been described as the limit to the living standards which the economy can provide to its workers. These schedules are illustrated in Fig. 15.18 where both are mapped against unemployment, as distinct from employment as in Fig. 14.9. The feasible real wage schedule may be described by Eq. (14.7) but in the case illustrated here $a_2 = 0$, so that the level of the feasible real wage is independent of the level of unemployment. The target wage may be described by Eq. (14.8) and its negative slope shows the restraining influence on the aspirations of wage bargainers exerted by the level of unemployment.[21] The intersection of the feasible real wage and target real wage schedules determines the level of the NAIRU.

From Eqs. (14.7) and (14.8) it follows that at a given and stable level of price expectations, where $P - P^e = 0$ (with the coefficients, a_3 and b_3, on the productivity variable, $K - L$, the same in both the price and wages equation), the size of the mark-ups and the factors in Z determine the level of the natural rate. A given rise in the target real wage, as reflected in a rise in b_0, raises the natural rate, a rise in the coefficient a_0 in the feasible real wage equation, shifts down the feasible wage schedule and increases the NAIRU, again a rise in wage pressure as measured by the variables in Z increases the NAIRU. What then are the factors underpinning Z? It has been suggested that these include welfare benefits, employment protection legislation (legislation making it more difficult for employers to dismiss workers) union power and

20. Hall, R.E. (1976) 'The rigidity of wages and the persistence of unemployment', *Brookings Papers on Economic Activity*, **2**, 301–35.
21. See Layard, P.R.G. (1986) *How to Beat Unemployment*, Ch. 3, Oxford University Press, Oxford, England; and the studies of Layard, P.R.G. and Nickell, S. (1987) 'Unemployment in Britain', in Bean, C., Layard, P.R.G., Nickell, S., (eds.), *The Rise in Unemployment*, Blackwell and Johnson, G.E. and Layard, P.R.G. (1986) 'The natural rate of unemployment: expectations and policy', in Ashenfelter, O. and Layard, P.R.G. (eds.), *Handbook in Labor Economics*, North Holland.

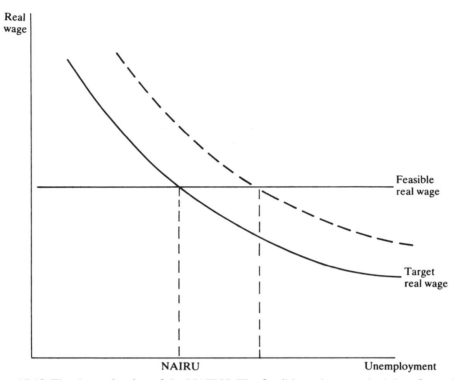

Figure 15.18 The determination of the NAIRU. The feasible real wage schedule reflects the real wage that the economy can deliver given the output of goods and services. The target real wage reflects the aspirations of wage bargainers, and its negative slope reveals how these are modified by unemployment. Intersection of the two schedules determines the natural rate of unemployment (NAIRU).

the degree of mismatch between available jobs and the skills of the unemployed. These are all factors implicit in Friedman's definition of the natural rate of unemployment detailed in footnote 9 above. An increase in any one of these might lead to an upward shift in the target real wage and hence to a rise in the NAIRU.

One of the the features of the early 1980s appears to have been a growth in the natural rate of unemployment. Table 15.12 presents one set of estimates as to how this has increased in most countries during the 1970s and early 1980s. Why should this be? A number of explanations have been proposed. Sluggish adjustment to the productivity slowdown in the United States and Europe in the 1970s and the increased incidence of government regulation of labor markets, via employment protection legislation, appear to be part of the explanation. In the United States it also appears that there have been changes in the natural rate as a result of changes in the composition of the labor force toward groups which exhibit higher equilibrium levels of unemployment;

Table 15.12 Estimates of the non-accelerating inflation rate of unemployment

Country	Time period	Actual unemployment rate (%)	Estimate of NAIRU (%)
France	1971–75	2.7	4.6
	1981–83	6.3	5.8
Germany	1967–70	1.0	0.8
	1981–83	6.3	5.8
Japan	1972–75	1.5	1.2
	1982–83	2.2	2.3
United Kingdom	1967–70	2.2	4.9
	1981–83	10.6	7.7
United States	1967–69	3.6	4.9
	1982–83	9.7	5.2

Source: Coe, D.T. and Gagliardi, F. (1985) 'Nominal wage determination in ten OECD countries', OECD *Economics and Statistics Working Paper 19*. OECD, Paris.

that is toward groups which engage in more job search and therefore exhibit higher quits and/or longer durations of unemployment.[22]

An alternative explanation of the rise in the natural rate suggests that a rise in the replacement ratio, described in chapter 3, has diminished the incentives to work. There has been a rise in the replacement ratio in a number of countries, but these generally occurred during the 1950s and early 1960s. However, the debate over the contribution of welfare benefits to unemployment has been particularly vigorous in the United Kingdom. It has been estimated at one extreme that a 10 percent reduction in benefit would have reduced the number unemployed by 700 000 when the total was 2.8 million. More typical estimates suggest that the increase in the natural rate due to the effects of benefits was between 55 000 and 80 000.[23] It has also been suggested that in Britain benefits were rather less stringently administered and that from the late 1960s social security benefits were more easily available.[24] The effect of unions on unemployment has been estimated to vary widely. Some researchers have found strong effects of unions in Britain although a more conservative estimate suggests that unions may have increased unemployment by around 3 percentage points over the 20 years to the mid-1980s.[25]

A major part of the rise in the natural rate in Britain appears to result from a rise in *structural unemployment*: shifts in the pattern of labor demand so that these now fit less perfectly the pattern of labor supply. Structural unemployment arises from a mismatch between the unemployed and job vacancies. It arises when the unemployed

22. These are the explanations offered by Johnson, G.E. and Layard, P.R.G. (1986), *op. cit.*
23. See Minford, P. (1983) 'Labour market equilibrium in an open economy', *Oxford Economic Papers*, **35**(4) for the largest estimate of the effects of unions and benefits and Nickell, S. and Andrews, M. (1983) 'Union real wages and employment in Britain, 1951–79', *Oxford Economic Papers* **35**(4) for a more typical estimate.
24. See Layard, P.R.G. (1983) *More Jobs, Less Inflation*, Grant MacIntyre.
25. See Layard, P.R.G. and Nickell, S. (1987), *op. cit.*

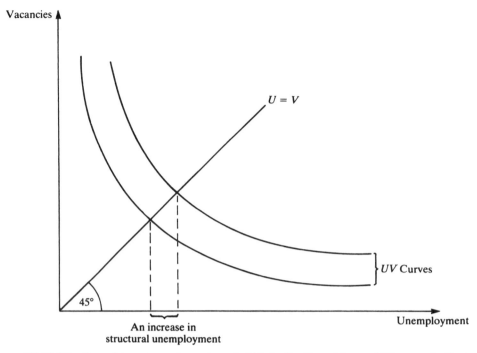

Figure 15.19 The Beveridge curve. An outward shift in the Beveridge or UV curve indicates an increase in the frictional and structural components of unemployment. Along the 45° line a given level of vacancies is matched by an equal level of unemployment. Outward movements represent reductions in labor market efficiency.

possess skills or live in geographical areas which are distinct from those in which the vacancies exist. The relationship between unemployment and vacancies is described by the *Beveridge curve*. This maps the level of vacancies or vacancy rate against the level of unemployment or unemployment rate. As we might anticipate such a mapping produces an inverse but non-linear relationship as depicted in Fig. 15.19. The shape of this curve reveals that no matter how high vacancies rise unemployment will never fall to zero and vice versa. An increase in structural unemployment is depicted by an outward shift of the Beveridge curve and this is just what has been happening in Britain, where the level of job vacancies in 1987 exceeded the average for the years 1979–80, even though in 1987 the unemployment rate was double that of the earlier years. It appears that although the demand for labor was rising, the unemployed seemed inappropriately equipped or located to fill the jobs that were emerging.

Hysteresis of the natural rate

Of greater signigicance in explaining the growth in the natural rate may be the notion of hysteresis:[26] the idea that unemployment causes unemployment. Above we drew the

26. See Cross, R. (ed.) (1987) *Unemployment, Hysteresis and the Natural Rate Hypothesis*, Blackwell, Oxford.

distinction between the actual and the natural, or equilibrium rate of unemployment. The notion of hysteresis proposes that the natural rate of unemployment follows the actual rate of unemployment with the result that there is no unique natural rate. From Eq. (15.8) we saw that when $\dot{Q}$ and π were constant

$$\dot{P} = \alpha(U - U^*) + \lambda \dot{P}^e \tag{15.8a}$$

The notion of hysteresis suggests that U^* at time t depends on past values of unemployment U_{t-1}. Thus Eq. (15.8a) may be rewritten as

$$\dot{P}_t = \alpha(U_t - \beta U_{t-1}) + \lambda \dot{P}_t^e \tag{15.11}$$

Where β represents the degree of dependency of the natural rate on past values of unemployment. If $\beta = 1$ full hysteresis occurs and there is no longer a unique U^*, the natural rate is equal to unemployment in the previous period. It is evident from Eq. (15.11) that full hysteresis implies that the inflation rate depends on the change in unemployment $(U_t - U_{t-1})$. Hysteresis suggests there is no unique historical equilibrium level of unemployment, no unique natural rate, but instead that there is a continuum of equilibrium rates, each one corresponding to a different time path for unemployment.

Why should unemployment cause further unemployment? We saw earlier in this chapter that the sharp fall in the flows out of unemployment in the early 1980s in the United Kingdom increased the mean duration of unemployment. Such an increase in mean duration might lead to a subsequent increase in unemployment if employers use unemployment duration as a sorting device. Employers may reason that those who have been unemployed for long periods have lost the 'work habit' or 'work ethic', or have skills that are no longer appropriate to employers' needs and thus they may fail to offer employment to the long-term unemployed. Where there has been a growth in long-term unemployment, this rise in duration may itself cause a further rise in the unemployment rate.

Insiders and outsiders[27]

An alternative explanation of changes in the NAIRU is offered by the distinction between insiders and outsiders. The term insiders is used to describe those with jobs while the term outsiders describes those without. More specifically the term insiders refers to those workers in jobs in which they possess a degree of market power. On this view the NAIRU is determined by the behavior of insiders and a growth in insider market power is reflected in a growth in the NAIRU. The market power possessed by insiders results from the transactions costs associated with swapping insiders for outsiders. It is expensive for firms to swap insiders for outsiders, due to the existence of hiring and training costs and, in consequence, firms are willing to pay their existing workforce a premium to retain their services. Even though the wages of insiders exceed the reservation wages of the unemployed, firms have no wish to employ outsiders;

27. See Lindbeck, A. and Snower, D. in Cross (ed.) (1987), *op. cit.* and Solow, R.M. (1985) 'Insiders and outsiders in wage determination', *Scandinavian Journal of Economics*, **87**, 411–28.

however, insiders' wages would not be expected to exceed the reservation wages of the unemployed by more than the hiring and training costs. It is clear that insiders have an inherent advantage over outsiders and they may use this to their advantage in wage negotiations. Indeed they may, as a deliberate bargaining tactic, amplify the costs associated with turning outsiders into insiders. Unions may be most adept at exploiting these opportunities and thus this offers a context for an active role by unions.

Important though the distinction between insiders and outsiders may be, it is, essentially, no more than a development of the logic of internal and career labor market theory. It emphasizes the significance of transaction costs, and the heterogeneity of workers, and suggests an important role for trade unions. Insider–outsider theories explore the implications of transaction costs theory for unemployment.

In this theory as with that of hysteresis, the NAIRU depends, at least in the short term, on the past history of unemployment. If unemployment has been falling, insiders face a decreasing probability of losing their jobs and they modify their behavior accordingly: they raise their wage demands. Wage and price inflation are inversely related to the rate of change of unemployment, not its level as posited in the simple Phillips relation, and where unemployment is stable insiders have little incentive to modify their wage demands. Only if unemployment has been rising and insiders face an increasing probability of losing their jobs will they lower their wage demands.

Insider theories of wage determination may be seen as downgrading the importance of changes in the external labor market. Recent empirical work has investigated these phenomena in the United Kingdom and Australia and found some support for this proposition.[28] The study of wage determination in Australia found that models incorporating labor utilization rates in the firm dominated a simple Phillips curve which included both price expectations and unemployment as explanations.

In the United Kingdom recent studies have found that wages depend on the average productivity of the firm and its financial position.[29] In particular there appears to be growing evidence that wage rates are positively related to lagged levels of company profitability.[30] Pay levels in Britain, it has been claimed, are shaped by 'an intricate blend of internal and external forces'. Unemployment appears to play only a small part in explaining wage change while wages paid by establishments elsewhere in the firm's area and firm profitability appear more important.[31] It has been concluded that wage determination in medium-sized to large companies in Britain is best seen as a kind of rent sharing 'in which workers appropriate a portion of profits and in which high

28. Gregory, R.A. (1987) 'Wages policy and unemployment in Australia', in Bean, C. Layard, R. and Nickell, S.J. (eds.), *The Rise in Unemployment*, Blackwell, Oxford; Nickell, S. and Andrews, M. (1983) 'Trade unions, real wages and employment in Britain: 1951–79', *Oxford Economics Papers*, **35**, 507–30.
29. See Nickel, S.J. and Wadhawani, S. (1987) 'Insider forces and wage determination', *London School of Economics*; Gregory, M., Lobban, P. and Thomson, A. (1987) 'Pay settlements in manufacturing industry, 1979–1984: a micro data study of the impact of product and labour market pressures', *Oxford Bulletin of Economics and Statistics*, **49**, 125–50.
30. Carruth, A.A. and Oswald, A.J. (1987) 'Wage inflexibility in Britain', *Oxford Bulletin of Economics and Statistics* **49**, 59–78; Rowlatt, P.A. (1987) 'A model of wage bargaining', *Oxford Bulletin of Economics and Statistics*, **49**, 347–72.
31. Blanchflower, D.G., Oswald, A.J. and Garrett, M.D. (1988) 'Insider power in wage determination', London School of Economics Centre for Labour Economics, Discussion Paper No. 319, August, p.45.

external unemployment weakens workers' bargaining strength'. In the United States researchers have also discovered a link between pay and profitability.[32]

SUMMARY

In this chapter we have focused on the issue of unemployment. This was *the* policy issue of the last half of the 1970s and first half of the 1980s in most major Western European industrial nations, but as the 1980s drew to a close concern over this issue was diminishing. Analysis of the nature of the unemployment experienced recently in the United States and Europe suggested that once again the labor market in the United States behaves very differently from that in Europe. The US labor market again appears much more flexible; the experience of unemployment is more general and its duration much shorter. Having said this, it was, nonetheless, clear that the experience of unemployment was still very far from equally distributed in most countries. The least educated, those in unskilled jobs and those from minority groups, suffered the highest unemployment rates in Britain and in the United States.

We examined competing explanations for unemployment and divided these theories into Keynesian and neoclassical theories. The former emphasized the involuntary nature of unemployment and the latter its voluntary nature. We did not attempt to arbitrate between these competing explanations, but merely tried to show that elements in both have validity and afford insights into the problem. Frequently, explanations are categorized as equilibrium or disequilibrium explanations; we have not used this terminology although it could be argued that on most interpretations it is synonymous with the voluntary/involuntary split. Unemployment is voluntary, it is an equilibrium phenomenon, if the present institutional arrangements in labor markets and the price of labor reflect the conscious choices of individuals and there are no pressures to change these arrangements. Again, unemployment is involuntary, it is a disequilibrium phenomenon, where there are pressures to change existing arrangements and to adjust levels of pay. In both cases the focus is on the extent to which the situation can be said to reflect the conscious choices of labor market participants, and how effectively these choices are registered in the market place.

Any discussion of unemployment necessitates a discussion of wages. Prices and quantities are related in all markets and the market for labor is no different in this respect. The Phillips curve brought this relationship to the fore but in focusing exclusively on money wages was found to be deficient. The expectations augmented Phillips curve proved to be more soundly based theoretically, although it rested on a competitive view of labor markets. An alternative perspective was offered by a model in which firms *and* workers had some degree of market power. The distinction between insiders and outsiders also rested on the view that workers possessed some degree of market power. Both insider–outsider models and the idea of hysteresis suggested that the simple relationship between wage change and unemployment posited in the Phillips curve was no longer appropriate.

32. Dickens, W.T. and Katz, L.F. (1986) 'Inter-industry wage differences and industry characteristics', in Lang, K. and Leonard, J. (eds.), *Unemployment and the Structure of Labour Markets*, Blackwell, Oxford.

PRINCIPAL CONCEPTS

The following concepts have been developed in this chapter and students should ensure that they are familiar with them:

1. The Phillips curve.
2. The expectations augmented Phillips curve.
3. Implicit contracts.
4. NAIRU.
5. Hysteresis of the natural rate.
6. Insiders and outsiders.
7. Adaptive expectations.
8. Rational expectations.
9. The Beveridge curve.

QUESTIONS FOR DISCUSSION

1. Do you agree that unless the distinction between stocks and flows is fully understood we can never devise appropriate policies to deal with the problem of unemployment?
2. Do job search theories offer any insights into recent unemployment experience in Britain and the United States?
3. Does the statement that the market for labor is a 'buyers' market', while the market for goods is a 'sellers' market' tell us anything about the nature of unemployment?
4. Would you agree that in order for unemployment to remain below the natural rate the government has continually to fool workers about the true rate of inflation?
5. Does implicit contract theory explain wage rigidity?
6. How do the notions of hysteresis and the distinction between insiders and outsiders inform our understanding of the determinants of wage inflation?
7. Can unions cause unemployment?

FURTHER READING

The 1980s saw an outpouring of books on unemployment. There are many very good ones among these, but the student is unlikely to be in a position to sample them all. The ones I recommend therefore offer summaries of the diverse and voluminous literature on the subject and/or have offered important yet accessible insights into the nature of the problem.

One of the best is by Sinclair, P.J. (1987) *Unemployment: Economic Theory and Evidence*, Blackwell. Bean C., Layard, P.R.G., and Nickell S.J. (eds.) (1987) *The Rise of Unemployment*, Blackwell, and Cross R. (ed.) (1987) *Unemployment, Hysteresis and the Natural Rate Hypothesis*, Blackwell, are also extremely helpful. A more advanced but again interesting treatment is to be found in Layard, P.R.G. and Johnson, G.E. (1986), in Ashenfelter O. and Layard P.R.G. (eds), *Handbook of Labor Economics*, North Holland.

APPENDIX 15A A MODEL OF UNEMPLOYMENT IN A UNIONIZED ECONOMY[A.1]

To illustrate the relationship between the union mark-up, the level of union density and the unemployment rate consider the following model. Suppose that the wage in the unionized sector W^U exceeds that in the competitive sector W^C by a positive mark-up, m. Then:

$$\frac{W^U}{W^C} = 1 + m \tag{15A.1}$$

For the homogeneous category of labor considered here this mark-up generates a queue of individuals for union jobs. If we adopt the assumption that the only way to find a union job is to search while unemployed then the present discounted value of being unemployed, V^U, is given by

$$V^U = (1 - \phi)B + \phi W^U \tag{15A.2}$$

where ϕ represents the probability of finding a union job at wage W^U while B represents the level of welfare benefits received while unemployed. This can be rearranged to show that the job finding rate ϕ given by:

$$\phi = \frac{V^U - B}{W^U - B} \tag{15A.3}$$

Now consider a position of equilibrium. Equilibrium in the union sector is described by a position in which the number of unemployed job seekers, U, expressed as a proportion of union employment, N^U, is equal to the proportion of union workers who leave their jobs, Q, divided by the job finding rate, ϕ. That is:

$$\frac{U}{N^U} = \frac{Q}{\phi} \tag{15A.4}$$

which by substituting in Eq. (15A.3) can be expressed as

$$\frac{U}{N^U} = \frac{Q(W^U - B)}{(V^U - B)} \tag{15A.5}$$

Now if the queue is in equilibrium people will be indifferent about joining the queue, that is the present value of not searching given by the wage in the competitive sector, W^C, will equal the present value of being unemployed V^U. That is $V^U = W^C$ and by substituting W^C into Eq (15A.5) we obtain

$$\frac{U}{N^U} = \frac{Q(W^U - B)}{(W^C - B)} \tag{15A.6}$$

A.1. This represents a simplification of the model proposed by Layard and Johnson (1986), *op. cit.*

Now if we divide the right-hand side through by W^c we obtain:

$$\frac{U}{N^U} = \frac{Q(W^U/W^C - B/W^C)}{(1 - B/W^C)} \tag{15A.7}$$

but of course from Eq. (15A.1) $W^U/W^C = 1 + m$ so that if, for simplicity, we let $\alpha = B/W^C$ then by substituting 15A.1 into 15A.7 and simplifying we obtain:

$$\frac{U}{N^U} = \frac{Q(1 + m - \alpha)}{1 - \alpha} \tag{15A.8}$$

and by further simplification this reduces to

$$\frac{U}{N^U} = \frac{Q + Qm - \alpha Q}{(1 - \alpha)} \tag{15A.9}$$

and

$$\frac{U}{N^U} = \frac{Qm}{(1 - \alpha)} + Q = Q\left[\frac{m}{1 - \alpha} + 1\right] \tag{15A.10}$$

Equation (15A.10) shows that the ratio of the unemployed to unionized workforce, U/N^U, is higher the higher is the union mark-up. Now of course the overall unemployment rate, U_r, depends on the proportion of workers who are unionized, that is on overall union density, D, and $D = N^U/N$ and $N = N^U/D$ so that $U_r = U/N + U$. U_r, is given by:

$$U_r = \frac{U}{\dfrac{N^U}{D} + U} \quad \text{or} \quad \frac{1}{\dfrac{N^U}{U} \times \dfrac{1}{D} + 1} \tag{15A.11}$$

This can be expressed in terms of the union mark-up by substituting Eq. (15A.10) into Eq. (15A.11)

$$U_r = \frac{D}{\dfrac{1 - \alpha}{Qm} + \dfrac{1}{Q} + 1} \tag{15A.12}$$

That is the higher is union density the higher is the union mark-up and the higher is the unionized quit rate, then the higher is the overall rate of unemployment.

Such a model shows how unemployment varies with the size of the unionized sector and the size of the union mark-up under the assumption that unions negotiate superior terms and conditions of employment. The superior union wage induces some individuals to engage in a search for a unionized job. Unemployment in this model is of the voluntary search variety and hence such a model does not provide a complete explanation of the levels of unemployment experienced in most Western European countries in the 1970s and first half of the 1980s.

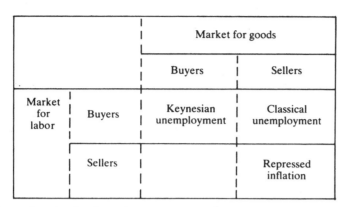

Figure 15B.1 Buyers' and sellers' markets and types of unemployment

APPENDIX 15B   KEYNESIAN AND CLASSICAL UNEMPLOYMENT

Keynesian unemployment is characterized by rationing in both the goods and labor markets; unemployment is due to lack of effective demand. These markets might be described as a *buyer's market*, for sellers of both labor and output are rationed. Sellers in both cases would like to sell more but are constrained by what buyers will purchase. This Keynesian case with a buyer's market in both labor and product markets suggests a way of identifying the different types of unemployment we have discussed[B.1] and this is shown in Fig. 15B.1. Thus Keynesian unemployment occurs where labor and product markets can be described as buyers' markets. Classical unemployment, on the other hand, occurs where firms are able to sell all they can supply in the market for goods, and the product market is therefore a seller's market, but sellers of labor are unable to sell all they would like and therefore labor operates in a buyer's market. A third state, in which demand exceeds supply in all markets, can be identified and this is described as repressed inflation. Finally, there also exists a state in which the goods market is a buyer's market and the labor market a seller's market but this is not very interesting: for output is determined in the short run by labor supply and since the demand for labor by firms is then rationed they cannot have a higher output than they sell: therefore they cannot be considered rationed sellers. The above shows that the notion of rationing can be adopted to explain both Keynesian and classical unemployment, but as this typology makes clear they each rest on very different views about the behavior of markets.

B.1. See Malinvaud E., (1977) *The Theory of Unemployment Reconsidered*, Blackwell, Oxford, England.

AUTHOR INDEX

The letter 'n' following a page number indicates that the name will be found in a footnote.

Subject index